T0394441

Terminology throughout History

Terminology and Lexicography Research and Practice (TLRP)

Terminology and Lexicography Research and Practice aims to provide in-depth studies and background information pertaining to Lexicography and Terminology. General works include philosophical, historical, theoretical, computational and cognitive approaches. Other works focus on structures for purpose- and domain-specific compilation (LSP), dictionary design, and training. The series includes monographs, state-of-the-art volumes and course books in the English language.

For an overview of all books published in this series, please see
benjamins.com/catalog/tlrp

Editors

Marie-Claude L' Homme
University of Montreal

Kyo Kageura
University of Tokyo

Volume 24

Terminology throughout History. A discipline in the making
Edited by Kara Warburton and John Humbley

Terminology throughout History

A discipline in the making

Edited by

Kara Warburton
Université du Québec à Trois-Rivières | Termologic

John Humbley
Université Paris Cité

John Benjamins Publishing Company
Amsterdam / Philadelphia

™ The paper used in this publication meets the minimum requirements of the American National Standard for Information Sciences – Permanence of Paper for Printed Library Materials, ANSI z39.48-1984.

DOI 10.1075/tlrp.24

Cataloging-in-Publication Data available from Library of Congress:
LCCN 2025007549 (PRINT) / 2025007550 (E-BOOK)

ISBN 978 90 272 2029 5 (HB)
ISBN 978 90 272 4486 4 (E-BOOK)

John Benjamins Publishing Company · https://benjamins.com

Table of contents

Acknowledgements

The editors extend their thanks to all those who contributed directly or indirectly to this historical account of terminology as a discipline.

Thanks go first and foremost to the directors of the collection, in particular to Professor Marie-Claude L'Homme, for their confidence in the viability of the project, their encouragements and their support and advice over what has turned out to be a lengthy period.

The two anonymous evaluators are to be specially thanked for the enormous work they took on, analysing the individual chapters and advising on the general orientation of the enterprise. The editors are grateful for their constructive remarks and suggestions, often shedding new light on points of theory which had initially not been sufficiently explored.

Thanks also are conveyed to the authors of the chapters. They have contributed the essential ingredients of the history of terminology, coming from different disciplinary horizons as well as from countries with differing research traditions, thereby enriching the final outcome.

The editors would also like to thank their colleagues who, without being authors, listened patiently and gave advice and encouragements. Particular thanks go to Professor Sue Ellen Wright for her judicious suggestions and to all those colleagues who, without being authors, listened patiently and gave advice and encouragements. Thanks are also extended to Emma Warburton who provided valuable editing services.

John Humbley would also like to express his heartfelt thanks to Professor Natalie Kübler for her unfailing support over quarter of a century, in particular as director of the Université Paris Cité research team CLILLAC-ARP. In 2025 this research group will be reconstituted as ALTAE, headed by Professor Mojca Pecman, who, together with Professor Stéphane Patin, director of the Applied linguistics faculty (EILA), are also warmly thanked.

Finally, we wish to acknowledge the contribution of Philippe Selosse and his colleagues (Angela Axworthy, Bernard Colombat, Martine Furno, Violaine Giacomotto-Charra and Jacqueline Vons) regarding the Renaissance period. Although ultimately their chapter could not be incorporated, we gained essential knowledge which enabled us to at least partially recognise this important period in the Introduction, and we look forward to their forthcoming publication.

Kara Warburton, John Humbley
Université du Québec à Trois-Rivières | Termologic, Université Paris Cité

Terminology throughout history
An introduction

John Humbley & Kara Warburton

How have textile fibres, which make up the greater part of our clothing, evolved over the centuries? There are various ways of approaching the history of this vital resource. One of them is through language. Klara Dankova (2023), for example, focusing on the words used to name the various fibres and the techniques associated with textiles, has recently analysed the successive innovations in their production and use, noting in particular the change from a natural to a synthetic base. Taking the language used in historical texts as an entry point and singling out the terms used to denote the innovations, the linguist provides a novel perspective for understanding the history of fibres. It is true that historians of science and technology have long used language as a means to identify trends, but the study of the terms used has rarely been the main focus or primary tool. This approach — diachronically studying changes in terminology as a means of understanding history — has recently become the subject of innovative research, which can be called the history of the terminology of the various sciences or technologies involved. But to carry out this research, several interlinking methodologies are involved, in particular those of terminology itself: relating concepts with their linguistic expression, constructing a concept system, accounting for synonymy and variation, searching for distinctive features, and so on. Just as history has its own methods, terminology as a field of enquiry has in recent times been constituted into what may be claimed to be a discipline, and a discipline which has been taking shape for longer than had previously been recognised. It is the ambition of this collective work to trace the evolution of the practice and the discipline of what is now known as *terminology*.

A discipline can be described for the purposes of this research as an autonomous area of study characterised by a clearly-defined articulated theoretical basis. Other features associated with disciplines concern their institutional characteristics, such as chairs in higher education, conferences, periodicals. As well as theoretical development, disciplines can also have practical applications. Indeed, in many cases, a discipline may emerge when practical experience is theorised, as would seem to be the case for terminology. It should also be noted that disciplines

https://doi.org/10.1075/tlrp.24.intro

are highly dynamic entities, which take form, develop and may whither, phases that may be embodied in terminological manifestations.

As this collective volume endeavours to demonstrate, the time has come to address the need to trace the history of terminology as an endeavour, a field of enquiry, perhaps even, a discipline. Sixty-three scholars involved in working with terminology have taken up what turns out to be the considerable challenge to document, analyse and illustrate how thinking about terms has evolved over time, in different geographical and social contexts and in particular the ways in which language is used to elaborate and to convey specialised knowledge.

Part of the challenge lies in determining just what terminology *is*. Terminology has indeed been envisaged as a practice, a methodology and, more controversially, as an identifiable discipline. The gauntlet was thrown down more than thirty years ago, when one of the leading experts of the time claimed the following:

> There is no substantial body of literature which could support the proclamation of terminology as a separate discipline and there is not likely to be. Everything of importance that can be said about terminology is more appropriately said in the context of linguistics or information science or computational linguistics.
>
> (Sager 1990: 1)

As will be seen in the following, terminology, like several other language-based pursuits, has both a practical and a theoretical dimension and, if it is not yet a fully-fledged discipline, as the 31 chapters of this volume attest it certainly has the ambition to become one.

Terminology: An emerging discipline

In spite of what Sager claimed, there is much evidence of terminology constituting not only a well-defined and often an indispensable practice, but also part of a theory of knowledge going back to Antiquity (Antia 2001). It is not only legitimate to consider that terminology is more than a set of practices or methods for working with units of meaning; it is also an emerging discipline, and, at the same time, a discipline with a past. From the practical point of view, terminology work has proved to be a fundamental component of such activities as industrial standardisation, which need to agree on definitions and the way naming is carried out. That is why the methods of creating, documenting, and managing terminologies are at the heart of many activities having little or nothing to do with language as such, in particular in classification and standardisation, as illustrated by ISO (International Organization for Standardization) and by its predecessor, ISA. From the 1970s, theories and practices relating to envisioning and working with terminology resources of various kinds have also been a subject taught in universities, in particular in Europe and in Canada, often in conjunction with courses in specialised translation but also in their own right in degree programs and research contexts. Terminology also plays an important part in technical writing and specialised documentation in general, though it may not always be explicitly recognised as such in this context (Gouadec 2005). This is in fact one of the paradoxes of terminology as an object of reflection: it is accepted as an important component of such activities as standardisation, translation, indexing and documentation, yet its most fundamental function is probably that of conveying specialised knowledge peculiar to any scientific or technical discipline, or even commercial activity (companies and organisations have their own "terminology"). In this sense, terms may be seen as shorthand for specialised knowledge. The terminological issues involved, in particular the drafting of coherent definitions, are often handled by the domaine experts themselves in ways established in the discipline (peer-edited journals, etc.), so there may be no practical need for a terminologist to intervene. This does not mean, however, that the processes of description, definition and naming, all part of the scientific process, are not worthy of epistemological attention, and who is better suited for this than the transdisciplinary-oriented terminologist? Indeed, this was the view espoused by the figure often regarded as the founder of terminology as a discipline, Eugen Wüster (Wüster 1974), who defined it as a "border area" (nowadays he would have probably used the metaphor of the interface) between linguistics, logic, ontology, information technology and natural science, i.e. a discipline between the disciplines.

Terminology is thus thought of here as an emerging discipline and as such, it shares a number of features with other recently established branches of language-based studies, namely the two related fields of translation studies and lexicography.

Translation has an even longer history than terminology as a recognised occupation, though not necessarily as a profession and even less so as a field of study. Its quest to secure status as a discipline involved finding a name, an umbrella term encompassing both practical and theoretical dimensions, training, as well as research. The common denominator generally agreed upon is *translation studies* in English, *Traduktionswissenschaft* in German and *traductologie* in French, and courses are on offer at institutes of higher learning under these titles in countries where these languages are spoken. Part of the drive for the change of status consisted in adding to the contemporary practice of translation a vast programme of studies focusing on translation as it was conceived throughout history. It is not by chance that one of the foremost researchers on the history of translation and translation studies, Jean Delisle, is also the author of what is most probably the first history of terminology as a profession (Delisle 2008), in this case limited to Canada. The avenues of research opened up by this pioneering work was one of the inspirations for the present volume.

Other researchers, especially from related fields such as knowledge organisation, consider that terminology has not come as far as translation studies in establishing its epistemological groundwork. Hjørland (2023), for example, states:

> A clear analysis of, and alternative to, "positivism" seems not to have been developed in terminology, somewhat in contrast to the closely related field of translation, where pragmatism, critical theory, hermeneutics, semiotics, and feminist epistemology are among the alternative views.

Lexicography is another practice that has much in common with terminology although it could be claimed that its disciplinary status is less in question. It developed during the Renaissance, but, like terminology, it has only been theorised and taught at universities for the last half century. A quick browse through leading journals such as the *International Journal of Lexicography* will reveal a high proportion of studies focusing on the past, not only on the contents of dictionaries and methods of dictionary making, but also on the role of dictionaries as mirrors of society. Specialised lexicography can be considered not only as a form of terminology, but also as a precursor, in that it incorporates as many milestones in the evolution of thought on how to encapsulate and reuse specialised knowledge.

Varying viewpoints on the early history of terminology

The word *terminology* (or equivalent) was first attested in the major European languages in the 19th century, so it would be tempting to start the history of the discipline with the emergence of the term itself. There are however cogent reasons for beginning either earlier or later. There is a good case for beginning well into the 20th century, in 1931, for example, with Eugen Wüster's pioneering thesis (Wüster [1931] 1970), which not only investigated theory as well as practice and established links with the linguistics of the day, but also created schools of study, in particular in German-speaking Central Europe, in the Soviet Union and in other countries too, including France (Candel 2022) and Canada (Delisle 2008). For the first time, there was a structured movement to research terms not only in different subject fields, but also as a manifestation of an autonomous intellectual pursuit. But there is also a strong case for taking into account the predecessors of modern terminology theory and practice, both the makers of specialised dictionaries or glossaries and, more importantly, those thinkers who in their different fields questioned the relationship between specialised knowledge and the use of language to express it. This latter approach has been the option taken here: to put terminology in the broader context, not merely as a predecessor to contemporary theories and practices, but also as coherent systems of representations of specialised knowledge in their own right. The first section of this book thus gives a succinct description of terminological thought before the 20th century.

This approach nonetheless poses certain difficulties. As terminology was not named before the 19th century, its early manifestations figure in historical documents under various guises. For example, in the middle of the 18th century, Diderot's thinking of what we would now consider questions of terminology were grouped together as the Language of the arts[1] (*"la langue des arts"* — see Chapter 3). The hypothesis that will be adopted here is that terminological thought of the past can be apprehended through its components. According to this supposition, features considered fundamental in the first elaborations of terminological theory, and notably as formulated later by Wüster, can be searched for in the practices of the past.

Among the first methods typifying terminology research and which gradually served to distinguish terminology from lexicology is the onomasiological approach, which takes the concept as the starting point and investigates its features to ultimately construct an appropriate term to name it. This method may be accompanied by reflections on how the concept is formed, on issues of classification and how language can be used to reflect a particular vision of the world or of a specialised area. The adequacy of the concept-to-name relationship also leads to thought on synonymy and how, at least in normative environments, it can be avoided — if that is indeed a tenable goal — or at least kept in check. Relations with lexicography are important too, as the need to document the linguistic markers of concepts in dictionary entries leads to explicit consideration of features that emerge as "terminological." Michel van der Yeught (2012: 17–19) suggests that the "dictionarisation" of a subject field — the need to order its terms in the form of a dictionary or glossary — may be a sign of the recognition of that field as a discipline itself, and its institutionalisation in the form of a "terminography."

The common thread underlying thoughts about terminology, however, is reflections on how language can — or cannot — express specialised knowledge. These considerations go back to Aristotle, whose conception of the definition by intension, passing through many historical phases, became the basis of terminological practice as typified in foundational modern reference works, such as the ISO standards.

---

1. Note that *arts* has substantially changed meanings over the centuries in both English and French, and in the 16th and 17th century included both the noble arts such as painting and the mechanical arts, comprising both traditional crafts and what were to become technologies in the 19th century.

Phases in the development of terminological introspection

This book roughly adopts a chronological order for the history, or indeed the pre-history, of the discipline of terminology, starting from the Ancient World, then passing on through the Middle Ages to the Enlightenment, when most of the defining criteria were set in place. The 19th century marks important advances and announces the developments in theory and methodology that took shape in the 20th century. The second section of the book focuses on early approaches to what ultimately shapes terminology from a methodological and theoretical perspective and paves the way to disciplinary status. The third and final section surveys terminological activities as carried out in selected countries or groups of countries throughout the world.

Early history

Aristotle's questions on the relations between language and knowledge were also raised in Roman times, as is shown in Michèle Fruyt's chapter, which addresses terminology in Antiquity, with a focus on Latin. This chapter demonstrates the natural division of man-made classifications with unambiguous categories and the use of metaphor to categorise natural phenomena, progressing from the known, and going on to understand and to name the less known. Interestingly, the use of metaphor would become later an essential naming strategy for certain language communities in modern times, as is shown in subsequent chapters.

In the West, Latin was the language of scholarly writing through the Middle Ages and well into the Renaissance. Terminology was thus elaborated in this language. Special attention has been paid to the complex process of transferring terminology from Latin into the vernacular languages, starting from the Middle Ages, through the Renaissance up to the age of Enlightenment, illustrated here through the example of French. French has been chosen from among European languages to exemplify this transfer process partly because it is particularly well documented and partly because, as a Romance language, it long remained beholden to Latin, but was at the same time different enough from the parent language that specific solutions had to be found to cross-lingual challenges. Joëlle Ducos, Michèle Goyens, Inge Fourneau and Fleur Vigneron show how Latin terminology, itself sourced in part from Greek, often via Arabic, was gradually transferred into French, with special attention paid to how French terminology came into being both in a recognised practice, namely medicine, and also in what was not yet a discipline, namely the study of plants, later known as botany. The authors identify several practices in terminology work of that early period that foreshadow principles that scholars, centuries later, would claim distinguish terminology from lexicology, in particular the onomasiological approach and the documentation of hierarchical relations. Term creation methods, later known as neology, were also developed during this period. It is also interesting to note that during this period the "problem" of synonymy was recognised, but even its purpose for effective communication, particularly through the vernacular to reach a broader public, was also understood.

The contributions to terminological reflection and practice that can be credited to the Renaissance period, important as they are, are not covered in this book, as they are the subject of the 2024 issue of *Le français préclassique*, by Philippe Selosse (ed.) (2024). However, exchanges with the latter have shed some light on this question. The Renaissance witnessed a substantial increase in scientific and technical knowledge in various disciplines, such as mathematics, anatomy, philosophy and the natural sciences, accompanied by a desire to transmit this knowledge to a wider public. The recognition of the importance of popular vernaculars for disseminating knowledge manifested through the emergence and documentation of terms in the vernaculars alongside their existing classical (Greek or Latin) counterparts. The new printing medium allowed "terminologists" of the time — scholars, domain experts, interested individuals — to present and discuss terms in the form of nomenclatures, glossaries, and annotated documents of various kinds. It was also common practice to use texts, when available, as source material to identify terms, meanings, and usage, foreshadowing modern corpus-based approaches. At the same time, phenomena such as polysemy, synonymy, and homonymy were recognised, documented, and reflected upon. This period was also one of intense lexicographic production, and lexicography began to acquire the status of a distinct discipline, complete with its own "terminology." In the Romance languages, however, such as French (see Selosse 2024), most term creation still occurred in Latin — so that new terms in the vernacular tended to be translations or transpositions from Latin and Greek.

Thought on logic and grammar over the 17th century paved the way for what would become the principles of terminology practice in the 20th. The *Port-Royal Logic* of 1662 drew notably on Descartes for metaphysics and set out the principles for the two fundamental dimensions of the terminological definition, namely intension (the category of the concept, and the set of semantic features that distinguish it from related concepts) and extension (those entities that instantiate the concept) (Depecker 2023:178). In researching the origins of terminological thought, care must be taken to identify disciplines, such as philosophy, which explore the ways scientists view the world.

The 17th and 18th centuries saw the emergence of so-called universal dictionaries, starting, for French, with Furetière's dictionary of 1690, described by Alain

Rey (1979: 4) as a veritable terminological resource,[2] in that it focussed on concepts which are apprehended through words. Specialised lexicography played an important part in the establishment of new domains of science and what would later be known as technology, as M. van der Yeught (2012) has pointed out. The terminology that permeated these dictionaries is thus an important instrument in the advancement of science and specialised practice in general. This and other specialised dictionaries led up to the *Encyclopédie* (1752–1772) by Diderot and d'Alembert, which embodied much terminological thought and sketched out the specificity of language for special purposes, as Maria Teresa Zanola explains in Chapter 3. She outlines the important conceptual shift, through advancements in encyclopaedism, from "nomenclature" to "terminology" that occurred during this period. This leads to her well-substantiated claim that terminology as a distinct product and practice came of age with Linnaeus' nomenclature of botany and especially in Lavoisier's naming of chemical concepts. Monoreferentiality and univocity became guiding principles for achieving systematicity in terminographic works of this period. The use of images to represent concepts also became popular, foreshadowing the semiotic dimension of terminology advocated by the philosopher C.S. Peirce in the late 1800s (see Chapter 5). The similarity between the chemist Guyton de Morveau's criteria for naming (precision, transparency, systematicity, etc.) and the term quality criteria commonly recognised today, is uncanny. Challenges of terminology implantation, and the role of society at large in its success, were also recognised.

The coming together of much research into the nature of terminology and of terminologies which characterised the 18th century did not lead to a significant concerted study of terms as such in the 19th. There was considerable work done of a terminological nature, but it was dispersed, as are modern-day investigations into the status of terminology at the present time. The English polymath William Whewell is generally credited with defining terminology in a form recognisable today, drawing on the scientific nomenclatures already mentioned, as Beatrice Ragazzini illustrates in Chapter 4. Ragazzini takes stock of 19th century thought on terminology and investigates issues of naming, defining and describing various cloud formations — a subject of great interest at the time — in a way that lent itself to systematic classification.

The philosophical approach to terminology was taken up by such thinkers as Charles Sanders Peirce, whose logico-semiotic approach is exposed in Chapter 5 by Claudia Stancati. Studying the terminology of philosophy, Peirce placed what he called "ethics" in the highest regard: the correct, conscious, and shared use of

---

2. Furetière's practice was already terminological and not just lexicographical, since his viewpoint was extra-linguistic and his ambition universalist (Rey 1979: 4).

terms, thus bridging the semantic, cognitive, and social dimensions, and antici-
pating aspects of modern socioterminology.

Specialised dictionaries, already important vectors of terminological practice
from the Enlightenment on, took on particular significance from the end of the
19th century with the creation of Captain Paasch's nautical dictionary, which foreshadows in practice many of the principles put forward in a more theoretical form
by Wüster. Marc van Campenhoudt, in Chapter 6, explains how this frequently
reedited dictionary includes visual representations of concepts, using illustrations embodying semantic distinctions which would be further developed much
later, including meronymic relations. With "conceptual equivalence" the driving
principle, Paasch's multilingual entries adopted a concept-oriented structure that
would later become the standard for terminological resources. Paasch was not the
only specialist lexicographer of his time to adopt a concept-oriented approach:
the use of functional illustrations characterised much of the early 20th century
work, notably in the hands of the leading lexicographer of technical dictionaries,
Alfred Schlomann (Schlomann Lowe and Wright 2006), to whom Wüster would
acknowledge a debt. As with Paasch, Schlomann's work was characterised by a
strictly onomasiological approach and assiduous use of illustrations, though without the depth of the marine dictionary's conceptual relations.

Developments in theory and methodology

Antia et al. (2005) see three periods in the efforts towards establishing terminology as a discipline. The first goes back to the *Wirtschaftslinguistik* movement or
the linguistics of economics (1920s and 30s), a forerunner to Language for Special Purposes (LSP) (Picht 1998), having its roots in the newly founded business
schools of Central Europe. These schools were primarily practice-oriented, but
backed by research from both the Prague linguists (see Kováříková, Chapter 9)
and Russian LSP research (Orel, Chapter 10). The second period ran from 1970
to 1990, with a strong rapprochement with linguistics, LSP, professional communication, text linguistics and pragmatics. The third period ran from the 1990s on,
where terminology is seen as a necessary component of technical translation and
began to make its entry into companies as an enabler of global marketing. As will
be seen, however, much of the contemporary development of terminology has
taken place outside the scope of translation.

To remain with the confines of a single volume, the editors of this book, with
its focus on disciplinary establishment, aimed to trace the history of terminology up to the 20th century, leaving for another publishing opportunity the significant contributions of megacorpora, artificial intelligence, and other modern

approaches to further shaping the discipline. However, in many chapters, this cut-off period was blurred, attesting to the challenges of documenting many differing situations where terminology has been theorised.

The major figure of terminology theory and most keen advocate of its status as a discipline was Eugen Wüster. Much has been written about his role in founding terminology and how he laid down the basic principles of what became known as the Vienna School of Terminology, with both supporters and opponents assessing the validity of his theoretical stance (see Myking 2001). There has been an upsurge in interest in Wüster's role in founding a theory of terminology, as evidenced not only by the chapters presented here and a pioneering thesis on the reception of Wüster's theories (Campo 2012) but also in a major reappraisal edited by Candel, Samain and Savatovsky (2022), the first two chapters of Faber and L'Homme (eds.) (2022) and research carried out in Trojar's thesis (2017).

Two chapters in the present volume highlight hitherto overlooked aspects of Wüster's thought concerning terminology. The first is Chapter 7, a study by Natascia Leonardi that focuses on the role artificial languages have played in the conceptualisation of terminology and more recently in artificial intelligence. The author brings out various parallels that exist between creating new and motivated terms and inventing a whole new language, which Wüster fully recognised. This chapter brings into focus the research carried out recently on this connection and its relation to the conception of Applied Linguistics as it was perceived between the wars.

Mitja Trojar, in Chapter 8, continues his previous work (Trojar 2017) by delving into Wüster's own writings and putting them into perspective with the history of ideas and linguistic theory. Focus is placed on Wüster's conception of linguistics in general and its relations with terminology. This chapter finishes with an analysis of one of the most controversial parts of terminological theory: the nature of the concept.

Apart from the so-called Vienna school of Terminology, two other schools stand out in the theoretical development of terminology which took shape after the First World War, namely as envisaged by the Prague School of Linguistics and the Soviet School of Terminology Science.

The Prague School was closely allied with structuralist linguistics characterised by the work of Trubetzkoy and his colleagues. Dominika Kováříková in Chapter 6 takes up the challenge of documenting this important link between general linguistics and terminology. The work of the Prague linguists demonstrates how the functional approach applied to language study in general was transferred to language for special purposes. This was an important step in addressing the need to equip the Czech language for the purposes of expressing science and technology, a primary function of terminology, found in other contexts, in particular that of the newly formed Soviet Union, where the focus was on multilingualism. The approach characterised by the Prague school was also an example of the perception of linguistics embracing topics such as the functions of language. This chapter brings together much work from the years between the wars, which have been previously scattered across publications written in languages that are not accessible to a global readership.

In her survey of terminology in the Soviet Union and later in Russia, Tatiana Orel in Chapter 10 distinguishes four main periods starting from the beginning of the 20th century. All are marked by a resolutely transdisciplinary approach based on linguistics, logic and philosophy, extending to mathematics and classification and, finally, encompassing different subject-matter disciplines. The leading figures of the first period were Dimitrij Lotte and Sergej Čaplygin, who, like Wüster, combined research on the nature of technical terminology with practice that was especially linked with standardisation. Contrary to what was to become the Vienna School of Terminology under the impetus of Wüster however, in both the Prague and Soviet schools terminology as a theory was considered an integral part of linguistics and not to be treated as something apart. The chapter also presents more recent developments in Russian terminology studies, in particular cognitive onomasiological modelling, which now dominates modern thinking.

Anne Condamines, Valérie Delavigne, François Gaudin and Aurélie Picton focus in Chapter 11 on two major developments in terminology theory that run contrary to Wüsterian principles: socioterminology and textual terminology. These two orientations have marked the way in which terminology has been envisaged not only in France, but also in other countries since the end of the 20th century. The authors stress the necessity of appraising terminology in its social context, the main objective of what has become a clearly defined area of study, that of *socioterminology* (Humbley 2018). They also chart the shift from onomasiological to predominantly semasiological analysis, which relies on the availability of large specialised corpora in machine-readable formats exploited by linguists in close collaboration with experts in the form of *textual terminology*. They explain how the use of language technology makes it possible to extract knowledge from texts using appropriate linguistic analysis.

These new interdisciplinary ways of approaching terminology led to the founding in 1993 of the Terminology and Artificial Intelligence network (TIA), which marked the involvement of terminologists in knowledge management and engineering. This collaboration in fact goes back to the field of documentation and the foundation in 1974 of the *International Classification* (now *Knowledge Organisation*) with the participation of Wüster, edited for 23 years by Ingetraut Dahlberg (Hjørland 2023). This orientation saw the founding in Germany in 1987 of the Terminology and Knowledge Engineering group (TKE: see Chapter 22) and continued, again in France, with Terminology and Ontology (TOTh), a series of conferences, workshops, and training schools founded by Christophe Roche. After a period of collaboration, terminology and knowledge engineering seem however to be going their separate ways, the TIA and TKE having both been dissolved, at least for the moment, thereby jeopardising this line of research into an important dimension of terminology. Hjørland (2023) argues that it is essential for terminology to address such epistemological questions if it is to advance in its theory.

One large chapter covers the essentials of terminological activity in the most active north American country in this connection, namely Canada. It was the French Canadians' *vif désir de durer* (de Villers 2005) which prompted massive efforts in terminology work so that the French-speaking community, especially, but not exclusively in Québec, could function linguistically in all sectors of society and in particular in employment. Aline Francoeur's Chapter 12 explores this important laboratory of language planning (known as *aménagement linguistique*). Efforts to ensure the use of French as the language of industry and public life throughout Québec were paralleled by terminology development at the federal level to guarantee the equal status of both French and English. To achieve these aims, Canada has actively engaged in the development of terminology resources, standards, and policies, as well as terminographic methods, particularly in neology. As Francoeur demonstrates, Canada, often in particular the province of Québec, can proudly claim a number of achievements: first in the world to offer a Master's degree in terminology (leading to the creation of PhD degrees), first to tackle the challenge of bridging common and civil law terminology, and first to coin the term *socioterminology* to reflect the unique social perspective of its methods. Two of the largest termbases in the world herald from Canada: TERMIUM, initially developed by the University of Montreal (as is reflected in the name) and now the nation's termbase, and the Grand dictionnaire terminologique of the Office québécois de la langue française. Regarding terminology theory, aside from Canada's substantial scholarly contributions to neology, mention must be made of Ingrid Meyer's knowledge-based approach to terminology and the Lexico-Semantic Theory developed by researchers at the Université de Montréal, illustrated by Marie-Claude L'Homme's work. These and other important Canadian contributions to terminology are acknowledged in passing here, as they were regrettably excluded from the chapter due to both space constraints and the desire to remain within the historical period mentioned earlier.

Spain is another country where terminological activity has been intense since the return of democracy, initially spurred on by the needs of terminology development for Catalan in the context of domain recuperation. In Chapter 13, Amparo Alcina highlights language planning activities, especially for Catalan, Basque and

Galician, but also takes stock of the considerable amount of research carried out in higher education. Institutional terminology bodies, both for Spanish and the other languages of Spain, have long been active in producing term resources and engaging in research. Indeed, Alcina highlights the theoretical contribution made by three linguists who have shaped terminology in Spain and beyond: Amelia de Irazazábal, María Teresa Cabré and Pamela Faber, all of whom have developed major research directions recognised the world over.

As an example of terminology activities in a Latin American country, Maria Pozzi describes developments in terminological theory and methodology in Mexico, emphasising efforts towards cooperation with different organisations practising terminology in various forms. Modern developments were initiated by three major projects going back to the 1970s: the dictionary of Mexican Spanish based on a vast corpus (the first linguistic corpus in Spanish), the creation of specialised translators' courses, and cooperation with European and Canadian terminology initiatives, in particular Eurodicautom (now IATE). The criteria to determine what terminology should be incorporated into a large language dictionary are discussed in detail here in the light of the Mexican experience.

Networking in terminology is by no means a Mexican preserve, but it is noteworthy that Spanish-speaking terminologists have been particularly active in international groupings. RITERM (Red Iberoamericana de Terminología) was founded in 1988 in Caracas and has been active in organising symposia in Spanish, Portuguese and Catalan. Since 2005 it has edited the biannual journal *Debate Terminólogico*. REALITER, which includes all the official Latin-based languages, was founded in Paris in 1993 as a "commission panlatine de terminologie."

Terminology cooperation and collaboration also has a regional dimension, illustrated in various forms throughout the present volume. One of the most successful is represented here by the Nordic countries. The very active Nordterm group has brought them all together, as Lotte Weilgaard Christensen and her colleagues report in Chapter 15. The Scandinavian experience has been both national and transnational: Danish terminology was for long linked to the two major business schools *(handelshøjskoler)* in Copenhagen and Aarhus, in the former where Heribert Picht (1998) in particular undertook to extend Wüster's theories to the terminology of economics, commerce, and law. It was also in Denmark where the "war" between lexicography and terminology broke out and was fought with vehemence for several decades, conveniently opening up options for specialised communication (see Bergenholtz, Kaufmann (2017)). Other Scandinavian countries pursued active national terminology policies, such as Norway with the oil industry.

Albina Auksoriūtė in Chapter 16 examines some important aspects that have been skimmed over in the past. Indeed, the years between the wars were marked by concern about terminological issues and considerable exchange took place, especially between Wüster and Soviet linguists, but certain important thinkers publishing in national languages went unnoticed on the international stage. This turns out to be very much the case for Stasys Šalkauskis, as Auksoriūtė makes clear here. Šalkauskis, like Peirce, was a philosopher and public educator who published a major dictionary of philosophy in Lithuanian as well as a dictionary of pedagogy, formulating term creation guidelines for the newly independent nation. He emphasised the close relationship between philosophy and linguistics, terminology being firmly attached to the latter.

Indeed, the first great success story of terminology, thanks to Wüster's tenacity, was in the field of standardisation, starting from ISA in the 1930s, reviewed up to the present day in Christian Galinski's Chapter 17. The forerunners of standardisation can be traced back to Antiquity, through the nomenclatures of the Enlightenment (see Chapter 3), but it was through the development of technology that terminology came into its own, with the founding of institutions such as ISO, the present-day successor to ISA and IEC, the International Electrotechnical Commission, which first met as early as 1906. Wüster was also the moving force behind the creation of the International Information Centre for Terminology, Infoterm, which played a key role in the terminological aspects of standardisation. The main thrust of Galinski's contribution is focused on terminology development on the international stage since 1945 and the efforts made to harmonise terminological standards in particular.

A theory of *Cultural Terminology* has been elaborated over a long period by Marcel Diki-Kidiri, who explains in his chapter why transferring terminology directly to languages with different histories and cultural references is largely a fruitless exercise and that the motivation for term creation is to be sought in each language's cultural heritage. This approach is theorised in the form of a perception grid consisting of concepts already integrated in the culture through which new realities can be apprehended, and which is not without recalling the use of metaphor in Latin, as illustrated in the first chapter.

Terminology the world over

It becomes obvious on reading the chapters on terminology development of the past centuries that although terminology had been a largely transnational preoccupation, during the 20th century distinctive national trends emerged. These tendencies are reviewed in the third section of this book, *Terminology the World Over*.

It has not proven possible to cover all countries and all branches of terminology in this initial survey, so some regrettably brief mention will be made here of important achievements which could not be included in the chapters of this section. Neither the United Kingdom as a whole (Chapter 31 covers Wales) nor the United States of America could be covered in spite of the important role that both have played in the history of the discipline.[3] For the former, mention should be made of two centres of higher education where terminology made significant progress. One was UMIST (University of Manchester Institute of Science and Technology), where Juan Carlos Sager was a professor until 1995. One of the most important scholars of "terminology science" (a denomination he abominated!), he worked first on language for special purposes (Sager, Dungworth and McDonald 1980) before publishing one of the most-quoted handbooks of terminology (Sager 1990). This publication paved the way for significant research, taking the form of books, articles and conferences, an important step, paradoxically, towards disciplinary status. He was also instrumental in the founding of the journal *Terminology*, and his inaugural article in the first issue focused on terminology in the history of knowledge representation. A few other British universities offered terminology courses, in particular the University of Surrey, where Khurshid Ahmad accomplished pioneering work in computerised terminology and Margaret Rogers in terminology for translation purposes. Terminology in Ireland should also have been rated a mention, both from the point of view of terminology work carried out in Gaelic, in particular in the form of a national termbank, and from the perspective of courses in higher education such as at Dublin City University.

In the United States leading figures include Sue Ellen Wright, particularly though not exclusively in the field of standardisation, and co-editor with Vienna-based Gerhard Budin (1997, 2001) of a major terminology management handbook, and Alan Melby, a pioneer in computer applications for translation, but more importantly for the theme of this book, the main impetus behind exchange formats such as MARTIF and TBX. Wright was also instrumental in establishing terminology courses and graduate research at Kent State University.

One other country notable for its absence in this collective work is Belgium, and regrettably so since terminology work there has a long history of innovative practice. As from the 1970s terminology was part of translators' training (a Belgian speciality!) in this trilingual country, first at the Institut Marie-Haps, founded in 1978 (Centre de terminologie de Bruxelles) and a little later at the Institut supérieur des traducteurs et interprètes (TERMISTI). The former not only produced the first large contingents of well-formed translator-terminologists but also fostered various forms of research, organising, for example, the first international

---

3. A valuable account of theoretical issues in terminology as they emerged in the United Kingdom and the United States of America can be found in Rogers and Wright (2006).

conference on diachronic terminology (de Schaetzen 1989). Moving into the 21st century, Schools of Translation were incorporated into universities and terminology work took on an increasingly theoretical dimension, with such linguists as Rita Temmerman of the Free University of Brussels, who struck a chord with practicing terminologists by caracterising terms as "units of understanding" and more generally in advocating a "socio-cognitive" approach. Her colleagues at the KU Leuven university, Frieda Steurs and Hendrik Kockaert, are well-known for their international outreach, the former as founder of NL-TERM, the Dutch-language terminology association and head of research in the Dutch-language institute, the latter in Qatar.

Rima Baraké and Andree Affeich describe the complex history and fabric of Arabic terminology since the end of the 19th century, starting with early developments in Egypt and Syria and continuing to the present across the 22 countries that comprise the vast Arab world. They explain the process of Arabisation, whereby attempts are made to increase the use of Arabic in various fields and terms are created for new concepts through processes such as morphological adaptation and transdisciplinary borrowing. Various academies and institutions are involved (see also Alsulaiman and Allaithy (eds), 2019), but due to decentralisation, the continued dominance of foreign languages in education, and the co-existence of a wide variety of Arabic dialects across a vast territory, among other factors, widespread implantation of uniform terminology has not been fully achieved. Terminological inflation (the uncontrolled proliferation of synonyms) is also said to be impeding communication, and the reasons why it is occurring are carefully analysed. The experience gained from these challenges will no doubt strengthen the Arabisation movement in the future.

One of the major fields of terminology cooperation is ideally illustrated by the activities of the European Union: here, not only is there major terminology collaboration between the national languages of all the member states, but also a unified treatment of terminology between the numerous European institutions, brought together in IATE (InterAgency Terminology Exchange) and described in Annamaria Fotos and her colleagues' Chapter 20. As has already been seen, standardisation is not only one of terminology's chief fields of action; it is one where international cooperation is key.

France has already been mentioned for pioneering activities in terminology, both practical and theoretical, from the Middle Ages on. By the middle of the 20th century a convergence of historical studies of specialised vocabulary had been established in Paris, paving the way for research in diachronic terminology. Among the works that resulted from this convergence mention is made of Matoré (1953: vocabulary of 19th century fashion), Quemada (1955: medical terminology), Wexler (1955: railway terminology) and Guilbert (1965, 1967: aeronautical and astronomical terminology). These scholars were influenced by sociological studies, which would later evolve into socioterminology (see Chapter 11). Breaking with the primarily lexicological approach of these specialised vocabularies, some academics with a translation background, such as Daniel Gouadec, introduced terminology courses to universities (Gouadec 1990) and organised groundbreaking training sessions (universités d'automne). By the 21st century terminology was primarily taught in conjunction with specialised translation. Parallel to these efforts, institutional terminology has been developed by various official bodies, whose aims and methods are analysed by Danielle Candel in Chapter 21. It should be pointed out that, as in Spain, there has been considerable overlap between academic and institutional terminology: for example, Bernard Cerquiglini and Loïc Depecker, former délégués généraux à la langue française, are both university professors of linguistics.

Europe has been the scene of much terminological activity and nowhere more so than in the German-speaking countries. Germany and Switzerland have a chapter each and Austria rates more than a passing mention in those chapters devoted to aspects of Wüster's work, but attention should be drawn to the role this country played in terminology on the global stage. The Austrian Standards Institute (ÖN, more recently ASI) for years hosted Infoterm, which held the secretariat of the terminology committee of ISO (TC37) from 1971 to 2020.[4] The University of Vienna has acted as custodian for the Wüster archives since 1996. The university's Translator-Interpreter Institute offers courses in terminology. Its director of many years, Gerhard Budin, is a leading scholar in the theory of terminology.

Klaus-Dirk Schmitz's account of terminology activities in Germany in Chapter 22 starts off by setting the stage in German-speaking countries between the wars with an emphasis on standardisation and on Eugen Wüster's contributions to both theoretical and practical terminology. His unique contribution, however, is to provide an insider's view of terminology networking from the "roaring 80s" onwards, as desktop computers, software localisation, markup languages, and other innovative developments drove changes, as well as creating opportunities for terminologists. As elsewhere, technical translation was a major sector for which terminology was deemed indispensable, but it was not the only critical factor: knowledge engineering also emerged as a particularly important application. The exceptionally active terminology associations and networks as well as training programs in German-speaking countries are given a thorough treatment in this chapter.

Greek contributions to terminology can be traced back to the Ancient World, but it was unfortunately not possible to include a chapter on the philosophical

---

4. From 2005 to 2019 the secretariat role was shared with the Standardization Administration of China (SAC) through a "twinning" arrangement. It was fully assumed by the SAC in 2020.

foundations of terminological thought and practice. Kostas Valeontis and his colleagues in Chapter 23 summarise the contribution that Ancient Greece made to the scientific and technical terminology of European languages. They then proceed to survey the creation of scientific terminology institutes starting in the 1920s, the methods used to create modern terminology, and the place that terminology took in the production of different types of dictionaries. Particular attention is paid to one of terminology's main applications, that of standardisation, though much still remains to be done.

Hungarian is the focus of Chapter 24 in which Ágota Fóris gives a full account of terminology development, especially in relation to language reform. As is well known, Hungary pursued a policy of linguistic autonomy through the 19th century, with repercussions for its efforts to develop its terminology. The major part of this chapter, however, is devoted to the history of Hungarian terminology over the 20th century. It was a time of great political upheaval, which fortunately did not prevent theoretical work — inspired by both Viennese and Soviet principles. Specialised dictionaries including up-to-date terminology have been produced, though specialised corpora tend to be less developed. From the late 20th century on, courses in terminology have been offered in universities.

Indonesia is the only representative of Asian languages that could be included,[5] but the efforts aimed at modernising its terminology have often been presented as one of language planning's success stories. In Chapter 25, Jérôme Samuel shows that the success is, however, relative, often achieved in spite of, rather than thanks to, official efforts.

Italy was perhaps slower off the mark in terminology work than Germany or France, but the association Ass.I.Term (Associazione Italiana per la Terminologia) has been active over the last thirty years, as Claudio Grimaldi (who has chaired the association since October 2023), recounts in Chapter 26. The balance in practical, vocational terminology and theoretical research has been achieved since universities have also been active in both practical aspects in LSP and in research, developing, among other aspects, a burgeoning interest in diachronic terminology.

The Macedonian language achieved official status at the end of the second world war, and in Chapter 27, Nikolche Mickoski gives credit to Blazhe Koneski, a leading linguist, for its codification. As is the case for the languages in other recently independent states, the modernisation of Macedonian has entailed the development of specialised vocabulary and terminology in general. One technique deployed to reduce the flood of foreign words to designate new concepts has been

---

5. It is of great regret that terminology in China and Japan could not be included. For Chinese, this is partly compensated by a special issue of the journal: *Revue d'aménagement linguistique* coordinated by Yang (2003).

the use of the rich stock of terms from folklore, an approach that mirrors that of Cultural Terminology described by Diki-Kidiri. Over 50 years ago, a commission also established a corpus-based process for terminology work complemented with semantic clustering along the lines of the seminal work by the Soviet terminologist, Lotte. Thus Macedonia adopted early on a hybrid of what are known today as the classical and text-based approaches. Additionally, even though Macedonia has been concerned with language planning, many synonyms have been tolerated in recognition of their "functional" role, a position now also largely recognised.

Slovak terminology thought and work is covered in Chapter 28 by Jana Levická and Miroslav Zumrík, who chart the course of terminology development, first before the creation of the state of Czechoslovakia, when both Czech and Slovak were grappling with their efforts to become official, national languages, then within the confines of the newly-formed state, when the overarching aim was bringing the terminology of the two language communities ever closer together. Since independence in 1993, the relations between these two closely related but autonomous languages have led to a dynamic situation that is analysed with examples of terminology development. The role of the linguist Ján Horecký in defining terminology as part of linguistics — as was the case for the Prague school — and in situating Slovak terminology in relation to Czech, is carefully analysed here.

In the only chapter (29) devoted to a particular African country,[6] the reader will discover how terminology has evolved in multilingual South Africa. Mariëtta Alberts addresses the conundrum of actively promoting all eleven official languages while continuing to develop English and Afrikaans terminologies at the same time. The chapter demonstrates how important terminology is in implementing language policy and underlines its interdependence: terminology work is never carried out in isolation of fieldwork. Issues of terminology training and natural language processing are also discussed.

Switzerland shares with France, but even more with Germany, many features of the way terminology work is organised especially in institutional settings, both public and private, national and international, as Bruno de Bessé, Aurélie Picton and Donatella Pulitano suggest in Chapter 30. The focus of this chapter is on the University of Geneva's terminology programme, examined from a didactic point of view, but also in relation to research and to professional organisation and prac-

---

6. For a more general perspective on African terminology, see the writings of Diki-Kidiri (Chapter 18) listed in this chapter, as well as those of Bassey E. Antia, in particular Antia (2000) and Antia and Kamai (2006), highlighting its importance in education. Mention should also be made of Messaoudi's (2023) studies in North Africa of functioning technolects and grassroots terminology.

tice in both public and private bodies. The link with terminological institutions outside Switzerland has also proven extremely fruitful.

The final chapter (31), though not the least, is devoted to terminology in Wales, focussing on one of Europe's minority languages, but also one of the more resilient, where terminology activism may well be a game-changer. Delyth Prys and her colleagues explain why, pinpointing the importance of education and political will in developing the terminology necessary to uphold the use of the language both in official life and in society at large.

To conclude, in this section and the former, developments in terminology theory and practice occurring in more than twenty countries have been appraised. That figure alone, coupled with the knowledge that activities and achievements in other areas could not be represented simply for practical reasons, attest to the global recognition of terminology both as a distinct discipline and as a field of study worthy of theoretical and methodological reflection.

Summing up

It is not surprising that this first effort to write the history of terminology as a practice and especially as an emerging discipline has brought out clearly contrasting features, some of which are foreseeable, others less so. Readers for example may notice slight variance among scholars in the use of key terms such as *univocity*, *ambiguity*, and *harmonisation*. These are the expected "growing pains" of an emerging discipline.

One aspect at the heart of the project has been to map out the timeline of the many attempts to account for what terminology is, and to analyse the outcome of those efforts. It is argued here that thought on terminology goes back much farther than had generally been acknowledged and notably before the word *terminology* or its equivalents were even first used. However, the points of reference used in the past are not those used in the present, which poses an epistemological challenge: to grasp thought on the relations between specialised knowledge and the language that expresses it as it related to the society of the time, while still retaining relevance to the way this relationship is understood today. The authors of the initial chapters use the tools of the history of science and culture to reveal to a modern-day readership the roles terms played in societies of the past.

In spite of this epistemological challenge, the writings assembled in this book amply demonstrate that the principles, methods, and theories of terminology as a discipline and as a practice have evolved over centuries through the accumulated contributions of thinkers and scholars the world over.

A second discovery has been the different conceptions that exist about what exactly terminology *is*. The study of the way terminology — both as elements of language and as a collection of practices aimed to understand, develop, and manage those elements — evolved in various countries brings to light at least one profound question: is terminology part of linguistics, the study of a subset of the lexicon or is it essentially extralinguistic, a method for apprehending knowledge though different codes, including language? These two broad conceptions of terminology run parallel, with the experts involved often seemingly unaware of or unconcerned by this dichotomy.

A third realisation is that terminology institutionally seems to be following a trajectory very similar to that of its sister disciplines — translation studies and lexicography — with which it has overlapping interests. From this perspective, it will be interesting to see how these three related disciplines gain credibility in higher education and in the language industry as a whole, or whether, on the contrary, they wither away through the effects of artificial intelligence or the like. However, terminology has one advantage over the other two — the excellent repurposability of terminology data as a digital resource. Terminology resources are already extensively used in modern natural language processing (NLP) applications and this trend is likely to continue. And all of a sudden, the artificial intelligence (AI) community has come to the realisation that semantically-structured knowledge representations (knowledge graphs, ontologies, taxonomies, semantic networks, etc.), when used alongside large language models (LLMs), can take AI to new unprecedented levels of performance and quality. What few of these new stakeholders realise, however, is that these types of resources are built according to long-standing principles of terminology as a discipline (such as concept orientation, onomasiological perspective, term autonomy, and the like). Given the growing number of applications, the future of terminology as a discipline is very bright indeed.

A fourth result is the realisation that terminology projects sometimes succeed, while others fail to live up to expectations. There are indeed shining examples of terminology playing a key role, as it did in restoring French as the language of workplace in Québec or in upholding multilingualism in Europe. Other less conclusive cases exist, such as Indonesia, where a certain level of terminological development has been achieved, in spite of the lack of support from official bodies. Likewise Arabic language institutions have faced near insurmountable challenges to bringing together the terminology of the many countries of the Arab world.

The fifth evidence which has emerged could be a gradual correction of gender balance in terminology studies. It is probably correct to speak of the founding fathers of terminology, as those close to Wüster and the Soviet school were of a largely male preserve. In later times, however, the change has been striking. For

Spain, for example, the founders of terminology are (or were) all women. Of the 63 authors in this book, 43 are women. Many of the leading thinkers of the more modern theories of terminology are also women, e.g. Condamines, Cabré, Faber, L'Homme, Pearson, Temmerman, and Slodzian, to name just a few.

The sixth outcome — which is possibly the most easily predictable — is that many questions remain and more research needs to be done. This may be the first book on the history of terminology. It certainly will not be the last.

References

Alsulaiman, Abied and Ahmed Allaithy (eds). 2019. *Handbook of Terminology, Volume 2. Terminology in the Arab world.* John Benjamins.

Antia, Bassey E. 2000. *Terminology and language planning.* Amsterdam: John Benjamins.

Antia, Bassey E. 2001. "Metadiscourse in Terminology: Thesis, Antithesis, Synthesis." *Terminology Science and Research*, 12/1–2: 65–84.

Antia, Bassey E, Gerhard Budin, Heribert Picht, Margaret Rogers, Sue Ellen Wright, and Klaus-Dirk Schmitz. 2005. "Shaping translation: A view from terminology research." *Meta* 5/4.

Antia, Bassey E. and Richard Kamai. 2006. "African issues in terminology. An Educational Perspective." In *Modern Approaches to Terminology*: 135–152.

Bergenholtz, Henning, and Uwe Kaufmann. 2017. "Terminography and Lexicography. A Critical Survey of Dictionaries from a Single Specialised Field." *Hermes* 10/18:91–125.

Campo, Angela. 2012. *The reception of Eugen Wüster's work and the development of terminology.* Thesis. Université de Montréal.

Candel, Danielle. 2022. "General principles of Wüster's General Theory of Terminology." In *Theoretical perspectives on Terminology*, ed. by Pamela Faber, and Marie-Claude L'Homme, 37–60. Amsterdam: John Benjamins.

Candel, Danielle, Didier Samain, and Dan Savatovsky (eds). 2022. *Eugen Wüster et la terminologie de l'école de Vienne.* Paris: SHESL.

Dankova, Klara. 2023. *Les fibres textiles entre synchronie et diachronie : études terminologiques.* Bern: Peter Lang.

de Schaetzen, Caroline (ed). 1989. *La terminologie diachronique.* Actes du colloque organisé à Bruxelles les 25 et 26 mars 1988. Paris : Conseil international de la langue française (CILF) et Ministère de la communauté française de Belgique.

de Villers, Marie-Éva. 2005. *Le Vif désir de durer. Illustration de la norme réelle du français québécois.* Montréal: Québec Amérique.

Delisle, Jean. 2008. *La terminologie au Canada. Histoire d'une profession.* Montréal: Linguatec.

Depecker, Loïc. 2023. "Terminologie : de la logique avant toute chose. L'exemple du terme de *catastrophe naturelle* dans le domaine des assurances." In *Alain Rey. Lumières sur la langue*, ed. by François Gaudin, 177–195. Paris: Champion.

Faber, Pamela, and Marie-Claude L'Homme (eds.). 2022. *Theoretical perspectives on Terminology.* Amsterdam: John Benjamins.

Gouadec, Daniel. 1990. *Terminologie : constitution des données*. Paris: AFNOR.

Gouadec, Daniel. 2005. "Terminologie, traduction et rédaction spécialisées." *Langages* 157: 14–24.

Guilbert, Louis. 1965. *La formation du vocabulaire de l'aviation*. Paris: Larousse.

Guilbert, Louis. 1967. *Le vocabulaire de l'astronautique*. Paris: Larousse.

Hjørland, Birger. 2023. "Terminology." *Knowledge Organization* 50, no. 2: 111–127.

Humbley, John. 2018, "Socioterminology." In *Languages for Special Purposes. An International Handbook*, ed. by John Humbley, Gerhard Budin, and Christer Laurén, 471–490. Berlin: de Gruyter.

Matoré, Georges. 1953. *La méthode en lexicologie*. Paris: Les belles lettres.

Messaoudi, Leila. 2023. *Les technolectes. Des traits identificatoires aux types savants et ordinaires en contexte plurilingue*. Rabat: Imprimerie Rabatnet. Preface: Pierre Lerat.

Myking, Johan. 2001. "Against prescriptivism? The 'socio-critical' challenge to terminology." *Terminology Science & Research*. 12 (1–2): 49–64.

Picht, Heribert. 1998. "Wirtschaftslinguistik: ein historischer Überblick." In *Fachsprachen/ Languages for Special Purposes*, ed. by L. Hoffmann, H. Kalverkämper, and H.E. Wiegand. Berlin: de Gruyter.

Quemada, Bernard. 1953. *Introduction à l'étude du vocabulaire médical (1600–1710)*. Paris: Didier.

Rey, Alain. 1979. "La Terminologie : noms et notions." *Que sais-je ?* n 1780.

Rogers, Margaret, and Sue Ellen Wright. 2006. "Approaches to terminological theories: the Anglo-Saxon approach." In Picht (ed.), *Modern Approaches to Terminological Theories and Applications*. Linguistic Insights, v. 36. 107–134. New York: Peter Lang.

Sager, Juan Carlos. 1990. *A Practical Course in Terminology Processing*. Amsterdam: John Benjamins.

Sager, Juan Carlos, David Dungworth, and Peter McDonald. 1980. *English special languages: principles and practice in science and technology*. Wiesbaden: Brandstetter.

Schlomann Lowe, Elisabeth, and Sue Ellen Wright. 2006. "The Life and Works of Alfred Schlomann: Terminology Theory and Globalization." In *Modern Approaches to Terminological Theories and Applications*, 153–161. New York: Peter Lang.

Selosse, Philippe. 2024. "Conclusion : de quelques particularités « terminologiques » des vocabulaires étudiés." In *Le français préclassique*, 26, 97–105. Paris: Honoré Champion.

Selosse, Philippe (ed). 2024. "La terminologie à la Renaissance." In *Le français préclassique*, 26. Paris: Honoré Champion.

Trojar, Mitja. 2017. "Wüster's view of terminology." *Slowenische Zeitschrift für linguistische Studien* 11: 55–84.

Van der Yeught, Michel. 2012. *L'anglais de la bourse et de la finance*. Paris: Ophrys.

Wexler, Peter. 1955. *La formation du vocabulaire des chemins de fer en France (1778–1842)*. Geneva: Droz.

Wright, Sue Ellen, and Gerhard Budin (eds). 1997, 2001. *Handbook of terminology management*. Vols. 1 & 2. Amsterdam: John Benjamins.

Wüster, Eugen. [1931] 1970. *Internationale Sprachnormung in der Technik besonders in der Elektrotechnik (Die nationale Sprachnormung und ihre Verallgemeinerung)*. Bonn: H. Bouvier und Co Verlag.

Wüster, Eugen. 1974. „Die allgemeine Terminologielehre — ein Grenzgebiet zwischen Sprachwissenschaft, Logik, Ontologie, Informatik und den Sachwissenschaften." *Linguistics* 12 (119): 61–106. In: Picht et Laurén (eds). 1993. *Ausgewählte Texte zur Terminologie.* Vienna: Termnet 331–376.

Wüster Eugen [1979] 1985. *Einführung in die allgemeine Terminologielehre und terminologische Lexikographie.* Wien, København: Infoterm, HHK.

Yang, Jian. 2003. *Aménagement linguistique en Chine, Revue d'aménagement linguistique,* 106. OLQF, Québec.

PART 1

Early history

CHAPTER 1

Terminology in Antiquity
An illustration from Latin

Michèle Fruyt
Sorbonne Université

Latin offers a wide range of terminology types, from the most unambiguous,
which are true nomenclatures (for institutions), to the most vague or
approximate (for natural categories), with intermediate zones where
different types cohabit in the same lexicon (as in Christian vocabulary). The
degree of imprecision of the terminologies is related to the nature of the
extralinguistic domain denoted and to its degree of remoteness from human
beings, depending whether it is man-made or belongs to nature. The
various types of terminologies documented in Latin are not specific to
Latin; they are still attested nowadays in various languages. The
terminologies of natural categories, however imprecise, have nevertheless
been re-used since the 18th century in the binomial nomenclatures of
modern sciences such as zoology created by the Swedish scientist Linnaeus.

Keywords: Latin, biunivocal terminologies, approximate terminologies,
Christian vocabulary, natural categories, geology, astronomy, aquatic
animals, scientific denominations, nomenclatures

1. Introduction

Like all languages conveying the knowledge and the entities of a given society, Latin
offers a plurality of types of terminology. Their nature and structure correlate with
the degrees of control and knowledge that the society and the linguistic community
have of the realia or extralinguistic entities. We deal here with the Latin of Antiquity, i.e. as it is represented from the earliest Latin texts in the Archaic period (3rd
century B.C.) through to the 6th and 7th centuries A.D. This corresponds to the
corpus of the important reference dictionary *Thesaurus Linguae Latinae*.

If the *realia* belong to a domain created by humans, they have direct knowledge and control over them. They create precise terminologies adapted to the
extralinguistic entities, organised according to dense lexical networks similar to

https://doi.org/10.1075/tlrp.24.01fru

modern scientific terminologies. But if the *realia* belong to a domain that humans know little about and have no control over, the denominations constitute only simple vocabularies and fuzzy or vague, approximate terminologies.

As a result, there is a range of terminology types in Latin, from true univocal nomenclatures at one extreme to approximate, fuzzy, vague terminologies at the other. Between the two extremes are mixed terminologies of varying degrees of precision, which are subject to the usual consequences of the polysemy of lexemes.

2.   Biunivocal terminologies

Since the names of Roman institutions were created by the Latin speaking community and by the members of Roman society in the same way that the institutions they name were, these names constitute relationships of biunivocity between the lexeme and the entity named.[1] This means that the term T_1 refers to one and the same extra-linguistic entity E_1 and that, conversely, this extra-linguistic entity E_1 is only named by this term T_1. The same situation is valid between E_2 and T_2, E_3 and T_3, etc.

This type of terminology is found in military, political and religious vocabularies, in kinship terminology, in the names of human beings according to their age and sex, in the measurements of weight, volume, length, surface areas, currencies, etc. Since these fields have a very strong tendency to be biunivocal still today, this continuity over time explains why, very often, Latin terminologies are especially important for the understanding of modern terminologies.

2.1   Institutions: Army, magistracy, religion

Military vocabulary is particularly precise for the various units of soldiers and the military hierarchy. The bi-univocity of this terminology is illustrated by Roman military units which are structured according to quantitative criteria, with each denomination corresponding without ambiguity to a specific unit. The organisation of the Roman army evolved over time. During the Roman Republic, for example, *legio* 'legion,' *cohors* 'cohort,' *manipulus* 'manipule' and *centuria* 'centuria' refer to precise quantitative units: a legion of 6,000 men contains 10 cohorts of 600 men, a cohort contains three manipules of 200 men and a manipule contains two centuries of 100 men.

The names of the types of soldiers are also univocally structured in generic and specific terms. Within a generic term are included several specific terms

---

1. The bi-univocity of terms denoting Roman institutions is limited by the chronological factor. It is only valid for a certain time period since institutions evolved over time.

that reflect the hierarchical structure of the named entities. The generic term *miles* plural *milites* 'soldiers, army'[2] includes *pedes* plural *pedites* 'infantrymen', as opposed to *eques* plural *equites* 'cavalry, horsemen'. There are also specific names for the *pedites* when drawn up in battle array: the *hastati* (youngest men, originally carrying an *hasta* 'spear') constitute the first line; the *principes* were the second line (older men), while the *triarii* were veterans (oldest men) functioning as a reserve in the third line. The soldiers of these three lines are all included in the term *legionarii* 'legionary solders'. This kind of hierarchical generic-specific lexical structure is usual in Latin as well as in modern languages, probably reflecting a cognitive approach to the creation of terminology common to all human beings.

In the political and legal domain, this bi-univocity is also observed in the naming of magistrates and the magistracies. For example, the terms *aedilis, quaestor, praetor, consul* refer unambiguously to the succession of functions in a magistrate's career. The terms *censor* and *dictator* refer to specific magistracies. Unlike the military terminology we have just seen, these terms are not organised according to a hierarchical structure with inclusion of specific sub-groups into more generic wider groups. These denominations constitute a series and there is an exclusive relationship between them, since if someone is *consul*, he cannot be at the same time *praetor, quaestor* or *aedilis*.

Senatus 'senate' and *senator* 'senator' also refer to specific concepts and *realia*, but, in this particular case, they display an inclusive structure involving a unit-group relationship since *senator* denotes a member or component unit of the group called *senatus*.

One can also show the univocal character of the denominations for other creations resulting from human activities, such as the religious festivals based on the name of a divinity (*Neptun-alia* 'The festival of Neptune').

The need for univocity also justifies the process of agglutination[3] that we find in denominative binomials, i.e. complex lexical units comprising two words joined together to form a single lexeme and a single denomination: *tribunus plebis* 'tribune of the plebs', *tribunus militum* 'military tribune'. To ensure the precision of its vocabulary, Latin also used its usual morphological processes, suffixation and nominal compounding.[4]

---

2. *Milites* plural may also function as the specific term 'infantry' when opposed to *equites* 'cavalry'.

3. This type of lexical creation by agglutination is well documented in modern languages: e.g. English *social security*, French *sécurité sociale*.

4. E.g. compounding in modern languages: English *kingfisher, twowheelers, multilingualism*. French *un rouge-gorge, les deux-roues, plurilinguisme*.

2.2   Social and kinship terminology

Society also needs an exact terminology for the vocabulary of kinship[5] and for naming human beings according to the relevant criteria of sex and age,[6] since it is these that situate individuals in society and define their social role. In this situation, terminology displays a legal dimension and a normative function.

These denominations are organised within a system where each element has a defined place in relation to the other elements of the system. This kind of lexical organisation is illustrated for human beings but also for domestic animals in the terminologies used by breeders. In the diachronic continuity towards the Romance languages, the referential value of some of these Latin words changed along with the evolution of the terms included in the system. When a term was not usable anymore (usually it became not distinctive enough for phonetic reasons), its void position, one that left a gap in the system, was filled by another term, which therefore underwent a semantico-referential shifting into the unoccupied position.

These changes often occur between specific and generic terms in both directions. For example, over the course of time, the generic Latin term *iumentum* 'beast of burden' became the specific term for 'female horse, mare' (giving French *jument*), since the ancient Latin word for 'mare' *equa*, became phonetically deficient in late Latin and later on disappeared from everyday use. Moreover, the specific term *caballus* 'riding horse or pack-horse' became the generic term for 'horse' in several Romance languages (French *cheval*) replacing Latin *equus* 'horse.' Similarly, the specific term *auunculus* 'maternal uncle' became a generic term for 'uncle' (French *oncle*).

For male human beings Latin provides logically-structured terms where the relevant feature is the progression due to age: *infans* 'baby, the one who does not speak yet,' *puer* 'child,' *adulescens* 'adolescent, young man,' *iuuenis* 'young man,' *senior* 'older, aging man' and *senex* 'old man.' These lexemes as well as the specific terms *uir* 'man, adult male' in contrast with a woman (*mulier, femina*) are included in the generic term *homo* 'human being' of either sex (literally 'inhabitant of the earth' from *humus* 'earth'); in its plural form *homines* means 'humankind, men, people' as opposed to *deus* 'deity, god.'

---

5. Some Latin kinship terms were inherited: *pater* 'father', *mater* 'mother', *frater* 'brother'. But Latin also developed its own vocabulary: e.g. *filius* 'son', *filia* 'daughter', *soror* 'sister'. The dissymmetry between paternal and maternal families (e.g. *auunculus* 'maternal uncle' and *matertera* 'maternal aunt', but *patruus* 'paternal uncle' and *amita* 'maternal aunt') increases the degree of precision.

6. Latin distinguishes between male and female human beings, but the network of age-related terms is denser for men because of their social and political role.

2.3   Measurement

The systems of measurement (weight, volume, length, surface) and units of currency, all creations of humans, also have precise denominations that enable quantification.

In measurements of length, we notice the processes of anthropocentrism and metaphorisation, since the denominations of human body parts are transformed into denominations of units of length: *digitus* 'finger, thumb,' *palmus* 'palm' (a unit of measurement of 4 inches derived from *palma* 'palm of the hand') and *pes* 'foot.' The salient feature retained for these parts of the body is their length.

Another use of metaphor will also be illustrated in relation to the vocabularies of natural categories.

3.   Terminologies and polysemy

In the vocabulary of arts and technology, all fields created by humans, Latin forged its own vocabulary through lexical creations, but the degree of precision is lower here because of the polysemy of the lexemes and their semantic evolution. This vocabulary takes up morphological elements inherited by Latin, as shown in the usual denominations for 'statue' (Duarte 2010): *signum, statua, simulacrum*. These terms have semantic specificities, but their semantic values evolve and enter into a relationship of parasynonymy or partial synonymy with other lexemes.

Signum, a term most often used for a statue, means: sign, concrete representation referring to something else. This etymological meaning explains why in archaic Latin *signum* denotes a particular statue: that of a deity (Dorothée 2002, 2006; Duarte 2010). The god is considered as present through his image which is this *signum* 'sign,' an entity referring to something else. But in classical times *signum* (Cicero) undergoes a semantic extension and can denote a statue in general. Dorothée (2006: 48) concludes that *signum* is characterised by the archiseme /Representation/.

Statua 'standing statue' of a human being (standing, seated, or on horseback by adding *equestris* 'equestrian') is related to *stare* 'to stand upright and still,' and it reflects an Indo-European root with the same meaning.

Simulacrum emphasises resemblance, reproduction and imitation, which comes from its formation, since it means literally: that by means of which one imitates, one reproduces. It is built on *simulare* 'to imitate, to make similar' with the instrumental suffix *-crum* (from *-c(u)lum* by dissimilation of /l/ into /r/; from the Indo-European instrumental suffix **-tlo-*). *Simulare* 'to make similar' is a denominative verb on *similis,-e* 'similar.' *Simulacrum* denotes a carved representation that may be that of a deity, but it is often also used in its etymological sense of 'representation' for a human being or an animal. The difference between *signum* for a god and *simulacrum* for an animal is visible in some texts. Because its fundamental meaning is 'identical reproduction,' *simulacrum* can enter into a relationship of parasynonymy and partial synonymy with *imago* 'representation, imitation, portrait, image.'

Unlike the above common terms, *sculptura* 'sculpture' is poorly attested and technical. Its suffix *-tura* is specialised for inanimate entities resulting from human activity, artefacts. The Latin *sculptura* was borrowed into French and English.

4. Mixed terminologies: Christian vocabulary

The creation of a Christian vocabulary appears in the texts of the 2nd and 3rd centuries C.E. with Tertullian and Cyprian, who use several means to forge new lexemes capable of denoting the new concepts and extralinguistic concrete realities of the new religion.[7] Some lexemes in Christian terminology offer a high degree of precision and are even univocal, but others have a lesser degree of precision because they increase the polysemy of pre-existing lexemes (Fruyt 2022).

4.1 The same signifier, but a change of referential value

A large number of terms denoting specifically Christian concepts and realities result from the re-use of pre-existing terms in Roman society and religion. The signifier remains the same, but the meaning and referential value of the word changes.

When two entities are considered equivalent in the two religions, Roman and Christian, Christian authors kept the existing word: e.g. for the divinity the (inherited) denomination *deus* 'God,' for the priests *pontifex, sacerdos*. However, we see a semantic adaptation followed by a semantic specialisation since they gave the term *fides* 'loyalty' a new meaning of 'Christian faith' (Lat. *fides* > Fr. *foi* 'faith') and they gave *pax* 'peace' the specific meaning of 'reconciliation with God.'

Sometimes underlying phenomena of interference from biblical Greek and Hebrew were involved: *uerbum* 'word' (in the plural 'words, utterance'; inherited) was re-used in the biunivocal proper noun (theonym) *Verbum dei* literally 'the Word of God,' i.e. 'Christ' (Fruyt 2022).

---

7. For the various conditions of lexical creation: Fruyt 2000, 2009, 2011-a, 2011-b.

4.2   Creation of new lexemes within Latin

On the basis of these previously existing Latin lexemes, Christian authors created entire 'families' of words using the usual productive suffixes and compounds, e.g. verbs and adjectives in °-*ficare*, °-*ficus* (*deificare* 'to deify', *deificus* on *deus* 'God'), agentive nouns in -*tor/-sor* derived from verbal stems (*confessor, interpolator, deificator*), process or quality nouns in -*itas* (*natiuitas, deitas*). This way of creating new vocabulary provided minimal innovation and change in the Latin lexicon, since both the basis of the words and the suffixes or compound types already existed in the language, where they were productive.

However, there are some sequences that are important innovations in the Latin lexicon. Some fundamental Christian concepts are denominated by biunivocal proper nouns (theonyms) whose signifier is a binomial of two pre-existing terms welded together according to the process of agglutination[8] into a single lexeme referring to a unique entity as a single referential unit: *Spiritus sanctus* 'the holy spirit', *Deus pater* 'God the Father', *filius Dei* 'the Son of God'.

4.3   The arrival of new signifiers: Borrowings from Greek

Christian vocabulary was increased by the arrival of new lexemes with new signifiers through borrowings from Greek. For its Christian vocabulary, Greek used the same process as Latin by taking pre-existing terms and turning them towards a new denotation which was specifically Christian. The Greek words underwent a semantic specialisation when used in Latin in a Christian context. These terms concern institutions, human events, festivals and ceremonies, sacraments, actions and behaviours that give rhythm to the life of Christians:

– *ecclesia* 'church' (< Greek ἐκκλησία 'the assembly of the people')
– *presbyter* 'priest' (from οἱ πρεσβύτεροι 'the elders, priests' New Testament; Gr. πρέσβυς 'aged, old'; Lat. *presbyter* > Engl. *priest*)
– *angelus* 'messenger, angel' (< Gr. ἄγγελος; Lat. *angelus* was borrowed in Engl. *angel*)
– *baptizare* 'baptise' (< Gr. βαπτίζω 'to dip, immerse someone in water', and New Testament 'baptise'; βάπτω 'to dip someone in water, wash')
– *prophetizare* 'to prophesy' (from Gr. προφητίζω), *propheta* M. 'prophet' (from Gr. προφήτης 'interpreter of the will of God' ; basis of *prophetare* 'to predict').

---

8. For the process of agglutination in lexical creation as opposed to compounding, see above notes 3 and 4.

4.4   Other uses of mixed terminologies

This type of mixed Latin terminology is observed not only in the specialised domain of Christianity. It is also predominant in philosophical, scientific and cultural discourse. A good example is the terminology of arithmetic and geometry. In the first place, this terminology uses pre-existing terms from the usual basic Latin vocabulary, increasing their polysemy to cover specialised values. Thus *intermissio*, which usually means 'to interrupt a continuity, to put something between two other things,' takes on the specialised value 'omission of a number in a series of numbers.' *Potentia*, which means 'power, might,' takes on the specialised meaning of 'power' to square a number (as in 3 to the power of 2) (Lecaudé 2010 and 2020). Secondly, this terminology borrows words from Greek: e.g. *cybus* 'cube' from Greek κύβος, *geometria* 'geometry' from Greek γεωμετρία (J.-Y. Guillaumin 2020: 161, 222, 94, 139).

5.   Approximate terminologies: Natural categories

The terminologies we will now examine can be described as: imprecise, fuzzy, vague, approximate. They occur for natural categories. By *natural categories* we mean atmospheric phenomena (Ducos 1998), soils and stones (Fruyt 2006, 2010), plants and trees (André 1956, 1985; Fruyt 2014), birds (André 1967), animals (terrestrial, aerial, marine) (Fruyt and Lasagna 2023), celestial entities, constellations (Le Boeuffle 1987).

These domains were not created by humans, who do not have control over them (or have only limited control). They are subject to natural forces without influence by humans. Moreover, these areas were poorly known to the Romans, who approached them with limited means of judgement. Their way of apprehending them was often based only on the senses. Compared to modern times, the Romans had only an empirical knowledge on the world, which varied according to the degree of proximity or remoteness of each domain of nature. As we do not have the same conceptualisation of the *realia* today for epistemic reasons (development of modern sciences), the Latin denominations seem to us approximate, lacking acuity and accuracy.

Unlike the domains of human institutions, natural categories do not give rise to univocal nomenclatures that form systems, but only to vocabularies, i.e. sets of lexemes referring to extralinguistic entities perceived as belonging to the same domain or class. In most situations, there is no univocal link between the lexeme and the denominated entity. A single lexeme can denote several entities and a single entity can be denoted by several lexemes. In addition to this semantico-referential vagueness, there are diastratic variations in the Latin lexicon (professional men vs. cultivated Latin authors) and diatopic variations whose extent is difficult to appreciate today.

Since the degree of accuracy and adequacy of lexemes, which defines the type of terminology, is a function of the degree of knowledge of the entity being named, the Romans were led to denominate the unknown by the known, the distant, poorly known extralinguistic entities by better-known closer ones. In these denominations, there is an underlying cognitive structure[9] and we are led to distinguish several extralinguistic zones, more or less close to humans. The degree of proximity or remoteness of these zones is relevant and this is what conditions the different naming processes observed in the Latin lexicon.

6.   Animals and plants of the first zone: Inherited terms

In the natural zone closest to man are domestic animals and those wild animals most frequently encountered, some plants (André 1956, 1985), and some birds (domestic fowl, wild birds like the eagle; André 1967). In this first zone, humans can have some control since they regulate the breeding of domestic animals, they cultivate certain plants and they use wild plants for their culinary or medical needs.

In Latin, domestic animals ('cow' *bos*, 'sheep' *ouis*, 'bee' *apis*, etc.) and some well-known wild animals ('wolf' *lupus*, 'fox' *uulpes*, 'mouse' *mus*, 'bird' *auis*, 'snake' *anguis*, 'fish' *piscis*) were often named by inherited terms present in other Indo-European languages (Brachet 2022). The denominations of the sun (Lat. *sōl*, Greek ἥλιος, Sanskrit *sūrya-s*), moon (Lat. *luna*, I.-E. root meaning 'light', literally 'that which shines'), cloud (*nubes*) and earth (*terra* etymologically 'the dry one') were inherited because their fundamental role for human life had been the same since the beginning of time.

7.   Geological and agronomic vocabulary

The vocabulary of soils and cultivable land presents a certain vagueness that reflects the empirical character of Roman knowledge and the *continuum* status of the object named (Fruyt 2006, 2010). Soils are usually mixtures of several materials or soil types in varying proportions. Farmers have little control over the nature

---

9. For cognitive phenomena in lexical creations: Fruyt 1998; and the articles in Fruyt and Valentin (eds.) 1998.

of soils, whose quality they can only seek to improve (e.g. by adding limestone in the form of chalk to soils that contain too much clay). For this reason, terminologies here are approximative with overlaps between terms.

7.1 A generic term

The generic term *terra* 'earth' displays a wide polysemy which is also found in other languages, notably in French (*terre*) and English (*earth*). This polysemy is probably linked to cognitive causes and to a chain of metonymies. The Latin *terra* has multiple meanings: earth substances, substances extracted from the ground, the surface of the earth, the ground, a country, a land, a solid part of the globe, a continent, the globe.

7.2 Specific terms

The vocabulary of geology in Latin is quite rich in specific terms and hyponyms (*creta, argilla, calx, pulla terra, harena, sabulum*), but it is a fluctuating and vague vocabulary. The continuous character (a *continuum*) of soil as a concrete entity has been interpreted and analysed differently in the lexicons of the various languages as a function of the different perceptions each group of speakers had of that *continuum*. For example, the English word *shale* has no exact correspondence in French and conversely the French *marne* has no exact correspondence in English (Foucaut and Raoult 1980/2000).

7.2.1 *Clay, chalk, marl*

The soils constituted by mixtures of clay and limestone in variable proportions are denoted in a vague way by three Latin terms *argilla, creta, marga* with overlaps in their semantico-referential value.

The Latin *argilla* denotes the matter and kind of soil called in English 'clay.' As *argilla* comes from a root denotating whiteness (as *argentum* 'silver,' a white metal), the term probably originally applied to very fine white clays like kaolin. The Latin *creta* 'chalk' can be presented as co-referential with *argilla* by Cato (*De agricultura* 40,2: *argillam uel cretam addito*). Clay and chalk are conceptualised in a somewhat vague manner since both terms are used to denote soils that are mixtures of clay and limestone in varying proportions, such as marl. Moreover, the links between *creta* 'chalk' and *marga* 'marl' are also unclear. *Marga* denotes, among other things, natural chalk (*creta*) and, conversely, some kinds of *creta* are considered kinds of *marga*.

Thus, *creta* can be co-referential with *argilla* and also denote 'marl,' a mixture of limestone and clay in variable proportions, sometimes with an excess of limestone or an excess of clay (these being soils of poor quality). Furthermore, Pliny the Elder classifies several kinds of soil named *marga*. They contain clays and chalk in the modern sense of these terms. These mixtures of clay and limestone are called *marga, marne, marl* in Latin, French and English respectively.

7.2.2 Limestone

The notion of limestone was created in the 18th century. Latin *calx* means above all 'lime,' a calcareous powder produced from the calcination of white calcareous stones in kilns and used in construction. *Calx* 'lime' was mentioned by Cato for the construction of a farm (Cato, *De agricultura* 14, 3–5) and for making lime in a kiln (16), as well as for the construction of the lime kiln (38).

But *calx* also denotes 'limestone' (*calx* or *calx lapis*), the white stone from which lime is made, as well as 'chalk' (a rarer meaning). This polysemy of *calx* is based on metonymy. Thus, *calx* denotes several forms under which the matter today called *limestone* can appear.

7.2.3 Sand

Sand is called *(h)arena* 'fine sand,' but the term became literary (with a specialisation for the sand in an arena) and was replaced by *sabulum* 'coarse-grained sand' and *sabulo* (for larger grains).

7.3 From Latin to French and English scientific terminology

Although the Latin agronomic vocabulary is often vague, nevertheless some Latin terms were borrowed by French scientific geology. A borrowing of the Latin signifier with a change of meaning is documented in Fr. *le solum* 'surface part of a parcel of land' (from Lat. *solum* 'ground,' originally 'lower part of something'), and Fr. *humus* 'matter resulting from organic decomposition' (from Lat. *humus* 'earth').

The reuse of a French term in the scientific vocabulary with semantic specialisation is also documented in Fr. *limon* from Lat. *limus* 'mud' with the French suffix *-on* (< Lat. *-ōn-*). To Lat. *limus* 'mud' (especially 'earth carried away by the water and deposited in the rivers'), French added today's technical geographical meaning. The notion of 'limon' did not exist in Antiquity. Fr. *limon* is translated by Engl. *mud* (a common term) and *silt* (a technical term).

Thus, changes of meaning occurred in the borrowings from Latin to French in the scientific terminology. But everyday language displayed continuity from Latin to French and other Romance languages.

7.4 Continuity in everyday vocabulary

The section on geological and agronomic vocabulary has shown that the Latin words for fundamental soils form a 'fuzzy' vocabulary. Indeed, the referential values of *argilla, creta, marga, calx* are not clearly distinguished in the Latin texts and they partially overlap. They can refer to the same entity, and, conversely, the same entity can be denoted or designated by these various terms.

However, this ancient terminology was useful enough to persist into some modern Romance languages as a result of phonetic evolution, without these languages needing to create new words: *argilla* > Fr. *argile, creta* > Fr. *craie, marga* > Fr. *marne* (and was borrowed in Engl. *marl*), *calx* > Fr. *chaux, sabulum* > Fr. *sable*. Moreover, Fr. *argile, chaux* and *sable* have retained in everyday language a referential value similar to that of their Latin ancestors.

7.5 The consequences of a lexical structure by inclusion

We have shown that, within both generic and specific terminology, the same term can function both as specific in relation to hierarchically higher terms and as generic in relation to hierarchically lower terms.

Marga 'marl' is a specific term when it is on the same level as *argilla* 'clay' and *creta* 'chalk,' but it becomes generic when Pliny the Elder posits the existence of six kinds of *marga* differentiated by their colour. Moreover, white *marga* (*alba marga*) is itself subdivided into several different products. In this classification by Pliny, the term *marga* thus appears at three different levels of the lexical hierarchy.

This type of structure by inclusion of specific terms in generic terms is fundamental as is shown by the fact that it has lasted over the centuries and is still used today.

8. The remote areas: Metaphorical denominations

The most distant zones from humans are the sea and the sky, two domains not well known to the Romans. As a result, the entities of these regions are named by different processes than the other areas. Geocentrism and anthropocentrism are quite understandable here since the human being is an inhabitant of the earth (the etymological meaning of Lat. *homo*) and since, as a general rule, one starts from the known to name the unknown (or the less known). This situation is reflected on the lexical level. The denominations go from the earth to the sky and from the earth to the sea. In these two remote areas, sky and sea, the naming processes reflect cognitive phenomena.

In the most remote areas, names created by metaphorical transfer dominate. The denominations for terrestrial entities are transferred and become denominations for celestial or marine entities perceived as similar (for metaphorical denominations in general: Fruyt 1989-a, 1989-b, 1992, 1993). This indirect denominative process consists in comparing the entity to be named with another entity already known and named. Then the pre-existing name of the known entity becomes the new name of the entity to be named. This process is based on the preliminary perception of a salient feature common to the two entities.

This denominative situation is similar to the cognitive mechanisms of metaphor, since the denomination is transferred from one domain to another, from one entity to another. This process consists of the following phases: (a) selection of a salient feature in the new celestial or marine entity to be named; (b) selection of the same salient feature in an already known terrestrial entity; (c) transfer of the name from the terrestrial entity to the celestial or marine entity.

This metaphorical naming process is dominant for aquatic animals, i.e. fish, crustaceans, echinoderms, shells (as we will see in §10.3) (Fruyt & Lasagna 2023, p. 100–102). Moreover, the metaphorical denominative transfer is generalised for constellations (as we will see in §9: *Draco, Anguis, Canicula, Aselli, Aquila*, etc.) (Fruyt & Lasagna 2023, p. 102–105 and 422–431).

As for the linguistic aspects of these vocabularies, we notice an absence of bi-univocity; the same lexeme can denote several entities and the same entity can be denoted by several lexemes.

9.   The furthest zone from humans: Astronomical vocabulary

The sky is the most distant zone from humans. The vocabulary of astronomy results from a transfer from the earth to the sky (Le Boeuffle 1987). The constellations are interpreted according to their approximate and perceived shape and their resemblance to terrestrial entities, which are essentially animals. The names of terrestrial animals were thus transferred to create the astronomical terms denotating the constellations.

It is sometimes difficult nowadays to find in the constellations the forms of the terrestrial animals selected by the Romans in the Latin lexicon, but we have some clues. For example, a text by Virgil shows that in the constellation of the Dragon or the Serpent (Lat. *draco* has both meanings), the salient features of the snake were to be found. *Anguis* 'snake' becomes the name of the constellation of the Dragon, which keeps the salient feature 'sliding', since it is described with the verb *elabor* 'to slide' and the context illustrates the features 'flexibility', 'curvature', 'sinuosity' (*flexu sinuoso*) characteristic of the snake (Virgil, *Georgics* 1, 244–245).

Many domestic animals have also lent their names to constellations and stars. The name of the dog and bitch *canis* is found in *Canicula* for the constellation of the (Great) Dog, where the suffix *-cula*, said to be a diminutive, denotes the resemblance to a dog (for this function of the diminutive suffix: Fruyt 1989-c, 2020). And the same suffix *-cula* shows its true diminutive function (smallness) when *Canicula* denotes the constellation of the Little Dog (Procyon, Greek Προκύων), also called *Canis minor* or *minusculus. Aries* 'ram' applies to the constellation Aries, *asinus* 'donkey' is used for *Aselli* (or *Asini*) 'Donkeys' stars of the constellation Cancer, *bos* 'bovine' for the zodiac Taurus, *equus* 'horse' for the boreal constellation Pegasus, *hircus* 'billy goat' for a comet, and for the constellation Capricorn (from Lat. *Capricornus*; from Lat. *caper* "male goat" and Lat. *cornu* "horn").

The situation is the same for constellations seen as representing wild animals encountered in everyday life. *Aquila* the eagle (bird) becomes the denomination of the Eagle, boreal constellation. *Lepus* 'hare' is the name of a southern constellation. The same transfer is documented for *lupus* 'wolf,' *uulpes* 'fox,' *mus* 'mouse,' *scorpio* and *scorpius* 'scorpion,' and *testudo* 'tortoise, carapace.'

There are also a few occurrences of a transfer from the sea to the sky, which shows that the sea was better known to the Romans than the sky. Some inhabitants of the sea are used to name celestial beings. It is the case of fish *piscis*, crab or crayfish *cancer*, whale *balaena* (or *balena, ballena*) and dolphin *delphinus* (a Latin term of Greek origin).

One can easily understand that a comet, because of the kind of trail it leaves in the sky and its long and thin shape, can be associated with the beard (body part) and therefore named *Barba*. It was also associated with the shape of a sword and given the Greek name for a sword that in Latin was then transliterated as *Xiphias* (Le Boeuffle 1987: 71, n°179 and 278, n°1321).

An exception to this orientation of the transfer is provided by *stella* 'star' which gives its name to *stella* 'starfish,' with a transfer from the sky to the sea, the salient common feature being a similarity of form.

10.   From earth to sea: Aquatic animals

We use the term *aquatic animals* here in the same way as Pliny the Elder in books 9 and 32 of his *Natural History*. This category includes fish, crustaceans, mollusks, various animals like sponges, starfish, worms, jellyfish, as well as marine mammals, 'sea monsters' (Février 2003; James-Raoul and Thomasset 2002), and tortoises (Fruyt and Lasagna 2023).

10.1   The link between the earth and the sea

The link between earth and sea is perceived as stronger than that between earth and sky. According to Latin authors, the two domains correspond and everything that is found on the earth (*terra, terrestris*) is also found in the sea (*mare, marinus*). The sea is perceived as the mirror of the earth. This conception, based on a philosophical concept, is mentioned, among others, by Seneca and Pliny the Elder (1st century A.D.). Pliny (*Historia naturalis* 9, 3) presents the sea as the nourishing power par excellence, as the place of unequalled forces, and as the place of birth of all kinds of monsters. This projection of terrestrial realities onto the sea has terminological consequences: marine entities are given the names of terrestrial entities deemed equivalent or similar.

There is thus a correlation between the terminological creativity of the linguistic community and the link that society has with the named entities. Societies and linguistic communities give a name to an entity when they need it. They name the entities when they are useful and used or, alternatively, when they are dangerous (for example among the fish, the ray and the shark, among birds, the eagle). Furthermore, the more useful an entity is, the more names it has. For example, the tuna fish, greatly appreciated in Roman gastronomy, is the fish that has the greatest number of names. There are also many names for common shellfish, especially mussels.

10.2   Formation of the denominations

The names of aquatic animals have various origins: some are inherited, others are borrowed (mainly from Greek and Gallic). For those that are created in Latin itself, one observes descriptive denominations which result from the perception of the linguistic community.

10.2.1   *Direct denominative process*

The basis of a denomination issued from a direct denominative process is the lexeme denoting the salient feature of the animal (for example *whiting*, name of a fish, from *white*). This situation is well documented when the salient feature is colour, for example in *aurata* 'royal sea bream, sea bream' literally 'the golden one' because the fish has a golden spot on its head (substantivation of the adjective *auratus* 'golden,' derived from *aurum* 'gold'). *Rubellio* is the name of an unknown fish with a reddish color (from *ruber* 'red'). The name of the river fish *barbus* 'barb' is derived from *barba* 'man's beard' and means literally 'the bearded one' since the salient feature of the fish consists of the filaments under the mouth.

10.2.2 *Indirect denominative process*

The most usual process is an indirect one, using an entity with similar features whose name is then transferred from the earth to the sea. These metaphorical transfers of names are not carried out at random. Aquatic animals are mostly named after terrestrial animals if they are perceived as living beings (fish, marine mammals). If the marine animal is a mammal, the transfer is also made from a mammal: *bos* 'bovine' is used for a large marine mammal (larger than the seal), while the seal, smaller, is named 'calf' *uitulus*. In this way, the difference of size between the ox (or cow) and the calf is respected when transferring to the sea.

In contrast, if the aquatic animal is perceived as inert and devoid of feeling, it takes the name of a terrestrial plant. Annelids (worms), jellyfish, squids, sponges, etc. are perceived as belonging to vegetation and named accordingly after terrestrial plants.

10.3   Starting point of the transfer

Cognitive aspects are shown by the identity of the entities from which the denominative transfers start; they start from terrestrial entities, which are mainly animals.

Domestic mammals are used for types of fish: *aries* 'goat,' *bos* 'bovine,' *canis* 'dog, bitch' (an unpleasant animal). Wild mammals for fish: *lupus* 'wolf' (aggressivity), *uulpes* 'fox,' *aper/apriculus* 'wild boar,' *mustela* 'weasel.' *Mus* 'mouse' denominates three animals: a fish, a sea monster and a turtle. *Lepus* 'hare' is used for a mollusk (without a shell); *leo* 'lion' and *elephantus* 'elephant' for the lobster (claws and antennae); *echinus* 'hedgehog' for the sea urchin (spines). As is to be expected, domestic mammals provide the names of marine mammals in Pliny.

Insect names occur in *locusta* 'grasshopper' (for lobster), *aranea* 'spider' (for *araneus/-ea* 'sting-fish'). The scorpion also gives its names to the 'sting-fish': *scorpio, draco, scorpaena.*

Bird names are used for fish when the salient feature is chromatic. Dark colour for *turdus* 'thrush,' *aquila* 'eagle,' *coracinus/coruus* 'crow,' *passer* 'sparrow,' *merula* 'blackbird.' *Hirundo* 'swallow' is used for a flying fish.

The names of objects are used when the form of the target animal is unusual (round, flat, long, etc.): *orbis* 'round surface' (for sunfish), *solea* 'sandal, sole' (for sole, dab, fish), *perna* 'ham' (mollusc), *gladius* 'sword' (swordfish), *pecten* 'comb' (shellfish), *rota* 'wheel' (fish), *serra* 'saw' (dangerous fish), *sudis* 'stake' (sea fish).

Marine animals take the names of plants when Pliny perceives them as inanimate or even as vegetal: *pastinaca* 'stingray' (with an elongated tail like the root of the parsnip), *hordeum* 'barley, barley grain' (for *hordeia*, an undefined shell-fish, stinging nettle), *cucumis* 'cucumber' (for an indeterminate echinoderm in the shape of a cucumber), *balanus* 'acorn' of the oak tree (for a sessile mollusk).

A body part (of humans and animals) is used for its shape or consistency in: *unguis* 'nail' and *dactylus* 'finger' (for a long shell), and *pulmo* 'lung' (for jellyfish). These names constitute a subclass, since the starting point is the part and not the whole by synecdoche. Body parts are also used when the target lexeme is formed by adding a suffix: *lingulaca* sole fish (on *lingua* 'tongue'), *dentex* dentate fish (on *dens, dent-* 'tooth'), *capito* grey mullet, European chub fish (on *caput* 'head'; a fish with a big head), Apuleius's creation *ueretilla* for a shell that does not exist (on *ueretrum* 'sexual parts of man and woman'), and *cornuta* for a marine mammal (*cornu* 'horn', the tusks of the walrus). The two different fish called *perca* — sea perch and river perch — are named after the stripes on their back.

The starting point for *torpedo* 'ray' (which paralyses its prey) is a psycho-physiological state of the human being or the animal, *torpor* 'torpor'.

Since this naming process from the known to the unknown, and especially from the earth to the sea, is widespread in many languages belonging to various linguistic families (Leblic 2002, Randa 2002), it does not depend on the languages involved but on the cognitive faculties of the people that do the naming.

10.4   Denominative metaphor in Latin authors

Latin authors (in particular Varro, Cicero and Quintilian) are familiar with metaphor as a figure of speech and a stylistic ornament. They denote the concept of metaphor with terms related to the verb *transfero* 'to transfer, to move from one place to another': *uerbum tralatum* 'a word transferred', i.e. 'in metaphorical use' (Cicero *De oratore* 3,161 and 3,149; *Orator* 92 and 202), *tralatio* 'transfer, metaphor' (Quintilian, *De institutione oratoria* 8, 2, 6).

Varro and Quintilian are aware that the process of metaphor also applies to denomination with names of fish and shellfish derived from earthly entities. Varro (*De lingua Latina* 5, 77, 3–5) uses the expression *uocabula translata* 'transferred terms' in this connection and continues as follows:

> The names of the fish are almost all taken from terms designating terrestrial things with which they have something in common, such as *anguilla, lingulaca, sudis*. Others are named after their colour, such as *asellus, umbra, turdus*; other names are taken from a particular feature, such as *lupus, canicula, torpedo*. In the same way for shellfish, some names come from the Greeks…, others are indigenous and are based on a resemblance, such as *pernae, pectunculi, ungues*. (our translation).

As can be seen from this text, the salient features perceived for fish are colour and behaviour and they are the same salient features that we also perceive today (mentioned above in 9.3 for *turdus, lupus, canicula, torpedo*). Varro also links fish with terrestrial entities in *asellus* (*asinus* 'donkey'), and *umbra* (*umbra* 'shadow'). He links shellfish with other terrestrial entities, the salient feature being the shape of the shellfish, in *perna* 'noble penshell' (*perna* 'ham'), *pectunculus* 'scallop' (*pecten* 'comb'), and *unguis* 'common piddock' (*unguis* 'nail').

Quintilian (*De institutione oratoria* 8, 2, 8) also speaks of *tralatio* in naming fish from birds and objects, citing *turdus* (for a dark-coloured fish) and *solea* (for a flat fish). Similarly, in his *Etymologies*, Isidore of Seville (6th–7th centuries), referring to the resemblance of aquatic animals to land animals, mentions the transfer of names.

10.5   The meanings of *piscis*

Piscis is the generic term for fish as found in Fr. *poisson*. But it also has a wider meaning for other marine animals in Plautus and Pliny the Elder (Fruyt and Lasagna 2023). In Plautus, in a culinary context, *piscis* extends to some food from the sea other than fish such as shellfish. For Pliny, the fact of living in the sea justifies his calling marine creatures other than fish *piscis*, the common feature being the environment and biotope.

However, contrary to what has been said elsewhere (e.g. de Saint-Denis 1947), *piscis* in Pliny does not extend to marine mammals. Pliny had a nuanced expression *forma piscium* where *forma* refers not to 'the form', but to more general elements relating to the biotope, i.e. the sea (Fruyt and Lasagna 2023).

The use of Fr. *poisson* in the general sense of 'aquatic animal,' as in Pliny, was maintained into the Middle Ages, notably for the whale and for 'marvelous fish,' i.e. sea monsters (Le Cornec 2012). Engl. *fish* also shows an extended referential value in the compounds *jellyfish, shellfish, cuttlefish*. They refer to aquatic animals that do not belong to the class called *fish* in the usual meaning of the term. But they are seafood (like in Plautus) and they live in the sea (like in Pliny).

Another generic term covering a large domain is *cancer*, used for all kinds of crabs and other crustaceans. The salient feature for this class is the *crusta* 'a not very hard carapace' that covers them (Fruyt and Lasagna 2023).

10.6   Borrowings from Greek

The borrowings from Greek constitute an important contingent which reflects the dependence of Latin on the Greek language in the cultural, technical and scientific fields in the broad sense. Some terms of Greek origin, borrowed by Latin in the pre-literary period, are no longer felt to be Greek and function in synchrony as fully Latin terms in everyday life, such as *ostrea* (or *ostreum*) 'oyster'. However, Pliny the Elder uses a large number of Greek terms constituting a learned technical vocabulary. Derived from Aristotle and other Greek authors, they would not have belonged to the everyday Latin language, but they serve Pliny's encyclopedic purposes.

11.   Formation of modern scientific vocabularies

Although the domains of natural categories do not constitute univocal lexical systems and provide only imprecise vocabularies, these vocabularies have nevertheless been re-used in order to create modern, scientific nomenclatures and terminologies. We have seen the borrowing of Latin words in the geological French vocabulary (Fr. *solum, humus*). This situation is generalised in botanical, zoological and especially in the scientific names of aquatic animals.

Pliny the Elder's lexemes were used for the creation of true scientific nomenclatures, where the relationship between the lexical unit and the extralinguistic entity named is univocal. The binomials created by Linnaeus in the 18th century are based on the vocabulary attested in Pliny (and some other authors, e.g. Ausonius from the 4th century A.D. for river fish). The Latin noun is used as the first element in Linnaeus's binomials, e.g. the sturgeon's scientific name is *Acipenser sturio* (Linnaeus 1758), from Lat. *acipenser* in Pliny and other authors. Lat. *pecten* — great Mediterranean scallop, pilgrim mussel, St. James's scallop — is maintained in its scientific binomial *Pecten jacobeus* (Linnaeus 1758).

Where modern scientists distinguish several animals bearing the same Latin name, that Latin name appears in all the scientific binomials as the first element. For example, Lat. *natrix* 'water snake' occurs in the binomials *Natrix natrix* (Linnaeus 1758) 'European grass snake', *Natrix tassellata* (Laurenti 1768) 'dice snake', *Natrix maura* (Linnaeus 1758) 'viperine water snake'.

Sometimes both elements of Linnaeus's binomial are Latin words from Antiquity. From Lat. *salmo* 'salmon' and *salar* 'trout', Linnaeus in 1758 created the scientific name for salmon, *Salmo salar*, which is still in use today.

12. Conclusion

We have described above several types of terminology in Latin, ranging from the most unambiguous to the vaguest, with intermediate zones where different types coexist in the same lexicon.

The degree of precision or imprecision in terminology is related to the nature of the extralinguistic domains named, depending on whether they are man-made or belong to nature, the latter being outside human control. The degree of (im)precision is also related to the degree of knowledge that the Latin linguistic community had of the domain and the elements included in it. And this knowledge itself depended on the proximity or remoteness of this domain to the people who created the name and to the earth on which they lived.

However, even these imprecise terminologies, despite their defects, offered sufficient adaptability to the entities denoted for modern science to have re-used them to good effect in scientific denominations since the 18th century.

References

André, Jacques. 1956. *Lexique des termes de botanique en latin*. Paris: Klincksieck.

André, Jacques. 1967. *Les noms d'oiseaux en latin*. Paris: Klincksieck.

André, Jacques. 1985. *Les noms de plantes dans la Rome antique*. Paris: Les Belles Lettres.

Brachet, Jean-Paul. 2022. "Noms d'animaux hérités en latin." *Revue des Etudes latines* 99, 2021: 1–9.

de Saint-Denis, E. 1947. *Le vocabulaire des animaux marins en latin classique*. Paris: Klincksieck.

Dorothée, Stéphane. 2002. "Aux origines de la notion de signe : les emplois de *signum* chez Plaute." *Revue de Philologie et d'Histoire ancienne* 76,1: 33–48.

Dorothée, Stéphane. 2006. *A l'origine du signe : le latin signum*. Paris: L'Harmattan.

Duarte, Pedro. 2010. *Le vocabulaire latin de la sculpture et de la peinture (1er siècle avant notre ère – 1er s. de notre ère)*. Thesis, University of Paris-Sorbonne, unpublished.

Ducos, Michèle. 1998. "Les phénomènes atmosphériques dans la poésie latine." In *Le temps qu'il fait au Moyen Âge. Phénomènes atmosphériques dans la littérature, la pensée scientifique et religieuse*, ed. by Joëlle Ducos, and Claude Thomasset, 139–150. Paris: Presses de l'Université de Paris-Sorbonne (PUPS).

Février, Caroline. 2003. "Le bestiaire prodigieux. Merveilles animales dans les littératures historique et scientifique à Rome." *Revue des Etudes latines* 81: 43–64.

Foucaut, A, and J.-F. Raoult. 1980 (2000, 5th ed.). *Dictionnaire de géologie*. Paris: Dunod.

Fruyt, Michèle. 1989-a. "Métaphore, métonymie et synecdoque dans le lexique latin." *Glotta* 67: 106–122.

Fruyt, Michèle. 1989-b. "Le rôle de la métaphore et de la métonymie en latin : style, lexique, grammaire." *Revue des Etudes latines* 67: 236–257.

Fruyt, Michèle. 1989-c. "Etude sémantique des 'diminutifs' latins : les suffixes *-ulus,-culus,-ellus, -illus* dé-substantivaux et dé-adjectivaux." In *Actes du 5e Colloque de Linguistique latine*, ed. by M. Lavency, and D. Longrée, in *Cahiers de l'Institut de Linguistique de Louvain* 15, 1–4: 127–138. Louvain-la-Neuve.

Fruyt, Michèle. 1992. "La dénomination par métaphore et métonymie en latin." In *Sens et pouvoirs de la nomination*, ed. by Suzanne Gély, 279–289. Montpellier: Public. Univ. Paul Valéry.

Fruyt, Michèle. 1993. "Les procédés de désignation dans les noms de plantes en latin." In *Les phytonymes grecs et latins.*, 135–190. Centre de Recherches comparatives sur les langues de la Méditerranée ancienne, LAMA n°12. Nice.

Fruyt, Michèle. 1998. "Les deux types de motivation dans certaines langues indo-européennes (français, latin,…)." In *Lexique et cognition*, ed. by Michèle Fruyt and Paul Valentin, 51–70. Paris: PUPS.

Fruyt, Michèle. 2000. "La création lexicale : généralités appliquées au domaine latin." In *La création lexicale en latin*, ed. by Christian Nicolas, and Michèle Fruyt, 11–48. Paris: PUPS.

Fruyt, Michèle. 2006. "La lexicalisation et la conceptualisation de la couleur dans les textes techniques et scientifiques latins." In *L'écriture du texte scientifique au Moyen Âge*, ed. by Claude Thomasset, 13–47. Paris: PUPS.

Fruyt, Michèle. 2009. "La creación léxica: consideraciones generales y su aplicación a la lengua latina." *Estudios clásicos* 136: 7–54.

Fruyt, Michèle. 2010. "La dénomination des sols et des terres cultivables en latin. L'apport du lexique latin à la connaissance des notions géologiques." In *Aux origines de la géologie de l'Antiquité au Moyen Âge*, ed. by Caude Thomasset, Joëlle Ducos, and Jean-Pierre Chambon, 27–73. Paris: Champion.

Fruyt, Michèle. 2011-a. "Word-Formation in Classical Latin," in *A Companion to the Latin Language*, ed. by J. Clackson, 157–175. Oxford: Wiley-Blackwell.

Fruyt, Michèle. 2011-b. "Latin Vocabulary." In *A Companion to the Latin Language*, ed. by J. Clackson, 144–156. Oxford: Wiley-Blackwell.

Fruyt, Michèle. 2014. "Aspects de la phytonymie en latin." In *L'expressivité du lexique médical en Grèce et à Rome. Hommages à Françoise Skoda*, ed. by Isabelle Boehm, and Nathalie Rousseau, 101–114. Paris: PUPS.

Fruyt, Michèle. 2020. "Le suffixe latin de diminutif : la distribution des allomorphes." In *Linguarum Varietas* 9, ed. by Paolo Poccetti, 125–145. Rome: Fabrizio Serra Editore.

Fruyt, Michèle. 2022. "Word-formation in Late Latin and the status of the Christian writers." In *Studies on Late and Vulgar Latin in the Early 21st Century*, ed. by Gerd V.M. Haverling, 77–92. Uppsala: Acta Universitatis Upsaliensis, Studia Latina Upsaliensia 37.

Fruyt Michèle, and Mauro Lasagna. 2023. *Les animaux aquatiques en latin: étude linguistique et sociétale*. Paris: L'Harmattan.

Fruyt, Michèle and P. Valentin (eds.) 1998. *Lexique et cognition*. Paris: PUPS.

Guillaumin, Jean-Yves. 2020. *Dictionnaire de la terminologie latine ancienne de l'arithmétique et de la géométrie*. Paris: Les Belles Lettres.

James-Raoul, Danielle, and Claude Thomasset (eds). 2002. *Dans l'eau, sous l'eau. Le monde aquatique au Moyen Âge*, Paris: PUPS.

Laurenti, Josephi Nicolai. 1768. *Specimen medicum*. Viennae (Harvard University, Museum of Comparative Zoology, Ernst Mayr Library).

Le Boeuffle, André. 1987. *Astronomie, astrologie. Lexique latin*. Paris: Picard.

Le Cornec, Cécile. 2012. "La dénomination des poissons merveilleux en français." In *Sciences et langues au Moyen Âge*, ed. by Joëlle Ducos, 419–432. Heidelberg: Universitätverlag Winter.

Leblic, Isabelle. 2002. "Classification des poissons dans quelques langues de Nouvelle-Calédonie." In *Lexique et motivation. Perspectives ethnolinguistiques*, ed. by V. de Colombel, and N. Tersis, 115–141. Paris: Peeters.

Lecaudé, Peggy. 2010. *La notion de puissance : les équivalents latins du grec δύναμις*. Thesis, University of Paris-Sorbonne, unpublished.

Lecaudé, Peggy. 2020. "Potentia." In *Le vocabulaire intellectuel latin. Analyse linguistique*, ed. by M. Fruyt, A. Ollivier, and T. Taous, 181–208. Paris: L'Harmattan.

Linnaeus, Carl 1758. *Systema naturae per regna tria naturae, secundum classes, ordines, genera, species, cum characteribus, differentiis, synonymis* (Editio decima, reformata) 1: I-IV: 1–824 (Laurentii Salvii, Holmiae). Stockholm.

Randa, Vladimir. 2002. "Perception des animaux et leurs noms dans la langue inuit (Canada, Groenland, Alaska)." In *Lexique et motivation. Perspectives ethnolinguistiques*, ed. by V. de Colombel, and N. Tersis, 79–114. Paris: Peeters.

CHAPTER 2

Terminology at the end of the Middle Ages in France

Joëlle Ducos[1], Michèle Goyens[2], Inge Fourneau[2]
& Fleur Vigneron[3]
[1] Sorbonne Université, EPHE, PSL | [2] KU Leuven |
[3] Université Grenoble Alpes

The Middle Ages were characterised by the emergence of European vernacular languages, which took their place beside Latin, hitherto the language of science practised by learned clerics and academics. Latin terminology was at the same time constituted by the integration of Greco-Latin and Arabic learning. This type of situation, where knowledge was often conveyed by translated and commented texts, paved the way for the creation of neologisms and linguistic innovations, in Latin as well as in the vernacular. This chapter examines the way terminologies and specialised lexical usages originated and developed, the social circles and the domains which promoted this expansion and the different coining and lexicalisation processes involved, focusing especially on French-speaking countries. After a general presentation of the medieval situation, two scientific domains will be analysed by way of example. The first is medicine, which gave rise to numerous Latin and French texts, and the second is botany, situated at the crossroads of common language and specialised uses. The medieval period is thus revealed as a veritable terminological laboratory, a time of linguistic experimentation serving the dissemination of science.

Keywords: Medieval French, Latin, medicine, botany, vernacular language

1.   Terminologies in the Middle Ages: Creation, translation and tradition

The medieval period is often presented as a kind of transition between Antiquity and the dawn of modern science from the 16th century onwards. The same holds for specialised languages and terminology: on the one hand, university scholars kept on producing terms and definitions following Greek and Arabic models, but on the other, specific medieval developments were taking place in terminology, and these have not been studied enough. The characteristics of a reflection on

https://doi.org/10.1075/tlrp.24.02duc

terminology were present, in Latin as well as in the vernacular languages,[1] and terminologies emerged in the different languages of Europe. This chapter will be dedicated especially to French by way of example.

1.1   A period of reflection on concepts and words

Medieval science, like philosophy, was based primarily on texts and commentaries rather than on an analysis of reality or experiments and was expressed in writings in various forms depending on the field. In addition to treatises and writings for practical purposes in astronomy, medicine or mathematics, the commentaries of authorities were essential sources for medieval terminology, because the *questiones* and *expositiones* were based on a precise analysis of each word used, in a translation — Greek-Latin or Arabic-Latin — or in a text written in Latin. The understanding of words, translated, copied or adapted, and of the terms created to denote new concepts, was central in scientific reflection and contributed to the creation of taxonomies and to the evolution and specialisation of terms. Defining and reformulating were basic steps of argumentation, and denominations or equivalencies were determined by these processes. For example, the nomenclatures of winds gave rise to extensive presentations as in the *Meteora* of Albert the Great (1251), where the author enumerated Greco-Latin names of winds in different traditions before presenting denominations that the author referred to as "usual." Meanings and forms of terms from natural philosophy were also analysed by scholars before becoming common: the Greek transliteration *antiperistasis* was not reserved for Greek-Latin translations but was often used in the commentaries of Averroes or Avicenna, where one would expect an Arabism instead. The scholars developed profound reflections about terminology, found new uses and carried out revisions based on conceptual definitions and taxonomies, such as Albert the Great (1251) who created a nomenclature of thunderclaps and redefined the existing lexicon of astronomy and natural philosophy. The discussion of Aristotelian and Platonic theories and their subsequent readings thus led to new meanings given to *impetus* (Weill-Parot, 2019: 299–314), which was essential to the theory of movement of 14th century Parisian natural philosophy and in particular to Johannis Buridanus' theory. The notion of *species* in Aristotle's commentaries and in treatises on optics also led to new definitions and to discussions, which showed the importance of the term in optics, and scholars attempted to further clarify the concepts involved. Defining a concept and giving it a label for a scientific theory, beyond the influence of authorities, was at the heart of medieval

1. On the relationship between Latin and the vernaculars, see *infra* §1.5.

reflection which developed a lexicon of *philosophia naturae*, adopted until the 17th century in texts but not, however, found in glossaries.

These terminological usages by scholars, based on the medieval practice of equivalence and explanatory glosses, were also present in French texts, especially in translations, where glosses providing definitions frequently appeared in translations of authoritative texts, as were the use of equivalence and other translation techniques: the translators sought multiple modes for the transmission of meaning, including neologisms, for example loanwords and semantic borrowings. From the 12th century to the 14th century, a rich lexicon was created and used in these texts, which attests to the remarkable capacity of the vernacular to express new concepts and scientific thought.

1.2 Lexical specificity

The specialised lexicon has often been marginalised by compilers of the dictionaries of medieval Latin and medieval French, but research carried out over the past decades, for Latin by the research projects of the New Du Cange[2] and for French the DMF 2023 (*Dictionnaire du Moyen Français*) and the DFSM (*Dictionnaire du Français Scientifique Médiéval*), has identified unmistakable instances of terminology, distinct from common language, both in Latin and in the vernacular. We can note however that at the end of the Middle Ages, for scientific French, terms were easier to identify, because one of the recognised criteria of domain specificity, the use of Greco-Latin bases (Kocourek:1991), was much more frequent during that period than before the 14th century. Thus, the importance of 13th century terms cannot be easily detected because of a preference for semantic rather than formal neology. For example, the language of mathematics of this period is characterised by the use of verbs from everyday language (*abattre* to denote subtraction, *assembler* to denote addition, *couper*, *garder*, etc.), the notable borrowings being for instance the names of Arabic origin *chiffre* 'figure,' designating at that time the number zero, or the names of geometric figures (*angle*, *figure*, *cône...*). Similarly, in astronomy, vernacular texts preferred *le Mouton* (Aries), *le cercle des bestes* (the zodiac), and *regart* rather than *aspect*. These uses in the first scientific vernacular texts made it difficult to identify terms as such, while their frequency of use and their repeated occurrence in many texts belonging to the same field indicated a terminology that was systematically practiced, which reveals a tendency to stabilisation beyond apparent hapaxes or idiolects, as can be seen in the DFSM.

---

2. *Nouveau Du Cange*, which is developed by IRHT (Institut de recherche et d'histoire des textes), Latin department.

1.3   Medieval directories, glossaries and terminologies

In the Middle Ages, glossaries, indices and other types of wordlists were widely used, and they are well-known by modern researchers. Biblical exegesis was the model for many wordlists and glossaries, whose aim was to foster understanding of the biblical text, such as the *Distinctiones*, several versions of which were produced from the 12th century onwards, which classified in alphabetical and/ or thematic order the words of the Scriptures. Moreover, the grammatical tradition of the Middle Ages, as illustrated by the *Liber glossarum* (late 8th century), reinforced this interest in vocabulary lists and glossaries. Many contained general words, but some were more specialised for example in the domains of plants, animals and precious stones. These works contributed to establishing traditions of nomenclatures in both Latin and French.

On the other hand, scientific treatises did not present vocabulary lists or glossaries: the tables of contents and the headings of the chapters were considered to be sufficient for the identification of terms and concepts. Encyclopedic texts often had indices to help the reader find important words and terms. The appearance of specialised glossaries, albeit with a didactic aim, became an important means of popularisation in the translations of the 14th century: certain French authors such as Nicole Oresme proposed a glossary of terms and neologisms (referred to as *forts mots*) with definitions at the end of their translations (1370–1372), and Olivier de la Haye accompanied his poem on the plague (1426) with a *Table par A B C*, where medical terms were explained. These were the first attempts to construct an alphabetical inventory to support specialised uses of French.

1.4   Scholars, academics and professionals

Medieval universities were the main producers of scientific terminology, since they maintained ancient Greco-Latin traditions and the contributions of Arabic science through translations and used them as a basis for their own creations. From the 13th century to the end of the Middle Ages, medieval scholars established terminological uses which were gradually imposed. However, it would be wrong to imagine that terminology development and use were limited to these scholarly circles: technical terms were in fact used in vernacular and in professional and lay communities, sometimes translated into Latin and often attested in historical, archival or even literary texts. For instance, the poem *L'Orloge amoureus* by Froissart (1368) contained a technical vocabulary of clockworking that was also present in an anonymous treatise dating from the middle of the 14th century (Singer 2005: 155–173). Similarly, a French manuscript, the *Carnet* by Villard de Honnecourt, gave an account of architectural vocabulary at the beginning of the 13th century (Wirth 2015; Ducos 2015): for example, *car-ole* (usually a 'dance in a ring, a round') designated a church ambulatory. The mathematical and geometric lexicon, used for monetary exchange or land sur-veying, was used by merchants and lawyers in their vernacular. Thus, French writing of mathematical and geometrical treatises by Nicolas Chuquet at the end of the Middle Ages was no exception. Similarly, the early attestation of vernac-ular medical vocabulary suggests non-clerical uses by surgeons, Jewish doctors and women.[3] Finally, the archives bear witness to names for techniques in crafts, in particular those of the iron industry, which are absent from scholarly texts (Verna 2017). The terminologies were therefore more than mere adaptations and copies of Latin terms, even if the attestations often appeared in non-scientific texts or on the fringes of science, and are, for this reason, more difficult to locate and understand.

1.5   Latin and vernaculars

For the sciences sanctioned by the universities, the fundamental role of Latin for generating terminological neologisms in vernacular languages is evident. Latin translations served as an intermediary for the understanding of Greek and Arabic texts and made use of Arabisms and Hellenisms. Latin was also the de facto lan-guage of science and philosophy. So in the prologues of his translations Nicole Oresme had to appeal for French to be considered a language of science. His ambition was that French might become the language of knowledge like Latin in relation to Greek. Latin terminology was also often present in French texts, mixed with French terms, especially in medical recipes and pharmacopoeia writ-ings, and used seemingly necessary xenisms, i.e. a foreign word used as such in a vernacular text. The *Dictionnaire du Moyen Français* and the DFSM confirm the importance of xenisms, integrated loanwords which adapted the Latin form to French morphology, and calques, i.e. borrowings of a phrase structure using native words during the 14th and 15th century. For example we see in Evrart de Conty's writings (cf. *infra* §2.3. and footnote 11) a clear opposition between three nomenclatures of the winds, that of "philosophers," which were comprised of Latin borrowings or Latin names (*auster/austre; eurus/eure; septentrion; aper-chie*), that of sailors attested for almost two centuries in Latin texts, which were based on wind directions (*su; su-suest; nort, nortwest...*), and that of common people (*bise, galerne, midi...*). The end of the Middle Ages was thus characterised by a growing diversity of uses, from the scholarly world to the ordinary speaker, promoted by the practice of crafts.

---

3. Jewish doctors were not clerics and were barred from the university.

However, before this period where Latinisms began to denote a certain level of knowledge, the relationship between Latin and French was not so unequivocal. In some linguistic areas, French coexisted with two other languages, such as in England where English, French and Latin were used. Here French, the language of scientific writings as evidenced by numerous treatises on plants and medicine, served as an intermediary between the vernacular language (English) and Latin, a learned and court language. In France however, during the 13th century, the authors of both translations and treatises sought less to copy Latin than to find linguistic resources in French. Mahieu le Vilain, the translator of Aristotle, is a good example: he tried different translations for *exhalatio, exalation, fumee, vapeur* before deciding on the French term *buee*, well attested elsewhere and therefore becoming an accepted term for the Aristotelian concept. To designate meteorological phenomena, he rejected the borrowings *impression* or *passion*, frequently attested in later centuries, and preferred a semantic borrowing with the neologism *emprainture*, formed on *empreindre*, equivalent of *imprimere,* and attested in the sense of 'embroidery'. Other authors used loan words, some of which had been attested earlier but in different senses and fields, like *generation, corruption, figure.*

This diversity of neologisms, which resulted in synonyms and a proliferation of terms in Latin and French, demonstrates that terminologies were not rigid, but emerged as a result of coinages by individuals or local communities, and produced semantic or conceptual networks which sometimes survived, sometimes disappeared, at least in the Middle Ages. From the 12th (for Latin) and the 13th (for French) until the 16th century, a form of standardisation was slowly emerging, while the writings of medieval sciences, demonstrating spectacular progress, increased in number. However, the later terminology was only partially inspired by these forms. For instance, it is well known that transliterations of Arabic, frequent in astronomy-astrology, medicine and mathematics, decreased considerably both in frequency and in number in the 16th century. The Middle Ages is therefore a period of emergence and creation, where terminological uses multiplied, first as idiolects, which sometimes became popularised but at other times disappeared. It is therefore necessary to make an inventory, domain by domain, to measure the extent and the structuring of terminology during this time. The cases of medicine and botany illustrate these tendencies very well.

2.   French medical vocabulary in the medieval period

2.1   Medicine from Antiquity to the Middle Ages

Modern medicine traces its origins to Ancient Greek medicine, as exemplified by Hippocrates. The initial belief that illness was a divine punishment and that healing was a gift from the gods was replaced by a physically based insight about health and disease. The humoral theory states that good health comes from perfect balance of the four humours: blood, phlegm, yellow bile, and black bile. Consequently, disease resulted from an improper balance of these four humours.[4]

Today many of the original Greek texts have been lost and are only known to us through their translations into Arabic, Syrian or Hebrew, which were elaborated as part of the development of Ancient Arab medicine during the Golden Age of Islam from the 8th century to the 14th century. Initially built upon tradition, Ancient Arab medicine was enriched with knowledge from Iran, India and finally Ancient Greek medicine. The most influential amongst these texts was *The Canon of Medicine* by Avicenna.[5]

Meanwhile, medicine in the west had come to a standstill, partly under the influence of Christianity with the Christus medicus. Care of the sick and the poor was entrusted to Christian charity within the monasteries.

The Ancient Arab medicine is an essential bridge for recovering the lost knowledge of ancient Greek medicine in the west. With the invasion of the Moors in Spain, the way to Europe was opened for Arab and Jewish doctors who brought with them the advanced knowledge of Ancient Arab medicine, including the Arabic translations of the original Greek texts.

In the meantime, medieval Europe regained interest in science. In the 9th century the Schola Medica Salernitana was founded as the first in a series of European medical faculties. Arabic medical texts were readily available and translation into Latin had begun. Gradually a canon of writings was produced which formed the basis of European medical education for centuries to come.[6]

---

4. For more information on the Hippocratic Medicine see a.o. Jouanna (1995).
5. For more information on the Ancient Arab Medicine see a.o. Strohmaier (1995).
6. For more information on the Schola Medica Salernitana see Ventura (2019).

2.2   Towards a French medical vocabulary

Used next to Latin during the Middle Ages, the vernacular positioned itself first as a language that was capable of expressing cultural and literary phenomena, and later as a language that could also express scientific knowledge. The first steps that were taken to express medical concepts in the French vernacular made use of translations from Latin, or sometimes from Arabic or Greek. The first translations emerged in the 13th century, and flourished from the 14th century onwards, and focussed on the most influential classical authors such as Hippocrates and Galen, or contemporary authors, such as Mondeville and Chauliac. There were also some texts composed directly in the vernacular, although not many until the 16th century.[7] This explains why a large part of the medical vocabulary appeared during the period of Middle French (1300–1550).

The task of the medical translator was far from easy. Indeed, translators had numerous difficulties when they needed to render medical knowledge in their mother tongue, knowledge that was often only available to a limited number of learned persons. Moreover, the appropriate vernacular term to express a specific medical concept was usually lacking, since science was expressed until then in the learned languages.

2.3   Translation techniques and the coining of a new vocabulary

When translating a Latin text, translators had to make choices with respect to the expression of medical concepts in their mother tongue. The first choice was to use native words, if available. But frequently, translators were dealing with concepts that lacked an appropriate expression in the vernacular because they were unknown to the common people. Translators had several choices then: they could create a new term using a process of transliteration, which would result in a term that is only transparent to the learned; or they could adapt a term from the source language to the morphological system of the target language, which results in the borrowing of a term, using language material or techniques of the foreign language (see *infra*). Some translators indeed preferred to create terms based on vernacular words. Van Tricht (2015) studied the French medical terminology of the Middle Ages used in eight medical or surgical treatises, and she showed the importance of differentiating between four medical domains:

---

7. For an overview of medical texts translated or written in the French vernacular, see the remarks in Jacquart (1998:265 ff.), and the information provided by Van Tricht (2015:119 ff.). A large part of these texts are integrated in the CHrOMed corpus, which is incorporated in the DMF 2023 and can be consulted via a search term in this dictionary. Cf. Goyens et al. (2023).

anatomy, physiology, pathology and therapeutics. Each domain reveals differences in the type of terms used by translators (for the concept of neologisms in medieval France, see Duval 2011).

So, when creating new medical terms, a translator could use two categories of coining techniques:[8] word formations using foreign language material or techniques, or native word formations (see above). The first involves borrowings from another language, usually Latin, or Greek via Latin,[9] of:

a.   a word form unchanged, also called *xenism*, as in *epiglotus* (< Latin *epiglotus* 'epiglottis')
b.   a word form that has been adapted to the morphological system of the target language, as is the case in the integrated loanword *adustion* (< lat. *adustio*, alteration of the humors due to warming; inflammation)
c.   a word combination, called *calque*, which follows the syntax of the source language while using native words, e.g. *dure mere* borrowed from Latin *dura mater*
d.   a semantic borrowing, where the meaning of the foreign word is adopted by an existing target language word; an example is *couture*, which in a non medical context means 'sewing,' but in the medical domain means 'cranial suture' from the Latin *sutura*.

The second category of term formation techniques makes use of elements of the native language. The first technique is *derivation*, usually via affixation, where an existing (native or borrowed) root or stem is provided with a prefix or a suffix in order to coin a new word; an example is *melancolieus* 'who has a complexion linked to black bile' derived from the noun *melancolie* 'black bile.' New words can also be coined by means of compounding, where simple lexemes are joined together. Both lexemes can be from the native language: *basjoes* 'jaw, the lower lateral part of the head,' from *bas* 'low' and *joe* 'cheek,' or *neu de la gorge* 'Adam's apple,' literally 'node of the throat'; one element can originate from a foreign language: *semence generative* 'sperm,' where *generative* is a loanword from Latin. Another type of neology involving the native language is *conversion* (also known as *zero-derivation*), where a morphological form remains the same, but changes

---

8. Different typologies have been proposed for neology in French; as is shown by Van Tricht (2015:74) referring also to Sablayrolles (2000:71), almost every lexicographer has proposed one, sometimes several typologies, reflecting the point of view of the researcher: word formation, semantic criteria, origin, etc.

9. Direct borrowings from Greek are rare in medieval French, but became frequent during the 16th century. However, many words of Greek origin were borrowed in medieval Latin, and then in medieval French; see for an example Dévière and Goyens (2018).

its grammatical category and meaning: for example, the present participle *cauterisant*, of the verb *cauterisier* 'to cauterise,' becomes an adjective in *medecine cauterisante* 'cauterising medicine,' or the adjective *melancolieus*, which becomes a noun designating the person who suffers from an excess of black bile. Finally, a neologism can be created through a change of meaning, via metaphor, metonymy, semantic extension or restriction. For example, the original meaning of *fontenele* 'fontanelle' is 'small fountain,' but in a medical context it refers to a membranous gap between the bones of the skull in babies and small children. This is an example of a metaphor, where the gap is compared to the basin of a spring (FEW III:679b). The case of *selle* 'faeces' is an example of metonymy; originating from Latin *sella* 'seat,' and later in addition 'saddle,' the term assumed in Old French the meaning of 'commode,' hence the expression *aller à la selle* 'to evacuate faeces,' which explains why *selle* was used in medicine to refer to faeces.[10]

Depending on the medical domain, new terms were coined following different patterns, as shown by Van Tricht's study (2015), in which she compares the medical terminology in Evrart de Conty's *Livre des Problemes*, a translation and commentary of the pseudo-Aristotelian *Problemata*, to that of a series of medical texts of the same period.[11] First, 38 percent of the terminology of anatomy used in this study is composed of native terms (like *bras* 'arm' or *ainne* 'groin'), with the remaining being newly coined. As was said earlier, this is not surprising, since terms for body parts are common in language. As to neologisms in this domain, generally speaking, 37 percent of them used elements from a foreign language, and 24 percent used native elements (Van Tricht 2015: 205).

Van Tricht's study (2015: 283) also shows that the terminology of physiology was composed of terms whose origin shows another distribution, where native terms were less frequent. They are found in only 17 percent of that vocabulary (e.g. *halener* 'to exhale,' or *orine* 'urine'). The neologisms were formed by using native elements (42 percent, e.g. compounds such as *matere de generation* 'sperm,' or *sanc menstrueus* 'menstrual discharge'), or foreign elements (38 percent, e.g. integrated loanwords such as *cole* 'yellow bile,' borrowed from Latin *chole*, which was in turn borrowed from Greek χολή).

---

10. Eponymy, a type of word formation where the name of a person, such as a scientist, is used to refer to a disease, does not yet appear in French medieval medical terminology.

11. Evrart de Conty's *Problemes* was translated from the Latin translation of the original Greek treatise by Bartholomew of Messina and from Pietro de Abano's commentary on that translation. For information on these texts, see Guichard-Tesson (1990), De Leemans and Goyens (2005). The first medical texts with which Evrart de Conty's terminology was compared were surgical texts and medical treatises (see Van Tricht 2015: 119–134). The comparison with these texts shows that Evrart de Conty's terminology is quite representative for the medical terminology of his time.

In the field of pathology, there were even fewer native terms (11,19 percent, as in *avugle* 'blind' from Latin *ab oculis*, and *fievre* 'fever' from Latin *febris*). More than half (54 percent) of the neologisms were coined from foreign elements (e.g. *apoplexie* 'apoplexy' borrowed from Latin *apoplexia*, which in turn borrowed it from Greek ἀποπληξία), and about a third (34 percent) were forms constructed from native elements (e.g. *borgneté* 'strabismus' derived from the adjective *borgne*; cf. Van Tricht 2015: 390).

The last domain studied, therapeutics, contained even fewer native words (10,84 percent, e.g. *jeuner* 'to fast,' from Latin *jejunare*, and *pourre* 'medicinal powder'). Most neologisms (69 percent) were coined from foreign elements (e.g. *adustion* 'cauter,' borrowed from Latin *adustio*, and *ptisane coulee* 'filtered tea made with barley,' a calque from Latin *ptisana colata*). Only 19 percent of the neologisms were constructions based on native elements (e.g. a verbal phrase such as *mouvoir par vomite* 'to purge by vomiting' or *confort* 'strengthening,' converted from the verb *conforter* 'to strengthen'; cf. Van Tricht 2015: 516–517).

To conclude this survey of terminology from different medical domains, it can be noted that varying proportions of native terms were used. Neologisms accounted for 80 to 90 percent of the terminology, and a foreign language, particularly Latin, was a major contributor of new terms. Anatomy is the only domain where native words comprised a large part of the terminology, more than a third, but where neologisms were also mainly coined with foreign, viz. Latin, elements. With the numerous translations from Latin treatises, and with all medical study and knowledge transmission carried out in Latin, this does not come as a surprise. Clerics, who knew and often translated Latin, would be familiar with a terminology where Latin stems are prominent. Nevertheless, how could translators make sure the terminology was understood?

Translators and authors adopted several strategies to integrate neologisms into their text. While some authors, such as Pierre Bersuire or Nicole Oresme, added a list of new words to their writings (see e.g. Lusignan 1986: 153–154), the most common method was the use of synonymic pairs and glosses (Duval 2011: 521–522). In a synonymic pair, the neologism was usually presented first, and then juxtaposed with a para-synonym, as in *la sanie ou la boe* referring to pus, where the first term is a loanword from Latin *sanies*, and the second the native word originally designating mud or dirt, and later putrefied matter (Van Tricht 2015: 405). Glosses are explanations of words, as in "fievres causonides, c'est a dire fievres ardans, de grant inflammation et de grant adustion" (Evrart de Conty, *Problemes*, BnF, fr. 24281, fol. 27v, l. 42; cf. Goyens and Dévière 2007: 277), where the clarification of *fievres causonides* is introduced by *c'est a dire* 'that is to say.'

Many medieval translators of scientific texts were aware that they were facing a difficult task: they needed to be faithful to the source text, but they also had to deliver a text in a clear, well-balanced language. Some translators, such as Jean d'Antioche, who translated rhetorical treatises at the end of the 13th century (Monfrin 1964:225; Lusignan 1986:168; Goyens 1994:177), or Evrart de Conty, who translated pseudo-Aristotle's *Problemata* (Guichard-Tesson 1990:140–141), even wrote about these challenges and expressly commented on the difficulties associated with the translation.

3.   French botanical terminology during the Middle Ages

Any historical discussion about terminology requires the existence of a scientific field, and yet botany is a field that did not constitute an autonomous discipline in the Middle Ages; universities did not teach it as such (Weijers and Holtz 1997). Moreover, the French noun *botanique* and the English noun *botany* were only first attested in the 17th century, in 1680 and 1696 respectively (TLFi, OED 1989). However, people were familiar with and interested in plants, although this was mainly via two identified scientific fields: medicine (Hunt 2008) and agriculture (Vigneron 2023). Unlike pharmacopoeia treatises, which are often referred to as *herbariums*, the writings on agriculture provide a more complete picture of plant-related terminology, beyond mere plant names, sometimes including definitions. Even if their focus was on the practical use of plants, the great encyclopaedias, which proliferated in Latin from the 13th century onwards, included separate books on plants, which is a clear indication of knowledge and interest (e.g. Ventura 2007). Finally, worth mentioning are the plant Sections 20 to 22 of pseudo-Aristotle's *Problemata*, which was translated into French around 1380 by Evrart de Conty,[12] who also added his own comments. Although botany was not strictly speaking a distinct field recognised by universities, there was nevertheless a specialised lexicon used in texts which displayed an outline of a botanical corpus. The texts were first written in Latin,[13] then, from the 13th and especially from the 14th century onwards, French translations appeared, which necessarily used a vernacular terminology. For example, the most well-known *herbarium* from medieval times, the *Tractatus de herbis* (Collins and Raphael 2003; Ventura 2009), was translated into French and widely distributed (see López Piñero et al. 2000–2001).

---

12. See footnote 11.

13. In medieval Latin, two major works were not translated into French: Albert the Great's *De Vegetabilibus* (Meyer and Jessen 1867) and Pierre d'Auvergne's *Sententia super librum* "De vegetabilibus et plantis" (Poortman 2003).

Moreover, medieval scholars produced self-contained glossaries to support translations from Latin to French, thereby initiating an approach that sometimes went further than the work of lexicographers, who arranged terms alphabetically. Indeed, some of these scholars proposed an onomasiological structure by including a dedicated section for plant names, or by dealing only with botany and products from the plant world for pharmacopoeia recipes. For example, the *Glasgow glossary*, in Latin and Anglo-Norman, groups plant names into two lists entitled *De herbis* (Hunt 1991: 401–419). Glossaries devoted exclusively to the botanical lexicon (*Synonyma herbarum*) were numerous in England in the 13th and 14th century, sometimes even adding to Latin and Anglo-Norman the corresponding designations in Irish (Galderisi 2011: 487–499; Hunt 1986; Hunt 1989a; Hunt 1989b; García González 2007). This attention to translation from one language into another might lead us to believe that the terminology was constructed and fixed. In fact, there was no stability, as synonymic networks emerged in both Latin and French without a preference for a specific term, but instead showing a succession of possible denominations. Texts translated into French were not exempt from this synonymy either. For example, the *Livre des prouffitz champestres et ruraulx* (henceforth referred to as LPCR), an anonymous translation of Pietro de' Crescenzi's *Liber ruralium commodorum*, alternates, depending on the chapter or even within the same title or sentence, between the use of *corulus* and *coudrier*, or *agnus castus* and *aignel chaste*. In the case of Latin words, the variety of borrowing techniques used resulted in synonymy, including xenisms (e.g. *corullus*, which appears only once in the LPCR) and borrowings or peregrinisms (e.g. *agnus castus* which is found in several French texts). Great caution is obviously required in this kind of distinction between xenisms and peregrinisms. While there is certainly some concern about the presence of such synonyms, these examples do reflect a difference between a foreign word that is perceived to be unusual, and a foreign word that is commonly used in French speech (Vigneron 2008: 29–30), a difference in usage and connotation that may have some purpose. Finally, the LPCR shows that integrated borrowings, i.e. borrowings respecting French morphology, are very common, for example *cucurbite* from the Latin *cucurbita*. Translators could thus create neologisms which would not necessarily be adopted into French. Similarly, *pommes puniques* and *pommes granates*, synonymous terms for 'pomegranates,' are respectively modelled on the Latin *mala Punica* and *mala granata*, but the latter is well attested in Middle French, whereas the former is not (Vigneron 2008: 32–34).

But more than plant names, which correspond to a need for reliable plant identification, it is rather the explicit relationships established between generic and specific terms that best testify to the establishment of botanical terminology in medieval French. In this respect, longer texts, which have more context, provide clearer evidence of the relationship between a hypernym and hyponyms than simple glossaries, which makes these types of texts particularly interesting for historical terminology research. For example, in the following text from the LPCR, the term *espece* is used to designate a plant as belonging to a group of plants: "L'en trouve trop d'especes de vignes et sont appellees par divers noms en diverses contrees et diverses provinces." (Vigneron 2023: 423)

The term *vigne* appears as a hypernym, and the text later cites many hyponyms presented as "especes de vignes." Moreover, interestingly, attention is also paid to local designations. This relationship between the general and the specific results in a fairly large number of compound nouns for plants. For example, in Evrart de Conty's *Livre des problemes*, we find the generic *ape*, and the text clearly indicates several hyponyms such as *ape renine* and *ape de ris* (Goyens 2005: 155–158). We can therefore see that the two modes of composition already existed: the hypernym supplemented by a relational qualifying adjective or by a complement of the noun.

Approaches that demonstrate classification are also worth highlighting, although one cannot really speak of a taxonomy for the medieval period. For example, the antonymous adjectives of Middle French *sauvage* 'wild,' on the one hand, and *privé* or *domestique* 'cultivated,' on the other hand, make it possible to identify two major categories in the plant world serving, in particular, to distinguish between tree species, such as the olive tree, presented as cultivated, and the oleaster, described as a wild olive tree (Laforêt 2021: "Arbres privés, arbres sauvages"). In the same vein, the two main categories of plants were designated by two terms, *herbes* and *arbres*, which had a classificatory value, despite the difficulty of clearly defining them, as some plants are found in one or the other category depending on the author (Vigneron 2010: 20–23). In the category of trees, we note the neological creation of *arbret* and *arbuste* in Middle French to designate a subcategory, *arbuste* being more of a hapax in the translation of Pietro de' Crescenzi's *Liber ruralium commodorum*, while *arbret* seems to be the term truly integrated into the French language of the 14th century (Vigneron 2010: 27–28). However, the latter is sometimes replaced by the locution *petit arbre*, which seems to be more commonplace. Admittedly, the terminology was not perfect in the sense that there was no single term for the category of cultivated plants and that neologisms such as *arbret* were not used systematically, but instead were sometimes glossed with a locution. However, this is not unique to the Middle Ages, since plant names in contemporary scientific botanical nomenclature also feature synonymy, for example according to either the Linnaeus or the Lamarck taxonomies. It is therefore relevant to underline the existence of a way of thinking that is not far from an ontology, because it is clear that the medieval scholars had a perception of the world which, starting from plants, proceeded from the generic to the specific when delimiting objects such as herbs and trees. The properties of these objects were described, as well as the relationships between them: for example, some trees were described as smaller than others, but were still related to the larger trees because they shared certain characteristics.

Beyond the naming of plants and their rough classifications, it is also important to consider the terminology of plant morphology and physiology, which can be found in agricultural treatises such as the LPCR or in encyclopaedias translated from Latin into French. Indeed, not only do these resources contain terms, they also, sometimes, include definitions, or elements of definitions, marking specialised use. Jean Corbechon's French translation *Proprietés des choses* (1372) of the Latin volume by Barthélemy l'Anglais includes such semantic descriptions. For example, the term *bois* 'wood' is referred to as a hard material of a tree, a feature that is generally known and is also mentioned in other sources (DFSM, *s. v. bois*, quote: Jean Corbechon). But whereas in other sources *bois* comprises the whole of the tree trunk, here a finer distinction is made by also describing the *mouelle* 'pith' in the *bois*, which, it is added, provides for the tree's nourishment. Thus a meronymic relationship is established between the term *bois* and *mouelle*. The term *bois* is also a meronym of *arbre* 'tree', as Jean Corbechon explicitly wrote that *bois* was a "partie de l'arbre" (one part of a tree).

4.   **Conclusion**

In medieval times, the effort to achieve scientific conceptualisation could be measured by the use of terms, in Latin as well as in French, even though some would be abandoned later. Some of the developments in this period, which would be taken up later in modern times, are worth pointing out, such as hierarchical conceptual relations and onomasiological structuring. The usual medieval synonymy was sometimes acted upon in a conscious way, as can be seen in some glossaries in particular, and dealing with synonymy is still one of the major issues in terminology today. In summary, most of the defining features of modern terminology were already present in the Middle Ages. Despite the risk of projecting anachronistic conceptions onto the past, the search for defining features of contemporary terminology in medieval treatises proves fruitful, showing the early contribution of this ancient period to the reflection on terminology as a discipline.

References

Collins, Minta, and Sandra Raphael (eds). 2003. *A Medieval Herbal. A Facsimile of British Library Egerton MS 747*. London: British Library.

De Leemans, Pieter, and Michèle Goyens. 2005. "La transmission des savoirs en passant par trois langues: le cas des *Problemata* d'Aristote traduits en latin et en moyen français." In *La Transmission des savoirs au Moyen Âge et à la Renaissance. Vol. 1. du XII*^{e} *au XV*^{e} *siècle*, ed. by Pierre Nobel, 231–257. Besançon: Presses universitaires de Franche-Comté.

Dévière, Elisabeth, and Michèle Goyens. 2018. "La médecine en traduction: Barthélémy de Messine, Pietro d'Abano et Évrart de Conty, un trio inextricable." In *Booldly Bot Meekly. Essays on the Theory and Practice of Translation in the Middle Ages in Honour of Roger Ellis*. The Medieval Translator — Traduire au Moyen Âge 14, ed. by Catherine Batt, and René Tixier, 341–359. Turnhout: Brepols.

DFSM: *Dictionnaire du français scientifique médiéval*, Sorbonne Université & Université Grenoble Alpes.

DMF: *Dictionnaire du Moyen Français*, version 2023. ATILF — CNRS & Université de Lorraine.

Ducos, Joëlle. 2015. "Terminologie médiévale française face au latin: un couple nécessaire?" In *Le Français en diachronie. Nouveaux objets et méthodes*, ed. by Anne Carlier, Michèle Goyens, and Béatrice Lamiroy, 133–160. Bern: Peter Lang.

Duval, Frédéric. 2011. "Les néologismes." In *Translations médiévales. Cinq siècles de traductions en français au Moyen Âge (XI*^{e}-*XV*^{e} *siècles). Étude et répertoire*, ed. by Claudio Galderisi, I, 499–534. Turnhout: Brepols.

FEW: von Wartburg, Walther. 1922. *Französisches Etymologisches Wörterbuch. Eine Darstellung des galloromanischen Sprachschatzes*. Bonn: K. Schroeder — Basel: R.G. Zbinden.

Galderisi, Claudio (ed). 2011. *Translations médiévales. Cinq siècles de traductions en français au Moyen Age (XI*^{e}-*XV*^{e} *siècles). Étude et répertoire*, vol. 2. Turnhout: Brepols.

García González, Alejandro. 2007. *Alphita*. Firenze: Sismel Edizioni del Galluzzo.

Goyens, Michèle. 1994. *Émergence et Évolution du syntagme nominal en français*. Sciences pour la communication 43. Bern: Peter Lang.

Goyens, Michèle. 2005. "Le lexique des plantes et la traduction des *Problèmes* d'Aristote par Evrart de Conty (c. 1380)." *Le Moyen français*, 55–56: 145–165.

Goyens, Michèle, Sylvie Bazin-Tacchella, and Gilles Souvay. 2023. "La dictionnairique au service de la morphologie : le *Dictionnaire du Moyen Français* 2020 et la base *Cormedlex.*" In *Regards croisés sur les dictionnaires à l'ère du numérique*, numéro des *ÉLA. Études de linguistique appliquée*, n° 211, juillet-septembre 2023, ed. by Anaïs Chambat, 335–348. Paris: Klincksieck.

Goyens, Michèle, and Elisabeth Dévière. 2007. "Le développement du vocabulaire médical en latin et moyen français dans les traductions médiévales des *Problemata* d'Aristote." In *La Traduction vers le moyen français*, ed. by Claudio Galderisi, and Cinzia Pignatelli, 259–281. Turnhout: Brepols.

Guichard-Tesson, Françoise. 1990. "Le métier de traducteur et de commentateur au XIVe siècle d'après Evrart de Conty." *Le Moyen français* 24–25: 131–167.

Hossfeld, Paul (ed). 2003. Alberti Magni opera omnia. *Meteora*, T.VI, 1. Aschendorff: Monasterii Westfalorum.

Hunt, Tony (ed). 1986. "The Botanical Glossaries in MS. London BL Add. 15236." *Pluteus* 4: 101–118, 139–150.

Hunt, Tony (ed). 1989a. "The Trilingual Glossary in MS London, BL Sloane 146, f. 69v-72r." *English Studies* 70/4: 289–310.

Hunt, Tony (ed). 1989b. *Plant Names of Medieval England*. Cambridge: D. S. Brewer.

Hunt, Tony (ed). 1991. *Teaching and Learning Latin in 13th-Century England*. Vol 1. Cambridge: D. S. Brewer.

Hunt, Tony (ed). 2008. *An Old French Herbal (Ms Princeton U.L. Garrett 131)*. Turnhout: Brepols.

Jacquart, Danielle. 1998. *La Médecine médiévale dans le cadre parisien. XIVe-XVe siècle*. Paris: Fayard.

Jouanna, Jacques. 1995. "La naissance de l'art médical occidental." In *Histoire de la pensée médicale en Occident. 1. Antiquité et Moyen Âge*, ed. by Mirko D. Grmek, and Bernardino Fantino, 25–66. Paris: Seuil.

Kocourek, Rostislav. 1991. *La Langue française de la technique et de la science. Vers une linguistique de la langue savante*. Wiesbaden: Oscar Brandstetter.

Laforêt, Alice. 2021. "'Tout arbre sauvage devient bon et privé par bon labourage.' Domestiquer l'arbre au Moyen Âge, de l'encyclopédiste au prédicateur." *Questes* 43: 57–73.

López Piñero, José María, Natacha Elaguina, Carlos Miranda García, and María Luz López Terrada (eds). 2000–2001. *Le Livre des simples médecines (fac-similé du ms. de la Bibliothèque nationale de Russie Fr. F. v. VI 1)*. Barcelona: M. Moleiro.

Lusignan, Serge. 1986. *Parler vulgairement. Les intellectuels et la langue française aux XIIIe et XIVe siècles*. Études Médiévales. Paris: Vrin, Montréal: Presses de l'Université de Montréal.

Meyer, Ernst H. F. and Carl Friedrich Wilhelm Jessen (eds). 1867. *Albert le Grand, De vegetabilibus libri VII. Historiae naturalis pars XVIII*. Berlin: G. Reimer.

Monfrin, Jean. 1964. "Humanisme et traductions au Moyen Âge." In *L'Humanisme médiéval dans les littératures romanes du XIIe au XIVe siècle*. Actes et Colloques 3, ed. by Anthime Fourrier, 217–246. Paris: Klincksieck.

OED 1989. *The Oxford English Dictionary*. Second edition by J.A. Simpson, and E.S.C. Weiner, vol. 2. Oxford: Clarendon Press.

Poortman, E.L.J. (ed). 2003. *Pierre d'Auvergne, Sententia super librum "De vegetabilibus et plantis."* Leiden: Brill.

Sablayrolles, Jean-François. 2000. *La Néologie en français contemporain*. Paris: Honoré Champion.

Singer, Julie. 2005. "L'horlogerie et la mécanique de l'allégorie chez Jean Froissart." *Médiévales* 49: 155–172.

Strohmaier, Gotthard. 1995. "Réception et tradition: la médecine dans le monde arabe et byzantin." In *Histoire de la pensée médicale en Occident. 1. Antiquité et Moyen Âge*, ed. by Mirko D. Grmek, and Bernardino Fantino, 123–149. Paris: Seuil.

TLFi: *Trésor de la langue Française informatisé*. ATILF — CNRS & Université de Lorraine.

Van Tricht, Ildiko. 2015. *Science en texte et contexte. La terminologie médicale française utilisée dans le Livre des problemes d'Evrart de Conty à la lumière du discours médical médiéval.* PhD dissertation, unpublished. Leuven : KU Leuven.

Ventura, Iolanda (ed). 2007. *Bartholomaeus Anglicus, De proprietatibus rerum*, vol. VI, liber XVII. Turnhout: Brepols.

Ventura, Iolanda (ed). 2009. *Ps. Bartholomaeus Mini de Senis, Tractatus de herbis (ms. London, British Library, Egerton 747).* Firenze: Sismel Edizioni del Galluzzo.

Ventura, Iolanda. 2019. "La 'Scuola medica Salernitana' e la sua produzione scritta: risultati e questioni aperte intorno ai 'maestri salernitani'." In *La medicina nel Basso*, 213–284. Spoleto: Fondazione Centro Italiano di Studi sull'Altro Medioevo.

Verna, Catherine. 2017. *L'Industrie au village. Essai de microhistoire (Arles-sur-Tech, XIVᵉ et XVᵉ siècles).* Paris: Les Belles Lettres.

Vigneron, Fleur. 2008. "Le lexique insolite dans le Livre des prouffiz champestres et ruraulx de Pierre de Crescens." *Recherches sur l'imaginaire. Écritures insolites* 33: 27–39.

Vigneron, Fleur. 2010. "L'arbre au Moyen Âge." In *L'Arbre au Moyen Âge*, ed. by Valérie Fasseur, Danièle James-Raoul, and Jean-René Valette, 19–32. Paris: PUPS.

Vigneron, Fleur (ed). 2023. *Le Livre des prouffitz champestres et ruraulx de Pierre de Crescens*, vol. 1: *Introduction et texte (livres I-VIII).* Paris: Honoré Champion.

Weijers, Olga, and Louis Holtz (eds). 1997. *L'Enseignement des disciplines à la Faculté des arts (Paris et Oxford, XIIIᵉ–XVᵉ siècles).* Turnhout: Brepols.

Weill-Parot, Nicolas. 2019. "Le projectile, l'aimant et la doctrine de l'*impetus* dans la physique du XIVᵉ siècle." In *De l'homme, de la nature et du monde*, 200–314. Genève: Droz.

Wirth, Jean. 2015. *Villard de Honnecourt, architecte du XIIIᵉ siècle.* Genève: Droz.

CHAPTER 3

Terminology in the 17th and 18th centuries

Maria Teresa Zanola
Università Cattolica del Sacro Cuore

What is nowadays referred to with the word *terminology* owes much to the
European tradition of lexicographical coding and linguistic-scientific
investigation that emerged in the 17th and 18th centuries. Such research was
carried out through the 'term' and 'nomenclature' paradigm, along with the
neological and communicative requirements of sciences, arts, and crafts.
This chapter illustrates the depth of the investigation which highlighted the
characteristics of terminology as well as its linguistic and cultural value and
aimed to attain communicative mediation between language and specialised
knowledge throughout these centuries.

Advancements in encyclopaedism and the birth of new scientific
languages triggered a conceptual shift from *nomenclature* to *terminology*:
therefore, the spheres of knowledge where the concept of terminology was
conceived will be explored. This interdisciplinary space where language and
technical and scientific knowledge were at play, where new concepts took
shape and opportunities for their communication grew, is examined here
with a focus on the following areas: the problems surrounding nomenclature and the classification of scientific and technical lexicons; the
production of technical and specialised dictionaries during the 17th century
and the first half of the 18th century; the debate on terminology in scientific
works of the time; and the contribution of the new chemistry of Lavoisier
and Guyton de Morveau to the development of terminology
systematisation.

Keywords: specialised lexicon, encyclopaedism, specialised lexicography,
knowledge transfer, Enlightenment

1.   Introduction

The modern concept of 'terminology' matured in linguistic and scientific thought
during the 17th and 18th centuries, as well as within European lexicographical and
encyclopaedic coding. During this period, the notions of *term* and *nomenclature*
were defined according to the neological and communicative needs of sciences,

https://doi.org/10.1075/tlrp.24.03zan

arts and crafts. Developments during this period enhanced the characteristics of the notion of terminology by emphasising its cultural value for communicative mediation between language and specialised knowledge.

French language historian Ferdinand Brunot (1930) posited three main phases in the development of scientific French in the 18th century. The first phase is that of the initial contact of science with its public, thanks to popularisers such as Réaumur and the Abbé Nollet. The second phase is that of the elaboration of a technical language and its dissemination through Diderot and d'Alembert's *Encyclopédie*. In the third phase, "under the influence of Condillac, a theory of systematic scientific language prevailed, of which the creation of Lavoisier's chemical nomenclature is a brilliant and decisive application" (Brunot 1930: 524; our translation).

The development of scientific language is that of its terminologies, whose role was fundamental in the construction and transmission of knowledge in 18th century Europe, as well as in the development of methods of analysis. These methods of analysis also emerged thanks to the scientific and technical developments in the arts and crafts: terminological activities intensified in response to urgent needs to describe and record the knowledge and know-how of craftsmen and manufacturers, as well as to improve the techniques themselves.

Scientific and technical innovators were the architects and creators of terminology: the creation of a specialised vocabulary became a means of technology transfer. Attention was paid not only to naming the concept or object, but also to defining it. It was understood that definitions help to clarify concepts in a given code. Moreover, order and clarity in the description of concepts lead to the possibility of the concepts being universally understood.

2. From nomenclature to terminology in Italy and France

In English, the first recorded use of the word *term*, meaning a word or phrase used in a limited or precise sense, was noted in the late 14th century. The Medieval Latin use of *terminus*, employed in mathematics and logic, is the reference point for its evolution in European languages. The first edition (1694) of the *Dictionnaire de l'Académie française* recorded *terme* in the sense of "ways of speaking which are peculiar to some art, to some science" (our translation), a definition which remained almost unchanged until Littré's dictionary (1873, *ad vocem*). The prefaces of 18th century scientific and encyclopaedic works demonstrate the extent to which these issues were debated: the deep theoretical, epistemological, and practical analyses constitute a frame of reference for terminological studies. These discussions focused on the fields of knowledge that saw the birth of the concept of *terminology*, an interdisciplinary area between language and technical and scientific knowledge, between new concepts and their dissemination, the traces of which are scattered throughout the history of French, Italian and more generally European culture. In this chapter we will focus on the following cases: (1) in 17th century Italy, the enrichment of the technical lexicon by Leopoldo de' Medici in the third edition of the *Vocabolario degli Accademici della Crusca*, (2) in 18th century France, the compilation of a specialised dictionary of artistic terms, and (3) the conceptual shift from *nomenclature* to *terminology* thanks to the birth of new scientific languages.

There is an abundance of examples showing how terminology became the subject of increased interest in Italy. Italian contributions to the vocabulary of architecture are a prime example of the construction of a specialised European vocabulary. There were also works that listed specific vocabularies of trades, such as Tomaso Garzoni's *La piazza universale di tutte le professioni del mondo* (1585). For his part, in the third edition of *Vocabolario degli Accademici della Crusca* (henceforth referred to as the Crusca Vocabulary), Leopoldo de' Medici set out to bridge the gap between the literary language, the language of academics and the language of economic and social life. Indeed, he applied the experimental method used in the natural sciences — learned from Torricelli and Galileo — to the study of language to launch his unprecedented endeavour to compile an inventory of the lexicon of the arts and crafts. This method involved a system of surveys and interviews with the craftsmen of Florence (Parodi 1975; Setti 2010: 21). Through oral sources (interviews) on the techniques and knowledge of the arts and crafts, Leopoldo de' Medici was able to collect valuable documentation on the terminology used in these fields (Setti 2010). This documentation permitted the extraction of terminological units for the classification in the *Crusca Vocabulary*, with the aim of ensuring their permanent preservation and the dissemination of knowledge. From 1650 onwards, Leopoldo de' Medici catalogued more than 9,000 technical terms, which were added to the artistic and technical terminology of the third edition (Accademia della Crusca 1691) of the *Crusca Vocabulary* (Zanola 2015; 2018a: 162–164). The accounts of the craftsmen illustrating the phases of their work reveal the terminological richness of their trades through the designations of, for example, procedures, instruments, and phases of work. These accounts constitute an authentic reference model for identifying the terminology of the arts and crafts (Zanola 2018b: 219–222).

Leopoldo de' Medici's papers on chemistry (Setti 2010: 130–162), which provided a clear and up-to-date synthesis of the knowledge on the subject, are also worthy of consideration. He explained the procedures of chemical experimentation of the time, using the terminology necessary to also deal with more general theoretical concepts (Setti 2010: 41). Each term is described as follows: first the origin of the term, with information on its etymology and geographical origin, followed by the Greek etymon; in some cases, the source of the information is indicated (Setti 2010: 130–131). These terms were also inserted into the third edition of the *Crusca Vocabulary* (1691), following a procedure that closely resembles that of modern times, i.e. building a corpus, extracting the terms from it, and then classifying the corresponding concepts according to lexicographical practices.

Systematic terminology research was carried out by Filippo Baldinucci in his *Vocabolario toscano dell'arte del disegno* (1681). In this work, he collected and arranged a wealth of terms, the fruit of extensive readings and fieldwork, in alphabetical order. Baldinucci aimed to promote an appreciation of Florence's artistic assets and to demonstrate what Tuscan masterpieces represented in the techniques and arts of the time. This art lexicon is linked to its sources: Baldinucci combined the artistic literature with the spoken vocabulary that he picked up in sculptors' and engravers' workshops. In the *Introduction* (1681:X), he apologised to the reader if his explanations were too long, but it was not a narrative to be read in the course of one sitting: "this effort of mine is not a history that you should read fluently […], it is a declaration of words, terms, qualities, and names of things" (our translation) for readers.

Baldinucci presented his art lexicon using entries that had already appeared in the second edition of the *Crusca Vocabulary* (Accademia della Crusca 1623) and included a concise definition of the common meaning of each term. Starting from this definitional base, he inserted technical details reflecting historical and erudite knowledge of the arts. Baldinucci's Vocabulary is considered an innovative work in the European context (Zanola 2015).

Throughout the 18th century, attention to terms and specialised lexicons was strongly linked to the debate on new terms and the concern for lexical clarity. This century culminated in an intense development that gave rise to the systematic nomenclature of botany and zoology, as well as the creation of chemical terms. It is precisely the scientists of the time, notably the naturalist Linnaeus and the chemists Lavoisier, Guyton de Morveau and Berthollet, who were the precursors of modern terminology, as their work established a rigorous system of nomenclature in the scientific fields (Zanola 2018b: 225–226).

In the following paragraphs, the conceptual shift from *nomenclature* to *terminology* is analysed through the emergence of new sciences — from alchemy to chemistry — and the ensuing systematisation of terminologies in scientific monographs and encyclopaedic works. This conceptual shift first became evident in the formation of new terms which were based on Greek-Latin roots in the case of anatomical nomenclature following the model of the Linnaean classification. Linnaeus created new terms according to a binomial nomenclature, i.e. the two-term naming system coining a unique two-word combination for every species. He used this system consistently for plants in the 1753 edition of his *Species*

Plantarum, and for animals in 1758 in the 10th edition of his *Systema Naturae*. These two dates are still considered milestones in scientific naming (Winston 2018: 1123).

Linnaeus and Lavoisier were the creators of a language that described a new science, botany and chemistry respectively, intended to be well conceived and well expressed: the constitution of a correct terminological framework marked the birth and development of innovation in these sciences (Grimaldi 2017; Grimaldi and Humbley 2021).

No terminological creation arises in a specific domain without expressive needs; on the contrary, the new term takes on the most appropriate forms to fulfil the communicative needs of that specific community of users/specialists. This creation of new nomenclatures mainly concerns scientific language and has a profound influence on the methods of formation of new terms: the aim is that technical and scientific language/terminology should be formed according to principles and methods that lead to the creation of coherent systems that are as monoreferential, precise and clear as possible.

Terminology can be examined from three angles: the scientific concepts themselves, the conceptual system that they comprise, and the terms that denote them (Rey 2010: 184–185). If we distinguish the linguistic notion of a word or lexical unit from the philosophical notion of a *name* — assuming that there is a relation between a naming sign and classes of designated objects — , the systematic dimension of the notion of *term* becomes apparent. *Term* implies a noun in the sense of *name* (even though it is not necessarily a noun, it can be a verb or an adjective, or a phrase that assumes one of these functions). It is therefore a noun in the sense of a designator given as a whole (Rey 2010: 184). The term *nomenclature* was confirmed in the 18th century to designate all the terms used in a science, an art or a technique. This was adequate for the classifications of Linnaeus, but it is *terminology* that corresponds to the creation of new terms by Duhamel du Monceau, Guyton de Morveau and Lavoisier. In *La physique des arbres* (1758), Duhamel du Monceau defined nomenclature as the science of plant names, a part of botany, "the true key" to botany, which consisted in knowing not just the names but the plants themselves. Order and clarity characterised the description of concepts and paved the way for a universally known language (Duhamel du Monceau 1758: III, our translation): "Nomenclature is [...] an important means of acquiring more useful knowledge: it is, so to speak, a vestibule that one must necessarily pass through before arriving in the rooms that make up the immediate usefulness of a fine house." This nomenclature was the "vestibule" to be crossed to reach the heart of the house: it was accessible thanks to classification establishing "general divisions and particular subdivisions."

The encyclopaedism of the 18th century highlighted the richness of the French craft and manufacturing tradition: during this century the coherent and comprehensive use of scientific language took shape (Zanola 2014: 32–35; 2018b: 225–230). Through teaching and popularisation, scientists introduced their listeners to new uses of language. The language of science was developed and became a part of science itself (Brunot 1930: 575–576): these issues of nomenclature were no longer secondary problems for scholars. On the contrary, these scholars felt the need to fine-tune the language by accepting or rejecting expressions that did not correspond exactly to their understanding of reality. We will further explore such considerations about terminology in the following paragraphs, through the analysis of lexicographic issues.

3. Descriptive methods in dictionaries and encyclopaedias

In the course of the 18th century, the need to describe the specialised terminology of science and technology led to the compilation of a large number of thematic dictionaries and dictionaries of science and technology, some the effort of a single scholar, others collaborative works.

At the request of Colbert, the Académie des Sciences undertook to compile a summary of "techniques" (crafts, trades, etc.) as early as 1675. At the beginning of the 18th century, under the direction of Réaumur followed by Duhamel du Monceau, the *Descriptions des arts et métiers, faites ou approuvées par Messieurs de l'Académie royale des sciences de Paris* were initiated in 1761, culminating in the publication of 50 volumes in 1782. This collection made a major contribution to the field of mechanics by describing all the methods and machines in use in the practice of the arts (Gille 1952: 28).

From 1751 to 1772, the thirty-five volumes of the *Encyclopédie ou Dictionnaire raisonné des Sciences, des Arts et des métiers*, edited by Diderot and d'Alembert, were published. The alphabetically arranged entries reflect the immense scientific, technical and technological achievements of the period (Darnton 1979). Other noteworthy works that were published in Europe were inspired by this encyclopaedic tradition including the works of Francesco Griselini for Italian (1768–1778) and of Father Terreros for Spanish (1786–1793) (Alvar Ezquerra 1987). The content of the *Encyclopédie* was continued in the *Encyclopédie méthodique*, a series of thematically-arranged dictionaries published by Panckoucke between 1782 and 1832 (Watts 1958; Rey C. 2014), each of which contained a standardised index that served as an access point for its contents. The range of disciplines, sciences and techniques described in these works is impressive.

The numerous technical and scientific vocabularies that were published in France in the course of this century are a rich source for the study of specialised lexicons. Examples of these include the dictionaries of agriculture by Liger (1703), of music by Sébastien de Brossard (1703), of commerce by Jacques Savary des Bruslons (1723–1730), of natural history by Valmont de Bomare (1764), of botany and pharmacy by Dom Nicolas Alexandre (1768), of botany by Bulliard (1797), and of physics by Sigaud de La Fond (1781), as well as numerous dictionaries of chemistry. Nor should we forget the specialised lexicographic works in English dating back from the Middle Ages to the Renaissance (Osselton 1999) and into the 17th and 18th centuries (Shapiro 2020).

All this terminological work recorded the peculiarities of variation due, on the one hand, to the variety of names and denominations used in various practices and innovations, and on the other hand to the desire for each trade to highlight its distinctiveness. Scientific terminologies appear to be more stable and homogeneous than terminologies from technical fields, which led to scientific terminologies being used to set the standards for reasoned principles of neology. Quemada (1978: 1153–1154) observed that these terminologies aimed to methodically construct systematic and hierarchical metalanguages, thus going beyond the purely denominative function of nomenclatures. Whether new terms are created or existing words are given new meanings, in the transition from word to term, thanks to the process of terminologisation, terminology is immediately used in texts in the fields concerned, which brings us back to the modern practices of contemporary analysis: the creation of the neologism, the definition of the term and its insertion into specialised discourse (which makes it possible to locate and extract it).

These lexicographical works were inspired by this systematic approach and offered the opportunity to develop useful and necessary methodological reflections for language exploration and the classification of terminology itself.

4.   Terminology in 18th century scientific and encyclopaedic works

The process of naming concepts is often the result of superimposed linguistic and technical interventions, which occur as the concept evolves. In the history of the formation of scientific and technical terminology, four main actors are involved: scholars, encyclopaedists, civil servants in charge of industrial activities and craftsmen. The cultural ferment surrounding techniques is the result of rich exchanges among these protagonists. These exchanges helped to establish a very dense and diverse fabric contributing to the development of modern technical and scientific knowledge and its terminologies (Zanola 2014: 76–79). The work that was carried out throughout the 18th century thus offers a detailed and thorough reflection on the terminological state of the arts and crafts, which reaches a degree of terminological standardisation.

In the Preface to the second edition of *Descriptions des Arts et métiers*, Jean-Élie Bertrand (1771:VII-VIII) pointed out that one of the great challenges in the description of the arts is the language of the craftsmen themselves. He therefore proposed a way to standardise terminology in order to reach a level of precision that enabled everyone to carry out all the processes of the arts.

As previously mentioned, Colbert also endeavoured to describe the arts (Swiggers 1984: 84). From 1732 onwards, at his initiative, the Académie des Sciences (1732–1734) published seven volumes describing various machines and inventions with the intent of inspiring further innovation. These machine tools, designed to produce objects for the court, aristocracy, and certain privileged families, were the result of technical and scientific experimentation, innovation and creativity, and represented the discoveries of the time: these purpose-built machines slowly developed into machines that triggered the Industrial Revolution. We will analyse technical terminology and machine construction as further examples.

The term *art* should be understood in the same sense it had at the time, i.e. that of the Greek term *technê,* meaning art, craft, technique or skill. In the *Encyclopédie*, Diderot added an important sub-entry entitled *De la langue des arts*, where he clarified that the *arts* were meant to designate *techniques*. In doing so he immediately highlighted one of the great difficulties in terminology, namely synonymy. He also noted the distinctions in naming that arise from degrees of hyponymy, all-part relations and diatopic variations, culminating in the wish for "elements of the grammar of the Arts" (Zanola 2014: 41–56). In the entry *Art*, Diderot pointed out the over-abundance of synonyms: some tools featured several names while others were only referred to generically (e.g., *gear, machine*). He concluded that it is common for craftsmen to invent new terms or to use an existing word with a new meaning: "The language changes to a great extent from one manufacture to another" (Diderot, D'Alembert 1751: *ad vocem*; our translation). Diderot's attempts at standardisation were expressed through two types of intervention (Zanola 2014: 43): firstly, by specifying the scope of adjectives and secondly, by deciding on the difference and/or similarity of the forms and uses of an instrument, a tool, a process, in order to come up with a term that distinguishes them and allows them to be named without confusion. Diderot stressed that the difficulty did not lie in the quantity of terms to be classified — neologisms to be introduced or superfluous synonyms to be eliminated — but in the desire and intention to define them precisely.

D'Alembert also admired machines, which were often anonymous technical and scientific discoveries, and did not fail to show his passion when he mentioned them in his *Discours préliminaire* (1751: I, XVIII). He set out to illustrate the method of constructing the machines, thus proposing a method of description that was a combination of the following elements (1751: LI; Proust 1982: 218–219):

- the terminological definition of the machine, with its basic characteristics
- a description of how it works (real instructions for use)
- the social function and role of machines in the evolution of technology
- the semiotic and functional value of the illustrations of the plates.

The authors of the *Encyclopédie* did not limit themselves to definitions (which alone would not allow the reader to understand how the machine works). They also used plates (*planches*) to visually represent the concept, object, operation, or technique. Diderot claimed that: "A look at the object or a picture of it says more than a page of text" (Friedmann 1953: 54; our translation). This again demonstrates that as early as the 18th century images were recognised as representations of concepts and of terms, a notion that carries forward in modern terminography.

In the *Encyclopédie*, machines were exemplified with rigour and great care (Zanola 2017). The 15 page description of the stocking machine best illustrates the method defined in the *Discours préliminaire*, i.e. visiting workshops, drafting specialised memoranda, constructing models, consulting existing technical literature, and assembling the machines themselves. The terminology is comprised mostly of common words employed with a new specialised meaning that is generic enough to be adequately adapted to many technical uses, yet at the same time perfectly clear. This text is a model for modern technical descriptions and operating instructions.

The difficulty that would normally be involved in explaining how a machine works is not based on terminological complexity, but rather on the fact that the mechanical succession of actions is not a mere transposition of human gestures (Jacomy 1990: 233). Thanks to the plates and their associated text, Diderot found a solution to the challenge of a manifold presentation that involved several intertwined elements at the same time.

The art of explaining a machine's operation requires a particular style as it constitutes a new genre of technical text, one with encyclopaedic references and therefore terminology. It could be seen as a forerunner of today's hypertext, an *ante litteram* database that shares a notional network and a common cultural vision.

5.   From alchemy to the chemistry of Lavoisier and Guyton de Morveau: The creation of a terminology

We now turn our attention to the field of chemistry, whose first lexicographical publications in French can be traced back to the 17th century. They include De Meuve's *Dictionnaire pharmaceutique ou apparat medico-pharmaco-chymique* (1677), the works of the king's pharmacist Nicolas Lémery (1697, 1698), and Thomas Corneille (1694), who prepared a supplement to the *Dictionnaire de l'Académie*, which was followed in 1708 by a *Dictionnaire universel géographique et historique* (Zanola 2010: 37). The first true French chemistry dictionary was that of Pierre-Joseph Macquer, chemist at the Royal Porcelain Factory in Sèvres, whose first edition (1766) was published anonymously. Macquer was not completely satisfied with his work, fearing that this science was "not very suitable for treatment in alphabetical order" (Macquer 1766:II, our translation). However, the collected terms show the evolved state of scientific description in this domain, which begins with a definition, followed by extensive explanations and references for further consultation, and continues with detailed examples and applications, all of which together form a vast repertoire of chemical knowledge (Zanola 2010: 45–48).

The idea of reforming the language of chemistry had already been proposed long before Lavoisier. Macquer and Baumé had begun to designate metallic salts by combining the names of the acid and the metal that constitute them (terminological blend became commonplace as a term formation method later). J.B.-M. Bucquet (1746–1780) and Fourcroy (1755–1809) applied the same principle to the field of mineralogy (Keirsaint 1968: 203).

The development of the nomenclature of chemistry illustrates the process of terminological creation: ideally the discovery of a concept is accompanied by the coining of a name to denote it. This is followed by systematisation of the nomenclature. Once the terminology is integrated into the language, the field of knowledge is more easily popularised (Zanola 2014: 114–128).

Chemical nomenclature, which to this point consisted of a veritable accumulation of fanciful names, thus needed to be replaced by a homogeneous, scientific nomenclature reflecting the chemical properties and characteristics of the various compounds (Viel 2006: 270). The words that were used — *Algaroth powder, Alembroth salt, Pompholix salt, phagedenic water, mineral turbith, colcothar, oil of tartar by default, oil of vitriol, arsenic butter, zinc flowers ...* — , actually border on the ridiculous. This is a classic case where the simultaneous establishment of a system of concepts, i.e. that of modern chemistry, and an associated linguistic system, together give rise to a new naming system known as chemical nomenclature.

In his *Mémoire sur les dénominations chimiques* (1782: 370) Guyton de Morveau explained why it was necessary to perfect the system and the rules to achieve a new nomenclature for chemistry. He condemned the fanciful names of alchemy and proposed names that evoke the component parts for chemical compounds and conform to their nature (1782: 371; our translation).

> The names of the entities which make up a Science or Art, which are its materials, its instruments, its products, constitute what is called its own language. The state of perfection of Language is an indication of the state of perfection of Science itself — it can only progress, it can only advance rapidly, if its ideas are represented by precise and well-determined signs, correct in their meaning, simple in their expression, convenient to use, easy to remember, preserving as far as possible, without error, the analogy which brings them together, the system which defines them and even the etymology which can be used to conjure them up.

The similarity between his criteria for a quality term — precision, accuracy, simplicity, accessibility (convenience), capacity for recall, transparency (preserving the analogy), and respect of the linguistic system — and that established by modern-day terminology theory, is uncanny. Guyton De Morveau continues by pointing out the complexity of attributes of chemical concepts, which in contemporary terminography are often represented in multi-dimensional ontologies and other concept representations.

> [...] Indeed, there is no science that requires more clarity, more precision, and it is agreed that there is none whose language is so barbaric, so vague, so incoherent. I say that no language requires more clarity; and to be convinced of this, it suffices to reflect on how many different states it must take into account for the same substance, sometimes united, sometimes separated, in this or that order, in this or that kind of composition, in this or that degree of combination, sometimes in an abstract manner, although it is not really isolated. How can we understand each other if we do not have the right terms to indicate these different states? This need becomes more apparent as the more objects there are to deal with multiply.

Guyton de Morveau established a coherent, precise, and unambiguous terminology, and designed a structured plan to communicate conceptual and linguistic novelties. First, he presented French and foreign chemists with tables summarising the methodical nomenclature he intended to adopt, but the spirit of the age was not yet favourable to such a project (Viel 1992; Anderson 1989). Having adopted this new way of conceiving chemistry, Guyton de Morveau undertook a complete work on chemical names with Lavoisier, Berthollet and Fourcroy. After eight months of lectures attended by several other members of the Académie des Sciences, Lavoisier introduced the basis for reforming and improving the *Nomenclature de la chimie* at the public session of the Académie on 18 April 1787, followed by a second memorandum on May 2.

In a communication to colleagues in 1782, Lavoisier acknowledged the effort that had already been made by Guyton de Morveau (Guyton de Morveau et al 1787: 3–4; our translation).

> He had not concealed from himself that it was not enough to create a language, which was still to be adopted, and that only convention could establish the scope of terms. He therefore believed that, before committing himself to the arduous task entrusted to him, it was necessary to make French chemists aware of the situation; to develop in their eyes the general principles which were to serve as a guide; to present them with tables of the methodical nomenclature which he proposed to adopt, and to ask for their consent, at least tacit. His memoir was then published in the *Journal de Physique,* and he had the modesty to crave, not the votes, but the objections of all those who cultivated chemistry.

Thus Guyton de Morveau not only recognised the social dimension of terminology implantation, he also incited creators of new terms to modesty: they must ask for consent, and invite objections. This was a true model of communication characterised by the intent to transfer and disseminate knowledge: for these scholars, words are true analytical methods by means of which it is possible to proceed from the unknown to the known (Guyton de Morveau et al 1787: 6). They pointed out that there are three elements in science: facts, ideas and words (13; our translation), as an anticipation of the Frege's triangle:

> We shall have [...] three things to distinguish in any physical science: the series of facts which constitute the science; the ideas which recall the facts; the words which express them. The word must give rise to the idea; the idea must paint the fact; these are three imprints of the same stamp and as it is words which preserve ideas and spread them, it follows that it would be impossible to perfect science if one did not perfect language. However true the facts were, whatever the truth of the facts, whatever the accuracy of the ideas they give rise to, they would still be transmitted as false impressions, if there were no accurate impressions to convey them.

Lavoisier considered that language should be a mirror of facts and corresponding ideas, so that everything was expressed clearly and precisely: "We cannot repeat too often that it is never nature or the facts she presents, but our reasoning that deceives us" (*ibidem*; our translation). Lavoisier's main idea was based on the fusion between theory and language, which he borrowed from the *Logique* of the Abbé de Condillac (1780). He drew three requirements from it:

- the need for a radical break with tradition
- the idea that the place of this break must be language, as it is language that can convey errors and prejudices, or, on the contrary, be the means for defending truth
- finally, the need to establish a close connection between facts, words and ideas.

Since language and knowledge are inseparable, only language can structure and organise the information that is acquired through meaning. If language is remade, science can be remade as well (Zanola 2014: 222). This terminological approach in new chemical terms makes one reflect on the fact that terminology in this field is no longer a simple nomenclature, but rather that, thanks to Lavoisier and his followers, it has contributed to building a new language for a new science (Zanola 2018b: 230). The *Méthode de Nomenclature* (1787) became a method for terminology formation. It should still be read today to remind us of the importance of clear, precise terminology and the benefits of logical-semantic consistency.

This terminology and its analytical method were immediately disseminated through translations (for Italian, Calloud 1790 and Dandolo 1791).[1] The creation of this terminology thus represents a model for the internationalisation of a lexicon: created in French, then spread to other languages with appropriate morphological adaptations.

Rey considers chemical terminology as the first modern scientific one: the parallelism between morphology and conceptualisation is complete in the field of chemical science, due to the simultaneous establishment of a system of chemical concepts and a linguistic system, in the form of a chemical terminology (2010: 181). The birth of terminology marks the birth of science itself.

6.   Conclusion

The revolution in practice and in thought concerning the scientific and technical use of words and the problems they pose came to a head in the 17th and 18th centuries, even though the issue had already been raised in Greek antiquity concerning the matter of the relation between word/term and concept. While the generalised approach to knowledge was increasingly inspired by the scientific method, in the 18th century the issue of the designation of and specialised discourse on new scientific and technical knowledge favoured the conscious development of terminology. The description of specialised fields therefore went hand

---

1. For more on the dissemination of Lavoisier's work in the United States, see Duveen and Klickstein 1954.

in hand with the identification of lexical/terminological units. During this century, the theoretical and descriptive principles of terminology as a practice were established and may be summarised in three main aspects (Zanola 2015, 2018a):

- the adequacy of the names of the concepts and notions of the sectors analysed
- the standardisation of terminological units through lexicons, glossaries and encyclopaedias
- the analysis of practices in the social functioning of terms and monitoring their dissemination for better transfer of knowledge.

The advancement of science is thus based on the adequacy of its language: the work on terminology carried out during the 18th century is as important as the observation and analysis of facts and phenomena. Logic is a favoured principle in terminology: the quest for an unambiguous and rigorous coordination between sign and meaning may find its application in efforts towards terminological unity during this period.

The terminological passion of the 18th century is therefore the testimony of a cultural choice, approaches of which distinguish guilds from academies, scholars from craftsmen, philosophers from the common folk. Thanks to the creation of terminology, its development, systematisation and description in the course of the 18th century, the process of building and transmitting knowledge has been able to flourish and progress, accompanied by fruitful and exciting debates.

References

Académie royale des sciences. 1732–1734. *Machines et inventions approuvées par l'Académie royale des sciences*. Paris : G. Martin, J.-B. Coignard fils, H.-L- Guerin.

Académie française. 1694. *Dictionnaire de l'Académie française* 1re éd. Paris.

Accademia della Crusca. 1623. *Vocabolario degli Accademici della Crusca*. Venezia: Bastiano de' Rossi.

Accademia della Crusca. 1691. *Vocabolario degli Accademici della Crusca*. 3 voll. Firenze: Stamperia dell'Accademia della Crusca.

Alexandre, dom Nicolas. 1768. *Dictionnaire botanique et pharmaceutique*. Paris: Didot.

Alvar Ezquerra, Manuel. 1987. "Presentación." In y Pando [1786–1793], *Diccionario castellano con las voces de ciencia y artes y sus correspondientes en las tres lenguas francesa, latina e italiana*, V–XVI. Madrid: Arco/Libros.

Anderson, Wilda C. 1989. "Scientific Nomenclature and Revolutionary Rhetoric." *Rhetorica* 7: 45–53.

Baldinucci, Filippo. 1681. *Vocabolario toscano dell'arte del disegno*. Firenze: Santi Franchi.

Bertrand, Jean-Elie (ed). 1771. *Descriptions des arts et métiers, faites ou approuvées par Messieurs de l'Académie royale des sciences de Paris*. Tome 1: *L'art du meunier, du boulanger, du vermicellier*. Neuchâtel: Imprimerie de la Société typographique.

Brunot, Ferdinand. 1930. *Histoire de la langue française des origines à nos jours. Le mouvement des idées et les vocabulaires techniques*, t. VI/1–2. Paris: A. Colin.

Bulliard, Pierre. 1797. *Dictionnaire élémentaire de botanique, ou Exposition par ordre alphabétique des préceptes de la botanique, et de tous les termes, tant françois que latins, consacrés à l'étude de cette science*. Paris: Imprimerie Crapelet.

Calloud, Pietro. 1790. *Metodo di nomenclatura chimica proposto da Morveau, Lavoisier, Bertholet e Fourcroy*. Venezia: Lorenzo Baseggio.

Corneille, Thomas. 1694. *Dictionnaire des arts et des sciences*. Paris: J.B. Coignard.

Corneille, Thomas. 1708. *Dictionnaire universel géographique et historique*. Paris: J.B. Coignard.

Dandolo, Vincenzo. 1791. *Trattato elementare di chimica. Presentato in un ordine nuovo dietro le moderne scoperte; con Figure. Recato dalla Francese nell'Italiana favella e corredato di annotazioni*, 4 voll. Venezia: Antonio Zatta e figli.

Darnton, Robert. 1979. *The Business of Enlightenment. A Publishing History of the Encyclopédie 1775–1800*. Cambridge: Belknap Press of Harvard University Press.

de Brossard, Sébastien. 1703. *Dictionnaire de musique, contenant une explication des termes grecs, latins, italiens et françois*. Paris: Ballard.

de Condillac, Abbé. 1780. *La Logique, ou les premiers Développemens de l'Art de Penser*. Paris: L'Esprit-Debure.

de Meuve, M. 1677. *Dictionnaire pharmaceutique ou apparat médico-pharmaco-chymique*. Paris: Laurent d'Houry.

Diderot, Denis, and Jean-Baptiste d'Alembert Le Rond. 1751–1772. *Encyclopédie ou dictionnaire raisonné des arts et des métiers par une société de gens des lettres*, 35 voll. Paris: Panckoucke.

Duhamel du Monceau, Henri-Louis. 1758. *La physique des arbres*. Paris: Guerin et Delatour.

Duhamel du Monceau, Henri-Louis (ed). 1761–1782. *Descriptions des Arts et métiers, faites ou approuvées par Messieurs de l'Académie royale des sciences*. Paris: Saillant & Nyon, Desaint, Imprimerie L. F. Delatour, Imprimerie Moutard, H.L. Guerin.

Duveen, Denis I., and Herbert S. Klickstein. 1954. "A Bibliographical Study of the Introduction of Lavoisier's *Traité élémentaire de chimie* into Great Britain and America." *Annals of Science* 10/4: 321–338.

Encyclopédie méthodique ou par ordre de matières par une société de gens de lettres, de savants et d'artistes. 1782–1832. 210 vol. Paris: Panckoucke, Liège: Plomteux.

Friedmann, Georges. 1953. "L'Encyclopédie et le travail humain." *Annales* VIII/1: 53–61.

Garzoni, Tomaso. 1585. *La piazza universale di tutte le professioni del mondo*. Venetia: Gio. Battista Somascho.

Gille, Bertrand. 1952. "L'Encyclopédie, dictionnaire technique." *Revue d'histoire des sciences et de leurs applications* V/1: 26–53.

Grimaldi, Claudio. 2017. *Discours et terminologie dans la presse scientifique française (1699–1740). La construction des lexiques de la botanique et de la chimie*. Oxford: Peter Lang.

Grimaldi, Claudio, and John Humbley. 2021. "How Metaphor Shaped Eighteenth Century Botanical Terminology in French." In *Variations on Metaphor*, ed. by Ilaria Rizzato, Francesca Strik Lievers, and Elisabetta Zurru, 128–142. Cambridge: Cambridge Scholars Publishing.

Griselini, Francesco. 1768–1778. *Dizionario delle arti e de' mestieri*. Venezia: Modesto Fenzo.

Guyton de Morveau, Louis-Bernard. 1782. "Mémoire sur les dénominations chimiques, la nécessité d'en perfectionner le système, les règles pour y parvenir, suivi d'un tableau d'une nomenclature chimique." *Observations sur la physique, sur l'histoire naturelle et sur les arts* 19: 370–382.

Guyton de Morveau, Louis-Bernard, Antoine-Laurent Lavoisier, Claude-Louis Berthollet, and Antoine — François de Fourcroy. 1787. *Méthode de nomenclature chimique*. Paris: Cuchet.

Jacomy, Bruno. 1990. *Une histoire des techniques*. Paris: Seuil.

Keirsaint, Georges. 1968. "Aperçu sur les nomenclatures en chimie." *Revue d'histoire de la pharmacie* 199: 203–206.

Lémery, Nicolas. 1697. *Pharmacopée Universelle, contenant toutes les compositions de pharmacie qui sont en usage dans la médecine*. Paris: L. d'Houry.

Lémery, Nicolas. 1698. *Traité universel des drogues simples mises en ordre alphabétique*. Paris: L. d'Houry.

Liger, Louis. 1703. *Dictionaire general des termes propres a l'agriculture*. Paris: Beugnié.

Littré, Émile. 1863–73. *Dictionnaire de la langue française*. Paris: Hachette.

Macquer, Pierre-Joseph. 1766. *Dictionnaire de Chimie*. Paris: Lacombe.

Osselton, Noel Edward. 1999. "English Specialized Lexicography in the late Middle Ages and in the Renaissance". In 2. *Halbband: Ein internationales Handbuch zur Fachsprachenforschung und Terminologiewissenschaft*, ed. by Lothar Hoffmann, Hartwig Kalverkämper, Herbert Ernst Wiegand, Christian Galinski, and Werner Hüllen, 2458–2465. Berlin — New York: De Gruyter Mouton.

Parodi, Severina (ed). 1975. *Inventario delle carte leopoldiane*. Firenze: Accademia della Crusca.

Proust, Jacques. 1982. *Diderot et l'Encyclopédie*. Genève-Paris: Slatkine.

Quemada, Bernard. 1978. "Technique et langage." In *Histoire des techniques*, ed. by Bertrand Gille, 1146–1240. Paris: Gallimard.

Rey, Alain. 2010. "Préalable à une définition de la terminologie." *Langues et Linguistique* 33: 175–185.

Rey, Christophe. 2014. *"Le Grand Vocabulaire françois" (1767–1774) de Charles-Joseph Panckoucke*. Paris: Honoré Champion.

Savary des Bruslons, Jacques. 1723–1730. *Dictionnaire Universel de commerce, contenant tout ce qui concerne le commerce qui se fait dans les quatre parties du monde*. Paris: Jacques Estienne.

Setti, Raffaella. 2010. *Le parole del mestiere. Testi di artigiani fiorentini della seconda metà del Seicento tra le carte di Leopoldo de' Medici*. Firenze: Accademia della Crusca.

Shapiro, Rebecca. 2020. "Seventeenth- and Eighteenth-Century English Lexicography." In *The Cambridge Companion to English Dictionaries*, ed. by Sarah Ogilvie, 114–126. Cambridge: Cambridge University Press.

Sigaud de La Fond, Joseph-Aignan. 1781. *Dictionnaire de physique*. Paris: Serpente.

Swiggers, Pierre. 1984. "Pré — histoire et histoire de l'Encyclopédie." *Revue historique* 271/1: 83–93.

Valmont de Bomare, Jacques Christophe. 1764. *Dictionnaire raisonné universel d'histoire naturelle*. Paris: Didot.

Viel, Claude. 1992. "Guyton de Morveau, père de la nomenclature (1736–1816)". In *Lavoisier et la révolution chimique. Actes du colloque tenu à l'occasion du Bicentenaire de la publication du "Traité Elémentaire de Chimie"* 1789, ed. by Michelle Goupil, Patrice Bret, and Francine Masson, 129–170. Paris: Sabix, École Polytechnique.

Viel, Claude. 2006. "Le Dictionnaire de chimie de Pierre-Joseph Macquer, premier en date des dictionnaires de chimie. Importance et éditions successives." *Revue d'histoire de la pharmacie* XCII/342: 261–276.

Watts, George B. 1958. "The Encyclopédie méthodique." *Publications of the Modern Language Association of America* 73/4: 348–366.

Winston, Judith E. 2018. "Twenty-First Century Biological Nomenclature — The Enduring Power of Names." *Integrative and Comparative Biology* 58/6: 1122–1131.

Zanola, Maria Teresa. 2010. "Histoire des sciences et des techniques, histoire des dictionnaires: quelques réflexions." *Les Cahiers du dictionnaire* 2: 37–52.

Zanola, Maria Teresa. 2014. *Arts et métiers au XVIIIe siècle. Études de terminologie diachronique*. Paris: L'Harmattan.

Zanola, Maria Teresa. 2015. "La terminologia, una galleria della lingua: arti, mestieri e saperi per la trasmissione della conoscenza." *La Crusca per Voi* 51/II: 2–8.

Zanola, Maria Teresa. 2017. "Machines et instruments scientifiques au XVIIIe siècle: définition, communication et transmission des connaissances." In *Autrement dit: définir, reformuler, gloser. Hommage à Pierluigi Ligas*, ed. by Paolo Frassi, and Giovanni Tallarico, 29–46. Paris: Hermann.

Zanola, Maria Teresa. 2018a. "Terminologie et diffusion des connaissances: un dialogue culturel et diachronique pour communiquer les métiers." In *La terminología, una necesidad de la sociedad actual*, ed. by Manuel González González, María-Dolores Sánchez-Palomino, and Inés Veiga Mateos, 159–180. Madrid: Iberoamericana — Vervuert.

Zanola, Maria Teresa. 2018b. "De 'nomenclature' à 'terminologie': un parcours diachronique (XVIIe–XVIIIe siècles) entre France et Italie." In *Terminology & Discourse / Terminologie et discours*, ed. by Jana Altmanova, Maria Centrella, and Katherine E. Russo, 217–233. Bern: Peter Lang.

CHAPTER 4

Exploring terminological processes in the 19th century

Beatrice Ragazzini
University of Bologna

This chapter describes terminological processes within the development of 19th century scientific knowledge. Taking the classification of cloud forms as an example, three terminological processes are analysed as they apply to the formation of 19th century scientific language i.e., term formation, term variation, and standardisation. These processes are presented through original quotations from primary sources and examined from the perspective of modern terminology theory. The formation of the nomenclature of clouds is set in the broader historical context of the 19th century construction of scientific disciplines and knowledge systematisation. The contribution of these processes to the progress of knowledge is discussed, as is the relevance of a diachronic perspective in the study of terminology.

Keywords: terminology theory, diachronic terminology, term formation, term variation, standardisation, cloud classification, 19th century, scientific language, scientific progress, nomenclatures

1. Introduction

This chapter examines the role of terminology, defined as the practice of naming, classifying, and describing concepts, as part of the development of scientific knowledge during the 19th century. Taking the subject of cloud forms as an example, we will illustrate the role of terminological processes when applied to a specific field of research i.e., the formation of the nomenclature of clouds. Starting with the first attempts at naming clouds at the beginning of the 19th century (Lamarck 1802; Howard 1803a), up to Arthur Clayden's (1905) proposed extension of the official nomenclature published in the *International Cloud Atlas* (Hildebrandsson et al. 1896), the history of the classification of clouds is presented as a succession of attempts at naming them. While Clayden's attempt is considered the end of a process, the diachronic perspective adopted in the description of the

https://doi.org/10.1075/tlrp.24.04rag

events will underline how research on the naming of clouds extended beyond the 19th century.

Considered in a broader historical context, the classification of clouds is one of many attempts to categorise and define natural phenomena and newly discovered entities during an era of intense interest in the organisation of knowledge at an international level (Yeo 1991; Daunton 2005 inter alia).

Following a brief account of the naming of cloud formations during the 19th century, three terminological processes are examined using examples relating to the formation of official terminology of clouds. First, these processes are briefly introduced in the perspective of modern terminology theory. Next, their application to the denomination of clouds is presented through citations from primary sources. To stress the relevance of these processes for the broader development of scientific knowledge, similar dynamics from other fields of study, such as architecture and mineralogy, will be briefly mentioned at the end of each section dedicated to the three terminological processes.

This analysis ultimately aims to demonstrate how the formation of specialised language, in this case the nomenclature of clouds, can be described as a collaborative practice composed of multiple processes and in which numerous actors were involved. Some of these processes are now identified as principles in modern terminology theory. Finally, the dynamics of formation of the nomenclature of clouds will be commented upon, and the relevance of applying a diachronic perspective in the study of terminology will be discussed.

2.   A century of naming and classifying

The classification of clouds emerged from a significant shift towards the formation of scientific knowledge during the 19th century. This process of systematisation of knowledge was established in the 17th century and lasted until the early 20th century. Defined as the "age of classification" (Yeo 1991: 26), this era saw, among other developments, the formation of scientific disciplines which organised the specialised knowledge of different fields of study into nomenclatures and classifications, some of which are still in use today (Daunton 2005). As Kuhn also pointed out (1976: 27), the 19th century was an age in which numerous disciplines became "professions with their own institutional forms." Among these forms, nomenclatures and conceptual classifications featured prominently.

Names and classifications were also linked to the need to categorise the unknown, as Delmas et al. (2010: VII) claimed, and "to encompass the multiplicity and diversity of the earth." The period between 1780 and 1850 was termed by Cunningham as the age of the "invention of science" (1988: 385). Indeed, quoting Foucault, Cunningham stated that science did not exist before the years around

1800 and, with reference to biology, that "the pattern of knowledge that has been familiar to us for a hundred and fifty years is not valid for a previous period" (Foucault 2005:139).

Influenced by pioneering studies on naming and classifying in botany and zoology during the 18th century and inspired by Carl Linnaeus' (1735) work on nomenclature, scholars in numerous fields of study that were previously considered to be unofficial areas of research began discussing their structure, and therefore, their nomenclature and conceptual classifications (Yanni 1997). This reflection involved both humanities and natural sciences. Apart from Linnaeus (1735), the work on scientific language was inspired by Diderot's (1751) *Encyclopédie* and Lavoisier's et al. (1787) *Méthode de nomenclature chimique*, as well as by his *Traité élémentaire de chimie* (Lavoisier 1789), and also by numerous other recently created dictionaries and encyclopaedias (Yeo 1991). As argued by Yeo (2003), this systematisation of knowledge was directly connected to the organisation of the language necessary to communicate new theories and discoveries among all members of the scientific community (see also Chapter 3).

The emergence of specialised journals and institutions dedicated to various disciplines and fields of knowledge was another relevant factor in the systematisation of knowledge (Yeo 1991) and in the process of the "professionalisation of science" (Ellis 2014:777). Research on the nomenclature of the human body was conducted in the field of medicine, while names for newly discovered physical entities and phenomena of the mind were also being explored (Crichton 1798).

Additionally, in specialised journals, experts discussed the nomenclatures of the arts, and classifications for the different historical periods of architecture (De Caumont 1825). At this time, experts in mineralogy were coining terms, partly to assert disciplinary independence from chemistry (Mohs 1825). In meteorology, which until then had not been recognised as a legitimate field of study, the study of clouds, winds and tides also led to the creation of new terms. These attempts towards knowledge organisation are reflected in the works produced by numerous experts who took an interest in scientific language and technical terms (Bentham 1817; Whewell 1840 inter alia). The naming of cloud forms is a prime example of such a terminological development.

More recently, scholars of the history of science have revisited and examined 19th century practices of naming and classifying that were popular with experts of the scientific disciplines at the time (Witteveen 2020), both from a general point of view, and from the perspective of specific disciplines (Case 2019; McOuat 1996), including that of clouds. Hamblyn (2002) reconstructed the trajectory of Howard's classification of clouds (1803a),[1] from his first proposal to the codification of the official nomenclature in the aforementioned *International Cloud Atlas*.

---

1. Henceforth referred to as Howard's classification or Howard's nomenclature.

Vasak (2014) examined the value of Howard's classification in the history of science, while Thornes (1984) recognised the influence of Howard's classification on 19th century painting and landscape representations, as did Stephens (2003), who went on to highlight the relevance of cloud classification to the formation of a system for the organisation of scientific knowledge. Moreover, from a historical perspective, the classification of clouds was critically relevant to the discipline of meteorology, proven in studies by the Royal Meteorological Society (Pedgley 2003), while the literary value of Howard's and Goethe's work on the nomenclature of clouds was described by Pinna (2007). Clearly, the establishment of cloud terminology was a model for the progress of terminologies in other fields.

However, the contributions of the work on cloud terminology to the development of modern terminology theory have not yet been recognised: that is what this chapter aims to do.

3.   Cloud classification in the 19th century

Attempts to classify cloud formations were made throughout the 19th century, following a few early attempts at naming and describing clouds the century before. As Hamblyn (2002) reported, the first classification of cloud formations was presented in 1802, when the French biologist Jean-Baptiste Lamarck published an article entitled "Sur la forme des nuages" in his journal the *Annuaire Météorologique* (Lamarck 1802). That same year, the English meteorologist Luke Howard presented a classification at an Askesian Society of London meeting which was published in the *Philosophical Magazine* (Howard 1803a; 1803b; 1803c). These two classifications will be presented in detail later.

As Hamblyn (2002) noted, while Lamarck's classification was immediately discarded, Howard's nomenclature caused an animated discussion among experts in various European countries, such as England, France, and Germany. The debate continued in numerous journals, such as the *Philosophical Magazine*, and *The Gentleman's Magazine* in England, as well as the German *Annalen der Physik* and the French *Journal de physique, de chimie, d'histoire naturelle et des arts*. Parallel to that debate, alternative nomenclatures were proposed in all the languages involved (Forster 1816; Ley 1894). Howard's terms even caught the attention of Goethe, a passionate meteorologist. A correspondence between the two experts has been documented, as well as some letters of appraisal by Goethe for the useful terms proposed by Howard, published as part of his *Werke* (Goethe 1834). Despite various attempts to replace or supersede Howard's Latin Nomenclature throughout the century, it became the most well-established terminology in the discipline.

The last decades of the 19th century saw an increasing necessity for a standardised and international nomenclature of clouds among the experts in Europe (Abercromby 1887; Hildebrandsson 1887). This necessity for standardised terms inspired the formation of a so-called Cloud Commission, a committee of experts of the International Meteorological Organisation which sought to codify the international nomenclature of clouds. As a result of their joint efforts, the standardised nomenclature was published in the aforementioned *International Cloud Atlas* in English, French and German by the end of the century. Ten terms were declared standard, and four of these were part of Howard's original nomenclature.

Interestingly, the evolution of the nomenclature continued after the publication of the official terms in the *International Cloud Atlas*, as new subvarieties of the standard ten types were discovered and described. Clayden's (1905) proposal for an extension of the official nomenclature was just one of many attempts to evolve the official terms. Inspired by previous classifications, such as that of Hildebrandsson (Hildebrandsson et al. 1890) and Ley (1894), Clayden defined subvarieties, or specifications to the official terms, which could "hardly be bettered" (Clayden 1905: 34). As an example, Howard's (1803a) class of clouds named "Cirrus" was further divided into nine subvarieties in Clayden's (1905: 155–156) classification, such as "Cirro-nebula" and "Cirro-filum" (ibid.). Indeed, Clayden's proposal can be seen as the culmination of a century of discussion and naming of cloud formations.

In this chapter, the analysis of the terminological dynamics of naming during this century will be limited to three main processes, each discussed from the perspective of modern terminology theory. The history of the classification of clouds is inspired by Hamblyn's reconstructions (2002).

3.1 Cloud terms at the beginning of the 19th century

3.1.1 *Term formation and neology*

Term formation is defined in the literature as the codification of denominations to identify specialised concepts (Myking 2020). A variant of term formation, "neology" is identified as the formation of terms for newly defined or discovered concepts (Humbley 2018). Described by Rey (1988, in Cabré 1999: 209) as a "dynamic field" which needs to be continuously updated in line with the evolution of knowledge, term formation has always been a primary concern of terminology theory (Sager 1990). The state of the art in term formation is discussed by Myking (2020), who questions the evolution of the process, affirming that the study of this procedure should become more "empirical" and less "normative" (ibid.: 8). Term formation is also described in the literature by the processes it involves. Rondeau

(1984: 123) distinguishes two types of neologisms: "néonymes d'origine," which are neologisms resulting from the naming of new concepts by their creators or originators, and "néonymes d'appoint," which are neologisms resulting from a process of borrowing or translating from the source language into another or creating an original neologism in a language other than that of the concept's origin. Sager (1997: 27) similarly conceptualises primary and secondary term formation. Both scholars emphasise the difference between a first process which consists in naming previously unnamed concepts, and a successive process of naming variation for already named and classified concepts.

According to these authors, while the first process is related to the formation of both new terms and concepts, or neologisms, secondary term formation deals with the naming of already existing concepts and can thus be considered a form of variation. Neology is described as a variant of term formation (Humbley 2018), referring to the denomination of newly discovered concepts. At the same time, secondary term formation is usually believed to occur when a term is borrowed or adapted from another language for an already named concept (Sager 1997). Additionally, term variation is defined as the presence of multiple denominations for the same concept (Freixa 2022). Secondary term formation is connected to term variation, since terms are imported from another language, and at the same time translation equivalents of the same terms are proposed in the target languages. Concurrently, term variants from within the same language are also possible.

Moreover, the relevance of naming for the advancement of knowledge is noted by Sager (1990: 60) as part of the process of "terminologisation." Thus, the formation of terms for newly discovered or defined concepts is referred to in the literature as neology (Humbley 2018). Humbley (ibid.) further investigates the evolution of theories on neology, while Kageura (2022) questions the features of the formation of new terms as part of a detailed attempt to describe rules and patterns of systematicity in the dynamics of term formation. As for its definition, Cabré (1999) describes neology as the appearance of a new term, which coincides with the appearance of a new concept. However, quoting Boulanger (1989; in Cabré 1999: 203), "neology cannot be easily defined" due to multiple factors, such as "society, the dictionary makers and the political situation" (ibid.) which are nowadays involved in the process.

How the definition of a term differs from the definition of a concept is also worth mentioning. As Myking (2020: 11) states, quoting the ISO 704 standard: "A term is a designation consisting of one or more words representing a general concept in a special language in a specific subject field" (ISO 704, 2002: 34). The definition of a term is compared in the literature to that of a definition or of an illustration as descriptors of a concept (Faber 2009: 128). Finally, Sager underlines the importance of the scientist's intentions and motivations, as well as the "social responsibility for facilitating communication and the transfer of knowledge" in the process of term formation (Sager 1997: 25). This will become relevant in the examination of nomenclatures in the following sections.

3.1.2   The first cloud nomenclatures

The first phase of naming cloud forms took place at the beginning of the 19th century starting with Lamarck's nomenclature of five types of clouds in 1802, mentioned earlier. Howard's contribution, entitled "On the modifications of clouds; and on the Principles of their Production, Suspension and Destruction" (1803a) was published in the *Philosophical Magazine* the following year. Table 1 compares these two classifications.[2]

Indicating the interest in the classification of meteorological phenomena at the time, Lamarck (1805b) presented a more detailed classification of clouds grouped into twelve types in 1805, accompanied by specific definitions. Published in his own journal (ibid.), the article was preceded by a classification of the states of the sky (Lamarck 1805a). In this work, Lamarck underlined the importance for emerging sciences to define their own terms as linguistic expressions of their principles (Lamarck 1805a: 101):

> In every emerging science, one is forced to create terms, or compound words, to express in a concise manner a series of inter-related ideas or facts that would otherwise only be expressable by means of description. It is clear that such descriptions would not serve well to document observations.

Despite the fact that they were published at virtually the same time and on the same subject, Lamarck's and Howard's nomenclatures were significantly different. With reference to the "intentionality" in term formation, as defined by Sager (1997: 25), communication and knowledge transfer at an international level was one of Howard's main concerns in forming his terms, leading him to choose Latin and English. Presumably with the same aim, Lamarck, in contrast, thought that providing Latin or English equivalents of his terms was not necessary, as French was international enough for an official nomenclature.

Beyond language, the main difference between the two classifications was the form of the terms. Howard's denominations of cloud formations were substantives (nouns) coined for the purpose of classification and then combined with one another. On the other hand, Lamarck's were more similar to descriptions, composed of the substantive *nuage*, and associated with different adjectives.

---

2. Gedzelman (1989: 381) states that the two classifications were developed "independently." I have indeed found no evidence of a connection between Howard and Lamarck, or that they were aware of one another's activity.

Table 1. Lamarck's and Howard's classifications of cloud forms

Lamarck	Howard
Celle des nuages en voile 'That of the clouds in voile'[a]	Cirrus — Def. Nubes cirrata, tenuissima, quae undique crescat. 'Parallel, flexible or diverging fibres, extendible in any or in all directions.'
Celle des nuages attroupés 'That of the clustered clouds'	Cumulus — Def. Nubes cumulata, densa, sursum crescens. 'Convex or conical heaps, increasing upwards from a horizontal base.'
Celle des nuages pommelés 'That of the dappled clouds'	Stratus — Def. Nubes strata, aquae modo expansa, deorsum crescens. 'A widely extended, continuous, horizontal sheet, increasing from below.'
Celle de nuages en balayures 'That of the clouds in sweeps'	Cirro-cumulus — Def. Nubeculae densiores subro tundae et quasi in agmine appositae. 'Small, well defined roundish masses, in close horizontal arrangement.'
Celle de nuages groupés 'That of the clouds in groups'	Cirro-stratus — Def. Nubes extenuata sub-concava vel undulata. Nubeculae hujus modi appositae. 'Horizontal or slightly inclined masses, attenuated towards a part or the whole of their circumference, bent downward, or undulated, separate, or in groups consisting of small clouds having these characters.'
	Cumulo-stratus — Def. Nubes densa, basim planam undique supercrescens, vel cujus moles longinqua videtur partim cumulata. 'The cirro-stratus blended with the cumulus, and either appearing intermixed with the heaps of the latter or superadding a wide-spread structure to its base.'
	Cumulo-cirro-stratus vel Nimbus — Def. Nubes vel nubium congeries pluviam effundes. 'The rain cloud. A cloud or system of clouds from which rain is falling. It is a horizontal sheet, above which the cirrus spreads, while the cumulus enters it literally and from beneath.'

a. Unless otherwise specified, all translations are provided by the author.

Furthermore, Howard also associated symbols with his terms. This was to facilitate annotation in notes of the states of the clouds (Vasak 2014).

Lastly, as Clayden (1905) would later suggest, a key feature of Howard's proposal was that it was composed of four basic cloud forms, which, in combination with one another, could describe all other types of clouds that had been observed by that time. As reported by Hamblyn (2002), in the following years as Lamarck's nomenclature was discarded, Howard's terms gained popularity and were discussed internationally throughout the 19th century (Forster 1811; Poey 1863). Howard continued to publish and explain the nomenclature in further works (e.g., 1818, 1843 (first published in 1937)). As knowledge about cloud formations developed, there was a need to extend Howard's initial nomenclature. However, Howard's original terms were retained as the core.

Work on classification and naming such as Howard's also took place in other disciplines. Demonstrating the interdisciplinary character of the research on naming at the time, a similar dynamic as the one described for the nomenclature of clouds can be recognised in the classification of minerals (Werner 1774) and of the periods of medieval architecture (De Caumont 1825). All these disciplines witnessed increased activities at the time in the process of describing and naming what were, until then, unnamed entities.

3.2   The development of cloud nomenclatures

3.2.1   *Alternative naming proposals*

Term variation played a key role in the development of the nomenclature of clouds. Three aspects of this phenomenon are described in the following paragraphs. First, alternative denominations of Howard's originally defined concepts which were formed by other scholars, are illustrated. While further refining the concepts, these alternatives represented an advancement of knowledge on the subject. Second, term translation is argued by the author to be a form of variation, since, while Howard's Latin terms are maintained, their equivalents and definitions are translated into French and German respectively. In this process of translation, term variation is identified with the existence of the original Latin terms from Howard's nomenclature, and the translation equivalents and definitions proposed in the target languages i.e., French and German.

The suitability of terms to denote concepts and allow communication at an international level was tested by the translation of Howard's terms into French and German i.e., into other cultures and languages. Lastly, term variation is considered in relation to the progress of knowledge, which is particularly relevant for this chapter.

Term variation has generally been regarded as a phenomenon to be discouraged in classical terminology theory. As Léon Araúz and Cabezas Garcia (2020: 214) recall, bi-univocal correspondence of term and concept was an essential feature of terminology for Wüster (1979) and of the Vienna School's prescriptive theory of terminology (see also Chapter 8). Only later did successive theorists come to recognise term variation as a relevant phenomenon which could not be disregarded in specialised language. Indeed, while specialised language needed to be agreed upon among the scholars of the discipline, for efficient communication, terminological variation began to gain importance in more descriptive and sociolinguistic approaches, as a "greater degree of variability" was accepted (Bowker and Hawkings 2006: 100). Quoting Pihkala (2001), Faber (2009: 113) also describes how the focus of socioterminology on the social and situational use of terminology sought to account for term variation. Term translation is argued by Léon Araúz and Cabezas Garcia (2020: 215) to be a form of term variation in an interlinguistic context. Interlinguistic contact may motivate term variation (Freixa 2022), addressing the presence of terms in multiple languages for the same concept, and the "equivalence" among multiple translations of terms is addressed in other works (Léon Araúz and Cabezas Garcia 2020: 215). Moreover, term translation in specialised language is also investigated as a form of variation by multiple authors (Fernández Silva et al. 2011; Léon Araúz and Cabezas Garcia 2020).

Other aspects of terminological variation investigated in the literature included its causes (Bowker and Hawkings 2006 inter alia), as well as its role in the formation of knowledge (Pecman 2012; 2014). Among others, Pecman (2014: 1) describes the connection between term variation and knowledge formation, defining variation as a "cognitive device" for the construction of knowledge, and Humbley and Picton (2017) reflect on the connections between field-specific knowledge and terminological activity. Specifically, the authors underline how experts could "fall back onto domain specific knowledge" (ibid.: 2) when forming terms, owing to their knowledge of the specialised domain. The same relation between domain-specific knowledge and terminology is examined by Sager (1994: 7), who defines terms as "means of knowledge transfer" while addressing term variation as a form of secondary term formation. Moreover, according to the theories of terminology of the last decades (Sager 1990; 1997), terms are always used in context. Each context involves multiple factors which motivate the choice of a specific variant. By seeing terms in their context, the monosemic and mononymic relation of concept and term prescribed by traditional terminology theory (Wüster 1979) should probably be reconsidered as influenced by the context in which this relation is established. At the same time, the arbitrary use of term variants, presumably motivated by contextual factors, should be reevaluated (Bowker and Hawkins 2006).

3.2.2   *Alternative nomenclatures and translations*

The nomenclature of clouds began to be subject to term variation for several reasons. First, variants to Howard's terms were proposed by other experts as part of the discussion that followed his proposal in 1803. Second, as the discussion extended into languages other than English, variants were created by way of term translation.

As Hamblyn (2002) reports, the discussion of Howard's nomenclature started the same night as it was proposed. Indeed, scholars immediately noticed the revolutionary nature of Howard's terms, as he presented the principles governing the combination of the four main types of clouds. The choice of Latin terms and the usefulness of the nomenclature were also immediately perceived as necessary for the development of research in the field of cloud studies. The following year, the same experts commented on the proposal in the *Philosophical Magazine*.

However, Howard's terms were destined to achieve much wider success than within the scientific community in London, and the discussion also expanded in specialised journals in other languages. As Howard's nomenclature was immediately translated into German and French, the discussion continued in the famous *Annalen der Physik* (Howard 1805). There, Howard's Latin terms were maintained, while their English definitions were translated into German. Other experts also published on the subject including Cotte (1804) and Brandes (1810). Cotte (1804: 279) defined the nomenclature of clouds as a "science des mots" separate from a "science des faits" (ibid.) to which Cotte claims it should lead. Indeed, Cotte distinguished clearly between the evolution of scientific language at the time, and the development of the knowledge it was connected to. In 1815, in the *Annals of Philosophy*, the discussion of the nomenclature of cloud formations became particularly intense, as Howard himself provided some explanations, and further definitions, of his own terms. Shortly thereafter, in 1817, Christopher Johnson proposed two additional varieties of clouds to be added to Howard's nomenclature i.e., a "Lanceolate cloud" and a "Triangular cloud" (Johnson 1817: 216).

As previously mentioned, term variants also resulted from translations of Howard's Latin terms. Commenting on Howard's terms and providing illustrations for the different types of clouds, Thomas Forster (1816) proposed an alternative nomenclature of clouds, based on an English translation of Howard's terms in *The Gentleman's Magazine*. Examples of Forster's (1816: 132) alternative terms were "Curl-Cloud" for "Cirrus" and "Stacken-Cloud" for "Cumulus". There, he questioned the use of Latin for technical terms, as this might hinder the diffusion of knowledge among non-experts:

> The habit of the English writers of borrowing from other tongues the greatest part of their technical words, especially those which are used for the Sciences, is one of the causes why Natural History is not so much known to the generality of the people [...] They told me that they could never remember the technical terms, which were made up of Latin or Greek words, which they did not understand; and wished that names could be given to Meteorological Phenomena, which are formed out of our own tongue. (1816: 131)

Goethe's contribution to the success of Howard's nomenclature in Germany is particularly noteworthy (Hamblyn 2002; Pinna 2007). The German author presumably became acquainted with Howard's nomenclature through a translation that appeared in the *Annalen der Physik* (Howard 1815). As suggested by Pinna (2007), Goethe complimented the English meteorologist in an epistolary exchange for a much-needed classification of clouds, as stated in his collected *Werke* (1834: 196): "Ich ergriff die Howardische Terminologie mit Freude, weil sie mir einen Faden darreichte, den ich bisher vermisst hatte" ('I grasped the Howardian terminology with joy because it presented me with a thread I had been missing').

In his 1834 work, Goethe dedicated a chapter to the form of clouds according to Howard and to his terminology. He also made an honorary tribute to Howard in a poem dedicated to his effort in naming. In Pinna's words (2007: 39), the poem represented a sort of "literary translation in verses of Howard's doctrine," which exemplified Goethe's interests in meteorology and poetry.

To conclude, it seems worthwhile to mention other disciplines in which similar dynamics took place. Regarding the process of term variation, the field of electrodynamics, where Ampère (1816) and Faraday (1832) discussed naming alternatives for physical entities in French and English respectively, followed a similar trajectory to that of the formation of the nomenclature of clouds. Additionally, similar attempts at improving the existing classification of winds were proposed in the mid-19th century (Smyth 1849). A form of intersemiotic translation was involved in the process, where terms were associated with symbols to identify different levels of wind strength. Term variation was also a part of the discussion and revision of the original nomenclatures proposed at the beginning of the century in various disciplines.

3.3   The role of standardisation

3.3.1   *The standardisation process*

Defined by Wüster (1979) as the aim of the General Theory of Terminology (GTT) with engineering, technology and science, standardisation was initially a main concern of terminology theory, as well as a fundamental process behind efficient communication and the advancement of knowledge (Johnson and Sager 1980: 81–82) (see also Chapter 8).

However, in recent decades, the prescriptive Wüsterian interpretation of standardisation as based on the notion of a monosemic and mononymic fixed correspondence between the concept and the term has lost strength, with the discipline embracing a more descriptive view, one more connected to the reality of language use and a broadening interest in other disciplines. This view entails interpretation of language planning as more akin to harmonisation (Gilreath 1992), or "normaison" in socioterminology to quote Gaudin (2005: 85), rather than strict standardisation. Recent theories of terminology have also reevaluated the role of speakers in determining the forms of language, seeing standardisation as an agreement on meanings shared by a community of users (Gilreath 1992). Similarly, Faber (2009: 113) defines standardisation as a "chimera" that is impossible to achieve, since language is in a constant state of change.

As described in Chapters 3 and 10, the concepts nowadays referred to as nomenclature and terminology were discussed between the 17th and 18th century, following the communicative needs of the emerging sciences. There are two main aspects which should be highlighted when it comes to the role of standardisation in the formation of an official nomenclature. The first is how the official nomenclature relates to the traditional knowledge of a community of users, who collaborate in the creation of standards (Galinski and Weissinger 2008). The second is the role of standard terms as "references" (Leonardi 2009: 41) in the codification of further knowledge and specialised language.

As Johnson and Sager state (1980: 87), terms that are traditionally used by a community of speakers can be said to belong to a "structured system of knowledge" of that community, who then ratify this knowledge in the form of standards. This shared knowledge is also described in the literature as objective (Wüster 1979) as opposed to the subjective view of each member of the community. As Cabré (1999) states, as ambiguous terminology led to communication issues, 19th, and early 20th century experts started to regulate terminology in their respective areas and to become directly involved in the process of standardisation. Additionally, the role of regulatory bodies in the creation of standards became central, as official terms were referred to as "the correction of a sociolinguistic situation and the choosing of a specific term as a reference form" (Cabré 1999: 195). Sager (1994: 1) also addresses the role of experts in the codification of official terms. Described as "custodians" of the collective knowledge, these experts agreed on a "social norm," or common knowledge of a community which should be organised into publicly available standards (Johnson and Sager 1980: 84).

The proliferation of variants and expansion proposals in official nomenclatures illustrated the use of standard terms as means of reference for the further development of knowledge (Leonardi 2009). Once the official terms were defined, following a standardisation process, they became the main means of reference in discussions among experts. These official terms were then used in the creation of new terms, or terminological variants, which, to be understood and constructed, needed to be described to the scientific community using standardised concepts and terms already known to all. The appearance of term variants and naming alternatives seemed to naturally follow the process of standardisation, as standard terms were needed for communication among experts and for the further development of knowledge, and they also allowed the creation of term variants to further describe concepts.

3.3.2   *The International Cloud Atlas*

A significant milestone in the formation of the nomenclature of clouds is the standardisation of terms in the *International Cloud Atlas* (Hildebrandsson et al. 1896), henceforth referred to as the Atlas. Led by a group of experts known as the Cloud Commission of the International Meteorological Committee, this publication standardised the nomenclature of clouds into ten official types of clouds (Hamblyn 2002). The official nomenclature was based on Howard's classification and published in Latin, English, French and German. As an example, the first three official cloud types were named "Cirrus", "Cirro-stratus" and "Cirrocumulus" (Hildebrandsson et al. 1896), as in Howard's (1803a) original nomenclature. In this process of standardisation, the importance of the terms traditionally used to describe clouds, which were originally derived largely from Howard's nomenclature, is undeniable. Indeed, when these terms became standardised in this Atlas, Howard's terms had already been part of the traditional language of the discipline for almost a century. Interestingly, the publication of the Atlas was preceded and followed by articles and volumes dedicated to variants and expansions of Howard's nomenclature. This demonstrated how term standardisation was part of a process of language development, which seamlessly accompanied the evolution of the discipline.

The Atlas was the result of joint efforts to define an international classification of cloud forms. Even though most terms were already in use, a shared international nomenclature was not available. The Atlas is the result of an intense process of terminology standardisation at an international level. Additionally, it was influenced by attempts to expand Howard's nomenclature, such as the one by Hildebrandsson and colleagues (Hildebrandsson et al. 1890), which featured a nomenclature in Latin, English, French and German, and Ley (1894). Specifically, in a chapter entitled "Classification, Nomenclature and Description of Clouds," Ley defined a nomenclature of clouds based on Howard. In doing so, he notably stressed the importance of traditional terms, which, more than a century after their introduction, were still fundamental to knowledge development in the discipline and communication among experts. Among others, examples of Ley's (1894: 26) Latin and

English terms were "Cumulus" or "Heap Cloud", and "Cumulo-rudimentum" or "Rudiment". Indeed, several years later, in 1896, the efforts of the international committee focused on standardising, in the Atlas, an extended version of Howard's nomenclature, which had meanwhile become widely used.

In the discussion among experts leading to the publication of the international nomenclature in the Atlas, some noteworthy considerations on the nature of terms and the usefulness of an international nomenclature were put forward. A few papers presented at the meetings of the Cloud Commission were published in the *Quarterly Journal of the Royal Meteorological Society*. There, two of the contributors to the codification of the official nomenclature, Ralph Abercromby and Hugo Hildebrandsson, from England and Sweden respectively, shared their concerns about the nomenclature and the criteria for the classification of clouds. As an example, Abercromby underlined the importance of both standardisation and tradition in terminology:

> My primary idea — on which Prof. Hildebrandsson entirely concurred — is that the name of a cloud is of far less importance than that the same name should be applied to the same cloud by all observers; and also, that the existing names should be retained, only that the form they are applied to should be more precisely defined. (1887: 155)

The publication of the Atlas did not end the discussion. Further attempts at specification and expansion of the official nomenclature were published in the following years, such as Clayden (1905). Specifically, the chapter of Clayden's (1905: 155–156) volume entitled "Cloud Nomenclature" proposed an expansion of the official nomenclature from the Atlas into 16 types of clouds, in which subvariants of the official terms were defined, such as "Cirro-stratus-nebulosus" and "Cirro-stratus-communis." In a noteworthy foreword to his newly proposed varieties, Clayden specified that if new forms of clouds were discovered, the nomenclature could be further extended:

> During our survey of these groups, we have found that some of them include clouds of many shapes, which must be due to the very diverse conditions. [...] if observations are to be made on the occurrence of these special kinds, with a view to arriving at a thorough understanding of the circumstances to which they owe their forms, it becomes necessary to devise a code of names and symbols whereby an interchange of ideas and records may be rendered possible. Specific names have been proposed as each form was considered, and it only remains to sum them up concisely. Subsequent observation, particularly in other climates, may show that further additions should be made; but if the principle of specific names be once admitted, it will be easy to fill any omission. (1905: 155)

Clayden also declared that the time had come for a more detailed nomenclature of clouds to match the progress of knowledge. He also encouraged the introduction of additional categories of clouds not as a substitution, but as an extension of Howard's original nomenclature.

While Clayden's work is the culmination of this reconstruction of the history of cloud terms, it also represents the beginning of further discussions on the nomenclature. The terminological history recalled herein is part of a much longer history, that of the formation and development of knowledge about clouds.

As already mentioned for the previous processes, standardisation was not limited to meteorology at the time. A similar need for standardisation resulted in the formation in 1838, by the British Association for the Advancement of Science (BAAS), of a Committee for the Revision of the Nomenclature of the Stars, with original members William Whewell, John Herschel, and Francis Baily (Herschel 1843). Standardisation efforts in both meteorology and astronomy aimed to organise their official nomenclatures and were characterised by the publication not only of standardised terminologies, but also of the discussions among the experts involved. This seems interesting from the perspective of terminology theory, where a diachronic perspective on terminological processes should be encouraged. With reference to the analysis of cloud terminology, the use of this perspective is motivated by the importance to study the historical and social context of term formation, as well as the dynamics occurring among experts, and the practices through which terms were formed.

4.   Discussion and conclusion

This chapter has outlined the contribution of terminology as the practice of naming, defining, and classifying concepts to the construction of the progress of scientific knowledge during the 19th century. It has illustrated three terminological processes as applied to the construction of specialised knowledge and exemplified through the history of the formation of the nomenclature of clouds.

After an overview of the existing literature on terminology theory, the application of these processes to the naming of cloud forms was analysed in an international perspective and set in a broad historical context. The classification of clouds was illustrated as part of a wider discussion on the organisation of scientific knowledge, in which many disciplines were involved (Daunton 2005; Yanni 1997). Indeed, similar initiatives were occurring simultaneously in other fields of study, such as minerals (Werner 1774) and architecture (De Caumont 1825).

The first and most detailed terminological process examined was term formation, as connected to neology and the formation of the first nomenclatures of clouds at the beginning of the 19th century.

The second process was term variation, which was described through three different aspects: the proposal of alternative denominations for the already named cloud forms, intended also as a means towards the advancement of knowledge, and the possibility of term translation into other languages. Lastly, the third process analysed was the standardisation of terms in an official nomenclature, which was published at the end of the century in Latin, English, French, and German.

As a final reflection, the importance of a diachronic perspective in the study of terminological processes should be recognised (Dury and Picton 2009). These processes should be studied with reference to the context in which they took place. If examined in a diachronic perspective, the evolution of the nomenclature of clouds could be further reconstructed. This would be done under the assumption that names for the types of clouds were further proposed and discussed and that examining a period beyond that covered by this chapter (1802–1905) would lead to a better understanding of how these processes developed over time.

The processes presented in this chapter were considered part of a "dynamic process of language development" (Johnson and Sager 1980: 100). Indeed, we have seen how the formation of the official nomenclature of clouds was both a dynamic and a collaborative process in which multiple factors and actors were involved. It was the result of decades of discussion and proposals in different languages which led to the formation of new terms. These terms first became widely used within meteorological discourse communities in different languages, and then official. In a process such as that described by Kuhn, these terms, as part of the specialised language of meteorology, were a shared property of a scientific community, and should therefore be studied in this context:

> Scientific knowledge, like language, is intrinsically the common property of a group or else nothing at all. To understand it we shall need to know the special characteristics of the groups that create and use it.   (Kuhn 1970: 210)

Consequently, from a terminological perspective, terms and nomenclatures should be studied as the result of a continuous process of defining and naming, which presumably never ends, and should always keep pace with the advancement of knowledge.

References

Abercromby, Ralph. 1887. "Suggestions for an International Nomenclature of clouds." *Quarterly Journal of the International Meteorological Society* 13 (62): 154–166.

Ampère, André-Marie. 1816. "Essay d'une classification naturelle pour les corps simples." *Annales de Physique et de Chemie* 1 (2): 295–394.

Bentham, Jeremy. 1817. *Chrestomathia Part II, containing Appendix Nr. 5, being an Essay on Classification and Nomenclature.* London: Payne and Foss.

Bowker, Lynne, and Shane Hawkins. 2006. "Variation in the Organization of Medical Terms. Exploring Some Motivations for Term Choice." *Terminology* 12 (1): 79–110.

Boulanger, Jean-Claude. 1989. "L'évolution du concept de NEOLOGIE. De la linguistique aux industries de la langue." In: *Terminologie diachronique.* Actes du colloque 7 (Brussels, March 1988), ed. by Caroline de Schaetzen, 193–211. Paris : Conseil internationale de la langue française.

Brandes, Heinrich W. 1810. "Einige Bemerkungen über Hrn. Prof. Gerstners Theorie der Wellen, über Beobachtungen Ramonds, das Barometer betreffend und über die Wolken." *Annalen der Physik* 34: 343–351.

Cabré, M. Teresa. 1999. *Terminology: Theory, Methods and Applications.* Amsterdam: John Benjamins.

Case, Stephen. 2019. "A "confounded scrape": John Herschel, Neptune and Naming the Satellites of the Outer Solar System." *Journal for the History of Astronomy* 50 (3): 306–325.

Clayden, Arthur W. 1905. *Cloud Studies.* London: John Murray.

Cotte, Louis. 1804. "Des observations météorologiques faites à Paris et à Montmorenci pendant les constitutions lunaires, boréales et australes de l'ans XII (1803–1804)." *Journal de physique, de chimie, d'histoire naturelle et des arts* 59: 278–279.

Crichton, Alexander. 1798. *An Inquiry into the Nature and Origin of Mental Derangement. Comprehending a Concise System of the Physiology and Pathology of the Human Mind.* London: T. Cadell Junior.

Cunningham, Andrew. 1988. "Getting the Game Right: Some Plain Words on the Identity and Invention of Science." *Studies in the History and Philosophy of Science* 19 (3): 365–389.

Daunton, Martin (ed). 2005. *The Organization of Knowledge in Victorian Britain.* Oxford: University Press.

de Caumont, Arcisse. 1825. *Essai sur l'architecture religieuse du moyen age. Principalement en Normandie.* Caen: Chalopin fils.

de Lamarck, Jean-Baptiste. 1802. "Sur la forme des nuages." *Annuaire météorologique* 3: 149–164.

de Lamarck, Jean-Baptiste. 1805a. "Spectacle du ciel." *Annuaire météorologique* 6: 97–112.

de Lamarck, Jean-Baptiste. 1805b. "Nouvelle définition des termes que j'emploie pour exprimer certaines formes des nuages qu'il importe de distinguer dans l'annotation de l'état du ciel." *Annuaire météorologique* 6: 112–142.

Delmas, Catherine, Christine Vandamme, and Donna Spalding Andreolle. 2010. *Science and Empire in the Nineteeth Century: A Journey of Imperial Conquest and Scientific Progress.* Newcastle upon Tyne: Cambridge Scholars Publishing.

Diderot, Denis, and Jean le Rond d'Alembert (eds). 1751. *Encyclopédie, ou dictionnaire raisonné des sciences, des arts et des métiers*. Paris: Briasson, David, Le Breton, Durand.

Dury, Pascaline, and Aurélie Picton. 2009. "Terminologie et diachronie : vers une réconciliation théorique et méthodologique ?" *Revue française de linguistique appliquée* XIV (2): 31–41.

Ellis, Heather. 2014. "Knowledge, Character and Professionalisation in Nineteenth-century British Science." *History of Education* 43 (6): 777–792.

Faber, Pamela. 2009. "The Cognitive Shift in Terminology and Specialized Translation" *MonTI. Monografías de Traducción e Interpretación* 1: 107–134.

Faraday, Michael. 1832. "Experimental Researches in Electricity." *Philosophical Transactions of the Royal Society* 122: 125–162.

Fernández-Silva, Sabela, Judit Freixa, and M. Teresa Cabré. 2011. "A Proposed Method for Analysing the Dynamics of Cognition through Term Variation." *Terminology* 17(1): 49–73.

Forster, Thomas. 1811. "The New Nomenclature of Clouds explained." *The Gentleman's Magazine* 81 (2): 112–114.

Forster, Thomas. 1816. "Specimen of a new Nomenclature for the Meteorological Science." *The Gentleman's Magazine* 86 (1): 131–132.

Foucault, Michael. 2005. *The Order of Things. An archaeology of the human sciences*. London and New York: Routledge.

Freixa, Judith. 2022. "Causes of Terminological Variation." In *Theoretical Perspectives on Terminology. Explaining Terms, Concepts and Specialized Knowledge*, ed. by Pamela Faber, and Marie-Claude L'Homme, 399–420. Amsterdam: John Benjamins.

Galinski, Christian, and Reinhard Weissinger. 2008. "Terminology Standardisation and Translation Standards." *Magyar Terminologia* 3 (1): 8–20.

Gaudin, François. 2005. "La Socioterminologie." *Langages*, 39 (157). La terminologie : nature et enjeux: 80–92.

Gedzelman, Stanley D. 1989. "Cloud Classification before Luke Howard." *Bulletin of the American Meteorological Society* 70 (4): 381–395.

Gilreath, Charles T. 1992. "Harmonization of Terminology: An Overview of Principles." *International Classification* 19: 135–139.

Hamblyn, Richard. 2002. *The Invention of Clouds. How an Amateur Meteorologist Forged the Language of the Skies*. London: Picador, Pan Macmillan.

Herschel, John. 1843. "Report of the Committee consisting of Sir J. Herschel, Mr Whewell, and Mr Bailey, for Revising the Nomenclature of the Stars. August 14, 1843." *Reports of the British Association for the Advancement of Science*. 13th Meeting: 292.

Hildebrandsson, Hugo H. 1887. "Remarks Concerning the Nomenclature of Clouds for Ordinary Use." *Quarterly Journal of the International Meteorological Society* 13 (62): 148–154.

Hildebrandsson, Hugo H., Wladimir Köppen, and Georg von Neumayer. 1890. *Wolken-Atlas, Atlas des Nuages, Cloud Atlas, Moln-Atlas*. Hamburg: Gebr. Besthorn.

Hildebrandsson, Hugo H., Albert Riggenbach, and Léon Teisserenc de Bort. 1896. *International Cloud Atlas, Atlas international des Nuages, Internationaler Wolkenatlas*. Paris: Gauthier-Villars et fils.

doi Howard, Luke. 1803a. "On the Modifications of Clouds; and the Principles of their Production, Suspension and Destruction." *Philosophical Magazine* XVI (62): 97–107.

doi Howard, Luke. 1803b. "On the Modifications of Clouds; and the Principles of their Production, Suspension and Destruction." *Philosophical Magazine* XVI (64): 344–357.

doi Howard, Luke. 1803c. "On the Modifications of Clouds; and the Principles of their Production, Suspension and Destruction." *Philosophical Magazine* XVII (65): 5–11.

doi Howard, Luke. 1805. "Über die Modifikationen der Wolken." *Annalen der Physik* 21: 137–159.

doi Howard, Luke. 1815. "Versuch einer Naturgeschichte und Physik der Wolken." *Annalen der Physik* 51 (1): 1–48.

Howard, Luke. 1818. *The Climate of London deduced from Meteorological Observations made at Different Places in the Neighbourhood of the Metropolis.* London: W. Phillips.

Howard, Luke. 1843. *Seven Lectures on Meteorology.* London: Harvey and Darton.

doi Humbley, John, and Aurélie Picton. 2017. "Introduction." In *Multiple Perspectives in Terminological Variation*, ed. by Patrick Drouin, Aline Francoeur, John Humbley, and Aurélie Picton, 1–11. Amsterdam: John Benjamins.

Humbley, John. 2018. *La néologie terminologique.* Limoges: Lambert-Lucas.

ISO 704 2002: *Terminology work — Principles and methods, 3rd edition*, Switzerland: ISO.

Johnson, Christopher. 1817. "Observations on Clouds." *Annals of Philosophy* 9: 216–219.

doi Johnson, Robert L., and Juan Sager. 1980. "Standardization of Terminology in a Model of Communication." *International Journal of the Sociology of Language* 23: 81–104.

doi Kageura, Kyo. 2022. "Terminological Growth." In *Theoretical Perspectives on Terminology. Explaining Terms, Concepts and Specialized Knowledge*, ed. by Pamela Faber, and Marie-Claude L'Homme, 457–475. Amsterdam: John Benjamins.

Kuhn, Thomas S. 1970. *The Structure of Scientific Revolutions.* Chicago: The University of Chicago Press.

doi Kuhn, Thomas S. 1976. "Mathematical vs Experimental Traditions in the Development of Physical Science." *The Journal of Interdisciplinary History* 7 (1): 1–31.

Lavoisier, Antoine L., Louis-Bernard Guyton de Morveau, Claude-Louis Bertholet, and Antoine-François de Fourcroy. 1787. *Méthode de nomenclature chimique.* Paris: Cuchet.

Lavoisier, Antoine L. 1789. *Traité élémentaire de chimie.* Paris: Cuchet.

Léon Arauz, Pilar, and Melania Cabezas Garcia. 2020. "Term and Translation Variation of Multi-word Terms." In *Análisis multidisciplinar del fenómeno de la variación fraseológica en traducción e interpretación / Multidisciplinary Analysis of the Phenomenon of Phraseological Variation in Translation and Interpreting*, ed. by Pedro Mogorron Huerta. *MonTI Special Issue* 6: 210–247.

Leonardi, Natascia. 2009. "Terminology as a System of Knowledge Representation: an overview." In *La ricerca nella comunicazione interlinguistica. Modelli teorici e metodologici*, ed. by Stefania Cavagnoli, Elena Di Giovanni, and Raffaella Merlini, 37–52. Milano: Franco Angeli.

Ley, William C. 1894. *Cloudland. A Study on the Structure and Characters of Clouds.* London: Edward Stanford.

Linnaeus, Carl. 1735. *Systema naturae, sive regna tria naturae systematice proposita per classes, ordines, genera, & species.* Leiden: Apud T. Haak.

doi McOuat, Gordon. 1996. "Species, Rules and Meaning: The Politics of Language and the End of Definitions in 19th century Natural History." *Studies in History and Philosophy of Science* 27 (4): 473–519.

Mohs, Friedrich. 1825. *Treatise on Mineralogy, or the Natural History of the Mineral Kingdom.* Edinburgh: Constable and Co.

doi Myking, Johan. 2020. "Term Formation: Is There a State of the Art?" *Terminologija* 27: 6–30.

Pecman, Mojca. 2012. "Tentativeness in Term Formation. A study of Neology as a Rhetorical Device in Scientific Papers." *Terminology* 18 (1): 27–58.

Pecman, Mojca. 2014. "Variation as a Cognitive Device. How Scientists Construct Knowledge through Term Formation." *Terminology* 20 (1): 1–24.

doi Pedgley, David E. 2003. "Luke Howard and his Clouds." *Weather* 58: 51–55.

Pihkala, Teija. 2001. "Socioterminology." *Terminfo* 2001 (1). Summaries, Nordterm 2001.

Pinna, Giovanna. 2007. "Météorologie poétique. Les nuages chez Goethe." In *Nues, nuées, nuages*, ed. by J. Pigeaud, 39–50. Rennes: Presses Universitaires.

Poey, Andrès M. 1863. "Sur deux nouveaux types des nuages observés à la Havane et dénommés PALLIUM (pallio-cirrus et pallio-cumulus) et FRACTO-CUMULUS." *Comptes Rendus Hebdomadaires des Séances de l'Académie des Sciences* 56: 361–364.

Rey, Alain. 1988. "Dictionnaire et néologie." *Actes du Colloque Terminologie et technologies nouvelles*, 279-289. Québec: Gouvernement du Québec.

Rondeau, Guy. 1984. *Introduction à la terminologie.* Montreal: Gaëtan Morin.

doi Sager, Juan C. 1990. *A Practical Course in Terminology Processing.* Amsterdam: John Benjamins.

doi Sager, Juan C. 1994. "Terminology: Custodian of Knowledge and Means of Knowledge Transfer." *Terminology* 1 (1): 7–15.

doi Sager, Juan C. 1997. "Term Formation." In *Handbook of Terminology Management*, Volume 1, ed. by Sue Ellen Wright, and Gerhard Budin, 25–41. Amsterdam: John Benjamins.

doi Smyth, Charles P. 1849. "An Attempt to Improve the Present Methods of Determining the Strength and Direction of the Wind at Sea." *Transactions of the Royal Society of Edinburgh* 16: 455–462.

doi Stephens, Graeme L. 2003. "The Useful Pursuit of Shadows: The Study of Clouds has Profoundly Influenced Science and Human Culture and Stands Poised to Lead Climate Science Forward Again." *American Scientist* 91(5): 442–449.

doi Thornes, John E. 1984. "Luke Howard's Influence on Art and Literature in the Early Nineteenth Century." *Weather* 39 (8): 252–255.

Vasak, Anouchka. 2014. "Cumulus, Cirrus, Stratus." *Géographie et cultures* 85 : 9–34.

Von Goethe, Johann W. 1834. "Wolkengestalt nach Howard." In *Werke*. Vollständige Ausgabe. Stuttgart und Tübingen: J. G. Gottascher Buchhandlung: 195–246.

Werner, Abraham G. 1774. *Von den äußerlichen Kennzeichen der Fossilien.* Leipzig: Crusius.

Whewell, William. 1840. *Aphorisms Concerning Ideas, Science and the Language of Science.* London: Harrison and Co.

doi Witteveen, Joeri. 2020. "Linnaeus, the Essentialism Story and the Question of Types." *Taxon* 69 (6): 1141–1149.

Wüster, Eugen. 1979. *Einführung in die allgemeine Terminologielehre und terminologische Lexikographie.* New York: Springer.

Yanni, Carla. 1997. "On Nature and Nomenclature: William Whewell and the Production of Architectural Knowledge in Early Victorian Britain." *Architectural History* 40: 204–221.

Yeo, Richard. 1991. "Reading Encyclopaedias: Science and the Organisation of Knowledge in British Dictionaries of Arts and Science 1730–1850." *Isis* 82 (1): 24–49.

Yeo, Richard. 2003. "Classifying the Sciences." In *Eighteenth-Century Science*, ed. by Roy Porter, 239–266. Cambridge: Cambridge University Press.

CHAPTER 5

Peirce and philosophical terminology
Between theory and ethics

Claudia Stancati
University of Calabria

Contemporary terminology emerged between the end of the 19th century and the beginning of the 20th, a development made manifest in the growing number of international conferences. This movement toward standardisation and internationalisation of sciences and technologies also involved the humanities and philosophical disciplines. The theories and ethics of terminology are all aspects of this movement in which Charles Sanders Peirce, starting from his semiotic perspective, was a major protagonist. Peirce was a prolific coiner of philosophical neologisms, an active collaborator on general and specialised dictionaries, and he considered the conscious and precise use of technical language as a matter of capital importance for the sciences in general and for philosophy in particular, one of the pivots of the work of every scientific community.

Keywords: sign, ethics, epistemology, philosophy

1. The language of philosophy: An international problem

By the second half of the 19th century the processes of internationalisation of exchanges had gradually come to embrace all areas: from technology to science, including human sciences, psychology, anthropology, legal and social disciplines and philosophy itself. A series of international conferences, organised between 1900 and the Great War,[1] attest to the cosmopolitan atmosphere in which national traditions adhered to by European philosophers and intellectuals could be compared. In this context were born or consolidated fundamental journals for the development of philosophical culture, such as: *Mind* (1876), the

---

1. For example: International Conferences of Philosophy: Paris 1900, Geneva 1904, Heidelberg 1908, Bologna 1911.

https://doi.org/10.1075/tlrp.24.05sta
© 2025 John Benjamins Publishing Company

Revue de métaphysique et de morale (1893) and *Scientia* (1907). Within a geopolitical situation strongly marked by nationalisms, conferences, journals and epistolary exchanges were initiatives aimed at intellectual cooperation, contributing to the ever-widening dissemination and accessibility of all knowledge. Many of these initiatives and organisations were to regain strength after the war and the creation of the League of Nations.

The establishment of a philosophical terminology was an integral part of this process, sometimes even its driving force. In fact, the idea of a dictionary of philosophical terms goes back to the 17th century at least (see Goclenius 1613), but the intellectual field, characterised by a deep reflection on the epistemological statutes of the sciences and by an intense activity aimed at their classification (Stancati 2018), made that period fundamental for scientific and, in particular, philosophical terminologies.

In the 17th century the discussion on philosophical terminology mainly dealt with the theme of a universal language. Logicians, mathematicians and linguists analysed this topic as a quest for, on the one hand, an establishment of a new mathematical and logical symbology, and, on the other hand, a language of global communication

In this respect, a universal language is a philosophical project but it implicates linguistic, semiotic, ethical and political issues of all kinds (Eco 1993: 10). At the dawn of the 20th century, the ease of communication and the growth of economic and political relations forced collaboration between states and between scientists, experts and technicians of all kinds. These needs were addressed by the projects of International Auxiliary Languages, which are artificially created from existing natural languages, simplifying their structure and making them accessible and neutral (Couturat and Leau 1903, 1907). Esperanto is probably the best known and most used among the International Auxiliary Languages. In the early years of the 20th century, the Austrian engineer Eugen Wüster (1931) suggested Esperanto, since it is a planned language, as a starting point for the systematisation of a technical language (see also Chapter 7). Indeed, its structural regularity would allow technical language to be rationalised and the formation of neologisms to be adequately controlled, which is significant in fields characterised by constant lexical inventions or redefinitions (Samain 2022).

In 1879 the German philosopher Rudolf Eucken (the winner of the 1908 Nobel prize for literature), published a first essay on the history of philosophical terminology: *Geschichte der philosophischen Terminologie im Umriss*. In 1896 the editorial board of the journal *Mind* announced the Welby Award for an essay on the causes of obscurity in philosophical language, which went to Ferdinand Tönnies for his essay *Philosophical Terminology*, published in three issues of *Mind*, in 1899 and 1900. In Italy, in 1899, Giovanni Vailati published an essay on language in the history of science and civilisation and discussed it during the Congress of Philosophy in 1900.[2]

In France, the logician Louis Couturat and the philosopher André Lalande, who thought that philosophers were a category of specialists in the study of the domain of the Being, started the collective compilation of the *Vocabulaire technique et critique de la philosophie* as one of the tasks of the Société française de philosophie in 1900. The aim was to allow philosophy and "moral" sciences to define their problems and scope of activities and achieve the goal of a "nomenclature inexpugnable comme celle des mathématiques ou de la chimie" (Lalande 1903: 368; Stancati 2003). According to Couturat and Lalande, in order to create a universal scientific language, which is the expression of collective thought, it is necessary to abandon the illogical multiplicity of languages, with the aim of sharing thoughts and words. As Lalande stated during a discussion with Henri Bergson throughout a session of the Société française de Philosophie (23 May 1901), the *Vocabulaire* is not written only for philosophers as "créateurs" (Lalande 1901: 100), but also for what he calls the "clientèle philosophique: élèves, savants, ouvriers, gens du monde" (Lalande 1901: 102). In this way, Lalande was able to show that he is aware of the responsibility of intellectuals toward the society in which they operate and the scientific communities within which they work.

In the United States, these guiding principles inspired the work of James Baldwin for the *Dictionary of Philosophy and Psychology* (1901–1905), in which Charles Sanders Peirce collaborated.[3] There were several connections between French and American philosophers at that time. Baldwin taught at the École Pratique des Hautes Études from 1913 and died in Paris in 1934. For his part Peirce, after the foundation of the Metaphysical Club in Cambridge (Massachusetts) in 1871, published two important articles in the *Revue philosophique* founded by Théodule Ribot, including "Comment rendre nos idées claires?" (1878).

---

2. Giovanni Vailati, a pragmatist philosopher close to Peirce's positions, was a collaborator of the logician Giuseppe Peano. In this essay (1899), Vailati showed the importance of distinguishing definitions from propositions, that is, from assertions on objects, in sciences and showed also the relevance of metaphor in scientific terminology.

3. C.S Peirce, *Collected Papers of C.S Peirce.* 1931–1958. 8 vols., Hartshorne, C., Weiss, P., Burks A. edd., Cambridge (Mass.): Harvard University Press, quoted as CP; here CP 5.388–5.393. Budin (2006) mentions Peirce as one of the forerunners of terminology theory amongst nineteenth and early twentieth century philosophers. Savatovsky (2022: 29) notes the creation of dictionaries of philosophy in the late 19th century in particular that of Baldwin, as paving the way for twentieth century terminology work.

2.   Peirce: Philosophy, terminology, lexicography

Peirce is universally known to have been the founder of Semiotics and Pragmatism, but his work concerning the theoretical elaboration of philosophical and scientific terminology has received much less attention.[4] From a theoretical point of view, terminological discourse is fundamental because at the terminological level the role of philosophy as a discipline matches the specific nature of pragmatism as a current of thought for which the theory of signs is very important.[5] Moreover, Peirce carried out important lexicographic activity both for Baldwin's *Dictionary of Philosophy and Psychology*, of which he edited the more than 100 entries field-marked Logic, and for the *Century Dictionary* (1889–1891), edited by the linguist William Dwight Whitney.

By the early 1860s, as his thoughts further developed, Peirce focused on the use of univocal and precise expressions to communicate his ideas by giving new definitions to words or even by creating new terms when he believed it was essential. In fact, the very definition of his own philosophical conception as *pragmatism* and then as *pragmaticism*, to mark its specificity, is absolutely emblematic (CP 5.414).[6] Peirce's work seems to lay the foundation for one of the fundamental principles of terminology, which emphasises the precision and practicality of language for communication purposes among specialists, since they require terms to be unambigous.

Peirce focused his theorical reflection and his terminological and lexicographic work on three general dimensions: the logico-semiological dimension, the historical dimension of the scientific communities that worked on defining their own technical terminology, and the ethical dimension of the symbolic behaviour of individuals. Therefore, regarding these dimensions, the terminological

---

4. A couple of exceptions are Oeheler 1981 and Ketner 1981, dedicated to Peirce's contribution on terminology and lexicography. Both noted that Peirce's ethics of scientific terminology belongs to a historical tradition that through Bacon refers back to some passages of Locke's *Essay*. For both, when Peirce writes that science is a social process, what he means is that scientific discovery is grounded in a communitarian dimension. And, from the recognition that scientific terminology is meaningful only in virtue of its social nature, it follows that every individual speech act may have important social consequences. There is "an ethics of words" precisely because our personal linguistic conduct may harm the whole community of inquirers.

5. The passages which are primarily considered here are taken from the *Collected Papers* named *The Ethics of Terminology* (CP 2.219–26; EP 2: 263–266), and the passage 5.413 Philosophical Nomenclature. These provide an overview of the results of Peirce's long journey of monitoring his own symbolic practices, and his general reflection on the very nature of philosophy and science.

6. Peirce eschewed the classical pragmatist development to the point of giving to his own position a new name, *pragmaticism*.

ethics of philosophy proposed by Peirce is placed in a crucial theoretical framework: the correct, conscious and shared use of terms, which Peirce calls ethics to emphasise its importance, implies above all a definition of the tasks and objects of philosophical activity itself. The use of correct terminology also involves a double comparison: first, between the use of the language of philosophy and of other sciences; second, between the linguistic practices of philosophy and the use of ordinary language. Generally, "it is desirable for any branch of science that it should have a vocabulary furnishing a family of cognate words for each scientific conception, and that each word should have a single exact meaning" (CP 2.222). However, it is equally important to remember that the conception of precision collides with the fact that symbols are conventional signs by their own nature. Furthermore, terminology is part of the history and development of the sciences, and is defined by the debate and consensus within a given community of research:

> Every symbol is a living thing, in a very strict sense that is no mere figure of speech. The body of the symbol changes slowly, but its meaning inevitably grows, incorporates new elements and throws off old ones. But the effort of all should be to keep the essence of every scientific term unchanged and exact, although absolute exactitude is not so much as conceivable.   (CP 2.222)

Peirce's terminological work is based on a fundamental epistemological presupposition, which is the importance of unity between sciences. This view is close to Wüster's terminological perspective which would emerge later, interpreted as an interdisciplinary interface ("Grenzgebiet") between logic, ontology, linguistics and information sciences. Terms are language units, cognitive elements and means of communication (Wüster 1981 [1974]).

Wüster did not know Peirce's work, so the influence is indirect but nevertheless "Peirce's thoughts found their way into object theory, definition theory and other components of terminology theory" and Peirce's categorisation (Firstness, Secondness, Thirdness) proved "a very robust grill for phenomenological descriptions of science and technology" (Budin 2006: 26).[7]

According to Peirce, laboratory practice and experimental approaches do not preclude reflections on the general scientific method and its objects, as he experienced himself (he was a Harvard graduate in chemistry). Peirce considered philosophy a "department of Positive Science" (CP 5.120), which requires revisions and

---

7. It would seem that Wüster had no direct knowledge of Peirce's work. Savatovsky (2022: 153) does claim that Peirce figures as a hapax in Wüster's thesis (1931), but in fact the Peirce mentioned in the index of the thesis is not C. S. Peirce, but someone else who worked for General Electric. Wüster did not mention C.S. Peirce in his thesis, though he does quote a few references to logical positivism. Other terminologists, however, have noted resemblances to some aspects of terminology in Peirce's work, see: Ivanovic (2020).

convergence in the terminological field, like all other scientific disciplines. For this reason, he constantly compared philosophical terminology with that of other sciences, considering that philosophical terminology was established in the same period (late 19th and early 20th centuries) by deep and shared revisions. With regard to redefinition of the philosophical nomenclature, Peirce believed that philosophical research should learn from the example of natural sciences, where researchers cooperate in their experiments until general consensus is reached in the community. The field of philosophy requires a scientific terminology which can be created through a process that must be both ethical and scientific, to ensure that new concepts are proposed along with their own univocal and generally accepted terms. After all, according to Peirce, the language of philosophy is characterised not only by the similarities that it has with the languages of natural sciences, but also by their differences. The main difference concerns the use of terms of ordinary language in a philosophical context, an observation that can be found in the works of Vailati (1899) and Lalande (1901) which Peirce also recognised:

> The ideal terminology will differ somewhat for different sciences. The case of philosophy is very peculiar in that it has positive need of popular words in popular senses not as its own language (as it has too usually used those words), but as objects of its study. It thus has a peculiar need of a language distinct and detached from common speech [...]. It is good economy for philosophy to provide itself with a vocabulary so outlandish that loose thinkers shall not be tempted to borrow its words. [...] The first rule of good taste in writing is to use words whose meanings will not be misunderstood [...]. This is particularly true in logic, which wholly consists, one might almost say, in exactitude of thought.   (CP 2.223)

As previously noted, Peirce applied his theories precisely to the language of logic in the entries written for the dictionary edited by Baldwin.

Throughout his writings, from the 1860s and until after 1900, Peirce elaborated several lists of principles and rules, and this justifies the merit that he ascribes to himself of having defined the term *code of terminology*. These rules generally recommended the use of terms in the senses in which they first became scientific to ensure the stability of reference and the semantic distinction on several levels; that is to say, both between technical and ordinary languages, and between different conceptions of different philosophers. Describing the origin of a philosophical term and the historical development of its use was very important to Peirce and it is also one of the cornerstones of Baldwin's dictionary, as will be shown.[8] Among his lists of principles and rules, the most detailed is probably

---

8. For instance, during a debate with Sidgwick on terminology, he states that "yet in Baldwin's Dictionary, where accuracy of definition ought to have been the first consideration [...], looseness of speech and looseness of thought are wife and husband" (CP 8.169).

the one that Peirce draws up for a syllabus, as he calls it, which he had prepared and then printed at his own expense as a supplement for the series of Lowell Lectures held at Cambridge in 1903. That list is included in *The Ethics of Terminology*, where he suggests for example:

> To take pains to avoid following any recommendation of an arbitrary nature as to the use of philosophical terminology. To avoid using words and phrases of vernacular origin as technical terms of philosophy. [...] For philosophical conceptions which vary by a hair' s breadth from those for which suitable terms exist, to invent terms with a due regard for the usages of philosophical terminology and those of the English language but yet with a distinctly technical appearance. Before proposing a term, notation, or other symbol, to consider maturely whether it perfectly suits the conception and will lend itself to every occasion, whether it interferes with any existing term, and whether it may not create an inconvenience by interfering with the expression of some conception that may hereafter be introduced into philosophy. Having once introduced a symbol, to consider myself almost as much bound by it as if it had been introduced by somebody else; and after others have accepted it, to consider myself more bound to it than anybody else. To regard it as needful to introduce new systems of expression when new connections of importance between conceptions come to be made out, or when such systems can, in any way, positively subserve the purposes of philosophical study. (CP 2.226)

Peirce's analysis also entails a comparison between different languages, which are evaluated according to their contributions to philosophical terminology and their proximity to the terminology of scholastic philosophy of the Middle Ages. Since it is accurate in logic and reason and due to its proximity to scholastic terminology, according to Peirce, English is claimed as the superior philosophical language, (even though it lacks other desirable qualities which are present in German or French).

Peirce also felt that the revolution brought about by the establishment of a philosophical terminology, through which each term should be confined to a single meaning free from vagueness, fits into a framework in which:

> Philosophers will find themselves confronted with a Babel such as zoölogists and botanists have had to contend with; and scientific progress will be hampered until something like uniformity of usage has been attained. What is to be done? Shall we go on, *laissant faire*, until we find our terminology in an inextricable snarl, and then call in an Alexander to cut the knot with some Volapük system? (CP 8.169)

Peirce appeals to "the dictate of our glorious Anglo-Saxon genius" (CP 8.169) to guide this process inspired by the work of the scholastic philosophers of the Middle Ages who have been able to elaborate the principles of formation of terms:

> The scholastic terminology forms a system at once precise and elastic. New terms can be constructed in accordance with the principles of it which may be understood by any one who is acquainted with these principles. This system, together with the accretions which it received in the seventeenth century, has the characters of a somewhat obsolete but yet universal language; it is not confined to the philosophers of any particular nation, but is equally the possession of all. It is the basis of the actual English terminology, and has even passed in great degree into ordinary English speech.
>
> (review of Noah Porter's *The Human Intellect*, 1869 W:274)

These remarks suggest to Peirce that it is of great importance to maintain the scholastic structure of English philosophical terminology as it passed through the English vernacular of the 18th century, since it is, according to him, "the best of all languages, modern or ancient for modern philosophical purposes" (MS 434:5, 1902), because it was "the most logically exact of any" (W 2:266, 1903). Even the form of philosophical texts attracts his attention, but the crucial point is the philosophical vocabulary, its adequacy and extension. It is precisely his review of Baldwin's *Dictionary* that provides him with the opportunity to clarify his thoughts on this point:

> Philosophy cannot become scientifically healthy without an immense technical vocabulary. We can hardly imagine our great-grandsons turning over the leaves of this dictionary without amusement over the paucity of words with which their grandsires attempted to handle metaphysics and logic. Long before that day, it will have become indispensably requisite, too, that each of these terms should be confined to a single meaning which, however broad, must be free from all vagueness. This will involve a revolution in terminology; for in its present condition a philosophical thought of any precision can seldom be expressed without lengthy explanations. Already, when philosophy is only just beginning to resemble science, the influx of new terms is getting to be considerable. One of the chief purposes of this dictionary seems to have been to fix the use of them.   (CP 8.169)

Along with the many edited or revised entries for the *Century Dictionary*, the entries edited by Peirce for the *Dictionary of Philosophy and Psychology* (1901–1905) — either alone or with Baldwin himself, and, rarely, together with other contributors — constitute a significant contribution to determining a philosophical terminology. In these entries, the links with scholastic philosophy, as previously mentioned, are evident. Some entries are closely related to semiotic conceptions and pragmatist doctrines. After all, both John Dewey and William James were among the consulting editors, together with other prominent cultural personalities. The Preface to the first volume of Baldwin's *Dictionary* corresponds completely with Peirce's conceptions. Recalling the works of Welby and Tönnies, Baldwin declares that an international working committee has been put together in the absence of an International Academy. Baldwin claims that the purpose of the Dictionary is "doing something for the thinking of the time in the way of definition statement and terminology," and, at the same time, "to serve the cause of education" (Baldwin, I, vii). Rather than acting in a prescritive way, he aimed "to understand the meanings which our terms have, and to render them by clear definitions [...] and to interpret the movements of thought through which the meanings thus determined have arisen." That is the reason why many entries of his dictionary are discussed from the historical point of view, which allows us to understand what is "really vital in the development of thought" (Baldwin, I, vii). The only authority the dictionary invokes is what Durkheim, quoted by Baldwin, calls "force of social constraints" (viii).[9]

3.   Terminology practices and scientific ethics

We have seen how Peirce's work fits into the international context of intense work on epistemology, the definition of objects and the classification of sciences. His is a process in which scientific terminologies are an ultimate aim and, at the same time, the indispensable means for reaching it. He places his ideas within general and shared reflections on scientific terminologies and lays the foundation for future developments in the field of terminology. Peirce is aware that terminologies are related to the nature of the subject matter for which they are developed and, regarding the evolution of each discipline, they vary depending on the different languages in which they are expressed. It is clear today that within legal, philosophical, literary fields and the like words must be defined and used in order to explain the underlying conceptual systems in which notions are related to an explicit system of values (Rey 1992: 63; Savatovsky and Candel 2007). Peirce's reflections on philosophical and scientific terminology fully reflect this perspective.

According to Peirce, all progress on knowledge is linked to the ability to think as a community, which is the common practice of research. The advancement of knowledge "cannot go far except by collaboration; or, to speak more accurately, no mind can take one step without the aid of other minds" (CP 1.220). It is a question of standardising, as much as possible for philosophy, the symbolic practices of individual researchers; since symbols are not individual, but social. Therefore,

---

9. With regard to general lexicography, Baldwin refers to *Century* and *Standard* dictionaries (xiv).

> no one can deny that there is an ethics of words, and especially of scientific words. Words have their rights as well as their duties, which must not be trampled upon. There is an ethic of words, because words are a social institution. Science too, is a social business, and cannot prosper without a common understanding of how word shall be used.
> (MS 1537:34, 1900)

It is now understandable why Peirce defines his theoretical reflections and his terminological and lexicographic practice as "ethics," since also science and its symbols are essentially public and shared, and the responsibility is not only collective, but also individual, and it helps to identify the theoretical positions in the field:

> It is an indispensable requisite of science that it should have a recognized technical vocabulary composed of words so unattractive that loose thinkers are not tempted to use them, and a recognized and legitimated way of making up new words freely when a new conception is introduced, and that it is vital for science that he who introduces a new conception should be held to have a duty imposed upon him to invent a sufficiently disagreeable series of words to express it. I wish you would reflect seriously upon the moral aspect of terminology.   (CP 8.301)

To conclude, Peirce's terminological reflection presents those same general elements which would later inspire the foundation of contemporary terminology, quite born around the same historical period and in the same cultural context. From a linguistics point of view, Peirce's work is based, on the one hand, on the rigorous definition of terms, and, on the other hand, on the conscious and motivated creation of neologisms. Furthermore, Peirce also believes that the ethical perspective of a transparent and appropriate communication among scientists and specialists in the same field is delineated through a more general definition of concepts in a system and through the individuation of different objects.

References

Peirce, Charles Sanders. *Collected Papers of C.S Peirce*. 1931–1958. 8 vols. Ed. by C. Hartshorne, P. Weiss, and A. Burks. Cambridge (Mass.): Harvard University Press. Quoted as CP.

Peirce, Charles Sanders. *The Writings of Charles S. Peirce: A Chronological Edition*. 1980–2000. 6 vol. Ed. by M. Fisch, C. Kloesel, E. Moore, and N. Houser. Bloomington: Indiana University Press. Quoted as W.

Peirce, Charles Sanders. *Annoted Catalogue of the Papers of Charles S. Peirce*. 1967. Ed. by I. R. Robin. Amherst: University of Massachusetts Press. Quoted as MS.

Baldwin, James Mark (ed). 1901–1905. *Dictionary of Philosophy and Psychology*, 3 vols. New York: The Macmillan Company.

Budin, Gerhard. 2006. "Prospects of a Philosophy of Terminology." In *The Theoretical Foundations of Terminology Comparison between Eastern Europe and Western Countries: Proceedings of the Colloquium held on 18 August 2003 in Conjunction with the 14th European Symposium on Language for Special Purposes*, ed. by Gerhard Budin, Christer Lauren, Heribert Picht, Nina Pilke, Margaret Rogers, and Bertha Toft, 21–21. Baden-Baden: Ergon Verlag.

Couturat, Louis, and Leopold Leau. 1903. *Histoire de la langue universelle*. Paris: Hachette.

Couturat, Louis, and Leopold Leau. 1907. *Les nouvelles langues internationales*. Paris: Hachette.

Eco, Umberto. 1993. *The Search for the Perfect Language (The Making of Europe)*. Oxford: Basil Blackwell.

Eucken, Rudolf. 1879. *Geschichte der philosophischen Terminologie im Umriss*. Leipzig: Von Veit & Comp.

Goclenius, Rudolf. 1613. *Lexicon philosophicum quo tanquam clave philosophiae fores aperiuntur*. Frankfurt, Becker, anastatic reprint. Frankfurt 1613 and Marburg 1615. Hildesheim: Olms, 1980.

Husserl, Edmund. 1913. "Ideen zu einer reinen Phänomenologie und phänomenologischen Philosophie. Erstes Buch: Allgemeine Einführung in die reine Phänomenologie." In *Jahrbuch für Philosophie und phänomenologische Forschung*. Halle: Max Niemeyer.

Ivanovic, Marija. 2020. "Eugen Wüster's Sign Typology, Some Observations." In *TOTh 2019. Terminologie & Ontologie: Théories et Applications*, ed. by C. Roche, 143–160. Chambéry: Presses Universitaires Savoie Mont Blanc.

Ketner, Kenneth Laine. 1981. "Peirce's Ethic of Terminology." *Transactions of the Charles S. Peirce Society* 17, 4: 327–347.

Lalande, André. 1901. "Propositions concernant l'emploi de certains termes philosophiques." *Bulletin de la Société française de philosophie* I, 3: 98103.

Lalande, André. 1903. "Les récents dictionnaires de philosophie." *Revue philosophique de la France et de l'étranger* 56 : 628648.

Oehler, Klaus. 1981. "The Significance of Peirce's Ethic of Terminology for Contemporary Lexicography in Semiotics." *Transactions of the Charles S. Peirce Society* 17, 4: 348–357.

Rey, Alain. 1992. *La terminologie: noms et notions*. Paris: Presses Universitaires de France.

Samain, Didier. 2022. "Wüster et la question de l'espéranto : un regard d'ingénieur." In *Eugen Wüster et la terminologie de l'école de Vienne*, ed. by Danielle Candel, Didier Samain, and Dan Savatovsky, 173–214. Paris: SHESL (HEL Livres, 2).

Savatovsky, Dan and Danielle Candel (eds). 2007. "Genèse de la terminologie contemporaine (sources et réception)." *Langages* 168.

Savatovsky, Dan. 2022. "Introduction. Wüster en contexte." In *Wüster et la terminologie de l'école de Vienne*, ed. by Danielle Candel, Didier Samain, and Dan Savatovsky, 7–87. Paris: SHESL.

Stancati, Claudia. 2003. "Une page d'histoire de la lexicographie en France et en Italie." In *History of Linguistics 1999*, ed. by Sylvian Auroux, 303–318. Amsterdam: John Benjamins.

Stancati, Claudia. 2018. *Linguistica e classificazione delle scienze*. Torino: L'Harmattan.

Tönnies, Ferdinand. 1899–1900. "Philosophical Terminology." *Mind NS* VIII 31: 467–490, 32: 289–332, IX 33: 46–60.

Vailati, Giovanni. 1899. *Alcune osservazioni sulle questioni di parole nella storia della scienza e della cultura*. Torino: Bocca.

Whitney, William Dwight (ed). 1889–1891. *The Century Dictionary*. New York: The Century Company.

Wüster. Eugen. 1931. *Internationale Sprachnormung in der Technik, besonders in der Elektrotechnik*. Berlin: VDI Verlag.

Wüster, Eugen. 1981 [1974]. "L'étude scientifique de la terminologie, zone frontalière entre la linguistique, la logique, l'ontologie, l'informatique et les sciences des choses." In *Textes choisis de terminologie I : Fondements théoriques de la terminologie*, ed. by Guy Rondeau, and Helmut Felber, 55–113. Québec: Université Laval — GIRSTERM.

CHAPTER 6

Paasch, pioneer of modern terminography

Marc Van Campenhoudt
Université libre de Bruxelles

From Keel to Truck is a vast trilingual (English, French, German) dictionary
that was highly successful in the late 19th century. To complete the work,
author Heinrich Paasch builds on a long tradition of marine dictionaries
and develops an original terminographical method which would
foreshadow 20th-century theory for the discipline of terminology. His
highly structured book prefigures terminological knowledge bases: a
monosemic approach, reliance on semantic relationships, and close
attention to divergences between languages.

Keywords: terminography, marine, ontology, semantic network,
dictionaries, equivalence

1.   Who is Heinrich Paasch?

Johann Heinrich Friederich Paasch was born in Dahme (Schleswig-Holstein) on
January 7, 1835, and died in Antwerp on March 25, 1904. The son of a fisherman,
according to his own words, he spent little time in school and taught himself
much of what he knew. At the young age of 15, Paasch enlisted in turn in the German and Danish navies. He would later sail as a deckhand, and then as an officer,
on German, Dutch, American and Russian merchant ships. A master mariner at
27, Paasch settled in Antwerp in 1870, and, in 1873, became a surveyor to Lloyd's
Register of Shipping in the city. This position, which he held until 1898 according to Lloyd's Register archives, gave him exposure to and experience in standards
relating to the marine industry and its terminology. In 1885, he became a Belgian
citizen. At the end of his life, he was a vocal advocate for the development of a
Belgian merchant navy.

In 1885, Paasch rises to international fame by self-publishing a trilingual
(English, French, German) marine dictionary entitled *From Keel to Truck, De
la quille à la pomme de mât, Vom Kiel zum Flaggenknoff*. The dictionary, still
modest in length at that time, saw huge success and was followed in 1890 by a

https://doi.org/10.1075/tlrp.24.06van

second publication, the *Illustrated Marine Encyclopedia*, written in English. In this encyclopaedia, the author introduces original methods of systematic classification, which he later applied to the second and third editions of his trilingual dictionary (published in 1894 and 1901 respectively). This would significantly add to the length of the work. With some 10,000 copies sold worldwide during the author's lifetime, the dictionary owes its success to its highly detailed illustrations, its inclusion of the latest industrial revolution technologies (see also Chapter 17), the breadth of its corpus (over 11,000 concepts),[1] and the accuracy of the equivalences offered (around 14,000 terms per language). A successful terminographer, Paasch had no children, and would become benefactor of his and his wife's neighbouring home villages.

Paasch's seminal work, *From Keel to Truck* (hereafter FKTT), marks a fundamental milestone in the history of specialised multilingual dictionaries, but in the world of terminology, Paasch's masterpiece is often left unmentioned. Indeed, an in-depth study of this book reveals a methodology that is both rigorous and original, and that prefigures the foundations of modern terminology while foreshadowing the evolution towards terminological knowledge bases. Breaking with the tradition of alphabetical ordering, the author groups terms by subject area, classifying them in systematic order based on specific semantic relationships: types, parts, location, etc. In addition, he takes great care to offer reliable translations and to this end, accounts for conceptual divergences between languages, adopting an original descriptive methodology that is underpinned by precise and highly innovative principles that herald the science of algorithms. While Paasch does include standardised terms, he never takes the easy way out by claiming authority, but rather mentions many synonyms.

Unfortunately, Paasch did not leave behind any theoretical writings. After his passing, his dictionary was updated by an international team that would ultimately add Spanish and Italian (in the 1908 and 1937 editions). However these contributions would be made without successfully respecting the author's original intentions (see Section 3). This likely explains why Eugen Wüster (1981: 74–76) refers to more recent dictionaries as precursors, such as those authored by Schlomann (1906–1932) and the International Electrotechnical Commission (IEC 1938). And yet, Paasch had developed, as early as 1894, a much more elaborate

---

1. For convenience, we use the word *concept* (adjective *conceptual*) to designate a multilingual unit of understanding (Temmerman 2000), which is necessary for establishing equivalences in a polyglot dictionary. It corresponds to the notion of terminology records in an approach that respects conceptual differences between languages (see 3.4). We also use *term* to designate any specialised linguistic sign. It can be a single word or a multiword. It may be monosemic or polysemic in a language.

terminographical methodology, which remained unequalled until Wüster's dictionary, *The Machine Tool*, published in 1968.[2]

2.   The precursors of Paasch in the maritime area

Of course, terminographical activity did not start with Eugen Wüster and the precursors he mentions on occasion. Much more distant origins are worth considering, as shown in Part 1. Terminologists and translators are often unaware that glossaries can be found in technical texts as early as the 15th century, and that terminography — or at least specialised lexicography — predates general lexicography (Van Campenhoudt 2016:579). What's more, lexicologists and philologists readily concur that multilingual — often specialised — glossaries have existed for longer than monolingual dictionaries (Quemada 1967:37–73, 567ff).

As early as the 17th century, various nautical dictionaries were published in the languages of major maritime powers (English, French, Dutch, and Spanish). As demonstrated by Villain-Gandossi (1999:40–46), specialised lexicographical activity in the French maritime area started very early compared to the history of general language dictionaries: the first known maritime dictionary was published in 1636 (Cleirac), while the first significant dictionary in this domain (with around 2,500 headwords) was compiled by Desroches in 1687. The first lexicographical work in the maritime field preceded therefore, by a few decades, the earliest monolingual French general language dictionaries, the first of which appeared at the end of the 17th century.[3]

Our study of multilingual maritime dictionaries published in the 19th century[4] does not reveal any particular trends or patterns in compilation techniques (Van Campenhoudt 2003). These books follow different methodologies, each exploring its own path as it attempts to solve the problem of establishing equivalence.

First, we note with interest that the first marine dictionary mentioned (Cleirac 1636) presents itself as a list of terms grouped in subdomains: navigation, weather, hazards, shipwrecks, etc. This systematic organisation — which is also used in the marine section of Jacques Ozanam's *Dictionnaire mathématique* (1691) — is found in at least two 19th-century multilingual dictionaries: the *Polyglossarium*

---

2. For a methodical comparison of Paasch (1901) and Schlomann (1932), see Van Campenhoudt (1996a:364–370 and 1997).

3. Richelet (1680), Furetière (1690), Corneille (1694), Ménage (1694) and Académie française (1694).

4. We will not look at monolingual dictionaries, even if they include equivalences towards target languages, such as Augustin Jal's excellent *Glossaire nautique* (1848).

Nauticum (1847), a dictionary in ten languages, albeit of limited breadth (around 770 concepts), and Paasch's dictionary (1885–1901), referred to in this chapter.

In the 19th century, Carel Roest (1842) and Karl Pieter ter Reehorst (1865) opt for a columned layout, which allows the reader to find equivalents by a simple horizontal lookup. This layout — also used by Paasch — will meet with great success in the 20th century. However, it allows reversing language pairs only if final indices are included, which was not the case in Roest and ter Reehorst's dictionaries. These works only recognised the language presented in the first column as the source language, and thus these books are considered *multi-bilingual*, never *multilingual*.[5]

Heinrich Tecklenborg (1870) does not establish direct equivalences between the entries in different columns, but rather presents a translation system based on matching numbered entries using German as an intermediary, thus granting it the (dangerous) status of pivot language.

As for Landolt (1865–1871), Dabovich (1883), and Boom (1888), they each opted for a vertical layout in which the term in the source language is immediately followed by its equivalents. This system also required indices, but the three authors preferred to experiment with techniques that allowed for the direct reversal of language pairs. These formatting styles offered as many books (Landolt) or sections (Boom) as there were source languages, or listed terms in all source languages as headwords (Dabovich). These choices reflect a clear awareness of the equivalence issue, even if the authors did not succeed in resolving all the difficulties encountered.

With the exception of the *Polyglossarium Nauticum* (1847), which follows the order of its illustrations, all dictionaries order terms based on the alphabet in a specific language, and no author offers true systematic arrangements comparable to those of Paasch (see 3.5). And yet, a topic-based ordering system ensures accurate equivalences according to context. Still, Dabovich (1883) experiments with ordering entries based on a breakdown of the German terms, which can sometimes lead to satisfactory groupings of types and parts.

None of the books provide definitions, except Roest's dictionary (1842) for Dutch and French terms and Tecklenborg's (1870) for German. Already in the 19th century, dictionaries included equivalences in different languages without providing any additional semantic information, a practice that continued into the following century. And because this information is essential in order to confirm

---

5. A truly multilingual dictionary allows all source and target languages to be swapped (the number of translation directions follows the formula L^2-L, where L is the number of languages). So, FKTT includes 3 languages and proposes 6 translation directions (3^2-3). A multi-bilingual dictionary allows only one source language, typically English nowadays (the formula is $L-1$).

equivalence, translators find themselves forced to browse monolingual dictionaries to ensure the accuracy of their output. Once again, in this area, Paasch — whose dictionaries in the very least defined generic terms (see 3.2) and systematically included illustrations (see 3.3) — offered a refreshing exception to the trend.

A critical point to note is that the dictionary most similar to Captain Paasch's is undeniably also the oldest, the *Polyglossarium nauticum*. Compared to the marine dictionary developed by Paasch, this work included more languages, but was shorter in length. Like FKTT, this work relied on a significant number of illustrations. It was also the only dictionary of the time not to be alphabetised. Instead, the entries were ordered according to the numbering and indexing of the full-page illustrations. As it is entirely based on references to physical realities, it respects equivalence *de facto*, by dividing polysemous terms into as many homonymous terms. Comparatively, in Paasch's book the illustrations allow the reader to visualise a reality and verify an equivalence, but they are certainly not the foundation of Paasch's terminographical method (see 3.3 and 3.4.3). The simple labelling technique used in the *Polyglossarium nauticum* made it impossible to establish equivalence for more abstract concepts, such as those relating to winds, currents, or maritime insurance. Therefore, this book could not have played more than an incidental role in the development of the original methodology that made FKTT so successful.

3.   Paasch's methodology

3.1   Two key dates: 1890 and 1894

Paasch's terminographical work extends from 1885 to 1901, according to the publication dates of his dictionary. Over the course of sixteen years, his method evolved significantly, and this is apparent in later editions. Despite its considerable success, the first edition of FKTT (1885) was dedicated to English conceptualisation, with terms ordered alphabetically in the English language. Coincidentally, English was the working language used at Paasch's employer, Lloyd's Register. Still, the original title already conveyed the idea of a systematic inventory from the bottom of the keel to the masthead (truck) (around 5,400 concepts covered). In addition, it features subdomains, a layout in columns, illustrations (without cross-references or trilingual captions), and an index for each language.

In 1890, Paasch published the *Illustrated Marine Encyclopedia*, entirely in English. A resolutely encyclopaedic book with a very high proportion of definitions (around 85%), the dictionary covered some 3,800 concepts and included 100 full-page illustrations showing 3,660 parts. All of this content would ultimately be included in the trilingual dictionary. Paasch inaugurated a system of references leading to these numbered illustrations, and followed principles of systematic classification based on semantic relationships between concepts (see 3.5.1). These references would be featured again, with more improvements, in the second edition of the trilingual dictionary, published in 1894.

As was the case of the first dictionary, the terms in the *Illustrated Marine Encyclopedia* were imbued with an English conception of the maritime world. Four years later, however, with the transition from the monolingual encyclopaedia to the trilingual dictionary, Paasch enriched the former's English nomenclature by including the ways in which the German and French languages conceptualise the world of sailing.[6] To this end, he followed a rigorous principle of conceptual equivalence (PCE) (see 3.4.1), based on monosemy, which guaranteed an exact translation regardless of the source and target languages. This means English was no longer a pivot language.

The increase in the number of concepts (around 7,690) in the dictionary's second edition is in part due to the transition from polysemy to monosemy (which implies homonymy, see 3.4), to the notable increase in the number of hyponyms — which were previously listed as addenda to the definitions — and to taking into account idiomaticity. It can be stated with certainty that all features of Paasch's method are already present in this 1894 edition. The third edition (1901) is characterised by a further increase in the size of the corpus (rising to around 11,700 concepts), including in the Miscellaneous section, where many concepts referring to abstract realities were added.

It can reasonably be argued that major principles of monolingual conceptual terminography (see 3.4) were implemented by Paasch as early as 1890 in his English encyclopaedia, and that more complex principles of multilingual conceptual terminology were implemented in 1894. This is notably earlier than any dates recorded in most terminology manuals. This fact serves to illustrate how the field of terminology is often denied its own fascinating history.

3.2   The terminological record: Precursor to digital models

The terminological record used by Paasch follows a rigorous structure that foreshadows digital models of the future. It is organised by subdomain, and is often based on semantic relationships (see 3.5.1). Its microstructure is as follows:

---

6. We shall see in Section 3 various examples of these divergences which touch on the concept of multidimensionality (Bowker 1992).

Main entry term; synonym(s) if applicable
Definition
Specification of the types of ships concerned
Cross-reference to another concept
Cross-reference to an illustration
Note
Example
Idiomatic expression

The Main entry term (in bold) is a simple or complex term, selected first based on criteria not specified by the author, but likely related to usage. It may be followed by additional information between brackets, such as the relevant holonym, an actant, a complement, a defining feature, etc. Main entry terms for concepts that belong to both subdomains Wooden Ship and Iron or Steel Ship are preceded by an asterisk. There is no limit to the number of synonyms, which are also in bold. Paasch does not provide a rationale explaining the order in which synonyms are presented.

Definitions are generally intensional, but can also be meronymic or metalinguistic. The extension is delimited by the imperatives of equivalence (see 3.4.1). Many hyponyms do not have their own definition, as their hyperonym is already defined and said hyponyms are often categorised based on relevant semantic traits (see 3.5.1). Some definitions are followed by encyclopaedic elaborations, or even practical examples. In certain cases, the definition is replaced by just a mention between brackets (holonym, context, etc.).

The specification of the types of ships concerned proves useful when co-hyponyms differ in certain languages depending on the type of ship (see 3.4.2). Many such cases where hyponymic relations are not common to all languages are indeed related to this kind of subdivision criteria.

A cross-reference to another concept is used in exceptional cases, when a different concept classification could have been used depending on the conceptual network. It is also used for related concepts, duplicates, and words in the same lexical family. The other conceptual relationships are provided by the macrostructure itself (see 3.5.1).

Cross-references to full-page illustrations (see 3.3) specify the page number and the item on that page; there are as many cross-references as there are specific representations of the concept in different illustrations. Conversely, each illustrated item is associated with a concept described in the systematic section.

Notes are sparse, providing additional encyclopaedic information when they do appear. Examples, provided mostly for non-nouns, are utterances that illustrate the usage of terms; they are indented, placed under their headword. Idiomatic expressions have separate entries. Their classification is based on the English language, as they typically appear following a term encountered in the English idiom. If they have definitions, the idiomatic expressions themselves are presented in bold, as they are considered to be concepts on their own (e.g, *hard a lee!, mainsail haul!* or *to be in stays*; see Van Campenhoudt 1994b).

The record structure is identical for each of the dictionary's three languages. All fields are optional, except for the main entry term. Each record corresponds to a concept whose boundaries are determined by the constraints of equivalence (see 3.4). Many are ordered based on semantic relationships (see 3.5.1), which foreshadows the concept of a terminological knowledge base (Meyer et al. 1992). A sample, specifically the ontology of *yards* (the marine concept), would later be digitised in the Termisti software application, whose novel architecture enabled the management of Paasch's conceptual relationships (Blampain et al. 1992).

FKTT is, in addition, easy to represent in a Terminological Markup Language (TML) that adheres to the "concept — language — term" architecture defined in the ISO 16642 (2017) standard, *Terminological Markup Framework (TMF)*. In order to demonstrate this, we encoded the FKTT using a custom-designed TML, with a Document Type Definition (DTD), to specify the structure and the data categories (Van Campenhoudt 2022). The modelling principles observed in Paasch's dictionary and subsequently used in our Termisti software application were then applied to the *Hydrographic Dictionary* (IHO 1994–1998) during the MLIS-Dhydro project (Descotte et al. 2001). The TMF architecture, created at the initiative of Laurent Romary (Romary 2001, Romary and Van Campenhoudt 2001), drove changes in the architectures of many databases,[7] and is a direct descendent of Paasch's terminographical method as much as, if not more than, of the Vienna School.

Figure 1 shows the tree structure of Paasch's dictionary. The main limitations of this DTD were related to the encoding of the semantic network, due to recurring gaps in terminological data category registries and reference TMLs at the time of the research (see Van Campenhoudt 2018). Using standards that are designed more for ontologies, such as the Web Ontology Language (OWL) and the Simple Knowledge Organization System (SKOS), would likely have allowed a more faithful encoding of the semantic network that underlies Paasch's dictionary.

---

7. One example is the early versions of Multiterm software, which required the definition to be placed under a term. Similarly, IATE's current architecture meets the requirements of the TMF standard better than Eurodicautom.

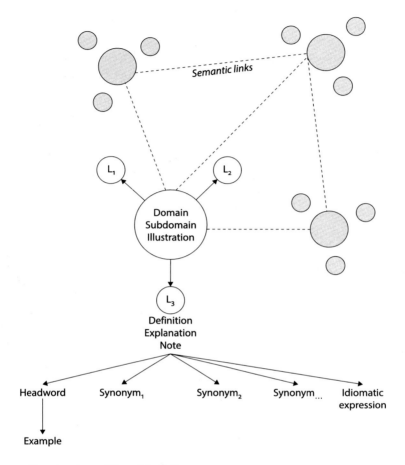

Figure 1. The structure of Paasch's dictionary

3.3   Illustrations

The dictionary's third edition (Paasch 1901) includes 109 full-page illustrations, with 3,750 parts designated by captions in three languages. The terminological records include cross-references to specific illustrations. The illustrations follow the systematic section and cover a large number of parts and ship types. Each item is numbered, and captioned in each of the three languages. The illustrations play a fundamental part in representing concrete realities and showing how languages conceptualise them, sometimes in divergent ways (see 3.4.3 and Figure 9).

As the dictionary's title indicates, the overall descriptive trajectory of the illustrations is "from keel to truck," i.e. from the bottom to the top. This is, however, only a general trend. To the extent possible, the numbering system is first based on spatial criteria that take into account conceptual relationships used in the systematic classification. Parts that are physically distant can be brought together through the numbering system, in order to highlight their common type. Similarly, spatial proximity itself can be used to associate the various parts of a given device.

3.4   An interlinguistic conceptual network

Each entry in the dictionary is devoted to a single concept. This means that the dictionary was initially designed as a multilingual inventory of concepts, not an inventory of terms. Its purpose is to represent how each reality in the nautical domain is conceptualised in each language, sometimes in ways that diverge. The dictionary does not claim to set a standard, although certain terms are mentioned as being standardised.[8]

3.4.1   *The principle of conceptual equivalence (PCE)*

Within each subdomain (e.g. "Machines," "Equipment: Standing-rigging," "Equipment: Running-rigging," etc.), concepts are linked together through a network of semantic relationships. In order to be used by translators, this conceptual network includes concepts that are specific to each of the languages in the dictionary (English, French, and German). In this sense, we refer to it as *interlinguistic*.

The equivalence between terms in two languages (L_1 and L_2) requires an acknowledgement of their ability to refer to the same concept. This principle of conceptual equivalence (PCE) can be expressed as follows:

> If A in L_1 is equivalent to α in L_2, and if A in L_1 is equivalent to ß in L_2 while α in L_2 is not synonymous with ß in L_2, this probably means that A in L_1 has two meanings that should be differentiated using two separate nodes in the network.
>
> $$L_1\ L_2$$
> concept 1: A α
> concept 2: A ß

Separating polysemous terms into homonyms is a natural consequence of applying the PCE.[9] This separation does not occur if differences in meaning do not go hand

---

8. Paasch mentions terms standardised by ship classification societies such as Bureau Veritas or Germanischer Lloyd. See Chapter 17 on international efforts during the 19th century.

9. Monolingual dictionaries generally use the criterion of etymology to separate homonyms. This etymological criterion is equivalent to using conceptual systems specific to foreign languages for creating homonymous terms that guarantee equivalence, whatever the etymology

in hand with differences in equivalence, unless accounting for hyponymic relationships in the macrostructure implies a transition from polysemy to homonymy
(Figure 2).

Pilotage. The skill or knowledge of a pilot respecting coasts, rivers, channels, currents, etc.	**Pilotage.** La connaissance d'un pilote des côtes, fleuves, courants, etc.	**Lootsenkunde.** Die Kenntniss eines Lootsen in Betreff der Küsten, Flüsse, Strömungen, des Fahrwassers u.s.w.
[...]	[...]	[...]
Pilotage. The money paid for the services of a pilot.	**Droits de pilotage.** Contributions perçues pour les services rendus par les pilotes.	**Lootsengeld.** Das, für die Dienste eines Lootsen gezahlte Geld.
[...]	[...]	[...]
Pilot-office. The building or the rooms in a sea-port, in which the Pilot-master and assistants conduct the business in connection with pilotage.	**Pilotage.** Bureaux de l'Administration du Pilotage dans un port, où l'inspecteur du pilotage et ses assistants dirigent les affaires se rapportant au pilotage des navires.	**Lootsenwesen.** Gebäude, in welchem sich die Büreaus einer Lootsenbehörde befinden und woselbst alle dieses Fach betreffenden Angelegenheiten erledigt werden.

(Paasch 1901:512)

Figure 2. Homonym separation according to the PCE

Of course, the strict application of the PCE means that the presence of a
synonym in one of the languages is enough to justify the principle of separating
homonyms, in accordance with the law on establishing nodes in the monolingual
network, on which this principle is based (Levrat and Sabah 1990:93). This is
shown in the Figure 3.

In many cases, including the example in Figure 3, separating homonyms is all
the more justified when the concepts involved belong to different subdomains and
are therefore not related. Furthermore, acknowledging conceptual links corrobo-
rates the need to distinguish multiple concepts based on the PCE. If a term can
be classified in two different "type of" (generic) tree structures, it may cover two
different concepts.

(e.g. *log = bûche, log = loch, log = livre de bord, log = registre,* etc.). Most bilingual dictionaries offer
equivalents in the context of polysemy; genuine multilingual polyglot dictionaries, such as
FKTT, offer equivalents in the context of homonymy.

Breakwater. A structure of timber; iron or steel plates, say from one to four feet in height according to the size of the vessel, fitted across forecastle-decks (notably of large steamers) to break the force of any sea shipped over the bows.	**Brise-lame.** Construction en bois, en fer ou en acier, ayant une hauteur de un à quatre pieds selon la grandeur du bâtiment, fixée en travers d'un pont de gaillard (notamment sur les grands steamers) pour briser les lames ou pour diminuer la force de celles-ci lorsqu'elles s'élèvent sur l'avant du navire.	**Brechwasser.** Ein Gefüge von Planken, eisernen oder stählernen Platten, je nach der Grösse des Schiffes, ein bis vier Fuss hoch, welches quer über ein Backdeck (besonders bei grossen Dampfern) angebracht ist, um die Gewalt der über den Bug stürzenden Wellen zu brechen.

(Paasch 1901: 43)

Breakwater. A stone-wall built up from the bottom of the sea, at the entrance of a bight, etc., to form a harbour, or to shelter one.	**Brise-lames.** Sorte de digue (ou mur de pierres) érigée sur le fond de la mer en avant d'un port et qui s'élève jusqu'audessus des eaux, pour amortir la violence des vagues, et protéger le port.	**Wellenbrecher; Brechwasser.** Eine am Eingange einer Bucht u.s.w. vom Grunde der See aufgebaute, deichähnliche Mauer, an welcher sich die Gewalt der Wellen bricht.

(Paasch 1901: 424)

Figure 3. Synonymy is addressed by the PCE

It should be noted that Paasch also distinguishes homonymous concepts, even abstract ones, based on their semantic content and not on a divergence between languages (Figure 4).

Course. The direction, over sea, from one point of land to another.	**Route.** Chemin à parcourir par voie de mer, de l'un point de terre à un autre.	**Kurs; Curs.** Die Richtung über See, von einer Landspitze zu einer anderen.
Course. The direction in which a vessel sails by compass.	**Route.** La direction qu'un navire suit d'après la boussole.	**Kurs; Curs.** Der Kompasstrich, auf dem ein Schiff segelt, um einen bestimmten Ort zu erreichen.

(Paasch 1901: 443)

Figure 4. Example of semantic divergence involving homonymy

3.4.2 *Towards a multiplication of the number of concepts?*

The PCE guarantees that each language may serve, in a given situation, as either the source language or a target language, a principle that has been recommended in ISO standards. However, as most linguists know, the semantic equivalence of terms between languages is not always bi-directional in this manner. For example, a term in one language may have a broader extension than its supposed equivalent in another. Such is the case with the German terms *Lootsenkunde, Lootsengeld* and *Lootsenwesen* (Figure 2), which cover three different concepts (skill of a pilot, money paid to a pilot, and pilots' building). In English, *pilotage* covers the first two concepts, but in French, *pilotage* covers the first and the third. In each of these languages, *pilotage* covers two different meanings and the terms are approached as two distinct lexico-semantic units, i.e. homonyms, rather than as one polysemic instance. A similar situation is found in Figure 3 with *breakwater*: English uses two homonyms, whereas the other two languages have adopted terms that differ only in status (here synonym in German and graphical variant in French). These examples demonstrate a basic principle of lexical semantics whereby renouncing polysemy, especially in terminology work where univocity is an underlying principle, results in the creation of homonyms.

Paasch seems to have understood and applied this principle systematically in FKTT, which does not resort to standardisation, borrowing, neologism, or paraphrasing to resolve issues related to equivalence. However, the increase in the number of concepts designated by homonyms is often curtailed by interesting regulating mechanisms (see Van Campenhoudt 1994a, 1996b, and 2001). Before summarising these mechanisms, we will first describe how Paasch exploits many hyponymy relationships in his systematic classifications (see 3.5.1.1).

Hyperonyms possess all the semantic traits of their hyponyms, and may replace them in discourse in a context of equivalence or synonymy (for example, use of the term *rodent* will avoid repetitive use of the term *mouse*). Paasch systematically and methodically uses hyperonyms to refer to hyponyms when one or several languages have more specific concepts. This conceptual void, which is well known in general language[10] and referred to as a *lexical gap*, is frequent in a maritime context. In his trilingual dictionary, which is oriented towards equivalence, Paasch systematically eschews describing hyperonyms that have no equivalent (they simply disappear), and duplicates them as homonymous equivalents of the co-hyponyms (Figure 5). Each homonym, of course, matches part of the hyperonym's extension. We refer to this isolated phenomenon in Paasch's work as *hyperonomasia*, and it implicitly results from the PCE (see Figure 5). Logically,

---

10. For instance, *mouton* [FR] = *sheep* or *mutton* [EN] and *dedo* [ES] = *toe* or *finger* [EN].

this same phenomenon emerged during the digitisation of the *Hydrographic Dictionary* (IHO 1994–1998, see Van Campenhoudt 2001: 194ff.).

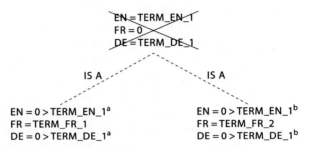

Figure 5. Hyperonomasia mechanism[11]

More elaborately still, through the PCE, Paasch attempts to systematically resolve cases of conceptual intersection between languages by creating a record dedicated to a "virtual concept" that does not exist in the involved languages. This virtual concept guarantees the equivalence by reducing the semantic features, for each language, to those of the common extension, and systematically resorts to hyperonyms.[12]

For instance, on three- and four-masted ships, the sequence of masts from stern to bow is not conceptualised in the same way in different languages (Figures 6 and 7). In French, a main-mast is added in the middle in order to create a four-masted square-rigged ship: there is a front main-mast (2nd mast) and a rear main-mast (3rd mast), while the last mast remains the mizen mast. In English and German, the 3rd mast keeps its name (*mizen mast, Kreuzmast*) and a new name is given to the 4th mast (*jigger mast, Jiggermast*). Logically, all sails located on these masts are conceptualised in divergent ways: the French *cacatois de perruche* is either the *mizen royal* or the *jigger royal* in English, depending on whether the ship has three masts or four. Similarly, the sail can be either the *Kreuz Royal* or the *Jigger Royal* in German (Figures 6 and 7). Figure 8 provides a practical illustration of this theoretical case.

In the tree structure presented in Figure 8, concept [4] illustrates exactly the same hyponymous concept that is created by borrowing hyperonyms that are distinct, but have perfectly compatible semantic traits: the left-hand side of the tree

---

11. Terms without equivalents at the level of the hyperonymous concept are only used as homonyms to designate all hyponymous concepts. The left-hand side of Figure 8 provides a practical illustration of this theoretical case.

12. See the examples of *reach* and *bras de mer* in the *Hydrographic Dictionary* (Van Campenhoudt 2001: 202–203).

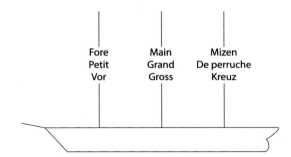

Figure 6. Sails of a three-masted square-rigged ship

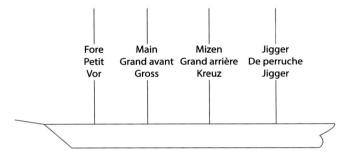

Figure 7. Sails of a four-masted square-rigged ship

distinguishes two types of *mizen royal = Kreuz Royal* depending on the mast's position (the criterion used in French); the right-hand side distinguishes two types of *cacatois de perruche* depending on the number of masts (the criterion used in English and German). In FKTT, the semantic network is interlinguistic: it keeps only concepts that originate from hyperonomasia, including one (identified by number [4] in Figure 8) that exists in none of the languages with such a restrictive extension.

In addition, the mechanism of the PCE fits an algorithm that can be calculated using matrices that include defining traits as +, -, or o. It was previously demonstrated in the *International Journal of Lexicography* (Van Campenhoudt 2001) that the same semantic matrices could be used to calculate equivalences in the *Hydrographic Dictionary* (IHO 1994–1998). The application of the Dhydro system to FKTT was later discussed by Janssen (2002:143–150), who preferred a componential approach inspired by John Sowa's lattices (1993) and Ganter and Wille's formal concept analysis (1996).[13]

---

13. The *International Journal of Lexicography* devoted a volume to this approach (Janssen 2004 and Van Campenhoudt 2004), and the journal *Languages* published a joint summary (Janssen and Van Campenhoudt 2005).

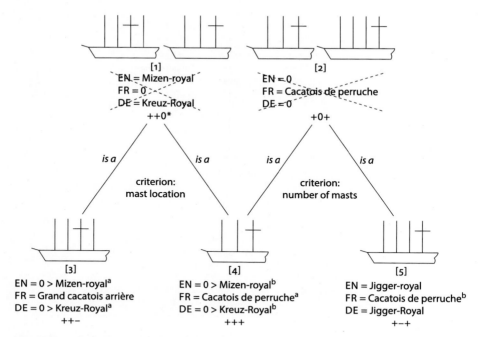

Figure 8. Hyperonomasia with virtual concept creation[14]

3.4.3 *Equivalence in illustrations*

On the full-page illustrations, equivalences are shown for each numbered part. This empirical solution of equivalence using terms as labels produces results that agree with principal theories at the core of Paasch's work: conceptual gaps are addressed by hyperonomasia, and partial overlaps result in records dedicated to virtual concepts that guarantee equivalence in cases of intersection. And the dictionary's macrostructure does indeed rely on the hyponymic relationships between those concepts.

In fact, illustration and denomination of referents empirically lead to an identical solution to that offered by the PCE. In Figure 9, which is directly inspired by the colour division problem proposed by Lyons (1968: 56ff.), each box corresponds to each of the sails referred to in each language by a different term. This means that each box represents the extension of this term in a particular language. By confronting the various divisions, we can see that in a trilingual dictionary, three different "concepts" or units of understanding must be used in order to encompass the three possible referents (Van Campenhoudt 1994a: 67–69).

---

14. The asterisk indicates multilingual semantic features: 3rd sail, 3rd mast, last mast (only specified at hyponym level).

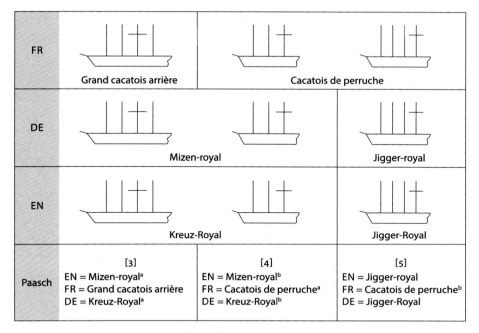

FR			
	Grand cacatois arrière	Cacatois de perruche	
DE			
		Mizen-royal	Jigger-royal
EN			
		Kreuz-Royal	Jigger-Royal
Paasch	[3] EN = Mizen-royal[a] FR = Grand cacatois arrière DE = Kreuz-Royal[a]	[4] EN = Mizen-royal[b] FR = Cacatois de perruche[a] DE = Kreuz-Royal[b]	[5] EN = Jigger-royal FR = Cacatois de perruche[b] DE = Jigger-Royal

Figure 9. Application of Lyons' schema (1968: 57).
The bracketed numbers correspond to Figure 8.

3.5   The macrostructure

Most subdomains encompass a number of concepts as part of a homogenous conceptual network that is simultaneously built on both a *type-of* relationship and a *part-whole* relationship. Parts of a ship that elude these subdomains are gathered in the Sundries subdomain. Concepts that refer to more abstract realities (actions, states, observable phenomena, etc.) are placed in the Miscellaneous and Mechanical expressions subdomains.

Heinrich Paasch liked to classify things in a rational order. In this respect, he is a child of the scientific and technical 19th century (see Chapter 4). Within each subdomain, concepts are arranged in a systematic order based on conceptual links. When this is not possible, the macrostructure lists the English main entry terms in alphabetical order (see 3.5.2).

3.5.1   *Systematic ordering*

3.5.1.1   *Hierarchical relationships*[15]

The type-of hyponymic relationship structures many entries, as a hyperonymous concept is immediately followed by its hyponyms, which are themselves classified based on *coordinate* relationships (see 3.5.1.2). Nested hierarchies can, of course, occur.

If, starting from a single hyperonym, multiple hyponymic families are observed depending on the nature of subdivision criteria used, then co-hyponyms are grouped based on said criteria (for instance, three families of wedges are distinguished: material-based, mast-based or deck-based). If a hyperonym is separated into distinct homonyms, each hyponym is placed under the proper hyperonymous concept. This is evidence of a solid and carefully considered methodology.

The meronymic part-whole relationship is also leveraged. To the extent possible, parts that can fit into specific types (bolts, rods, angle-bars, etc.) are grouped based on type-of relationships, rather than enumerated alongside other items in the mechanisms of which they are a part. Indeed, it is often easier to find ordering criteria for co-hyponyms than for co-meronyms (Van Campenhoudt 1996c).

Cruse (1986: 163–164) calls *super-meronyms* meronyms (e.g. *wing*) inherited from a hyperonym (*bird*) and *hypo-holonyms* hyponyms (e.g. *parrot*) which inherit meronyms (*wing*) from their hyperonym (*bird*). In a multilingual context, meronyms can be super-meronyms or hypo-meronyms, depending on the language. For example, *point de drisse* is a meronym for *sail* only in French, and it has no equivalent in English or German. We need to descend to the level of hyponyms (*triangular sail* or *gaff sail*) and choose the correct hypo-meronym as the equivalent, in strict application of the PCE (see Figure 10). Where possible, classifying the parts according to the hyponymy relationship provides the most regularity in the macrostructure, while justifying the proposed equivalences (Van Campenhoudt 1994: 140ff. and 1996c: 62–64).

If necessary, meronyms of the concept previously treated as a hyperonym are listed following the co-hyponyms. The type-of presentation is used, among others, for the description of very limited subdomains such as Anchor, Capstan, Winch, Windlass, etc.

---

15. Here we adopt the distinction between vertical — or hierarchical — and horizontal — or coordinate — relationships, established by Wüster (1974, French translation).

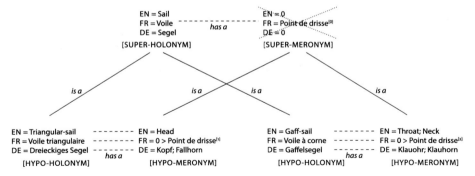

Figure 10. Meronyms involved in a hyponymic relationship through application of the PCE

3.5.1.2   *Coordinate relationships*

When the typology allows for it, co-hyponyms are classified according to a horizontal — or *coordinate* — relationship, immediately linked to the subdivision criterion which allows the reader to distinguish them in the type-of tree structure, especially using a spatial (front-behind, above-below) or temporal (precedes-succeeds) relationship.

The possibility to exploit these relationships often results in recurring layout models, including chains, cyclical ordering, helical ordering, and scale (Cruse 1986: 189 and 192–195), as well as antonymy, depending on criteria relating to time, space, number, or size (Figure 11).

Morning watch.	**Quart du jour.**	Morgenwache; Tagwache.
Fore-noon-watch.	**Quart de huit heures à midi.**	Vormittagswache.
After-noon-watch.	**Quart de midi à quatre heures.**	Nachmittagswache.
Dog watch.	**Quart de deux heures; Petit quart.**	Abendwache; Plattfuss.
First watch.	**Quart de huit heures à minuit.**	Erste Wache.
Middle watch.	**Quart de minuit à quatre heures.**	Mittelwache.

(Paasch 1901: 576)

Figure 11. Helical ordering of concepts[16]

---

16. The temporal relationship follows the 24 hours of the day before passing to the next day. *Morning watch*: between 4 and 8 am, *dog watch*: between 4 and 6 pm.

3.5.1.3   *Example of systematic ordering*

An example of macrostructure modelling for topsails is shown in Figures 12 and 13. It features homonyms related to the PCE, e.g. *main-topsail, mizen-topsail* (EN); *grand hunier, perroquet de fougue* (FR); *Gross-Toppsegel, Gross-Marssegel* (DE). Hyponymous concepts are arranged under the appropriate homonym and ordered based on subdivision criteria that correspond to coordinate relationships: front-behind at the 2nd level (*main — middle — mizen — jigger*), below-above at the 3rd level (*lower — upper*). Obvious to a sailor consulting the dictionary, these classifications guarantee the completeness of the equivalences. They are made accessible to translators, from any language, through indices.

topsail (*main hyperonym*)
    [...]
        cohyponyms (front-behind relationship)
            main topsail 1
                cohyponyms (below-above relationship)
                    lower main topsail 1
                    upper main topsail 1
            main topsail 2
                cohyponyms (below-above relationship)
                    lower main topsail 2
                    upper main topsail 2
            main topsail 3
                cohyponyms (below-above relationship)
                    lower main topsail 3
                    upper main topsail 3
             main topsail 4; lug main topsail
            middle topsail
                cohyponyms (below-above relationship)
                    lower middle topsail
                    upper upper topsail
            mizen topsail 1 (front-behind relationship)
                cohyponyms (below-above relationship)
                    lower mizen topsail 1
                    upper mizen topsail 1
            mizen topsall 2
                cohyponyms (below-above relationship)
                    lower mizen topsail 2
                    upper mizen topsail 2
            mizen topsail 3: lug mixen topsail
            jigger topsail
            etc.

Figure 12. Ordering followed by Paasch in Figure 13 (homonyms are numbered)

Equipment.	Équipement.	Ausrüstung.
Sails.	*Voiles.*	*Segel.*
Lower-fore-topsail (Schooner).	**Petit hunier fixe** (Goëlette).	**Vor-Untertoppsegel** (Schooner).
Upper-fore-topsail (Schooner).	**Petit hunier volant** (Goëlette).	**Vor-Obertoppsegel** (Schooner).
Fore-topsail; Lug-fore-topsail (Chasse-marée) See Pl. 93.4.	**Hunier de misaine** (Chasse-marée). Voy. Pl. 93.4.	**Vor-Toppsegel** (Chasse-marée). Siehe Pl 93. 4.
Main-topsail. See Pl. 83–83.	**Grand hunier.** Voy. Pl. 83–83.	**Gross-Marssegel** Siehe Pl. 83–83.
Lower-main-topsail. See Pl. 88[3].17, 85. 41 & 89. 13.	**Grand hunier fixe** Voy. Pl. 83. 17, 85. 41 & 89.13.	**Gross-Untermarssegel.** Siehe Pl. 83 17, 85. 41 & 89. 13.
Upper-main-topsail. See Pl. 83. 18, 85. 42 & 89. 14.	**Grand hunier volant.** Voy. Pl. 83. 18, 85. 42 & 89.14.	**Gross- Obermarssegel.** Siehe Pl. 83. 18, 85. 42 & 89. 14.
Main-topsail (Four-mast-Ship, Four-, or Five-mast-Barque). See Pl. 84. 52 & 56.	**Grand hunier avant** (Quatre-mâts carré, Quatre-mâts-barque ou Cinq-mâts-barque). Voy. Pl. 84. 52 & 56.	**Gross-Marssegel** (Viermast-Schiff, Vier-, oder Fünfmast-Bark). Siehe Pl. 84. 52 & 56.
Lower-main-topsail (Four-mast-Ship, Four-, or Five-mast-Barque). See Pl. 84. 52, 86. 37 & 87. 40.	**Grand hunier fixe avant** (Quatre-mâts carré, Quatre-mâts-barque ou Cinq-mâts-barque). Voy. Pl. 84. 52, 86. 37 & 87. 40.	**Gross- Untermarssegel** (Viermast-Schiff, Vier-, oder Fünfmast-Bark). Siehe Pl. 84. 52, 86 37 & 87. 40.
Upper-main-topsail (Four-mast-Ship, Four-, or Five-mast-Barque). See Pl. 84. 56, 86. 40 & 87. 44	**Grand hunier volant avant** (Quatre-mâts carré, Quatre-mâts-barque ou Cinq-mâts-barque). Voy. Pl. 84 56, 86. 40 & 87. 44	**Gross-Obermarssegel** (Viermast-Schiff, Vier-, oder Fünfmast-Bark). Siehe Pl 84. 56, 86. 40 & 87. 44.
Main-topsail (Schooner).	**Grand hunier** (Goëlette).	**Gross-Toppsegel** (Schooner).
Lower-main-topsail (Schooner).	**Grand hunier fixe** (Goëlette).	**Gross-Untertoppsegel** (Schooner).
Upper-main-topsail (Schooner).	**Grand hunier volant** (Goëlette).	**Gross-Obertoppsegel** (Schooner).
Main-topsail; Lug-main-topsail (Chasse-marée. See Pl. 93. 5.	**Grand hunier** (Chasse-marée). Voy. Pl. 93. 5.	**Gross-Toppsegel** (Chasse-marée). Siehe Pl. 93. 5.
Middle-topsail (Five-mast-Vessel). See Pl. 87. 41 & 45.	**Grand hunier central** (Navire à cinq mâts). Voy. Pl. 87. 41 & 45.	**Mittel-Marssegel** (Fünfmast-Schiff). Siehe Pl. 87. 41 & 45.
Lower-middle-topsail (Five-mast- Vessel). See Pl. 87. 41.	**Grand hunier fixe central** (Navire à cinq mâts). Voy. Pl. 87. 41.	**Mittel-Untermarssegel** (Fünfmast-Schiff). Siehe Pl. 87. 41.
Upper-middle -topsail (Five-mast- Vessel). See Pl. 87. 45.	**Grand hunier volant central** (Navire à cinq mâts). Voy. Pl. 87. 45.	**Mittel-Obermarssegel** (Viermast-Schiff). Siehe Pl. 87. 45.

Equipment.	Équipement.	Ausrüstung.
Mizen-topsail (Ship). See Pl. 83. 25 & 26.	**Perroquet de fougue** (Trois-mâts carré). Voy. Pl. 83. 25 & 26.	**Kreuz-Marssegel** (Vollschiff). Siehe Pl[.] 83. 25 & 26.
Lower-mizen-topsail (Ship) See Pl. 83. 25.	**Perroquet de fougue fixe** (Trois-mâts carré) Voy. Pl, 83. 25.	**Kreuz-Untermarssegel** (Vollschiff). Siehe Pl. 83. 25.
Upper-mizen-topsail (Ship). See Pl. 83. 26.	**Perroquet de fougue volant** (Trois-mâts carré). Voy. Pl. 83. 26.	**Kreuz-Obermarssegel** (Vollschiff). Siehe Pl. 83. 26.
Mizen - topsail (Four-mast-Ship, (Four-, or Five-mast·Barque). See Pl. 84. 53 & 57 & 87. 42 & 46.	**Grand hunier arrière** (Quatre-mâts carré, Quatre mâts-barque ou Cinq-mâts-barque), Voy. Pl. 84. 53 & 57 & 87.42 & 46.	**Kreuz- Marssegel** (Viermast-Schiff, Vier-, oder Fünfmast-Bark). Siehe Pl. 84. 53 & 57 & 87. 42 & 46.
Lower-Mizen-topsail (Four-mast-Ship, Four-, or Five-mast-Barque). See Pl. 84. & 53 & 87. 42.	**Grand hunier fixe arrière** (Quatre-mâts carré. Quatre-mâts-barque ou Cinq-mâts-barque). Voy. Pl. 84. 53 & 87. 42.	**Kreuz- Untermarssegel** (Viermast-Schiff, Vier-, oder Fünfmast-Bark). Siehe Pl. 84. 53 & 87. 42.
Upper-mizen-topsail (Four-mast- Ship, Four-, or Five-mast-Barque). See Pl. 84. 57 & 87. 46.	**Grand hunier volant arrière** (Quatre-mâts carré, Quatre-mâts-barque ou Cinq-mâts-barque. Voy. Pl. 84. 57 & 87. 46.	**Kreuz-Obermarssegel** (Viermast-Schiff, Vier-, oder Fünfmast-Bark). Siehe Pl. 84. 57 & 87. 46.
Mizen-topsail; Lug-mizen-topsail (Chasse-marée). See Pl. 93. 6.	**Hunier de tapecul** (Chasse-marée). Voy. Pl. 93. 6.	**Treiber-Toppsegel** (Chasse-marée). Siehe Pl. 93. 6.
Jigger-topsail (Four- mast-Ship). See Pl. 84. 54 & 58.	**Perroquet de fougue** (Quatre-mâts carré). Voy. Pl. 84. 54 & 58.	**Jigger-Marssegel; Besahn-Marssegel** (Viermast-Schiff). Siehe Pl. 84. 54 & 58.

Figure 13. Ordering of topsails in accordance with the methodology (Paasch 1901: 339)

3.5.2 *Alphabetical ordering*

3.5.2.1 *General principle*

When it is difficult, or even impossible, to follow systematic models, the classification is based on the form of English headwords and on the possibility of grouping terms by lexico-semantic families. To this end, for organising multi-word terms, the headword is the primary key. This enables the grouping of all concepts that are referred to in English using terms that have the same headword with the same meaning (e.g. *capstan* in Figure 15). If the headword is carefully selected, this procedure offers the advantage of consolidating a large number of hyponyms, meronyms, and related concepts. In addition, it enables many concepts to be classified in the subdomain without resorting to pseudo-logical groupings. Alphabetical ordering based on English headwords is a good complement to arrangement principles based on conceptual relationships. Lastly, the PCE guarantees equal treatment of languages, with English having no pre-eminence beyond the ordering used.

3.5.2.2 *Typical structure*

Terms are ordered alphabetically by the language in the first column, i.e. English (see Figures 14 and 15), and in the case of multi-word terms, based on the headword. Terms with the word + headword structure are generally co-hyponyms or concepts belonging to successive levels of hyponymy (word + word + headword). Once they have all been listed, the next terms are those with words to the right, i.e. those with a headword + word structure, which generally refer to co-meronyms or related concepts. Other meronyms, with a word + *of a(n)/of the* + headword structure are usually positioned last.

```
                    Headword
        A           Headword
    A   A           Headword
    B   A           Headword
A   C   A           Headword
B   C   A           Headword
        B           Headword
        C           Headword
    A   C           Headword
    B   C           Headword
        D           Headword
                    Headword   A
                    Headword   B
                    Headword   C
                    Headword   D   A
                    Headword   D   B
                    Headword   Z
    A of a          Headword
    B of a          Headword
    C of a          Headword
                    etc.
```

Figure 14. Alphabetical ordering principles in English

	capstan		
after	capstan		
double	capstan		
jeer	capstan		
main	capstan		
steam	capstan		
	capstan	bar	
	capstan	bar	hole
	capstan	barrel	
	capstan	pawl	
	capstan	pawl	head
	capstan	pawl	rim
	capstan	spindle	
	capstan	spindle	collar
	capstan	spindle	socket
	capstan	whelp	
	capstan	whelp	chock
drum-head of	capstan		

Figure 15. Terms comprising *capstan* (Paasch 1901: 253)

3.6   The indices

At the end of the dictionary, an index for each of the three featured languages can be found. The reader is directed to a page number, as concepts are unfortunately not numbered. The indices do not break down complex terms, which are simply ordered alphabetically.

In addition, all terms that occur in an entry (main entry term, synonyms) are not necessarily listed in these indices. Considering that the systematic entries favour an ordering based on the type-of relationship, it seems superfluous to index certain terms that follow the general models of hyponym formation.

4.   An innovative method rather than a school

We have found some of the author's archives at the Maritime Museum in Antwerp. They only concern his life and the dissemination of his dictionary. Despite our efforts, we could not locate Heinrich Paasch's working documents. However, following a long and meticulous analysis, we are convinced that Paasch built and perpetually improved upon his dictionary by developing strict and highly innovative methodological principles.

Only his passing can explain why he was not able to teach these principles to the Italian and Spanish contributors for the fourth edition, published posthumously (1908), much less to those who collaborated on the final edition, published in 1937. Unfortunately also, the individuals involved in updating and translating the dictionary were unaware of, and therefore could not properly draw on, the sophistication of the theoretical model that was critical to much of Paasch's work. Sadly, Paasch's successors were harbingers of the tragedy that has afflicted far too many dictionaries and large databases of the 20th and 21st centuries by equating terminology work with translation of a source language, a process that superimposes the source language's own perceptual interpretation of concepts onto other languages. These posthumous editions, which did not systematically apply his principles, were nonetheless widely distributed. That fact may have led theorists of terminology to fail to recognise the significance of Paasch's contribution to the field, and cause them to favour the standardisation approach that followed.

Although Paasch was neither an academic nor a terminologist in the classical sense, he managed to produce an innovative, deeply reflected, and rigorously structured terminographic work that merits our admiration today. In any case, during his time, the academic world would probably not have been ready to theorise his specialised multilingual dictionary, lacking the contemporary theories we have today to understand his groundbreaking approaches. Terminologists now accept that their discipline is the result of an evolutionary process, and are therefore bound to consider all contributions to the historical development of their field. Accounts such as this one unequivocally demonstrate that through his innovative, carefully considered and highly structured work, Paasch was the first to develop methods that later would define Terminology as a discipline. Let us read his dictionary, and find inspiration in his ethics: to show respect for the diversity of languages and its variable usages.

Acknowledgements

We would like to acknowledge the valuable contribution of our translator, Simon Kroeger. We would also like to thank the editors for their valuable guidance.

References

Blampain, Daniel, Philippe Petrussa, and Marc Van Campenhoudt. 1992. "À la recherche d'écosystèmes terminologiques." In *L'environnement traductionnel. La station de travail du traducteur de l'an 2001. Universités francophones. Actualité scientifique*, ed. by André Clas, and Hayssam Safar, 273–82. Sillery & Montréal: Presses de l'Université du Québec et AUPELF-UREF.

Boom, D.-J. 1888. *Zeemans woordenboek in vier talen [...]*, 2nd ed. 's-Gravenhage: De gebroeders Van Cleef. Paris: Challamel Aîné.

Bowker, Lynne. 1992. *Guidelines for Handling Multidimensionality in a Terminological Knowledge Base*. Ottawa: University of Ottawa. PhD Thesis.

Cleirac, Estienne. 1636. *Explication des termes de marine employez dans les édicts, ordonnances et reglemens de l'Admirauté*. Paris: M. Brunet.

Cruse, D. Alan. 1986.(1991=reprint). *Lexical Semantics*. Cambridge: Cambridge University Press.

Dabovich, P. E. 1883. *Dizionario tecnico e nautico di marina. Italiano, Tedesco, Francese ed Inglese [...]*. Trieste: Julius Dase.

Descotte, Sylviane, Jean-Luc Husson, Laurent Romary, Nadia Viscogliosi, and Marc Van Campenhoudt. 2001. "Specialized Lexicography by Means of a Conceptual Data Base: Establishing the Format for a Multilingual Marine Dictionary." In *Maritime Terminology: Dictionaries and Education, Proceedings of the Second Conference on Maritime Terminology*, ed. by J. Vainio, 63–81. Turku: University of Turku.

Desroches. 1687. *Dictionnaire des termes propres de marine [...]*. Paris: A. Auroy.

Ganter Bernhard and Rudolf Wille. 1996. *Formale Begriffsanalyse: Mathematische Grundlagen*. Berlin: Springer Verlag.

IEC. 1938. *Vocabulaire électrotechnique international = International Electrotechnical Vocabulary*. Paris: Comité électrotechnique français.

IHO. 1994, 1996, 1998 *Hydrographic Dictionary. Diccionario Hidrográfico. Dictionnaire hydrographique*. 5th ed. Monaco: International Hydrographic Organization.

ISO 16642. 2017. *Computer applications in terminology — Terminological markup framework*. 2nd ed. Geneva: International Organization for Standardization.

Janssen, Maarten. 2002. *SIMuLLDA: a Multilingual Lexical Database Application using a Structured Interlingua*. PhD thesis. Utrecht: Universiteit Utrecht.

Janssen, Maarten. 2004. "Multilingual Lexical Databases, Lexical Gaps, and SIMuLLDA." *International Journal of Lexicography* 17(2): 137–54.

Janssen, Maarten, and Marc Van Campenhoudt. 2005. "Terminologie traductive et représentation des connaissances: l'usage des relations hyponymiques." *Langages* 157 (1): 63–80.

Landolt, Heinrich Mathias Friedrich. 1865–1871. *Dictionnaire polyglotte de termes techniques militaires et de marine [...]*. Leiden : E.J. Brill.

Levrat, Bernard, and Gérard Sabah. 1990. "'Sorte de', une façon de rendre compte de la relation d'hyponymie/hyperonymie dans les réseaux sémantiques." *Langages* 25 (98): 87–102.

Lyons, John. 1968. *Introduction to Theoretical Linguistics*. Cambridge: Cambridge University Press.

Meyer, Ingrid, Lynne Bowker, and Karen Eck. 1992. "COGNITERM: An Experiment in Building a Terminological Knowledge Base." In *Euralex '92 Proceedings I-II. Papers submitted to the 5th EURALEX International Congress on Lexicography in Tampere, Finland*, ed. by Hannu Tommola, Krista Varantola, Tarja Salmi-Tolonen, and Jurgen Schopp, I-159–172. Studia Translatologica Ser. A vol. 2. Tampere: University of Tampere.

Paasch, Heinrich. 1885. *From Keel to Truck — De la quille à la pomme de mât — Vom Kiel zum Flaggenknopf [...]*. 1st ed. Antwerp: Ratinckx frères.

Paasch, Heinrich. 1890. *Illustrated Marine Encyclopedia*. Antwerp: the author.

Paasch, Heinrich. 1894. *From Keel to Truck — De la quille à la pomme de mât — Vom Kiel zum Flaggenknopf [...]*. 2nd ed. Antwerp: H. Paasch; Hamburg: Eckardt & Messtorff; London: Fisher.

Paasch, Heinrich. 1901. *From Keel to Truck — De la quille à la pomme de mât — Vom Kiel zum Flaggenknopf [...]*. 3rd ed. Antwerp: H. Paasch; Hamburg: Eckardt & Messtorff.

Paasch, Heinrich. 1908. *From Keel to Truck — De la quille à la pomme de mât — Vom Kiel zum Flaggenknopf — De quilla a perilla — Dalla chiglia al pomo dell'albero. Dictionnaire de marine anglais-français-allemand-espagnol-italien [...]*. 4th (post mortem) ed. Paris: Augustin Challamel.

Paasch, Heinrich, and Louis Bataille. 1937. *De la quille à la pomme du mât — From Keel to Truck — Vom Kiel zum Flaggenknopf — De Quilla a Perilla — Dalla Chiglia al Pomo dell'Albero [...] établi d'après l'ancien dictionnaire du capitaine Paasch [...]* 5th (post mortem) ed. Paris: Société d'éditions géographiques maritimes et coloniales ; London: George Philip.

Polyglossarium Nauticum. 1847. Hamburg: H.G. Voigt.

Quemada, Bernard. 1967. *Les dictionnaires du français moderne, 1539–1863. Étude sur leur histoire, leurs types et leurs méthodes*. Paris, Bruxelles, and Montréal: Didier.

Roest, Carel. 1842. *Het marine stoomwerktuig beschreven in den vorm van een woordenboek in de Nederdiertsche, Fransche en Engelsche talen*. Amsterdam: G. Hulst van Keulen.

Romary, Laurent. 2001. "Un modèle abstrait pour la représentation de terminologies multilingues informatisées TMF (Terminological Markup Framework)." *Cahiers Gutenberg* 39–40: 81–88.

Romary, Laurent, and Marc Van Campenhoudt. 2001. "Normalisation des échanges de données en terminologie: les cas des relations dites conceptuelles." In *Actes des 4es Rencontres terminologie et intelligence artificielle (Nancy, 3–4 mai 2001)*, 77–86. Nancy: INIST-CNRS.

Schlomann, Alfred. 1906–32: *Illustrierte Technische Wörterbücher*, 17 vol. München und Berlin: R. Oldenbourg.

Sowa, John F. 1993. "Lexical Structures and Conceptual Structures." In *Semantics and the Lexicon*, ed. by James Pustejovsky, 223–262. Studies in Linguistics and Philosophy. Dordrecht: Springer Netherlands (Kluwer).

Tecklenborg, Heinrich. 1870. *Internationales Wörterbuch der Marine über alle in Verkehr Vorkommenden Technischen Ausdrücke [...]*. 2 vol. Bremen: Joh. Georg Heyse.

Temmerman, Rita. 2000. *Towards New Ways of Terminology Description: The Sociocognitive Approach*. Amsterdam: John Benjamins.

Ter Reehorst, Karl Pieter. 1865. *The Mariner's Friend, or Polyglot Indispensable and Technical Dictionary [...]*. 2nd ed. London: Taylor.

Van Campenhoudt, Marc. 1994a. *Un apport du monde maritime à la terminologie conceptuelle multilingue : étude du dictionnaire du capitaine Heinrich Paasch "De la quille à la pomme du mât" (1885–1901)*. 2 vol. Paris: Université Paris XIII. PhD Thesis.

Van Campenhoudt, Marc. 1994b. "Idiomaticité et gestion de données terminologiques : une approche conceptuelle." *Meta* 39(1): 97–106.

Van Campenhoudt, Marc. 1996a. "'De la quille à la pomme de mât' : le capitaine Paasch, sa vie, son œuvre." *Le Chasse-Marée* 95: 24–33.

Van Campenhoudt, Marc. 1996b. "Réseau notionnel, intelligence artificielle et équivalence en terminologie multilingue: essai de modélisation." In *Lexicomatique et dictionnairiques, IVes journées scientifiques du réseau thématique Lexicologie, terminologie, traduction*, ed. by André Clas, Philippe Thoiron, and Henri Béjoint, 281–306. AUPELF-UREF and F.M.A.

Van Campenhoudt, Marc. 1996c. "Recherche d'équivalences et structuration des réseaux notionnels: le cas des relations méronymiques." *Terminology* 3(1): 53–83.

Van Campenhoudt, Marc. 1997. "Évaluation des terminographies multilingues: le dictionnaire nautique du capitaine Paasch face au dictionnaire aéronautique de l'ingénieur Schlomann." In *Les dictionnaires spécialisés et l'analyse de la valeur, actes du colloque organisé en avril 1995 par le Centre de terminologie de Bruxelles (Institut libre Marie Haps)*, ed. by A. Hermans, 75–115. Peeters: Leuven, and Louvain-la-Neuve.

Van Campenhoudt, Marc. 2001. "Pour une approche sémantique du terme et de ses équivalents." *International Journal of Lexicography*, 14(3): 181–209.

Van Campenhoudt, Marc. 2003. "L'évolution des dictionnaires de traduction du domaine maritime au XIX siècle: aux sources de 'De la quille à la pomme de mât'." *Chronique d'histoire Maritime* 52: 83–97.

Van Campenhoudt, Marc. 2004. "Réseau sémantique et approche componentielle des bases de données multilingues." *International Journal of Lexicography*, 17(2): 155–160,

Van Campenhoudt, Marc. 2016. "Terminologie et langues spécialisées dans les pays de langue romane." In *Manuel de traductologie*, ed. by Jörn Albrecht, and René Métrich, 589–616. Berlin: De Gruyter.

Van Campenhoudt, Marc. 2018. "Standardised Modelling and Interchange of Lexical Data in Specialised Language." *Revue française de linguistique appliquée*, 22(1): 41–60.

Van Campenhoudt, Marc. 2022. DTD and Schema of the Dictionary "From Keel to Truck": Heinrich Paasch 1901.

Van Campenhoudt, Marc. 2022. "DTD and Schema of the Dictionary 'From Keel to Truck': Heinrich Paasch 1901." *Di-fusion [italics]: institutional repository of the Université libre de Bruxelles.*

Villain-Gandossi, Christiane. 1999. "De Robert Estienne à Heinrich Paasch : la place du vocabulaire maritime dans les dictionnaires plurilingues." In *Maritime Terminology: Issues in Communication and Translation. Proceedings of the First International Conference on Maritime Terminology (Brussels, 15–16 May 1998)*, ed. by Newman Daniel Lawrence, and Marc Van Campenhoudt, 22–46. Brussels: Éditions du Hazard.

Wüster, Eugen. 1968. *The Machine Tool*. London: Technical Press.

Wüster, Eugen. 1974. "L'inversion d'un rapport notionnel et les symboles correspondants utilisés en lexicographie" = "Die Umkehrung einer Begriffsbeziehung und ihre Kennzeichnung in Wörterbüchern". Translated by INFOTERM. *Nachrichten für Dokumentation*, 25(6): 256–263.

Wüster, Eugen. 1981. "L'étude scientifique générale de la terminologie, zone frontalière entre la linguistique, la logique, l'ontologie, l'informatique et la science des choses." In *Textes choisis de terminologie. Vol. I : Fondements théoriques de la terminologie*, ed. by Guy Rondeau, and Helmut Felber, 55–113. Québec: Université Laval — GIRSTERM.

PART 2

Developments in theory and methodology

CHAPTER 7

Terminology science, international languages, and knowledge communication

Natascia Leonardi
University of Macerata

Eugen Wüster, the founder of terminology science, is considered in this study as part of a long tradition of interventions in natural languages aiming at improving their representative and communicative efficiency. From the invention of artificial language systems (in 17th century Europe), through language planning (from the 19th century onwards) this tradition continues in contemporary formalised models developed in Natural Language Processing that are at the basis of Artificial Intelligence applications. International artificial/auxiliary languages are recognised to have a key role in the birth of terminology as a scientific discipline.

Keywords: artificial language, Esperanto, knowledge formalisation, conceptual framework, specialised language

1. Introduction

The history of terminology as a discipline originates with Eugen Wüster's systematic elaboration of a method for improving specialised communication both at national and international levels. Wüster's earliest major publications appeared in the 1930s, during a time of widespread scientific and technological advancement. The chronological collocation opens up the way to a consideration of the background and the dynamic communication network that had already characterised the field of specialised knowledge in the previous centuries (Section 2). Wüster's solution to communication problems is deeply rooted in his knowledge of contemporary linguistic theories and of interlinguistics, as he was an expert in Esperanto, an international constructed language, and had started to contribute to its lexicography before devoting himself to the development of a theory and practice of terminology (Section 3).

In the present analysis the panorama of "linguistic construction" provides the premise for tracing a line back to the 17th century. This epoch was charac-

https://doi.org/10.1075/tlrp.24.07leo

terised by an enthusiasm for the creation of improved languages which might favour direct and unequivocal communication, especially among scientists. But this line of continuity can be also traced forward, into the 20th century, when similar strategies started to be used for managing natural language comprehension and translation via computational systems.

In our perspective, language construction that aims to optimise communicative efficiency is closely related to the concept of *formalisation*, intended primarily as an *instrument* for making available a model that may guarantee complete regularity in each facet of linguistic systems. The necessity to systematically organise and communicate specialised content is a common thread that connects the long tradition of language construction with the history of terminology. The basic assumption underlying the picture presented here is the idea that an "artificial" linguistic code can be used within a community. It translates into the following commitments: the elaboration of a regular (formal) model based on systematically defined concepts shared by specialists (rather than on variable lexical items), and the planning of a "grammatical" (mostly morphological) system which can guarantee the highest degree of regularity and transparency for the expression of concepts and their relations (Sections 3.1 and 3.2).

Language creation — and its *artificiality* — utilises strategies that vary depending on the aims driving the planning of new codes. In the case examined here the similarities between different approaches to language construction and/or language planning are so numerous that they can actually support the parallelism between traditional attempts at building a universal language and the modern planning and description of an improved code for specialised communication. In this perspective, universal language projects and terminology are considered as plans for elaborating an international and unequivocal linguistic device that might allow the correct communication of knowledge. Their commonalities also match the more recent need to identify what might be defined as an *inter-lingua*, namely, a formalised scheme that can support computational strategies of (multi-) linguistic computational management. Here a stronger accent will be put on the line of continuity running backwards in time to allow an interpretation of Wüster's terminology work within a historical progression. This also includes, but does not start with, the traditional reading provided in the terminology literature that identifies 18th century scientific nomenclatures as direct antecedents of the birth and consolidation of terminology as a discipline.

A preliminary terminological clarification is needed, because in the present analysis the designations *specialised languages* and, more generally, *specialised communication* are used as inclusive terms for the various possible fields of specialisation. In fact, the development of the interpretative line focuses first on 17th century *new science* or *new philosophy*, closely connected with technology, which at that time was viewed as applied sciences; a further facet in this early context is represented by the languages of trade and commerce. The evolution towards the foundations of terminology moves the focus onto a partly different object, more directly related to the technical and commercial needs of modern communication. At the beginning of the 20th century, the languages of science or *scientific languages* — as they were designated at the time — were acknowledged a more stable status than in the previous period in the international academic panorama, and were identified as *specialised languages*.[1]

The trait that remains constant is the search for a regular linguistic code, namely a formalised system that can guarantee a proper degree of precision in communication, possibly also in international relations. Depending on the period and the aims, the code is sought through a regularisation of natural languages or the construction of artificial ones (Bausani 1974; Eco 1995; Vickery 2000).

2.   The emergence of new science and technology, and the language issue

The decisive thrust towards the search for an efficient and shared language emerges from the need for a linguistic code capable of breaking down the cognitive and communicative limits imposed by existing languages, mainly in specialised fields (sciences and techniques), and commercial contexts (Burke 2004). However, it is necessary to make a distinction between those that are generally indicated as *linguae francae* or *international languages* and those planned as *languages of knowledge*. The latter are also oriented towards clarity and communicative economy, but are mainly focused on the correctness and transparency of the content transmitted, at national and international levels (Eco 1995; Vickery 2000).

Linguistic invention can be associated with specialised communication, also in different epochs. So, the representation and transmission of specialised knowledge is correlated to the 17th century search for a philosophical perfected language as well as to international languages, either artificial or standardised planned in more recent times (cf. Section 3). The adjective "philosophical" is used in the prominent project presented by John Wilkins (Section 2.1), but given the time in history, the meaning must be interpreted as relating to the new knowledge

---

1. Therefore, in this study the designation *specialised languages* is used instead of *Languages for Special Purposes* (LSPs), recognised in the modern period as a well-established term. *Specialised languages* is considered more appropriate to the discussion of this concept in the historical contexts analysed here. Moreover, *specialised languages* is often correlated here with concepts such as *specialised communication, specialised knowledge, specialised content*.

produced by the new sciences. Therefore, "philosophical" is to be read as a synonym for "scientific."

As Slaughter highlights with a focus on Renaissance England, "for the most part the motivation of the language projectors was more scientific than linguistic; their concern was more with nature than with language" (Slaughter 1982: vii). Indeed, during the Renaissance period new sciences started to emerge, thanks to the so-called Scientific Revolution, which was driven by a new approach to understanding nature (Dear 2001; Henry 2008). Slaughter's statement can be extended and adapted to later periods characterised by the evolution of science and technology. The linguistic implication in Slaughter's text refers to what could be defined as the study of language — especially an artificial one — mainly for the sake of everyday communicative needs. In fact, the scientific dimension (which is behind many of the artificial language projects throughout history) is prominent in several of the works devoted to this subject, especially in the 17th and 18th centuries. More specifically, the focus on lexical definition, shared by many plans of this type, is interpreted there in light of a classificatory system oriented towards meaning or concept organisation or to both. New science and new philosophy in that period focused on the *knowledge of nature* (i.e. reality), be it *empirical* in the Baconian tradition, or *logic-rationalistic* in that of Descartes.

The communication problem is linked to the emerging recognition that vernacular languages were also valid for scientific communication; in this role they still coexisted with Latin during that period. The transmission of knowledge, mainly in written form, among specialists in different countries and among the academies developing all over Europe, at first often also required the translation (and/or reporting) of essays and private correspondence, and then later on of learned journals (Ornstein 1928; Vickery 2000: 72–81).[2] Hence, the problem of communication in science goes far beyond the international dimension, as it is first of all related to the coexistence of different languages within the individual countries. Over time, Latin began to lose its monopoly as the language of choice for scientific communication and vernaculars needed to be structured and regulated in order to fulfil the role that had recently been recognised for them. This is what, for example, the *Port-Royal Grammaire générale et raisonnée* (1660) set out to do.

But even far beyond linguistic restructuring, new codes are conceived so that they can be easily acquired and used to communicate with precision, especially in scientific matters. Beginning in the 17th century numerous projects unfolded in the panorama of constructed or invented languages. These designations can be

---

2. On the role of the printing press, and of journals and books Eisenstein (1979: 460) states: "Periodical publication is thus viewed as a further extension of the kind of scientific reporting that had previously been conducted by handwritten correspondence" (cf. Gibson 1982).

used to include international linguistic codes and artificial languages of knowl-edge.[3] The common aim of these varieties is to facilitate national and international communication, the basic difference being in the level of rigour and precision they may reach in order to represent and transmit the content that has to be com-municated. Therefore, a distinction clearly emerges between international auxil-iary languages and the languages of science.[4] The former are conceived to favour communication through systems that are as neutral as possible with respect to national languages, while the latter are meant to make scientific/technical com-munication precise, unequivocal, and consistent within the same community of specialists, whether national or international. Furthermore, attention to the reg-ularity and simplicity of linguistic structures, and the ease of acquisition of the expressive code prevail in international languages, whereas in specialised lan-guages the dimension of the conceptual content and its clear and unambiguous correlation with the expression are dominant aspects.

2.1   The philosophical language: A universal language of science

Here John Wilkin's *An Essay Towards a Real Character and a Philosophical Lan-guage* (1668) will be considered as a paramount model of its contemporary and later universal language projects. Fleming (2017) interprets it, and particularly the "real character" presented there, as a 17th century predecessor of the contempo-rary infosphere, and one of the "two scholarly halves" with respect to Gottfried Wilhelm Leibniz's *characteristica universalis* (Fleming 2017: 20). Hence, the writ-ten code proposed by Wilkins in the *Essay* is considered there a precursor for the organisation and management of computational (linguistic) information at a global level. In the present study, it is interpreted as a model for standardised international communication driven by advancements in science, and made pos-sible by the formalisation techniques available at that time. Indeed, the focus here is rather on the delineation of a conceptual framework as the basis of an improved system of communication.

If compared to other similar attempts, the *Essay* presents a complete linguistic analysis and planning that is not accomplished in other works. Eco defines it as "the most complete project for a universal and artificial philosophical language that the seventeenth century was ever to produce" (1995: 238). And indeed, it is

---

3. Secret codes are also a part of this tradition, but will not be considered for the purpose of this paper (cf. e.g. Ellison 2017).

4. By (international) *auxiliary language,* what is intended here is an artificially constructed code conceived to facilitate communication; auxiliary languages can be distinguished in *a priori* and *a posteriori* languages or mixed systems (cf. Laycock and Mühlhäusle 1990: 460–466).

the only one that provides a concrete description of a linguistic system, covering semantics, grammar, pronunciation, and graphic coding. But Wilkins' project focuses on the lexicon, which he actually intended as a system for defining concepts rather than lexemes. Indeed, he clearly distinguishes the reference *Alphabetical Dictionary of the English Language* from the defining *Tables of the Universal Philosophy* devoted to conceptual arrangement (Wilkins 1668). In the *Essay*, the *Alphabetical Dictionary* was composed by William Lloyd and because of the approach used, it may be parallelled to a technical terminology, were it not for its focus on the overall lexicon rather than on a delimited knowledge domain. For each single semantic sense identified, it is given a code composed of the abbreviations of the main classificatory levels of the Tables. In fact, it is also a fundamental key for accessing the specific conceptual definitions provided in the Tables via a hierarchically structured path of component concepts.

Wilkins describes the *Tables of the Universal Philosophy* as a "regular enumeration and description of all those things and notions to which names are to be assigned" (1668: 22). The collection is organised in a structured hierarchical scheme, inspired by the categorisation models available at that time, namely Aristotelian categories and the Baconian encyclopaedic knowledge paradigm. In Wilkins' Tables a series of formal devices graphically render the principles of concept dependence and their mutual relationships. The classificatory canons identified by Wilkins as the basics of knowledge organisation consist first of all in a hierarchical arrangement complemented by a thematic distribution of the items. The hierarchy, which is visually represented by a system of braces and indentation, gives an account of the relationships of inclusion (i.e. dependence) between the items. This device reproduces the classical categorial principles of *genus proximum* and *differentia specifica*, according to which the more general elements occupy a higher level in the structure, and transmit their properties to the *particulars* that are collocated on lower levels. Braces render graphically the differences that characterise the items included in the hierarchy. In Wilkins' schemes differences illustrate distinctions which do not always imply opposition, so they cannot be identified with logical disjunctions but rather indicate a generic lack of coincidence; indeed, they can even show a relationship of affinity. Since the *Essay* provides an all-encompassing image of knowledge, the overall hierarchy is subdivided into thematic sections which are devoted to specific subjects, identified by the more general elements of the classification (Wilkins 1668: 23).

The *Essay* outlines as a new *book of nature*, a revised *organon*. But, at the same time, it lays the foundations for the scientific classification emerging at the time. It should be remembered here that the *Essay* is a collaborative project, proposed and backed by the then-rising Royal Society of London for Improving Natural Knowledge. The sections devoted to matters more strictly scientific — i.e.

animals and plants — were compiled by two specialists, Francis Willoughby and John Ray respectively. Indeed, the scientific bearing of the *Essay* is clear and all-encompassing, as is its orientation towards standardisation. One example among others, is the elaboration of a standard system for weights and measures based on the decimal metric system (Wilkins 1668: 191–192). This model is widely considered by specialists to be the origin of the measurement system introduced in France in the 18th century, from which the present international standard sprang (e.g. Williams 2020: 79).

A more thorough discussion of this work is beyond the scope of the present analysis, but some further specifications are necessary. The *Essay* is conceived to include "all things and notions," and is open to further integrations of concepts and modifications of the relational structure to account for increased knowledge — especially of the "Natural bodies," i.e. animals, plants, and minerals. The relational definition system is devoted to the overall vocabulary, nevertheless the emphasis is certainly on a scientific system of definition, especially oriented towards natural sciences. In the *Epistle Dedicatory* to the Royal Society that commissioned the work, Wilkins hopes that the possible errors in the text will be corrected by a group of members of the Society, and specifies that both the classificatory scheme and the universal language are open to modification due to new scientific discoveries (Wilkins 1668: *Epistle Dedicatory*, passim, 69, 166–167).

The core idea is to create a formalisation obtained through a defining network of concepts and relations. This model is intended to overcome the obstacles of natural languages in national and international communication. Even though the basic assumption is that evidence shows languages to be problematic for scientific communication, Wilkins' approach is far from ignoring their intrinsic cultural implications. As will be the case with Wüster's approach to standardising terminology, the specific cultural, hence linguistic, instances are neither denied nor ignored. On the contrary, it might be synthesised that the plurality of linguistic varieties and their variations are at the basis of a need to identify a single regular communicative medium.

3.   From universalism to terminology

The delineation of scientific and technological disciplines had been accomplished by the end of the 19th century. This period marks the beginning of the planning of auxiliary languages as well as their adaptation to the modern sciences and to everyday communication with an international dimension (Chartier and Corsi 2000; Burke 2004; Garvía 2015: 7–17). The need for a shared specialised language is clearly outlined by Couturat and Leau (1903: vii-viii), in particular through mentioning the Association internationale des Académies (1899–1912). This association promoted collaboration among the scientific academies in Europe and gradually in the rest of the world. The need of these institutions for a regularised system for designating and communicating the terms of the various scientific disciplines is acute, as is clearly stated in a report on the establishment of this association (Darboux 1901). Couturat and Leau in their Préface (1903) explain the necessity for an international auxiliary language, which was also required and promoted by the Délégation pour l'adoption d'une langue auxiliaire internationale, founded in 1901 with support from the academies of the aforementioned association. They also report the *Statut* of this delegation (Couturat and Leau 1903: ixx-xx) and, as a premise, they discuss the example of Volapük. In this way they address the need for an international language, one that could remain fixed and stable notwithstanding its diffusion among communities of speakers. In fact, as they highlight, Volapük failed to accomplish the aim it was designed for, i.e. to be unitary and standardised without impositions of a superior organism, but for a free choice of the community of specialists and the ensuing general acceptance by the rest of the speakers. As Couturat et al. (1910: 9) synthesise:

> The fact is that science, philosophy, and technology are constantly waging a fierce battle with existing languages. What they want is a language as simple and clear as the fundamental laws of nature, as logical as the precision of experiment, and as many-sided as the complexity of the facts which it has to describe.

At a time when the effects of the industrial revolution were clearly visible, and the connections inside and then outside of Europe had started to improve, scientific exchange is no longer the sole driver of international communication. As a matter of fact, the emergence of Esperanto as an international auxiliary code is grounded in the need for specialised communication in different areas, from the sciences to industry, craft, and tourism:

> This action plan was understood and approved, because in two years the *Delegation* received more than 130 endorsements from International Congresses, or from Societies of scholars, traders, industrialists, tourists, workers, some of whom were international, and others based in France, Belgium, Switzerland, England, Germany, Sweden, Russia, Austria, Italy, Spain, Bulgaria, the United States, and the Argentine Republic.   (Couturat and Leau 1903: xxii-xxiii, our translation)

Specialised knowledge is certainly one of the common threads connecting the history of terminology to the tradition of language construction. Slaughter (1982) focused on universal languages and taxonomy, namely systems of knowledge organisation and representation (cf. Section 2). Almost at the same time, Hüllen (1984; 1989; 2009) was among the first linguists to explicitly highlight the continuity between universalism, specialised languages, and terminology. He does so through the image of the taxonomical system, which the author directly connects to the lexicographic model of the thesaurus. He then refines his interpretation by explicitly pointing to a continuity of universal language projects with terminology (Hüllen 1989: 241–245). Hüllen speaks of a "Wilkinsian thesaurus paradigm" identified as the framework that associates 17th century plans for a universal language with modern terminology. In the panorama of interlinguistics — as language planning (Tauli 1968: 167) — and Esperantology, the conceptual knowledge network is seen as a bridging element between Early-Modern universal language plans and the birth of a modern terminological discipline (e.g. Blanke 1985; Gobbo 2020).

3.1   Wüster, Esperanto and terminology

Wüster was an Esperantist before becoming an engineer, a company manager, and the founder of modern terminology. In most studies on terminology his commitment in the Esperantist movement is not mentioned; among the few exceptions are Cabré (1999: 165), Temmerman (2000: 21), Samain (2010; 2023), and Humbley (2022; 2023). Whereas, in the context of language planning studies, Budin (1994: 86–87), Tonkin (2015), and Trojar (2017) acknowledge this connection. The elaboration of Wüster's theory is more generally considered as the result of his commitment to his family business (which he was to continue to manage throughout his life) and his studies in electrical engineering (Kingscott 1998: 14; Lang 1998: 627; Cabré 1999: 167; Zanola 2018: 27). But, part of his early education also consists in learning a new language, an international and auxiliary language, Esperanto, which he approached in 1913 during his youth. Within a couple of years, he mastered the language, and would later translate and publish fables by Gotthold Ephraim Lessing into Esperanto (Blanke 1996: 315–316).

Blanke synthesises Wüster's literary translation work into Esperanto, showing a continuity in the following years, until 1922, and a clear shift into Esperantist specialised lexicology and lexicography as early as in 1923 (1996: 316). Wüster (1923) composed a terminology of mechanical engineering, as well as a bilingual, encyclopaedic Esperanto-German dictionary. The latter was published only in part during his lifetime (Wüster 1923–1929), and demonstrates his dual interest in lexicology and interlinguistics.[5] In 1924, Wüster introduced his thoughts on the possible application of Esperanto as a specialised international language, and further developed these ideas in the section of his doctoral thesis (1931) devoted to a description of the main auxiliary languages, and in particular of Esperanto. The

---

5. For further publications by Wüster on Esperanto and specialised language cf. Blanke (1996: 316) and for the posthumous publication of the notes by Wüster on the remaining part of the dictionary cf. Wüster (1994) and Blanke (1996: 321–322).

fact that this section covers almost one third of the overall text indicates the relevance of Esperanto in the development of Wüster's theory of terminology (cf. also Samain 2023).

Hence, in 1931 Wüster would begin to express his terminological ideas systematically. The role that conceptual and linguistic regularisation and standardisation played in the planning of international auxiliary languages — and of Esperanto in particular — is one of the aspects that were, and still remain, central in terminology research and applications (Cabré 1999:194–213; Humbley 2023). Essentially, Wüster was attempting to delineate a theory and a methodology which could circumvent the communication problems inherent in language use, within both national and international communities of specialists. As Cabré states, "[he] was a staunch advocate of a single language for scientific and technical communication" (2003:167). Nevertheless, he was also acutely aware of the difficulties that actual communication — both general and specialised — presents in attempting to adhere to rigid, superimposed rules aiming at complete univocity and standardisation. Mutual correct comprehension is guaranteed by the regularity and clarity of the concept defining system and the morphology rules provided in his theory. This is the same strategy adopted by Wilkins in his Tables of knowledge and in the lexical construction norms for his universal language.

In fact, it is true that the relational network of concepts that characterises terminology has antecedents in scientific classification, as mentioned in contemporary studies on terminology. But there are also at least two aspects that need to be considered. First of all, these studies were preceded by and partly modelled on the knowledge schemes produced in the previous tradition of conceptual and linguistic systematisation, including universal language projects. We can hint here at Carolus Linnaeus' familiarity with John Ray's scientific classifications, even though Linnaeus' primary focus is on the classifications produced after Ray's collaboration with Wilkins (Stevenson 1947:254). The origin of 18th century scientific nomenclatures based on classificatory systems is traced back to Wilkins' and the Royal Society's approach to new sciences by Rossi (1997:278–281) and Zingales (2010:71–72). Secondly, the lexical and morphological rules based on agglutination and developed to increase clarity and transparency can be seen as more closely related to the strategies of language planning, which are also focused on maximum transparency and correspondence between content and expression, rather than being inherently characteristic of scientific nomenclatures.

Wüster's posthumous work (1991) contains not only statements on terminological principles and terminographic guidelines that might be interpreted as *radical*, as Cabré (2003:166–167) highlights, but also more moderate views on what can be considered the problematic aspects of a normalised terminological system. Indeed, Wüster was aware of the features that hinder univocity and absolute precision, but also of the fact that these are constituent parts of every linguistic system used by all communities, including those of specialised languages (see also Chapter 8). The reference here is, for example, to synonymy,[6] the context-dependence of terms, and the validity of a descriptivist approach in lexicological as well as terminological studies and applications (Wüster 1991: 87; 90; 97).

These preoccupations relating to the nature of language and its influence in specialised communication can be traced back to Wüster's deep knowledge of linguistic (Humbley 2022: 17–19) and lexicographic issues, and of the dominant theories of the times (cf. Wüster 1931; 1974; 2003; 2004). In his opening address at the Infoterm Symposium, Wüster (1976) highlights the parallels between the theories of four European figures whose work was related to founding and promoting the principles of terminology, particularly as regards the model of a relational definition system. The experts mentioned are the German Alfred Schlomann (for the onomasiologically structured specialist dictionary model), the Genevan structuralist Ferdinand de Saussure (for his *system of concepts* model), the Russian engineer Ernst Drezen, identified as the promoter of international terminology standardisation in Russia, and the "polyglot English information scientist, J. Edwin Holmstrom" (Wüster 1976: 34) who promoted the formation of an international terminology office within UNESCO, from which Infoterm originated. Wüster's linguistic interests are demonstrated by the numerous references in his writings to contemporary and historical linguistic works, as Laurén and Picht (2001: 31) point out.

Wüster attributes an essential function to the clear-cut identification of concepts, their properties, and their relationships, which allows terminographers (as well as lexicographers) to develop a valid and efficient system of knowledge representation. He explicitly refers to "systematic [i.e. onomasiological] dictionaries":

> [...] the knowledge of the structure of meanings inevitably leads to the demand for systematic dictionaries. And this applies to the general language as well. Ferdinand de Saussure was indefatigable in pointing out that a concept can be delimited only by both saying what it is and what it is not. In no other way can this partial similarity of concepts be presented so clearly as by placing similar concepts side by side in a dictionary.
>
> (Wüster 2004: 297)

Most universal language projects focus on the lexicon and on morphology rather than on the complete restructuring of the grammar as a whole, at least during the centuries considered in this study. This can be explained by the language planners' desire to guarantee a regular delineation and transmission of the core items in human communicative interaction, namely data, information, and knowledge.

---

6. For a discussion of synonymy in Wüster's work and the use he makes of it see Candel (2004).

This urge for a correct conceptual communication favours the identification of systems that may help the precise representation of conceptual items and their relevant mutual relations. This strategy goes together with the proposal for a regular system of designations which can directly convey the content via the expression, either one that is natural and restructured, or one that is artificial.

Wüster is familiar both with natural and artificial formalisation systems, therefore terminology as a discipline shows that it is more than a part of a specialised national language, or of a scientific relational scheme expressed by internationally valid nomenclatures. Terminology blends the idea of defining schemes of interrelated concepts, which are regarded as being shared by humans, with the possibility of designating them universally within the different national languages. This possibility clears the way for a conceptual/semantic system which can also represent the basis of computational management of the semantics of natural languages. It is on this defining system that direct and unequivocal (specialised) communication relies.

3.2   Wüster, logic, and linguistics

Wüster (2003: 287) considers the identification of a clear-cut relational framework of concepts as the cornerstone of any language, both natural and artificial. In fact, following de Saussure's idea of *langue*, he believes that this framework constitutes a shared repository that guarantees mutual understanding among humans, whose mental knowledge is based on culturally and linguistically specific "subjective concepts," namely "concepts which exist in the heads of individual human beings — associated with designations or other signs" (2003: 286). These concepts "have a common core which constitutes the basis for mutual communication and comprehension; these are the 'objective concepts' of the shared language" (ibid).

So, since there is a common *matrix* of concepts which are shared by the speakers of a language, it is possible to identify these concepts univocally, and assign them a specific designation in the different languages in order to produce a precise communicative vocabulary (Wüster 2003: 270–276). This lexical inventory is a specialised one in Wüster's view (1931), whereas it is a general one in universal/international codes (such as Wilkins' *Essay* or Esperanto), and is computationally manageable in contemporary linguistic Artificial Intelligence applications.[7]

The conceptual framework delineated by Wüster is characterised by a structure which parallels that of taxonomy, and has remarkable antecedents in traditional logic. Hence, in Wüster's view, logic should not be disregarded by

---

7. For a discussion on ontology and knowledge graphs related to semantics in Natural Language Processing cf. among others Garg et al. (2022).

linguists, as it can provide significant methods of concept organisation and definition for other disciplines:

> Logic [...] has definitively established in what relation concepts can stand to each other and how, on the basis of these relations they can be so ordered that they form a conceptual field, a concept system.   (Wüster 2004:286)

More specifically, the conceptual relations that Wüster identifies as relevant for logic (and semantics) consist in hierarchical dependencies; to these, part-whole, and membership relations are added as relevant principles for systematisation (Wüster 2004:286–287). Hence both linguistics and terminology can borrow and adapt the relational conceptual model, which is based in logic, in order to improve their systems of content description and representation. He specifies that "[a]n analogous [to linguistics] division of labour with respect to logic is indicated for terminology" (288). Regarding the attempts made in linguistics in this area, Wüster quotes the 1952 study of Hallig and Wartburg (*Begriffssystem als Grundlage für die Lexikographie: Versuch eines Ordnungsschemas*) which aimed to delineate a relational system as a basis for a lexicographic product.

Wüster parallels the internal and external structures of concepts with those of linguistic meanings; he states that: "Every concept can be expressed as a combination of other concepts, especially as the combination of a superordinate concept with additional concepts of characteristics. In this way, every concept is simultaneously a constituent of a structure and itself a structure" (Wüster 2004:287). This strategy is analogous to that adopted by Wilkins in his *Essay* (cf. Section 2.1).

Wüster also highlights a correspondence between the principles of logic (and semantic) relations and de Saussure's idea of *valeur*: "De Saussure's *valeur* and the form of the meaning of a word in general is [...] the position of the word meaning within a system of concepts" (Wüster 2004:287; 1976). In this way he relates the concept organisation that is used in logic to the linguistic theories of meaning, and proposes a solution to the "personality splits of scholarship" which, in his view, exist between linguistics and logic (2004:294). For Wüster this break is epitomised by the figures and works of the de Saussure brothers. On the one hand, the linguist Ferdinand represents the interest of linguistics in the structure of *langue* with a relational system in which socially shared conceptual *valeurs* are established. On the other hand, the mathematician and Esperantist René embodies the position of "those who concern themselves with the logic of composite words, that is [...] terminologists and language planners" (294).

The principle of morpho-semantic composition in the formation of words is widely applied in artificial language plans, and has a basic role in terminology. This is because a precise identification (obtained through unambiguous definition) of units endowed with a specific morphological function and semantic value grants the transparency and univocity both of simple and complex lexical units which belong to any type of planned language. This approach is coincident with de Saussure's view of *relative motivation* of the linguistic sign. Wüster explains this point as follows:

> The explicit structure of a concept is provided — even though not fully — by those member concepts which are expressed by word elements (=morphemes) of the given sequence of words. For the complete identification of the explicit structure, the conceptual relations which remain unexpressed between the expressed conceptual elements are also required. The implicit structure of a concept is determined by its characteristics — they, too, are concepts — and by the place which the concept occupies in the world of concepts of the respective language.
>
> (2004:283)

Indeed, Wüster's Esperantist activity affected his commitment to regulating specialised language terminology. His early work on the compilation and publication of the Esperanto-German encyclopaedic dictionary was a landmark in his later research in terminology: "But before the author started to exploit the larger possibilities of action in the field of special languages, he spent four years of his life exclusively on systematically comparing and delimiting the meanings of the most frequent words of the most important Indo-European languages" (Wüster 2004:293). The reference is to his own work on Esperanto conceived in the 1920's, at the beginning of his research activities, as an international code for specialised communication (cf. Section 3.1).

4. Modern developments and tentative conclusions

In the history of thought and of (specialised) language studies, one of the fundamental elements is the focus on a rigorous architecture for defining core knowledge concepts, shared or possibly sharable, by all human beings. For this reason, the approach delineated here traces a line of continuity throughout distinct projects of conceptual and linguistic formalisation. In different epochs there is evidence of a constant search for a system where common, shared knowledge may be regularly managed to guarantee national and international communication, be it general, specialised, or both. This search is conducted with different "technologies" in the various periods, from Wilkins' Tables, to Wüster's relational concept definition, and to modern and contemporary developments of schemes that may identify and manage core concepts in computational applications.

Wilkins' model has been associated — together with Peter Mark Roget's *Thesaurus* (1852) — with the later computational frameworks which culminated in the Princeton *WordNet* lexical database, and led to developments in Information Technology and computational applications for Natural Language Processing. This association can be found in studies devoted to general or specialised lexicography. A correct interpretation of Wilkins' Tables would see how they anticipate onomasiological lexicography — as Roget (1852: xxviii–xxix) himself also recognises (Hanks, 2016: 108–109). But in some cases, the *Tables* are viewed in the context of (modern) scientific accuracy of definition or of efficiency for computational applications. The way in which this connection is made is sometimes even unfair. Occasionally, the mocking *El idioma analítico de John Wilkins* by Jorge Luis Borges (1952) is mentioned when discussing universal language projects, and Wilkins' in particular (cf. Fleming, 2017: 175; 253).[8] In other cases, the focus shifts away from what is recognised here as the main formalising attempt of this work, as happens in Fleming (2017), where Wilkins' text is related to computational applications primarily due to its artificial code, the Universal Characters. In that perspective, the pre-modern ontology of the Tables is defined as "a bit of a mess" (Fleming 2017: 181).

However, the formalising model of concept definition univocally associated to lexical items in the *Essay* and its *Dictionary* represents a very important facet of Wilkins' book in the panorama of specialised language studies. If Wilkins' artificial expressive code is left aside, the parallel between his theoretical statements on "universal" knowledge representation with Wüster's elaboration of terminology principles is even more direct. Indeed, Wüster himself set aside Esperanto as a valid international specialised language precisely when he decided to focus on the elaboration of a general theory of terminology. The systematic scheme of concept description and its international bearing which characterise terminology are at the basis of the relevance that this discipline has had for the field of Natural Language Processing via ontologies and knowledge graphs. The intention here is to illustrate the role of identifying a common system of core concepts as the magic key to make languages mutually comprehensible via assumed shared knowledge.

The frameworks of knowledge organisation outlined until the first half of the 20th century are analogous to the models developed in the decades that followed

---

8. The text by Borges is renowned for the following passage, clearly critical towards Wilkins' classification: "These ambiguities, redundancies, and deficiencies recall those attributed by Dr. Franz Kuhn to a certain Chinese encyclopedia called the *Heavenly Emporium of Benevolent Knowledge*. In its distant pages it is written that animals are divided into (a) those that belong to the emperor; (b) embalmed ones; (c) those that are trained; (d) suckling pigs; (e) mermaids; (f) fabulous ones; (g) stray dogs; (h) those that are included in this classification; (i) those that tremble as if they were mad; (j) innumerable ones; (k) those drawn with a very fine camel's-hair brush; (l) etcetera; (m) those that have just broken the flower vase; (n) those that at a distance resemble flies" (Borges 1999: 231).

for the computational management of information. In this later perspective, natural or artificial languages are not conceived as being managed by humans, but by machines. Nevertheless, the underlying model for managing conceptual knowledge remains the same (at least in part) in Artificial Intelligence research. What can be seen as a path from artificial language creation to computational language management at present seems to be based on the need to find a compromise between what would be the best conceptual model for natural language(s) management and what can actually be provided to machines so that they can manage natural languages and human knowledge, even though as yet not in a completely satisfactory, or perfect, way.

References

Bausani, Alessandro. 1974. *Le lingue inventate. Linguaggi artificiali, linguaggi segreti, linguaggi universali*. Roma: Ubaldini.

Blanke, Detlev. 1985. *Internationale Plansprachen*. Berlin: Akademie — Verlag.

Blanke, Detlev. 1996. "Zur Plansprache Esperanto und zur Esperantologie im Werk von Eugen Wüster." In *Sprachnormung und Sprachplanung. Festschrift für Otto Back zum 70. Geburtstag*, ed. by Heiner Eichner, Peter Ernst, and Sergios Katsikas, 311–329. Wien: Edition Praesens.

Borges, Jorge Luis. 1999 [1952]. *Otras Inquisiciones. El idioma analítico de John Wilkins*. In *Jorge Luis Borges. Selected Non-Fictions*, ed. by Eliot Weinberger, Esther Allen, and Suzanne Jill Levine, 229–232. London: Penguin.

Budin, Gerhard. 1994. "Language Planning and Terminology Planning. Theories and Practical Strategies." In *International Conference on Terminology Science and Terminology Planning. In Commemoration of E. Drezen (1892–1992) (Riga, 17–19 August 1992) and International IITF — Workshop Theoretical issues of terminology science. Riga, 19–21 August 1992*, ed. by Jennifer Draskau, and Heribert Picht, 85–93. Vienna: TermNet Series 4.

Burke, Peter. 2004. *Languages and Communities in Early Modern Europe*. Cambridge: Cambridge University Press.

Cabré, Maria Teresa. 1999. *Terminology. Theory, Methods and Application*. Amsterdam: John Benjamins.

Cabré, Maria Teresa. 2003. "Theories of Terminology. Their Description, Prescription and Explanation." *Terminology* 9 (2): 163–199.

Candel, Danielle. 2004. "Wüster par lui-même, Les fondements théoriques de la terminologie." In *Des fondements théoriques de la terminologie*, ed. by Colette Cortès, 15–31. Paris: Cahiers du CIEL.

Chartier, Roger, and Pietro Corsi (eds). 2000. *Sciences et langues en Europe. Une conférence organisée par le Centre Alexandre Koyré*. European Communities.

Couturat, Louis, and Léopold Leau. 1903. *Histoire de la langue universelle*. Paris: Hachette.

Couturat, Louis, Otto Jespersen, Richard Lorenz, Wilhelm Ostwald, and Leopold Pfaundler (eds). 1910. *International Language and Science. Considerations on the Introduction of an International Language into Science.* London: Constable & Co.

Darboux, Gaston. 1901. "Association internationale des Académies." *Journal des savants* 1: 5–23.

Dear, Peter. 2001. *Revolutionizing the Sciences: European Knowledge in Transition, 1500–1700.* Basingstoke, Hampshire: Palgrave.

Eco, Umberto. 1995. *The Search for the Perfect Language.* Oxford: Blackwell.

Eisenstein, Elizabeth L. 1979. *The Printing-press as an Agent of Change. Communications and Cultural Transformations in Early-modern Europe.* Vol. II. Cambridge: Cambridge University Press.

Ellison, Katherine. 2017. *A Cultural History of Early Modern English Cryptography Manuals.* London: Routledge.

Fleming, James D. 2017. *The Mirror of Information in Early Modern England. John Wilkins and the Universal Character.* London: Palgrave/Macmillan.

Garg, Muskan, Amit Kumar Gupta, and Rajesh Prasad (eds.). 2022 *Graph Learning and Network Science for Natural Language Processing.* CRC Press, 2022.

Garvía, Roberto. 2015. *Esperanto and its Rivals. The Struggle for an International Language.* Philadelphia: University of Pennsylvania Press.

Gibson, Sarah S. 1982. "Scientific Societies and Exchange: A Facet of the History of Scientific Communication." *The Journal of Library History (1974–1987)* 17 (2): 144–163.

Gobbo, Federico. 2020. *Introduction to Interlinguistics.* Munich: GRIN.

Hanks, Patrick. 2016. "Definition." In *The Oxford Handbook of Lexicography*, ed. by Philip Durkin, 94–122. Oxford: Oxford University Press.

Henry, John. 2008. *The Scientific Revolution and the Origins of Modern Science.* 3rd ed. Oxford: Palgrave/Macmillan.

Hüllen, Werner. 1984. "Bischof John Wilkins und die Fachsprachen unserer Zeit." *Fachsprache* 6 (3–4): 115–122.

Hüllen, Werner. 1989. *Their Manner of Discourse. Nachdenken über Sprache im Umkreis der Royal Society.* Tübingen: Narr.

Hüllen, Werner. 2009. *Networks and Knowledge in Roget's Thesaurus: From Ancient to Medieval.* Oxford: Oxford University Press.

Humbley, John. 2022. "The reception of Wüster's General Theory of Terminology." In *Theoretical Perspectives on Terminology. Explaining Terms, Concepts and Specialized Knowledge*, ed. by Pamela Faber, and Marie-Claude L'Homme, 15–35. Amsterdam: John Benjamins.

Humbley, John. 2023. "Wüster et l'aménagement linguistique." In *Eugen Wüster et la terminologie de l'école de Vienne*, ed. by Danielle Candel, Didier Samain, and Dan Savatovsky, 119–140. Paris: SHESL (HEL Livres, 2).

Kingscott, Geoffrey. 1998. "Tribute to the Founder of Terminology: 1998 Marks the Centenary of Eugen Wüster's Birth." *Language today* 11: 14–19.

Lang, Friedrich H. 1998. "Eugen Wüster — zum 100. Geburtstag. Ein Elektrotechniker als Terminologe." *Elektrotechnik und Informationstechnik* 115 (11): 625–628.

Laurén, Christer, and Heribert Picht. 2001. "Terminologie aus linguistischer Sicht." *Terminology Science & Research: Journal of the International Institute for Terminology Research* 12 (1–2): 30–40.

Laycock, Donald, and Peter Mühlhäusle. 1990. "Language Engineering: Special Languages." In *An Encyclopedia of Language*, ed. by Neville E. Collinge, 456–472. London: Routledge.

Ornstein, Martha. 1928. *The Role of Scientific Societies in the Seventeenth Century*. Chicago: Chicago University Press.

Roget, Peter M. 1852. *Thesaurus of English Words and Phrases, Classified and Arranged so as to Facilitate the Expression of Ideas and Assist in Literary Composition*. London: Longman, Brown, Green and Longmans.

Rossi, Paolo. 1997. *La nascita della scienza moderna in Europa*. Roma/Bari: Laterza.

Samain, Didier. 2010. "Eugen Wüster. De l'espéranto à la terminologie." In *Cultures et lexicographie*, ed. by Michaela Heinz, 279–296. Berlin: Frank & Timme.

Samain, Didier. 2023. "Wüster et la question de l'espéranto: un regard d'ingénieur." In *Eugen Wüster et la terminologie de l'école de Vienne*, ed. by Danielle Candel, Didier Samain, and Dan Savatovsky, 173–214. Paris: SHESL.

Slaughter, Mary. 1982. *Universal Languages and Scientific Taxonomy in the Seventeenth Century*. Cambridge: Cambridge University Press.

Stevenson, Ian. 1947. "John Ray and his Contributions to Plant and Animal Classification." *Journal of the History of Medicine and Allied Sciences* 2 (2): 250–261.

Tauli, Valter. 1968. *Introduction to a Theory of Language Planning*. Uppsala: Almqvist/Wiksell.

Temmerman, Rita. 2000. *Towards new Ways of Terminology Description. The Sociocognitive Approach*. Amsterdam: John Benjamins.

Tonkin, Humphrey. 2015. "Language Planning and Planned Languages: How can Planned Languages Inform Language Planning?" *Interdisciplinary Description of Complex Systems* 13 (2): 193–199.

Trojar, Mitja. 2017. "Wüster's View of Terminology." *Slovenski jezik — Slovene Linguistic studies* 11: 55–85.

Vickery, Brian. 2000. *Scientific Communication in History*. Lanham, Md.: Scarecrow Press.

Wilkins, John. 1668. *An Essay Towards a Real Character and a Philosophical Language*. London: Gellibrand and Martin Printer to the Royal Society.

Williams, Jeffrey. 2020. *The Search for the Absolute. How Magic Became Science*. San Rafael: Morgan & Claypool.

Wüster, Eugen. 1923. *Maŝinfaka Esperanto-Vortaro prielementa. (La maŝinelementoj; maŝinoj; plej gravaj esprimoj el la konstrukciado kaj teknologio) Deutsche Ausgabe. (Esperanto-Deutsch und Deutsch-Esperanto mit Zahlenverweisen)*. Leipzig: Hirt & Sohn.

Wüster, Eugen. 1923–1929. *Enzyklopädisches Wörterbuch Esperanto — Deutsch — Enciklopedia vortaro esperanta — germana*, bd. 1–4: A — korno. Leipzig: Hirt.

Wüster, Eugen. 1924. *Esperanto und der Techniker. Die Bedeutung der Welthilfssprache Esperanto für den Techniker, ihr Wesen und ihre Ausbreitung seit dem Weltkriege*. Berlin/Dresden: Esperanto-Verlag Ellersiek & Borel, 2. Aufl.

Wüster, Eugen. 1931. *Internationale Sprachnormung in der Technik. Besonders in der Elektrotechnik (Die nationale Sprachnormung und ihre Verallgemeinerung)*. Berlin: VDI.

Wüster, Eugen. 2003 [1959/1960]. "The Wording of the World Presented Graphically and Terminologically." *Terminology* 9 (2): 269–297.

Wüster, Eugen. 2004 [1959]. "The Structure of the Linguistic World of Concepts and its Representation in Dictionaries." *Terminology* 10 (2): 281–306.

Wüster, Eugen. 1974. "Die allgemeine Terminologielehre. Ein Grenzgebiet zwischen Sprachwissenschaft, Logik, Ontologie, Informatik und den Sachwissenschaften." *Linguistics* 119 (1): 61–106.

Wüster, Eugen. 1976. "International Activity in Terminology: 75 Years of Research — Foundations and Challenge for the Rest of the Century." In *International Co-operation in Terminology. Proceedings of the First Infoterm Symposium*, 32–36. München: Verlag Dokumentation.

Wüster, Eugen. 1991. *Einführung in die allgemeine Terminologielehre und terminologische Lexikographie*. 3. ed. Bonn: Romanistischer Verlag.

Wüster, Eugen. 1994. *Enciklopedia Vortaro Esperanto — Germana. Korno — Z (Enzyklopädisches Wörterbuch Esperanto — Deutsch. Korno — Z. Manuskript. Mit einer Einführung von Detlev Blanke. Darin enthalten: Hans-J. Plehn: Enciklopedia Vortaro Esperanto — Germana. Korno — L. Bearbeitung des Manuskripts von Eugen Wüster*. Microfilm. Wien: Österreichische Nationalbibliothek/IEMW.

Zanola, Maria Teresa. 2018. *Che cos'è la terminologia*. Roma: Carocci.

Zingales, Roberto. 2010. "Nascita ed evoluzione del linguaggio chimico." *Quaderni di Ricerca in Didattica (Science)* 1: 61–84.

CHAPTER 8

Wüster's ideas on language, linguistics and terminology

Mitja Trojar
Research Centre of the Slovenian Academy of Sciences and Arts

The chapter analyses some of Wüster's fundamental texts in order to faithfully document his ideas about language and terminology, language and technical languages, the relation between general language and technical languages and his understanding of concepts. By analysing and commenting on quotations from Wüster's major works, it explores certain social, historical and other factors that determined Wüster's thinking about languages and focuses on how Wüster used metaphors to construct his theory of terminology. The chapter also investigates the cornerstone notion of Wüster's theory: the *concept*.

Keywords: Eugen Wüster, General Theory of Terminology, Vienna School of Terminology, Esperanto, technical languages

1. Introduction

Eugen Wüster is an influential figure in the field of terminology, notably credited with being the founder of the General Theory of Terminology. Initially, the field of terminology was largely dominated by his approach and by other schools of terminology strongly influenced by Wüster's theory (cf. Laurén and Picht 1993). The 1980s, the 1990s and especially the early 2000s brought a critical reappraisal of the ideas attributed to Wüster, the Vienna School of Terminology and/or any other traditional approach to terminology. To name just a few of the better known: Slodzian 1993, Rastier 1995, Pearson 1998, Cabré 1999, Temmerman 2000, Gaudin 2003, L'Homme 2004, and later by Faber and López Rodríguez 2012. These criticisms levelled against Wüster, his General Theory of Terminology or any other traditional theory of terminology, can be said to be part of the so-called "competition game" in the market of linguistic ideas. The previously dominant approach is particularly exposed to criticism. But the past two decades have also seen a rekindled interest in the work of Eugen Wüster: the reception

https://doi.org/10.1075/tlrp.24.08tro

of his work and the scrutiny of his ideas from the perspective of the history of linguistics and of terminology. These new writings emphasise the need to re-evaluate Wüster's ideas within the social, historical and economic circumstances in which they were conceived. For example, Campo's (2012) survey showed the reception of Wüster's work in English, French and Spanish academic articles was largely positive, Humbley (2004, 2022a) reviews the reception of Wüster's work in the French-speaking areas and within emerging approaches to terminology and attitudes towards specific issues relevant to the field of terminology (e.g. the primacy of the concept). A recently published volume containing proceedings of a symposium on Wüster held in 2006 (see Candel, Samain and Savatovsky 2022) is particularly enlightening as to the philosophical, cultural, linguistic and historical contexts in which Wüster's ideas were framed. Candel's research (2004, 2007, 2017, 2022) is revealing as she engages in careful reading of Wüster's texts to observe his reformulation strategies showing the evolution of his ideas on terminology.

In order to fully comprehend Eugen Wüster's ideas about language and terminology, it is indispensable to put them in their historical context and consider basic landmarks of Wüster's personal and professional life: rarely are biographies so revealing about the scientist's motivations and ideas as in Wüster's case. For this reason, the first section of the chapter presents basic biographical information on Eugen Wüster. The second section focuses on how Wüster's idea of economy (efficiency) translated into his theory of terminology. The third section examines a key issue: Wüster's notion of *concept*.

2.   Wüster's life and work

Eugen Wüster was born in Wieselburg (Lower Austria) on October 3, 1898.[1] His father, Eugen Bernhard Wüster, and his uncle managed a tool-manufacturing company Wüster & Co., founded in 1889 in Wieselburg. Wüster studied electrical engineering at the Charlottenburg Technical University in Berlin and completed his undergraduate degree in 1927. In 1928 he joined his father's company as a partner and later became its sole owner. In 1931 he was awarded a PhD degree for his thesis *Internationale Sprachnormung in der Technik besonders in der*

---

1. Our account of Eugen Wüster's life and work is based on Wüster ([1941] 2001, [1952] 2001, 1968, 1970, 1974), Felber (1973), Felber and Krommer-Benz (1979), Felber and Lang (1979), Lang, Lang and Reiter (1979), Felber (1980, 1998a, 1998b), Lang (1998a, 1998b, 1998c), Infoterm (2004), Blanke (2008) and Budin (2022).

Elektrotechnik (*International Standardisation of Language in the Field of Engineering, Especially Electrical Engineering*) from Stuttgart Technical University. His thesis was published as a monograph in 1931 and was translated into Russian in 1935 (see also Chapter 10).[2] The Russian translation was the decisive impulse that gave rise to the proposal made by the Soviet Union to establish Technical Committee (TC) ISA 37 "Terminology" with the International Federation of the National Standardizing Associations (ISA). After the war (in 1947) ISA was relaunched as the International Organization for Standardization (ISO); its Terminology TC being dissolved in 1949 due to inactivity. Wüster's endeavours to reestablish this committee bore fruit in 1951 when ISO/TC 37 was set up. He held the position of Secretariat until 1971 on behalf of the Austrian Standards Institute. Much of the work for this committee was carried out in Wieselburg by Wüster and his colleagues; Wüster not only devoted much of his time to terminological activities, he also provided his own funds for them.[3] In 1971 Wüster's terminology centre in Wieselburg evolved into the International Information Centre for Terminology (Infoterm), which was founded by UNESCO through a contract with the Austrian Standards Institute. Wüster was also a university teacher: in 1955 he started lecturing on woodworking machines and tools at the Agricultural University in Vienna (Wüster 1952), from 1972 to 1974 he lectured on his General Theory of Terminology at the University of Vienna. Eugen Wüster passed away on 29 March 1977.

In addition to the activities described above, Wüster collaborated with the International Electrotechnical Commission on the International Electrotechnical Vocabulary before and after WWII. Wüster also produced a bibliography of monolingual terminological resources (1955/1959, Wüster et al. 1979) and compiled a dictionary of terms used in the field of machine tools (1967, 1968). Wüster was an Esperanto enthusiast (see Chapter 7 in this volume) and a proponent of planned languages in general (he was fluent in both Esperanto and Interlingua). Between 1923 and 1929 he published an encyclopaedic Esperanto-German dictionary (1923a) and an Esperanto-German dictionary of machine elements (1923b). Between 1958 and 1971 Wüster was the president of the Austrian Society for Documentation and Information. He authored over 500 publications (cf. Lang, Lang and Reiter 1979, Felber 1998a). One of his best-known works, *Einführung in*

---

2. The 2nd edition of the monograph was published in 1966 and the 3rd edition in 1970. An abridged version of the monograph was published in 1934, which was translated into Esperanto in 1936.

3. Wüster's business was essential to conducting terminological activities as it served as a source of funds and thus kept terminological activities running.

die allgemeine Terminologielehre und terminologische Lexikographie, was posthumously published in 1979 (1st ed.).[4]

The diversity and span of the fields Wüster actively engaged in is impressive. To call Wüster "the founder of modern terminology," as he is typically dubbed, is not wrong, but the epithet does not do him justice: his thinking did indeed centre on terminology, but reached far beyond. In addition to being a theoretical terminologist and a practical terminographer, he was also an Esperantist, advocate of planned languages, translator, lexicographer, (electrical) engineer, language planner, linguist, semiotician, information science expert, documentalist, standardisation expert, industrialist, editor, and university professor. His vast practical experience and thorough knowledge of a multitude of fields allowed Wüster to develop his theory of terminology, which bears the mark of his entrepreneurial concern for economy and probably also of his personality traits.

Wüster, as described by his colleagues, was disciplined, hard-working, sparing with words (to the extent that he was often perceived as haughty and aloof), meticulous (as he paid the utmost attention to details, which is why he was considered by some as intolerant) and utterly thorough. Felber and Lang further describe another trait of Wüster's personality:

> In his work Wüster always had economy on his mind. However, economy was often only reached if the participants in the communication process were willing to learn the basics. Without such a learning process the discussions did not seem productive to him and therefore uneconomical.   (Felber and Lang 1979: 18)[5]

The pursuit of this economy (*Wirtschaftlichkeit*) was however not solely a feature of Wüster's personality and a guiding principle of his actions. (Linguistic) economy was also one of the principles that he incorporated in his theory of terminology, (linguistic) economy thus paralleling (cost-)effectiveness of the material means of communication. In a paper dealing with telecommunications, Wüster argues:

> A telecommunications engineer should apply the same standards of precision and economy to his wording and terminology as he uses in constructing his material means of communication. In other words: communications engineering should be completed with language engineering.   ([1948] 2001: 1)

---

4. See Wüster (1985). The 3rd edition was published in 1991. The manuscript was being prepared by Wüster in 1972–1974, but remained unfinished. Helmut Felber revised the manuscript, completed it and prepared it for publication.

5. All the quotations in this chapter have been translated by the author unless indicated otherwise.

The following section examines, among other things, how Wüster applied precision and economy to different levels of language structure. The section offers commentaries on quotations from Wüster's works (especially from his thesis (1931)) in order to elucidate his views on language and terminology.[6]

3.   Wüster's linguistic pragmatism

Wüster's concern for economy, efficiency, *Wirtschaftlichkeit*, in language regularly resurfaces in his writing. One such instance is the critique of natural language and the problem of selecting the best language for international communication. In order to understand his stance on the matter of planned languages it is worthwhile to look into a metaphor[7] (comparison) he introduces to contrast planned languages with natural languages. In the introduction to one of his early works, *Enciklopedia Vortaro Esperanta-Germana* (1923), natural language is equated with a catalogue.

> Language is a catalogue of the world. It is a notebook of a nation, in which generation after generation inscribe their memories of the world. It grows together with the range of the nation's experience, the notebook becomes a card index of memories of the world: a card index, which was created from individual records and has changed owners countless times; the drafting of notes, the format, the material, the ordering of index cards — all this with no firm guiding principles. Some things are eliminated as they are no longer of any use, some things are provisionally patched up. However, a thorough rearrangement on the basis of the state of experience is impossible. You only have one card file and you cannot let it slip out of your hands. This is natural language. It bears the stamp of chance, which has dominated its development.
>
> Then came Ludwig Zamenhof. He took what was essential and useful in the languages of the European-American cultural sphere and what they had in common and created a new language out of it. This was Esperanto with its 16 rules without exception and its few hundred basic words.   (1923a:[6])

Natural language is compared to a disorderly card file index whose development is most significantly influenced by chance, rather than by any coherent set of

---

6. This method has been used to analyse Wüster's texts, e.g. Candel 2004, Trojar 2017, Humbley 2022b.

7. In his writings Wüster used a number of metaphors to construct a certain conception of language. These metaphors helped him not only to present the complex and abstract notion of language in more concrete and simplified terms, but also to highlight a certain aspect of it, as well as to express his ideological position on (natural or technical) language; it is for this reason his metaphors are so interesting and revealing.

principles. By contrast, Esperanto, a planned language, is the result of a deliberate human effort, which does not suffer from the same deficiencies as natural languages since it is highly regular. Wüster, himself a keen Esperantist, thus presents a rather harsh critique of natural languages:[8] as being highly irregular, harder to learn and thus less economical.

Wüster's attitude towards Esperanto and other planned languages as opposed to natural (national) languages was fundamentally shaped by his personal experience with learning foreign languages. He (1931: 391–392) recounts how he bought an Esperanto textbook at the age of 15 and absorbed it within a week. Only a few days later he participated in an Esperantist convention in Wrocław: he was stupefied as he could understand almost everything that was being said in Esperanto, all the more so because he had studied French and Italian for considerably longer, but was not able to understand much more than a few words. Wüster was quick to underscore one of the Esperanto's advantages:

> The fact that you can learn to speak Esperanto without a teacher is linked to the fact that *in use* Esperanto is also very convenient: if an expression for any concept is not available, you can in most cases easily create one.
>
> (1931: 392, emphasis in original)

Wüster's personal experience with Esperanto being easy to learn had a profound impact on his conception of language planning.[9] If language A is easier to learn than language B, then one needs to invest less time in order to learn language A; language A is therefore more economical than language B. This is precisely the kind of reasoning Wüster used in assessing the adequacy of various planned and natural languages to become the sole language of international communication. After examining a number of languages — Latin, English, Esperanto, Volapük, Ido, Occidental, Latino sine flexione — Wüster's selection process boils down to the choice between Esperanto and English.

---

8. This critique of language, however, cannot be directly linked to the views held by the Vienna Circle (*Wiener Kreis*). As Savatovsky (2022a, 2022b) points out, Wüster was not a member of the Vienna Circle and the inclination to logical positivism is most visible in his later articles, especially those from the 1960s. Nonetheless, Savatovsky (2022b: 154) recognises three aspects logical positivism and terminology have in common: language reform and the parsimony principle, the question of nominalism and the problem of the real definition.

9. See Humbley (2022b) for a discussion of Wüster's views on language planning. Note that Chapter 8 of the *Internationale Sprachnormung in der Technik* is dedicated to the choice of the *international language* (*internationale Sprache*), which Wüster also calls *world language* (*Weltsprache*) or *auxiliary language* (*Hilfssprache*; auxiliary language not necessarily being a planned language), i.e. a language used for communication among nations speaking different (national) languages. Selecting a language best suited for international communication can be and should be considered a language-planning activity.

Wüster (1931: 404) presents a scenario in which Esperanto is the international auxiliary language and English is only intended to be read by non-native English speakers: such a scenario would save around 50 percent of effort for schoolchildren. The adoption of Esperanto would therefore be remarkably more economical in terms of the work invested in learning the world auxiliary language than choosing any other natural language.[10] Esperanto presents itself — or rather, is presented by Wüster — as the most economical language for international communication.[11]

It is now easier to see how and why Wüster's personal experience with Esperanto and his interest in planned languages shaped his views of languages, both planned and technical. The true appeal of Esperanto for Wüster was its economy. However, economy was not just some random quality that his personality happened to possess and prize so highly. Economy is one of the two defining features of an engineer. The opening paragraph of Wüster's thesis explains what engineering is and what sets an engineer apart from a theoretical chemist and physicist:

> Engineering is the economical application of the laws of nature. On the basis of his knowledge of nature the engineer creates material devices that are intended to satisfy a human need as fully as possible and yet as cheaply as possible. The *application*, the creative drive on the one hand, and the parsimony of means, the *economy* on the other, distinguish the activity of an engineer from that of a physicist and theoretical chemist.   (1931: 1, emphasis in original)

Wüster, an engineer by training and an active industrialist, considered his own profession as inextricably tied to the economy of means, *Wirtschaftlichkeit*; being economical, frugal with means is part and parcel of being an engineer. In the above quotation, he thus first links the idea of economy to engineering. In the paragraphs that follow, he explains the significance of technical language for an engineer and

---

10. Economy is not the only factor in Wüster's consideration of the suitability of the selected auxiliary language, the selection must also be *fair*. He (1931: 411) expresses his fears rather bluntly: "Esperanto is not only called for because of economy, but just as much because of fairness. Should English be selected as the world auxiliary language, the other nations will be culturally degraded to the status of an English colony."

11. Esperanto's vocabulary being largely derived from (Indo-)European languages, Wüster did acknowledge the fact that Esperanto is harder to learn for speakers whose mother tongues are other than (Indo-)European languages. For example, Wüster (1931: 391) cites a report adopted by the League of Nations in 1922, which states that European and American children learn Esperanto in a year, whereas East-Asian children learn it in two years (both groups learning it at a rate of two class periods per week). However, the report also states that learning Esperanto is still significantly easier for East-Asian children than learning European languages, which require six years of learning (with 4 to 5 class periods of language training per week). Wüster concludes that Esperanto is 7 times easier for a Japanese child to learn than European languages.

links technical language to economy: He makes it clear that technical language (*Zwecksprache*[12]) is one of the non-material, social tools engineers need to perform their work and emphasises the need for this tool to be economical.[13]

> Engineering work requires various auxiliary tools. Not all of them are material. Before the engineer's creation is made visible and tangible, it exists only in the imagination of its mental creator and initially only in its basic form. Individual parts of the plan must be gradually developed, the matured plan must be made known to intellectual coworkers and later on to fellow manual workers. Even if the creation is eventually ready for use, various ideas must be exchanged about it, ideas that only an engineer is capable of thinking.
>
> The development of the plan by its creator and communication between everyone involved in the creation and the use of the work require a tool that captures and conveys thoughts (concepts). There are several such non-material tools; they are subsumed under the names "sketch," "sign" and "language." These are the *main social tools* (Hellmich [...]) of an engineer; like all his tools, he must consider them "from the perspective of economy" [...].
>
> (1931: 1, emphasis in original)

Wüster introduces economy as a criterion to assess language. This is what makes the above passage so revealing: not only does it show how he conceived of technical language (as a tool), it also demonstrates the power of metaphors in theory building: the tool metaphor is far from being a mere stylistic embellishment in his writing; he uses it to introduce his concern for economy into his theory of technical language making the need for linguistic economy some sort of a "natural" consequence of the metaphor. His reasoning can be reformulated as a syllogism: two premises ((1) technical language is a tool, (2) tools must be assessed with regard to economy) and a conclusion to be drawn from them (therefore technical language, too, must be assessed with regard to economy). This syllogism may in turn be interpreted in its stronger version: technical language is a tool, tools must be *made* economical, therefore technical language must also be made economical — a

---

12. Following the distinction made by philosopher Anton Marty (1847–1914), Wüster opposes *Zwecksprache* (the engineer's technical language which is merely a means for communicating truths and facts) to *Edelsprache* (higher literary language that conveys pleasant notions). Wüster attributes these terms to Theodor Steche and limits his discussion to *Zwecksprache*, see Wüster 1931: 1, cf. Collinson 1931: 229 (Collinson translates *Edelsprache* as 'higher literary language' and *Zwecksprache* as 'technical language'). Note that Wüster also uses the term *Fachsprache* ('special language', 'technical language', 'language for specific/special purposes'). The term *technical language* is used throughout this chapter to refer to the language described in Wüster's theory.

13. Wüster's (self-)image as an engineer can thus be considered as one of the major sources of his pragmatic, functional views of technical language.

reading which also opens the way to prescriptive (standardisation) activities. The *technical-language-is-a-tool* metaphor is a pure ideological choice; it is a means he uses to justify making (linguistic) economy the cornerstone of his theory; considering technical language as a tool is by no means a logical necessity. Wüster was perfectly aware of the power of metaphors as he was choosing his metaphors carefully and deliberately. In his discussion of objections raised against planned languages (one of the objections being "Language is an organism that cannot be created artificially," 1931: 350) he dismisses the *language-is-a-living-organism* metaphor since he had earlier subscribed to another metaphor. Wüster argues:

> The view that language is an *"organism,"* which lives its own life like living creatures, was abandoned by modern linguistics long ago; nonetheless this view can still be encountered in debates over the question of planned languages, especially in non-specialist ones.   (1931: 351, emphasis in original)

Wüster felt compelled to reject the *language-is-an-organism* metaphor: if language were an organism with its own independent life, it might prove difficult or impossible to be interfered with. This would run counter to the core idea of his theory that (technical) language should be (re)designed in order to be rendered as economical as possible.

In order to be able to assess the quality of technical language at different levels of language structure, Wüster introduces yet another metaphor, this time comparing language to a vehicle (see the next quotation). Note that the *technical-language-is-a-vehicle* metaphor should not be seen as contrary to the *technical-language-is-a-tool* metaphor, rather, it can be considered as its expansion and/or elaboration (i.e. vehicle is a type of tool).

> Technical language is a vehicle [...]. A certain input of physical and mental energy ensures the transmission of a certain quantity of ideas from human to human. Linguistic signs are comparable to vehicles that carry the load of ideas. The *evaluation criterion* [...] for technical language is hence the relation between performance and energy consumption. Among several means of transport that carry the same load, provided their purchase price is the same, the best is the one that exhibits the lowest energy consumption and the lowest loss of load. In language low energy consumption is called *convenience* and low "loss of load" is called *precision*; a means of communication is all the more precise, the more the ideas actually evoked in the partner are in line with the intended set of ideas.
>   (1931: 85, emphasis in original)

Wüster further specifies that linguistic convenience and precision are requirements that are often contrary to one another. In the case of language the purchase price for an individual is the energy spent in order to learn a language, whereas the other requirement is the ease of using the language. He also discusses how convenience and precision manifest themselves at different levels of language structure (see Table 1).

Table 1. Quality features of language (Wüster 1931: 86, adapted)

Quality Features of Language		
Quality feature → Language factor ↓	Convenience	Precision
written form	concision, ease	discriminability
relation between written form and sound form	one-to-one relation	
sound form	concision, ease	discriminability
conceptual form	concision	
relation between linguistic form and meaning	one-to-one relation	
	few word elements	each concept named
	intelligible conceptual form	
meaning	sharpness, fitness for purpose	

For example, a concise written form is more convenient than a long one as it requires less time and effort to be read and written. However, a written form should not be so concise as to endanger discriminability.[14] As far as the relation between written form and sound form is concerned, the ideal relation is a one-to-one correspondence between sound form and meaning, which means that as few expressions as possible should be ambiguous or have synonyms. Wüster argues that homonyms are detrimental as they impair precision — the interlocutor does not always know which of the co-occurring meanings is actually intended. Nonetheless, he admits that homonyms cannot always be avoided. Later in the thesis, he softens his position with regard to unambiquity by introducing the notion of *relative unambiguity*. He explains this concept using the following example.

> If the thunder rolls [*rollt*] or a laundrywoman mangles [*rollt*], one knows unambiguously what is meant. However, if one hears of a *rollendes Flugzeug*, one should be in doubt as to whether it is still running on the taxiway [...] (part of the airfield) or it is already flying and inclining around the longitudinal axis [...]. It is only if the location (ground or air) of the airplane is evident from the context that the German expression *rollen* is unambiguous when applied to an airplane.
>
> Adapted from (Wüster 1931: 95–96)

---

14. Discriminability is the quality of a given written/sound form to be easily distinguished from other written/sound forms.

Relative unambiguity refers to unambiguity that is created by the context, i.e. the context disambiguates the senses of an expression (term). What is particularly interesting in the previous quotation is that Wüster identifies and describes two types of contexts:[15] the first example "*der Donner oder eine Waschfrau rollen*" illustrates what nowadays would be called co-text, verbal context, comprising the part of the text co-occurring with the word in question (specifically two possible subjects of the verb *rollen*), whereas the second example (*rollendes Flugzeug*) makes reference to the situational context and the speaker's/hearer's knowledge of the situation (specifically the location of the airplane). He not only acknowledged context, but also attached significant importance to the capacity of context to disambiguate senses. There is another passage in *Internationale Sprachnormung in der Technik* in which Wüster (1931: 49) comments on the ambiguity of determinative compounds; the number of interpretations of compounds, such as the German compound term *Kupferverlust* 'copper loss,' is theoretically infinite: *Kupferverlust* in principle denotes a loss that bears any relation to copper (e.g. loss of copper, loss caused by copper). Wüster goes on to assert:

> The number of *meaningful* options is however finite. "Verlust unter Kupfer" ['loss under copper'], for example, does not seem to belong among them. The *context* — sentence context or other circumstances — eliminates more of the options that make sense without context [...]. Only rarely is more than one single meaningful option left [...]. However, the expert alone is capable of identifying meaningful options and making the inference from the context; the term is somewhat deficient (in a given case) if such an inference is necessary.
>
> (1931: 50, emphasis in original)

Wüster again emphasises the power of context (of both identified types of contexts) to disambiguate ambiguous terms. Nevertheless, the power of context is not unrestrained: only a field expert with sufficient specialised knowledge may be able to make use of the context(s). However, ambiguity is not always eliminated. For example, if there is not enough context, it may be harder (if not impossible) to disambiguate terms. He describes the following situation:

> However, there are also cases in which context is not sufficient for *disambiguation*. For example, on a list of goods in a trade fair catalogue it is not readily apparent whether German *Federn* is intended to mean "elastische Federn" (springs), "Vogelfedern" (for pillows or hats), "Schreibfedern" [pens] or "Federkeile" [keys without taper]. One can then help oneself, as has been done above, by adding some closer determination which stands in for the otherwise present sentence context.   (Adapted from Wüster 1931: 107, emphasis in original)

---

15. Cf. Hartmann and James (2002: 29, entry *context*).

Context is thus not always accessible or sufficiently clear to render the term unambiguous; for this reason, Wüster offers a strategy of adding short semantic descriptions of terms that help the reader select the intended reading (sense).

Synonyms, too, affect the convenience of technical language: they unnecessarily burden the memory (especially in learning a foreign language) and cause confusion (particularly with beginners in a certain field of study who expect different designations to refer to different, rather than the same, concepts). Again, Wüster admits that synonymous compounds with a different semantic structure (*Begriffsform*) are frequently inevitable, i.e. when they convey different views of the same concept, such as the German words (terms) *Kochsalz* ('common salt') and *Natriumchlorid* ('sodium chloride') (1931:96). His words testify again to his realistic views of synonymy and polysemy in terminology:

> Also in terminology the desire for complete one-to-one correspondence between the term and concept must remain a pious hope. This follows from the fact alone that the *number of concepts* in a given field is roughly a *thousand* times greater than the *number of word roots*. This imbalance may be partly reduced by combining word elements and creating figurative meanings, but can by no means be eliminated. Additionally, figurative meanings are already a form of ambiguity.
>
> (1991:87, emphasis in original)

Wüster's consideration of linguistic convenience and precision permeates his entire writing. He inspects all levels of language structure (phonetic form, word-formation, semantic structure), always assessing structures from the perspective of convenience and precision. However, he had a very realistic view of language and language use; for example, his acknowledgement of the power of context to disambiguate terms certainly makes him a linguist well ahead of his time.

The following section discusses Wüster's most significant contribution to the field of terminology: his theory of concepts.

4.   Wüster's ideas on concepts

The concept of *concept* (*Begriff*) is a pivotal notion in Wüster's theory of terminology.[16] This concept allows Wüster to focus on the semantic structure of terms and their mutual relations; it also enables him to observe semantic phenomena

---

16. Wüster's notion of *concept* has been much discussed (and criticised) within the field of terminology, see, for example Candel (2004, 2022), Humbley (2004, 2022a), Oeser (2022), Budin (2022). Most notable criticisms against Wüster's theory of concepts include Slodzian (1993), Rastier (1995), Zawada and Swanepoel (1994), Temmerman (2000), Gaudin (2003).

across different languages. It is also what makes his theory decidedly onomasio-logical. His definition of *concept* is logical, making reference to logical notions, as he adopted the definition as established in logic. In his thesis Wüster points out:

> (Technical) language is a system of acoustic signs (linguistic designations) to which representations (*concepts, meanings*) are assigned. Linguistic messages are divided into sentences. A sentence is the expression of a logical proposition, i.e. it consists of a subject and a predicate [...]. The subject is a representation of which something is asserted; the predicate is a representation that is asserted of the subject. For exam-ple, in the sentence *alle Taschenlampen werden durch Trockenelemente gespeist* ['*all flashlights are powered by dry cells*'] the part *alle Taschenlampen* is the subject and the rest is the predicate. The smallest group of sounds to which a distinct represen-tation can be assigned is called a word element [...]. The subject of the example sen-tence thus consists of word elements *all, e, Tasch, en, Lamp, en*. In the following, *concept* will be understood as any representation that does not contain subject and predicate at the same time.   (1931: 11, emphasis in original)

In the previous passage Wüster cites two authors: logician Kurt Joachim Grau and linguist Hermann Paul. Grau (1921: 38) describes the established analysis in logic in which the proposition [*Urteil*] is divided into two parts: logical subject and log-ical predicate; the sentence [*Satz*] being the linguistic expression of the propo-sition. In contrast, Paul's (1920: 121–150) perspective is that of a linguist as he is concerned with the definition of sentence [*Satz*] in linguistics; his definition of the sentence can be said to be largely psychological.[17] Paul presents a bipartite divi-sion of the sentence into at least two elements: subject and predicate.

What is important to note with regard to Wüster's definition of concept, being essentially logical, is that it does not limit the concept to a specific field of knowl-edge (scientific discipline), which he also subtly indicates by enclosing *technical* [*Zweck-*] in parentheses and by juxtaposing *concepts* and *meanings* in the first sentence of the quotation. From the perspective of logic, it is in principle irrele-vant whether one deals with ordinary (general-language) concepts or with spe-cialised (scientific) ones; for example, Grau (1921: 24–26), the logician referred to by Wüster, considers *Mensch* 'human', *Napoleon* (proper noun), *wachsen* 'to grow', *Elektrizität* 'electricity' all as concepts.[18] Although Wüster is primarily concerned with technical language and its expressions (terms), the examples he provides in his dissertation clearly show that he does not restrict the term *concept* (*Begriff*) to denote specialised (scientific, technical) concepts exclusively.

---

17. Paul (1920: 121) defines the sentence as a linguistic expression of associated representations in the soul [= *Seele*] of the speaker and a means of generating such association of representa-tions in the soul of the hearer.

18. *Electricity* being an example of a specialised concept.

Examples of general-language concepts in his *Internationale Sprachnormung* include, for example, *Nachmittag* 'afternoon' and *Orange* 'orange'. Moreover, Wüster also uses the term *concept* to refer to grammatical concepts, i.e. those that express grammatical relations, such as linguistic elements used to express inflections.[19] His own use of the term *concept* (*Begriff*) in the *Internationale Sprachnormung in der Technik* (1931) thus clearly shows that he conceived of specialised concepts and general-language concepts as being all — concepts.

There is however an oft-cited passage in Wüster's posthumous *Einführung in die allgemeine Terminologielehre und terminologische Lexikographie* (1991) that may make it seem as though there were a fundamental difference between concepts (represented by terms) and meanings of words in general language. Wüster argues:

> In terminology the realm of concepts is considered independent of the realm of designations (=terms). Therefore terminologists talk about *concepts*, whereas linguists talk about *word meanings* in relation to general language. For terminologists a terminological unit consists of a *word* to which a concept as the meaning is assigned. Most contemporary linguists, however, consider the word as an inseparable unit made up of word form and word meaning.
>
> (1991: 1–2, emphasis in original)

The above statement can be interpreted on two levels. Firstly, there is the terminological level: Wüster describes different terminologies linguists and terminologists use to refer to the same entity (*concepts* vs. *meanings*). There is however another level that does not pertain to structural differences between concepts and meanings, but rather has to do with methodological differences between terminology and linguistics (lexicology, lexicography): his perspective is that of a terminologist involved in standardisation at national and international levels, where the content of concepts may be negotiated among field experts, new concepts and new terms may be created and where concepts may sometimes be renamed. From this perspective, terms and concepts allow for a higher degree of intervention from terminologists and standardisation experts than words would typically receive from descriptive (and even prescriptive) linguists: typically, linguists do not invent new meanings or designations. The key point here is the act of assigning a term (being an orthographic / phonological *word*) to the concept: this is a deliberate act performed by field experts and/or terminologists. In this respect, the intervention of field experts and/or terminologists is normal, in such settings concepts and terms

---

19. Wüster (1931: 71) says: "A concept with a grammatical function is a derived concept." Wüster (1931: 13) defines *conceptual derivation* (*Begriffsableitung*) as a linguistically manifested structure of concepts built from other concepts that represents the inner linguistic form of a word.

can (are expected to) be interfered with.[20] If one considers the sphere of concepts as independent from the sphere of terms, one can easily justify creating a new term for an existing concept or assigning an existing term to a new concept.

If the two disciplines, terminology and linguistics, are considered methodologically the way Wüster considered them, then there is indeed a stark contrast between terminology, which actively engages in shaping and creating its objects of investigation, and linguistics, which normally takes existing thought-sound relations for granted and merely aims to describe them. According to Wüster, terminology as an applied science (a science which is not interested in merely producing descriptions) is only possible if the postulate of inseparability of concept and sound form is eliminated. In standardisation settings, in which much effort is invested into unification of standards and terms, the separability of concepts and terms thus becomes a necessary theoretical and methodological premise that enables the making of *Soll-Norm* at the national and international levels.

There is another passage that clearly shows that Wüster did not conceive of meanings and concepts as two different entities. On the contrary: for Wüster *concepts* (as defined in classical logic and psychology) coincide with *meanings* of words.

> As defined in classical logic and psychology the *concept* is the mental summation (conceptus) of individual — material or immaterial — objects on the basis of common characteristics. The lexical meanings of a word are simply the concepts associated with this word. This mode of viewing the question does not conflict with the linguistic custom of speaking by preference of meaning or content [*Inhalt*] rather than of concept; it simply complements it. Incidentally, a concept need not be the content of a single word, but may stand for an entire group of words.
>
> ([1963] 2004: 286, translated by Juan C. Sager)

Wüster could hardly have expressed his views of concepts more clearly: word meanings are concepts, too. The distinction between *meanings* and *concepts* does indeed reflect two different terminological traditions, that of terminology and that of linguistics. It is also noteworthy that he believed linguistics would benefit considerably if it adopted conceptual analysis developed by logicians:

---

20. Wüster (1991: 2–3, 4, 139–141; 35) distinguished between the so-called *Ist-Norm* (implicit linguistic rules determined by the actual linguistic usage created through the unhindered development of language) and *Soll-Norm* (explicit linguistic rules laid down or designations selected by relevant experts, e.g. by a terminology standardisation committee, and intended to influence linguistic usage). In technical languages the enforcement of *Soll-Norm* (prescribed rules and terms) quite quickly turns *Soll-Norm* into *Ist-Norm*.

Recognising these facts, the delimitation of linguistics from logic would have to look as follows: Linguistics takes over from logic the knowledge of the possible relations between concepts, or, using the words of the reporters to the Congress of Linguisticians, the knowledge of the possible forms of word meaning. Naturally, such a takeover must be undertaken critically, which means leaving the necessary space for adaptation and development of the borrowed material. It is, however, solely the task of linguistics to represent the concepts provided by the words of a given language, i.e. the substance of word meanings, in the form of conceptual systems, i.e. to establish the relations actually existing between word concepts. Naturally, only with respect to the general language. If linguistics, at least applied linguistics, does not undertake this task it will remain undone.

([1963] 2004: 287, translated by Juan C. Sager, translation adapted by the author)

What Wüster asserts here is that linguistics will be unable to perform the semantic analysis of the general-language vocabulary unless it adopts methods of conceptual analysis from logic (like terminology did in order to analyse specialised concepts). This shows that he believed that meanings of general-language vocabulary not only can be, but rather must be described using the same apparatus as used in the field of terminology to describe specialised concepts.

Wüster was very well aware of the fact that terminology was far ahead of linguistics as far as semantic analysis is concerned, at least in its practical, lexicographic (terminographic) aspect. In order to accentuate the progress made in the field of terminology (processing and arrangement of terms in systematic, rather than alphabetical order), he contrasted two terminological dictionaries from the beginning of the 20th century:

And right after the turn of the century a year-long, almost dramatic battle erupted between the alphabetic and systematic methods. Shortly after 1900, the Association of German Engineers (VDI) decided to create a monumental dictionary called *Technolexikon*. A young philologist recommended by the publisher Langenscheidt was appointed as the leader of the work. Between 1902 and 1905, 3.6 million term records were collected. It goes without saying that *Technolexikon* was supposed to be laid out in alphabetic order.

In 1906, an engineer, equally young, Alfred Schlomann published a small *systematic* dictionary on machine elements. It contained six languages and included pictures. This novel solution came as a real bombshell. In 1907 the VDI board calculated that 40 more years would be required in order to make *Technolexikon* ready for print using the existing method. A report by Arnold Schröer from English studies at the University of Cologne, who referred to himself as a lexicographer, came out in favour of Schlomann's method. As a result, VDI abandoned the work on *Technolexicon*; it had already devoured half a million German marks.

([1974] 2001: 145, emphasis in original)

For Wüster, the failure of *Technolexicon* and the triumph of Schlomann's dictionary testified to the superiority of the systematic method, i.e. the systematic arrangement of terms in dictionaries, over the philological (alphabetical) approach. Linguistics could thus benefit greatly if it borrowed concepts and methods from logic (and terminology). Despite this belief, Wüster — the perspicacious linguist that he was — did perceive certain qualitative differences between specialised (scientific) concepts, that terminology deals with, and everyday (general-language) concepts investigated by linguistics. The above-quoted passage continues with a review of the application of the systematic method in general-language lexicography, with Wüster bemoaning the slow and uneven progress made up to that point and speculating on the reasons for that:

> This begs the question why in general language the implementation of theoretically so firmly justified demands has lagged so far behind. The reason probably lies in the following: general-language words have very many meanings and shades of meaning and many meanings are not clearly delimited. It thus appears unsuitable — at least for practical purposes — to rip apart networks of meaning in the presentation of general language. On the other hand, it is obvious and has always been common practice to restrict a terminological dictionary to a single specialised field. That is why a term that appears in a terminological dictionary can only ever have one or a few meanings.   ([1974] 2001: 146–147)

Wüster acknowledges the differences between clearly defined specialised concepts and fuzzy meanings of general language. This is remarkable in itself. His observation on ordinary concepts not being clearly delimited comes at a time when criticisms of the so-called classical theory of concepts were only beginning to emerge in psychology.[21] Nonetheless, as shown above, he recommended that conceptual analysis from logic be used in linguistics (lexicography): having a semantic theory, however imperfect it may be, is infinitely better than having none at all. Even with regard to specialised concepts, he was far from being naïve, he knew that not all specialised concepts are clearly delimited (i.e. defined) *per se*. Instead, it is through arduous scientific work that the strict delimitation of concepts is achieved:

> Some concepts from everyday life defy any clear delimitation; for example, it is impossible to give a generally valid definition of when a body *is standing* [German *steht*] and when it *is lying* [German *liegt*] [...]. Mechanics has adopted designations *Wucht* [lit. '*force*'] and recently *Ruck* [...] ['*jerk*'] from general language, but not without giving them a sharper interpretation; they are completely defined

---

21. And in philosophy before that, see, for example, Margolis and Laurence (1999) for a collection of readings on concept theories.

as "kinetic energy" and "derivative of acceleration with respect to time". Nobody has yet succeeded in defining the folk meaning of *work* [German *Arbeit*]; it was only through a forcible modification of the extension of the concept that mechanics was able to attain the necessary sharpness of meaning of its most important concept.   (1931: 114)

Here, Wüster again contrasts everyday concepts and specialised concepts, the former being difficult if not impossible to define, whereas the latter become defined through scientific work, specifically, through making changes to their extensions.

Wüster mentions other instances of specialised concepts that even scientists find difficult to define: e.g. the distinction between German terms *Stahl* 'steel' and *Schmiedeeisen* 'wrought iron' (1931: 109); the distinction between *suffixes* and *endings* (1931: 12); the distinction between two concepts of his own theory, i.e. *constituted concepts* (concepts created consciously and explicitly) and *grown concepts* (concepts created subconsciously and implicitly) ([1959/60] 2003: 285–286), where he admits that there is "no firm borderline" between them. This shows that he knew very well that not all specialised concepts are clearly delimited (and perhaps even cannot be).

In fact, Wüster's well-known programmatic assertion regarding terminology work ("It aims at strict delimitation between concepts," 1991: 1) is in line with his intimate knowledge of concepts: Wüster did not claim that specialised concepts are strictly delimited (defined) *per se*, however, he conceived of the emerging field of terminology as an auxiliary discipline helping other disciplines to delimit their concepts. He believed that strict delimitation of concepts is the culmination of scientific work:

> Strict, scientific delimitation of concepts is easily feasible only on the basis of systematic arrangement; the alphabetical arrangement common in philological works is more suited for research on the mere phonetic form of expressions.
>   (1931: 207)

Even though this passage is really about the superiority of the systematic arrangement in terminography, it reveals that he equated strict (terminological) delimitation of concepts with scientific delimitation of concepts. From this perspective, it is easier to understand why terminology as a discipline facilitating specialised communication *should* aim at strict delimitation between concepts: the terminological perspective ensures that scientific concepts are well-formed.

Wüster's conception of *concepts* can be said to be remarkably multifaceted: to recap, his definition of *concept* stems from logic ("representation that does not contain subject and predicate at the same time"). However, he did not confine the concept to the sphere of logic, the concept is simultaneously a psychological entity: He argues that concepts are mental objects, whose being is not determined in time and only exist in the heads of people ([1959/60] 2003: 271). From the perspective of linguistics, the notion of *concept* coincides with the notion of (lexical) meaning: concepts are meanings, the term *concept* being favoured by terminologists and the term *meaning* being preferred by linguists. Wüster acknowledged that general-language concepts are fuzzy and sometimes impossible to define. He admitted that the same is true of certain specialised concepts, but believed concepts that are clearly delimited are (more) scientific. The distinction between the *concept* and *meaning* is simply a matter of the semiotic perspective: semasiologically speaking, the sign has a meaning, onomasiologically speaking, the concept is called by a certain name (sign).[22] Additionally, he also restricted the concept to denotative meaning: terminologists deal with concepts (i.e. the conceptual content) and typically need not take connotations into account.[23] Wüster's view of concepts as reflected in his assertions about concepts and his own usage of the term testifies to his penetrating insights into the semantics of both general and technical languages.

5.   Conclusion

Eugen Wüster was a fascinating personality with many interests and talents. He is widely credited with being the founder of the field of terminology; to consider him a terminologist is not incorrect, but far too narrow. In addition to his many professions and roles, he was perhaps first and foremost an observant linguist with a deep understanding of the functioning of the general language and technical languages. He not only had first-hand experience in learning foreign languages and planned languages, but he was also intimately familiar with recent advances in linguistic theory of the time. Even nearly a century after the publication of his dissertation, Wüster's works and ideas appear fresh and may serve as a source of inspiration for modern theories of terminology. However, this can only be the case if Wüster is read, reread, reflected upon and appreciated in his historical context.[24]

---

22. "If a sign concept is permanently assigned a designating concept, i.e. in the language system, the latter is called the '*meaning*' of the sign. In the inverse direction one says the concept 'is called' such and such." ([1959/60] 2003: 292, translated by Juan C. Sager).

23. "There is a certain circumstance that makes it easier for terminologists to get by with the term "concept": for them the meaning of a term is exhausted in the denotative meaning, also called "conceptual meaning". Typically, "connotations" are removed." ([1974] 2001: 137).

24. This contribution was created within the framework of the research programme P6-0038 funded by the Slovenian Research and Innovation Agency.

References

Blanke, Wera. 2008. *Esperanto — Terminologie und Terminologiearbeit*. New York: Mondial.

Budin, Gerhard. 2022. "Wüsters Allgemeine Terminologielehre — ein Grenzgebiet zwischen Sprachwissenschaft, Logik, Ontologie, Informatik und den Sachwissenschaften." In *Eugen Wüster et la terminologie de l'école de Vienne*, ed. by Danielle Candel, Didier Samain, and Dan Savatovsky, 243–294. Paris: Société d'histoire et d'épistémologie des sciences du langage.

Cabré, Maria Teresa. 1999. *Terminology. Theory, Methods and Applications*. Amsterdam: John Benjamins.

Campo, Ángela. 2012. *The Reception of Eugen Wüster's Work and the Development of Terminology*. PhD thesis. Montréal: Université de Montréal.

Candel, Danielle. 2004. "Wüster par lui-même." In *Des fondements théoriques de la terminologie, Cahiers du CIEL 2004*, ed. by Colette Cortès, 15–32. Paris: Centre interlangue d'études en lexicologie.

Candel, Danielle. 2007. "Terminologie de la terminologie. Métalangage et reformulation dans l'Introduction à la terminologie générale et à la lexicographie terminologique d'E. Wüster." *Langages* 168 (4): 66–81.

Candel, Danielle, 2017. "Eugen Wüster (1898–1977). 'Terminologie et variation'". In *Terminologie et ontologie : théorie et applications. Actes de la conférence TOTh 2012*, ed. by Christophe Roche, 21–37. Chambéry: Université Savoie Mont Blanc.

Candel, Danielle. 2022. "General Principles of Wüster's General Theory of Terminology." In *Theoretical Perspectives on Terminology: Explaining Terms, Concepts and Specialized Knowledge*, ed. by Pamela Faber, and Marie-Claude L'Homme, 37–59. Amsterdam: John Benjamins.

Candel, Danielle, Didier Samain, and Dan Savatovsky (eds). 2022. *Eugen Wüster et la terminologie de l'école de Vienne*. Paris: Société d'histoire et d'épistémologie des sciences du langage.

Collinson, William Edward. 1931. "Neue Wege zum reinen Deutsch. Von Theodor Steche." *The Modern Language Review* 26 (2): 229–231.

Faber, Pamela, and Clara Inés López Rodríguez. 2012. "Terminology and Specialized Language." In *A Cognitive Linguistics View of Terminology and Specialized Language*, ed. by Pamela Faber, 9–31. Berlin, Boston: De Gruyter Mouton.

Felber, Helmut. 1973. "Eugen Wüster — a Pioneer in Terminology." *Babel* 19 (4): 182–185.

Felber, Helmut, and Friedrich Hans Lang. 1979. "Würdigung der Person und des Wissenschaftlers." In *Terminologie als angewandte Sprachwissenschaft. Gedenkschrift für Univ.-Prof. Dr. Eugen Wüster*, ed. by Helmut Felber, Friedrich Lang, and Gernot Wersig, 15–28. München: K. G. Saur Verlag.

Felber, Helmut, and Magdalena Krommer-Benz. 1979. "Das internationale Informationszentrum für Terminologie (Infoterm) — ein Brennpunkt der internationalen Terminologiearbeit." In *Terminologie als angewandte Sprachwissenschaft. Gedenkschrift für Univ.-Prof. Dr. Eugen Wüster*, ed. by Helmut Felber, Friedrich Lang, and Gernot Wersig, 70–86. München: K. G. Saur Verlag.

Felber, Helmut. 1980. "In Memory of Eugen Wüster, Founder of the General Theory of Terminology." *International Journal of the Sociology of Language* 23: 7–14.

Felber, Helmut. 1998a. "Eine erweiterte Wüster Bibliographie (1931–1977)." In *Eugen Wüster (1898–1977). Leben und Werk. Ein österreichischer Pionier der Informationsgesellschaft. Eugen Wüster (1898–1977). His Life and Work. An Austrian Pioneer of the Information Society*, ed. by Erhard Oeser, and Christian Galinski, 235–323. Vienna: TermNet.

Felber, Helmut. 1998b. "Weltweite terminologische Tätigkeiten zwischen 1965 und 1985. (WÜSTERs Lebenswerk)." In *Eugen Wüster (1898–1977). Leben und Werk. Ein österreichischer Pionier der Informationsgesellschaft. Eugen Wüster (1898–1977). His Life and Work. An Austrian Pioneer of the Information Society*, ed. by Erhard Oeser, and Christian Galinski, 69–104. Vienna: TermNet.

Gaudin, François. 2003. *Socioterminologie. Une approche sociolinguistique de la terminologie.* Bruxelles: Éditions Duculot.

Grau, Kurt Joachim. 1921. *Grundriß der Logik*. 2nd ed. Lepzig: B.G. Teubner. Wiesbaden: Springer Fachmedien.

Hartmann, Reinhard R. K., and Gregory James. 2002. *Dictionary of Lexicography*. New York: Routledge.

Humbley, John. 2004. "La réception de l'oeuvre d'Eugen Wüster dans les pays de langue française." In *Des fondements théoriques de la terminologie, Cahiers du CIEL* 2004, ed. by Colette Cortès, 33–52. Paris: Centre interlangue d'études en lexicologie.

Humbley, John. 2022a. "The Reception of Wüster's General Theory of Terminology." In *Theoretical Perspectives on Terminology: Explaining Terms, Concepts and Specialized Knowledge*, ed. by Pamela Faber, and Marie-Claude L'Homme, 15–35. Amsterdam: John Benjamins.

Humbley, John. 2022b. "Wüster et l'aménagement linguistique." In *Eugen Wüster et la terminologie de l'école de Vienne*, ed. by Danielle Candel, Didier Samain, and Dan Savatovsky, 119–139. Paris: Société d'histoire et d'épistémologie des sciences du langage.

Infoterm. 2004. *Thirty Years of Infoterm*.

L'Homme, Marie-Claude. 2004. *La terminologie : principes et techniques*. Montreal: Presses de l'Université de Montréal.

Lang, Anneliese, Friedrich Hans Lang, and Rosa Reiter. 1979. "Bibliographie der Arbeiten Wüsters auf den Gebieten der Terminologie, Dokumentation, Klassifikation, Normung und Sprachwissenschaft." In *Terminologie als angewandte Sprachwissenschaft. Gedenkschrift für Univ.-Prof. Dr. Eugen Wüster*, ed. by Helmut Felber, Friedrich Lang, and Gernot Wersig, 29–57. München: K. G. Saur Verlag.

Lang, Friedrich Hans. 1998a. "Eugen Wüster — Erinnerungen eines Zeitzeugen." In *Eugen Wüster (1898–1977). Leben und Werk. Ein österreichischer Pionier der Informationsgesellschaft. Eugen Wüster (1898–1977). His Life and Work. An Austrian Pioneer of the Information Society*, ed. by Erhard Oeser, and Christian Galinski, 27–67. Vienna: TermNet.

Lang, Friedrich Hans. 1998b. "Eugen Wüster — His Life and Work until 1963." In *Eugen Wüster (1898–1977). His Life and Work. An Austrian Pioneer of the Information Society*, ed. by Erhard Oeser, and Christian Galinski, 13–26. Vienna: TermNet.

Lang, Friedrich Hans. 1998c. "Eugen Wüster — zum 100. Geburtstag. Ein Elektrotechniker als Terminologe." *Elektrotechnik und Informationstechnik* 115 (11): 625–628.

Laurén, Christer, and Heribert Picht. 1993. "Vergleich der terminologischen Schulen." In *Ausgewählte Texte zur Terminologie*, ed. by Christer Laurén, and Heribert Picht, 493–539. Vienna: TermNet.

Margolis, Eric, and Stephen Laurence (eds). 1999. *Concepts: Core Readings*. Cambridge, Mass.; London: MIT Press.

doi   Oeser, Erhard. 2022. "Eine evolutionäre Deutung der Theorie der Terminologie von Wüster." In *Eugen Wüster et la terminologie de l'école de Vienne*, ed. by Danielle Candel, Didier Samain, and Dan Savatovsky, 295–310. Paris: Société d'histoire et d'épistémologie des sciences du langage.

Paul, Hermann. 1920. *Prinzipien der Sprachgeschichte*. 5th edition. Halle (Saale): Verlag von Max Niemeyer.

doi   Pearson, Jennifer. 1998. *Terms in Context*. Amsterdam: John Benjamins.

Rastier, François. 1995. "Le terme : entre ontologie et linguistique." *La banque des mots* 7: 35–65.

doi   Savatovsky, Dan. 2022a. "Introduction. Wüster en contexte." In *Eugen Wüster et la terminologie de l'école de Vienne*, ed. by Danielle Candel, Didier Samain, and Dan Savatovsky, 7–87. Paris: Société d'histoire et d'épistémologie des sciences du langage.

doi   Savatovsky, Dan. 2022b. "Wüster/Carnap: Vienna School/Vienna Circle. Terminology between Linguistics and Philosophy of Language." In *Eugen Wüster et la terminologie de l'école de Vienne*, ed. by Danielle Candel, Didier Samain, and Dan Savatovsky, 141–172. Paris: Société d'histoire et d'épistémologie des sciences du langage.

Slodzian, Monique. 1993. "La V.G.T.T. (Vienna General theory of terminology) et la Conception Scientifique du Monde." *Le Langage et l'Homme* 28 (4): 223–232.

doi   Temmerman, Rita. 2000. *Towards New Ways of Terminology Description: The Sociocognitive Approach*. Amsterdam: John Benjamins.

Trojar, Mitja. 2017. "Wüster's View of Terminology." *Slovenski jezik / Slovene Linguistic Studies* 11: 55–85.

Wüster, Eugen. 1923a. *Enciklopedia Vortaro Esperanta-Germana. Enzyklopädisches Wörterbuch Esperanto-Deutsch*. Leipzig: Ferdinand Hirt and Sohn.

Wüster, Eugen. 1923b. *Maŝinfaka Esperanto-vortaro. Prielementa. Maschinentechnisches Esperanto-Wörterbuch. Der Grundbegriffe*. Leipzig: Ferdinand Hirt and Sohn.

Wüster, Eugen. 1931. *Internationale Sprachnormung in der Technik besonders in der Elektrotechnik*, 1st ed. Berlin: VDI-Verlag.

Wüster, Eugen. 1934. *Grundzüge der Sprachnormung in der Technik*. Berlin: VDI-Verlag.

Wüster, Eugen. [1941] 2001. " Die sprachliche Gemeinschaftsarbeit der deutschen Technik während der letzten fünf Jahre." In *Jahrbuch der deutschen Sprache* 1. 218–225. Reprinted in: *Terminologie und Wissensordnung. Ausgewählte Schriften aus dem Gesamtwerk von Eugen Wüster*, ed. by Heribert Picht, and Klaus-Dirk Schmitz, 391–400. Vienna: TermNet.

Wüster, Eugen. [1948] 2001. "Sprachtechnik und Nachrichtentechnik." In *Österreichische Zeitschrift für Telegraphen-, Telephon-, Funk- und Fernsehtechnik* 2 (5–6). 102–107. Reprinted in: *Terminologie und Wissensordnung. Ausgewählte Schriften aus dem Gesamtwerk von Eugen Wüster*, ed. by Heribert Picht, and Klaus-Dirk Schmitz, 1–10. Vienna: TermNet.

doi   Wüster, Eugen. 1952. *Die Herstellung der Sägeblätter für Holz. Eine Betriebsführung für Sägewerker und andere Sägenfachleute*. Vienna: Springer-Verlag.

Wüster, Eugen. [1952] 2001. "The Coming Concentration of International Terminology Work." In *Review of Documentation* 19 (1). 1–7. Reprinted in: *Terminologie und Wissensordnung. Ausgewählte Schriften aus dem Gesamtwerk von Eugen Wüster*, ed. by Heribert Picht, and Klaus-Dirk Schmitz, 401–416. Vienna: TermNet.

Wüster, Eugen. 1955/1959. *Bibliography of Monolingual Scientific and Technical Glossaries*. Vol. 1: National standards. Vol. 2: Miscellaneous sources. Paris: Unesco.

Wüster, Eugen. [1959/60] 2003. "The Wording of the World Presented Graphically and Terminologically." In *Sprachforum* 3/3–4. 183–204. Translated by Juan C. Sager. Terminology 9/2. 269–297.

Wüster, Eugen. [1963] 2004. "The Structure of the Linguistic World of Concepts and its Representation in Dictionaries." In *Proceedings of the 3rd Congress of International Federation of Translators*. 415–443. Translated by Juan C. Sager. Terminology 10/2. 281–306.

Wüster, Eugen. 1967. *Grundbegriffe bei Werkzeugmaschinen. Deutscher Ergänzungsband zu dem Grundwerk — The Machine Tool: An Interlingual Dictionary of Basic Concepts — Dictionnaire Multilingue de la Machine-Outil: Notions fondamentales (Mehrsprachiges Wörterbuch in Sach- und Abc-Folge, mit Begriffsbestimmungen und Abbildungen)*, 1st ed. London: Technical Press.

Wüster, Eugen. 1968. *The Machine Tool. An Interlingual Dictionary of Basic Concepts Comprising An Alphabetical Dictionary and A Classified Vocabulary with Definitions and Illustrations. English-French Master Volume*, 1st ed. London: Technical Press.

Wüster, Eugen. 1970. *Internationale Sprachnormung in der Technik besonders in der Elektrotechnik*, 3rd ed. Bonn: Bouvier.

Wüster, Eugen. 1974. *The Road to Infoterm*. Pullach bei München: Verlag Dokumentation.

Wüster, Eugen. [1974] 2001. "Die Allgemeine Terminologielehre — Ein Grenzgebiet zwischen Sprachwissenschaft, Logik, Ontologie, Informatik und den Sachwissenschaften." In *Linguistics* 119. 61–106. Reprinted in: *Terminologie und Wissensordnung. Ausgewählte Schriften aus dem Gesamtwerk von Eugen Wüster*, ed. by Heribert Picht, and Klaus-Dirk Schmitz, 131–174. Vienna: TermNet.

Wüster, Eugen, Helmut Felber, Magdalena Krommer-Benz, and Adrian Manu. 1979. *International Bibliography of Standardized Vocabularies = Bibliographie internationale du vocabulaires normalisés = Internationale Bibliographie der Normwörterbücher*, 2nd ed. München: K.G. Saur.

Wüster, Eugen. 1985. *Einführung in die allgemeine Terminologielehre und terminologische Lexikographie*, 2nd ed. Copenhagen: Fachsprachliches Zentrum.

Wüster, Eugen. 1991. *Einführung in die allgemeine Terminologielehre und terminologische Lexikographie*, 3rd ed. Bonn: Romanistischer Verlag.

Zawada, Britta E., and Piet Swanepoel. 1994. "On the Empirical Adequacy of Terminological Concept Theories — The Case for Prototype Theory." *Terminology* 1 (2): 253–275.

CHAPTER 9

The Prague School of Terminology

Dominika Kováříková
Charles University

This chapter explores the theoretical development of Czech terminology, particularly through the influence of the Prague Linguistic Circle (PLC), which has shaped Czech linguistic thought since its establishment in 1926. The PLC's emphasis on functional and structural linguistics has significantly contributed to the development of Czech terminological theory, leading to a distinctive focus on the linguistic dimension of terminology. While external factors such as the building of national identity, political shifts and more recent trends like globalization and technological advancement have also played important roles, the core developments have been driven by linguistic innovation. The chapter traces this evolution from the 19th century to the present day. Key to this development is the perception of the term not merely as a unit of knowledge but as a lexical item within a structured language system.

Keywords: terminology, terminography, Prague Terminology School, Prague Linguistic Circle, functional and structural linguistics

1. Introduction: Prague Terminology School and other schools

The Prague Terminology School is regarded as one of four principal terminology schools (Vienna, Moscow, Prague, and Québec).[1] The name Prague (alternatively Czechoslovak) School was introduced by G. Rondeau (Bozděchová and Kocourek 2018: 101). Among the so-called traditional terminology schools, the Prague School is known as one that focuses the most on the linguistic dimension of terminology.

In the first half of the 20th century, representatives of the Vienna, Moscow, and Prague Schools knew about each other's works. They shared an interest in many topics, namely standardisation and successful communication among professionals (Bozděchová 2009), optimal term formation, and systematic terminology. However, as Wüster, Drezen, and Lotte shared the basic approach to terminology in that

---

1. H. Picht names the Nordic School as the fifth school of terminology (Picht 2011: 13).

https://doi.org/10.1075/tlrp.24.09kov

they focused on the concept as a unit of knowledge and had seen terminology as inherently multidisciplinary (Picht 2011), the Czechoslovak approach was more linguistic (Kocourek 2013). The *term* was considered an item of a modern language lexicon rather than a unit of a larger system of concepts within a discipline or a profession. In short, terms were perceived more as lexical items characteristic of specialised texts than units of knowledge.

Nevertheless, the Prague School has not been entirely uniform throughout the century of its development, and we can identify three main approaches (see also Bozděchová and Kocourek 2018: 100):

1. The classical Prague Terminology School orientation on the linguistic aspect of terms and terminology: the objective is to describe the terms as linguistic (lexical) items as well as their function in specialised text.
2. Terminology as a multi-disciplinary field of study involving linguistics, logic, ontology, and individual domains (similar to Wüster's approach).
3. Linguistics in the service of terminology planning and standardisation.

Although the linguistic approach did not always prevail in Czech terminological studies, terms have always been understood as lexical items (Filipec 1974) that are part of the language system, with a special status in specialised texts. This linguistic perception of terms is based on the functional and structural linguistics tradition of the Prague Linguistic Circle (PLC).

In the functional and structural linguistic framework characteristic of the PLC, (1) the elements of the language system are examined as related phenomena (structuralism), and (2) the language fulfills a variety of functions (functional approach) reflected in the linguistic description through the use of functional styles. The functional styles of standard language (standard Czech is the formal register of Czech), among them professional and academic functional language, were described in 1932 by B. Havránek.

The authority and prestige of linguistic inquiry in the Czechoslovak cultural context resulted from the 19th-century struggle for national independence, the Czech and Slovak National Revival. A crucial constituent of this national identity was and still is a fully developed modern language that can perform all its functions: everyday communication, construction of literary texts, and also professional and academic communication.

This chapter focuses on political and cultural periods, because terminology theory and practice yielded to political ideologies to a certain degree. We briefly cover the period of National Revival in the 19th century, followed by the First Czechoslovak Republic (1918–1938) and by the post-war period and Communist Party rule (1945–1989). The final section covers the period of the modern democratic system (1989 — present day).

2.   Origins of Czech terminology: The Czech National Revival

Historical events in the 19th century and the beginning of the 20th century, and the cultural climate of that period, led to widespread interest in Czech terminology. The National Revival affected this period in many European countries and was a powerful influence on Czech culture. The revivalists saw language as a pillar of national identity. The Czech identity was determined in opposition to the German language; therefore, German influence on the Czech language was systematically eliminated, especially by Czech purists (Engelhardt 2001). In terminology, this purism manifested by translating and calquing German terms and creating neologisms. The Czech language was carefully cultivated by the revivalists in order to be able to perform all the functions of a modern language: everyday communication, literary expression, specialised communication, and administrative funtions. Czech had been used for everyday communication for centuries, but specialised texts were almost exclusively written in German or Latin until the 1820s, and there was a desire for this to change.

Starting in the 19th century, attempts were made to promote Czech terminology by publishing both general language dictionaries and terminological dictionaries, the most prestigious of which was Josef Jungmann's *Czech-German dictionary* [*Slovník česko-německý Josefa Jungmanna*] (1835–1839), comprising about 120,000 entries. Jungmann and his coworkers extended the vocabulary of language for specific purposes by using translations into Czech, creating calques and adopting lexical items from other Slavic languages and neologisms (Jedlička 1948).

Terminological dictionaries were also published in various fields, including philosophy, mathematics, logic, botany, medicine, law, administration, commerce, metallurgy, music, physical education (later affected by military terminology), and in trades such as tailoring and shoemaking (Jedlička 1948; Janata 2020).

In 1853, Pavel Josef Šafařík published an influential German-Czech dictionary of scholarly terminology for secondary schools (Šafařík 1853) containing 15,000 key terms from sciences, arts, engineering and commerce.

Against this historical context, the first half of the 20th century saw increased interest in the Czech lexicon and terminology. In 1918, the fight for Czech national identity culminated in the establishment of the Czechoslovak Republic (the Slovak language and identity did not reach full emancipation until the 1950s and 1960s).

3.   1918–1939: The first Czechoslovak Republic

In 1918, the Czechoslovak Republic declared its independence from the Austro-Hungarian Empire. One of the pillars of national identity was a functioning Czech language in all areas of human communication, including scholarly communication. Opposition towards the German language in general and also towards German elements in the Czech language was evident in Czech linguistics, especially in efforts to replace old German terminology with Czech equivalents. The platform for these puristic efforts in the early years of the new republic was the linguistic journal *Our Speech* [*Naše řeč*].

As will be shown later, the Czech and Slovak languages were not equal. By law, the official language of the new republic was designated as Czechoslovak, which encompassed two distinct variants: Czech and Slovak (Levická 2019). However, it is important to note that Czech and Slovak have indeed been separate languages. In practice, the Czech language was promoted, and it was expected that the two languages would assimilate in favor of Czech over time. This prediction proved wrong starting in WWII and continuing in the 1950s and 1960s when the emancipation of the Slovak language was achieved; terminology was crucial in this process.

In linguistics, the primary influence of this period was the Prague Linguistic Circle (PLC), established in 1926. With the functional and structural linguistic approach, purist efforts faded, and the contemporary theory of language culture focused on standard language and its functions.

Besides the PLC, several other factors strongly influenced linguistic studies in the period of the First Czechoslovak Republic, especially the study of lexis and terminology as crucial components of any modern language. Among them were two significant endeavors with a major consequence for contemporary terminology. Even before the emergence of the independent republic, the Office for the Dictionary of Czech Language [Kancelář Slovníku jazyka českého] was established in 1911, and the *Czech Language Dictionary* itself (Příruční slovník jazyka českého) — a significant work with 250,000 entries — was published between 1935 and 1957. During this dictionary's design and compilation, Czech lexicographers frequently discussed terminology in linguistic journals such as *Our Speech* [Naše řeč] (published since 1916), *Word and Word Art* [Slovo a slovesnost] (published since 1926 as a PLC platform), and *Our Administrative Czech* [*Naše úřední čeština*] (focusing mainly on railway terminology, published between 1921 and 1933).

In the same period, researchers and professionals from many disciplines, among them several members of the PLC, were preparing the *Otto's Encyclopedia of the New Era* [Ottův slovník naučný nové doby], published between 1930 and 1943. Tens of thousands of entries in the Encyclopedia were terms, including the entry *Terminology* written in 1941 by B. Havránek and containing one of the first definitions of the term in the Czech tradition. As with most encyclopedias, this work, as a non-linguistic resource, focuses on terms as units of knowledge (similarly to Wüster's perspective), rather than as units of the lexicon.

Following the establishment of the Czechoslovak Republic in 1918, there was a strong national effort to develop and strengthen various sectors of society. This upsurge of nationalism was reflected in the deliberate advancement of multiple fields, which in turn required the creation of suitable tools, with vocabulary (terminology) being among the most important. Terminology was developed across many areas, but one that stands out is the military, as it had only recently gained independence from Austria-Hungary.

To summarise, the 1920s and 1930s witnessed significant growth in the development of terminology and terminography across numerous disciplines, professions, crafts, and trades.

4.   Prague Linguistic Circle and terminology

The Prague Linguistic Circle (PLC) (Pražský lingvistický kroužek) was established in 1926 as a group of scholars interested in the synchronic study of language. Its principles were presented at the First International Congress of Slavists in Prague in 1929 in their program statement (Mathesius et al. 1929). Among notable members were Vilém Mathesius, Roman Jakobson, Nikolay Trubetzkoy, Sergei Kartsevsky, Bohuslav Havránek, Josef Vachek, L. V. Kopeckij, Jan Mukařovský, and Vladimír Skalička. These linguists focused on synchronic linguistic analysis as a continuation of Ferdinand de Saussure's *Cours de linguistique générale* (1916). The PLC was officially disbanded in 1952 for political reasons and again re-established in 1995.

The functional and structural linguistic approach was adopted by representatives of the PLC. They believed that all elements of language are interconnected within the language system as a whole, and that the language system is founded on the relationships between its units, which are often referred to as *oppositions*. As Čermák and Hajičová (2003) noted, every language unit is composed of a unique set of oppositions. In accordance with this approach, scholarly and specialised texts are intellectual rather than emotional, and they are primarily written rather than spoken, as they aim to communicate information rather than focus on form (which is the function of poetry) (Mathesius et al. 1929).

The linguists of the PLC emphasised the functionality of language in various situations, as well as the needs of the language community. This approach recognises that language serves multiple communicative functions, and the choice of linguistic elements is determined by their specific function. In a collective statement in 1958, former PLC linguists summarised that "[t]he linguists belonging to the Prague School saw an essential feature of language systems in the functional tasks of language, in its practical application" (Vachek 1964: 464).

The program of the PLC (Mathesius et al. 1929) stated that standard Czech (the formal register of Czech that was still developing during that period), as opposed to the commonly-spoken language, should employ a more intellectual lexicon, especially terminology, to convey higher-level concepts. Standard Czech should be able to express complex abstract ideas and ensure clear, precise communication of scientific, philosophical, religious, social, political, and legal concepts. Throughout the Czech linguistic tradition, terms have been regarded as significant elements of the lexicon, with a strong focus on their linguistic properties rather than solely as units of knowledge.

In an article examining the functional differentiation of standard language and language culture, Bohuslav Havránek (1932)[2] distinguishes four functions or purposes of standard language:

1. everyday communication (conversation) — spoken language, less official texts, and therefore less need for intervention
2. expert communication (communication in practical professions) — almost strictly standard language, mostly context-independent, characterised by use of so called *words-terms* (with the meaning established through convention among experts in the given field)
3. theoretical communication (scholarly communication) — strictly standard language, context-independent, characterised by use of so called *words-concepts* (with a precise and unambiguous meaning in any context)
4. esthetic/poetic function (literary texts).

Terminological studies have relevance in two of these language functions, expert communication and theoretical communication, since they both necessitate a succinct yet comprehensive form and are used to convey precise, accurate, and exact information.

In his entry on *terminology* in the *Otto's Encyclopedia* (1941), Havránek became one of the pioneers in providing a definition of *term* in the Czech language. This entry established certain aspects of what constitutes a term that had a significant impact on Czech terminology studies and are still referenced today (e.g. Poštolková et al. 1983; Bozděchová 2009; Čermák 2010). A term is characterised as a fixed (stable) expression, its meaning is strictly conceptual without expressivity or pragmatic features, and it is precise and unambiguous. According to Havránek, a term

---

2. In this text, Havránek cites Wüster's *Internationale Sprachnormung in der Elektrotechnik* from 1931, only one year after its publication.

should ideally have a word-formation capacity, meaning it should be able to easily generate other terms through derivation (Havránek 1941).

The Prague Linguistic Circle had members who were also active in the field of terminography. In 1930, Trubetzkoy and his colleagues presented a systematic terminology of phonology at the International Phonological Meeting, subsequently published in an article (Jakobson et al. 1931: 309–323). This work introduced terms such as *phonology, markedness, binary opposition,* and *distinctive feature.* The most notable terminographical project undertaken by a PLC member was Vachek's *Dictionnaire de Linguistique de l'École de Prague* (1960), which will be discussed in greater detail later in this chapter.

5.   Definitions of "term" in the classical era

During the classical era of Czech terminology (1920s to 1960s), there was intense interest in defining the notion of "term." The earliest definitions of the notion of *term* in Czech have been extensively described in the literature (Kocourek 1965; Roudný 1977; Bozděchová 2009, 2017; Bozděchová and Kocourek 2018), as they played a significant role in shaping the understanding of this concept. The following paragraphs will focus on these early definitions.

The first definition of *term* in the Czech tradition was written by PLC member L.V. Kopeckij and is based on B. Havránek's characterisation (Havránek 1932). Kopeckij defined the term as a word that has a precise and unambiguous meaning in a specialised text and is recognised as pertaining to a particular field, even if it appears in an informal context (Kopeckij 1935: 121).

Havránek's definition of *term* from *Otto's Encyclopedia* (Havránek 1941: 1074) was similar to Kopeckij's as it was based on the same characteristics. They both differentiated between *proper terms,* which have a specialised meaning even in non-specialised texts (e.g., *diabetes mellitus,* always referring to a medical condition), and *automatised words* (or *automatised multi-word units*) that only have a specialised meaning in specialised texts, but non-specialised meaning in other types of texts (e.g., *bond* in chemistry vs. general use). While both proper terms and automatised words were viewed as specialised lexical items, the label "term" was only applied to the former.

In his 1948 study about Josef Jungmann's terminology, Jedlička considered both types (terms and automatised words) as "terms" and defined them as lexical-semantic items fulfilling expert and scholarly language functions. A term is established by a definition, convention, or codification (Jedlička 1948: 31). Having a defined meaning remains one of the distinguishing characteristics frequently cited in definitions of "term."

In 1951, Vl. Šmilauer pointed out that terms, as typical intellectualised words, label the "pure" concept; their meaning is precisely determined and defined, and is context-independent (Šmilauer 1951: 6). K. Sochor, in his practical manual for terminologists, defined *term* as a lexical item; it labels a concept from a specific field of knowledge and is a constituent of its terminology system. Terms are the building blocks of specialised texts and are precise and unambiguous (Sochor 1955: 8–10). K. Hausenblas (1962) defined *term* as a naming unit having a specific meaning in a particular field of knowledge. Like A. Jedlička, Roudný (1977) also emphasised the formal aspect of terms rather than their semantic aspect.

Almost simultaneously, R. Kocourek and J. Machač reached a similar conclusion, i.e. that terms have two main characteristics: their specific conceptual meaning and their function in specialised texts (ensuring that professionals can share and understand information accurately). Both regard other features as less significant or typical only under certain circumstances (Kocourek 1963: 32; Machač 1964: 66). After 1964, the notion of *term* was defined by several other Czech linguists (more in Bozděchová 2017). Most definitions enumerate similar features such as system character, stability, conceptual meaning and the existence of a definition.

6.   The period of 1945–1989

Immediately after the Second World War (until the spring of 1948), efforts to re-establish the original pre-war situation in Czech linguistics, both in research and in resuming international relations, were initiated. These efforts were interrupted in 1948 by the coup d'état, which established a totalitarian regime; Czechoslovakia joined the Soviet power bloc. Between 1948 and 1989, the country was ruled by the Communist Party of Czechoslovakia, which dominated not only the political scene but also interfered in all cultural areas and academia. The study of linguistics was no exception: especially in the 1950s, linguists were compelled to renounce structuralism and quote Marr's and later Stalin's linguistic theses (more on the political pressures in Czech linguistics in Dvořáčková 2017). Although the established functional and structuralist linguistic orientation was officially considered undesirable during this period, B. Havránek, a co-founder of the Prague Linguistic Circle, remained one of the leading figures in Czech linguistics during the 1950s and 1960s. The functional approach to text types and the systematic linguistic perspective were retained, and terminology continued to be discussed in the context of Havránek's functional style of specialised texts and as a component of the linguistic system. Terms were viewed as components of the lexicon, interconnected with other elements of the language.

Terminology was one of the areas of linguistics in which the ideologies of the time were very much reflected, namely

1. the centralisation of power, including the centrally planned economy
2. rapprochement of nations (bringing nations closer together), especially nations of the Soviet power bloc
3. more generally, the progress of humanity towards a better world order and rejection of the old.

The centrally planned economy promoted technical fields, particularly heavy industry, and it also required prompt and complete terminology standardisation to achieve a full understanding among professionals. For those reasons, the original theoretical and practical linguistic focus of Czech terminology shifted towards a more standardised, system-based approach. This non-linguistic perspective viewed terms as fixed labels within specific technical disciplines, focused primarily on their role in ensuring clarity and consistency across national and international norms. This trend is apparent in terminology work during the whole period, until the 1980s. The existing terminology associated with the previous social order, namely in the military and administrative fields, was officially reassessed, and new terminology for areas such as centrally planned production was created (Kuchař and Roudný 1965). In the context of the growing terminologies in technical and other fields and with the shift towards standardisation, the linguistic contribution to terminology focused on word formation, adoption, and other processes of terminology enrichment.

Despite this general trend, one of the most dynamic periods of Czech terminology was during the 1960s when it thrived thanks to collaboration with well-organised and active Slovak terminologists (cf. Zumrík and Levická's chapter in this volume). Although Slovak terminology was well developed both theoretically and practically during the 1950s under the leadership of J. Horecký (Levická 2019), in the 1960s there was political pressure for the convergence of the two languages, particularly in the field of terminology. This effort was in part linked to the ideology of bringing the nations closer together that was adopted in the early 1960s by the Communist Party of the Soviet Union. The two national languages were to develop together in the field of terminology, and especially the newly emerging Slovak terminology was to mirror the Czech one. The practical motivation for this policy was to foster very close economic relations between the two nations and facilitate effortless and effective communication between professionals.

6.1   Terminology department of the Czech Language Institute

After the Second World War, the Czech Language Dictionary Office (Kancelář Slovníku jazyka českého) became the Czech Language Institute. The terminology department of the Institute provided linguistic consultancy assistance to the Office for Standardisation in the production of standards. Linguists affiliated with this department participated in dozens of terminology committees for various fields (Tejnor 1968). Karel Sochor produced a handbook of practical guidelines for members of terminology committees who lacked a linguistic background (Sochor 1955).

According to Roudný, the role of consulting linguists in terminology committees was to provide guidance to committee members on linguistic aspects of the naming process, such as the appropriateness of chosen names and the correctness of new term formations in accordance with the standard language (Roudný 1977: 247–248). In comparison with the previous era, the role of linguists was weakened: previously they evaluated terms, and definitions, within the broader discipline of terminology in all its dimensions.

6.2   Czechoslovak Commission for Linguistic Terminology

In 1955, the International Committee of Slavists was established, whose aim was to build on the pre-war cooperation of Slavists in Europe and around the world. The Committee continued its work in the tradition of the First International Congress of Slavists that took place in Prague in 1929. In 1958, the Fourth International Congress of Slavists was held in Moscow, where its Terminology Commission was established alongside other committees.

In 1959, the Czechoslovak Commission for Linguistic Terminology (Československá terminologická komise) was established as a focused branch of the Terminology Commission (Jedlička 1960). Under its supervision, several major dictionaries of linguistic terminology were published. Most notably, the *Dictionnaire de linguistique de l'École de Prague* by Josef Vachek (in collaboration with Josef Dubský) was published in 1960. This dictionary summarises the terminology of the Prague Linguistic Circle. It also contains citations from 154 texts (monographs and articles) by more than 30 authors representing the PLC (Čermák and Hajičová 2003). The original version of the dictionary contained terms in French, while the English version was published in 2003 (Vachek 2003), and the Czech version in 2005 (Vachek 2005).

Another such dictionary was the *Dictionary of Slavic Linguistic Terminology* [Slovník slovanské lingvistické terminologie] (1977 and 1979), in which more than two thousand linguistic terms were translated into English, French and German, in addition to nine Slavic languages. This particular dictionary was created within the International Committee of Slavists.

6.3   Czech-Slovak terminology

In the 1960s, Czech and Slovak terminology, namely the controversial question of their convergence, were a major topic for political reasons. In the 1950s, there had been great progress in Slovak terminology, following similar progress of Czech terminology in 1920s and 1930s. A terminology department was established at the Slovak Language Institute in 1950, and in 1956, Ján Horecký published a book on Slovak terminology. The book presents a theoretical examination of terminology and the function of terms as stylistically marked lexical items, as well as a historical overview of Slovak terminology.

In 1962, the Central Czechoslovak Committee of Terminology [Ústřední terminologická komise ČSAV] was established with the intention of enforcing greater collaboration, and the *Czechoslovak Terminology Journal* [Československý terminologický časopis] (CTJ) replaced the *Slovak Professional Terminology* [Slovenské odborné názvoslovie] as the official terminology journal.

Czech and Slovak communities did not share the same enthusiasm about harmonising terminology. Whereas on the Slovak side it was considered political interference in a prospering discipline with a well organised framework and its own publishing platform (Levická 2019), this period is perceived as very fruitful by Czech terminologists: thanks to vigorous cooperation between the two sides, mutual learning in both practical and theoretical issues could be achieved (Bozděchová and Kocourek 2018).

6.4   Czechoslovak Terminology Journal

Czechoslovak Terminology Journal [Československý terminologický časopis] (CTJ) was published between 1962 and 1966 in 30 issues. Similar to its predecessor, *Slovak Professional Terminology* journal, practical terminology articles were dominant, including reports from individual committees. However, the journal also published several key Czech theoretical texts, alongside a number of Slovak theoretical articles. Translations of texts by Soviet and other foreign researchers regularly appeared as well. Furthermore, Czech-Slovak language relations was a recurring theme in the journal, especially in the program statements by Bělič (1962), Horecký (1963), and the editorial board (i.e. *Principles of coordination of Czech and Slovak terminology* [Zásady koordinácie českej a slovenskej terminológie], 1964).

Important Czech theoretical texts include the journal article by K. Hausenblas (1963), which focuses more generally on the lexicon of specialised texts. Hausenblas considered terms lexical units functioning as elements of text with their own tendencies and behavior, rather than as ideal and standardised items with designated properties. In contrast with dictionaries or standards which feature terms in a highly controlled environment, in authentic texts it is not always easy or even possible to distinguish between terms and non-terms. Hausenblas therefore distinguishes *semi-terms*, i.e. units that are not entirely clear as terms or non-terms. Many of these semi-terms are now referred to as *academic words*, which are common across academic disciplines. This topic was further developed by Bečka (1972) and Kováříková and Kovářík (2021).

Hausenblas, more generally, also summarises aspects of terminological research as follows:

1. the term as a name of a phenomenon of reality (term-concept-phenomenon relation)
2. the term as a component of the terminological system (the relation of the term to other terms in the field)
3. the term as a component of a professional text (relation to other types of linguistic phenomena, lexical, grammatical, and other)
4. the position of the term in the vocabulary of the language (the relationship between terms and non-terms).

Other theoretical works in the CTJ include articles on the need to consistently distinguish between terms as units of terminology and names as units of nomenclature (Blatná 1964), on the relativity of the term's independence of the context (Man 1965), on the existence of synonyms in terminology (Kocourek 1965) and on Czech and Slovak definitions of *term* (Kocourek 1965).

The theoretical works published in the CTJ over the five year period were quite influential in the following decades of Czech terminology research.

6.5 Terminology studies and L. Drozd

Following the discontinuation of the CTJ journal, Czech terminology articles were featured in other linguistic journals, mainly *Slovo a slovesnost* and *Naše řeč*. The *Terminology Studies* [Terminologická studie] series, published between 1966 and 1976 in six volumes, with Vladimír Brand and later Lubomír Drozd as chief editors, served as another publishing platform. The series consisted mainly of articles about terminology written in Russian, English, German, and French, along with a few in Czech.

L. Drozd is an internationally recognised terminologist who published in Czech and German. Alongside his German colleague, W. Seibicke, he authored a book about the language of science and technology (Drozd and Seibicke 1973), which featured a preface by E. Wüster. Wüster noted that the study of terminology is a part of lexicology[3] but at the same time he referred to terminology as a transitional area between linguistics and professional disciplines.

The authors stressed the importance of terms for scientific and technical reflection, viewing them as a prerequisite and a condition for it. In addition to terminology, the book covers various aspects of professional texts, including characteristic syntactic features, distinctions between professional and non-professional language, terminologisation and determinologisation, and the evolution of individual terms over time.

6.6   Quantitative approach to terminology

In the 1960s and the following decades, quantitative linguistic research was supported by the Communist Party. One of the contributors to the frequency dictionary of Czech (Jelínek et al. 1961), J. V. Bečka, began to explore the vocabulary of academic texts. Motivated by the needs of teaching university level Czech as a second language course for students from politically allied countries, Bečka, a pioneer of term extraction as it is known today, examined the possibilities of term recognition based on the quantitative features of lexical items in academic and specialised texts, such as frequency and distribution in texts and across disciplines. Bečka (1972, 1973) identified three types of lexical items: terms (e.g. *hydrochloric acid*), general language words (e.g. *large, to read*), and academic words (such as *to examine, analysis, research*).

V. Vlková (1976, 1978), another terminology researcher, also adopted a quantitative approach by examining terms in texts (rather than terms as ideal representations of knowledge). She found that terms constitute roughly 20% of academic and professional texts and that the natural sciences and technical fields contain a higher proportion of terms than the humanities and social sciences.

The Five-Language Dictionary of Quantitative Linguistics [Pětijazyčný slovník z kvantitativní lingvistiky] (Těšitelová et al. 1970) reflects the focus on quantitative linguistic research during the period. The dictionary features entries such as *frequency dictionary, type-token, absolute frequency, entropy,* and *dictionary richness,* with translations of Czech terms into English, French, German, and Russian.

6.7   Terminology as a linguistic vs. independent discipline

Since the 1950s, most Czech terminologists have regarded linguistics as a discipline that offers fundamental linguistic and methodological tools for scholarly

---

3. In his review of the book Filipec (1974) commented that this fact "is ... self-evident in our country" (translated by the author).

pursuits in terminology. Linguists were often in the position of advisors, overseeing whether newly formed terms were created according to appropriate linguistic principles (cf. Bozděchová and Kocourek 2018: 100).

To aid terminologists from non-linguistic disciplines, B. Poštolková, M. Roudný, and A. Tejnor's concise work *Czech Terminology* [O české terminologii] (1983) served as a guide, similar to K. Sochor's handbook (1955). Tejnor believed that terminology was an interdisciplinary field that required input from experts in different areas, including linguists and logicians (Tejnor 1968: 23). According to him, linguists offer comprehensive knowledge of the lexicon, along with lexicographic expertise that can be utilised to develop specialised dictionaries and terminology standards.

In the context of linguistics in the service of terminology, Tejnor also emphasises the fundamental importance of the principles of word formation for terminology creation and standardisation, and his view is echoed in other studies (e.g., Poštolková, Roudný, and Tejnor 1983; Poštolková 1984; Bozděchová 2009).

7. A brief history of Czechoslovak standardisation

Standardisation efforts in Czechoslovakia can be traced back to the early years of the Republic, evolving significantly through the 20th century. This section outlines key developments, organised into distinct periods to present a clear chronological view.

7.1 Early efforts (1920s–1930s)

The movement toward terminology standardisation began shortly after the establishment of the Czechoslovak Republic in 1918. In the 1920s, the Czechoslovak Electrotechnical Association (Elektrotechnický svaz československý) and the Czechoslovak Standardising Association (Československá normalizační společnost) published initial regulations and standards across various technical fields. These early efforts laid the groundwork for more comprehensive standardisation practices.

7.2 Post-World War II developments

Following World War II, Czechoslovak linguists and terminologists became familiar with the international efforts led by Technical Committee 37 of the International Organization for Standardization (ISO/TC 37). Czechoslovakia soon became a participating member of ISO/TC 37, aligning its national standards with broader international norms.

7.3   Standardisation in the Communist era (1948–1989)

During the Communist era, particularly from the late 1940s to the 1980s, standardisation efforts were shaped by the centralised planning model. Terminology work in this period focused heavily on creating uniform terms across various disciplines to support the planned economy. Institutions such as the Office for Standardisation [Úřad pro normalizaci] played a critical role, ensuring consistency across national and international standards. This trend continued throughout the Communist period, reflecting the political and economic priorities of the time.

7.4   The modern era and legacy of standardisation

The emphasis on terminology standardisation persisted until the 1980s, leaving a lasting impact on how technical and professional language was developed and used in Czechoslovakia. The Czech Standards Institute [Český normalizační institut] continues to oversee standardisation activities, maintaining the legacy of these historical efforts.

8.   Czech terminology after 1989

In 1989, there was a radical change in the political situation in Czechoslovakia with the fall of communism. The ideologies and principles of the previous era were abandoned, including the focus on heavy industry and technical fields, as well as centralisation in general, and these changes affected terminology research.

The role of linguists underwent a gradual redefinition, shifting from their responsibility of refining language to one of depicting language phenomena and speaker perception. This paradigm shift, along with the global trend towards a communicative and pragmatic approach in linguistics, also had an impact on the linguistic analysis of terminology (Bozděchová 2017). With the help of extensive corpora, it became possible to observe the typical characteristics of terms in texts.

Another universal phenomenon associated with terminology is the substantial influence of English as a lingua franca in the academic arena, particularly in the field of information technology (Kocourek 2001b).

8.1   Terminology at linguistic conferences

Czech terminology has been significantly influenced by direct international contact through coordinating terminology panels at the XV and XVII International Congress of Linguists held in Quebec City in 1992 and Prague in 2003.

The 2003 terminology panel at the Prague conference, which was reported on by Freixa (2003) in the *Terminology* journal, was coordinated by Rostislav Kocourek and Svatava Machová. It was a continuation of the long international discussions about the theory of terminology. In Prague, R. Kocourek, M. T. Cabré, R. Temmerman, M.-C. L'Homme, and others discussed the theory of terminology from various perspectives. Kocourek focused on recent theoretical proposals and their positive influence on the traditional theory of terminology. Cabré argued for a descriptive rather than prescriptive approach to terminology, and J. Šabršula, in the tradition of the Prague Terminology School, focused on the status of terminology within the language system.

A series of Czech conferences, Termina, demonstrated the continued interest of Czech linguists in terminology. Four conferences were held between 1994 and 2004, with the majority of the presentations focusing on practical or specific terminological or terminographic issues. Additionally, several noteworthy theoretical studies were presented, including works by Filipec (1995), Čermák (2001), Jelínek (2001), and Kocourek (2001a, 2001b).

8.2   Modern terminology studies

Since 1989, several influential linguistic studies have been published that are in line with the Prague Terminology School tradition. These studies examine terminology in connection with lexicology and lexicography, viewing the term as a specific type of lexical item.

S. Machová's chapter in the *Handbook of Lexicography* [Manuál lexikografie] (Machová 1995) is a significant study examining the theoretical and practical aspects of terminography. Comparing lexicographers and terminographers, Machová notes that terminographers often introduce and standardise terms while lexicographers describe stabilised and commonly-known items. She addresses the challenge of distinguishing between terms and non-terms in specialised texts, stating that such distinctions can only be made in the context of a specific text or discipline. Machová also identifies two categories of terms based on Wayne D. Cole's (1991) work: *prescriptive terms*, defined for use by professionals in sciences and technology, and *pseudo-prescriptive terms* (descriptive terms in Cole's work), commonly used in humanities and social sciences where definitions are subject to negotiation and interpretation (Machová 1995: 144).

During this period, R. Kocourek, an internationally respected terminologist, published various studies. Some of his works focused on the history of Czech terminology (Kocourek 2001a, 2013; Bozděchová and Kocourek 2018), while others, typically in French, explored the theory of terminology (Kocourek 1989, 1991). In his book on scientific and technical terminology, *La langue française de la technique et de la science*, Kocourek defines *term* as a fundamental unit of specialised text that requires a definition (Kocourek 1991). A lexical item only becomes a term if it is repeatedly used in professional texts and represents a clearly defined concept. In his earlier work, Kocourek provided his definition of *term* as a "defined word or a multi-word unit" (1965: 21). In his later work (1989), he introduced the concept of *semantic explications* as more detailed and specific information that may supplement or replace a definition in some cases.

In 2009, I. Bozděchová conducted a study on contemporary terminology with a focus on collocational terms in medicine. This study included an overview of terminology theory and history, with a specific emphasis on the Prague Terminology School and popular topics in Czech terminology. Bozděchová identified key characteristics of terms commonly cited by Czech terminologists, such as precision of meaning, unambiguity, the existence of a definition, and stylistic and pragmatic unmarkedness (Bozděchová 2009: 29). Additionally, Bozděchová highlighted the importance of a textual approach to terms, a feature of Czech terminology since the 1960s (Hausenblas 1963; Kocourek 1991; Machová 1995; Filipec 1995; Čermák 2001).

The research performed by D. Kováříková in 2017 aimed to identify the typical quantitative and distributional features of terms in order to provide a solid foundation for automatic term extraction. This approach was inspired by Bečka's (1972) work and research on automatic term recognition (ATR), which was prominent in the field of terminology research in the 2000s and 2010s (e.g. Kageura et al. 2004). The availability of large corpora of contemporary written Czech in the Czech National Corpus (www.korpus.cz) made it possible to research quantitative term features. Data mining methods used for ATR confirmed Bečka's initial findings that terms can be reliably identified in texts using relatively simple quantitative criteria such as frequency, frequency ratio (risk ratio), and distribution (Kováříková 2017).

Furthermore, Kováříková's study investigated non-terms commonly found in academic texts, which resulted in the creation of the Czech Academic Word List (Kováříková and Kovářík 2021).

9.   Conclusion

The development of Czech terminology has always been heavily influenced by the social climate and political situation. During the interwar period, the formation of Czech national identity was a major driving force behind terminology studies. Following 1948, the political orientation towards the values of the Soviet Union greatly impacted Czech terminology, placing a strong emphasis on centralisation and technology. In modern times, advancements in technology and globalisation have opened up new possibilities for language processing, leading to a renewed focus on texts and the adoption of new theoretical and methodological approaches in terminology and linguistics.

The traditional Prague Terminology School is closely associated with the Prague Linguistic Circle and functional and structural linguistics. Terminology has consistently been seen as a sub-discipline of linguistics, developed in the context of language cultivation. Terminology studies were closely linked to the most significant linguistic work of the time, namely the monolingual dictionary *Příruční slovník jazyka českého*.

In the post-war period, the linguistic theory of terminology was further developed, focusing on the characteristic features of terms. However, terminology studies of the time were often dedicated to the service of terminology standardisation, with terminologists-linguists commonly serving as advisors to field professionals.

In modern times, what characterised the traditional Prague Terminology School remains largely unchanged. Even today, terminological research is closely linked to linguistics and linguistic theories. The linguistic orientation and treatment of terms as lexical items are still essential aspects of Czech terminology.

Funding

This work was supported by the European Regional Development Fund project "Beyond Security: Role of Conflict in Resilience-Building" (reg. no.: CZ.02.01.01/00/22_008/0004595).

References

Bečka, Josef Václav. 1972. "The Lexical Composition of Specialised Texts and its Quantitative Aspect." *Prague Studies in Mathematical Linguistics* 4: 47–64.

Bečka, Josef Václav. 1973. *Lexikální složení českých odborných textů technického zaměření. Díl 1. Úvodní studie.* Praha: SPN.

Bělič, Jaromír. 1962. "Za upevňování kontaktu mezi češtinou a slovenštinou na poli terminologie." *Československý terminologický časopis* 1: 1–6.

Blatná, Libuše. 1964. "Termín — terminologie, název — nomenklatura." *Československý terminologický časopis* 3: 340–345.

Bozděchová, Ivana. 2009. *Současná terminologie (se zaměřením na kolokační termíny z lékařství)*. Praha: Karolinum.

Bozděchová, Ivana. 2017. "Prague School of Terminology." In *Polskie i europejskie nurty terminologiczne. Seria Studi@Naukowe 38*, ed. by Marta Małachowicz, and Sambor Grucza, 108–120. Warszawa: Uniwersytet Warszawski.

Bozděchová, Ivana, and Rostislav Kocourek. 2018. "O novodobém vývoji a principech české terminologické práce." In *Слов'янське термінознавство. Кінця хх — початку ххі століть*. Міжнародна колективна монографія, редактор Вікторія Іващенко, 74–88. Kiev.

Čermák, František. 2001. "Termín a frazém (Případ překrývání a periférie dvou nominativních oblastí)." In *Termina 2000. Sborník příspěvků z II. konference 1996 a III. konference 2000*, ed. by Milan Žemlička, 31–36. Praha: Galén.

Čermák, František, and Eva Hajičová. 2003. "Introduction: Prague School of Linguistics in its Classical Time and Today." In Josef Vachek, *Dictionary of the Prague School of Linguistics*, ed. by Libuše Dušková, 1–23. Amsterdam: John Benjamins.

Čermák, František. 2010. *Lexikon a sémantika*. Praha: NLN.

Cole, Wayne D. 1991. "Descriptive Terminology: Some Theoretical Implications." *Meta: Journal Des Traducteurs* 36 (1): 16–22.

Drozd, Lubomír, and Wilfried Seibicke. 1973. *Deutsche Fach- u. Wissenschaftssprache. Bestandsaufnahme — Theorie — Geschichte*. Wiesbaden: Brandstetter.

Dvořáčková, Věra. 2017. "'Bez Havránka si nikdo ani neškrtl.' Poválečné vztahy katedry českého jazyka pražské filozofické fakulty a akademického Ústavu pro jazyk český." *Acta Universitatitis Carolinae: Historia Universitatis Carolinae Pragensis* 57 (1): 105–122.

Engelhardt, G. 2001. "Český a německý purismus z konce 19. století." *Naše řeč* 84 (5): 235–244.

Filipec, Josef. 1974. "Nové kompendium o odborném jazyku a terminologiiium." *Slovo a slovesnost* 35 (3): 195–198.

Filipec, Josef. 1995. "Funkce odborného a běžného lexika v odborných textech a v lexikálním systému." In *Termina 94*, ed. by Milan Žemlička 37–46. Liberec: TU v Liberci a Ústav pro jazyk český AV ČR.

Freixa, Judit. 2003. "Workshop on the Theory of Terminology: XVIIth International Congress of Linguists Prague, Czech Republic, July 28, 2003." *Terminology* 9 (2): 317–319.

Hausenblas, Karel. 1962. "K specifickým rysům odborné terminologie." In *Problémy marxistické jazykovědy*, ed. by Jaromír Bělič, and Lubomír Doležel, 248–262. Praha: Ústav pro jazyk český AV ČR.

Hausenblas, Karel. 1963. "Termíny a odborný text." *Československý terminologický časopis* 2: 7–15.

Havránek, Bohuslav. 1932. "Úkoly spisovného jazyka a jeho kultura." In *Spisovná čeština a jazyková kultura*, ed. by Bohuslav Havránek, and Miloš Weingart, 32–84. Praha: Melantrich.

Havránek, Bohuslav. 1941. "Terminologie." In *Ottův slovník naučný nové doby*, ed. by Bohumil Němec. Praha: Novina.

Horecký, Ján. 1956. *Základy slovenskej terminológie*. Bratislava: Vydavateľsvo SAV.

Horecký, Ján. 1963. "Nová etapa v koordinácii českej a slovenskej terminológie." *Československý terminologický časopis* 2: 1–7.

Jakobson, Roman et al. 1931. "Projet de terminologie phonologique standardisée." *Travaux du Cercle linguistique de Prague* 4: 309–323.

Janata, Michal. 2020. *Zrod české terminologie*. Praha: Malvern.

Jedlička, Alois. 1948. *Josef Jungmann a obrozenecká terminologie literárněvědná a linguistická*. Praha: Česká akademie věd.

Jedlička, Alois. 1960. "Ustavení Čs. terminologické komise při Čs. komitétu slavistů." *Slovo a slovesnost* 21 (2): 158–160.

Jelínek, Jaroslav, Josef V. Bečka, and Marie Těšitelová. 1961. *Frekvence slov, slovních druhů a tvarů v českém jazyce*. Praha: SPN.

Jelínek, Milan. 2001. "O potřebě verbonominálních spojení v intelektualizovaných textech vůbec a odborných zvlášť." In *Termina 2000. Sborník příspěvků z II. konference 1996 a III. konference 2000*, ed. by Milan Žemlička, 204–211. Praha: Galén.

Kageura, Kyo, Béatrice Daille, Hiroshi Nakagawa, and Lee-Feng Chien. 2004. "Recent Trends in Computational Terminology." *Terminology* 10 (1): 1–21.

Kocourek, Rostislav. 1963. *Anglická zemědělská terminologie*. Dissertation thesis.

Kocourek, Rostislav. 1965. "Termín a jeho definice." *Československý terminologický časopis* 4: 1–24.

Kocourek, Rostislav. 1989. "Définition, sémantique lexicale et théorie linguistique." *ALFA* 2: 26–50.

Kocourek, Rostislav. 1991. *La langue francaise de la technique et de la science*. Wiesbaden: Brandstetter.

Kocourek, Rostislav. 2001a. "Terminologie a odborná lingvistika na přelomu století: směry, vývoj a posun cílů." In *Termina 2000. Sborník příspěvků z II. konference 1996 a III. konference 2000*, ed. by Milan Žemlička, 12–30. Praha: Galén.

Kocourek, Rostislav. 2001b. "Terminologické anglicismy: příčiny jejich vzniku, jejich lingvistická povaha a místo v slovní zásobě." In *Termina 2000. Sborník příspěvků z II. konference 1996 a III. konference 2000*, ed. by Milan Žemlička, 196–203. Praha: Galén.

Kocourek, Rostislav. 2013. "Slovo k jazykovědnému studiu terminologie." In *Čeština v pohledu synchronním a diachronním. Stoleté kořeny Ústavu pro jazyk český*, ed. by Světla Čmejrková, Jana Hoffmannová, and Jana Klímová, s. 41–47. Praha: Karolinum.

Kopeckij, Leontin V. 1935. "O lexikálním plánu hospodářského jazyka." *Slovo a slovesnost* 1 (2): 120–122.

Kováříková, Dominika. 2017. *Kvantitativní charakteristiky termínů*. Praha: NLN.

Kováříková, Dominika, and Oleg Kovářík. 2021. *Akalex. Online application*. Praha: FF UK.

Kuchař, Jaroslav, and Miroslav Roudný. 1965. "České odborné názvosloví v uplynulém dvacetiletí." *Naše řeč* 48 (3), 133–143.

Levická, Jana. 2019. "Slovenská terminológia v kontexte jazykovo-spoločenskej situácie 60. rokov 20. storočia." In *Človek a jeho jazyk 4. Terminologické inšpirácie profesora Jána Horeckého*, ed. by Jana Levická, and Miroslav Zumrík, 23–43. Bratislava: Veda.

Machač, Jaroslav. 1964. "Odborná terminologie ve výkladovém slovníku." *Československý terminologický časopis* 3: 65–75.

Machová, Svatava. 1995. "Terminografie." In *Manuál lexikografie*, ed. by František Čermák, and Renata Blatná, 137–157. Praha: H&H.

Man, Oldřich. 1965. "Termín a kontextové vztahy." *Československý terminologický časopis* 4: 80–84.

Mathesius, Vilém et al. 1929. "Thèses présentées au Premier Congrès des philologues slaves." *Travaux du Cercle linguistique de Prague* 1: 5–29.

Ottův slovník naučný nové doby. 1930–1943. Praha: Ottovo nakladatelství/Novina.

Pětijazyčný slovník z kvantitativní lingvistiky. 1970. Ed. by Marie Těšitelová et al.. Praha: Strojírenský informační ústav.

Příruční slovník jazyka českého. 1935–1957. Praha: Státní nakladatelství.

Picht, Heribert. 2011. "The science of terminology: history and evolution." *Terminologija* 18: 6–26.

Poštolková, Běla. 1984. *Odborná a běžná slovní zásoba současné češtiny*. Praha: Academia.

Poštolková, Běla, Miroslav Roudný, and Antonín Tejnor. 1983. *O české terminologii*. Praha: Academia.

Roudný, Miroslav. 1977. "Z historie českých definic." *Slovo a slovesnost* 38 (3): 237–240.

Šafařík, Pavel Josef. 1853. *Německo-český slovník vědeckého názvosloví pro gymnasia a reálné školy*. Praha: Kalveské knihkupectví.

Slovník česko-německý Josefa Jungmanna. 1835–1839. Praha.

Slovník slovanské lingvistické terminologie. Díl I. a II.. 1977, 1979. Ed. by Alois Jedlička. Praha: Academia.

Šmilauer, Vladimír. 1951. *Zásoba slovní a význam slov*. Praha: Státní nakladatelství učebnic.

Sochor, Karel. 1955. *Příručka o českém odborném názvosloví*. Praha: Nakladatelství Československé akademie věd.

Tejnor, Antonín. 1968. "Normalizace terminologie jako součást péče o kulturu spisovného jazyka." *Slovo a slovesnost* 29 (3): 303–312.

Vachek, Josef, and Josef Dubský. 1960. *Dictionnaire de Linguistique de l'École de Prague*. Utrecht: Spectrum Editeurs.

Vachek, Josef (ed). 1964. *A Prague School Reader in Linguistics*. Bloomington: Indiana University Press.

Vachek, Josef, and Josef Dubský. 2003. *Dictionary of the Prague School of Linguistics*. Amsterdam: John Benjamins.

Vachek, Josef, and Josef Dubský. 2005. *Lingvistický slovník Pražské školy*. Praha: Karolinum.

Vlková, Věra. 1976. "Charakteristika slovní zásoby odborného stylu z hlediska kvantitativního." *Slovo a slovesnost* 37 (4): 318–328.

Vlková, Věra. 1978. "K problematice tzv. multiverbizačních spojení, zvláště v odborném stylu." *Slovo a slovesnost* 39 (2): 106–115.

"Zásady koordinácie českej a slovenskej terminológie." 1964. *Československý terminologický časopis* 3: 129–143.

CHAPTER 10

Terminology science of the Soviet Union and Russia

Tatiana Orel
University of Ottawa

This chapter describes four periods of terminology science development in the Soviet Union and Russia from the beginning of the 20th century to the beginning of the 21st century. It includes the description of major orientations and methodologies of the Soviet/Russian terminology school and analyses the work of the most prominent scholars who influenced the advancement of this science. We also present the state-of-the-art of cognitive-communicative terminology with the implementation of cognitive-onomasiological modeling reflecting the achievements of traditional terminology science and cognitive linguistics. This chapter also traces the evolution of Soviet/Russian terminology science and the transformation of its research landscape which resulted in the cognitive-communicative paradigm that has produced the interplay of methodologies for developing ontological systems based on cognition, communication, and anthropocentrism.

Keywords: terminology science, Russian terminology school, cognitive-onomasiological modeling, cognitive-communicative terminology science, cognitive terminology, theory of nomination

1. Introduction

Terminology science in the Soviet Union and Russia has been evolving for over a century. It can be considered an independent science that originated from the intersection of four major scientific disciplines encompassing numerous domains (Leitchik 2007):

1. Linguistics (theory of nomination, theory of communication, theory of text, theory of languages for specific purposes, standardisation theory, psycholinguistics, sociolinguistics, and cognitive linguistics)
2. Logics and philosophy (i.e., methodologies)

https://doi.org/10.1075/tlrp.24.10hum

3. Mathematics (informatics, classification theory, etc.);
4. Subject matter disciplines including natural, technical and social sciences (biology, physics, chemistry, medicine, etc.).

However, despite its long history and the significant contribution of Russian terminologists, its scientific achievements are not widely known among the communities of terminologists in other countries. Thus, this chapter aims to demonstrate the history of Soviet/Russian terminology science, leading to its current trends within the cognitive-communicative paradigm that has produced the interplay of methodologies for developing ontological systems for translation, applied linguistics, semantic webs, content and information management systems.

2.   Four periods in the development of Russian terminology science

There are four periods in the history of the development of the Soviet/Russian terminology school (Leitchik, Shelov 2003; Leitchik 2007; Golovin, Kobrin 1987; Tatarinov 1994; Grinev-Griniewicz 2008) spanning the past hundred or so years.

Prior to discussing the formation of the Soviet/Russian terminology school per se, it is important to acknowledge the contributions of the *preparatory period* (1780–1920), also called the *proto-scientific period* (Grinev-Griniewicz 2008). During this period the first terminological dictionaries used for translation were compiled. One of the most prominent figures of that period was Pavel Florensky, a philosopher, mathematician, theologian, and linguist. He tragically died during Stalin's repressions, and his groundbreaking manuscripts *Termin* ('The Term') (1917–1922) and *Imena* ('The Names') (1926) were published only at the end of the 20th century (Florensky 1998). According to Alekseeva (2009; 2019), his philosophical ideas about the notion of *term* were very advanced as he perceived the term as a product of thought, comprising a compressed text of science and serving as a tool of cognition (Florensky 1998). He also investigated the etymological and semasiological background of the notion *term* and introduced the concept of its systematicity (Alekseeva 2019).

During the *first period* (1930s–1960s) of the development of the Russian/Soviet school of terminology, the essential principles of terminology theory and methods were formed. The major achievements of that time are associated, first of all, with experts in the sphere of engineering, namely Lotte (1931; 1932; 1936; 1961) and Drezen (1932; 1936), who are primarily known for founding the principles of terminology standardisation and internationalisation as a means of aligning terminology with the pace of technological and industrial progress.

According to Tatarinov (1994) and Grinev-Griniewicz (2008), in 1928, D. S. Lotte began to conduct research in the sphere of scientific and technical terminology and, in 1933, he founded the Technical Terminology Committee at the Academy of Sciences of the USSR. Lotte (1931) adopted the prescriptive approach to terminology, recognised the importance of a correctly constructed terminology, and promoted research of phenomena such as synonymy, polysemy and homonymy in order to enable terminologists to eventually eliminate their "negative" products (e.g., synonyms, polysemes, and homonyms). At the same time, he recognised the value of the descriptive approach to characterise the features of existing terminologies. Lotte also focused on identifying a concept's salient features to clarify and better define it in order to position the concept in a conceptual system before proceeding with any additional terminology work. He also laid out the orientations of terminology research: formal linguistic, technical-semantic and phonetic, where not only the forms and meaning of terms were in the research focus, but also their functions.

Lotte (1932) established the following objectives in the sphere of technical terminology: collection and systematisation of terminological materials, research on the formation and development of terms in the Russian language, comparison of Russian and foreign terminologies, term creation methods, contraction of long forms, experimental research into the perception and internalisation of terms (e.g., conducting surveys among professionals in different fields), and application of research carried out abroad into the standardisation of terminology.

Lotte (1932) also created a conceptual system of the terms of terminology science, reflecting a language subsystem. For instance, *terminonositel* was introduced to denote an object and concept designated by a particular term. Another example is *terminoelement* (Lotte 1936), signifying a constituent part of a term that carries meaning.

Moreover, Lotte was the founder of Soviet/Russian theoretical terminography (1932; 1961) and created a German-Russian automotive dictionary (1936) based on onomasiological principles, which further stimulated his pursuit of a scientific definition of *translation unit*. Lotte (1961) also focused on the issues of terminological equivalence in the multilingual context of translation, the creation of new terms and the methods of registering common translation solutions in bilingual terminological dictionaries.

Meanwhile, Drezen (1932; 1936), who was a specialist in Esperanto, records management, engineering and linguistics and who published about 200 papers, also made an enormous contribution to Soviet/Russian terminology science with 18 publications devoted to terminology (Tatarinov 1994). He was also a victim of Stalin's repressions, so many of his works were not published until the end of the 20th century.

Having been influenced by the works of Wüster (1931) and Lotte (1931; 1932), Drezen supported the idea of terminology standardisation based on the principles of *proportional internationality*, meaning the development of national languages along with their preparation for an international language, for example, Esperanto. In addition, Drezen (1936) focused on term precision, indicating a full and clear definition of the concept expressed by a term as well as the relation between term precision and monosemy. He also described term requirements that were not of conceptual but rather of axiological nature, for instance, briefness, lightness, clarity, precision, discernability, simplicity, monosemy, etc. He believed that undesirable features of a terminology (e.g., synonymy, polysemy, and homonymy) could be eliminated or mitigated by rationally constructed definitions of terms.

Drezen's spectrum of interests also involved the structure of scientific and technical language and its relation to literary language, figurative language in scientific literature, borrowings, word order in term combinations, and other properties. Unfortunately, his conclusions were never synthesised into one coherent work (Tatarinov 1994).

Despite the predominantly prescriptive approach to the nature of the term, Drezen (1936) arrived at some conclusions through the gnoseological viewpoint (the role of terms in scientific knowledge and cognition), whereby he stated that it was less important to improve the form of a term than to enhance the quality of the corresponding concept by achieving clarity and precision. This can be viewed as one of the first attempts to research a term from the perspective of human thought.

At the same time, Reformatskiy (1952), Vinogradov (1947) and Vinokur (1939) introduced terminology science as a branch of general linguistics. They posed the problem of defining the notion of a term and identified the main features that distinguish terms from the words of general language. These features were monosemy, precision, briefness, and lack of ambiguity and emotionality. They also contributed to the development of the concept of terminology, its organisation as a system, term-formation principles and models, resulting in the emergence of Soviet/Russian terminology science based on engineering and linguistic approaches. Until the 1970s, there was a division in the perception of terminology science that (a) the conceptual system of a domain represented by a terminology is within the competency of a professional expert, whereas (b) the questions of terminology structure and formation relate to the competency of a linguist (Grinev-Griniewicz 2008).

An important milestone of that time was the differentiation between the notions of *nomenclature* and *terminology* as two different types of special lexical units, where nomenclature is a separate class and not a sub-type of terminology (Grinev-Griniewicz 2008: 260). Thus, Vinokur defined nomenclature as "a system of abstract and arbitrary signs" (1939: 8 — our translation).[1] Without elaborating on what these signs were, Reformatskiy (1952) and Vinokur (1939) emphasised that a nomenclature was a means of designating objects without a particular relation to the demands of theoretical thought. Consequently, a nomenclature was considered as a group of specialised names, i.e., *nomens*, connected with the designation of objects not in the act of thinking but in the act of perception and representation (Grinev-Griniewicz 2011).

However, at the same time, Akhmanova (1966: 6) distinguished a terminology as a group of specialised lexical units that served to designate general notions of a specific scientific domain, and a nomenclature as a group of specialised lexical units that served to designate individual notions, i.e., concrete objects, of this domain. Later, Grinev-Griniewicz (2008: 38) clarified the ideas of Reformatskiy (1952) and Vinokur (1939), adding that a nomenclature was an abstract system of signs in the sense that a nomen is not an expression of meaning but a label for a particular object whose signifying function is ignored. In this way, the scholars indicated the abstract nature of a nomen.

In the 1950s and 1960s, according to Leitchik and Shelov (2003), the majority of terminology studies shifted their focus from the investigation of a term and terminology as core concepts to the linguistic behavior of terms in literary texts and in the mass-media (Andreev 1965; Akhmanova 1969; Kandelaky 1977; Piotrovskiy 1952; Reformatskiy 1952). Since literary texts abound with tropes, expressive phrases, idiomatic phraseology, and overall, with stylistics, even terms, being part of this context, are "ignited stylistically" (Reformatskiy 1952: 20).

In addition, 1964 saw the creation of the All-Union Scientific Research Institute of Technical Information, Classification and Coding (a branch of Gosstandard and known as VNIIKI). This institute worked on standardising scientific and technical terminology at the state level (Felber and Budin 1989). Later, in the 1970s, it developed standardisation methodologies, standards for terminology work, and a system of terminology control as well as reference databases of terms. Since 2004, it has been known as Federalnoye Agentstvo po Tehnicheskomu Regulirovaniyu i Metrologii (the Federal Agency for Technical Regulation and Metrology (Rosstandard)) (Kazarina 2008).

Despite the significant advances in terminology science at that time, Alekseeva (1998: 11) validly points out that the theories of a term had axiomatic features and could not be considered as theories per se as they were not useful in resolving the problems associated with the controversial nature of a term expressed in synonymy, polysemy, homonymy, etc. Also, Golovin and Kobrin (1987: 28) noted that studies that were conducted in the first period of Soviet/Russian terminology

---

1. All translations in this chapter are by the author.

science were valuable and necessary for the science of language but were unable to reveal the true nature of a term. According to Tatarinov (1996), research in the field of terminology was, until the 1980s, conducted within the philological, functional-stylistic, and diachronic approaches:

> In Russia, there has long been a tradition of paying careful attention to terms, which, however, did not go beyond the scope of translation and lexicographic activities, during which compilers of specialised dictionaries and translators of scientific works treated terms as very specific words but did not attempt, as we would now say, to penetrate the theoretical essence of the term.
>
> (Tatarinov 1996: 6)

Thus, the first period is noted for the emergence and formation of the foundations of terminological theory and practice.

The *second period* (1970s–1990s) is characterised by further development of terminology theory, methodology and practice as well as by distinguishing terminology science as an independent scientific discipline with its objectives and challenges. As Grinev-Griniewicz (2008) points out, such scholars from the spheres of linguistics, logics and information science as Kondrashev (1971), Averbuh (1986), Gerd (1976), Golovin (1972), Danilenko (1976), Leitchik (1974; 1989), Superanskaya et al. (1989), Khajutin (1972), Marchyuk (1988) and others contributed significantly to the field of terminology science as a discipline by:

- developing the notions of *term, terminology,* and *nomenclature* with the establishment of the criteria related to nomens
- developing term-formation models based on the methods of linguistic statistics
- addressing challenges of terminological database automation and providing guidance for terminological editing
- elaborating methods for creating information-retrieval thesauri
- describing, structurally and semantically, specific terminology systems
- standardising scientific and technical terminology.

At that time, in Soviet/Russian linguistics, the term *terminology* had two meanings: (1) a group of words and word combinations that designate specialised or professional objects and concepts; (2) a branch of linguistics that studies groups of terms, their grammatical organisation and laws of functioning (Golovin and Kobrin 1987: 7). Thus, it was proposed to differentiate the meanings of this term by using the term *terminology* ('*terminologia*' in Russian) for the first meaning, while a new term, *terminology science*, ('*terminovedeniye*' in Russian) was introduced for the second. Leitchik (1989: 365) defined the latter as follows: "a complex scientific discipline whose subject matter is terms and their groups in the form of terminological systems and terminologies, as well as the regularities of formation, construction, functioning and use of these groups of terms".

Manerko et al. state that the separation of these two key terms can be considered a landmark for Russian terminology science since "it acquired its own methodological principles and well-established meta-language apparatus for future investigations" (2014: 17). Soon after, Khajutin (1972) published the first textbook of Soviet/Russian terminology science.

Also, during this period, a term was defined as a word associated with a particular definition and assigned consciously to a specific scientific concept (Gerd 1976: 101). In other words, terminological meanings are established through a deliberate consensus.

Significant theoretical advancements were made regarding the definition and concept of a term. It also became evident that the processes of creating new terminological units did not receive sufficient attention in the Soviet/Russian terminology school since the focus was predominantly on studying terms as ready-made units (Leitchik 1989). Golovin (1972) questioned the requirements that terms were expected to meet (conciseness, unambiguity, absence of synonymy and homonymy, precise correlation with the expressed concept, lexical systematisation, etc.). In response to this criticism, Leitchik (1989) also stated that the requirements for a term can only be met in the lexical units of artificial languages created for the purposes of information systems; hence, "terms, as lexical units of LSP (Languages for Special Purposes), endlessly strive for the 'ideal state' but never achieve it" (Leitchik 1989: 17). In addition, numerous special types of lexical units were singled out: *terminoids*, i.e., lexical units from specialised domains whose meanings and definitions are still fuzzy, i.e., not well-defined and not well-established, leading to a lack of understanding or acceptance in a professional community (Khajutin 1972); *pre-terms*, i.e., lexical units from specialised domains that are temporarily used as terms to describe new concepts but that do not satisfy term requirements (Leitchik 1985); *quasi-terms*, i.e., pre-terms that are persistently used and become well-established in a terminology; *pseudo-terms*, i.e., lexical units from specialised domains that are used for imaginary concepts (e.g., *unicorn*) (Leitchik 1981); and *prototerms*, i.e., units from the general lexicon that are used during the early stage of a discipline's development and that eventually become terms as the discipline evolves. Prototerms often remain undefined in lexicographic works and function as layperson synonyms of scientifically established terms, which are usually accompanied by definitions (Grinev 1990; Grinev-Griniewicz 2011).

The 1970s and 1980s were the most intensive years for Soviet/Russian terminology science as it was during this period that its solid theoretical grounds were established. As a result, by the late 1980s, Soviet/Russian terminology science had become a separate complex discipline with a formed scientific apparatus, thoroughly described by Leitchik (1989).

The *third period* (from the end of the 1980s to the end of the 1990s) saw further development of Russian terminology science as an independent discipline with numerous research orientations. It is characterised by the production of textbooks, reference books, and systematic dictionaries of terms (Leitchik 2007). For instance, the most influential publications that impacted the Russian terminology science of the first three periods were featured in the four-volume collected works by Tatarinov (1994; 1995; 1999; 2003).

The most prominent scholars of this period include Grinev (1990), Golovin and Kobrin (1987), Leitchik (1989), Kiyak (1989), Superanskaya et al. (1989), Melnikov (1991), Marchyuk (1992), and Tatarinov (1996). The research was related to describing individual terminology systems, national and local terminologies, structural types of terms, term formation methods, and semantic fields. Historical, comparative and terminographic terminology studies were also a focus of research interests (Grinev-Griniewicz 2008). At the same time, these years were characterised by a significant decline in terminological research in Russia due to the socio-economic crisis of the country (Leitchik 2007). However, this period witnessed renewed reflection on the orientations of terminology science that had been formed in the previous 70 years. From this reflection emerged an interrelated terminographic terminology science and a terminology theory of text (a theory of text typology comprising a term analysis of text. i.e., from term to text and a text analysis of the term. i.e., from text to term) that have various foci including comparative, onomasiological, semasiological, typological, functional, historical, and domain specific (e.g., medicine) (Grinev-Griniewicz 2008).

At the same time, Russia started to contribute to terminology science at the international level by participating in international terminology conferences. In 1993, S.V. Grinev became chair of the working group Terminology Principles of the ISO Technical Committee 37, Language and Terminology, and he and other Russian colleagues actively participated in the development of international standards related to terminology.

As a result, the Russian terminology school accumulated extensive experience in studying many aspects of scientific and technical knowledge in various domains. This facilitated the *fourth period* (2000 – present), which is characterised by new orientations in this scientific discipline, made possible thanks to past achievements in terminology science, with an innovative view on the processes of cognition and communication (Leitchik 2007). Based on semantics, lexicology, cognitive psychology and cognitive linguistics, the *onomasiological* and *cognitive-communicative schools* are considered the leading schools of this period.

Such scholars as Serebrennikov (1988), Kolshansky (1990), Ufimtseva (1968), Gak (1972), Shmelev (1973), Arutyunova (1990), Koubriakova (1978; 2004) and others laid the groundwork for *onomasiological terminology science* based on semantics and lexicology, whereas the foundations of *cognitive-communicative terminology science* are presented in the works of Leitchik (2007), Novodranova (2000; 2014), Manerko (2000; 2002; 2003; 2022), Aleekseeva (1998), Alekseeva and Mishlanova (2019), Volodina (1993; 2000), and others.

3. Research orientations and methodology in Russian terminology science

3.1 20th century

Terminology science in Russia has been developing in multiple research orientations. In the 20th century, the primary research foci were on the areas of typology, comparative analysis, lexicography, and standardisation.

The *typological orientation* is concerned with distinguishing the general and specific features of terminology systems as well as developing universal parameters and general principles of terminological organisation.

The *comparative orientation* provides a methodology for comparative analysis of terms and terminology systems from the diachronic perspective resulting in implications for the theory and practice of translating specialised texts.

The *lexicographic orientation* is related to the compilation of dictionaries enhanced with hierarchical relations between terms and concepts in terminology systems to formalise semantic text processing, create keywords for information retrieval and storage and develop computer systems for knowledge representation and machine translation. In addition to these orientations in terminology science, the problems of terminological *standardisation* and *harmonisation* are investigated (Grinev 2000: 32–33).

Since Russian terminology science has an orientation towards linguistics, linguistic methodology, including semantic, formal and functional methods, is in the foreground of its development. These methods are applied in the research at the levels of terms and terminology systems. Leitchik (2007) identifies six major semantic and formal linguistic methods used in the 20th century that contributed to the development of the orientations in the 21st century. They include:

1. The historical-descriptive method, which demonstrates the process of establishing scientific and technical terminologies. It allows us to describe the processes of term creation and, by observing how terms and their variants change, reveal how the knowledge and theoretical basis of the corresponding

domain also changed. The historical-descriptive method entails describing formal or observable characteristics of specialised concepts as well as internalised cognitive representations. For example, Gerd (1976; 2005) diachronically analysed the Russian terminology system of ichthyology by modeling, in lexico-semantic groups, folk knowledge about fish (which features both regional and typological variation) among the people of the High North of the USSR. His findings about historical tendencies in the formation, development and transformation of ichthyology terminology provided insights into the evolution of new terminology systems. His research on productive means of term formation was also applied to terminology standardisation. Later, Kutina (1995) researched the history of Russian terminology of physics, astronomy, and geography. Through both studies (Gerd 1976; Kutina 1995), the conceptual evolution of these domains is shown, in the formation of which both observable and cognitively perceived features are demonstrated.

2. The method involving componential analysis of terms and terminology systems to identify common components of meaning (semes) among their interconnected units (Grinev-Griniewicz 2008).

3. The method of the artificial semantic language of RX-codes, as developed by the Ukrainian scholars Skorohodko (1970) and Pshenichnaya (1967) for information retrieval systems. The semes from the semantic analysis of definitions can thereby be obtained, establishing semantic similarity among the terms belonging to the same terminology system. A graph can be built using the data obtained from the analysis, reflecting the structure (frame) of a terminology or terminology system. It is based on the binary description of a 'thing' (X) and 'relation' (R) (Karaulov 1981).

4. The method of definitive analysis, which is based on a logic-linguistic analysis of definitions enabling the construction of a graph. This is different from the RX-codes method because it is based not on the extraction of semes from the structure of a term, but on the juxtaposition of features of the special notions appearing in the definitions of related terms (Shelov 2003).

5. The method of distribution analysis, which is based on examining the co-occurrences of a term in texts, including the texts of definitions. It also includes the methods of cluster analysis and fuzzy sets applicable to analysis of texts in related subject areas. This method enables the construction of terminology clusters within one terminology system (Shelov 1998).

6. The method of constructing formal elements (e.g., affixes or prefixes) of lexical units or derivatives belonging to one terminology system (Koubriakova 1978).

3.2   21st century

As noted above, the most recent orientations of the fourth period of the development of the Russian terminology school are the *onomasiological* and *cognitive-communicative* orientations, which emerged within the framework of the theory of nomination (Serebrennikov and Ufimtseva 1977, Koubriakova 1986, Humbley 2007).

In the theory of nomination, which studies the nominative function of language, the semasiological and onomasiological approaches are distinguished (Serebrennikov and Ufimtseva 1977). The semasiological approach studies the meanings of lexical units and analyses their designations only from the formal perspective. In contrast, the onomasiological approach involves the study of the relationship not so much between the object and its designation but between the meaning (concept) and the means of its expression. This relationship is particularly evident in the process of forming a new designation as a new linguistic sign from already existing language elements (Koubriakova 1986).

The onomasiological approach is associated with "clarifying how conceptual forms of thinking relate to each other, how designations are created, established, and distributed among different fragments of objective reality" (Volodina 1993: 10). According to Manerko, studying nomination in this context "...leads to a better understanding of how a person perceives, categorises and conceptualises various items of spatial, social and emotional experience..." (2004: 7).

Thus, the *onomasiological orientation* contributes to views on term formation as a specific naming process that results from cognitive processes and the mental experience of an individual. Based on the theory and methodology of onomasiology, onomasiological terminology science was born as the study of the nomination of specific concepts and of term formation. According to this principle, analysing existing forms of terms enables the most productive means and models of term formation to be established, which facilitates the development of term formation guidelines (Grinev-Griniewicz 2008).

Moreover, Koubriakova (2004) stated that the formation of derivatives (new words formed from another word or root) is based on the word-formation models having lexical and categorial foundations; thus, a derivative is a means of naming a new conceptual structure or "a quantum of knowledge" in order to make such a structure accessible to other people in the act of communication and the transmission knowledge.

A word formed by derivation is a compact form of a sign used for communication. Hence, cognition and communication determine how knowledge is "packed" in a derivative because knowledge structures behind each element of a derivation model are integrated into a unified structure of semantic information for the entire complex.

One of the most important advances in the onomasiological orientation can be considered *cognitive-onomasiological modeling*, as introduced by Manerko (2000). Cognitive-onomasiological modeling records the knowledge structures that are mental representations of human knowledge and experience, taking into account the value-oriented (pragmatic) logic that supports the created linguistic unit in speech (Manerko 2002: 97).

The relation between an object, a process or attribute, and predication, is considered a milestone in the advancement of onomasiology within Russian terminology science. These three entities determine word formation (Koubriakova 1986, 2004; Pozdnyakova 1999; Zabotkina 1991) and phrase formation (Manerko 2000, 2019$_{1,2}$, Drozdova 2003, Shevchuk 1985). This relation enabled the description of the nomination act with the help of specific linguistic models reflecting the transition from the concept of a designated object to its designation.

Thus, the study of any nominative unit (a derivative, compound word or word combination) is focused on three semantic components, connected with each other and placed in the deep structure of a name, the *onomasiological base*, *mark* and the connecting *predicate* (Koubriakova 2004, Pozdnyakova 1999, Manerko 2000). At the onomasiological level, one of the smallest units of meaning recognised in the semantic analysis is the *seme* (a constituent of the semantic structure of the linguistic sign). A seme functions either as an *onomasiological base* and denotes the class, gender, species, etc., to which the object belongs, or as an *onomasiological mark* that specifies the base. Moreover, semes are connected by the *onomasiological connective* (predicate) which represents the logical semantic relations between the onomasiological base and the onomasiological mark. Thus, the onomasiological model of any complex formation (a derivative, a compound lexical unit or a phrase) represents three interconnected semantic constants forming the conceptual structure, called a *proposition*, that is embedded in the deep structure of the designation and represents the conceptual basis of the process of naming. The *propositional relation* is the semantic relation between a lexical unit (e.g., derivative, compound, word combination) and the concept behind it.

For example, in the ThirdPlaceLearning (TPL) theory of intercultural communication (Orel et al. 2014, Alagic et al. 2016), the term *aligning* relates to the *process* of regulating a somatic-emotional state that is *used for* the *operation* of achieving a desirable state that is in turn conducive to productive communication. The onomasiological structure for the term *aligning* consists of the infinitive, *to align*, an instance of the OPERATION (onomasiological mark) concept; the suffix *-ing*, an instance of the concept PROCESS (onomasiological base); and the predicate BE USED FOR (onomasiological connective). They map the propositional relation [PROCESS — BE USED FOR — OPERATION].

The propositional structure is the most frequent type of conceptual organisation of knowledge, and it "denotes a particular operational structure of consciousness and/or a certain unit of knowledge stored in the human mind" (Koubriakova et al. 1996:137). Thus, humans utilise ready-made and developed knowledge structures to describe new knowledge (Koubriakova 2004).

Consequently, the study of knowledge representations of the propositional type is based on the cognitive-onomasiological modeling of complex nominative units. To understand the conceptual sphere of any discipline, it is essential to construct all its propositional relations because they will indicate what conceptual structures are stored in human memory based on interactions with the world and influences of scientific-technical knowledge. In this process of cognitive-onomasiological modeling, the concepts are logically represented, and they indicate fixed associations that are repeated within the whole terminology system. The predicates are constructed on the basis of meanings of lexical units and their definitions registered in glossaries, thesauri and contexts.

Thus, cognitive-onomasiological analysis sheds light on the regularities of a linguistic unit's usage in speech and written text since, in the process of nomination, the semantic and semiotic functions of language units are formed to reflect the elements of reality in speech acts.

As a result, cognitive-onomasiological modeling has dramatically influenced modern terminology science in Russia, which is now characterised by the paradigmatic shift towards the *cognitive-communicative* orientation (Novodranova 2000, 2014; Manerko 2014, 2016, 2019[1,2], 2022; Drozdova 2003; Alekseeva 1998; Alekseeva and Mishlanova 2019). That orientation aims to describe term semantics and terminology systems from the cognitive and functional perspectives, including cognition, cognitive processing, and communication processes. Accordingly, *cognitive-communicative terminology science* is based on the anthropocentric principle (Koubriakova 2004, Manerko 2000, Boldirev 2000, Novodranova 2000), which considers "different spheres of human knowledge in dynamic mental processes accompanying special communication" (Manerko 2019[1]:48).

This perspective has transformed Russian studies in terminology science by uncovering the cognitive mechanisms of knowledge processing in the minds of communication participants and by exploring the functional aspects of language use. The goal is to examine how social and cultural aspects of specialised discourse and human thinking influence communication by researching terms (Manerko 2019[1]). The main object of the research in cognitive-communicative terminology science is lexical units from specialised domains — i.e., terms as the most informative language units.

Thus, cognitive-communicative terminology science focuses on the general and scientific knowledge structures of an individual, which are reflected in numerous elements of mental constructs and communicated in professional discourse. In the cognitive-communicative orientation of terminology science in Russia, linguistic systems and their elements are not investigated separately but in the historical, social, cultural, physical and sensory contexts discovered through linguistic features (Manerko 2019₁,₂:2022). Moreover, these linguistic systems (in the form of terms) reflect the dynamic nature of background knowledge structures that results from the evolving nature of scientific activity (Novodranova 2000). Such a conceptual system is dynamic, reflecting changes in human life and society, and can change its form according to pragmatic purposes (Orel 2007).

The *methods* of terminology science in the cognitive-communicative paradigm combine the traditional methodologies accumulated previously by the Russian terminology school with multiple elements borrowed from the achievements of cognitive linguistics and cognitive science abroad. One of the methods includes analysing the *term definition* and possibly its *etymology* to identify its position in the hierarchical organisation of concepts belonging to a specific sphere of knowledge and to determine various aspects of human experience, for example, in the sensory, social or physical spheres.

The representatives of the Russian cognitive-communicative terminology science believe that in the description of terminology systems, various cognitive mechanisms influencing the formation of an entire conceptual system should be considered. A conceptual system is at the foundation of language representations reflected in the consciousness of an individual. Thus, *conceptualisation* and *categorisation* provide an opportunity to observe how an individual perceives their environment and what knowledge structures participate in the formation of linguistic representations. The conceptualisation process is aimed at distinguishing minimal informative units of human experience.

The categorisation process is directed at including similar units into larger groups — categories (Boldirev 2000). A category is always formed in relation to a particular knowledge sphere, whereas concepts organise into categories that are formed as knowledge structures in the interaction between humans and the world. For instance, within the most representative category of Artifacts of the English telecommunications terminology, the most productive onomasiological models, consisting of the concept 'Thing,' are [THING — BE USED FOR — OPERATION] and [THING — BE OF — TYPE (KIND)]. These models, reflecting the primary relationships between concepts, are used to define a device in terms of its function or describe its type (Orel 2007; Alagic et al. 2016).

Categories reflect the most common and essential features and relations representing reality phenomena based on human thought processes. The categorial analysis of nominative terminological units that are predominant in terminology systems and their distribution according to semantic categories helps to reveal the connections between a surface representation of a language and what is hidden from our observation, what remains in the depths of consciousness of an individual.

The categorial analysis of terminology reveals the fuzziness of categorial borders, their flexible structure and also the interaction of terms with each other. The fuzziness of categorial borders can be explained by the openness of classes and the dynamics of general and scientific knowledge and perceptions of humans in their interaction with the world (Orel 2007; 2008).

Following the method of analysing terminological definitions to construct a conceptual system of a specialised domain based on the principles of categorisation and conceptualisation, the next method refers to the previously discussed *onomasiological analysis* and *cognitive-onomasiological modeling*. It is used to describe nomination characteristics of terms, i.e., structural and semantic features, and their propositional relationships. As a result, cognitive-onomasiological modeling involves investigating the main relations among concepts and their prototypical propositional models in relation to a knowledge domain and as reflected in its terminology. This method also includes the analysis of the phenomena related to image schemas (Johnson 1987, Orel 2008, Manerko 2019[1]), conceptual metonymy and metaphor (Lakoff 1987; Johnson 1987, 1993; Alekseeva and Mishlanova 2019).

Image schemas can be described as non-propositional mental constructs, i.e., coherent gestalt-structures, reflecting part of human experience and cognition at the levels of perception, representation and organisation of events. Lakoff (1987) asserts that image schemas structure our experience pre-conceptually and also structure the concepts themselves. So, image schemas have two functions: they are concepts that possess their own directly comprehensible structure, and they are also used metaphorically for structuring complex concepts (Lakoff 1987).

Finally, these conceptual structures (categories, concepts, propositional models, image schemas, conceptual metonyms and conceptual metaphors) create the foundation for the final method of cognitive-communicative analysis — frame construction. *Frame analysis* (see also Chapter 13) reflects the process of recording, transmitting, receiving, and storing information. Accordingly, it includes the whole "package" of knowledge about a particular sphere of human activity. The term *frame* was first used by Minsky (1977) as a paradigm to understand visual reasoning and natural language processing. According to Fillmore (1977), a frame is an abstraction or an "idealisation" of an individually construable form of mental representation encompassing one's experience, knowledge, perception, etc. Incorporation of knowledge about a fragment of real life into a frame involves encoding information about it (participants, their behavior, etc.). In other words, a frame is a unified knowledge structure or specific schematisation of experience that provides a conceptual basis for a significant lexical corpus (Orel et al. 2014). Research of the knowledge organisation of any sphere of human activity through frame analysis is an effective way to study terminology systems, where a frame is a structural unit that helps us visualise the integration of concepts into an actual communicative situation. The frame of a knowledge sphere can perform three functions: (1) reflect the structure of a knowledge sphere, (2) result in knowledge sphere cognition, and (3) record knowledge in the human mind (mental representation) (Orel et al. 2014). Frame analysis facilitates examining a language as a mental formation generated by human thought and as an essential system of human knowledge representation. As a result, the frame's structure is a large, multi-component concept, representing "a package" of information.

Today many researchers from the Russian school of terminology science examine terminology systems within the cognitive-communicative paradigm to investigate the mechanisms of human mental processes and language activity in our interaction with the world. The most recent achievements of the Russian terminology school in developing the cognitive-communicative approach were published in *Terminology Science in Russia Today: From the Past to the Future* (Manerko et al. 2014).

The cognitive-communicative approach helps us conceptualise the connections between phenomena that exist in the symbolic representation of language and phenomena that are hidden from our observation deep within the human consciousness. This approach enables us to advance our understanding of the processes and mechanisms of human cognition.

4.   Conclusion

Developing in four stages over a period of more than a century, the Soviet/Russian terminology school continues to evolve, adapting to societal and technological changes. Like any other science, it has undergone a shift in its scientific paradigms that reflect the transition from a simple description and recording of empirical observations to explaining the processes of cognition and communication reflected in complex language phenomena. As a result, the shift in the scientific paradigms of Soviet/Russian terminology science has facilitated the development of new principles and methodologies, reflecting changes in the theoretical complexity of this scientific domain.

Thus, Soviet/Russian terminology science has moved beyond systematically describing terms as linguistic phenomena. The cognitive-communicative approach has enabled researchers to focus on explaining term formation principles and terminology systems within an anthropocentric framework, considering the discursive dynamism and extra-linguistic contexts with both common and specialised kinds of knowledge structures involved. The methodological variability of this cognitive-communicative terminology science contributes to the development of cognitive models of different mental mechanisms involved in professional communication. As a result, the interplay of methods from the traditional and cognitive-communication orientations of terminology science has enormous potential to provide new insights not only about the nature of terms and terminology systems but also about the construction of ontological systems required for knowledge engineering and information management. Moreover, the methods of cognitive-communicative terminology science enable us to identify discrepancies between the linguistic and conceptual realms of terminology and also to unify these two planes in an ontological system that can be used in designing multilingual databases, semantic webs, and content and information management systems. Consequently, the evolution of Soviet/Russian terminology science and the transformation of its research landscape resulting in the cognitive-communicative paradigm has produced the interplay of methodologies for developing ontological systems based on cognition, communication, and anthropocentrism.

References

Akhmanova, O.S.: Ахманова, О.С. 1966. *Словарь Лингвистических Терминов*. Москва: Советская энциклопедия.

Akhmanova, O.S.: Ахманова, О.С. 1969. *Синтаксис как Диалектическое Единство Коллигации и Коллокации*. 79–83. М.

Alagic, M., T. Orel, and G.M. Rimmington. 2016. "Toward dynamic representations of ThirdPlaceLearning." *Term Bases and Linguistic Linked Open Data: Terminology and Knowledge Engineering* 2015: 179–188. Copenhagen: CBS.

Alekseeva, L.M.: Алексеева, Л.М. 1998. *Проблемы Термина и Терминообразования: Учеб. Пособие по Спецкурсу*. Пермь: Перм. ун-т.

Alekseeva, L.M. 2009. "Interaction of terminology and philosophy." *Categorization and Conceptualization in Languages for Special Purposes and Professional Discourse Studies*: 40–46. Moscow: Ryazan.

Alekseeva, L.M.: Алексеева, Л.М. 2019. "Языковое провидение П.А. Флоренского." *Philological Studies*, 5: 82–86.

Alekseeva, L.M., and S.L. Mishlanova. 2019. "Metaphor from the Derivational Perspective." *Fachsprache. Journal of Professional and Scientific Communication Special Issue*: 3–21.

Andreev, N.D.: Андреев, Н.Д. 1965. "Методы статистико-комбинаторного анализа в действии и в перспективе." *Статистико-Комбинаторное Моделирование Языков*: 5–20. М.-Л.

Arutyunova, N.D.: Арутюнова, Н.Д. 1990. "Метафора и дискурс." *Теория Метафоры*: 5–32. М.

Averbuh, K.Y.: Авербух, К.Я. 1986. "Терминологическая вариативность: теоретический и прикладной аспекты." *ВЯ* 6: 38–49.

Boldirev, N.N.: Болдырев, Н.Н. 2000. *Когнитивная Семантика: Курс Лекций по Английской Филологии*. Тамбов: Изд-во Тамб. ун-та.

Danilenko, V.P.: Даниленко, В.П. 1976. "О месте научной терминологии в лексической системе языка." *ВЯ* 4: 64–71. М.

Drezen, E.K.: Дрезен, Э.К. 1932. Нормализация технического языка при капитализме и социализме. *Международный язык*, 7–8, 11–12.

Drezen, E.K.: Дрезен, Э.К. 1936. *Научно-Технические Термины и Обозначения и их Стандартизация*. М.: Стандартгиз.

Drozdova, T.V.: Дроздова, Т.В. 2003. *Научный Текст и Проблемы его Понимания (На Материале Англоязычных Экономических Текстов)*. Автореферат. Диссертации доктора филол. наук. М.: Институт языкознания РАН.

Felber, H., and G. Budin. 1989. *Terminologie in Theorie und Praxis*. Verlag: Gunter Narr; Tübingen.

Fillmore, Ch. J. 1977. "Topics in Lexical Semantics." In *Current Issues in Linguistic Theory*, ed. by R. Cole, 76–138. Bloomington: Indiana University Press.

Florensky, P.A.: Флоренский, П.А. 1998. *Имена*. Москва.

Gak, V.G.: Гак, В.Г. 1972. "К проблеме соотношения языка и действительности." *ВЯ* 5: 12–23.

Gerd, A.S.: Герд, А.С. 1976. "Терминологическое Значение и Типы Терминологических Значений." *Проблематика Определений Терминов в Словарях Разных Типов*: 101–107. Ленинград.

Gerd, A.S.: Герд, А.С. 2005. *Прикладная Лингвистика*. Санкт-Петербург: Издательство СПб. университета.

Golovin, V.N.: Головин, Б.Н. 1972. "О некоторых проблемах изучения терминов." *Вестник МГУ. Филология* 5: 49–59.

Golovin, B.N., and R.Y. Kobrin: Головин, Б.Н., Кобрин, Р.Ю. 1987. *Лингвистические Основы Учения о Терминах: Учеб. Пос. для Филол. Спец. Вузов*. М.: Высшая Школа.

Grinev, S.V.: Гринев, С.В. 1990. "Терминография: проблемы и перспективы." *Теория и Практика Научно-Технической Лексикографии и Перевода: Межвуз. Сб. Горький*: 17–23. Горьк. ун-т.

Grinev, S.V.: Гринев, С.В. 2000. "Терминоведение на пороге третьего тысячелетия." *Научно-Техническая Терминология (Научно-Реферативный Сборник)* 1: 31–34. М: ВНИИКИ.

Grinev-Griniewicz, S.V.: Гринев-Гриневич, С.В. 2008. *Терминоведение: Учебное Пособие для Студентов Высших Учебных Заведений*. Москва: Издательский центр «Академия».

Grinev-Griniewicz, S. 2011. "Terminological Methods in the History of Terminology Science." *Terminologija*: 27–42.

Humbley, J. 2007. "La nomination : présentation." *Neologica*: 13–17. Édition Garnier.

Johnson, M. 1987. *The Body in the Mind: The Bodily Basis of Meaning, Imagination, and Reason*. Chicago: University of Chicago Press.

Johnson, M. 1993. "Why Cognitive Semantics Matters to Philosophy." *Cognitive Linguistics* 4 (1): 62–74.

Kandelaky, T.L.: Канделаки, Т.Л. 1977. *Семантика и Мотивированность Терминов*. М.: Наука.

Karaulov, Y.N.: Караулов, Ю.Н. 1981. *Лингвистическое Конструирование и Тезаурус Литературного Языка*. Москва: Наука.

Kazarina, S.G.: Казарина, С.Г. 2008. "Стандартизационные процессы в терминологии." *Языковедение*, 4: 48–50.

Khajutin, A.D.: Хаютин, А.Д. 1972. *Термин, Терминология, Номенклатура: Учеб. пос.* Самарканд: Самарканд. гос. ун-т им. А. Навои.

Kiyak, T.R.: Кияк, Т.Р. 1989. *Лингвистические Аспекты Терминоведения: Уч. Пос.* Киев: Уч.-метод. кабинет по высш. обр. при Минвузе УССР.

Kolshansky, G.V.: Колшанский, Г.В. 1990. *Объективная Картина Мира в Познании и Языке*. М: Наука.

Koubriakova, E.S.: Кубрякова, Е.С. 1978. *Части Речи в Ономасиологическом Освещении*. Москва: Наука

Koubriakova, E.S.: Кубрякова, Е.С. 1986. *Номинативный Аспект Речевой Деятельности*. М.: Наука.

Koubriakova, E.S.: Кубрякова, Е.С. 2004. *Язык и Знание. На Пути Получения Знаний о Языке. Части Речи с Когнитивной Точки Зрения. Роль Языка в Познании Мира*. Москва: Языки славянской культуры.

Koubriakova, E.S., V.Z. Demyankov, Y.G. Pankratz, and L.G. Luzina: Кубрякова, Е.С. Демьянков, В.З., Панкрац, Ю.Г., Лузина, Л.Г. 1996. *Краткий Словарь Когнитивных Терминов*. Москва: Издательство МГУ.

Kutina, L.L.: Кутина, Л.Л. 1995. "Формирование Терминологии Физики в России (1966)." In *История Отечественного Терминоведения: Направления и Методы Терминологических Исследований (Очерк и Хрестоматия)* 2 (1), ed. by В.А. Татаринов. Москва: Московский Лицей.

Lakoff, G. 1987. *Women, Fire and Dangerous Things: What Categories Reveal about the Mind*. Chicago: The University of Chicago Press.

Leitchik, V.M.: Лейчик, В.М. 1974. "Номенклатура – промежуточное звено между терминами и собственными именами." *Вопросы Терминологии и Лингвистической Статистики*: 13-24. Воронеж.

Leitchik, V.M.: Лейчик, В.М. 1981. "Некоторые вопросы упорядочения стандартизации и использования научно-технической терминологии." *Термин и Слово*: 121–128. Горький.

Leitchik, V.M.: Лейчик, В.М. 1985. *Словник Терминов Терминоведения*. Москва.

Leitchik, V.M.: Лейчик, В.М. 1989. *Предмет, Методы и Структура Терминоведения*. Диссертация доктора филол. наук. М.: ИЯ АН СССР.

Leitchik, V.M., and S.D. Shelov. 2003. "Terminology: Where is Russian Science Today?" In *LSP & Professional Communication* 3: 82–109. DSFF / LSP Centre.

Leitchik, V. M.: Лейчик, В.М. 2007. Когнитивное терминоведение — пятый этап развития терминоведения как ведущей научной дисциплины рубежа XX-XXI веков. *Когнитивная Лингвистика: Новые Проблемы Познания*: сб. науч. тр. / под ред. Л.А. Манерко, 121–132. Институт языкознания РАН; Ряз. гос. ун-т имени С.А. Есенина. М.: Рязань.

Lotte, D. S.: Лотте, Д.С. 1931. Очередные задачи технической терминологии. Изв. АН СССР. Сер. VII, Отд-ие общ. наук, 7: 883–891. Ленинград.

Lotte, D. S.: Лотте, Д.С. 1932. Упорядочение технической терминологии. *Социалистическая Реконструкция и Наука*, 3: 139–140.

Lotte, D. S.: Лотте, Д.С. 1936. *Немецко-Русский Автомобильный Словарь*. Москва, Ленинград.

Lotte, D. S.: Лотте, Д.С. 1961. *Основы Построения Научно-Технической Терминологии*. Под ред. акад. И.И. Артоболевского. М.: Изд-во АН СССР.

Manerko, L. A.: Манерко, Л.А. 2000. *Язык Современной Техники: Ядро и Периферия: Монография*. Рязань: Изд-во РГПУ им. С.А. Есенина.

Manerko, L. A.: Манерко, Л.А. 2002. Когнитивно-дискурсивный аспект исследования номинативных единиц в современном английском языке. *Когнитивная Парадигма: Фреймовая Семантика и Номинация*. Межвуз. сб. науч. Статей 1: 97–111. Пятигорск: Изд-во ПГЛУ.

Manerko, L. A.: Манерко, Л.А. 2003[1]. "Истоки и основания когнитивно-коммуникативного терминоведения." *Лексикология. Терминоведение*. Стилистика: 120–126. Сб. науч. трудов. Москва-Рязань.

Manerko, L. A. 2004. "Nominative Units in Scientific English." *Terminology Science and Research* 15: 7–16.

Manerko, L. A., Klaus-Dieter Baumann, and Hartwig Kalverkamper (eds). 2014. *Terminology Science in Russian Today: From the Past to the Future*. Berlin: Frank & Timme.

Manerko, L. A. 2016. "Towards Understanding of Conceptualisation in Cognitive Terminology." *The Journal of University of SS Cyril and Methodius in Trnava*, 1(2): 129–170. Warsaw: De Gruyter Open.

Manerko, Larissa. 2019[1]. "Knowledge Structures and Ways of Their Description in Cognitive Terminology Research." *Terminologija (Vilnius)* 26: 47–72.

Manerko, Larissa. 2019[2]. "From Academic Discourse to the Construal of Scientific Cognition and Knowledge Structures." In *Specialized Discourses and Their Readerships*, ed. by David Banks, and Emilia Di Martino, 69–88. Singapore: Springer.

Manerko, Larissa. 2022. "Focusing on Cognitive and Communicative Perspective in Specialized Knowledge modelling methodology." In *Specialized Knowledge Mediation: Ontological and Metaphorical Modelling*, ed. by Ekaterina Isaeva, 3–39. Cham: Springer International Publishing.

Marchyuk, Y. N.: Марчук, Ю.Н. 1988. *Машинный Перевод как Информационная и Технологическая Реальность*. Москва.

Marchyuk, Y. N.: Марчук, Ю.Н. 1992. *Основы Терминографии*. Москва.

Melnikov, G. P.: Мельников, Г.П. 1991. *Основы Терминоведения: Учеб. Пос.* М.: Изд-во УДН.

Minsky, M. 1977. "Frame Theory." In *Thinking: Readings in Cognitive Science*, ed. by P. N. Johnson-Laird, and P. C. Wason, 355–376. Cambridge: Cambridge University Press.

Novodranova, V. F.: Новодранова, В.Ф. 2000. "Когнитивные науки и терминология." *Научно-Техническая Терминология* 2: 68–69.

Novodranova, V. 2014. "Cognitive Terminology is 10 Years Old." In *Terminology Science in Russia Today: From the Past to the Future*, ed. by L. Manerko, K-D. Baumann, and H. Kalverkämper, 99–108. Forum für Fachsprachen Forchung. Berlin: Frank & Timme.

Orel, T. 2007. "Terminology Analysis by Means of Frame Construction." *XVI European Symposium on Language for Special Purposes (LSP) "Specialized Language in Global Communication"*: 119–121. Hamburg: University of Hamburg.

Orel, T. 2008. "The Method of Terminology Description by Means of Image Schemas." *Cognitive Linguistics: New Issues of Cognition*. The Institute of Linguistics of the Russian Academy of Sciences and Ryazan State University. Moscow, Ryazan.

Orel, T., M. Alagic, and G. M. Rimmington. 2014. "Concept System Analysis of the ThirdPlaceLearning Theory." *Terminology and Knowledge Engineering* 2014. Berlin.

Piotrovskiy, R. G.: Пиотровский, Р.Г. 1952. "К вопросу об изучении термина." *Вопросы Грамматического Строя и Словарного Состава Языка*, 18 (2): 21–36.

Pozdnyakova, E. M.: Позднякова, Е.М. 1999. *Словообразовательная Категория Имен Деятеля в Английском Языке (Когнитивный Аспект Исследования): Монография*. Тамбов: Изд-во ТГУ им. Г.Р. Державина.

Pshenichnaya, L. E.: Пшеничная, Л.Э. 1967. "Представление значения термина в информационнно-поисковой системе Института кибернетики АН УССР." *НТИ* 2(8).

Reformatskiy, A. A.: Реформатский, А.А. 1952. "Лингвистические Вопросы Перевода." *Иностранные Языки в Школе*, 6: 20–45.

Serebrennikov, V. A.: Серебренников, Б.А. (ed). 1988. *Роль Человеческого Фактора в Языке. Язык и Картина Мира*. М: Наука.

Serebrennikov, V. A., and A. A. Ufimtseva: Серебренников, Б.А. и Уфимцева, А.А. 1977. *Языковая Номинация (Виды Наименований)*. Москва, Наука.

Shelov, S. D.: Шелов, С.Д. 1998. *Определение Терминов и Понятийная Структура Терминологии*. Санкт-Петербург: Издательство СПб. университета.

Shelov, S. D.: Шелов, С.Д. 2003. *Термин. Терминологичность. Терминологические Определения*. Санкт-Петербург: Издательство СПб. университета.

Shevchuk, V. N.: Шевчук, В.Н. 1985. *Военно-Терминологическая Система в Статике и Динамике*. Автореферат диссертации доктора филол. наук. М.: Ин-т языкознания АН СССР.

Shmelev, D. N.: Шмелев, Д.Н. 1973. *Проблемы Семантического Анализа Лексики (На Материале Русского Языка)*. М.: Наука.

Skorohodko, E. F.: Скороходько, Е.Ф. 1970. *Лінгвістічні Основи Автоматизації Информаційного Пошуку*. Київ.

Superanskaya, A. V., N. V. Podolskaya and N. V. Vasiljeva: Суперанская, А.В., Подольская, Н.В., Васильева, Н.В. 1989. *Общая Терминология: Вопросы Теории*. М.: Наука.

Tatarinov, V. A.: Татаринов, В.А. 1994. *История Отечественного Терминоведения: Классики Терминоведения (Очерк и Хрестоматия)*. Москва: Московский Лицей.

Tatarinov, V.A.: Татаринов, В.А. 1995. *История Отечественного Терминоведения: Направления и Методы Терминологических Исследований (Очерк и Хрестоматия)* 2 (1). Москва: Московский Лицей.

Tatarinov, V.A.: Татаринов, В.А. 1996. Исторические и Теоретические Основания Терминоведения Как Отрасли Отечественного Языкознания. Диссертация доктора филол. наук. Москва.

Tatarinov, V.A.: Татаринов, В.А. 1999. *История Отечественного Терминоведения: Направления и Методы Терминологических Исследований (Очерк и Хрестоматия)* 2 (2). Москва: Московский Лицей.

Tatarinov, V.A.: Татаринов, В.А. 2003. *История Отечественного Терминоведения: Аспекты и Отрасли Терминологических Исследований (1973–1993) (Хрестоматия)* 3. Москва: Московский Лицей.

Ufimtseva, A.A.: Уфимцева, А.А. 1968. *Слово в Лексико-Семантической Системе Языка.* М.: Наука.

Vinogradov, V.V.: Виноградов, В.В. 1947. *Русский Язык: Грамматическое Учение о Слове.* М.: Учпедгиз.

Vinokur, G.O.: Винокур, Г.О. 1939. "О некоторых явлениях словообразования в русской технической терминологии." *Труды Московского Института Истории, Философии и Литературы: Сборник Статей по Языковедению*: 3–54. Москва.

Volodina, M.N.: Володина, М.Н. 1993. *Национальное и Интернациональное в Процессе Терминологической Номинации.* М.: Изд-во МГУ.

Volodina, M.N.: Володина, М.Н. 2000. *Когнитивно-Информационная Природа Термина (На Материале Терминологии Средств Массовой Информации).* М.: Изд-во МГУ.

Wüster, E. 1931. *Internationale Sprachnormung in der Technik Besonders in der Elektrotechnik.* VDI Verlag.

Zabotkina, V.I.: Заботкина, В.И. 1991. *Семантика и Прагматика Нового Слова (На Материале Английского Языка).* Автореферат доктора филол. наук. М.

CHAPTER 11

Socioterminology and Textual terminology

From texts to uses of terms

Anne Condamines, Valérie Delavigne, François Gaudin
& Aurélie Picton
University of Toulouse Jean-Jaurès | Sorbonne Nouvelle University |
University of Rouen | University of Geneva

This chapter describes a part of the history of terminology, through the
narrative of the emergence of two schools of thought in France:
Socioterminology and Textual terminology. The authors of this chapter
make no claim to represent French terminology *per se*. They seek to reflect
on how terminology as a discipline has evolved in France. After
contextualising the birth of these two theoretical approaches, the authors
discuss their similarities and differences. This "comparative profile"
highlights the proximity of the theoretical and methodological positions of
Socioterminology and Textual terminology. The last section summarises
these positions and offers reflections on the future of these two approaches,
as well as on the future of terminology itself as a discipline.

Keywords: Socioterminology, Textual terminology, corpora, specialised
discourse, applied linguistics

1. Introduction

The aim of this chapter is to outline the near concomitant emergence in France of
two terminological approaches, Socioterminology at the end of the 1980s, and Textual terminology at the beginning of the 1990s, and to demonstrate how theoretically and methodologically close they are.[1] The beginnings of Socioterminology
stem from an epistemologically critical position regarding a theory of terminology which, oriented towards translation and standardisation (see Chapter 17 for
a glimpse on the history of standardisation), formulated the idealist dream of an

---

1. We refer interested readers to Condamines and Picton (2022) and Gaudin and Delavigne
(2022), which detail the theoretical foundations of the two approaches discussed in this chapter.

https://doi.org/10.1075/tlrp.24.11con

unambiguous language, fixed in its uses, which devalued the description of actual usage in the multiplicity of real interactions (Gambier 1987, Gaudin 1989). Textual terminology adopts an equivalent position and, in its early days, very quickly tackled the terminology needs within companies by associating with automatic language processing (Bourigault and Slodzian 1999).

The objective here is not to trace an exhaustive and representative history of terminology in France or elsewhere, but rather, to share experiences, views, and reflections of researchers on the evolution of these two approaches (see for instance Chapter 21 for a view on the evolution of the official framework of terminology in France). It is obvious that the development of Socioterminology and Textual terminology is part of the global evolution of a discipline that has become critically important and involves many researchers and key trends all over the world. To begin with, a history of the beginnings of each of these trends is traced in this chapter. The historical contexts in which Socioterminology, in the late 1980s, and Textual terminology, in the early 1990s, emerged are described. The second part synthesises the main theoretical foundations upon which these two trends have been built. Finally, the conclusion offers a cross-perspective of Socioterminology and Textual terminology and a reflection on what connects and distinguishes them. These elements contribute to opening up the discussion on the theoretical evolution of terminology and possible future perspectives.

2.   Historical background

2.1   Socioterminology

Since the 1980s and 1990s, work initiated in Quebec in response to the needs of its language policies has called into question certain terminological practices and theoretical presuppositions (Martin 1993, Rey 1988) (see also Chapter 12). Issue 157 of *Langages*, published in 2005, reported on these various developments (Depecker 2005). In this context, Socioterminology and Textual terminology are both part of a movement that has seen the development, in linguistics, of corpus-based approaches to describe actual discourse and recognise the diversity of discourse communities.

Socioterminology developed in the 1990s at the University of Rouen, which was active in sociolinguistics. It was while working with a German partner on a bilingual computerised dictionary of bioindustry terms, Biolex, that Louis Guespin and François Gaudin became interested in terminological theory, which at that time centred on the work of Eugen Wüster. The documentary and standardisation practices which characterised terminology at the time proved inapplicable in the interdisciplinary field of the bioindustries (Gaudin et al. 2017). The texts of the corpus used, which involved negotiating emerging terms between experts of different domains and regulating meanings, were described by Guespin as interface discourse. At the time, Rouen was a major centre for sociolinguistics, headed by Marcellesi. Co-author with Gardin of a reference handbook of sociolinguistics (1974), he and Guespin put forward the concept of glottopolitics (Guespin and Marcellesi 1986), which would turn out to be important for terminology in the language planning context. Gardin also headed a pioneering workgroup known as Language and Work (Borzeix and Fraenkel 2001), which influenced and finally incorporated sociolinguistic work in terminology (Gardin et al. 1994).

This team of scholars and researchers had studied under Jean Dubois (1920–2015) and Louis Guilbert (1912–1977), both linguists and lexicographers and the latter also well-versed in terminology (Guilbert 1973). They gave a distinctly sociolinguistic orientation at the scientific level and a materialist one at the philosophical level, to what was later to be called *Socioterminology*, and even sometimes the *Rouen School*. The dissertations and theses that were later defended at this university were clearly influenced by these orientations (Humbley 2018).

The term *Socioterminology* appeared at the beginning of the 1980s in texts by Jean-Claude Boulanger (1981) from Canada, Pierre Lerat (1984) from France, and Monique Slodzian (1986) from the former USSR. In a paper presented in 1986 at the Colloquium on Fertilisation in Romance Languages, Yves Gambier (1987) contributed further to its principles. A specialist in interactional linguistics, Gambier moved to Finland after defending a thesis at the University of Rouen, shortly before terminology became the focus of the team with which he had worked for a year. The impetus was there. The various studies that followed focused on language practices, usage mechanisms and the dynamics of the functioning of terms and their circulation. They attempted to account for the diversity of usage, whether oral, which is often neglected in terminology, or written (Gaudin 1993, 2003).

2.2 Textual terminology

Textual terminology was developed in the early 1990s in two different contexts, by researchers whose orientations quickly converged. On the one hand, in Paris, Didier Bourigault and Monique Slodzian, who were both involved in teaching language engineering at the Centre de Recherche en Ingénierie Multilingue (CRIM) of the Institut National des Langues et Civilisations Orientales (Inalco), immediately adopted a perspective of terminology that was based on corpus analysis. Bourigault developed Lexter, a terminology extraction software, for his thesis. Slodzian, a translator and specialist in Russian linguistics at Inalco, was familiar with the theories of terminology from Russian scholars (Slodzian 1986,

1989) and had also met Louis Guespin. Her work and philosophy aligned with the interpretative perspective of François Rastier which considers that meaning is not given but constructed in context (Rastier 1987).

Meanwhile, in Toulouse, a terminology project was carried out in the framework of the joint Matra Marconi Space and Toulouse Institute of Computer Science Research (IRIT) laboratory, called Action Recherche et Application Matra IRIT en Interface Homme Système (ARAMIIHS) in the framework of the European Eurolang project. The aim was to compile Matra Marconi Space (MMS) terminology and adapt it for use in a computer-assisted translation tool. To carry out this project, Anne Condamines was hired as a post-doctoral fellow at the CNRS (French National Center for Scientific Research). Her background was twofold. During her PhD in Linguistics at IRIT, Condamines had acquired expertise in syntax and semantics and in computerised language processing and knowledge engineering. In this project, the analysis of a satellite maintenance corpus had shown that only 15% of the terms used in the MMS documentation were listed in the terminology repositories of the Délégation générale à la langue française et aux langues de France (DGLFLF, known by then as DGLF, for Délégation générale à la langue française) (DGLF). It seemed essential to base the investigations on data produced by the editors themselves (namely corpora).

With the help of computer scientists at ARAMIIHS, the team, made up of linguists, computer scientists and domain experts, began to develop tools to help in the exploration of specialised corpora, starting with a sort of rudimentary concordancer (Condamines and Amsili 1993). In this context, Bourigault and Condamines, created the research group Terminology and Artificial Intelligence (TIA) in 1993, financed by the CNRS which leading researchers such as Nathalie Aussenac-Gilles and Valérie Delavigne soon joined. Later, colleagues from the information and communication sciences brought additional insight to the work in a new working group named ASSTICCOT (Aussenac-Gilles and Condamines 2007).

At that time, tool-based approaches were just beginning to develop. The Translator's Workbench Project (Kübler et al, 1995), financed by the European Community, led to the development of tools, focused on translation, integrating terms analysis. The aforementioned working groups and the TIA conferences, which took place every two years until 2015, helped to bring people with shared interests together. Linguists interested in terminology, computer scientists and knowledge engineers collaborated to build networks of concepts from corpora. Their objective was to build terminological knowledge bases or ontologies (which, in the research group, were considered to be more or less equivalent), through the use of *knowledge rich contexts* (Meyer 2001, Marshman 2022). Gradually, other needs emerged. It was thus necessary to broaden the focus to the updating of these evolving terminology knowledge bases and, consequently, to diachronic variation

(Picton 2009, 2018), the importance of which for terminology research had already been highlighted, particularly by advocates of Socioterminology (Rey 1979, Gaudin 1996, 2003). This achievement paved the way for considering the social uses of terms (Gaudin 1995), the diversity of norms (Gambier et al. 1991) and the process of determinologisation (Meyer and Mackintosch 2000, Humbert-Droz 2021), as well as the role of multidisciplinarity (Condamines and Dehaut 2011) or diastratic variation (Picton and Dury 2017).

As for automatic language processing, it evolved towards deep learning methods, which only work on large volumes of texts. Linguistics-oriented terminology on the one hand, and computer science-knowledge engineering on the other hand, subsequently partly drifted apart (Condamines and Picton 2022).[2]

It can thus be said that Textual terminology developed on five principles: (1) the use of real corpora, (2) the creation or use of tools to explore them, (3) a linguistic analysis of how terminology functions, (4) accounting for needs other than those of a translational nature, and (5) close collaboration with domain specialists, who help to ensure that the analysis is well grounded.

This historical overview has highlighted the privileged links between Socioterminology and Textual terminology and described the circumstances that contributed to their convergence: the exchange of ideas between Slodzian, Guespin, Gaudin and Bourigault, Delavigne's involvement in the TIA group, and recognition of changing needs and environments. Reflecting on the same concepts, encountering the same aporias and seeking social utility are the common points that brought them together.

3.   Theoretical foundations

Since their emergence, Socioterminology and Textual terminology have followed converging paths and complementary philosophies, which is reflected in their theoretical foundations. We select five of them here: (1) a reaction to classical theoretical proposals, (2) an objective to describe actual use, (3) a contribution to methodological responses, (4) an intrinsic need to describe variation, and (5) a need to reappraise the notions of "domain" and "expert." These theoretical foundations are described in the following paragraphs.

---

2. Several works are still exploring the links between languages for special purposes and NLP, for example (to name but a few): Aussenac-Gilles (2017), Drouin et al. (2018), González Granado (2021).

3.1   A reaction to classical theoretical proposals

When Louis Guespin and François Gaudin, both sociolinguists, first came to grips with the terminological theory generally accepted at the time (General Theory of Terminology or GTT, Wüster 1981), they were perplexed as Guespin recalled in his article in *Les cahiers de linguistique sociale* (1991). The GTT was developed in the 1930s by Eugen Wüster, who dreamt of a stability of relations between words and *notions* (Rey 1979), which would later become *concepts*. Wüster insisted on the biunivocity of the term and its monosemy in relation to a domain, and placed the principle of onomasiology at the heart of the terminological working process, even though he himself did not actually use the word *onomasiological* (Candel 2004). These presuppositions were open to challenge, becoming the starting point for epistemological reactions in both Socioterminology and Textual terminology circles. Of course Wüster's early ideas must be considered in the context of the period, and can be viewed from a more nuanced or contrasting perspective (see Chapter 8).

The first challenges to the theoretical principles of the GTT, by advocates of both Socioterminology and Textual terminology, targeted the postulates of the biunivocity of the term, of the monosemy linked within a domain, and of the principle of a conceptual approach coupled with an onomasiological working method (Gambier 1987, Gaudin 1989, Condamines 2018a, Condamines and Picton 2022). In particular, the onomasiology-semasiology opposition, which is typical of German semantics, was not common in French linguistics. These presuppositions revealed their limitations for terminological planning (Depecker 1997). A *tree diagram* recommended by an onomasiological approach can sometimes be useful for organising work (Dubuc 1992, Pecman 2018), but does it reflect language use? Nothing is less certain. However, if a tree diagram is not constructed, criteria must be established to study the uses of terms in a semasiological approach.

From the point of view of Socioterminology, challenges to classical theory and methodology were also voiced in the model of glottopolitics which points out the spontaneous emergence of local norms. Guespin (1993) emphasises the process of *normaison* which corresponds to the spontaneous emergence of local norms, since any language ensemble that enables inter-comprehension has its own systemic norms. Guespin contrasts *normaison* and *normalization* (or standardisation). The latter, which corresponds to the level of institutional norms, influences spontaneous norms. The interactional perspective influenced most of the thinking on the question of institutional standards on spontaneous norms. It always places lexical forms within the exchanges in which they take place, and in which it is sometimes necessary to facilitate inter-comprehension, often by harmonising terminologies.

Members of the TIA group began to reflect on these principles from the dual perspective of linguistics and knowledge engineering. It became clear that there were many needs in the field of terminology and that the existing approaches, inspired by the so-called "classical" theoretical principles, did not always make it possible to meet them. Indeed, until the 1980s, theoretical and methodological approaches were far removed from the realities of actual language use and user needs, particularly for documentation management. Researchers subsequently developed systematic and reproducible methods of corpus constitution and anchored their work in linguistics.

The need to consider actual language use, as well as the emergence of new methodological approaches, have thus consolidated the theoretical program common to Socioterminology and Textual terminology.

3.2 A common objective: To describe actual use

Socioterminology, by virtue of its descriptive perspective, borrows from socio-linguistic or ethnographic methodologies: interviews and observations added to the corpus. In general, in sociolinguistics, field work and surveys are core to the methodology. On this point, the sociolinguistic analysis applied to terminology by Monica Heller (1982) remains exemplary as it shows the need for field studies in order to gain a better understanding of the mechanisms of lexical usage in companies, and particularly of factors relating to term motivation and resistance to terminological changes. The evidence drawn from fieldwork presented a challenge for classical terminology, which had to be adapted to consider the way language is actually used and the mental representations of speakers involved in a situation of communication (Gaudin and Delavigne 1997, Delavigne 1996). In the same way, thinking about lexicographical aspects made it possible to produce a more detailed description of terms.

Textual terminology, on the other hand, has focused on the needs identified either by domain language experts (translators, technical writers), who are the primary users of terminology resources/recommendations, or by experts in the field, who are the users of documents written by language experts. Whether it is a question of building terminology resources (Bourigault et al. 2004, Condamines 2018b), updating them (Condamines et al. 2004, Picton 2009), or describing the passage of terms from a given domain into the general language (Condamines and Picton 2014), the objective of analysing the linguistic phenomena at stake has led Textual terminology to develop a thorough reflection on tool-based methodologies that can be applied to specialised corpora, as well as on the close collaboration with experts.

Since they reflect different perspectives, Socioterminology and Textual terminology could be perceived as taking different positions regarding the role of linguists and their societal involvement. In fact, driven by a desire to describe language, both approaches above all aim to understand how expert knowledge and linguistic phenomena combine to arrive at a mutual understanding, either between experts or between experts and non-experts. As can be seen, both approaches are primarily concerned with transmitting meaning.

3.3   A contribution to methodological responses

The difficulties encountered in the subject fields explored by Textual terminology and Socioterminology led their advocates to challenge the methodologies of classical terminology theory, and methodological adaptations were required in order to take actual usage into account.

In the case of work inspired by Sociolinguistics, there is a desire to consider the way speakers think about the terms they are using (Gaudin and Delavigne 1997, Delavigne 1996, 2001). Socioterminology has thus come to use the methods of discourse analysis in placing terms in contexts of language production, circulation, reception and interpretation which constrain usage. From sociolinguistics, it has borrowed methodologies in which field work and surveys are central (Gaudin and Delavigne 1997). In this sense, the morpheme *socio-* is indeed a truncation of *sociolinguistics.*

Textual terminology has developed its reflections around the constitution and exploration of text corpora, initiated at a time when corpus-based lexicology was in full swing in Great Britain (Sinclair 1996) and principles and methods (for example in the retrieval of definitions) could easily be adapted for the analysis of French specialised corpora. One question was particularly central in this perspective: that of the representativeness of the corpora (Biber 1993, Sinclair 1996, Habert 2000) according to the objective of the study. In this context, Textual terminology has built a systematic methodology where corpora are constituted according to the context of the study and the need expressed by the experts (both domain language experts and field experts). Candidate-terms extracted by term extraction tools (e.g term extractors such as TermoStat, Drouin 2003) are the starting point for the analysis of the corpora. The focus on terms makes it possible, on the one hand, to question the relationship between the term and the concept it denotes or is presumed to denote and, on the other hand, to use tools, whether they are dedicated to terminology (i.e. term extractors or relation extractors) or are more general purpose (concordancers, taggers). The study of terms allows one to enter the corpus by orienting the analysis in another mode than the sole discursive aspect. Terms are studied according to different linguistic features, such as frequency and other quantitative data, the presence of denominative variants and, above all, the term's distribution. The approach is thus clearly in line with Firth's linguistic approach (1957), although developed in Textual terminology through a broader understanding of the notion of context, which can be understood as syntactic dependencies, as well as window-based contexts (bag of words) or as knowledge-rich contexts (Skuce and Meyer 1990, Meyer 2001, Condamines and Picton 2022). Subject-field experts (domain language experts and/or field experts) are involved throughout the analysis, from the initial request to the validation of the results. The aim is to combine the skills of linguist-terminologists on the functioning of language with those of the subject-field experts in order to propose an interpretation of the data, in a co-construction process. The validation of the results has two facets. On the one hand, the interpretation proposals are based solely on the language regularities produced by the discourse community and the results make it possible, at least in part, to meet the initial need whether expressed by field operators or language experts. On the other hand, the results must fit into the overall paradigm of linguistics, and contribute to scientific thought of the disciplines (linguistics and terminology) (Condamines and Picton 2022).

In the same manner as discourse analysis, Socioterminology increasingly makes use of corpora, which have become easier to build and process through access to web content and technologies and corpus analysis tools. Like related disciplines, it has benefited from advances in corpus linguistics and the widely available large-scale data.

From the point of view of Textual terminology, the anchoring in linguistics is more clearly seen in lexical semantics and corpus lexicology, whereas from the point of view of Socioterminology, an interpretative semantics (Rastier 1995) anchored in discourse analysis prevails. It should be noted that Socioterminology is distinguished by its interest in language issues in relation to the use of language by the general public. From a methodological point of view, this has been reflected, from its very beginning, in the emphasis placed by Socioterminology on the oral dimension, which is the essence of interactions and the mode by which terms are naturally circulated. Apart from a few semiotically specific units such as symbols and other mathematical formulae, terms indeed circulate mainly orally. If the objective is to construct terminologies that are closer to usage, it is necessary to consider the actual linguistic phenomena at stake, in other words, to look at exchanges that mobilise all forms, sometimes different from strictly oral ones, in multiple registers, such as digital discussion forums.

The anchoring principles of Socioterminology and Textual terminology therefore complement each other and are mutually supportive (Delavigne et al. 2022).

3.4   An intrinsic need to describe variation

When confronted with corpora, terminology researchers could not help but observe that variation is a natural phenomenon in languages for special purposes (LSP).

Variation was observed through socioterminological surveys, corpus analysis and exchanges with experts. In accordance with the notion of sociolinguistic anchoring, the hypothesis that the appearance of a given term variant or discursive reformulation does not occur by chance was proven in various subject fields explored by researchers in Socioterminology. And according to the demands and needs expressed by companies (such as drafting of technical documentation, archiving, information retrieval...), the textual approach quickly revealed links between variations and different communicative situations, by pointing to, for example, a dependency on textual genres (Condamines 2008), i.e. a framework which combines the communicative situation and linguistic norms in which any real exchange takes place (Bakhtin 1984). The evidence made manifest through textual terminological analysis (developed on the basis of different applied needs) has assisted in highlighting the richness and complexity of dialectal variation, and participated in legitimising in particular the analysis of the diachronic dimension (and specifically the short diachronic, Picton 2014, 2018), as well as the diastratic dimension in specialised discourse (Humbert-Droz 2021, González Granado et al. 2022).

With respect to describing the meaning of terminological units, socioterminological work on various specialised vocabularies has highlighted the relevance of conducting a social analysis of the circumstances of the term's circulation or distribution (Gentile 2003, 2007, Alrashidi 2016) and the ways they are used in the workplace (Nguyen 2013). Approaches to semantic analyses implemented a modular and relational description of meaning (An Vo 2014, Baudouin 2008, Tran 1999) inspired by the pioneering work of Pierre Lerat (1988). In Textual terminology, the question of term variation has been thoroughly discussed in terms of speakers' varying points of view on the same linguistic unit (Condamines & Rebeyrolle 1997, Condamines et al. 2021).

3.5   Towards a reappraisal of domain and expert

The construction and use of corpora, which are not simply random data but rather constructs, is challenging for both Textual terminology and Socioterminology as approaches, the main issue being how to collect texts according to the point of view of the analysis. Even for studies restricted to LSPs, corpus design cannot be reduced to a simple confirmation of belonging to a domain (Gaudin 1995, Delavigne 2022) which is assumed to pre-exist the analysis. Dividing content into domains is difficult, and hardly objective, even with documents that adhere to strict standards. The results of efforts to divide content into domains will vary according to the objective of the study. As a consequence, it is sometimes difficult to devise a terminology that all parties agree on.

Thus, domains, a useful notion in documentation, were thought of as spheres of activities, a notion taken from Bakhtin, which seemed more adequate to describe their porous nature and the absence of clear boundaries, difficulties which did not allow domains to be a serious theoretical tool. The notions of usage and interaction challenged the orthonymic perspectives of classical terminology theory, even in apriori standardised vocabularies (Gaudin 2023). Variation was evident in all corpora. Even aeronautics, a sector with highly regulated communications, proved to be porous to speakers' needs for differentiation, with airplane pilots even using nicknames for airports (Lopez 2013).

The effectiveness of using domain as a classificatory device also depends on the expert, who is responsible for delimiting what falls within a sector of experience (Otman 1993, see 3.2.) or not. The expert plays a key role in ensuring the relevancy of the resources offered. The evolution and plurality of the expert's role(s) in terminology work has also been highlighted, from being a repository of domain knowledge to an active partner in the analysis (e.g. Bourigault and Slodzian 1999). From a diachronic perspective, the relevance (or even the possibility) of a *retro-diagnosis* (Picton 2018) on the terms and knowledge of experts remains problematical.

Apart from broader issues that the notion of expertise raises in terminology (such as: what type of expertise? for whom? for which purpose?), the actual participation of experts in the circulation of terms should be clarified. In what way can they be *guarantors* of the terms in use? The notion of *deference*, as used in social epistemology (Origgi 2004), allows us to rethink the theorical problem of expertise (Gaudin and Nicolae 2017), and has been taken up by both Textual terminology and Socioterminology.

4.   Synthesising insights: Paving the way to new dialogues

This historical account of the emergence of Socioterminology and Textual terminology has identified numerous points of convergence. Moreover, these two approaches have in common a clear break with the classical GTT.

The two approaches share their disciplinary anchorage in linguistics, which means that terminology studies cannot be isolated from linguistics and that *terms* as objects of observation cannot be radically differentiated from *words* (see Chapter 9). This perspective is not that of the Wüsterian vision of terminology, which aimed to keep terms away from the risks of variation due to the effects of context; the objective was to maintain a stable link between *term* and *concept* in order to limit problems of transmission and understanding. Of course, Wüster's pioneering reflections must be considered in the context of the period, when standardisation was an international concern, leading Wüster himself to even campaign for Esperanto as a universal language (1924).

In accordance with this disciplinary anchorage in linguistics, Socioterminology and Textual terminology have followed the trajectory of linguistics and the development of corpora. Concurrently, as these two approaches expanded, they sought to introduce systematic methodologies. Both orientations seek to acknowledge authentic language use, including the semiotic dimension specific to terminology, which resides in its relationship to knowledge. From this point of view, both approaches are inspired by corpus linguistics. The interaction with natural language processing and knowledge engineering has been fundamentally enriching, and has prompted questions on the role of tools. In fact, the evolution of tools in the exploration of specialised corpora has become a central issue.

Regarding methodological aspects, Socioterminology and Textual terminology are similar on many points. Both approach the construction of corpora according to the problem at hand or the terminological resource to be constituted. Both use terms as the entry point for studying corpora, and both use, to varying degrees, Natural Language Processing (NLP) tools. A term is considered to be a linguistic unit that circulates and is subject to various inflected forms according to the interactions and types of discourse in which it is actualised. Regarding terms, the domain expert is not sufficient to determine usage. Observing the way speakers negotiate the meaning of the words they use in the texts reveals the different strategies they use to adapt their terms to their readers. Once we focus on usage, more flexible descriptive models make it possible to observe the relations associating a referent (in the world) with a linguistic expression, which can differ in different discourse communities (Alrashidi et al 2018).

Ultimately, all these questions are closely linked to the concept of the terminological unit, and to the differences between the semiotics of the term and that of the linguistic sign. However, the term, as a unit of knowledge that allows us to understand and act, is conceded a status, at least provisional, by a specific discourse community. Its sociolinguistic characteristics often bring it close to what was once called professional jargon. The connections between Textual terminology, Socioterminology and interpretative semantics led to the adoption of François Rastier's definition of a concept as a "normed meaning" (Rastier 1995, 2010).

The choice of *meaning*, as a concept derived from linguistics, is clearly motivated in this definition: it places the term firmly in linguistics and not in cognitive psychology. Finding the right term to represent a concept is not orthonymy, which would refer to a choice of label for a referent, but rather the aim is to understand how meaning is regulated within the discourse community of experts concerned. This regulation is manifested by mostly perceptible variations in the discursive environment of the terms. This emphasis on terms as gateways into texts has favoured interaction with NLP specialists whose tools operate on the basis of the retrieval of forms. By considering various properties such as grammatical category, statistical comparison with general language (non-specialised) corpora, idiosyncratic distribution and others, these forms can be considered as candidate terms. Linguist-terminologists have then to confirm or reject these candidates as terms and to integrate them into their studies.

These perspectives have led experts/researchers in both Socioterminology and Textual terminology to study different types of variations, and in particular to work on the diachronic aspect of vocabularies (Candel and Gaudin 2006, Picton 2018) and on diastratic variation (Picton and Dury 2017), which is a common way to find out how terms effectively circulate in discourse.

The study of authentic discourse and its associated social demands gives terminological work an often application-oriented dimension. For a long time, terminology was considered a field of applied linguistics, and therefore of little interest to theoretical linguists (with the exception of Mounin 1972). In fact, terminology evolved out of a response to a need, and due to this response being unsatisfactory, space was made for other approaches, methods, and perspectives to be considered. Louis Guespin made the application-oriented aspect a defining feature of Socioterminology, emphasising that beyond descriptive studies, social utility lies at the very heart of the socioterminological project in a "glottonomic" perspective. He summarised the concept as follows: "Glottonomy proposes, following the analysis of a particular language situation, the modalities of an intervention on language practices specific to this situation" (1985: 26) (our translation). We can thus acknowledge that terminology is also a form of applied linguistics, i.e. a situated science (Condamines and Narcy-Combes 2015), which allows us to restore the credibility of this approach, whose concerns have long been considered ancillary to those of theoretical linguistics. Applied linguistics is also practical linguistics.

Socioterminology has thus been given a double vocation: "on the one hand to describe, on the other hand to inform" (Gaudin 1990: 178). In the same way, this application-oriented dimension is inscribed from the outset in Textual terminology, whatever the applications envisaged, whether they emerge from the world of industry with the construction of terminological knowledge bases or controlled languages (Condamines 2020), or whether they are related to the evolution of knowledge, the transfer of knowledge between different speakers and mechanisms linked to the circulation of terms, such as determinologisation (see Humbert-Droz, 2021).

Although applied linguistics in France was once linked to teaching, the scope of the field has now broadened to include other types of applications. In the field of terminology, applications have diversified, from the production of dictionaries to assistance in technical writing or the creation of databases. Applied linguistics also helps to solve problems relating to popularization (see for example Delavigne 2012, 2019a, 2019b).

It is probably the nature of the corpus considered that most distinguishes Socioterminology from Textual terminology. Although they both focus on uses and aim to produce resources beyond simple descriptions, the natural inclination of Socioterminology draws it towards themes related to socio-political issues. Studies on the evaluation of terminology policies and the implantation of terms are closely linked to the sociological analysis of discourse communities and their behaviour.

Finally, it should be noted that the development of Socioterminology and Textual terminology is part of the global evolution of a discipline whose importance has become crucial. Terms are omnipresent in 21st century communication practices (think of COVID, Lerat 2021) and at the same time we have seen a proliferation of studies and a diversification of currents of thought, all more or less similar to the two orientations that are the focus of this chapter. In the last thirty years, theoretical positions have evolved: different teams are now working in France and throughout the world on specialised corpora with the help of tools, without necessarily claiming explicitly to espouse any particular theoretical position. The use of corpora has become widespread. Thus, it can be concluded that terminology today cannot ignore the importance of texts of all types, nor can it neglect the social dimension of language exchanges.

Acknowledgements

We would like to thank the editors of this book for their suggestions to improve the quality of this chapter.

References

Alrashidi, Badriyah. 2016. *Un problème de terminologie médicale au Koweït : la vulgarisation autour du diabète*. Ph.D. dissertation, University of Rouen.

Alrashidi, Badriyah, Valérie Delavigne, and François Gaudin. 2018. "La référenciation des termes: perspectives socioterminologiques." In *Terminologie et ontologie. Théories et applications*, ed. by C. Roche, 35–50. Presses Universitaires Savoie Mont-Blanc.

Aussenac-Gilles, Nathalie. 2017. "Semantic Relations at the Machine Learning Era: Where are the (Good Old) Patterns Gone?" In *Workshop Information Retrieval in Terminology Using Lexical Knowledge Patterns*. Bergen, Norway: IITR.

Aussenac-Gilles, Nathalie, and Anne Condamines. 2007. "Corpus et terminologie." In *La redocumentarisation du monde*, ed. by R. T. Pedauque, 131–147. Toulouse: Cepadues Editions.

Bakhtin, Mikhaïl. 1984. *Esthétique de la création verbale*. Paris: Gallimard.

Biber, Douglas. 1993. "Representativeness in Corpus Design." *Literary and Linguistic Computing* 8(4): 243–257.

Borzeix, Anni, and Béatrice Fraenkel. 2001. *Langage et travail. Communication, cognition, action*. Paris: CNRS Éditions.

Boulanger, Jean-Claude. 1981. "Compte-rendu de L'aménagement linguistique du Québec de Jean-Claude Corbeil." *Terminogramme* 7–8: 11–12.

Bourigault, Didier, Nathalie Aussenac-Gilles, and Jean Charlet. 2004. "Construction de ressources terminologiques ou ontologiques à partir de textes : un cadre unificateur pour trois études de cas." *Revue d'Intelligence Artificielle (RIA)* 18(1): 87–110.

Bourigault, Didier, and Monique Slodzian. 1999. "Pour une terminologie textuelle." *Terminologies Nouvelles* 19:29–32.

Candel, Danielle. 2004. "Wüster par lui-même." *Cahiers du CIEL*: 15–31.

Candel, Danielle, and François Gaudin (eds). 2006. *Aspects diachroniques du vocabulaire*. Mont Saint-Aignan: Publications des Universités de Rouen et du Havre.

Condamines, Anne. 2008. "Taking *genre* into Account for Analyzing Conceptual Relation Patterns." *Corpora* 8: 115–140.

Condamines, Anne. 2018a. "Nouvelles perspectives pour la terminologie textuelle." In *Terminology and Discourse*, ed. by J. Altmanova, M. Centrella, and K. E. Russo, 93–112. Bern: Peter Lang.

Condamines, Anne. 2018b. "Terminological Knowledge Bases." In *The Routledge Handbook of Lexicography*, ed. by P. Fuertes-Olivera, 335–349. London: Routledge.

Condamines, Anne. 2020. "Towards an Ergonomic Linguistics. Application to the Design of Controlled Natural Languages." *International Journal of Applied Linguistics*. Wiley Online Library.

Condamines, Anne, and Pascal Amsili. 1993. "Terminology between Language and Knowledge: an Example of Terminological Knowledge Base." In *Terminology and Knowledge Engineering* 93, ed. by K.-D. Schmitz, 316–323. Frankfurt: Indeks Verlag.

Condamines, Anne, and Nathalie Dehaut. 2011. "Mise en œuvre des méthodes de la linguistique de corpus pour étudier les termes en situation d'innovation disciplinaire : le cas de l'exobiologie." *Meta* 56(2), 266–283.

Condamines, Anne, Julie Humbert-Droz, and Aurélie Picton. 2021. "Néologie par déterminologisation : Méthode de repérage et catégorisation en corpus dans le domaine de la physique des particules." In *La néologie des langues romanes : Nouvelles dynamiques et enjeux*, ed. by M.Villar Díaz, J.C. de Hoyos, P. Dury, J. Makri-Morel, and V. Renner, 287–304. Bern: Peter Lang.

Condamines, Anne, and Francis Narcy-Combes. 2015. "La linguistique appliquée comme science située." In *Cultures de Recherche en Linguistique Appliquée*, ed. by F. Carton, J.-P. Narcy-Combes, M.-F. Narcy-Combes, and D. Toffoli, 209–229. Paris: Riveneuve Éditions.

Condamines, Anne, and Aurélie Picton. 2014. "Des communiqués de presse du Cnes à la presse généraliste. Vers un observatoire de la diffusion des termes." In *La néologie en langue de spécialité*, ed. by P. Dury, J.C. de Hoyos, J. Makri-Morel, V. Renner, and M.B. Villar Diaz, 165–188. Lyon: CRTT.

Condamines, Anne, and Aurélie Picton. 2022. "Textual Terminology: Origins, Principles and New Challenges." In *Theoretical Approaches to Terminology*, ed. by M.-C. L'Homme, and P. Faber, 219–236. Amsterdam: John Benjamins.

Condamines, Anne, and Josette Rebeyrolle. 1997. "Point de vue en langue spécialisée." *Meta* XLII (1). 174–184.

Condamines, Anne, Josette Rebeyrolle, and Annie Soubeille. 2004. "Variation de la terminologie dans le temps : une méthode linguistique pour mesurer l'évolution de la connaissance en corpus." In *Proceedings of the European Association for Lexicography conference* (EURALEX 2004), 547–557.

Delavigne, Valérie. 1996. "Problèmes d'enquêtes en socioterminologie." In *Proceedings of Secondes journées internationales de Terminologie*, 163–178. Université du Havre.

Delavigne, Valérie. 2001. *Les mots du nucléaire. Contribution socioterminologique à une analyse des discours de vulgarisation.* PhD dissertation, University of Rouen.

Delavigne, Valérie. 2012. "Peut-on 'traduire' les mots des experts? Un dictionnaire pour les patients atteints de cancer." In *Dictionnaires et traduction*, ed. by M. Heinz, 233–266. Berlin, Frank & Timme.

Delavigne Valérie. 2019a. "Littératies en santé et forums de patients: des formes d'ergonomie discursive." In *Éla. Études de linguistique appliquée. Littératie en santé: une approche linguistique* 195: 363–381.

Delavigne Valérie. 2019b. "Les mots du cancer: le partage des termes pour l'élaboration d'une culture périmédicale." In *Comunicació, llenguatge i salut / Comunicación, lenguaje y salud. Estratègies lingüístiques per millorar la comunicació amb el pacient / Estrategias lingüísticas para mejorar la comunicación con el paciente*, ed. by R. Estopà, 153–183. Barcelona: Institut de Linguistica aplicada. Universitat Pompeu Fabra.

Delavigne, Valérie. 2022. "La notion de domaine en question. À propos de l'environnement." *Neologica. Néologie et environnement* 16: 27–59.

Delavigne, Valérie, Aurélie Picton, and Emma Thibert. 2022. "Socioterminologie et terminologie textuelle: l'expertise en questions." *8ᵉ Congrès mondial de linguistique française* 138: 04012.

Depecker Loïc (ed). 1997. *La mesure des mots: cinq études d'implantation terminologique.* Mont-Saint-Aignan: Presses universitaires de Rouen et du Havre.

Depecker Loïc (ed). 2005. *La terminologie: nature et enjeux. Langages* 157.

Drouin, Patrick. 2003. "Term Extraction using Non-technical Corpora as a Point of Leverage." *Terminology* 9(1): 99–115.

Drouin, Patrick, Natalia Grabar, Thierry Hamon, Kyo Kageura, and Koichi Takeuchi. 2018. "Computational Terminology and Filtering of Terminological Information: Introduction to the Special Issue." *Terminology* 24: 1–6.

Dury, Pascaline, and Aurélie Picton. 2009. "Terminologie et diachronie: vers une réconciliation théorique et méthodologique?" *Revue Française de Linguistique Appliquée* 13 (2): 31–41.

Firth, John Rupert. 1957. "Applications of General Linguistics." *Transactions of the Philological Society* 56: 1–14.

Gambier, Yves. 1987. "Problèmes terminologiques des pluies acides: pour une socio-terminologie." *Meta* 32–3: 314–320.

Gambier, Yves, François Gaudin, and Louis Guespin. 1991. "Terminologie et polynomie." In *Les langues polynomiques*, PULA, no. 3/4, Actes du Colloque international CORTI 90: 202–217.

Gaudin, François. 1990. *Terminologie: des problèmes sémantiques aux pratiques institutionnelles.* PhD. dissertation, University of Rouen.

Gaudin, François. 1993. *Pour une socioterminologie: des problèmes sémantiques aux pratiques institutionnelles.* Mont-Saint-Aignan: Publications de l'Université de Rouen.

Gaudin, François (ed). 1995. "Usages sociaux des termes : théories et terrains." *Meta* 40–2: 193–329.

Gaudin, François. 1996. "Terminologie : l'ombre du concept." *Meta*, 41–4 : 604–621.

Gaudin, François. 2003. *Socioterminologie. Une approche sociolinguistique de la terminologie.* Bruxelles: Duculot.

Gaudin, François. 2023. "L'orthonymie, un concept à facettes." In *Alain Rey. Lumières sur la langue*, ed by F. Gaudin, 169–175. Paris: Honoré Champion.

Gaudin, François, and Valérie Delavigne. 1997. "L'enquête en terminologie : point de la question et propositions." *Terminologies nouvelles* 16: 37–42.

Gaudin, François, and Valérie Delavigne. 2022. "Founding Principles of Socioterminology." In *Theoretical Approaches to Terminology*, ed. by M.-C. L'Homme, and P. Faber, 177–196. Amsterdam: John Benjamins.

Gaudin, François, and Cristina Nicolae. 2016. "La référenciation en socioterminologie : réflexions à partir de l'astronomie." *Repères DoRiF*, 10.

Gentile, Ana Maria. 2003. "Les gallicismes dans le discours de la psychanalyse en langue espagnole. Essai de description socioterminologique." *Cuadernos de Lenguas Modernas* 4–4: 109–155.

Gentile, Ana Maria. 2007. *La circulation sociale du discours de la psychanalyse en langue espagnole.* Ph.D. dissertation, University of Rouen.

González Granado, Nicolás. 2021. *A Glimpse into Terminology Research with R: Two Experiments Exploring Diastratic Variation in a Large Specialised Corpus.* Masters dissertation, University of Geneva.

González Granado, Nicolás, Aurélie Picton, and Patrick Drouin. 2022. "De l'analyse statistique à l'apprentissage automatique : le langage R au service de la terminologie." *Études de linguistique appliquée*, 4(208) : 447–467.

Guilbert, Louis. 1973. "La spécificité du terme scientifique et technique." *Langue française* 17: 5–17.

Guespin, Louis. 1991. "La circulation terminologique et les rapports science, technique, production." *Cahiers de linguistique sociale, Terminologie et sociolinguistique* 18:59–80.

Guespin, Louis. 1993. "Normaliser ou standardiser." *Le Langage et l'Homme*, XXVIII/4: 213–222.

Guespin, Louis, and Jean-Baptiste Marcellesi. 1986. "Pour la glottopolitique." *Langages* 83: 5–34.

Habert, Benoît. 2000. "Des corpus représentatifs: de quoi, pour quoi, comment ?" In *Linguistiques sur corpus. Études et réflexions*, ed. by M. Bilger. *Cahiers de l'université de Perpignan* 31: 11–58.

Heller, Monica. 1982. *Le processus de francisation dans une entreprise montréalaise : une analyse sociolinguistique*. Montréal: Office de la langue française.

Humbert-Droz, Julie. 2021. *Définir la déterminologisation : Approche outillée en corpus comparable dans le domaine de la physique des particules*. PhD. dissertation, University of Geneva / University of Toulouse.

Humbley, John. 2018. "Socioterminology." In *Languages for Special Purposes. An International Handbook*, ed. by J. Humbley, G. Budin, and C. Laurén, 417–490. Berlin: de Gruyter.

Kubler, Marianne, Khurshid Ahmad, and Gregor Thurmair (eds). 1995. *Translator's Workbench. Tools and Terminology for Translation and Text Processing*. New York: Springer Nature.

Lerat, Pierre. 1984. "Lexicologie des institutions." In *Sociolinguistique des langues romanes. Actes du XVIIe congrès International de linguistique et de philologie romanes*, 251–259. Université de Provence.

Lerat, Pierre. 1988. "Terminologie et sémantique descriptive." *La banque des mots*, no. spécial, éd. CILF : 11–30

Lerat, Pierre. 2021. "La lexiculture experte sur un plateau." In *Termes en discours. Entreprises et organisations*, ed. by V. Delavigne, and D. de Vecchi, 141–159. Paris: Presses de la Sorbonne Nouvelle.

Lopez, Stéphanie. 2013. *Norme(s) et usage(s) langagiers : le cas des communications pilote-contrôleur en anglais*. Ph.D. dissertation, University Toulouse 2.

Marcellesi, Jean Baptiste, and Bernard Gardin. 1974. *Introduction à la sociolinguistique: la linguistique sociale*. Paris: Larousse.

Marshman, Elizabeth. 2022. "Knowledge Patterns in Corpora." In *Theoretical Approaches to Terminology*, ed. by M.-C. L'Homme, and P. Faber, 291–310. Amsterdam: John Benjamins.

Martin, André. 1993. "Théorie de la diffusion sociale des innovations et changement linguistique planifié." In *L'implantation du français. Actualisation d'un changement planifié*, ed. by A. Martin, and C. Loubier. 11–55. Montréal: OLF.

Meyer, Ingrid. 2001. "Extracting Knowledge-Rich Contexts for Terminography: A Conceptual and Methodological Framework." In *Recent Advances in Computational Terminology*, ed. by D. Bourigault, M.-C. L'Homme, and C. Jacquemin, 279–302. Amsterdam: John Benjamins.

Meyer, Ingrid, and Kristen Mackintosh. 2000. "When Terms Move into our Everyday Lives." *Terminology* 6(1): 111–138.

Nguyen, Thi Huyen Trang. 2013. *Analyse de l'usage du vocabulaire des matériaux de construction et description terminologique vietnamienne-française*. Ph.D dissertation, University of Rouen.

Origgi, Gloria. 2004. "Croyance, déférence et témoignage." In *La philosophie du langage*, ed. by J. Proust, and E. Pacherie, 167–184. Paris: Ophrys.

Otman, Gabriel. 1993. "Le talon d'Achille de l'expertise terminologique." *La banque des mots*, numéro spécial, 75–87.

Picton, Aurélie. 2009. *Diachronie en langue de spécialité. Définition d'une méthode linguistique outillée pour repérer l'évolution des connaissances en corpus. Un exemple appliqué au domaine spatial.* Ph.D. dissertation, University Toulouse Jean-Jaurès.

Picton, Aurélie. 2014. "The Dynamics of Terminology in Short-Term Diachrony: A Proposal for a Corpus-based Methodology to observe Knowledge Evolution." In *The Dynamics of Culture-bound Terminology in Monolingual and Multilingual Communication*, ed. by Rita Temmerman, and Marc Van Campenhoudt, 159–182. Amsterdam: John Benjamins.

Picton, Aurélie. 2018. "Terminologie outillée et diachronie : éléments de réflexion autour d'une réconciliation." *ASp* 74:27–52.

Picton, Aurélie, and Pascaline Dury. 2017. "Diastratic Variation in Language for Specific Purposes. Observations from the Analysis of two Corpora." In *Multiple Perspectives in Terminological Variation*, ed. by P. Drouin, A. Francoeur, J. Humbley, and A. Picton, 57–79. Amsterdam: John Benjamins.

Rastier, François. 1987. *Sémantique interprétative*. Paris: Presses universitaires de France.

Rastier, François. 1995. "Le terme: entre ontologie et linguistique." *La banque des mots* 7: 35–65.

Rastier, François. 2010. *Sémantique et recherches cognitives*. Paris: Presses universitaires de France.

Rey Alain. 1988. "Les fonctions de la terminologie: du social au théorique." In *Actes du sixième colloque OLF-STQ de terminologie. L'ère nouvelle de la terminologie*, 87–108. Québec: OLF.

Sinclair, John. 1996. "Preliminary Recommendations on Text Typology." *EAGLES Document EAG-TCWG-TTYP/P.*

Skuce, Douglas, and Ingrid Meyer. 1990. "Terminology and Knowledge Engineering: Exploring a Symbiotic Relationship." In *Proceedings of the 6th International Workshop on Knowledge Acquisition for Knowledge-Based Systems*, 29/1–29/21. Calgary: SRDG Publications, University of Calgary.

Slodzian, Monique. 1986. "Présentation. La terminologie en URSS: aperçu sur ses développements en Europe Centrale." *Slovo*, 8: 38.

Slodzian, Monique. 1989. "Les nouveaux horizons de la terminologie spécialisée : apports de l'école soviétique de terminologie." *La licorne* 15: 507–512.

Tran, Duc Tuan. 1999. *La terminologie médicale vietnamienne*. Ph.D. dissertation, Université de Rouen.

Wüster, Eugen. 1924. *Esperanto und der Techniker. Die Bedeutung der Welthilfssprache Esperanto für den Techniker, ihr Wesen und ihre Ausbreitung seit dem Weltkrieg*. Berlin und Dresden: Esperanto-Verlag Ellersiek & Borel G.m.b.H.

Wüster, Eugen. 1981. "L'étude scientifique générale de la terminologie, zone frontalière entre la linguistique, la logique, l'ontologie, l'informatique et la science des choses." In *Textes choisis de terminologie. Fondements théoriques de la terminologie*, ed. by G. Rondeau, and H. Felber, 57–114. Québec: Université Laval: GIRSTERM.

CHAPTER 12

Terminology in Canada
A language planning journey

Aline Francoeur
Université Laval

This chapter delineates the emergence of terminology activities in Canada in the early 1900s, and goes on to cover the major turning points in the development of the discipline and profession up to the end of the 1980s. It shows how terminology became a key tool in carrying out Canada's official bilingualism policy, providing the French terms needed to translate increasingly specialised texts from English to French. It also illustrates the pivotal role terminology played in the extensive campaign led by the Quebec government in the 1970s and 1980s to make French the official language of business, administration, and commerce in the province of Quebec. Lastly, it touches on the francisation of the common law vocabulary, another milestone in the history of terminology in Canada.

Keywords: French, English, language planning, translation, Quebec francisation campaign, Office québécois de la langue française, Translation Bureau, legal terminology, common law, bijuralism

1. Introduction

Terminology as a discipline and profession enjoys an enviable status in Canada, and there is nothing accidental about that. Reading through Jean Delisle's magisterial book *La terminologie au Canada: histoire d'une profession* (2008), one quickly realises that a tremendous amount of work, dedication, and commitment went into the development of a distinctively Canadian expertise in this field. One also discovers that streams of practice that came to be seen as two distinct terminology schools or approaches — one grounded in translation, the other, in language planning — actually emerged and evolved hand in hand in response to the same challenging situation: a growing demand for French terms.

Various factors concurred to create this demand, which by the late 1960s and early 1970s reached a critical point. Joining forces and resources, professional

https://doi.org/10.1075/tlrp.24.12fra

translators and linguists, along with translation and linguistic scholars, engaged in the colossal undertaking of filling lexical gaps in major sectors of activity where French terminology was not readily available. They learned and sharpened their terminology skills through practice, producing hundreds of English-French glossaries and vocabularies, and building substantial term banks. The insights gained from this wealth of experience provided the basis for methodological guides, textbooks, university courses and even degrees in terminology, and ultimately brought terminology to the high level of expertise that has become the Canadian standard. All this in a span of some 40 years, from the early 1950s to the late 1980s. Those banner years will be the main focus of this chapter. Likewise, we will concentrate mostly on two areas of Canada, namely the Ottawa region and the province of Quebec, which grew into thriving hubs of terminological activity. But first, to put things into context, let us briefly look at the country's linguistic landscape.

2.   Canada's linguistic landscape

Originally peopled by First Nations and Inuit societies, colonised by the French in the 16th century, and finally conquered by the British in the 17th century, Canada covers a vast land divided into ten provinces and three territories. New Brunswick, Nova Scotia, Ontario, and Quebec were the original four provinces of the Dominion of Canada as established in 1867, to which were later added six more provinces: Manitoba (1870), British Columbia (1871), Prince Edward Island (1873), Alberta (1905), Saskatchewan (1905) and Newfoundland (1949),[1] as well as three territories: Northwest Territories (1870), Yukon (1898), and Nunavut (1999).

Language policies are deeply rooted in Canadian political and legal institutions. With the enactment of *The British North America Act* on July 1, 1867 (known since 1982 as the *Constitution Act*), which established the Canadian federal state and outlined the distribution of powers between the federal government and the provincial legislatures, provisions were made for English-French bilingualism in both Canada's and Quebec's parliaments. A century later, in 1969, the *Official Languages Act* extended English-French bilingualism to the entire federal administration, making Canada an officially bilingual country.

It is important to know, however, that Canada's bilingualism is first and foremost political and institutional; as Sherry Simon (2014: 47) puts it, it is meant "to ensure that the government and governmental services speak two languages to its citizens." Indeed, data from the 2021 national census confirm what Linda Cardinal

---

1. The province of Newfoundland was officially renamed Newfoundland and Labrador in 2001.

Figure 1. Canadian provinces and territories (Hogweard 2020)[2]

(2004:100) wrote at the turn of the millennium about bilingualism in Canada: "The theory may be bilingualism but the practice is increasingly one of unilingualism."

With merely 18% of the population who can conduct a conversation in both official languages,[3] Canada can accurately be described as "a bilingual country full of unilingual people" (Hamilton 2010:12) or, to be more precise, full of people whose first — and only — language is English, as the bilingualism rate of the Francophone population is more than five times that of the Anglophone (47.6% compared to 9.0%). Canadians whose mother tongue is neither French nor English have for their part an English-French bilingualism rate that is, at 11.5%, slightly higher than that of the Anglo-Canadians. As it is, most Canadians who are fluent in both official languages — i.e., 59.2% — reside in Quebec, the one province where

---

2. Hogweard. 2020. "Map of Canadian provinces and territories." Wikimedia Commons [public domain].

3. All statistics in this paragraph are from Statistics Canada 2022a.

French is the majority language. English is thus Canada's dominant language, and by far. Three Canadians out of four, i.e., 75.5%, report it as their first official language, compared to 21.4% for French. French is mostly spoken in Quebec, and, to a lesser extent, New Brunswick.

To sum up, "Canada could [...] be defined as a vast country inhabited by a great variety of ethnolinguistic groups communicating with one another through intermediaries who are translators and interpreters" (Delisle 1984: 6) and, we should add, terminologists. The bulk of translation work is done from English to French in order to serve the purpose of official bilingualism, but translation and interpretation from English to other languages are also necessary to address the needs of the diverse communities that make up the Canadian linguistic mosaic.[4] As for terminology, professional activities are almost exclusively centred on the English-French language combination, the main focus being, once again, to support institutional bilingualism in Canada, and, in Quebec, to secure the position of French as the one official language.

3.   Early forays into term compilation: From Quebec City to Ottawa

Jean Delisle (2008) identifies 1902 as the starting point in Canada of multiple attempts at collecting and defining terms, without established methods or training, yet with a sense of admirable principles nonetheless. Setting the scene for terminology practice as we know it today, initiatives typical of this period were motivated by the desire to counteract the massive influence of the English language on the French vocabulary, an influence that resulted in the proliferation of English technical terms and anglicisms.

Appropriate French terms needed to be made available, and that is what Canadian pioneers of terminological research set out to do.

Joseph-Évariste Prince, a lawyer and professor of social economy at Université Laval, in Quebec City, led the way with a study of 153 French railway terms that was published in a series of nine instalments from 1902 to 1903 in the *Bulletin du parler français au Canada*.[5] Garnered from seven sources — three monolingual French dictionaries, two treatises, and two pieces of legislation,

---

4. Some 210 languages were reported as mother tongues in the 2021 national census, of which more than 70 are indigenous languages (Statistics Canada 2022a).

5. This Bulletin was published by the Société du parler français au Canada, a learned society newly founded by Adjutor Rivard and Stanislas Lortie, and consisting of representatives of Quebec City's intellectual elite. Under the auspices of Université Laval, the Société devoted itself to the study, defense, and illustration of the French language in Canada.

all originating from France — the alphabetically arranged terms were for the most part accompanied by an English equivalent, an explanation (definition) or a sentence showing the way the term was used (a context), sometimes also a list of words with which it would normally combine (collocations). Usage notes were occasionally included, along with the source(s) of the information (i.e. the name of the author of the document consulted). In short, the typical information expected to be found in a modern terminology resource was there, and, as seen in Figure 2 (Prince 1903: 89), the author showed a clear concern for adopting a methodical and well-structured layout.

> **Garde-barrière** *(gateman).* — Pour surveiller les passages à niveau.—PICARD.
> **Gardiennage** *(guardianship).* — Entretien. Manœuvre des aiguilles et des signaux.—PICARD.
> **Garage** *(side tracking).*—Action de mettre un convoi, un wagon sur une voie ou dans une gare d'évitement. Voie de *garage*, voie dans laquelle on doit *garer* les wagons de service.—PALAA.
> **Garde-frein** *(breakman).*—On emploie aussi le mot serre-frein. *Garde-frein de queue (rear breakman)*: — ceux qui s'occupe du bon éclairage et du bon entretien des signaux d'arrière des trains.—PALAA.
> **Garde-ligne** *(section man).*—Qui surveille la ligne du chemin de fer.—GUÉRIN.
> **Gare de triage** *(terminal station).*—Gare spéciale comportant des voies nombreuses pour le classement des véhicules et la formation des trains.—PICARD.
> **Grille fumivore** *(start arrester).*—Appareil dont sont pourvues les machines locomotives pour consumer leur fumée.—PALAA.
> **Groupage** *(grouping).*—Réunion dans un même envoi de plusieurs colis.—SARRUT.

Figure 2. Excerpt from J.-E. Prince's study of railway terms

Had he known that he was laying the foundations of a new discipline, Prince would probably have been less modest about the value of his contribution. Indeed, he did not make much of his work, describing it as a mere compilation from various sources, and confiding that in using the alphabetical order, "the only one that is possibly suited for a work of this kind," his intention "was not, of course, to make a dictionary" (Prince 1902: 5; our translation).[6]

Similar studies by members of the Société du parler français au Canada were to follow, aimed at cataloging French terms related to modern inventions (railways, electricity, typewriting, etc.) or regional realities (maple syrup production, farmhouse building, etc.). These studies were the work of scholars or members of the clergy who were neither linguists nor lexicographers but shared an interest in the French language and made it their task to protect it from all "imperfections,"

---

6. All translations in this chapter have been done by the author.

such as anglicisms and English borrowings. That was, after all, the main purpose of the Bulletin.

In Ottawa, Canada's capital, French-Canadian translators from the federal government were the initiators of terminology productions. While promoting the use of a quality French language was a clear objective, they had an additional goal in mind: to share the fruit of extensive, time-consuming research done in the course of their everyday work of translating specialised texts. Two pivotal organisations on the Ottawa scene gave them the opportunity to do so: the Institut canadien-français d'Ottawa, one of many French-Canadian associations founded at the dawn of the 20th century, in order, as Delisle (2008:13) puts it, to block the assimilationist intentions of the Anglophone majority, and the Association technologique de langue française d'Ottawa, constituted in 1920 to "encourage the methodological production of technological works (called specialised glossaries today)" as well as to "establish a climate favorable to co-operation in research," and "purify the language of legislative and administrative documents produced by the federal government" (Delisle 1984:12).[7] Together, these organisations completed more than 120 terminological studies involving 63 different authors between 1920 and 1949 (Leduc 1985:16, quoted in Delisle 2008:16). Topics as varied as radio broadcasting, elevators, electric generators, insurance policies, and embroidery were covered. Many of these studies were published in *Les Annales*, the annual publication of the Institut canadien-français d'Ottawa, and most of them originated from individual translators who had developed the habit of recording terms on traditional handwritten file cards.

Many more fascinating forays into terminology were made in Canada by true "chevaliers de la refrancisation" (refrancisation knights), to use Delisle's felicitous expression (2008:42). Yet the examples given above suffice to bring out the primary functions that terminology would come to fulfill in Canada: to preserve and promote a minority language, standardise terms, and support translation activities.

---

7. These French-Canadian institutes and associations were mostly located in Quebec. Those located in Ontario contributed to the survival of the French language in that province. The Association technologique de langue française d'Ottawa, the oldest organisation of translators in Canada, started to operate under the name Association des traducteurs et interprètes de l'Ontario (ATIO) in 1962.

4.   The powerful influence of translation

Jean-Claude Boulanger (1984) and Pierre Auger (2001), well-known Quebec scholars in terminology, are among many experts who have highlighted the closely intertwined relationship between translation and terminology in the Canadian context.[8] Auger wrote, for instance:

> Translation — we cannot stress this point enough — has always "accompanied" terminology. Why is that so? A first main reason resides in the fact that terms are needed to translate specialised texts. A second is that terminology has always been an activity first incumbent upon translators. More important still, terminology evolved in the wake of the translation industry.   (Auger 2001: 86–87)

Unsurprisingly, translators were the architects of the first major terminological project launched in Canada, which resulted in the publication, in 1945, of the 1,016-page *Military Dictionary*, English-French, French-English. A team of nine translators from the federal Translation Bureau, assigned for the occasion to the Army Language Bureau, compiled this imposing piece of work under the supervision of Major Pierre Daviault, a leading figure in the history of translation in Canada. As recalled by Delisle and Otis (2016: 223), the project started in 1942; for over a year, it ran simultaneously with a sister project of the US War Department, whose staff had called on their Canadian counterparts to help prepare an English-French dictionary of military terms. The American dictionary, which was being compiled with the prospect of US landings in North Africa and France, appeared at the end of 1943; it contained 45,000 terms. The Canadian dictionary, published two years later, turned out to be more than twice the size, with some 100,000 terms, a great number of which were drawn from translators' personal term-files or collected from the abundance of military documents (instruction and maintenance manuals, periodicals, brochures on weapons handling, etc.) that had been translated from English into French since the beginning of the Second World War. In the preface, Daviault acknowledged that translated material and personal term-files were not the most reliable sources to use. However, just as the crafters of terminological studies that came before them, he and his team did what they could with the means they had.

   With regard to documentation, the means at the time were meager, if not pitiful, a situation that translators were confronted with on a daily basis. Their concern grew in parallel with the increasing volume of technical texts to be translated. Without proper reference material, how were they to find equivalents for

---

8. See also Kerpan (1975 and 1977), Gélinas-Surprenant and Hussman (1993), Williams (1994), and Delisle (1984 and 2008).

the innumerable English neologisms emerging in the wake of technical and scientific innovations? Even the best-intentioned translators would have been discouraged by the magnitude of the challenge. The fact is that "the research stage of the translation process," as terminological research was first known, was "regarded [by many] as a necessary evil" (Gélinas-Surprenant and Hussman 1993:25). Evil or not, it was a task that required considerable time and patience, let alone resourcefulness. To alleviate the burden, "[m]any public and private companies boasting their own teams of translators chose to assign one member of the team to full-time research and data-recording (so as not to duplicate efforts on previously search terms)" (26). This is, in a nutshell, how *terminologist* as a vocation first appeared, with the first terminologist roles taking shape in 1953 at the Translation Bureau of the Government of Canada, although the Association technologique de langue française d'Ottawa has to be credited with laying the groundwork for this historic step.[9]

As a matter of fact, the Association made the first attempt at rescuing Ottawa translators from the throes of term-seeking with the inauguration in 1953 of a lexicology centre where some 50 translators among its members would "devote one night a month [as volunteers] to the compilation of a central card index [...], and all federal government translators were invited to submit the results of their terminological research" (Delisle 1984:30). Less than a year later, Aldéric-Hermas Beaubien, Superintendent of the Translation Bureau, proposed to take the centre under the Bureau's wing to bring into existence, in December 1953, the first Terminology Service named as such in Canada. The beginnings were modest: Jacques Bernuy, a translator, was the sole employee (not yet called a *terminologist*, and Pierre Daviault, by then Beaubien's assistant, was in charge.[10] The Service's original mandate was to address the shortage of documentation and bring some coherence to administrative language. More precisely, Bernuy's duties included "making bilingual cards, drafting terminological bulletins and guidelines, gathering useful documentation, and answering requests for advice over the telephone" (Delisle 1984:31). Replace "bilingual cards" with "bilingual term records," and "over the telephone" with "by email," and you basically have here a modern terminologist's job description. Needless to say, no one in 1953 could have predicted that by 1970, the Terminology Service clients would have access to

---

9. With a staff of 252 translators, managers and support personnel in 1954–1955, the Translation Bureau was no doubt the country's largest employer of translators at the time, and it still is. As of October 2022, there were 695 translators, and 33 terminologists working for the Bureau (Boisvenue 2022).

10. The first occurrence of the term *terminologue* (the French for *terminologist*) identified by Delisle (2008:107) appeared in a job advertisement published by the Translation Bureau in 1967, in the daily newspaper Le Droit.

"more than 2,000 reference works, 120,000 bilingual index cards, 131 terminology bulletins, and 30 periodicals" (Delisle 1984: 43), or that by 1975 the Service would employ some 80 terminologists (Delisle 2008: 151), and operate what is still today one of the biggest term banks in the world, TERMIUM.

The creation of the Translation Bureau's Terminology Service is no doubt a significant and highly symbolic landmark for terminology in Canada. However, to gain ground and visibility, terminology would have to enter a wider range of work settings and fields. From the late 1950s onwards, the implementation of translation services in leading institutions and companies such as the Canadian National Railway Company, Bell Canada, and the Canadian Industries Limited (CIL), proved invaluable in providing "the impetus for what was to become a distinct profession" (Gélinas-Surprenant and Hussman 1993: 26). Indeed, as the Canadian translation industry continued to expand and get better organised, it became obvious that assigning terminology-related tasks to one particular member of a translation team was the way to go with regard to efficiency and term consistency, even in small-scale translation services.

5.   Renewed and strengthened efforts towards francisation

If translation was a catalyst for the development of terminology in Canada, it was not the only one. Beginning in the 1960s, concerns among the French-speaking population regarding the dominance of English resumed on an unprecedented scale, especially in the province of Quebec, where the Quiet Revolution was taking place in a spirit of emancipation and would lead to major social reforms. This time around, there was more at stake than language purity and correctness: it was about keeping French alive among the population. Over the years, low levels of literacy, combined with increased, sustained exposure to English, had taken a toll on the status of the French language. Thus, in the early 1960s,

> Quebec needed to regain control of the linguistic situation in order to ensure the vitality of the French language on its territory and to adapt it to modern commercial and technical realities. Indeed, a language that is used at home only, kept out of the workplace and of the world of commerce and finance, and completely supplanted by English in technical and cutting-edge sectors, has limited chances of survival.
>
> (Dubuc 2001: 17)

Such was the case that French, although still by far the majority language in Quebec, was at that point in a precarious position. From the mid-19th century, the rural exodus that came with industrialisation involved massive population movements to Montréal and a few other urban areas, where work could be found, which created the perfect conditions for English to make great headway into the lives of French Quebecers who, while living in rural villages, had been largely spared its influence.[11] Over time, in the cities, French Quebecers ended up working in companies and factories owned by Anglo-Canadians or Americans, where English was the language of internal communications, with foremen, managers, and bosses in general, and where everything technical or specialised — tools, pieces of machinery and equipment, supplies, procedures, etc. — bore an English name, for "the technology used in Quebec was from England or the United States, thus the vocabulary related to it was known, and assimilated in English" (Linteau 2000: 155).[12]

The Quiet Revolution marked the linguistic awakening of Francophones who, in the early 1960s, counted for approximately 65% of Montréal's population (Robert 2000: 240). Their tolerance began to erode with regard to having to work in English, or not being able to be served in French in shops and businesses across the city.[13] For the first time, language issues became prominent in the public sphere and moved up in the political agenda. Jean Lesage, leader of the Quebec Liberal Party and Premier of Quebec from 1960 to 1966, was quick to take action. On March 24, 1961, less than a year after being elected and in the context of the creation of a Ministry of Culture, he established the Office de la langue française (now known as Office québécois de la langue française, or OQLF), with the mandate to see to the correction and enrichment of the French language, both spoken and written.[14]

5.1 The OQLF: From a symbolic presence to the pivot of language planning

As recounted by Auger (2001: 81–82), the OQLF had a rather timid start, with very limited means at its disposal, and therefore a role that was more symbolic than instrumental. Language quality was the main priority in the early stage. The inaugural *Cahier de l'Office de la langue française* came out in 1965 under the title *Norme du français écrit et parlé au Québec*, with the lofty goal — in barely 8 pages of actual content — of establishing a norm that would apply to the different

---

11. Before the mid-19th century, the population of Quebec was largely rural. In 1850, for instance, less than 20% of people were living in cities. By 1931, this percentage had reached 60% (Linteau 2000: 158).

12. Quebec's economy became increasingly "dominated by English Canadian and American corporations. These corporations tended to present themselves with an English face not only to their own workers but to the public at large in the province" (Coleman 1984: 134).

13. One of the aims of the Quiet Revolution was to foster the growth of a new French Quebecer employer class.

14. In what follows, we will simply refer to this institution as OQLF, even though we will at times discuss periods when it was named Office de la langue française or Régie de la langue française.

aspects of the French language (morphology, syntax, phonetics, and lexicon) and would govern language usage in spheres such as public administration, education, law courts, religious practice, and the media (Ministère des Affaires culturelles du Québec 1965: 6). However small in size, this publication was deemed "very important" by the then Minister of Culture, Pierre Laporte, who wrote in his foreword: "If Quebecers want to continue to speak French, they must impose a rigorous linguistic discipline on themselves, and be constantly vigilant in applying it" (Ministère des Affaires culturelles du Québec 1965: 3).

Only a handful of vocabularies and glossaries were produced in the early years of the OQLF. From 1962 to 1969, short terminological studies were included on a regular basis in a periodical bulletin called *Mieux dire*. Terms were also occasionally discussed in a serial publication that had little to do with terminology in spite of its title, *Guide de terminologie*. Printed from 1962 to 1963 for a total of 12 issues, it is described by Delisle (2008: 47) as a compilation of notes about anglicisms and other usages deemed improper, presented along the puristic lines of "Ne dites pas... Dites plutôt" (Don't say this..., rather say that...).

Things took a fresh turn in November 1969 with the passing of Bill 63, or *Loi pour promouvoir la langue française au Québec*, Quebec's first language law. For the OQLF, this meant increased responsibilities, and with these came greater resources. The OQLF's mandate was refocused on language planning, more precisely on putting measures in place to counter the influence of English in the province and ensure that companies located in Quebec would operate in French. To quote Auger again (2001: 82), terminology came as a natural response to these new responsibilities. Thus were launched the famous *chantiers terminologiques*, those major projects led by the OQLF in the 1970s and 1980s to conduct terminology work in the main industrial and economic sectors represented in the province.

The efforts bore fruit: from its inception in 1961 to the end of the 1990s, the OQLF produced more than 200 glossaries and vocabularies (Maurais 1999: 283), established a systematic vocabulary of terminology (Boutin-Quesnel et al. 1979), and published several methodological guides, among which the *Guide de travail en terminologie* (Auger et al. 1973) and the *Méthodologie de la recherche terminologique* (Auger and Rousseau 1978), two works that are seminal in that they were a first attempt at describing a systematised approach to terminology work.[15] The OQLF also created a term bank, the Banque de terminologie du Québec (BTQ), now known as the Grand dictionnaire terminologique (GDT). As we shall

---

15. The *Guide de travail en néologie technique et scientifique* (Auger et al. 1974) and the *Méthodologie de la recherche terminologique ponctuelle* (Célestin, Godbout, and Vachon-L'Heureux 1984) are two other works worthy of note.

see in Section 7, Jean-Claude Corbeil was a major influence behind many visible achievements by the OLQF.

5.2 The Société Radio-Canada, another major actor in terminology's first hour

As pivotal as they were, the OQLF's *chantiers* were not the only initiatives of the sort. Other public institutions such as the Société Radio-Canada/Canadian Broadcasting Corporation and Hydro-Québec (the main electricity producer in Quebec), major private companies such as Bell Canada (a telephone company), and professional corporations such as the Institute of Chartered Accountants of Quebec, to name but a few, contributed decisively to the ongoing francisation process within their own spheres. The value of their pioneering work cannot be underestimated. In the following paragraphs, we describe the particular case of Société Radio-Canada, since it is where Robert Dubuc, who is viewed as Quebec's father of terminology, spent most of his fruitful career.

The Société Radio-Canada (SRC), the French-language component of Canada's national public broadcaster, was established in 1936, alongside the Canadian Broadcasting Corporation (CBC), the English counterpart. Although French programmes were broadcast by the SRC from the start, the dual institution, with its head office based in Toronto, operated essentially in English. This one-way bilingualism was blatantly prejudicial to the French-speaking employees who, even among themselves, had no way to discuss job duties, working conditions, management of operations, radio and television production and so on, with proper French terminology, since the only terms they had access to were in English. In 1959, in an effort to turn the tide, Philippe Desjardins, head of the translation services at the SRC/CBC's headquarters in Ottawa, appointed an ad hoc committee to translate all job titles used in the institution. It turned out to be an ambitious initiative: altogether, more than a thousand job titles were translated or adapted. This unique terminology experience was deemed fruitful enough for the committee to acquire a permanent status in 1960; named the Comité de linguistique de Radio-Canada, it remained active for some thirty years. Among its first members were two well-known figures: grammarian Jean-Marie Laurence, and Robert Dubuc.

Soon enough, this committee established itself as a major actor on the terminology scene, first through a bulletin launched in 1961 and called *C'est-à-dire*, which proposed short articles on various aspects of French grammar and usage. This bulletin was broadly distributed: two thirds of its readership was outside Radio-Canada, in institutions and private companies where translation was done, and in universities (Groupe de travail sur la qualité de la langue 2003: 6). What made it particularly popular were the *fiches* that were attached to it in the form of perforated index cards, grouped by six on a single sheet to fit into the bulletin but ultimately meant to be separated and filed into a cabinet or shoebox. Some of these *fiches* were intended to provide French equivalents for terms related to radio and television production, e.g. *angle shot, dolly out*. Others were aimed at correcting anglicisms or terms and expressions that were considered to be improper, e.g. *bureau chef* (a calque of *head office*), *châssis doubles* (a calque of *double windows*).

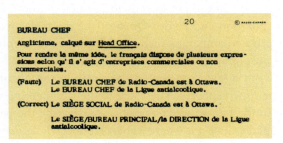

Figure 3. One of Radio-Canada's *fiches*

Jean-Paul Vinay (1962: 23), in a review of the bulletin, congratulates Radio-Canada for its initiative, which, as he put it, "will help to further improve a technical and semi-technical language that has lately made significant progress." The bulletin and its sought-after index cards were printed until 1994. Altogether, more than 7,000 cards were published (Corbeil 2012: 36). Not only did they establish elements of the structure of term records as we know them today, but they also foreshadowed the advent of term banks, inasmuch as they are a remarkable example of a widespread, rapid, and systematic enterprise of terminology dissemination, one of the first of its kind.

6.   Getting ready for terminology to take off

The substantial increase in terminological activities in the 1960s, whether they were carried out in Ottawa as part of Canada's bilingualism policy or in Quebec to promote the use of French in the workforce, made more visible than ever myriad methodological issues that continued in this now fast-developing field of practice. On a positive note, these issues also made terminology itself more visible, and, in due course, it caught the attention of translation and linguistics scholars, who were quick to realise that an emerging discipline with great potential for research and teaching was taking shape. Still, an additional step had to be taken before common working methods and clear guidelines could be defined. As it was, each group or individual engaged in terminology work was doing their best to tackle recurring challenges, without really knowing how things were done elsewhere. For terminology to take root and gain recognition both as a distinct profession and an academic discipline, terminologists had to unite, learn from each other's experience, and find common solutions to shared methodological problems. The occasion came in August 1965 as a direct outgrowth of an initiative taken a year earlier by the Society of Translators and Interpreters of Canada (STIC).

In the early 1960s, although a decade or so had passed since the creation of the Translation Bureau's Terminology Service, finding French terms remained difficult for most translators. A further attempt to alleviate the situation came from the STIC, which created a Documentation Commission in 1964. For Delisle (2008: 34), this is a pivotal moment in the history of terminology in Canada: in its mission statement, the Commission formulated principles that would end up shaping the profession. Those principles all pointed in the same direction: sharing resources and collaborating to develop the best practices and training in terminology.

A year later, in 1965, the STIC organised a five-day symposium to which were invited thirteen "translators and linguists who, by their profession or situation, had an active interest in the advancement of linguistics and terminology in Canada" (*La rédaction* 1965: 63). These guests were representatives from the Translation Bureau, the OQLF, SRC, STIC, Société des traducteurs de Montréal, the Canadian National Railway Company, the Canada Council for the Arts, Canada's Ministry of Agriculture, as well as the Université de Montréal and the Université Laval. For the first time, major actors in the field had a chance to sit at the same table to talk terminology. Translation scholar Jean Darbelnet, from Université Laval, acted as facilitator for the occasion. On the agenda were three items:

> (1) to make an inventory of available resources in those fields [linguistics and terminology]; (2) to explore ways of improving the coordination of terminology work, with regard to research but also at the level of terminology dissemination; (3) to study the possibility of creating, in the near future, a national centre for terminology and linguistics.   (*La rédaction* 1965: 63)

Those broad themes provided the starting point for addressing various theoretical and practical considerations: the importance of relying on original documentation rather than translations when researching terminology, the necessity — up to a point — of standardising terms, and the need to agree on the content of term records, among others (Delisle 2008: 36–37). It is also on that occasion that Jean-Paul Vinay, who was at the time director of the center for lexicographical research at Université de Montréal, suggested the revolutionary idea of an electronic word bank (Delisle 2008: 37).

This symposium brought consensus among practitioners and scholars as to what methodological gaps needed to be addressed, and how to plan for a sustained, more organised growth of this promising and fast-developing field of practice. By the same token, it also established a tradition of regular gatherings to discuss terminology methodology, best practices, and eventually theory.[16] According to Delisle (2008:171), forty-four such terminology events were held in Canada between 1970 and 1989, an average of two per year. The OQLF, the Translation Bureau, universities, and other major institutions took turns hosting these events. On many occasions, terminology specialists from abroad would join in, including Eugen Wüster, Helmut Felbert, Alain Rey, Roger Goffin, and Pierre Gilbert, to name but a few.

By the late 1960s and early 1970s, everything was thus set in place for terminology to take off in Canada: language laws reinforcing the status of French at the federal and provincial levels, a constant, surging demand for French terms due to an intensification of English to French translation and the francisation campaign initiated in Quebec, a strong interest for terminology among scholars in translation and linguistics, and the will to join forces to develop a methodology and tools, notably a term bank. Leading figures also emerged, to whom we owe many initiatives that in time solidly positioned terminology not only in the workplace, but also in university curricula and research centers, and later contributed to establishing the reputation of Canada on the international scene. Professor André Clas, from Université de Montréal, is one such figure, having revived in 1968 the idea of creating a Canadian term bank and taking the lead to see the project through (Delisle 2008:215; Bastin 2020). As noted above, this idea was proposed by Vinay in 1965, but it is Clas who provided the impetus needed to get things going. The Banque de terminologie de l'Université de Montréal (BTUM), which became TERMIUM in 1975 after being acquired by the Translation Bureau of the Government of Canada, was inaugurated in 1971 while Clas was the chair of the department of linguistics and modern languages.[17] A tireless promoter of terminology, Clas made sure to make plenty of room for it in *Meta*, the well-known translation journal that he edited for forty years (1967–2007).

For his part, Robert Dubuc, our national father of terminology, worked on all fronts: not only was he a prominent member of the linguistics committee of Radio-Canada, but he also set the stage for terminology training in Canada, being the originator of the first university course in terminology, and the author of "the

---

16. As Rondeau states (1980:158), terminology was a young discipline in the Canadian context, and elaborating theories was not a primary task for those involved in its initial development. Rather, urgent practical needs are what triggered these early terminological activities.

17. It is not possible to elaborate here on the origins and specificities of TERMIUM nor on those of the Banque de terminologie du Québec (Grand dictionnaire terminologique under its current name). Once again, one should consult Delisle (2008), who dedicates a 58-page chapter to these two "national jewels." See also Chapter 30 on the influence of these two term banks in the development of terminology databases in Switzerland.

first full-fledged textbook to be published in Canada on the subject of terminology" (Bowker 2017: 156), the *Manuel pratique de terminologie*, which ran through four editions from 1978 to 2002, and was adapted into English in 1997 under the title *Terminology: A Practical Approach*. Alongside Marcel Paré, Dubuc played a significant role in the early years of the BTUM, acting as chief terminologist for this gargantuan project that aimed "to provide clients with a remedy for the [...] dearth of reliable terminological documentation, its dispersion and its inaccessibility" (Dubuc 1972: 203).

But among the many individuals who were fully committed to the cause of terminology in the booming period from the late 1960s through the late 1970s, Jean-Claude Corbeil, "the pillar of francisation in Quebec" (De Villers 2022), unquestionably deserves special attention, inasmuch as his specific conception of language planning — and most particularly the central place that terminology occupies in that context — has very much shaped the way terminology has developed and been practised in Quebec.[18]

7.   Jean-Claude Corbeil's influence and legacy

After completing a Ph.D. in Linguistics at the Université de Strasbourg in 1966, Jean-Claude Corbeil took up sociolinguistics around 1968 while a professor in the linguistics department at the Université de Montréal. He developed a particular interest in issues such as the French language used in Quebec as compared to France and other Francophone countries, and the status of the French language in Quebec and Canada (Centre de recherche interuniversitaire sur le français en usage au Québec [n.d.]). This interest quickly took him away from his academic career: in 1971 he became the first linguistic director of the OQLF, a position he held until 1978 and through which he honed his sociolinguistic thoughts and found many occasions to put them into practice.

Corbeil entered the OQLF at a time when everything had yet to be done in Quebec in the area of language planning. As mentioned earlier, the first provincial language law, Bill 63, or *Loi pour promouvoir la langue française au Québec*, had been instituted in 1969 under Jean-Jacques Bertrand's Union nationale government, but it was left to the Liberal Party of Robert Bourassa, elected in April

---

18. Corbeil is also well-known for his *Dictionnaire visuel*, a dictionary that has been translated into thirty-five languages, distributed in more than a hundred countries, and sold some nine million copies over the years (Cajolet-Laganière 2022). Presumably the best-selling terminology work of all time, the *Dictionnaire visuel* was first authored solely by Corbeil in 1986, then coauthored with Ariane Archambault for later editions.

1970, to preside over its implementation. Two months after his election, Premier Bourassa made it clear that his government was "firmly determined to take all possible measures to secure the use of French in the workplace, everywhere in Quebec" (Corbeil 2007b: 149); in fact, this had been one of Bourassa's campaign promises. However, the government had no specific action plan, and the OQLF was not yet set up to take on additional duties.

A year passed before concrete actions were taken: in March 1971, Premier Bourassa appointed a new director of the OQLF, Gaston Cholette, entrusting him with the institution's reorganisation along the lines of the francisation dossier. Cholette wasted no time in recruiting collaborators who would help "create from scratch a francisation strategy" (Corbeil 2007b: 152). Hired as linguistic director in those unique circumstances, Corbeil found in his new function an ideal opportunity for promoting his idea of language planning, of which terminology was to become a central component.

Corbeil's language planning model is based on the postulate that interventions in language cannot be planned solely from a top-down perspective. Hence his proposal early on to replace the term *planification linguistique* that had hitherto been adopted in French as the equivalent of *language planning* by *aménagement linguistique*, which could be translated in English as *language management*, a term that was felt to be devoid of the authoritarian connotations often associated with state interventionism. For Corbeil, language planning is not meant to impose norms on language users, but rather to orchestrate, on the basis of their needs and in their own interest, a coordinated response to a sociolinguistic situation that needs to be redressed. Such a process requires detailed knowledge of the situation itself, and when two languages compete, an in-depth analysis of how each is actually used in a specific context.

Accordingly, if French was to replace English in Quebec's workplace, the strategic starting point that imposed itself, as Corbeil puts it (2007b: 152), was to examine the "communication circuit" in typical companies, in order to determine who communicates with whom, in which language and mode (written or oral) and for what purpose. Field study and surveys would thus be the course to take — a course that was not commonplace at the time, as sociolinguistics was still in its infancy. In other words, OQLF staff would have to go on-site to observe real-life business operations and communication dynamics to see if and how French was used, with the declared goal of finding ways to intensify and generalise its use at every level and in all aspects of the organisation's activities.

But first, the OQLF had to find companies that would agree to participate in its sociolinguistic experiment and thereby commit to making French the normal and everyday language on their premises. In fact, taking part in the study meant undergoing an actual francisation process, a process that would inevitably have broad implications for the company's operations and could potentially have — at least during the implementation phase — a negative impact on productivity or profits. As Corbeil recalls (2007b: 155), the francisation plan put forth by the provincial government was far from being popular in those days, and finding business owners or managers who would happily welcome the OQLF's personnel and work with them towards building a francisation strategy was an uphill task. Still, Cholette managed to convince thirteen companies to help lay the groundwork of the OQLF's francisation strategy.[19]

7.1   From language planning to terminology planning

The OQLF's observers soon realised that administrative and technical terminology was a stumbling block for most workers as the only terms they knew were English ones, which they would use even when communicating in French. From that point onwards, terminology became a major component of the OQLF's overall francisation strategy and a core area of activity for Corbeil and his team who subsequently focussed their attention on how terms become entrenched in language.

> We especially wanted to understand by whom and by what means terms are disseminated, and which routes they take to enter the usual vocabulary of those who speak the language. More precisely, we sought to discover the points (or nodes) where terms are chosen or created, and then put into circulation in various types of communications (mostly written but also oral) [...].   (Corbeil 2007a: 94)

Five major routes of terminology dissemination were identified: industrial communications (e.g. instruction manuals, staff training), administrative documents (e.g. job descriptions, collective agreements), commercial texts (e.g. advertisements, product catalogues), governmental materials (e.g. building and electrical codes, forms and information leaflets), and scientific and technical communications (e.g. teaching materials, scientific publications). Collectively, these "institutionalised communications" would need to be at the forefront of terminology planning efforts in Quebec (Corbeil 2007a: 95).[20]

---

19. Two banks (the Royal Bank of Canada and the Bank of Montreal), two refineries (BP and Golden Eagle), two pulp and paper companies (Domtar and CIP), a textile company (Dominion Textile), a retail business (General Cigar), and five factories (General Electric of Canada, Canada Packers, Canadian Industries, Canadian Johns-Manville and Noranda Metal Industries) (Corbeil 2007b: 155).

20. Unsurprisingly, the notion of "institutionalised communications" would form the background of Quebec's linguistic policy, since Corbeil participated in the elaboration of both the

Terminology remained central to Corbeil's conception of language planning, and in fact developed into a comprehensive terminology planning strategy drawn from the following premises:

> The creation of terminologies is a prerequisite to teaching specialised subjects [...]; it is a prerequisite to using a language at work, whether it be in public administration, industry, shops or offices; it is a prerequisite if any language is to serve as a language of science and technology [...]. Any modern language requires constant and systematic neological activity. A language that stops producing its own terminology is doomed to pass into folklore or be downgraded to second-class status [...]. Quebecers have had that experience: the generalised use of English had persuaded both Anglophones and a substantial proportion of Francophones that it was impossible to do anything serious in French because — so they believed — the French language did not have proper terminology. It will have taken ten years of terminology work to convince everyone to the contrary.
>
> (Corbeil 2007b[1989]: 429–430)

Just as, in Corbeil's view, language planning interventions require a concerted effort with members of the communities concerned, whose adherence to the process and participation in it alone can only ensure positive and durable results, terminology planning is not the sole business of terminologists. For Corbeil (2007b: 432), it is incumbent upon subject-field specialists to develop and maintain their own terminology. Therefore, terminologists should not monopolise the terminology planning process; their role should be one of guidance and support. Terminology planning should accordingly be a team effort, with specialists bringing in their understanding of the concepts and of the structural organisation of terms in their field, and terminologists contributing with their linguistic expertise regarding, for instance, term creation strategies and lexical borrowing, and their broad knowledge of lexicography and terminology resources.

7.2   Systematic terminology *à la Québécoise*

If providing workers with appropriate French terminology was a necessity with regard to francisation of the workplace in Quebec, it nonetheless represented a daunting challenge: not only did Corbeil and his team have to inventory the many English terms used to carry on day-to-day business operations, and concurrently devise a method for gathering the corresponding French terms, they also had to outline a strategy to effectively replace English terms by French terms in the workplace (Corbeil 2007a: 94). The task at hand had little to do with ad hoc term

---

Loi sur la langue officielle (Bill 22) and the *Charte de la langue française* (Bill 101) adopted by Quebec's National Assembly in 1974 and 1977 respectively.

research as performed in translation settings, and the valuable Canadian expertise that had been built in terminology in the previous decade or so was therefore not very helpful:

> [...] it quickly became clear that the extent of terminology needs was such that a new methodological approach was required, one that could be applied to large sets of terms and concepts [...] and could involve collaboration among professionals from various backgrounds (translators, linguists, subject-field specialists) working in the public, parapublic and private sectors. This is why Quebec came up with a specific methodology for terminology work.   (Corbeil 1985: 6)

This methodology is both systematic and comparative: systematic in that it allows for the treatment of groups of terms rather than isolated terms, and comparative in that it implies establishing separate lists of terms in each language (English and French) *before* comparing them to see convergences, divergences, and possible gaps in one language or the other. Gaps in French are then filled through neological creations, and thus the need for guidelines in this area.[21] Pierre Auger, in his introduction to the *Méthodologie de la recherche terminologique*, sketched out the basic tenets of the OQLF approach:

> Our approach [...] is oriented on terminology work done in two languages that we consider equally "competent" to designate technico-scientific realities, even though each of these languages is, in its own way, a reflection of a different and particular mapping of the world's realities. In fact, language allomorphism as revealed through terminology work demonstrates in an absolute way the necessity of a separate description [...] for each terminological system under study. It is only at the final stage that the two descriptions are compared and term equivalence is established through the concept. Gaps thus revealed in the target language [French in this case] are to be filled with neologisms.   (Auger 1978: 12)

Auger portrays the OQLF methodology, which he helped to develop,[22] as a middle ground between a typical translation-based approach to terminology and Eugen Wüster's General Theory of Terminology, which, incidentally, is also referred to as *systematic* (Auger 2001: 89) (see Chapter 8 on Wüster's Theory).[23] The OQLF

---

21. With regard to neology in terminology, Jean-Claude Boulanger, who was a terminologist at the OQLF from 1974 to 1984, and a professor of terminology and lexicology at the Université Laval from 1984 to 2011, was indisputably the leading expert in Canada. One of his publications (Boulanger 1986) presents a detailed account of the role of neology in Quebec's language planning policy.

22. Pierre Auger entered the OQLF as a linguist-terminologist in 1971, and held various positions between 1975 and 1987, among which that of director of the terminology division. From 1987 to 2009, he was a professor of terminology at Université Laval.

approach differs markedly from Wüster's: it is semasiological rather than onomasiological, which implies that it is corpus-based. Since the OQLF terminologists "start from the terms to go to the concepts" (Auger 1978: 12), their first task is to collect terms and other terminological data from a variety of sources that are representative of the subject-field being studied. As explained in the OQLF guide *Méthodologie de la recherche terminologique* (Auger and Rousseau 1978: 26–29), both written and oral sources are used, but "since only a portion of terminology is conveyed through oral language, written sources should serve as a basis" (29). This also demonstrates that the OQLF approach is in line with the principles of socioterminology (see Chapter 11 on this approach). Indeed, according to John Humbley (2018: 470), "the practice of socioterminology originated in Quebec, and it could be claimed that it was here that it was effectively and extensively practiced for the first time." This is also Boulanger's point of view. Boulanger, who coined the term *socioterminology* in 1981, considers that "socioterminology has long been tacitly present in the very concept of language planning," and prompts us to remember that the OQLF's first "terminological pursuits" were, after all, initiated by means of on-site fieldwork (Boulanger 1995: 195).

8.   Terminology enters universities

Another sign of the rising popularity of terminology in Canada during the 1970s and 1980s, and its legitimisation as a discipline in its own right, was the development of terminology courses in various colleges and universities across the country. Dubuc pioneered the teaching of terminology in Canada in 1969 at the Université de Montréal. Dubuc's course, offered in the context of a BA in Translation, was combined with a technical translation seminar to allow for hands-on training. It became an autonomous terminology course in 1973, but nevertheless remained anchored in a translation perspective (Delisle 2008: 272). Such was the case for the majority of terminology courses that came into existence in the following years. By the late 1980s, all undergraduate translation programmes in Canada included at least one terminology course (273), for a total of some thirty terminology courses altogether taught in colleges and universities throughout the country (Kennedy 1986).

A few universities in Quebec stood out at the time, adopting a sociolinguistic take on terminology rather than presenting it as a mere ancillary function of translation. The Université du Québec à Trois-Rivières (UQTR) was one of them. Under an agreement with the OQLF, a terminology course was offered as early as

---

23. Links can also be drawn with the Prague School of Terminology (see Chapter 9).

1972 to students from both the BA in Linguistics and in Translation. Auger, then director of the terminology division at the OQLF, was the initiator of this course in which terminology was introduced as an application of modern linguistics, a language-planning tool such as was being developed in Quebec. At the Université du Québec à Montréal (UQAM), where there was no translation programme, a Certificate in Terminology was inaugurated in 1980. The sole instance of its kind, it was entirely grounded in linguistics, with mandatory courses including an introduction to terminology, methods of terminology work, and terminology, computer science and documentation, among others, and optional courses covering the study of language, lexicology and lexicography, semiology and semantics, and language planning.[24] According to Delisle (2008:273), this programme was meant for anyone whose job necessitated having a good handle on technical and scientific language (e.g. translators, technical writers, and journalists). Unfortunately, it no longer exists.

Another noteworthy achievement, and one that shows that terminology in Canada was, by the late 1970s, gaining ground as a theoretical discipline, is the creation of two MA programmes in terminology, both offered in French. The honour for launching the first ever MA in terminology — that is, the first in the world — belongs to the Université Laval (Delisle 2008:275). Developed with the OQLF support in 1978, this programme was open to students with undergraduate degrees in Translation, Linguistics or other disciplines. According to the description provided by Elaine Kennedy (1986), it included ten courses and an internship, all mandatory, as well as research credits. Its name, MA en terminologie et traduction, and the list of courses covering general terminology, translational terminology and terminological neologism, among others, show that it was a combination of translation-oriented and linguistics-oriented terminology. The second programme, the MA en linguistique appliquée: terminologie, was started at Université de Montréal in 1981, but came to an end in the late 1990s. Designed for graduates in translation or linguistics, it included three mandatory terminology courses on theory, practice, and the use of computers, complemented by electives in translation, lexicology, machine translation, computational linguistics, or translation theory, among others.

The introduction of terminology in Canadian university curricula in the 1970s and early 1980s coincided with the publication of the first methodological guides and textbooks. Apart from Dubuc's book and the OQLF publications mentioned earlier, another book, *Introduction à la terminologie*, was published at the time by professor Guy Rondeau, from Université Laval. It went through two editions (1981 and 1984), the first subsidised by the OQLF, and the second featuring

---

24. See Kennedy 1986 for a complete description of the programme.

a preface by Corbeil. Commenting on that work, Lynne Bowker (2017:157) draws attention to the fact that Rondeau used it "to posit some theoretical foundations for terminology and to inventory some of its applications around the world," and that in doing so, Rondeau's book "[i]n many ways [...] complemented the existing practical Canadian works on terminology."

9.   Common law in French: Another Canadian milestone

This chapter would not be complete without an overview of one more terminological accomplishment, namely the francisation of common law, which was prompted by yet another situation specific of Canada: *bijuralism*. Canada's colonial history not only fostered the recognition of two official languages, but also the co-existence of two legal systems: the English common law and the French civil law. Following the founding of New France in the 16th century, the civil law tradition "became firmly rooted in the territory that would later become part of Canada" (Gaudreault 2006:206). With the British conquest that followed and the Royal Proclamation of 1763 came the imposition of common law in all matters. However, as the French-speaking inhabitants continued to observe their former rules and customs when dealing among themselves, the civil law tradition survived in the colony (by now called Quebec by the British) and was eventually reinstated by the British Parliament with the Quebec Act of 1774 for matters pertaining to property and civil rights. In the meantime, criminal and penal matters, and public matters generally, remained under the common law regime. Thus was born Canada's dual legal system.

Provisions for bijuralism were preserved in the *Constitution Act of 1867*, when powers and responsibilities were divided between the federal government and the provinces. It was established that the Parliament of Canada would legislate "first and foremost in the area of public law," which would be "governed by common law principles" (Levert 2004:153), while matters of private law would be dealt with at the provincial level.[25] As a result, the province of Quebec continued to be governed by civil law in matters of private law, while in all the other provinces and in the territories, common law would apply throughout, in both private and public matters.

The co-existence within a single state of two legal systems and the resulting interaction between the two are likely in themselves to pose a particular challenge, even when legislative powers are — on paper — clearly distributed. In the Canadian

---

25. Note that under the Constitution, the Parliament of Canada "has full legislative jurisdiction over the territories, although it has delegated much of this power to the territorial legislatures through devolution" (Brideau, Brosseau, and Lowenger 2022:1).

context, for instance, "it happens fairly often [...] that laws enacted by the Parliament of Canada touch on concepts or notions involving private law," and the federal government "is even on occasion required by the Constitution to legislate on matters that definitely fall within the private law domain, such as bankruptcy legislation" (Levert 2004: 153). As we know too, legal issues per se "intermix and transcend domains in legal situations which are often complex and multifaceted," and they "take no account of the separation of legislative powers" (McLaren 2017: 8).

The level of challenge is multiplied when you add legislative bilingualism to the equation, that is, the obligation to adopt and publish statutes in both official languages. In Canada today, this obligation exists for the federal government, but also for the governments of Manitoba, New Brunswick, Ontario, and Quebec, where provincial laws have come to be enacted in both English and French as certain constitutional obligations towards minority-language communities were acknowledged (Labelle 2016: 134). Another important aspect of this complex situation is that "once a bilingual statute is enacted pursuant to a constitutional obligation, both the French and the English versions are authentic and have equal authority in law" (McLaren quoted in Biel 2015: 14).

9.1 Bijuralism and bilingualism *à la Canadienne*[26]

Adding bilingualism to bijuralism creates four legal audiences in Canada: Francophones under civil law, Francophones under common law, Anglophones under civil law, and Anglophones under common law (Levert 2004). What does that imply in practice? Not only that each audience should have access to legislative texts in the official language of their choice, but also that they should find in those texts "wording and terminology corresponding to the legal system in effect in their respective province or territory" (158). Easier said than done when there is no established terminology for a particular legal system in one of the two official languages... which was the case until recently for common law in French, as "the terminology network of common law evolved exclusively in English over the course of several centuries" (McLaren 2017: 2).

Yet, Canada's federal government has been able to follow through with its constitutional obligation of legislative bilingualism since 1867. How could that be? Lionel A. Levert (2001: 6–7) provides a clear answer to this question:

---

26. Heading inspired from the title of a lecture given in February 2017 by jurilinguist Louis Beaudoin at Quebec House, the Quebec Government Office in London, UK. The complete title of the lecture was: Common Law in French and Civil Law in English — Bijuralism and Bilingualism à la canadienne!

> Until the 1970s, all acts were drafted in English and then translated into French by translators who were not recognised as having any particular skills in law and who were usually forced as a result to convey the message of the English version very slavishly. Since they did not have any current resources concerning the common law in French or the civil law in English, the expression of the interaction between federal law and private law was based on makeshift equivalents that they devised on the basis of the available resources and without concern for the problems of interpretation that could result in some parts of the country. [...] [T]he English version of the federal statutes tended to reproduce the terminology and concepts of the common law while the French version derived its terminology from civil law sources.

Although this approach may have been enough to meet the requirements of legislative bilingualism, there was a serious drawback to it: "two of the four audiences mentioned above were ignored, namely Francophones living outside Quebec who are subject to common law and Quebec Anglophones who are subject to civil law" (Levert 2001: 7). These neglected audiences were in fact the two official Canadian minority language communities; their members would not be familiar with the terms and concepts embodied in federal legislation as they differed from those of the legal system in effect in the provinces where they lived.

Producing an adapted English version of the federal statutes for Anglophones living in Quebec, that is to say a version written along the lines of the civilian legal tradition, was a real possibility, since "Quebec's civil law has been 'bilingual' for a long time and has developed its own English vocabulary" (Levesque 2016: 722–723). Indeed, the very first version of Quebec's Civil Code which came into force in 1866, namely *The Civil Code of Lower Canada*, was bilingual.[27] Producing an adapted French version for the Francophones living in majority English-speaking provinces and territories governed by common law was another story.

9.2   Jurilinguists to the rescue

The lack of appropriate French terminology to express common law concepts was brought to full light in the mid-1970s, when the provinces of New Brunswick, Ontario, and Manitoba began translating their own statutes into French, and when common law started to be taught in French at the Université de Moncton

---

27. There is no doubt, however, that the Paul-André Crépeau Centre for Private and Comparative Law (formerly known as the Quebec Research Centre of Private and Comparative Law) founded in 1975 by professor Paul-André Crépeau from McGill University's Faculty of Law, has played a major part in describing the English terminology of Quebec private law and in making it available through valuable resources published in the context of its Private Law Dictionaries and Bilingual Lexicons project.

and the University of Ottawa. Because federal statutes had traditionally been translated from English to French using civil law terminology, there was no common law vocabulary in French to rely on, and consequently terms were forged "in an ad hoc fashion as and when needed" (McLaren 2017: 3). The resulting body of terms had evolved "any old how, in an approximative fashion, in order to fulfill one-off needs, without uniformity between the provinces and territories and the federal government, and without scientific foundation" (4). This lack of uniformity became "a major threat to the integrity and the intelligibility of the langage of common law in French," argues Karine McLaren, present director of the Centre de traduction et de terminologie juridiques (CTTJ) at the Université de Moncton. She adds:

> Whereas in English legal notions were expressed by terms capable of universal use, whose meaning was defined and recognised, in French the multiplicity of terminological "solutions" or equivalents which were more or less approximate and which existed here and there in Canada made their expression in French fraught with difficulty and uncertainty.   (McLaren 2017: 3)

The time was ripe to develop a standardised French common law vocabulary that "judges, legislators, lawyers, authors, law professors, translators: those whose task is to express the law" (McLaren 2017: 6) could depend on.[28] The CTTJ, established in 1979 by the Université de Moncton Faculty of Law to support the teaching of common law in French, spearheaded this major move.[29] Under the guidance of founding director Gérard Snow, a jurist, jurilinguist, and certified translator, the CTTJ implemented a rigorous working method to start the francisation of common law vocabulary afresh. The aim was to build the French terminology on the same conceptual network as the English, in order to achieve an exact correspondence between the two. This way, each French term would

---

28. As pointed out by André Labelle (2016: 135), "it was [also] time to take drafting in both official languages seriously." Canada's Department of Justice took a proactive stance in that respect in 1978, switching from translation to an innovative co-drafting approach. This approach involves two legally-trained, bilingual drafters, one with French as first language and the other, English; "each drafter is expected to comment on the text of the other drafter, and each has the responsibility of ensuring that both texts are consistent with each other" (Levert 2004: 155). Because "legislative drafters are not by definition language experts," jurilinguists also participate in the process (Levert 2004: 156). The government of New Brunswick also turned to co-drafting, while the other Canadian jurisdictions that legislate in both official languages still resort to translation (McLaren quoted in Biel 2015: 14–15).

29. The Faculty of Law of the Université de Moncton itself broke ground in 1978, being the first university in the world to offer a Bachelor of Law programme (LL. B.) in common law taught entirely in French.

"occupy exactly the same place given to the corresponding English term in the legal system, failing which it is the legal system itself which is modified" (4). Such a method involved "a thorough analysis of [each term's] particular place and function within the legal notional network" of common law; hence the work would have to be "accomplished by expert jurilinguists" (4), that is, linguists or translators who have knowledge of the language of the law.[30]

Two years into this arduous and intricate enterprise, the CTTJ became the driving force of the Program for the Integration of Both Official Languages in the Administration of Justice (POLAJ), a national programme introduced in 1981 by Canada's Department of Justice "to improve access to justice in both official languages by promoting, among other things, the creation of tools for the people who draft legislation" (Levert 2001: 8).[31] Since POLAJ's major responsibility is to coordinate and support efforts towards the development and standardisation of common law in French, the tools created under its auspices are to a large extent terminological in nature, and primarily meant to disseminate the recommendations of a standardisation committee that was in due time formed by POLAJ. These tools are of major importance, as they are

> used by legal professionals to offer legal services to justice system users; to teach common law in French; to support language training of professionals in the justice field; to provide legislative drafters with the legal vocabulary necessary to draft laws in both official languages; and to provide legal translators, court interpreters and stenographers with a reliable vocabulary for expressing the law in the other official language.   (McLaren quoted in Paradis 2017: 29)

The CTTJ was productive right from day one. Even before POLAJ was implemented, the Moncton-based team published the initial volume of the *Vocabulaire anglais-français et lexique français-anglais de la common law*, the very first English-

---

30. Jean-Claude Gémar defines jurilinguistics as a practice and discipline at the crossroads of law and linguistics (2005 and 2011), a "crucible in which legal languages, translation, terminology, lexicography, comparative law, linguistics, and semiotics intermix" (Gémar quoted in Girard 2022: 467). It has taken shape "in the last quarter of the twentieth century and in the wake of translation," and "Canada has, for reasons related to its history, languages and legal traditions, acted as a pioneer in [its] development" (Gémar 2005: n.p.). An emeritus professor at the Université de Montréal and the Université de Genève, where he taught legal translation and jurilinguistics, Gémar coined the French term "jurilinguistique" and used it for the first time, with its English equivalent, in the title of a collective work he edited in 1982: *Langage du droit et traduction: essais de jurilinguistique/The Language of the Law and Translation: Essays on Jurilinguistics* (Gémar, quoted in Girard 2022: 464).

31. POLAJ has since been renamed Promoting Access to Justice in Both Official Languages (PAJLO).

French terminological publication on the common law as a system of private law (Delisle 2008: 310). More volumes were to follow, covering the main areas of private law (civil procedure, law of property, law of trusts, law of succession, law of contracts, law of torts, etc.) and introducing many French neologisms that were created as part of the standardisation process. Term creation was indeed frequent, as it was "necessary to introduce into the [French] language significant legal terms that simply [did] not exist in that language" (McLaren 2017: 2). The jurilinguists at CTTJ resorted to both semantic and formal neology: some terms from the civilian tradition were "recycled and integrated into the conceptual network of the common law," a few archaisms "were given a new life, such as 'tenance' for 'tenancy'," and new terms stemming from existing French morphemes were coined (Snow 2002: 187).

Another example of the fine work done at the CTTJ is the *Juridictionnaire*, a compendium of difficulties and expressions typical of the French legal language as it is used in the Canadian context. Compiled by jurilinguist Jacques Picotte and published from 1991 in a series of volumes, this work is now available online via the CTTJ website and integrated as well into the writing tools offered by the Translation Bureau on the online Language Portal of Canada. Last but certainly not least, JURITERM, a bilingual term bank created in 1993 which now contains "over 18,000 entries in every field of private common law, including the complete standardised French vocabulary of the common law" (CTTJ [n.d.]), is clearly the jewel in the crown of the CTTJ.[32]

Although the CTTJ's achievements are the result of a collective effort, Gérard Snow, its founder and director for thirty years, is largely acknowledged as the inspiration behind it all. The fact that he was awarded in 2007 the highest Canadian civilian honour — the Order of Canada — for his "immeasurable" contribution "to the integration of the French language in the practice of common law in New Brunswick and elsewhere in Canada" (The Governor General of Canada website [n.d.]) says a lot about the national importance of his work. Likewise, there is no question for Delisle (2008: 311–312) that Canada attained international recognition with regard to common law in French thanks to Snow's exemplary dedication to the cause.[33]

---

32. JURITERM can be consulted for free from the CTTJ's website. Apart from conducting research and publishing terminological resources, the CTTJ offers translation, revision, drafting, and consulting services. It has also compiled and maintains an exhaustive bibliography of jurilinguistic works published in French. As of October 2022, this bibliography contained 56 pages and covered works published from 1847 to this day.

33. Snow's dedication has not wavered over the years. Among other things, he co-authored in 2010 the first general French common law dictionary, *La common law de A à Z* (Vanderlinden, Snow, and Poirier 2010), a work that covers nearly 3,000 concepts and includes an English-

Two other jurilinguistic centres contributed to the standardisation of the French vocabulary of common law in the context of POLAJ. The Centre for Legal Translation and Documentation (CLTD), cofounded in 1981 by the University of Ottawa and the Association des juristes d'expression française de l'Ontario (AJEFO), "has been helping to develop a body of French terminology for Ontario legislation and the common law since its earliest days" (CLTD 2022a). Its role is "to create the legal documentation needed for practicing law and delivering legal services in French, primarily in Ontario, but also in the other common law provinces and territories" (CLTD 2022a). The CLTD has compiled various lexicons over the years. Of particular interest is the *Lexicon of Ontario Statutes and Regulations*, which contains close to 50,000 English terms and their French equivalents, all taken from the statutes and regulations of Ontario, many accompanied by examples of phrasing (CLTD 2022b). More recently, in 1998, it produced a *Legal Glossary of Federal Statutes* which contains some 85,000 English entries collected from the statutes of Canada, with their French equivalents (CLTD 2022c).

For its part, the Institut Joseph-Dubuc, known since 2011 as the Centre de ressources en français juridique (CRFJ), was established in 1984 at the Université de Saint-Boniface, in Manitoba, to develop work tools and provide continuing language training for French-speaking legal practitioners from Western and Northern Canada, and later from the Maritime provinces as well. The CRFJ is broadly known for its workshops on legal terminology, which are part of a national legal terminology training programme that it offers in more than ten cities to a varied clientele: Crown counsel, judges, clerks of the court and other officers of the court, associations of French-language legal practitioners, law firms, translators, etc. (Blais 2009: 14). The CRFJ is also active in compiling terminological resources and making them freely available. For example, as of December 2022, it offers close to 60 bilingual glossaries of terms and expressions used under common law, with themes spanning from impaired driving to tax law, intellectual property, DNA, and terrorism and national security. Worthy of mention are also hundreds of linguistic capsules about French legal terms or expressions displayed as a browsable list on its website.

Apart from the CTTJ, the CLTD, and the CRFJ, McGill-based Paul-André Crépeau Centre for Private and Comparative Law as well as the Translation Bureau of the Government of Canada are part of POLAJ's standardisation committee (McLaren 2017: 3).

French index. A second edition, revised and expanded, was published in 2017. This work represents a concrete implementation of terminological principles.

10.   Conclusion

In 1984, Guy Rondeau explains as follows his decision to publish a revised, updated edition of his *Introduction à la terminologie* only three years after the first:

> the evolution of terminology as a discipline — in its theoretical, methodological, and pragmatic aspects as well as in its territorial expansion — is so fast that it becomes necessary to provide an update not every ten years, but rather every two years.
> (Rondeau 1984: xl)

Indeed, things moved very fast, as giant steps were taken during the 1970s and 1980s to gather French terms and to disseminate them on a large scale through glossaries, vocabularies, and term banks, while concurrent efforts were made to develop and implement concerted working methods, reflect on theoretical considerations, and create university courses and programmes in terminology. The number of terminologists — now proudly bearing this title — grew rapidly in those two decades, especially with the creation of TERMIUM and the BTQ. According to Delisle (2008: 151), up to 80 terminologists were working for the Translation Bureau in 1975, and 70 for the OQLF. About 20 Montréal-based companies also had their own terminology services. There were thus between 150 and 200 practising terminologists in Canada by the mid-1970s. By the turn of the 1990s, terminologists were formally recognised as a professional body in the provinces of Ontario, New Brunswick, and Quebec.[34]

As we have seen, terminology has played a key role in the official bilingualism policy of Canada, in bringing French to the forefront in Quebec businesses, industries, and commerce, and in developing a standardised vocabulary of common law in French. During the period covered in this chapter, terminology work primarily served the French language and, as a professional activity, it was mainly concentrated in the vicinities of the federal government in Ottawa and the greater Montreal urban area in Quebec. However, over time, it has come to cover more ground, in various respects. For instance, terminology is part of the solution to protect and strengthen the Inuit language (see Government of Nunavut and Nunavut Tunngavik Incorporated 2005, and Government of Nunavut 2013). A formal *Inuktutisation* campaign is under way in Nunavut, one of the government's strategic priorities being to "promote the use of Inuktut in the workplace," and

---

34. The certified terminologist title is a reserved title in all three provinces. It was granted in 1989 in Ontario and New Brunswick, respectively through the Association of Translators and Interpreters Act and the Corporation of Translators, Terminologists and Interpreters of New Brunswick Act, and in 1992 in Quebec, through the creation of the Corporation professionnelle des traducteurs et interprètes agréés du Québec (CPTIAQ), which became the Ordre des traducteurs, terminologues et interprètes agréés du Québec (OTTIAQ) in 2000.

"to collaborate with the Inuit Uqausinginnik Taiguusiliuqtiit [a language authority created by the Legislative Assembly of Nunavut] in developing and implementing standard terminology in Inuktut" (Government of Nunavut [n.d.]: 5).[35] Such an initiative demonstrates that Canada continues to be fertile ground for terminology work, and that there is still room for fresh, new activities.

References

Auger, Pierre, Bruno de Bessé, Bernard Salvail, Jean-Marie Fortin, and Anne-Marie Beaudoin. 1973. *Guide de travail en terminologie*. Québec: Office de la langue française.

Auger, Pierre (ed). 1974. *Guide de travail en néologie technique et scientifique*. Québec: Office de la langue française.

Auger, Pierre. 1978. "Introduction." In *Méthodologie de la recherche terminologique, Pierre Auger, and Louis-Jean Rousseau*, 11–12. Québec: Éditeur officiel du Québec.

Auger, Pierre, and Louis-Jean Rousseau. 1978. *Méthodologie de la recherche terminologique*. Québec: Éditeur officiel du Québec.

Auger, Pierre. 2001. "La méthodologie de la recherche terminologique de l'Office de la langue française: sa place dans l'enseignement et la formation au Québec." *Terminogramme* 101–102: 81–91.

Bastin, Georges. 2020. "André Clas — Une vie consacrée à la traduction, la terminologie et la lexicologie." *Meta* 65 (2): 499–520.

Biel, Łucja. 2015. "Translator's Corner. Łucja Biel Interviews Karine McLaren, Director of the Centre de traduction et de terminologie juridiques (CTTJ), Université de Moncton, Canada." *The Journal of Specialised Translation* 23: 12–17.

Blais, François. 2009. "Canada's Jurilinguistic Centres." *Language Update/L'Actualité langagière* 6 (4): 14.

Boisvenue, Karine. 2022. *Info en RH demandée*. Email sent to Aline Francoeur. October 5, 2022.

Boulanger, Jean-Claude. 1984. "La situation de la terminologie au Québec." *Lebende Sprachen* 29 (1): 19–22.

Boulanger, Jean-Claude. 1986. "La néologie et l'aménagement linguistique du Québec." *Language Problems and Language Planning* 10 (1): 14–29.

Boulanger, Jean-Claude. 1995. "Présentation : images et parcours de la socioterminologie." *Meta* 40 (2): 194–205.

Boutin-Quesnel, Rachel, Nycole Bélanger, Nada Kerpan, and Louis-Jean Rousseau. 1979. *Vocabulaire systématique de la terminologie*. Québec: Office de la langue française.

Bowker, Lynne. 2017. "How Information Science Helped to Shape the Emerging Field of Terminology in Canada (1973–81)." *Canadian Journal of Information and Library Science* 41 (3): 151–168.

---

35. Inuktut is the Inuit language as it is spoken in Arctic communities throughout Canada (Pirurvik Centre and the Government of Nunavut).

Brideau, Isabelle, Laurence Brosseau, and Allison Lowenger. 2022. *The Distribution of Legislative Powers: An Overview*. Ottawa: Library of Parliament.

Cajolet-Laganière, Hélène. 2022. *Jean-Claude Corbeil. Le linguiste Jean-Claude Corbeil nous quitte*. Centre de recherche interuniversitaire sur le français en usage au Québec, Faculté des Lettres, Université de Sherbrooke.

Cardinal, Linda. 2004. "The Limits of Bilingualism in Canada." *Nationalism and Ethnic Politics* 10 (1): 79–103.

Célestin, Tina, Gilles Godbout, and Pierrette Vachon-L'Heureux. 1984. *Méthodologie de la recherche terminologique ponctuelle : essai de définition*. Québec: Office de la langue française.

Centre de recherche interuniversitaire sur le français en usage au Québec (CRIFUQ). [n.d.]. "Biographie." *Site en hommage à Jean-Claude Corbeil*.

Centre de traduction et de terminologie juridiques. [n.d.]. *Description of Juriterm*. Université de Moncton, Faculté de droit.

Centre for Legal Translation and Documentation. 2022a. *The CLTD*.

Centre for Legal Translation and Documentation. 2022b. *Lexicon of Ontario Statutes and Regulations*.

Centre for Legal Translation and Documentation. 2022c. *Legal Glossary of Federal Statutes*.

Coleman, William D. 1984. "Social Class and Language Policies in Quebec." In *Conflict and Language Planning in Quebec*, ed. by Richard Y. Bourhis, 130–147. Clevedon: Multilingual Matters.

Corbeil, Jean-Claude. 1985. "Préface." In *Vocabulaire systématique de la terminologie* [new edition], Rachel Boutin-Quesnel et al.., 5–7. Québec: Les Publications du Québec.

Corbeil, Jean-Claude. 2007a. "Le rôle de la terminologie en aménagement linguistique: genèse et description de l'approche québécoise." *Langages* 168: 92–105.

Corbeil, Jean-Claude. 2007b. *L'embarras des langues. Origine, conception et évolution de la politique linguistique québécoise*. Montréal: Québec Amérique.

Corbeil, Jean-Claude. 2012. "Radio-Canada et le raffermissement linguistique." In *La télévision de Radio-Canada et l'évolution de la conscience politique au Québec*, ed. by Denis Monière, and Florian Sauvageau, 27–37. Québec: Presses de l'Université Laval.

Delisle, Jean. 1984. *Bridging the Language Solitudes. Growth and Development of the Translation Bureau of the Government of Canada, 1934–1984*. Ottawa: Secretary of State.

Delisle, Jean. 2008. *La terminologie au Canada. Histoire d'une profession*. Montréal: Linguatech.

Delisle, Jean, and Alain Otis. 2016. *Les douaniers des langues. Grandeur et misère de la traduction à Ottawa, 1867–1967*. Sainte-Foy: Presses de l'Université Laval.

de Villers, Marie-Éva. 2022. "Jean-Claude Corbeil, pilier de la francisation." *Le Devoir*, 29 janvier.

Dubuc, Robert. 1972. "Termium: System Description." *Meta* 17 (4): 203–219.

Dubuc, Robert. 2001. "La francisation terminologique, le plus beau fleuron de l'Office de la langue française." *Terminogramme* 101–102: 17–24.

Gaudreault, Marie-Claude. 2006. "Canadian Legislative Bijuralism: An Expression of Legal Duality." *Commonwealth Law Bulletin* 32 (2): 205–219.

doi Gélinas-Surprenant, Hélène, and Edna Hussman. 1993. "Terminology: A New Profession in a Canadian Context." In *Standardizing Terminology for Better Communication: Practice, Applied Theory, and Results*, ed. by Richard A. Strehlow, and Sue Ellen Wright, 22–29. Ann Arbor: American Society for Testing and Materials.

doi Gémar, Jean-Claude. 2005. "De la traduction (juridique) à la jurilinguistique. Fonctions proactives du traductologue." *Meta* (50) 4: n.p..

doi Gémar, Jean-Claude. 2011. "Le droit traduiras? Jurilinguiste seras! De quelques raisons dirimantes…" *Équivalences* 38 (1–2): 71–109.

doi Girard, Marie-Hélène. 2022. "Entrevue: Jean-Claude Gémar 'dans tous ses états'." *Meta* 67 (2): 462–477.

Government of Canada. 2021. "The Constitutional Distribution of Legislative Powers." *The Federation at a Glance*.

Government of Nunavut. [n.d.]. *Iviqtippalliajut: In the Process of Falling into Place*. 2018–2023. [Iqaluit]: Government of Nunavut.

Government of Nunavut, and Nunavut Tunngavik Incorporated. 2005. ᓯᓚᐅᑉ ᐊᓯᔾᔨᕈᑦᑎᕐᓂᖓᓄᑦ ᑕᐃᒍᖤᓕᕆᓂᖅ / Hilaup Aalannguqtirninganut Taiguuhiliqiniq/Terminology on Climate Change. [Iqaluit]: Government of Nunavut, and Nunavut Tunngavik Incorporated.

Government of Nunavut. 2013. *Terminology on Human Anatomy*/ᑎᒥᐅᑉ ᑭᓱᒃᑐᑎᒪᖕᒌᑦ ᑕᐃᒍᔾᔨᖏᑦ/*Timiup Kisukuttilimaangita Taiguusingit/Timimi Kituuyaakhait Taidjutait/Terminologie anatomique*. [Iqaluit]: Government of Nunavut.

Groupe de travail sur la qualité de la langue. 2003. *Un français de qualité: une priorité pour Radio-Canada*. Montréal: Société Radio-Canada.

Hamilton, Grant. 2010. "Translation in Canada." *The ATA Chronicle* 39 (10): 12–15.

doi Humbley, John. 2018. "Socioterminology." In *Languages for Special Purposes*, ed. by John Humbley, Gerhard Budin, and Christer Laurén, 469–488. Berlin: De Gruyter Mouton.

Kennedy, Elaine. 1986. "What's in a Program?" *Circuit* 13: n.p.

doi Kerpan, Nada. 1975. "La terminologie de l'entreprise." *Meta* 20 (1): 71–74.

doi Kerpan, Nada. 1977. "Histoire de la terminologie au Canada et au Québec." *Meta* 22 (1): 45–53.

doi Labelle, André. 2016. "What Ever Happened to Legislative Translation in Canada?" *Statute Law Review* 37 (2): 133–143.

La rédaction. 1965. "Rencontre de traducteurs et de linguistes à Stanley House (STIC)." *Journal des traducteurs/Translators' Journal* 10 (2): 63–65.

Leduc, Dominique. 1985. "L'Association technologique de langue française d'Ottawa." In *L'ATIO: Rétrospective 1920–1980*, ed. by D. Leduc, and B. Daigle, 11–24. Ottawa: École de traducteurs et d'interprètes.

Levert, Lionel A. 2001 [1999]. "Harmonization and Dissonance: Language and Law in Canada and Europe. The Cohabitation of Bilingualism and Bijuralism in Federal Legislation in Canada: Myth or Reality?" In *The Harmonization of Federal Legislation with the Civil Law of the Province of Quebec and Canadian Bijuralism. Booklet 1: Bijuralism and Harmonization: Genesis*, 5–10. Ottawa: Department of Justice Canada.

doi Levert, Lionel A. 2004. "Bilingual and Bijural Legislative Drafting: To Be or Not To Be?" *Statute Law Review* 25 (2): 151–164.

Levesque, Frédéric. 2016. "Le bilinguisme législatif et le bijuridisme dans les lois fédérales, les provinces de common law et les territoires canadiens: l'exemple des obligations *joint and several.*" In *Un regard québécois sur le droit constitutionnel: mélanges en l'honneur d'Henri Brun et Guy Tremblay*, ed. by Patrick Taillon, Eugénie Brouillet, and Amélie Binette, 719–742. Cowansville: Éditions Yvon Blais.

Linteau, Paul-André. 2000. "La nouvelle organisation économique et sociale." In *Le français au Québec: 400 ans d'histoire et de vie*, ed. by Michel Plourde, 154–162. Montréal: Éditions Fides/Les Publications du Québec.

Maurais, Jacques. 1999. *La qualité de la langue: un projet de société. Rapport préparé par Jacques Maurais.* Québec: Conseil de la langue française.

McLaren, Karine. 2017. *The Standardization of the French Vocabulary of the Common Law: The Cornerstone of Access to Justice in French.* Moncton: Centre de traduction et de terminologie juridiques, Faculty of Law.

Ministère des Affaires culturelles du Québec. 1965. *Norme du français écrit et parlé au Québec.* Cahiers de l'Office de la langue française, No.1. Québec: Ministère des Affaires culturelles.

Paradis, Denis. 2017. *Ensuring Justice is Done in Both Official Languages. Report of the Standing Committee on Official Languages.* Ottawa: House of Commons.

Pirurvik Centre, and the Government of Nunavut. [n.d.]. "What is Inuktut?" *Inuktut Tusaalanga.*

Prince, Joseph-Évariste. 1902. "Terminologie. Les chemins de fer." *Bulletin du parler français au Canada* 1 (1): 5–8.

Prince, Joseph-Évariste. 1903. "Terminologie. Les chemins de fer." *Bulletin du parler français au Canada* 1 (5): 88–89.

Robert, Jean-Claude. 2000. "La langue, enjeu politique du Québec." In *Le français au Québec: 400 ans d'histoire et de vie,*" ed. by Michel Plourde, 239–246. Montréal: Éditions Fides/Les Publications du Québec.

Rondeau, Guy. 1981. *Introduction à la terminologie.* Montréal: Centre éducatif et culturel inc.

Rondeau, Guy. 1984. *Introduction à la terminologie.* Deuxième édition. Chicoutimi: Gaëtan Morin éditeur.

Simon, Sherry. 2014. "Official Bilingualism: Fair Exchange?" In *Fifty Years of Official Bilingualism: Challenges, Analyses and Testimonies*, ed. by Richard Clément, and Pierre Foucher, 47–52. Ottawa: University of Ottawa Press.

Snow, Gérard. 2002. "Le *use* de la *common law* : étude terminologique." *Meta* 47 (2): 186–197.

Statistics Canada. 2022a. *While English and French are still the main languages spoken in Canada, the country's linguistic diversity continues to grow.*

Statistics Canada. 2022b. *Mother tongue, provinces and territories, 2016 and 2021.*

The Governor of Canada website. [n.d.]. "Mr. Gérard Snow." *Honours. Recipients.*

Vanderlinden, Jacques, Gérard Snow, and Donald Poirier. 2010. *La common law de A à Z.* Cowansville: Yvon Blais/Brussels: Bruylant.

Vinay, Jean-Paul. 1962. "Review of *C'est-à-dire...* Publication du Comité de linguistique de Radio-Canada, Montréal, Vol. I [1961+]. Polycopié 8 1/2 x 11; Fiches 3 x 5, en feuilles perforées." *Journal des traducteurs/Translator's Journal* 7 (2): 23.

Williams, Malcolm. 1994. "Terminology in Canada." *Terminology* 1 (1): 195–207.

CHAPTER 13

Terminology in Spain and its place in the world

Amparo Alcina
Universitat Jaume I

This chapter explores the evolution of terminology in Spain, tracing its journey from early stages to contemporary practices. Key institutions, influential figures, and foundational theoretical frameworks that have shaped the discipline are examined. The role of the Real Academia Española and other scientific institutions in standardising terminology is highlighted. The contributions of scholars such as Amelia de Irazazábal and the impact of political and cultural changes on terminology development are analysed.

The chapter delves into key theoretical perspectives, including Teresa Cabré's Communicative Theory of Terminology and Pamela Faber's Frame-based Terminology. These theories offer valuable insights into the cognitive and communicative aspects of terminology. Finally, the chapter emphasises the growth and diversification of terminology research in Spain, with the establishment of new research groups and the integration of terminology into various academic and professional fields.

Keywords: terminology, specialised translation, communicative theory of terminology, frame-based terminology

1. Overview of terminology development in Spain

This chapter will explore how terminology as a discipline evolved in Spain, starting with the publication of the early vocabularies, which are of interest because of their inclusion of terms, and continuing until the present where a wide range of research groups and institutions are interested in examining terminology and developing applications and resources.

The compilation and study of scientific and technical vocabulary in Spanish has a long tradition dating back to the work undertaken by the Real Academia Española (RAE) since it was established in 1713. The RAE's technical vocabulary committee was composed of distinguished scientists with a special sensitivity to

https://doi.org/10.1075/tlrp.24.13alc

language. Moreover, the science academies also took an interest in terminology. For example, the terminology committee of the Real Academia de Ciencias Exactas, Físicas y Naturales de España (RAC) published the first edition of the 'scientific and technical vocabulary' in 1983, thanks to the efforts of Ángel Martín Municio.

The Consejo Superior de Investigaciones Científicas (CSIC) also worked hard in defence of Spanish terminology and its practical application, while focusing on upholding a uniform standard that would prevent a multiplicity of terms for the same concept (Criado de Val 1984). Manuel Criado de Val and Amelia de Irazazábal were closely involved with enhancing awareness about the methods of terminology work and the importance of defending terminology in Spanish at that time.

On the other hand, the nature of terminology development in Spain cannot be understood without considering the nation's cultural and linguistic plurality. The establishment of democracy and enactment of the Spanish constitution of 1978 led to the political recognition of linguistic diversity, and the creation and promotion of institutions that would safeguard the various languages of the state, which were subsequently acknowledged as co-official. That means that Catalan, Valencian, Basque and Galician have official status and are legally recognised for use in government, education, and other official domains alongside Spanish in their respective autonomous communities. Institutions such as terminology centres and language academies (TermCat, AVL, UZEI and Termigal) were set up to coordinate strategies for language planning and terminological normalisation for Catalan, Valencian, Basque and Galician, respectively, which had endured marginalisation from social and professional life and from industrial and scientific development during the Spanish dictatorship (1939–1974) (Siguán 1996, Cabré 1996).

The introduction of university studies in translation and interpreting, and the compulsory inclusion of terminology as a subject, led to the presence and expansion of this discipline across Spain, resulting in a considerable rise in the number of subject specialists, research projects, doctoral theses and publications on terminology. Particularly noteworthy is the work of the Pompeu Fabra University Institute for Applied Linguistics (IULA), directed by Teresa Cabré. Set up in 1994, the institute has made great advances in terminology training and dissemination.

Furthermore, researchers, lecturers and specialists cooperated through international networks to develop terminology. Set up in 1998, RITerm, the Red Iberoamericana de Terminología, coordinates and encourages cooperation in terminology. Created in 1996, the Realiter network focuses on Romance languages.

The Spanish Association for Terminology, AETER (Asociación Española de Terminología), founded in 1997, brings together researchers, lecturers and professionals, as well as businesses and institutions, to develop and promote terminology as a discipline, stimulate the creation of much-needed terminological resources and disseminate existing ones. Every year, the association organises a terminology conference during which advances in the discipline are reported and researchers have the chance to exchange information about their projects. In 2001, the Catalan Society for Terminology, SCATERM, was set up to promote and disseminate terminology in Catalan. This association publishes the journal *Terminalia*, which contains scientific articles, reviews and other interesting information about terminology.

The great theoretical contributions to terminology that originate in Spain stem from Teresa Cabré's Communicative Theory of Terminology and from Pamela Faber's Frame-based Terminology. These theories have had and continue to have wide recognition and international prestige.

Every year, many meetings, conferences, courses and congresses are organised in Spain, providing researchers with the chance to share their contributions to the discipline and to exchange information about their projects. In addition to universities, various bodies and foundations are involved in matters related to terminology.

2.   Early scientific vocabulary in Spanish

The study of terminology in Spanish has been approached by experts from the various scientific, technical and legal areas of lexicography. Many of these people have launched projects and concentrated their efforts on initiatives that, in many cases, have received the support of important individuals and institutions. However, either because of political and/or economic reasons, these efforts have not come to fruition until recent times.

The *Tesoro de Covarrubias* (Covarrubias 1611), the first general Spanish dictionary that saw the light of day in 1611, contains references to the importance of the lexicon of specialised fields, such as medicine, because of the need for accuracy. The creation and development of terms in Spanish in the 17th and 18th centuries was channelled through the translations of scientific works. In the sciences, early scientific works were written and circulated in Latin. From the 18th century onwards, however, publications began appearing in vernacular languages. In medicine, for example, these works are mostly translations of either French documents or of French translations of English documents (Gómez de Enterría and Gallardo 2010). The translators were medical doctors, schooled in the humanities and sensitive to literary and linguistic accuracy. These texts are therefore a source of neologisms and contribute to enriching scientific language in Spanish (Gómez de Enterría 1999, Gómez de Enterría and Gallardo 2010).

Throughout the 18th century, there was a growing tendency towards the creation of neologisms with foreign words being adapted to the vernacular. Moreover, towards the end of the century, there was also resistance to the abandonment of Latin, given its value as the international language of science. At an international level, the first classifications and nomenclatures appeared in chemistry, botany and zoology, and learned procedures for creating new words were laid out, thereby increasing the value of nomenclatures. Thus, in the early 19th century, a translation of a botanical text reveals the translator's preference for using international, Greek or Latin-based terms and nomenclatures over Spanish terms. The justification was that these terms facilitated the acquisition of science and made it common to all learned nations. The various denominations underwent a period of fluctuation, and the coexistence of both (foreign and Spanish terms) led to the propagation of the phenomenon of denominative and conceptual variation. See also Chapters 2 and 3, which trace the early development of terminology in other countries.

In 1847, the Real Academia de Ciencias Exactas, Físicas y Naturales, also referred to as Real Academia de Ciencias (RAC) was founded, and it was agreed that one of the institution's tasks should be to compile a dictionary of the terms used in all branches of the sciences encompassed by the institution. Several shifts in Spanish history delayed the project until 1921, when the scientist Leonardo Torres Quevedo, a member of the RAE, promoted these tasks with the support of such acclaimed colleagues as Santiago Ramón y Cajal (winner of the Nobel Prize for Medicine in 1906) and the close cooperation of several scientific corporations in Spanish-speaking Central and South America. Under the presidency of Torres Quevedo, volume one of the *Diccionario Tecnológico Hispanoamericano* was published (1930).

In 1983, the first edition of the *Vocabulario Científico y Técnico* was published by the Real Academia de Ciencias in response to the statutory commission it had received on its foundation in 1847. At the public presentation of this dictionary in 1984, Ángel Martín Municio defined it as "the careful integration of science, technology and language, which, naturally, has required lexicological technique, rigorous data and scientific concepts."[1] Martín Municio also highlighted the fact that 13,000 terms do not emerge "from the arbitrariness of a few, but from the agreement and cooperation of many." The working method was "by groups consecutively arranged and divided up into: academics, terminology committee, specialist groups, area consultation groups, general circulation in the academy journal, and the lexicological group" (Real Academia de Ciencias 2013). In successive editions, new lexicographical norms were adopted, symbols were included for entries and

---

1. All translations in this chapter are those of the author.

the section of Spanish — English and English — Spanish equivalents was added. In the prefaces of the various editions, insistence was placed on promoting Spanish and on the need to include terms comprised of more than one word, as well as synonyms and neologisms which are part of the language of science.

3.   Promotion of terminology as a discipline (1970–1994)

In the 1970s, several initiatives were launched in an attempt to coordinate Spanish scientific and technical terminology, and to standardise scientific language. Amelia de Irazazábal, a graduate in chemical sciences with a heightened awareness of language, was the driving force behind the most of these initiatives. Considerable interest was shown in the computerisation of existing terminologies, especially regarding their applications in documentation and documentary languages. The arrival of foreign terminologies, in particular from the Anglo-Saxon world, was viewed with great concern and there was talk of "an invasion of terms" and of the "deterioration of Spanish" (Irazazábal 1993). Hence the emergence of initiatives such as FITRO (Fonds International des Terminologies Romanes), which fostered joint coordination efforts between countries with Latin-based languages, and Hispanoterm (Centro de Terminología Científica y Técnica en Español), a collaboration between Spain and Latin American nations. Also during this period, contact was made with the terminological initiatives in Central Europe. In 1984, the CSIC's Instituto Miguel de Cervantes published the Spanish version of H. Felber and H. Picht's book on methods of terminography and principles of terminological research, with an introduction by Criado de Val (Felber and Picht 1984). See also Chapters 8 and 17, which explain similar concerns and terminological activities from that time.

Through research institutes and groups (ISOC, ICYT and TermEsp) and thanks to the endeavours of scientists like Criado de Val and de Irazazábal, the CSIC designed research programmes around Spanish terminology, its adaptation, standardisation and harmonisation, group coordination, terminology training and dissemination. The need for language protection policies for terminology in Spanish and the other co-official languages was raised and defended in several forums and publications.

These activities continued in the 1980s and 90s. Furthermore, collaboration began with developers of the European Commission's terminology database, Eurodicautom, to incorporate terms in Spanish. In 1987, the Madrid Manifesto, which expressed concern for the deterioration of Spanish, was signed at the closing ceremony of the I Exposición de Lingüística Informatizada y Terminología Científico-Técnica, held in Madrid (Irazazábal 1993). Within the framework of the

TermEsp group, a Spanish scientific language database, also named TermEsp, was designed. It was created to contain terminology in the languages of Spain (Castilian Spanish, Catalan, Basque and Galician), as well as equivalents in French, English and German, and was made available online.

From 1988 onwards, de Irazazábal organised and directed introductory courses on terminology at the CSIC, to counter the lack of terminology specialists in several areas of translation and interpreting, knowledge transfer, and international commerce and industry. Later, Irazazábal went on to teach in numerous courses given by various Spanish universities, such as those of Granada, Alcalá de Henares and Comillas, thereby consolidating her position as a leading figure in this field.

Amelia de Irazazábal was the author of over fifty glossaries, thesauri, books and articles, and participated in numerous research contracts in the public and private sectors. Along with colleagues in Unión Latina, she edited a catalogue of terminological resources in Spanish. In 2003, Infoterm awarded her the Eugen Wüster Prize.

Her articles reflect her continued concern about the deterioration of Spanish because of the uncontrolled incorporation of numerous Anglo-Saxon terms imported with the technologies and processes to which they refer, along with badly coined or unnecessary borrowings. Another of her concerns was the lack of relations and coordination between Spanish groups working in terminology. Finally, she was concerned by the absence of appropriate policies governing language and terminology that would determine focus areas for research (Irazazábal 2004). Hence, many of her efforts were dedicated to arranging scientific meetings, working with institutions and establishing collaborations.

The dictionaries and vocabularies that were published under her leadership reflect her interest in standardisation, language planning and the recent application of technologies.

Another outcome of this period was the beginning of a collaboration with Latin America, which led to the creation of RITerm in 1988 in Caracas, Venezuela. Irazazábal held positions of executive secretary and honorary president of RITerm (Mayoral Asensio and Gallardo San Salvador 2012, Cabré 2012).

4. The expansion period (1994–2002)

As a result of the intense awareness-raising work by Amelia de Irazazábal from her research group TermEsp, along with the collaboration and enthusiasm of the faculty at the translation schools — including Natividad Gallardo and Roberto Mayoral (University of Granada) — and the support of international figures in terminology (Mayoral Asensio 1991), terminology became a compulsory subject in translation studies. In 1991, the first Latin American Colloquium on the teaching of terminology was held in Granada, bringing together terminology specialists from Spain, Latin America and Europe, to exchange opinions about the objectives, contents and professional profiles that such training would need to encompass.

During that period, the Spanish university system underwent considerable change, and many new public and private universities were established. Translation and interpreting achieved recognition in higher education, becoming degree studies in 1994. The fact that the subject of terminology was compulsory, with a minimum duration of 80 class hours, coupled with the introduction of the new degrees in translation and interpreting at numerous universities, led to a high demand for university lecturers and researchers with terminology training.

At the same time, several terminology manuals were published, followed by the publication in 1991 of Irazazábal's *Curso de Introducción a la Terminología* (Irazazábal 1991). This coursebook aimed at spreading the principles of the General Theory of Terminology as well as the work of the ISO TC/37 committee. See also Chapters 8 and 17 about this theory and activities of this committee.

In 1992, *La terminologia. La teoria, els mètodes, les aplicacions* was published in Catalan. Teresa Cabré, the author, was a renowned lexicographer and linguist who had conducted research at the University of Barcelona and had served as the director of TermCat, the Centre de Terminologia de Catalunya, from 1982 to 1988. This major work addresses general and contextual issues, theoretical aspects of terminology as an interdisciplinary field, the foundations of terminology (including specialised languages, the terminological unit and specialised documentation), the practice of terminography (international principles and standards, materials, and working methods), terminotics (contributions from computer science, language industries, terminological databases and other resources), terminological standardisation and neology, and finally, professional terminology and the role of language services.

The publication of Cabré's book, first in Catalan (1992) and later in Spanish (1993), French (1998), and English (1999), had a great impact and provided a significant boost to terminology as a discipline in Spain. In 1993 and 1995, the publisher Fundación Germán Ruipérez also produced the Spanish translations of Juan Sager's *A Practical Course In Terminology Processing* (Sager 1990) and Arntz and Picht's *Einführung in die Terminologiearbeit* (Arntz and Picht 1989), which, along with Cabré's book, were used as textbooks in translation and interpreting studies at Spanish universities for some time.

In this context of growing demand for terminologists, in 1994, at the behest of Cabré, Pompeu Fabra University set up the Institute for Applied Linguistics

(IULA), which she went on to direct for a long time. The institute's main objectives and activities revolve around research, training and dissemination of specialised language and terminology.

The Institute rapidly became a benchmark in the field of terminology and specialised languages, not only in Catalonia, but also in Spain and Latin America. It regularly held numerous activities for training and scientific transmission in relation to terminology, which were attended by experts of international renown in various specialist fields as well as university lecturers, researchers and students. These included conferences, seminars, training courses and doctoral degrees. The works presented at these events have been published in book collections by Edicions de l'IULA (Pompeu Fabra University), and are regarded as highly prestigious in Spain and as genuine reference works. This publisher is responsible for the following series: *Activitats* (covering the presentations and results of seminars, talks and sessions of a scientific sessions), *Conferències* (lectures by renowned specialists in doctoral courses), *Materials* (disseminating research results through lexicographical, terminological, computational or educational resources), *Monografíes* (university textbooks, themed monographs or selected texts, original or translated, related to applied linguistics research), *Tesis* (publishing theses defended in the Institute's doctoral programme), and *Coedicions* and *Coautories* (collaborative research outcomes with other institutions). Also issued by this publisher are translations into Catalan of works by classical authors in the field of terminology and specialised languages such as Wüster, Hoffman and Lotte, among others (see also Chapters 8 and 10, which show how the work in different regions has been shared over the years). Most of these collections contain research done by members of the IULA.

Since its creation, the IULA has attracted and welcomed the talent of numerous university students from Latin America who have undertaken their doctoral studies and defended their theses on specialised languages and terminology and who have gone on to form their own teams in their countries of origin, or have completed further research at the Institute. All that has undoubtedly encouraged academic and research relations in Spain and Latin America.

Later, in 1996, these various initiatives supporting Spanish terminology would establish links with the terminology network for Romance languages, REALITER. Another significant milestone was the creation in 1997 of the Asociación Española de Terminología (AETER) in Madrid. AETER was established on the initiative of individuals and institutions interested in the study of terminology and specialised languages and in the creation and consultation of terminological resources in Spanish and the other languages of Spain. The board of directors included Ángel Martín Municio, Amelia de Irazazábal and Teresa Cabré. Martín Municio was elected as the first president.

The intense research activity undertaken at the IULA, in addition to prior experience at TermCat, undoubtedly planted the seed for a new way of approaching terminological studies and works, one that is different from the standardising view advocated by the General Theory of Terminology (GTT). Thus, from 1992 onwards, aware of the difficulties of applying the principles of the GTT and concerned with equipping terminology with the theoretical and methodological foundations needed to underpin its autonomy as a discipline, Cabré began to develop what would become the Communicative Theory of Terminology. Her works, articles and conferences would later be included in a volume entitled *La terminología. Representación y comunicación* (Cabré 1999) and in another volume recently published in English entitled *Terminology. Cognition, Language and Communication* (2023).

At many conferences all over Spain and Latin America, Cabré talked about the theoretical and practical problems of the GTT and set out the principles of her Communicative theory. Internationally, other scholars from areas such as sociolinguistics and cognitive linguistics voiced similar concerns about the GTT (e.g. Gaudin 1995, Temmerman 2000). These new perspectives were taken into account in terminology research and applications in Spain.

The Communicative Theory of Terminology gained wide circulation and acceptance in Spanish and Latin American academia. However, despite its development and dissemination, the GTT, with its well established principles and methodology, continued to hold influence and prestige, particularly because of the works of Amelia de Irazazábal and her disciples and colleagues. Irazazábal remained committed to advocating for the creation of a Spanish terminology committee in the Spanish Association for Standardization and Certification (AENOR), which would serve as the mirror committee for ISO TC/37. Finally, in 2005, AENOR established Technical Committee 191 for terminology, thanks to the efforts of AETER. Guadalupe Aguado de Cea, author of the renowned *Diccionario Comentado de Terminología Informática* (Aguado de Cea 1994), has also actively participated in the Spanish committee CTN-UNE 191 and ISO TC/37.

Amelia de Irazazábal passed away in 2004. Many colleagues expressed their deep admiration not only for her remarkable professional accomplishments as well as her generosity (Mayoral Asensio and Gallardo San Salvador 2012, Cabré 2012).

4.1   The Communicative Theory of Terminology

The Communicative Theory of Terminology (henceforth CTT) arose because of the need to respond to the problems raised by the principles of the GTT, which has a focus on standardisation. The CTT was conceived as a language theory, one which integrated linguistic, cognitive and communicative aspects, following earlier proposals by Sager (1990). According to this approach, terminological units — the primary focus of study within terminology — are lexical units that form part of natural language and are distinguished by their use in various types of communication (see also Chapter 9 for a similar view from the Prague Circle). These lexical units are activated as terms when used in appropriate contexts and situations, which is known as the principle of adequacy. Therefore, the pragmatic conditions (domain, theme, way of addressing the theme, text type, sender, receiver and situation) are the factors that determine a selection of features in the meaning transmitted as content in a specific lexical unit. For that reason, it is important to distinguish between general and specialised knowledge. Specialist speakers are competent in both types of knowledge. However, these types are not internalised separately in the mind. The CTT emphasises the need to address variation in terminological units. From a descriptive perspective, terms are not invariable either in form or content. Popularisation of specialised units needs to be accounted for just as terminologisation of units of general language and pluriterminologisation, namely, the insertion of units from one domain into another. Concepts, inseparably linked to form, vary according to their adequacy for the type of communication. This theory therefore goes against many of the postulates of the GTT, such as the goal of univocity of terms. The aims of the CTT are to describe and explain terms and their functioning on a linguistic, cognitive and communicative level. The 'model of doors' (Cabré 2000, 2023: Ch. 1) or the 'Polyhedricity Principle'(Cabré 2008, 2023: Ch. 4) synthesise the idea of terminology as an interdisciplinary area of knowledge. In the words of Cabré:

> The conception of terminology as a necessarily interdisciplinary area of knowledge, which deals with terms and integrates the cognitive, linguistic, semiotic and communicative aspects of terminological units, leads us to propose what we call 'the model of doors'. It is a theory that makes it possible to deal with terms multidimensionally. [...] the Principle of Polyhedricity [...] according to which terms are interdisciplinary units composed of distinct sides or facets, each one corresponding to a level of analysis.   (Cabré 2023: 15, 89)

5.   Diversification of groups and linguistic perspectives (2002–2012)

By around 2002, the critical mass of lecturers and researchers dedicated to terminology and specialised languages in Spain had grown. They then began to organise into research groups based on common interests, prior training or social and economic context, among others. In general, these were small university-based groups that led to a proliferation of research concentrations, applications and domains within Spanish terminology. In some cases, the theoretical assumptions, objectives, methodologies, and subject matter of these groups were very different, enriching both the diversity of approaches and the types of outcomes produced. The various groups focused on objectives including term formation or neology, the study of cognitive aspects of language or the application of language technologies. During this period, these groups would grow, progressively release their results, and eventually give rise to a broad and consolidated outlook around 2012, which continues today, as we shall see below.

From the perspective of the discipline's foundations, both the GTT and the CTT continue to exert influence today. Additionally, at least one more theory has emerged. From 2002 onwards, Faber's Frame-based Theory began to take shape and was subsequently consolidated in *A Cognitive Linguistics View of Terminology and Specialized Language,* published in 2012.

In the following section, we will describe the activities of Pamela Faber and the group of researchers she coordinated, whose work examining terminology from a linguistic and cognitive perspective culminated in the Frame-based Terminology Theory and, in one way or another, would influence other groups at the same time.

5.1   Frame-based Terminology

In the late 1990s, at the University of Granada, Pamela Faber began a line of research in terminology with a linguistic and cognitive approach. A disciple of the lexical grammarian Martin Mingorance (Mingorance 1998), Faber continued her research, teaching and professional activities in lexicology, linguistics, lexical grammar, translation, and interpreting. Around 2000, the research project "OncoTerm: a bilingual system of information and oncological resources" signalled the beginning of a series of research projects centred on the study of terminology in the cognitive processes of translation.

Initially, Faber focused on cognitive neuroscience, psycholinguistics and cognitive linguistics to guide her research in terminology. On the one hand, she concentrated on the cognitive processes related to the management of the conceptual lexicon (Givón 1995) and, on the other, on the cognitive processes entailed in translation, in which terminological competence would fit as a module within a model of translation competence (Hurtado Albir 1999). The modular structure of memory, information processing, and the mechanisms of memory access and storage play an important role in these cognitive processes.

Regarding cognitive processes, according to Givon, the conceptual lexicon stores shared knowledge about our physical, cultural and mental universe. It is made up of a network of interconnected nodes, where the activation of one node activates other nodes nearby. Concepts represent conventionalised experiences, which can be divided into categories of entities, events, properties and relations (Givón 1995). Faber extends this idea to terminology, proposing that the acquisition of specialised knowledge requires the assimilation of prior cognitive structures and their expansion into more specific levels (Faber 2002).

Terminological competence is said to consist of the storage of specialised knowledge in memory, the automatisms inherent to terminological access, creativity in the formation of terms and the translator's ability to solve knowledge acquisition problems during the translation process. The translation process involves more contextual associations than other cognitive processes as well as global patterns of textual correspondence.

Hence research in OncoTerm focused on the analysis of specialised knowledge structures and the textual structures in which they appear. Knowledge structures or category templates are the result of analysing concepts and their relations. These templates are obtained through a corpus linguistics methodology by extracting terms and their contexts from specialised texts and improving extraction methods. Terms in context are the basis on which to analyse concepts and their various types of relations, not only hierarchical relations, such as generic-specific or part-whole, but also any other relation that links a concept to other domain concepts.

Moreover, conceptual structures reveal highly diverse relations that, in many cases, are specific to the domain. In the first project, which examined the oncological domain, the 'medical event' was developed as a framework or template composed of macrocategories linked by conceptual relations specific to the domain. The macrocategories template became more detailed as the project advanced. Thus, the medical event revealed, among others, macrocategories such as Agent-1, Agent-2, Process, Disease, Outcome and others. The medical event led to categories such as Disease-Agent, Gene or Cancer-Cell as specific to Agent-1; Specialist, Oncologist or Pathologist as specific to Agent-2; or Affect, Diagnose, Invade as specific to Process (Faber 2002).

At the same time, one objective of the project was to create an information system specifically designed for translators in a specialised field. OntoTerm (Moreno 2002) was created for that purpose. This application enabled the structuring and storing of conceptual and terminological information, respectively. A knowledge base, which is different from a terminological database, was designed to integrate the premises of artificial intelligence (AI).

A significant core of researchers, in addition to Pamela Faber, collaborated on the OncoTerm project. The publication of *Investigar en Terminología* (Faber and Jiménez 2002), which presents the main results of this project, was a major milestone for terminology in Spain. On the one hand, the aim and results of the project offered an approach to terminology that connected more completely with the assumptions of cognitive theories on language and translation. On the other, this new approach included the possibility of systematically developing aspects of the meaning of terms by providing an analytical method, based on linguistics, and an efficient tool, based on AI.

Over the years, this new approach has had far-reaching repercussions for terminology research in Spain and in Europe. Many research groups have introduced research using specialised corpora, ontologies for structuring specialised knowledge and the analysis of terminological competence in relation to translation processes. However, the Frame-based Theory has sometimes lacked the recognition that it undoubtedly deserves, perhaps because of the influence and the widespread dissemination of the CTT in Spain and Latin America.

Nevertheless, as the years have gone by, thanks to a long series of national and international research projects, the success of this new cognitive and text-based theory of terminology is now undeniable. Following the OncoTerm project, the research group headed up by Pamela Faber, later officially known as the Lexicon research group, has undertaken numerous research projects with important results in the form of influential publications, researcher training and the supervision of doctoral theses.

The Lexicon research group continued to explore the cognitive and linguistic approach, always obtaining excellent results and, with time, a national and international reputation. Within the framework of various projects, research was extended to other domains, such as coastal (PuertoTerm, MarcoCosta) and environmental engineering (ECOSISTEMA, RECORD, CONTENT), as well as that of medicine (VARIMED, COMBIMED) (Cabezas-García and León-Aráuz 2023, León Aráuz, Reimerink, and Faber 2009, López Rodríguez et al. 2010, Tercedor Sánchez, López Rodríguez, and Prieto Velasco 2014). The knowledge database tool OntoTerm became obsolete, and currently results are shown online.

From the theoretical perspective, the assumptions of Martín Mingorance's Lexical Grammar were gradually integrated into Fillmore's frame theory and his concept of frame (Fillmore 1985), giving rise to the Frame-based Terminology theory (Faber 2012). This theory encompasses a linguistic approach that includes explanations, methodologies and resources for researching terms from linguistic levels, including the syntactic and semantic, and from the cognitive perspective for developing knowledge structures as networks of interrelated concepts. These structures are also visually represented. The development of cognitive aspects and tools like domain events and frames has provided the basis for studying figures of speech such as metaphor and metonymy in specialised domains, highlighting how specialised language and conceptual structures facilitate the learning of new concepts and new domains and contribute to scientific advancement in the sense already outlined in the philosophy of science.

Undoubtedly another significant contribution is the design and use of tools based on AI principles for organising the knowledge structures underlying terms. With the arrival of the internet and online tools, the OntoTerm application gave way to online knowledge databases such as EcoLexicon. The EcoLexicon knowledge base represents the concepts of the environment in an interconnected network of relations specific to the domain. Visually, EcoLexicon is a network of concepts in the form of nodes connected by arcs, which represent the relations. Likewise, the concepts are connected by arcs with their denominations in several languages (Faber, León and Prieto 2009, Gil-Berrozpe and Faber 2017). See Chapter 11 for more discussion about knowledge bases.

6.   Consolidation of research in terminology (2012 to the present)

Some of the groups have brought together lecturers with a background in languages or linguistics. Their research focuses on the formation of the lexicon, its linguistic features and phraseology, the evolution of terms and the role of neology within this evolution or the history of specialised language (Alcina and Gamero Pérez 2002, Gallardo San Salvador 2003, García Palacios and Fuentes Morán 2002, Guerrero Ramos and Pérez Lagos 2002, Guerrero Ramos and Pérez Lagos 2020). In other cases, also with a language profile, researchers have contributed a translation approach, which involves working with languages like English (Alcaraz Varó and Hugues 1997, Alcaraz Varó 1998, Alcaraz Varó, Hughes, and Campos 1999, Alcaraz Varó et al. 2005).

The topics chosen are also varied and often reflect the socioeconomic context of the university in which they are located, such as agriculture, cheesemaking, viticulture, fishing, ceramics, and so forth (Civera García 2002, Ibáñez Rodríguez 2020, Losey León and Corpas Pastor 2023, Monterde Rey 2013, Roldán Vendrell 2013, Sanz Espinar and Berlanga de Jesús 2022).

As for theoretical and methodological perspectives, aside from the previously mentioned theories, other approaches are having some influence in Spanish circles: Knowledge-based Terminology from Canada (Meyer, Eck, and Skuce 1997, Bowker 1997, see also Chapter 12), which has guided the work of the Tecnolettra research group led by Amparo Alcina at Jaume I University (Alcina 2009, 2024), and the approach of specialised lexicography and the functional theory of lexicography (Bergenholtz and Tarp 1995) on which the work of the International Centre for Lexicography led by Pedro Fuertes-Olivera at the University of Valladolid (Fuertes-Olivera and Tarp 2014) is based.

Some studies display great methodological singularity, such as the work on the fine leatherwork terminology of Ubrique (García Antuña 2014), which entailed recording an oral corpus of the specialised lexicon used by the artisan workers, as there were no written sources for this manual and artisanal craft.

In addition to the foundations and methodology of terminology, the computer tools used in these studies — such as terminological databases, ontologies, corpus analysis software, term extraction tools and a combination of these with computer-aided translation programs, machine translation and translation memories — have been explored by several research groups, in particular Lexicon at the University of Granada, Tecnolettra at Jaume I University, Tradumática at the Autonomous University of Barcelona and Lexytrad at the University of Málaga, as well as the IULA at Pompeu Fabra University.

7.   Conclusion

In this chapter we have attempted to reflect on the main events, figures and activities that have led to the current state of terminology in Spain. We have shown that there are many entities and research groups dedicated to terminology, and that they have made highly significant contributions to the discipline.

The importance of language and translation studies at the university level and the coexistence of several official languages has tipped the evolution of the discipline of terminology towards a largely descriptive and linguistic approach.

The development of terminological resources in different socioeconomic areas has contributed to improving specialised communication, including translation. This development has in turn contributed to a greater knowledge of the discipline itself and to explaining many aspects of language functioning and the cognitive processing involved. For all this, we can conclude that the work of terminology researchers and teachers in Spain has achieved a prominent place internationally.

References

Aguado de Cea, Guadalupe. 1994. *Diccionario comentado de terminología informática*. Paraninfo.

Alcaraz Varó, Enrique. 1998. *Diccionario de términos jurídicos : inglés-español, spanish-english*. 3rd ed. Barcelona: Ariel.

Alcaraz Varó, Enrique, Brian Hughes, and Miguel Ángel Campos. 1999. *Diccionario de términos de marketing, publicidad y medios de comunicación: inglés-español, Spanish-English*. Barcelona: Ariel.

Alcaraz Varó, Enrique, Brian Hughes, José Mateo Martínez, Chelo Vargas Sierra, and
Adelina Gómez González-Jover. 2005. *Diccionario de Términos de la Piedra Natural e
Industrias Afines. Inglés-Español. Español-Inglés.* Barcelona: Ariel.

Alcaraz Varó, Enrique, and Brian Hugues. 1997. *Diccionario de términos económicos,
financieros y comerciales: inglés-español = Spanish-English.* 2nd ed. Barcelona: Ariel.

Alcina, Amparo. 2009. "Metodología y técnicas para la elaboración de diccionarios
onomasiológicos." In *Terminología y Sociedad del conocimiento*, ed. by Amparo Alcina,
Esperanza Valero, and Elena Rambla, 33–58. Berne: Peter Lang.

Alcina, Amparo. 2024. "ONTODIC: A Model of Linguistic Knowledge Representation Based
on Description Logic." *Terminology.*

Alcina, Amparo, and Silvia Gamero Pérez (eds). 2002. *La traducción científico-técnica y la
terminología en la sociedad de la información, Estudis sobre traducció.* Castelló:
Universitat Jaume I.

Arntz, Reiner, and Heribert Picht. 1989. *Introducción a la terminología.* Madrid: Fundación
Germán Sánchez Ruipérez.

Bergenholtz, Henning, and Sven Tarp. 1995. *Manual of Specialised Lexicography: The
Preparation of Specialised Dictionaries.* Amsterdam: John Benjamins.

Bowker, Lynne. 1997. "Multidimensional Classification of Concepts and Terms." In *Handbook
of Terminology Management*, ed. by Sue Ellen Wright, and Gerhard Budin, 133–143.
Philadelphia: John Benjamins.

Cabezas-García, Melania, and Pilar León-Araúz. 2023. "Term and Concept Variation in
Climate Change Communication." *The Translator.*

Cabré, Teresa. 1992. *La terminologia. La teoria, els mètodes, les aplicacions.* Barcelona:
Empúries.

Cabré, Teresa. 1996. "La terminología en España: panorama general." *Terminometro* 2:6–9.

Cabré, Teresa. 1999. *La terminología: representación y comunicación. Elementos para una
teoría de base comunicativa y otros artículos.* Barcelona: Institut Universitari de
Lingüística Aplicada. Universitat Pompeu Fabra.

Cabré, Teresa. 1999. *Terminology. Theory, Methods and Applications.* Translated by
Janet Ann DeCesaris. Amsterdam: John Benjamins.

Cabré, Teresa. 2000. "Terminologie et linguistique : La théorie des portes." *Terminologies
nouvelles: Terminologie et diversité culturelle* 21:10–15.

Cabré, Teresa. 2008. "El principio de poliedricidad: la articulación de lo discursivo, lo
cognitivo y lo lingüístico en Terminología (I)." *Ibérica* 16:9–36.

Cabré, Teresa. 2012. "Nota en record d'Amelia de Irazazábal, sempre present en el meu record."
Terminalia 6:63–64.

Cabré, Teresa. 2023. *Terminology: Cognition, Language and Communication.* Amsterdam: John
Benjamins.

Civera García, Pilar. 2002. "Traducción científico-técnica y terminología en el sector de la
industria cerámica." In *La traducción científico-técnica y la terminología en la Sociedad de
la información*, ed. by Amparo Alcina, and Silvia Gamero Pérez, 167–176. Castelló:
Universitat Jaume I.

Covarrubias Orozco, Sebastian de. 1611. *Tesoro de la lengua castellana, o española.* Madrid:
Luis Sanchez.

Criado de Val, Manuel. 1984. "Introducción." In *Métodos de terminografía y principios de investigación terminológica*, ed. by Hispanoterm. Madrid: Consejo Superior de Investigaciones Científicas.

Faber, Pamela. 2002. "Investigar en Terminología." In *Investigar en Terminología*, ed. by Pamela Faber, and Catalina Jiménez, 3–24. Granada: Comares.

Faber, Pamela (ed). 2012. *A Cognitive Linguistics View of Terminology and Specialized Language*. Berlin: De Gruyter Mouton.

Faber, Pamela, and Catalina Jiménez (eds). 2002. *Investigar en Terminología*. Granada: Comares.

Faber Benítez, Pamela, Pilar León Araúz, and Juan Antonio Prieto Velasco. 2009. "Semantic Relations, Dynamicity, and Terminological Knowledge Bases." *Current Issues in Language Studies* 1 (1):1–23.

Felber, Helmut, and Heribert Picht. 1984. *Métodos de terminografía y principios de investigación terminológica*, ed. by Hispanoterm. Madrid: Consejo Superior de Investigaciones Científicas.

Fillmore, Charles J. 1985. "Frames and the Semantics of Understanding." *Quaderni di Semantica* 6:22–254.

Fuertes Olivera, Pedro, and Sven Tarp. 2014. *Theory and Practice of Specialised Online Dictionaries. Lexicography versus Terminography*. Berlin: Mouton De Gruyter.

Gallardo San Salvador, Natividad (ed). 2003. *Terminología y traducción: un bosquejo de su evolución*. Granada: Editorial Atrio.

García Antuña, María. 2014. "Algunas notas sobre el léxico específico de la piel." In *Terminología y comunicación científica y social*, ed. by Mercedes Roldán Vendrell, 155–180. Granada: Comares.

García Palacios, Joaquín, and Ma Teresa Fuentes Morán (eds). 2002. *Texto, Terminología y Traducción*. Salamanca: Ediciones Almar.

Gaudin, François. 1995. *Pour une socioterminologie. Des problèmes sémantiques aux pratiques institutionnelles*. Rouen: Université de Rouen.

Gil-Berrozpe, Juan Carlos, and Pamela Faber Benítez. 2017. "The Role of Terminological Knowledge Bases in Specialized Translation: The Use of Umbrella Concepts." In *Temas actuales en terminología y estudios sobre el léxico*, ed. by Miguel Ángel Candel-Mora, and Chelo Vargas-Sierra, 1–25. Granada: Comares.

Givón, T. 1995. *Functionalism and Grammar*. Amsterdam: John Benjamins.

Gómez de Enterría, Josefa. 1999. "Las traducciones del francés, cauce para la llegada a España de la ciencia ilustrada. Los neologismos en los textos de botánica." In *La traducción en España (1750–1830). Lengua, literatura, cultura*, ed. by Francisco Lafarga, 143–155. Lleida: Edicions de la Universitat de Lleida.

Gómez de Enterría, Josefa, and Natividad Gallardo. 2010. "Las versiones de Medicina y Botánica y la nueva terminología científica en el siglo XVIII." *Cuadernos del Instituto Historia de la Lengua* 4:55–75.

Guerrero Ramos, Gloria, and Fernando Pérez Lagos (eds). 2002. *Panorama actual de la terminología*. Málaga: Universidad de Málaga.

Guerrero Ramos, Gloria, and Fernando Pérez Lagos (eds). 2020. *Terminología, neología y traducción*. Granada: Comares.

Hurtado Albir, Amparo. 1999. "Objetivos de aprendizaje y metodología en la formación de traductores e intérpretes." In *Enseñar a traducir. Metodología en la formación de traductores e intérpretes*, ed. by Amparo Hurtado Albir, 8–58. Madrid: Edelsa.

Ibáñez Rodríguez, Miguel (ed). 2020. *Enotradulengua. Vino, lengua y traducción*. Berlín: Peter Lang.

Irazazábal Nerpell, Amelia de. 1991. *Curso de introducción a la terminología*. Madrid: Instituto de Información y Documentación en Ciencia y Tecnología (ICYT).

Irazazábal Nerpell, Amelia de. 1993. "La terminología científica. Su enseñanza en lengua española." *Política científica* 38: 52-58.

Irazazábal, Amelia de. 2004. "¿Podremos coordinar, al fin, la terminología científica en lengua española?." In *Ciencia, Tecnología y lengua española: la terminología científica en español*, 43–50. Madrid: Fundación española para la ciencia y la tecnología.

León Araúz, Pilar, Arianne Reimerink, and Pamela Faber. 2009. "Puertoterm & Marcocosta: A Frame-Based Knowledge Base for the Environmental Domain." *Journal of Multicultural Communication* 1:47–70.

López Rodríguez, Clara Inés, Pamela Faber, Pilar León Araúz, Juan Antonio Prieto Velasco, and Maribel Tercedor. 2010. "La Terminología basada en marcos y su aplicación a las Ciencias Ambientales: los proyectos Marcocosta y Ecosistema." *Arena Romanistica* 7 (10):52–74.

Losey León, María Araceli, and Gloria Corpas Pastor. 2023. *La terminología del dominio de la seguridad de la navegación marítima en inglés y en español*. Berlín: Peter Lang.

Martín Mingorance, Leocadio. 1998. *El modelo lexemático-funcional: El legado lingüístico de Leocadio Martín Mingorance*, ed. by Amalia Marín Rubiales. Granada: University of Granada.

Mayoral Asensio, Roberto. 1991. *Introducción*. Coloquio Iberoamericano sobre enseñanza de la Terminología, Granada.

Mayoral Asensio, Roberto, and Natividad Gallardo San Salvador. 2012. "Amelia de Irazazábal (1926–2004). Admirada Amelia." *Terminalia* 60–62.

Meyer, Ingrid, Karen Eck, and Douglas Skuce. 1997. "Systematic Concept Analysis within a Knowledge-Based Approach to Terminology." In *Handbook of Terminology Management*, ed. by Sue Ellen Wright, and Gerhard Budin, 98–118. Philadelphia: John Benjamins.

Monterde Rey, Ana María. 2013. "Estudio de la metáfora en los ictiónimos de Canarias una revisión actualizada con métodos terminológicos." *Revista de lexicografía* 19:31–54.

Moreno Ortiz, Antonio. 2002. "Representación de la información terminológica en OntoTerm: un sistema gestor de bases de datos terminológicas basado en el conocimiento." In *Investigar en Terminología*, ed. by Pamela Faber and Catalina Jiménez, 25-70. Granada: Comares.

Real Academia de Ciencias Exactas, Físicas y Naturales. 1983. *Vocabulario Científico y Técnico*. Madrid: España.

Real Academia de Ciencias. 2013. *Vocabulario Científico y técnico digital*.

Roldán Vendrell, Mercedes. 2013. *Diccionario de términos del aceite de oliva (DTAO)*. Madrid: Arco Libros.

Sager, Juan Carlos. 1990. *A Practical Course in Terminology Processing*. Amsterdam: John Benjamins.

doi San Martín, Antonio, Melania Cabezas-García, Miriam Buendía-Castro,
        Beatriz Sánchez-Cárdenas, Pilar León-Araúz, Arianne Reimerink, and Pamela Faber.
        2020. "Presente y futuro de la base de conocimiento terminológica EcoLexicon."
        Onomázein 49:174–202.

Sanz Espinar, Gemma, and Lorenza Berlanga de Jesús. 2022. "Representación del
        conocimiento especializado en bases de conocimiento francés-español: ámbito de los
        quesos." In *Universalidad y multiversalidad en literatura, lengua y traducción*, 171–185.
        Granada: Comares.

Siguán, Miquel. 1996. "España, país plurilingüe." *Terminometro* 2:3–5.

doi Temmerman, Rita. 2000. *Towards New Ways of Terminology Description. The Sociocognitive
        Approach*. Amsterdam: John Benjamins.

Tercedor Sánchez, María Isabel, Clara Inés López Rodríguez, and Juan Antonio Prieto Velasco.
        2014. "También los pacientes hacen terminología: retos del proyecto VariMed." *Panace@:
        revista de Medicina, Lenguaje y Traducción* 25 (39):95–103.

Vizuete y Picón, Pelayo, and Union Internacional Hispano-Americana de Bibliografia y
        Tecnologia Científicas. 1930. *Diccionario Tecnológico Hispano Americano*. Madrid: Arte y
        Ciencia.

CHAPTER 14

Terminology in Mexico
Reflections on theory and methodology

María Pozzi
El Colegio de México

This chapter recounts how modern systematic terminology has evolved in Mexico. It highlights three events that mark its beginnings: the project of the *Dictionary of Mexican Spanish* and how it dealt with terms, the first terminology courses and terminography projects, and the agreement between the Commission of the European Communities and El Colegio de México regarding Eurodicautom and Mexican-Spanish terminology. It then accounts for the expansion of terminology by means of the proliferation of courses, and a growing number of researchers and their contributions. Next, it describes the role of Mexico in international organisations and terminology networks. Finally, it analyses the challenges faced by Mexican terminologists and how the future may be envisaged.

Keywords: terminology in Mexico, terminography, international cooperation in terminology, theoretical terminology, applied terminology, terminotics

1. Introduction

According to Stala (2020: 226), lexicography has been practised in Mexico since the 16th century, when the first printing press arrived in the New World. Romero Rangel (2016: 1–6) states that the *Vocabulario en lengua Castellana y Mexicana* by Fray Alonso de Molina was the first bilingual dictionary published in the New Spain (today's Mexico) in 1555, its second edition appearing in 1571. It includes 16th century Spanish and Nahuatl vocabularies. Molina's objective for the publication of his dictionary was twofold, first, to help the missionaries in their evangelisation task and second, "to teach, indoctrinate and govern in the language of the Indigenous people"[1] (ibid.: 64).

---

1. All translations in this chapter have been done by the author.

https://doi.org/10.1075/tlrp.24.14poz
© 2025 John Benjamins Publishing Company

Two hundred years later, between 1786 and 1789, Antonio de Alcedo published the *Diccionario geográfico-histórico de las Indias Occidentales o de América*. It includes names of local flora and fauna as well as words referring to daily life in these territories (Kamenetskaia 2018: 627).[2]

Two hundred years later still, Mexican terminology became systematised, adopted rigorous theoretical and methodological positions, and made further contributions. The present work describes this recent history.

2.   The beginnings of systematic terminology in Mexico

Three events that took place at El Colegio de México (COLMEX) during the nineteen seventies and early eighties mark the beginning of modern systematic terminology work in this country: (1) the project to compile and publish the *Diccionario del español de México*, (2) the establishment of a translator training programme, and (3) the signing of an agreement between COLMEX and the Commission of the European Communities (CEC) regarding Eurodicautom and Mexican-Spanish terminology.

2.1   Dictionary of Mexican Spanish

The project to compile the *Diccionario del español de México* (DEM) directed by a very young Luis Fernando Lara was launched in 1973. The aim was to have a dictionary of Mexican Spanish that would reflect Mexico's own history and culture, in a similar way to that of the Webster dictionaries for American English. In the Introduction to the DEM, Lara (DEM 2010: 17–18) tells us that some of the initial issues that had to be addressed were firstly, how to identify Mexican Spanish vocabulary and secondly, how to compile it. Previous Mexican dictionaries were,

---

2. In addition to Spanish, there are 68 national indigenous languages in Mexico. In 2001, the *Ley General de Derechos Lingüísticos* was enacted to protect and regulate the linguistic rights of Mexican indigenous communities and peoples. Since then, various terminologies have been developed in some of these languages on topics of special interest for those communities. Some of these include the *Glosario de términos jurídicos empleados en la traducción de la Constitución política de los Estados Unidos Mexicanos al náhuatl de la Huasteca Potosina*; *diccionarios ilustrados de partes del cuerpo en chontal*, developed by the Instituto Nacional de Antropología e Historia (INAH). The Mexican Physics Society is developing scientific terminology in various indigenous languages; Patricia Méndez Zapata and Catalina Naumis (Méndez Zapata and Naumis 2015) studied the *Terminología del huipil triqui*, and Oscar Méndez Espinosa (Méndez 2019) the *Terminología de Geografía en zapoteco*. This is, however, a broad topic of study and research that could itself be the subject of an extended academic paper.

in fact, dictionaries of Mexicanisms, because the words included were those used in Mexico that were not registered in other Spanish dictionaries, especially those published by the Real Academia Española (RAE). Therefore, what was needed was a comprehensive dictionary of Spanish based solely on Mexican usage.

According to Lara (DEM 2010: 18–21) and Fernández Gordillo (2014: 68–69) there was some discussion about the best method to compile words used in Mexico regardless of whether they were used elsewhere. After analysing several possibilities, it was decided to set up a computer-based corpus containing carefully selected written and oral texts that would guarantee the best strategy to register a reasonable number of different words, their uses, and meanings. It is worth remembering that in those days computers were widely used for scientific calculations and for commercial data management, but the application of computers to the humanities in general and to linguistics, in particular, was still in its infancy. Also, in the early seventies, perforated cards were the standard means of data input, and computers accepted capital letters, numbers, and a few symbols such as #, @, $, /, (), +, but no lower-case letters, accents, or other diacritics or characters. Computer memory capacity (64 KB) was very small, and processing times were very long. However, that state-of-the-art technology offered by far the best option to establish and manage a corpus of contemporary Mexican Spanish (Corpus del español mexicano contemporáneo (CEMC)) in a manner that would allow the objective analysis of a large number of texts, the calculation of frequencies and other statistical measures, and the production of concordances for each occurring word to facilitate the identification of its meanings.

The following subsection provides an overview of the CEMC and highlights some of its terminology-relevant features.

2.1.1 *Corpus of contemporary Mexican Spanish*

A detailed description of how the CEMC was set up, together with its specifications and characteristics, can be found in Lara (DEM 2010: 19–22), Lara and Ham Chande (1979), Ham Chande (1979) and Fernández Gordillo (2014).

According to Lara (DEM 2010: 20), the main criteria for including a work in the CEMC were:

a. written by a Mexican author
b. published between 1921 and 1974
c. literary works from the National Library Report list of best-selling books
d. texts from the most widely available Mexican scientific and technical textbooks and specialised journals.

The CEMC consists of 996 texts, each one an extract of about 2,000 words from each work.[3] It has a total of 1,891,045 tokens and 64,183 types (DEM 2010: 21, Ham Chande 1979: 76, Fernández Gordillo 2014: 68). Each text was first classified according to language level: standard language in its two varieties, formal language and informal language, and non-standard language, Then, it was classified according to its genre into scientific, technical, literary, journalistic, dialectal texts, oral conversations, etc. For example, a medical text was classified as 'formal language — science,' and a conversation between uneducated children was classified as 'non-standard language — oral conversation.' A total of 180 scientific texts containing 346,313 tokens produced 26,487 types, and 102 technical texts containing 202,716 tokens yielded 17,836 types (Lara and Ham Chande 1979: 29–30, Ham Chande 1979: 76). Words contained in scientific and technical texts are a combination of terms and general language words.

Lara and Zahn (1973) list the specific criteria to include scientific and technical works in the CEMC:

a.   widely available semi-specialised scientific and technical journals
b.   user manuals for machines and other instruments
c.   textbooks
d.   theses and dissertations.

The CEMC was the first linguistic corpus of Spanish, designed and set up between 1973–74. It is an annotated corpus that includes a tag indicating the part of speech (POS) of each word. In those early days of computer-assisted lexicography, there was no machine-readable Spanish dictionary available that could be used for the automatic assignment of POS to words. Thus, the first parser for Spanish had to be designed from scratch; its main purpose was to automatically assign the corresponding POS tag to each word contained in the CEMC in the context where it occurred. For this, a team of linguists and mathematicians devised a set of linguistic rules to determine the POS for each word.[4] García Hidalgo (1979) gives a detailed account of how this parser worked, its results and how it facilitated the

---

3. Each text included in the CEMC was chosen according to the following process: (1) one page was randomly selected from each of the 996 works, (2) one paragraph was randomly selected from that page, (3) as many continuous full paragraphs as necessary were selected to obtain a maximum of 2,000 graphic words.

4. Some of the simplest rules are, for instance, an article (definite or indefinite) should normally be followed by a noun or an adjective, a personal pronoun should be followed by a verb. Others are much more complex, such as those used to disambiguate a word that could, in principle, be assigned two or more word classes, or those used to group different verb forms under the infinitive, or plural nouns under their canonical form.

identification of meanings, the writing of definitions, the identification of terms, the listing of concordances of any given word ordered by POS, and the calculation of several statistical measures.

2.1.2   *Preliminary studies to define the treatment of terms in the DEM*

According to Lara and Zahn (1973), traditional European lexicography had consistently avoided including terms in general language dictionaries because it was accepted that their usage was restricted to a small group of scientists and technologists, whereas the average speaker for whom general dictionaries were intended was thought of as a non-technical person who would not require, use, or be interested in terms of any kind. In addition, in the first half of the 20th century both linguists and early terminologists considered a term to be a mere label assigned to an object or a concept, therefore the definition of a term was conceived as a definition of the object or the concept it represents as opposed to the definition of a word whose meanings are the main object of description in general language dictionaries. However, Lara and Zahn (1973) state that by the end of the century the panorama was very different because the general population had become more familiarised with science and technology, and therefore needed to have access to that kind of information in general language dictionaries; this situation had already been addressed by some contemporary dictionaries mainly in the United Kingdom and North America. For Lara (DEM 2010: 24), the issue of how to handle scientific and technical terms in the DEM was important from the beginning of the work, as he states in the Introduction to the dictionary: "Our contact with the special vocabularies of science and technology led us to conduct the first studies of Spanish terminology in Mexico and to promote interest in this new field of applied linguistics." Further down (ibid.: 30) Lara continues: "We have paid special attention to technical terminologies that are commonly used in Mexico." In the case of scientific and technical terms, it was important to consult and follow the advice of specialists to ensure that the definitions offered were reliable and up to date.

The rest of this section describes how terminology was dealt with in the DEM.

Before starting the actual lexicographical work, several preliminary studies were carried out to define the positions to be adopted by the team of lexicographers regarding theoretical, general, and methodological issues. Two of them were particularly relevant for terminology. They focussed on four topics which, eventually, laid the foundation for the treatment of terms:[5] (a) what terms to include, (b) how to define terms, (c) when to add domain labels to terms, and

---

5. Lara and Zahn (1973) address the first three (a, b and c) and Valadez (1973) deals with the last one (d).

(d) how to deal with borrowed terms. The following subsections (2.1.2.1 to 2.1.2.4) are based on or adapted from the information provided in Lara and Zahn (1973) and Valadez (1973).

2.1.2.1   *What terms the dictionary should include*

Lara and Zahn (1973) identified and analysed three alternatives: the first one refers to the distinction between terms that depend on the extralinguistic reality and words that do not. This distinction led to two types of dictionaries, the encyclopaedic and specialised dictionaries that provide information on real-life objects or concepts and the general language dictionary that provides word meanings. Clearly, a dictionary containing both words and some terms can benefit from the latter approach as it also highlights the differences between a strictly linguistic definition and a terminological one.[6] The second alternative refers to the level of specialisation of the term in question, since it is evident that highly specialised terms should not find a place in a general language dictionary, but semispecialised terms, i.e. those with a lower level of specialisation and thus closer to the general language are expected to be included as are terms that have become general language words. The main problem in this case was where to draw the line because a term can be semi-specialised to some people and specialised or not specialised at all to others. The third alternative refers to the use of the term within a community which is reflected in its frequency and more importantly, in its extension of use.

With the results of this study, it was decided that the DEM would include scientific and technical terms that met the following criteria:

a.   terms that are widely used in the national community.
b.   general and semi-specialised terms, but not highly specialised terms.
c.   terms that belong to the domains of science and technology that are important in present-day Mexico.
d.   terms recommended by top Mexican scientists and technologists.

Examples of terms in the latest online edition of the DEM (2024) include *fracking*, *drone*, *integral (Mat)*, *integral (Geom)* and *resonancia magnética (Fís)*.[7]

---

6. These are discussed in 2.1.2.2.

7. Fracking, drone, integral (*Mat.*), integral (*Geom.*) and magnetic resonance (*Phys.*) respectively.

2.1.2.2 *How terms should be defined*

The second topic (Lara and Zahn 1973) focused on a contrastive study of definitions of semi-specialised terms in some of the main dictionaries of Spanish (*Diccionario de la Lengua Española* (1970) — DRAE), English (*Webster's Third New International Dictionary of the English Language* (1966) — W III), and French (*Dictionnaire alphabétique et analogique de la langue française — Petit Robert* (1965 — PR), and *Dictionnaire du Français Contemporain* (1971) — DFC).[8] The result, not surprisingly, was inconsistent across the dictionaries analysed. Some of them leaned towards the writing of proper terminological definitions, while others tried to maintain a linguistic orientation.[9] Table 1 shows two examples (water and aspirin) of how terms were defined in DRAE, W III, and DFC/PR. These definitions have since been updated.

These definitions, as analysed by Lara and Zahn (1973), present interesting features because each dictionary had to find the right balance between linguistic and terminological definitions. For water/*agua*/*eau*, the DRAE chose to provide its chemical composition and physical characteristics, though some of them are not necessary for the definition or even true. W III provides a mixture of information, some of which can be part of the meaning of the general language word, and some can be part of the semi-specialised term. DFC, on the other hand, provides a linguistic definition with no hint of being a semi-specialised term.

In the case of aspirin/*aspirina*/*aspirine*, establishing the right balance was even more complex. DRAE, W III, and PR highlight aspirin's white colour, in tablet form (except for DRAE), and having analgesic and antipyretic properties, in line with a general language definition. In addition, DRAE and W III also add that aspirin is a crystallised compound, and all three dictionaries give its chemical composition. From the analysis of these definitions, it is evident that 'aspirin' is a semi-specialised term.

The position taken by the DEM, according to Lara and Zahn (ibid.), was twofold: (a) "In order to preserve the work within general language dictionaries,

---

8. These editions correspond to the latest editions available in 1973, at the time when this study was conducted.

9. A linguistic definition provides one or more meanings of a word, that is to say, it records what the average speaker understands by that word and how it is used in everyday life situations. A terminological definition relies on extralinguistic reality, it provides the characteristics of the concept usually stated in a more technical form. Depending on the actual text not everyone is able to understand it unless the user has some previous knowledge of the specific domain. In practice, however, it is not always possible to differentiate one from the other, but sometimes it is very clear when a terminological definition has been provided in a general language dictionary. (See in Table 1 the definition of *aspirina* (aspirin) found in all three dictionaries, DRAE, W III and PR).

Table 1. Definition of water and aspirin in Spanish, English and French general language dictionaries

Dictionary	Word/ Term	Definition
DRAE (1970)	*agua* (water)	Cuerpo formado por la combinación de un volumen de oxígeno y dos de hidrógeno, líquido, inodoro, insípido, en pequeña cantidad incoloro y verdoso en grandes masas, que refracta la luz, disuelve muchas sustancias, se solidifica por el frío, se evapora por el calor y, más o menos puro, forma la lluvia, las fuentes, los ríos y los mares.
		(A body formed by the combination of one volume of oxygen and two of hydrogen, liquid, odourless, tasteless, colourless in small quantities, and greenish in large masses, which refracts light, dissolves many substances, solidifies by cooling it, evaporates by heating it and, more or less pure, forms rain, springs, rivers, and seas.)
W III (1966)	water	The liquid that descends from the clouds as rain, forms streams, lakes, and seas, issues from the ground in springs, and is a mayor constituent of all living matter and that when pure consists of an oxide of hydrogen H_2O or $(H_2O)x$ in the proportion of 2 atoms of hydrogen to one atom of oxygen and is an odorless, tasteless, very slightly compressible liquid which appears bluish in thick layers.
DFC (1971)	*eau* (water)	Liquide incolore, inodore, sans saveur à l'état pur, le plus commun dans la nature.
		(A colourless, odourless, tasteless liquid in its pure state, the most common in nature.)
DRAE (1970)	*aspirina* (*farm.*) (aspirin)	Cuerpo blanco cristalizado en agujas y muy poco soluble en agua. Lo constituyen los radicales de los ácidos acético y salicílico y se usa como antirreumático y antipirético.
		(A white body crystalised in needles and very slightly soluble in water. It is made up of the radicals of acetic and salicylic acids and is used as an antirheumatic and antipyretic.)
W III (1966)	aspirin	1. A white crystalline compound $CH_3COOC_6H_4COOH$ of salicylic acid used especially in tablet form as an antipyretic and analgesic like the salicylates but producing fewer undesirable effects — called also — acetylsalicylic acid.
		2. A tablet of aspirin.
PR (1965)	*aspirine* (aspirin)	Acide acétylsalicylique, remède analgésique et antithermique.
		(Acetylsalicylic acid, analgesic and antithermal remedy.)

the definition of each term should consider the difference between its meaning (linguistic) and its referent (extra-linguistic)"; and (b) domain specialists would be asked to draft the definitions of semi-specialised terms to make sure these are technically correct.

In practice, definitions of terms with a lower level of specialisation are more linguistically oriented, while semi-specialised terms, when convenient or possible, provide a meaning for the word when used in general language, and an appropriate terminological definition is given for the term. Example (1) shows how DEM (2024) defines *planeta* (planet).

(1) planeta s m
   1. Cuerpo celeste que no emite luz propia y gira alrededor del Sol, como la Tierra, o de otra estrella[10]
   2. (*Astron*) Cuerpo celeste del sistema solar que se caracteriza por tener una gravedad propia, capaz de haberle dado una forma relativamente esférica y por haber despejado las regiones por donde corre su órbita; así, son planetas desde Mercurio hasta Neptuno[11]

In (1), the first definition corresponds to the meaning of *planeta* as a general language word, whereas the second clearly corresponds to the concept *planeta* in the domain of Astronomy. The first one shows 'planet' as used by children and average speakers (general language word), while the second one is an adaptation of the definition of 'planet' provided by the International Astronomical Union (specialised term) as used by specialists and highly educated speakers.

Example (2) shows the terminological definition of *neutrino* (neutrino) in the domain of Physics.

(2) neutrino s m
    (*Fís*) Partícula subatómica del grupo de los leptones, sin carga eléctrica y de masa tan pequeña que su interacción con las demás partículas es mínima, de manera que puede atravesar cualquier materia sin apenas interactuar con ella[12]

In (2) DEM provides only one definition because there is no general language meaning associated to *neutrino*.

---

10. A celestial body that does not emit its own light and revolves around the Sun, like the Earth, or another star.

11. (*Astron*) A celestial body of the solar system characterised by having sufficient gravity, by being capable of assuming a relatively spheric shape, and by having cleared the neighbourhood around its orbit; thus, the planets are from Mercury to Neptune.

12. (*Phys*) Subatomic particle of the group of leptons, without electric charge and with such a small mass that its interaction with other particles is minimal, such that it can pass through any matter without hardly interacting with it.

2.1.2.3   *When domain labels should be used and how to assign them*

The third topic focused on finding how domain labels are used in DRAE (1970) and *Diccionario general ilustrado de la lengua Española* (1961) — VOX, what terms were assigned a domain label, and how these labels were assigned. The result (Lara and Zahn 1973) showed a considerable variation both in terms of the number of domain labels used and how these were assigned. DRAE identifies 138 domains some of which are further divided in subdomains, as in medicine: surgery, embryology, anatomy, gynaecology, etc. VOX, on the other hand, only identifies 58 domains.

DEM defined 60 domain labels corresponding to scientific and technical fields and some traditional Mexican arts and crafts. Since the DEM is a general language dictionary, it was decided that terms would only have a domain label when the specialised definition differed from the general language meaning. Example (3) shows two semi-specialised terms in mathematics, *número partitivo* (partitive number) and *número primo* (prime number), the first one of which does not require a domain label whereas the second, does.

(3)   a.   número partitivo
       Número que expresa parte de una unidad, como mitad, cuarto, quinto, onceavo, quinceavo, veinteavo, etc[13]
       In this instance, the definition does not require special mathematical knowledge, therefore it does not have a domain label.
       b.   número primo (*Mat*)
       Número que solamente es divisible por sí mismo y por la unidad, como 5, 7, 101, etc[14]
       In this case, the domain label is necessary because some semi-specialised mathematical knowledge is required to understand the definition.

2.1.2.4   *How borrowed terms should be treated*

In her study of 1973, Valadez describes two opposing approaches regarding the acceptance of borrowed words and terms in Spanish.[15] The first one, more traditional, rejects the inclusion and usage of terms coming from other languages, and proposes to translate or adapt them to make them look like natural Spanish words, as in the case of some international units, such as joule, watt, volt, ohm, etc, which were adapted into Spanish as *julio, vatio/wat, voltio,* and *ohmio* respectively.

---

13. A number that expresses a part of a unit, such as half, fourth, fifth, eleventh, fifteenth, twentieth, etc.

14. A number that is divisible only by 1 or by itself, such as 5, 7, 101, etc.

15. For this work I have adapted Valadez's text to deal only with terms.

The second one, more liberal, considers that borrowed terms enrich the language, and therefore their use should not only be accepted but even encouraged, especially for international terms, as this facilitates communication. Modern-day examples might include *business-to-business e-commerce, software,* and *switch,* borrowed from English, and *diskette* from French.

There are, however, many terms imported from different languages which are actually used in Mexican Spanish that reflect both approaches. What usually happens is that borrowed terms coexist with a varying number of Spanish forms, as in the case of *fracking* which is widely used in Spanish in its original English form together with the Spanish equivalents *fracturación hidráulica, fractura hidráulica, hidrofractura* and *hidrofracturación.*

The DEM's position towards borrowed words in general is to include those that have already been assimilated into Mexican Spanish and are widely used.

As to the form in which borrowed terms were included in the Dictionary, again, the preferred form was determined by its use within the community, i.e., as a direct loan (*drone, software*), or adapted, to reflect its natural pronunciation in Spanish (*beisbol, basquetbol, futbol*). Sometimes though, the preferred form is a loan translation, as in *rascacielos* (skyscraper), and *resonancia magnética* (magnetic resonance).

This detailed description of the decisions behind the treatment of terms in the DEM provides an insight into the careful design and consistent methodology followed by the DEM. Fifty years on, it still serves as a model for general and specialised lexicography in Mexico and other Spanish-speaking countries.

2.2 Translator training programme

The Programa para la Formación de Traductores (PFT) offered by the Centre for Linguistic and Literary Studies represents an important stepping stone in the history of Mexican terminology. It began in 1969 as a seminar on translation from English and French into Spanish in response to the concerns of Tomás Segovia, the great poet, translator, and writer, about the overall quality of translations in Mexico. He wanted translators to become aware of the language, to feel the language, to get to know the language, to enjoy working with languages and, equally as important, to immerse themselves in the cultures involved. By 1974 the seminar became a two-year diploma course specialising in literary translation. At the same time, it was evident that Mexico needed to produce high-quality specialised translations, thus the importance of including a two-semester terminology course in the curriculum. Since there was no one with the necessary knowledge or experience to teach the subject, in 1976 Jacques Goetschalckx, Head of the Terminology Bureau of the Commission of the European Communities (CEC) was invited to teach an intensive course to lecturers and students, and the following year this course was taught by Anne Boisvert, from the University of Montreal and terminologist at the Translation Bureau, Public Works and Government Services Canada. Although the main aim of these courses was to teach translators how to systematically and rigorously solve the terminology problems faced while translating specialised texts, they also included theory and methodology as well as practical work focused on how to produce mono- and multilingual specialised glossaries and vocabularies. As a result of these courses, in 1977 the first translation-oriented terminology works were produced in Mexico, sponsored by the CEC, which included six multilingual glossaries and vocabularies; several years later, a multilingual term bank containing the students' work was created (Hernández 2022: 8).

The first ever symposium dealing with terminology in Mexico, the Simposio sobre Traducción y Terminología, took place in November 1979 in Mexico City (Hernández 2022: 8). And in 1989 the Centre for Demographic and Urban Studies in collaboration with the PFT published a glossary of environmental terms (Sánchez and Guiza 1989), sponsored by UNESCO.

In 2004, the diploma course in translation became a Master's degree in Translation Studies. Its main purpose is to produce high quality translators and translation researchers. It has three basic orientations: annotated translation, translation studies and terminology. At the time of writing, this course is in the process of being upgraded to become a PhD in Translation Studies.

The terminology courses offered by COLMEX shaped most terminology courses currently available in Mexico as part of the translation curricula of public and private educational institutions.

2.3   Agreement between CEC and COLMEX on Eurodicautom

As a result of Jacques Goetschalckx's visit, in 1980 COLMEX and the CEC signed a collaboration agreement by means of which, in exchange for having unlimited access to Eurodicautom, COLMEX would provide terminology in Spanish. A copy[16] of Eurodicautom was installed and students and lecturers provided equivalents in Mexican Spanish for a few thousand terms contained in Eurodicautom. However, when in January 1986 Spain joined the CEC, it became only natural that Spanish terminology contained in the European term bank should come from

---

16. The copy of Eurodicautom installed in Mexico consisted of the actual physical tapes and Winchester disks with the original PL/1 files as well as the database contents. It is worth remembering that at the time, it was customary to develop *ad hoc* software for database management systems from scratch.

Spain and its various institutions and not from a single non-European Spanish-speaking country. Consequently, the CEC-COLMEX agreement ended.

Nevertheless, after all these years terminology work took off in Mexico as will be seen in the following sections.

3. The expansion

From the mid-nineties, slowly but steadily, terminology has been developing in Mexico mainly in the form of courses, theoretical and applied research, and terminotics.

3.1 Terminology courses

Several Mexican institutions have been offering terminology courses for some years now. Most of them are taught within the framework of translation programmes, while others offer the possibility of selecting translation courses that include a module on terminology in the last year of undergraduate studies in modern languages. There is also a one-year postgraduate course leading to a diploma in terminology offered by the Instituto Superior de Intérpretes y Traductores.

Today, terminology for translators is taught at no fewer than fifteen institutions of higher education. Also, Leticia Leduc, a freelance translator and terminologist, has been tirelessly teaching terminology to translators and interpreters for the past thirty-odd years in the framework of the Mexican associations of translators and interpreters.

Three universities teach terminology courses as part of their undergraduate or postgraduate programmes in linguistics or applied linguistics. Although initially there were just a handful, the number of students working in terminology related topics for their dissertations and theses has been steadily growing.

Furthermore, two permanent seminars on lexicology, lexicography and terminology are held at COLMEX and the Universidad Nacional Autónoma de México (UNAM), where research projects are regularly presented and discussed.

From the early nineties some twenty-five Mexican students have chosen terminology or terminotics as their primary research topic for their PhD degrees in linguistics, applied linguistics, computational linguistics, translation, computer science, or library science, and many more are in the process of completing them. That number is far exceeded by those currently working towards their master's or bachelor's degrees. Some students have pursued their postgraduate degrees abroad, mainly at the University of Manchester Institute of Science and Technology (UMIST), the University of Manchester, the Universitat Pompeu Fabra —

Barcelona, Universidad Complutense de Madrid, and Université d'Avignon; others have obtained their degrees from Mexican universities.

3.2   Researchers and topics of interest

Over the last few decades terminology research, both theoretical and applied, has expanded in Mexico. This was partly due to the first students who obtained their PhDs in computational linguistics and linguistics whose main research topic was terminology or terminotics. The first two, María Pozzi and Gerardo Sierra, worked with Juan Sager and Jock McNaught at UMIST. Both Sager and McNaught greatly contributed to shaping the current research activities related to terminology and terminotics in Mexico. Thanks to their encouragement, Sierra founded, in 1999, the Grupo de Ingeniería Lingüística (GIL) at UNAM's Engineering Institute, and on her return from the United Kingdom back in 1992, Pozzi started developing the corpus of scientific texts in Mexican Spanish at COLMEX.

On the home front, Ana María Cardero was the first Mexican linguist to obtain her PhD with a thesis related to terminology. She founded the Seminar of lexicology, lexicography, and terminology at UNAM and established a linguistics-oriented terminology research group.

There are currently around twenty terminology researchers working in Mexican universities. Their main research topics include theoretical terminology, philosophy of terminology, neology and other linguistic aspects of terms, specialised corpus design, term banks, terminography and children's terminography, terminology standards, ontologies, terminotics, terminology in Mexican sign language and terminology in some indigenous languages.

3.3   Evolving theories and their influence on Mexican terminology

This section would not be complete without a brief account of how the theoretical positions of Mexican terminologists have evolved and how this has influenced newer design and development of applied terminology projects.

Since systematic terminology started to be practised in the country, theoretical positions adopted by Mexican terminologists have evolved in almost every respect. Section 2 described how the treatment of general and semi-specialised terms in the DEM were based on the best linguistic and lexicographic practices available at that time. From the mid-seventies to the mid-nineties, the General Theory of Terminology (GTT) was adopted as the leading theoretical framework which resulted mainly in prescriptive rather than descriptive works. This was only natural because the GTT was, by far, the most influential theory at that time.

However, since the beginning of the nineties, terminology, both theory and practice, started to evolve everywhere. Several scholars expressed concerns about some shortcomings of the GTT, especially those related to its idealised and reductionist nature (Cabré 1999: 113–116) and proposed that each communicative situation required a different approach and appropriate solutions to achieve effective communication based on the specific domain and the actual participants involved. Together with her group at the Universitat Pompeu Fabra, Teresa Cabré went on to develop the Teoría Comunicativa de la Terminología (TCT) which follows a descriptive approach to terminology as opposed to the GTT's prescriptive approach. Previously, Sager (1990: 5) had stated that because terminology is so heavily dependent on language and culture, standardisation as originally envisaged by the GTT was not always possible or even desirable. Temmerman's sociocognitive approach to terminology (2000) provided a newer framework where prototypes play a significant role in understanding and defining concepts. These positions have exerted the greatest influence on Mexican terminology and have contributed to shaping newer theoretical positions that in turn have determined current research and applications.

By the end of the nineties, Pozzi (1999) questioned the idea that a concept is comprised of a *unique* and *universally-recognised* set of essential characteristics. She proposed instead that essential characteristics attributed to a concept can vary from person to person depending on their perspective and experience. She thus acknowledges degrees of concept variation. There are not many works on the philosophy of terminology; however, Lara (2001a: 176–182) has made important contributions to this field, suggesting a linguistic approach to understanding the relationship between concept-object-sign. He also proposed (2001b: 220) four layers of meaning that allow us to locate the cultural and universal character of the specialised term: (a) prototype formation, (b) stereotype formation, (c) verbal meaning formation, and (d) specialised meaning delimitation.

Mexico has carried out some pioneering works in terminotics. Among them, a methodology to produce an onomasiological dictionary (Sierra 1996), where users input a set of words that ideally form part of the definition of a concept and, as output, they are presented with a list of terms (the definiendum) ordered by probability of a successful match. Also, Wikipedia was used to automatically validate term candidates (Vivaldi et al. 2012) by means of Wikipedia's own internal structure. More recently, systems for the automatic extraction of definitions and defining contexts in Spanish (Aguilar et al. 2016, Dorantes et al. 2017) and for the automatic extraction of examples (Lázaro 2015) have been successfully developed. In addition, several faculties and institutes of UNAM are currently developing terminologies related to their own specific interests, as in the case of the Instituto de Investigaciones Estéticas, where Molina (2024) coordinates the Terminological Treasure of Arts and Archaeology in Mexico (TTAAM) which provides 18,000 definitions of terms related to the history of art and archaeology in Mexico. And Glandy Horita (2005) developed the terminology of ethology at the Facultad de Medicina Veterinaria y Zootecnia.

In another project, a multi-layered general science dictionary is being created at COLMEX, where users are presented with tailored information based on their profile.[17] Finally, there is an initiative to develop terminology for specific domains, including those related to the Covid-19 pandemic, in Mexican sign language (Cruz and Palacios (in press)).

4.   International cooperation

International cooperation in terminology is paramount for its efficient development. From the time Mexican researchers began working in terminology, they understood the importance of taking part in joint projects with international organisations, terminology networks, universities, national government agencies and specific individuals abroad. The following subsections (4.1–4.3) describe the collaboration of Mexican researchers in international terminology activities.

4.1   ISO/TC 37 language and terminology

ISO/TC 37 Language and Terminology, brings together a large number of terminology experts from countries around the world. Its scope has been extended to include the publication of international standards not only related to terminology, but also to natural language processing, translation, interpreting and other language-based activities in the multilingual information society. Furthermore, ISO/TC 37 is one of ISO's nine horizontal technical committees, which means that all other technical committees are required to follow some of its core standards (ISO 704, ISO 10241–1, ISO 16642, ISO 30042) to document or exchange their own terminology.

Unlike several ISO national member bodies that are private, Mexico's standards body, the Dirección General de Normas (DGN) is a public directorate

---

17. These include 6–12, 13–15, 16–18-year-old children and the average general speaker. Definitions and other information provided vary according to the individual user profile. For example, the dictionary stores several levels of definitions and displays the most appropriate one for the user: definitions for children are oriented to helping them to understand the concept and are accordingly written; illustrations are age-appropriate, interesting additional information is included for school-age children, as are some explicit applications of the concept. For the average adult speaker definitions are more formal but always oriented for the non-specialist. (Pozzi 2022)

within the Ministry of Trade and Industry. Mexico became the first Spanish-speaking participating member (P-member) of ISO/TC 37 in 1994. Since then, the Mexican team has been headed by María Pozzi, who has been active in most of the working groups of its five subcommittees.

4.2   Unión Latina

Unión Latina was an international organisation whose members included countries that had at least one national or official Latin language. One of the four directorates under the Secretariat-General was the Directorate of Terminology and Language Industries (DTIL) headed by Daniel Prado for many years until Unión Latina ceased to exist in January 2012 due to financial difficulties. However, it must be acknowledged that it played a decisive role in the promotion of all aspects of terminology not only in Mexico but in several Latin countries, especially in the Americas and Europe. Two international terminology networks, the Red Iberoamericana de Terminología (RITerm) and the Red Panlatina de terminología (Realiter) were created to bring terminologists together with the aim of participating in joint projects of common interest.[18]

4.2.1   *Red Iberoamericana de Terminología (RITerm)*

In the words of Teresa Cabré (2012: 82), "to talk about Ibero American terminology inevitably leads to talking about Daniel Prado." He was instrumental in the creation of RITerm and the promotion of terminology as a discipline of study in Latin America. Furthermore, he introduced, organised, and promoted terminology in several countries of the region, including Spain and Portugal, and more importantly, he helped groups of terminologists to establish contact with each other and to collaborate in the development of joint projects. From the time of its creation back in 1988, thanks to Prado's initiative, and with the sponsorship of Unión Latina, UNESCO and Infoterm, Mexican terminology greatly benefited from RITerm. The few isolated groups of terminologists working in the country came together and shared knowledge and experience. Joint projects with other Spanish, Catalan and Portuguese-speaking countries started to develop, using a unified methodology. That was the time when terminology established itself in the region in a more systematic way. A biennial RITerm symposium has been held

---

18. See Chapter 15 (Weilgaard Christensen et al.) to reinforce the importance of regional associations for terminology development, in this particular instance, Realiter and RITerm, and Nord term, the association of organisations and societies in the Nordic countries which are engaged in terminology work, training and research.

ever since at different locations within Latin America, Spain and Portugal. Mexico has hosted two of them in 1996 and 2020/2021).

RITerm promoted and supported several activities, among which the following three stand out: (a) terminology training programmes, (b) RITerm Joven which used to finance high quality joint research projects proposed by young terminologists from three or more countries, and (c) the development of a collaborative term bank (RITerm-BD) containing data of common interest. Prado, as head of DTIL, provided infrastructure, logistics, organisational skills, ideas, know-how and sometimes funding that resulted in the rapid development of terminology in this part of the world.

Mexico was a founding member of RITerm and has been active ever since. Elena Lozanova (COLMEX, Mexico) was the first RITerm Joven recipient of funds for her project to develop a termbase of environmental law phraseology in three languages. The other students participating in this project came from Catalonia, Colombia, and Brazil, and the languages covered were Catalan, Portuguese, and two varieties of Spanish.

The role played by Teresa Cabré who, together with Daniel Prado shaped the world of theoretical and applied terminology not only in Mexico but also in other Latin American countries, should be recognised and praised. Prado's pragmatic approach, enthusiasm and efficiency combined with Cabré's academic strength and stamina resulted in a success story. Their joint effort to transmit their passion for terminology to linguists, documentalists, translators, and computer scientists was not in vain. Most countries in the region are now seriously working in one or more aspects of terminology. Together, they organised courses, seminars, conferences, workshops, and joint international projects. Many students continued their postgraduate studies in Barcelona under the supervision of Cabré and her colleagues at Universitat Pompeu Fabra.

As part of RITerm's activities to promote terminology, Prado, together with the Office québécoise de la langue française (OQLF), organised terminology courses in several Latin American countries including Mexico. For some of these countries, it was their first contact with the discipline. Without Prado and Cabré, and therefore, RITerm, terminology in Latin America would be very different today.

4.2.2 *Red Panlatina de Terminología (Realiter)*

Realiter was founded in Paris, in December 1993. Once again, Daniel Prado, at the time head of DTIL, played a decisive role in its creation and development. Its original aim was to connect individuals, institutions and organisations involved in terminology work in countries having at least one Latin national or official language. It was conceived to produce a series of terminography products, including specialised lexicons and vocabularies in the network's languages: Catalan, French, Galician, Italian, Portuguese, Romanian, and Spanish, as well as English. One of its first projects, led by Louis-Jean Rousseau, was to establish a set of common methodological principles on which to base the collaborative work to produce these lexicons. More than 35 panlatin lexicons or vocabularies have been published online and/or in printed form in a wide range of subject fields. Most include the Mexican Spanish variant provided by Mexican members of Realiter.

Realiter organises a yearly scientific conference where members present the results of research projects as well as newer theoretical or methodological advances in terminology. Mexico has regularly been attending these conferences.

María Pozzi served on the executive board of Realiter from 2002 until 2019; she oversaw the Mexican Spanish version of the Panlatin lexicons and was its liaison officer to ISO/TC 37.

4.3   Universities, government agencies, and institutions

Mexican terminology researchers have been welcomed as visiting scholars in several universities, government agencies and other institutions. Among them, the Universitat Pompeu Fabra, UMIST, the University of Manchester, the National Centre for Text Mining, the Centro de Información y Documentación Científica (CINDOC) in Madrid, the Université d'Avignon, the University of Harvard, the Translation Bureau of Public Services and Procurement Canada,[19] the Office québécois de la langue française (OQLF), and various South American Universities. There are still some joint projects being developed with terminologists working at some of these universities.

As part of this international cooperation, Mexico has hosted several conferences, symposia and workshops dealing with specific aspects of terminology, specialised translation, and special languages.

5.   Challenges and the future of terminology in Mexico

Although terminology work in Mexico has been steadily growing and diversifying, there are still many challenges to overcome.

Efforts are ongoing to convince the Mexican government to set up a national centre for terminology and to develop a national term bank, to manage, harmonise and develop various terminologies in Mexican Spanish. Awareness needs to be raised among the private sector about the importance of terminology. This

---

19. Formerly Public Works and Government Services Canada.

requires the elaboration of solid business case arguments. Because there are no terminology policies in Mexico, the terminology of several domains, especially of newer technological ones, is disorganised. Finally, there is a fair amount of disagreement with respect to neologisms: On the one hand, the rules established by the RAE, regardless of the actual use of a term in the Mexican community, continue to be applied. On the other, some people are more concerned with achieving faster and better communication in the Mexican context, so they readily adopt English terms without question. However, most people are merely concerned with being understood. Consequently, it is sometimes possible to identify a large number of synonyms representing a single concept.

However, as always, with great challenges there are also great opportunities. Terminology work is conducted by a select group of people, including academic researchers, language engineers, translators, interpreters, lexicographers and documentalists. Some original research projects have been awarded government and university grants which have resulted in a series of useful applications with important social impact. Postgraduate students have also benefited from government grants to study terminology-related topics in top European universities, mainly in Catalonia, France, and the United Kingdom amongst others.

In short, terminology in Mexico has come a long way from the state it was in fifty years ago, and although not everything has gone according to what the first terminologists originally had in mind, the future looks promising, as the number of terminologists and interesting research projects has steadily increased.

Funding

I wish to thank the Consejo Nacional de Ciencia y Tecnología (CONACYT) for the generous funding of this research which was conducted within the framework of the project: El vocabulario básico científico de México. Un estudio de sus características, componentes y difusión (No. CB-2013–220528-H).

References

Aguilar C., O. Acosta, G. Sierra, S. Juárez, and T. Infante. 2016. "Extracción de contextos definitorios en el área de biomedicina." *Procesamiento del Lenguaje Natural* 57: 167–170.

Cabré, Teresa. 1999. *La Terminología. Representación y Comunicación*, Barcelona: Institut Universitari de Lingüística Aplicada.

Cabré, Teresa. 2012. "Daniel Prado, el Pilar Fundamental de la Terminología Iberoamericana." *Debate Terminológico* 8:82–83.

Cruz Aldrete, Miroslava, and Niktelol Palacios Cuahtecontzi. (in press). "Terminología de la salud en LSM: A propósito de COVID-19." In *Inclusión y terminología en la sociedad actual*, ed. by N. Palacios, M. Pozzi, and G. Sierra. Mexico City: El Colegio de México.

DEM. 2010. *Diccionario del Español de México*, dir. by L. F. Lara. Mexico City: El Colegio de México.

DEM. 2024. *Diccionario del Español de México*, El Colegio de México.

DFC. 1971. *Dictionnaire du Français Contemporain*. Jean Dubois et al.. Paris: Larousse.

Dorantes M.A., A. Pimentel, G. Sierra, G. Bel-Enguix, and C. Molina. 2017. "Extracción automática de definiciones analíticas y relaciones semánticas de hiponimia-hiperonimia con un sistema basado en patrones lingüísticos." *Linguamatica* 9 (2): 33–44.

DRAE. 1970. *Diccionario de la Lengua Española*. Real Academia Española, 19a ed. Madrid: Espasa-Calpe.

Fernández Gordillo, Luz. 2014. "La lexicografía del español y el español hispanoamericano." *Andamios. Revista de Investigación Social*, 11(26): 53–89.

García Hidalgo, María Isabel. 1979. "La formalización del analizador gramatical del DEM." In *Investigaciones lingüísticas en lexicografía*, ed. by Luis Fernando Lara, Roberto Ham Chande, and Ma. Isabel García Hidalgo, 85–156. Mexico City: El Colegio de México.

Ham Chande, Roberto. 1979. "Del 1 al 100 en Lexicografía." In *Investigaciones lingüísticas en lexicografía*, ed. by Luis Fernando Lara, Roberto Ham Chande, and Ma. Isabel García Hidalgo, 41–83. Mexico City: El Colegio de México.

Hernández, Tania. 2022. "De la Formación en Traducción y Traductología en El Colegio de México." *Lingüística Mexicana. Nueva Época*, 4 (2): 7–14.

Horita, Glandy. 2005. *Terminología de etología aplicada, integración conceptual y descripción lingüística*, Universidad Nacional Autónoma de México, Master's Dissertation, unpublished.

Kamenetskaia, Sofía. 2018. "El léxico de la Nueva España en el Vocabulario de Antonio de Alcedo." *Nueva Revista de Filología Hispánica* (NRFH), 66 (2): 627–649.

Lara, Luis Fernando. 2001a. "Conceptos" y jerarquía de términos." In *Ensayos de Teoría Semántica: lengua natural y lenguajes científicos*, 175–207. Mexico City: El Colegio de México.

Lara, Luis Fernando. 2001b. "Término y cultura: hacia una teoría del término." In *Ensayos de Teoría Semántica: lengua natural y lenguajes científicos*, 209–248. Mexico City: El Colegio de México.

Lara, Luis Fernando, and Jetta Zahn. 1973. "El tecnicismo en el léxico del español mexicano. Posiciones posibles." In *Monografía No. 8*, Diccionario del Español de México. Mexico City: El Colegio de México (unpublished).

Lara, Luis Fernando, and Roberto Ham Chande. 1979. "Base Estadística del Diccionario del Español de México." In *Investigaciones Lingüísticas en Lexicografía*, 5–39. Mexico City: El Colegio de México.

Lázaro, Jorge. 2015. *El Ejemplo en Terminología. Caracterización y Extracción Automática*. PhD Thesis (unpublished). Barcelona: Institut Universitari de Lingüística Aplicada. Universitat Pompeu Fabra.

Méndez Espinosa, Oscar. 2019. *La Terminología de Geografía en Zapoteco: una Nueva Perspectiva para las Escuelas de Oaxaca, México*. Barcelona: Institut Universitari de Lingüística Aplicada. Universitat Pompeu Fabra. PhD Thesis (unpublished).

Méndez Zapata, Patricia Alejandra and Catalina Naumis. 2015. "Terminología del huipil triqui." *In XII Congreso ISKO España y II Congreso ISKO España-Portugal.* 10–20 November. Organización del Conocimiento para sistemas de información abiertos. Murcia: University of Murcia.

Molina Salinas, Claudio. 2024. *Tesoro terminológico de las artes y arqueología en México.* Ciudad de México: Instituto de Investigaciones Estéticas, UNAM.

Pozzi, María. 2022. "Design of a dictionary to help school children to understand basic mathematical concepts." In *Dictionaries and Society. Proceedings of the XX EURALEX International Congress,* ed. by A. Klosa-Kückelhaus, S. Engelberg, C. Möhrs, and P. Storjohann, 678–689. Mannheim: IDS-Verlag.

Pozzi, María. 1999. "The concept of 'concept' in terminology: a need for a new approach." In *Terminology and Knowledge Engineering,* ed. by P. Sandrini, 28–42. Vienna: TermNet.

PR. Robert, Paul. 1965. *Petit Robert — Dictionnaire alphabétique et analogique de la langue française.* Paris: Société de Nouveau Littré.

Romero Rangel, Laura. 2016. *El Vocabulario Castellano-Mexicano de Alonso de Molina: Estudio Lexicográfico.* Mexico City: El Colegio de México. PhD Thesis (unpublished).

Sager, Juan C. 1990. *A Practical Course in Terminology Processing,* Amsterdam: John Benjamins.

Sánchez, Vicente, and Beatriz Guiza. 1989. *Glosario de términos sobre medio ambiente.* Santiago: UNESCO.

Sierra Martínez, Gerardo. 1996. "Estructura semántica del léxico en un diccionario onomasiológico práctico." *Estudios de Lingüística Aplicada* 23/24: 417–425.

Stala, Ewa. 2020. "Historia de la lexicografía hispanoamericana." *Studia Iberystyczne* 19: 223–251.

Temmerman, Rita. 2000. *Towards New Ways of Terminology Description: The Sociocognitive Approach.* Amsterdam: John Benjamins.

Valadez, Carmen Delia. 1973. "El papel de las palabras provenientes de otras lenguas de cultura en el léxico de México. Posiciones posibles del DEM." In *Monografía No. 6.* Mexico City: Diccionario del Español de México, El Colegio de México (unpublished).

Vivaldi, Jordi, Luis Adrián Cabrera, Gerardo Sierra, and María Pozzi. 2012. "Using Wikipedia to Validate the Terminology Found in a Corpus of Basic Textbooks." In *Proceedings of the 8th Conference on Language Resources and Evaluation (LREC'12),* 820–827. Paris: ELRA.

VOX. 1961. *Diccionario general ilustrado de la lengua española.* Barcelona: Gili y Gaya, Spes.

W III. — Webster III. 1966. *Webster's Third New International Dictionary of the English Language,* unabridged, ed. by Philip Babcock Gove. Springfield: G. C. Merriam Company Publishers.

CHAPTER 15

The Nordic Terminology Community
Research and practice

Lise Lotte Weilgaard Christensen,[1] Hanne Erdman
Thomsen,[2] Bodil Nistrup Madsen,[2] Anna-Lena Bucher,[3]
Henrik Nilsson,[3] Claudia Dobrina,[3] Håvard Hjulstad,[5] Åsa
Holmér,[6] Johan Myking,[7] Anita Nuopponen,[8] Sirpa Suhonen,[9]
Anu Ylisalmi[9] & Ágústa Þorbergsdóttir[10]

[1] University of Southern Denmark | [2] Copenhagen Business School |
[3] The Swedish Association for Terminology | [4] The Swedish Centre
for Terminology TNC | [5] Standards Norway | [6] The Institute for
Language and Folklore | [7] University of Bergen | [8] University of
Vaasa | [9] The Finnish Terminology Centre | [10] The Árni Magnússon
Institute for Icelandic Studies

This chapter analyses and discusses the coherence of Nordic terminology
co-operation. The hub of this co-operation is the Nordterm network
initiated in 1976. Over the years, a bridge has been built from Nordterm to
each country and vice versa. We describe the development of Nordterm and
the history of terminology organisations in each of the Nordic countries,
and outline the research activities and the development of methodologies as
well as the teaching and training activities carried out in the Nordic
countries. Nordic term banks and terminology portals as well as contributions to the international terminology community are described. We also
explain how the conditions for terminology work in the region have
changed.

Keywords: Nordic terminology co-operation, terminology training and
teaching, terminology research, terminological data categories,
terminological format, concept system, formalisation, terminology work,
terminological management tool, term bank, terminology centre

https://doi.org/10.1075/tlrp.24.15wei

1.   Introduction

The aim of this contribution is to investigate and discuss how the Nordic terminology communities have historically been sources of mutual inspiration despite
varying language families and despite differing strengths and focuses of the individual countries in respect of terminology, whether in research, training, or practice. The coherence of Nordic terminology co-operation may, to a large extent, be
attributed to the existence of Nordterm, the Nordic terminology network. Moreover, when changes in the conditions for terminology work took place in the various countries, Nordterm turned out to function as an important centre ensuring
stability over the years. In addition, we see this contribution as an opportunity
to share the significant contributions of Nordic terminology activities in a joint
article. This is important because, to our knowledge, the latest joint articles were
published in the 1980s (Picht and Draskau 1985a; Nordterm Steering Committee
1988; Picht 1998), at a time when Nordterm had existed for just a decade.

The rest of the chapter is organised as follows: Section 2 describes the development of the Nordterm network, and Section 3 describes the history of terminology organisations in each of the Nordic countries. In Section 4, we provide an
overview of the research and development carried out in the Nordic countries in
respect of methodologies, organised by themes rather than by countries. Section 5
focuses on term banks, since most of the countries have central term banks or terminology portals. Section 6 contains an overview of teaching and training, and
finally, Section 7 describes Nordic contributions to the international terminology
community.

2.   Nordterm: The Nordic terminology network

The Nordic countries include Denmark, Finland, Iceland, Norway, and Sweden.
Moreover, the Faroe Islands and Greenland are both part of the Danish Realm,
while Åland is part of the Republic of Finland. Since 1973, Denmark, and since
1995, Finland and Sweden have been members of the EU. The official languages of
the area are Danish, Faeroese, Finnish, Greenlandic, Icelandic, Norwegian (with
two official written forms: Bokmål and Nynorsk), Sami, and Swedish.

Rooted in a long tradition of political, economic, and cultural co-operation,
Nordic co-operation is the world's oldest of its kind. It focuses on areas in which a
joint Nordic effort creates added value for the Nordic countries and their citizens.
The official Nordic co-operation takes place within the framework of the Nordic
Council of Ministers (formed in 1971), through which the Nordic governments
co-operate, and in the framework of the Nordic Council (formed in 1952), which
is the forum of co-operation of the parliamentarians.

Nordic co-operation in the field of terminology began in 1976 (Kristensen 1994: 72–73; Bucher 1994). Some of the underlying reasons for this co-operation were:

- An increased interest in special languages (LSP) and terminology in Europe and the Nordic countries.
- An increased need for research into special languages, in particular into their terminology.
- Denmark's entry into the EC as the first Nordic country in 1973. This led to a focus on special language translation and related terminologies in a wide range of areas.
- The existence of terminology centres in some of the Nordic countries. The overall purpose of these centres was to ensure that the Nordic languages retained their position and could function for communication in all domains.

In 1976, the first Nordic terminology meeting, marking the beginning of Nordterm co-operation, took place in Stockholm at the Swedish Centre for Technical Terminology (TNC); however, the initiative came from the newly formed Terminology Group at the Copenhagen School of Economics (later Copenhagen Business School, CBS), put into effect by its chairman, Gert Engel (Bucher 1994: 115–126). Recognising the important role played by TNC in Swedish society, he suggested that the first meeting be held there. The first meeting was attended by TNC, the Norwegian Council for Technical Terminology (RTT), the Finnish Terminology Centre (TSK), and the Terminology Group in Denmark. The participants perceived the meeting as meaningful, partly because it highlighted the different strengths and experiences of the different countries, and as a result, mutual exchange was considered valuable by everyone. There was a consensus that similar meetings should follow (Kristensen 1994: 72–73; Bucher 1994; Picht 1998: 2145). Over the years, Íslensk málnefnd (The Icelandic Language Council) and Sámi Giellagáldu (The Nordic Sami Institute) have joined Nordterm. Recently, Málráðið (The Language Council of the Faroe Islands) and Oqaasileriffik (The Language Secretariat of Greenland) have been granted observer status with voting rights (Nordterm Steering Committee 2021: 5).

An important decision made at the first Nordterm symposium in 1976 was that a working group was set up to develop a common training programme for persons with terminology as their main occupation, e.g. those active at the national terminology centres. The aim was to gather terminological expertise from the Nordic countries as well as from other European countries with the aim of exchanging experience and training opportunities. Creating a solid network of terminologically trained people would further the development of special language and terminology in each country. An initial two-week graduate course was held in Denmark in 1978. Other graduate courses followed in 1982, 1985, and 1990.

The Nordterm co-operation framework is relatively informal. However, in 1987, the need arose for a certain degree of formalisation. What had developed organically during the first decade needed governance, and consequently statutes were created. According to these statutes, the role of Nordterm as a Nordic forum and network in the field of terminology is (1) to promote Nordic co-operation in the field of terminology through joint projects, conferences, seminars, etc., and (2) to ensure the influence and participation of the Nordic countries in the field of terminology at an international level.

Nordterm has a steering committee whose responsibilities are, among others, to represent Nordterm externally and to coordinate activities. Its members are mainly representatives of the national terminology centres or organisations. Terminological activities are carried out through Nordterm working groups (Picht 1998: 2146). Currently, there are two: Terminology research and training and Terminology – digitalisation and tools.

A symposium is held every two years, with varying themes and topics, and hosting circulates among the countries. Lectures and presentations are held mainly in Nordic languages, which constitutes an important principle. Depending on the location, interpretation might also be required (e.g. of Finnish into and from Scandinavian languages).

At the Nordterm symposium in 2007, Heribert Picht (2007: 35–47) summarised the most central topics of terminology science covered by Nordterm over the years as follows:

1. Scientific/theoretical topics:
   – Terminology as a discipline
   – Terminological schools
   – General problems related to terminology research
   – Terminology theory as applied philosophy of science
2. Special language research in relation to terminology and specialist communication
3. Terminology work in a stricter sense:
   – Concept (concept analysis, concept modelling, dynamic concepts, objects)
   – Conceptual representation (sign models, terms, signs, words, neologisms, non-verbal representations, definitions)
   – Presentation and availability of terminological information (term banks, terminological representation of knowledge, dictionaries, term record formats, data categories)
   – Knowledge structuring (concept systems, concept relations, semantic networks, classifications, thesauri, ontologies)

Recently, i.e. after 2007, language policy issues with a focus on terminology have also been dealt with, for example at Nordterm 2015 (Þorbergsdóttir 2017a).

According to Jolkkonen (2008: 86–91), the continuation and development of the Nordterm co-operation network are motivated by two goals:

1. Strengthening the professional role of the terminologist
2. Contributing to knowledge development and upskilling of terminologists

Nordterm provides networking opportunities for researchers and practising terminologists and has definitely been beneficial for each individual country, just as Nordic co-operation in general has been in other areas. Some examples of projects and activities will be described in Sections 4.3, 4.7, 6.2, 7.1.

Similarly, in Chapter 14, Pozzi describes the international terminology networks, RITerm and Realiter. However, in contrast to the co-operation among the Nordic countries, in these cases the co-operation is rooted in their common languages, in particular Spanish.

3. History of terminology organisations in the Nordic countries

3.1 Denmark

The fact that in 1941, a Danish centre for technical terminology was established as part of a common Scandinavian initiative, is often overlooked by recent Nordic literature on terminology. However, in 1960, the centre ended its activities, probably due to the lack of a permanent coordinating body and support from industry and commerce (Kristensen 1941: 201–202; Picht 1988: 13; Spang-Hanssen 1972: 73; Kristensen 1994: 70).

The subsequent Danish terminology initiatives came in the early 1970s, after Denmark had become the first Nordic country to join the European Community (EC) in 1973 (Picht 1988: 13; Kristensen 1994: 68–70). The initiative originated from the Copenhagen Business School (CBS), where the language departments created a Terminology Centre (Terminologiafdelingen) in 1974 (Picht 1985: 4, 13; Kristensen 1994: 66). In the same year, the Terminology Centre organised a conference, to which institutions and companies with an interest in terminology work were invited (Picht 1985: 4; Kristensen 1994: 69–71). The conference led to the creation of the Terminology Group (Terminologigruppen), which has since been an umbrella organisation for terminology activities in Denmark. The main goal of the Terminology Group has been to promote Danish terminology work, and since 1976, it also represents Denmark in the context of Nordterm (Kristensen 1994: 71;

Picht 1985: 4). Members are primarily university institutions and other organisations, participating on a voluntary basis.

As emphasised by Picht (1985: 8), unlike the other Nordic countries, Denmark had no national terminology centre. Over the years, this situation has resulted in difficult conditions for terminology activities in Denmark. This was still the case at the end of the 20th century.

However, in the period 1998–2001, a comprehensive project, called the DANTERM centre contract (DANTERM-centerkontrakten), was initiated by CBS and SDU (University of Southern Denmark, until 1998 the HHS/Business School of Southern Denmark). In such a centre contract, private companies and public research institutions can apply for funding for establishing a national centre of expertise, and the DANTERM Centre (DANTERMcentret) was the first within the Humanities to receive this funding from the Danish Research Council (DANTERMcentret 2001: 5). The DANTERM Centre was established as a central part of the project. Moreover, three research institutions (CBS, SDU, and the Department into Institute for Business Information Technology in Kolding) as well as six major private enterprises participated in the project (DANTERMcentret 2001: 12; DANTERMcentret 2002). The aim of the project appears in its title: "Development of Methods and Tools for the Creation and Operation of Corporate Term Bases." After the conclusion of the project, the activities carried out at CBS were continued on a commercial basis by the DANTERM Centre. Today, after the closing down of language research and education at CBS in 2017–2019, only development and maintenance of the terminology management system i-Term[1] continue, carried out by the private company DANTERM Technologies, see Section 4.13.

3.2   Finland

The Finnish Terminology Centre is a non-profit association founded in 1974. The association was founded over concern for the Finnish language in the field of technology, as reflected in its name: Tekniikan Sanastokeskus, Finnish Centre for Technical Terminology. In 2004, the association changed its name to Sanastokeskus TSK, the Finnish Terminology Centre TSK, in order to reflect the fact that the Centre would henceforth offer expertise in other areas as well. In 2021, the name was shortened to Sanastokeskus.

Over the years, Sanastokeskus has become a national terminology centre offering a wide variety of terminological services. An important activity has been the development of vocabularies — a total of 106 have been published as of 2023.

---

1. https://www.danterm.dk/products/i-term-main.html

The first vocabulary was *Telesanasto* (Vocabulary of telecommunication, 1982). Tietotekniikan termitalkoot, 'the Finnish Group for IT Terminology,' started its work in 1999. The purpose is to define concepts and to give Finnish term recommendations for English IT terms. At the end of the past millennium, the banking business was subjected to major reforms and mergers in Finland as well as in other Nordic countries, and the inconsistency of terminology caused problems for translators. Therefore, the Terminology Centre worked on the harmonisation of banking and financial terminology in Finnish and Swedish, and partly in English. Pankki- ja rahoitussanasto, 'the Bank and Finance Term Bank,' has been available since 2002.

The role of the Terminology Centre in terminology projects ranges from giving advice on methodology to managing or carrying out large terminology projects. Finland's entry into the European Union in 1995 increased the need for terminology work in Finnish. From 1995 to 2002, the Terminology Centre and its subcontractors added more than 100,000 Finnish equivalents into the Eurodicautom term bank (Nykänen 1999). The Centre has also participated in working groups aiming at the semantic interoperability of IT systems used in the Finnish public sector.

The Centre has published guidelines concerning tools and methods applied in terminology work, most notably Heidi Suonuuti's (2001) *Guide to Terminology*. Suonuuti was the head of the Centre in 1978–1993 and chaired ISO/TC 37 from 1991 to 1997. This useful guide is based on her vast experience in practical terminology work and terminology standardisation. It has been translated into several languages including Chinese.

Since 1980, the Centre has published a newsletter, *Terminfo* (Ylisalmi 2010). In 1996, the Centre launched its website, offering practical information on terminology work.

The Centre has long-term co-operation partners both within and outside Finland. Thus, it works with the Institute for the Languages of Finland, the Translation and Language Division of the Finnish Prime Minister's Office, and the National Electrotechnical Standardization Organization, among others. As an example, the Centre participates actively in the work of ISO/TC 37 Language and terminology. Thanks to financial support it has received since it was founded in 1974, mainly from the Ministry for Education and Culture, the Centre has been able to offer terminology-related services to the public free of charge.

3.3   Iceland

Systematic terminology projects began in Iceland in 1919 when the Association of Chartered Engineers in Iceland (Verkfræðingafélag Íslands) appointed a terminology committee. Their work (in the form of glossaries without definitions characterised by the prevailing linguistic purification policy) was first published in the Association's periodical, then later as special issues listing trade terms as well as machine and shipping terms (Hilmarsson-Dunn and Kristinsson 2010: 222–223).

At first, there was no formal framework in Iceland to support the collection and coining of neologisms, so the initiative often came from individuals or interested parties. Independent terminology committees and individuals therefore became the standard working practice (Jónsson 2007: 158–159, 162).

The national authorities started to support neologism work in the 1950s when the Alþingi (the parliament) allocated funds for this endeavour (Halldórsson and Jónsson 1993: 16–23). A special commission for neologisms (Nýyrðanefnd) was established in 1960, and its successor, the Icelandic Language Council (Íslensk málnefnd), in 1964. Among its duties was taking over work on neologisms. Terminology work in Iceland has typically been neologism-oriented, with less focus on the analysis of conceptual systems (Hilmarsson-Dunn and Kristinsson 2010: 225).

The Icelandic Language Council co-operated with its Nordic partners from its establishment. One of the venues for Nordic co-operation was Nordterm. Icelanders working in the field of terminology attended courses in terminology in the 1980s held under the auspices of Nordterm. As a result, and especially after the establishment of the Icelandic Language Institute (Íslensk málstöð) in 1985, professional terminological methods were introduced. New terminological committees were established, and the Icelandic Language Institute collaborated with many of them. This resulted in the further development and invigoration of terminology work in Iceland. Over 50 terminology committees of various kinds have existed in Iceland, usually composed of subject matter experts who work on a voluntary basis on the terminology within their field, and direct public support was limited. The situation improved dramatically with the establishment of the Icelandic Language Fund (Málræktarsjóður) under the auspices of the Language Council in 1991. The main objective of the fund is to support terminology projects.

The Icelandic Language Institute also published a series of LSP glossaries and launched a publicly available, web-based term bank in 1997, into which the contents of most Icelandic LSP glossaries are imported. The Icelandic Language Institute merged with the Árni Magnússon Institute for Icelandic Studies (Stofnun Árna Magnússonar í íslenskum fræðum) in 2006. Pursuant to Icelandic Act no. 40/2006 pertaining to the Árni Magnússon Institute, it is among the duties of the institute to operate a term bank, see Section 5.3, and to provide other services and advice to terminologists (Þorbergsdóttir 2020: 338).

3.4 Norway

The following description is primarily based on unpublished documents from the archives of Rådet for teknisk terminologi (RTT, the Norwegian Council for Technical Terminology) (Myking, Hjulstad, and Dysvik 2018). During the last decades of the 19th century there was a growing interest in Norwegian technical language. At the time, practically all technical literature and higher-level education in technical fields was published in other languages, in particular German. In 1897, Den Norske Ingeniør- og Arkitektforening (the Norwegian Engineers' and Architects' Association) established a language committee. The task of the committee was collecting and organising material for a dictionary of technical words and designations. Some term lists were published in technical magazines, but most of the material remained unpublished. The committee received some government funding, but after a period of inactivity it was dissolved in 1912. The Norwegian Engineers Association (Ingeniørforeningen) recommended that efforts to establish Norwegian terminology should continue and should be moved to the Norwegian Institute of Technology (Norges Tekniske Høiskole, NTH) in Trondheim. From 1918 to around 1930, a number of initiatives were taken at NTH. In parallel with these initiatives, other terminology activities started, in particular at the Norwegian Institute of Technology (Norges Standardiseringsforbund, NSF). During the 1930s, terminology activities in other countries, particularly Sweden, impacted the work carried out in Norway.

In 1938, the Norwegian Council for Technical Terminology (Rådet for teknisk terminologi, RTT) was formally established following an initiative of the Norwegian Engineers' Association and with the support of the University of Oslo and NTH. The purpose of RTT was to work for clarity, unambiguity, and consistency in Norwegian terminology. Initially, the secretariat of RTT was located at the library of NTH in Trondheim. Its first main project was the elaboration of a technical dictionary of Norwegian entries and equivalent terms in English, French, Swedish, and German. Inspired by similar activities in Sweden, RTT also established working groups for specific technical subject fields. After World War II, there was an increasing need for an English — Norwegian technical dictionary. Most of the work of RTT was focused on the development of John Ansteinson's English-Norwegian and Norwegian-English Technical Dictionaries (Ansteinson 1948, 1954). RTT continued to collect and systematise Norwegian terminology. Starting around 1950, new independent terminology committees were established for specific subject fields. The formal structure of RTT was modified to include these committees. Due to insufficient funding, RTT ceased operations in 1955.

Teknisk Ukeblad (the technical weekly magazine) took over the work in 1956. RTT was formally re-established in 1957 in Oslo. Instead of focusing on one comprehensive technical dictionary, it developed separate glossaries for each sub-ject field. The series of 70 RTT glossaries probably became better known than the institution itself. Most of the glossaries have Norwegian term entries, Norwegian definitions, and term equivalents in other languages: usually English, German, and Swedish. Until the early 1980s, RTT developed terminology in only one of the official forms of Norwegian: Bokmål. In co-operation with the Language Council of Norway, RTT gradually added terms in Nynorsk to all its new glossaries, as well as to the machine-readable versions of previously published glossaries.

RTT continued to develop technical glossaries for various subject fields as the printed publication series *RTT-ordbøker* (RTT glossaries). In addition, it partici-pated in other terminology and dictionary projects. To enhance co-operation with other organisations interested in terminology and with the general public, the Foreningen for teknisk terminologi (FTT, the Norwegian Association for Techni-cal Terminology) was established in 1991.

The RTT and FTT ceased operations in 2001 due to lack of funding. Some of the terminology work has continued at the Language Council of Norway, while other activities are carried out at Standards Norway.

Until the early 1980s, terminological research played a rather modest role in Norway. One significant exception, however, was the Norwegian Project for Mul-tilingual Administrative Nomenclature (ADNOM), a co-operation between the universities of Bergen, Oslo, and Surrey in collaboration with the Ministry of For-eign Affairs (Chaffey et al. 1984).

In the 1980s, Norwegian oil exploration increased rapidly, making use of tech-nologies, and their related terminologies, imported from English areas. In the sociolinguistic and cultural climate of that epoque, there was concern for the fate of the national language, and consequently, terminology became a politi-cal issue. In 1983 and 1985, the large project Terminol was launched to ensure that oil exploration, drilling and production could be conducted in the Norwe-gian language through the extensive development of Norwegian term equiva-lents (Andersen and Myking 2018b). Terminological activities continued within the University of Bergen until 2000. A terminology research centre was estab-lished in 1989 under the name of the Norwegian Term Bank (Norsk Termbank). This centre attempted to raise the academic ambitions in this new discipline. Staff members were involved in Nordic (Nordterm) activities, and terminology pro-jects were conducted across a variety of domains, in particular medicine, in the 1990s (Andersen and Myking 2018a).

In the years following 2000, terminology activities have continued within the framework of the Language Council of Norway. The council has been assigned the responsibility to protect the Norwegian language. The official Norwegian language policy has been redesigned following the publication of an important whitepaper in 2008 and the passing of a new Language act in 2021. In this process, the importance of terminology has been officially recognised. A state-funded terminology gateway called *Termportalen* was established at the University of Bergen followed in 2023 by a government action plan to increase the efforts to prevent and eventually reverse the processes of domain loss (see Section 5.4 Norway).

3.5 Sweden

The Swedish Centre for Technical Terminology (TNC) was founded in 1941 as a result of technological developments starting at the beginning of the century. The main initiators were technicians, and there was strong support from large companies such as Asea (today ABB) as well as from the Royal Swedish Academy of Engineering Sciences. From the beginning, TNC's activities were centred around principles and methods for analysing concepts and terms, but it also created glossaries. A fundamental aim was to provide answers to terminology-related queries, based on solid principles, and to solve terminological problems (Bucher 2016: 72–99).

In the late 1960s, the increasing number of Swedish glossaries in various fields led to the use of computerised methods for processing, disseminating, and storing terminology. Thus, term bank development became an essential part of TNC's work. Terminological vocabularies were available on CD-ROM as early as 1987, and in 2009, Sweden's national term bank *Rikstermbanken* (Språkrådet, Institutet för språk och folkminnen) was launched on the Internet and made available to the public free of charge. The term bank is now hosted at the Institute for Language and Folklore, see below.

In the 1940s, TNC received state support for its activities. This enabled it to maintain its important role as Sweden's centre for terminological activities, which was of great benefit to society as a whole. Sweden's entry into the European Union in 1995 triggered a shift in focus towards more translation-oriented terminology work. In addition, TNC gained a central role during the early 2000s when the Swedish parliament focused on the role of language in society and passed the *Language Act* in 2009. The Language Act includes a clause stating that government bodies have a special responsibility to ensure that Swedish terminology within their various specialist areas is available, used, and developed (Kulturdepartementet 2009). From the beginning, TNC also co-operated with the Language Council and other organisations, such as the Swedish Academy. Following a major national survey, in 2005 TNC presented a comprehensive description of a national terminological infrastructure (TISS — Terminology InfraStructure in Sweden) comprising training, a terminology centre, and the national term bank (Nilsson 2010: 61–78).

Until its closure in 2018, TNC continued its activities and contributed academic articles and presentations to various symposia and publications. The closing of TNC was due to unfortunate circumstances where decisions were made by people without knowledge of terminology work and its benefits for society, and where no real impact analysis of such a closing was made by the government. Today, a consequence of this is a lack of overview and centralised responsibility for co-ordination of national terminological activities.

Since the closure of TNC, government funding for terminology activities has been transferred to the agency Institutet för språk och folkminnen (Isof) (the Institute for Language and Folklore). Part of the mission of Isof is to support terminology work within Swedish institutions and government bodies, but it cannot take on work for the private sector. Thus, the hub that TNC formed no longer exists.

Today, work on terminology-related issues is carried out by various agencies and associations. For example, the non-profit association Terminologifrämjandet (the Swedish Association for Terminology) (Nilsson, 2022:62–64) disseminates knowledge about terminology to some extent, and thus it functions as a reference point for terminology workers in Sweden.

4.   Research and development of methodologies and tools

4.1   Terminology schools and theories

In their writings, Laurén, Picht, and Myking (Laurén et al. 1998; Laurén and Picht 1993, 2006) have contributed to the theory and history of terminology by bringing together and comparing the different 20th century approaches — sometimes also called *terminology schools*, e.g. the so-called Vienna, Soviet, and Prague schools, and terminological approaches in Canada, Germany, and the Nordic countries. Their research has focused on the different views taken by those various approaches regarding elements of theory, such as the meaning of *concept* and *term*, and the relation between concept and term. They also discuss the differing views on terminology planning, standardisation, and other relevant topics. They conclude that differences among these approaches reflect different priorities and research traditions rather than fundamental theoretical differences (Laurén and Picht 1993).

The Danish terminologist Toft (2002) explored the theoretical aspects of a new terminology theory gradually emerging from the original Wüsterian basis, inspired in particular by the work of Robert de Beaugrande and Gerhard Budin (Beaugrande 1996; Budin 1994). With the aim of exploring and contributing to the theoretical basis of this emerging approach, she focused on the insights of modern Systems Theory and Cognitive Science and their implications for model creation in terminology. In later years, the metaphorical basis of those models became central to her work (Toft 2002, 2013).

In the 1990s, researchers at the universities of Bergen and Vaasa explored the relationship between terminology, sociolinguistics (Rangnes 1996), and even sociological theory (Sæbøe 1996) using empirical evidence from oil terminology, and also explored the potential of concepts such as motivation (Myking 1998) and socioterminology (Myking 2001) (for discussions of socioterminology, see Chapter 11). During the late 2010s, interest was turned towards a sociology of terminology with studies on the professional role of the terminologist and her/his functions. See also Chapters 7, 8, 9, 10, 12, and 22, the latter referring to the Nordic countries.

4.2   PDS — project for computational linguistics

During the 1970s, RTT collaborated with the the Project for Computational Linguistics (Prosjekt for datamaskinell språkbehandling, PDS), at the University of Bergen, in developing computational methods for developing terminology resources and glossaries. As the use of computers became more widespread and small computers grew more powerful, RTT developed its own software for managing terminology and developing glossaries. This software included a markup language for terminology records, later developed into the Nordic Terminology Record Format (NTRF).

The activities of PDS at the University of Bergen in the 1970s and 1980s resulted in a separate terminology activity: the Norwegian Term Bank (Norsk Termbank), mentioned in Section 3.4.

4.3   NTRF — Nordic Terminology Record Format

One result of the more technically oriented co-operation taking place within Nordterm is a markup format used for recording terminological data in term banks: the Nordic Terminology Record Format, NTRF. The central terminology institutions of Finland, Norway, and Sweden had been using slightly different, but basically compatible term record formats, and that compatibility was demonstrated in 1992 with the production of the CD-ROM Termdok version 3. The new format was based on ISO standards of the late 1990s and was also heavily inspired by SGML, in which text is broken down into discrete units delimited by tags according to the type of information it contains. NTRF functions in the same way and allows grouping and nesting of information units (Hjulstad and Eckmann 1999). The NTRF format was not only important for term bank development in the Nordic countries, but also played a role as an important predecessor to work carried out within ISO on formats such as MARTIF, GENETER, and later TBX (Nilsson et al. 2016). The format and its basic principles are still used today, although many institutions have converted to, or used, other formats, often XML or SKOS, or are working with wiki-based solutions.

4.4   The DANTERM concept

In 1975, the DANTERM project was initiated at CBS, with the aim of creating the linguistic and computational basis for a Danish term bank (Picht 1988:13; Kristensen 1994:74). This early DANTERM project should not be confused with the later DANTERM centre contract, mentioned in Section 3.1. At the beginning of the 1980s, as part of the DANTERM project, the DANTERM concept (Engel and Madsen 1985) was developed at CBS. The core of the DANTERM concept is the comprehensive data structure for entries in a term base, in which one entry comprises information on equivalent concepts and terms in a number of languages. Hence one entry contains

– language independent data categories (e.g. subject field),
– concept-related data categories (e.g. definition) made available for each language, to reflect that concepts are language-specific, see e.g. Hull et al. (1999), and
– term-related data categories (e.g. usage examples) likewise available for each synonym in a given language.

The DANTERM concept has been the basis of most of the term base development subsequently carried out in Denmark.

In Hull et al. (1999:76–79), it was proposed to record the language-specific concepts in separate concept entries with equivalence relations between them. This would allow for separate terminology work in each language, as described in ISO 704:2000. The proposal was repeated in Madsen and Thomsen (2016) but has never been realised in a terminology management tool.

4.5   Data categories

During the 1980s in Denmark, a group of lexicographers and terminologists, known as the DANLEX group, co-operated in developing a taxonomy of data categories for both terminology and lexicography (DANLEX Group 1987). The taxonomy was further developed and published as a Danish Standard in 1998 (DS 2394–1 1998). Finally, in connection with the DanTermBank project 2011–2015, it was integrated with the ISO data categories (DatCatInfo), as described in Madsen et al. (2012). The results are publicly available in an online database

(DanTermBank Data Categories), including diagrams showing the taxonomic organisation of the data categories, and it was concluded that the taxonomic structure...

> ... allows users to get an overview and easily identify individual data categories. This is important in order to provide an overview, both if a user wants to suggest new data categories, and if the set of metadata should be used for choosing data categories for a new terminological data collection.   (Madsen et al. 2012: 255)

4.6   The DANTERM subject-field classification

In the 1970s, an international working group met to discuss appropriate principles for a subject-field classification suitable for term banks. Its efforts resulted in a number of recommendations, but no common classification. In the 1980s, at the Nordic level and within the Nordterm framework, the results achieved in the 1970s were taken up again, but still did not result in a subject-field classification (Picht 1994: 115–117).

Following the earlier attempts, the development of a Danish subject-field classification for term banks was initiated in the late 1980s. A first version was published (DANTERM-Klassifikationsudvalget 1994), a result of joint efforts made by CBS and SDU (Picht 1994: 117, 121). The requirements to be met by the subject-field classification included the following: flexibility and manageability, as well as the possibility of adding topics for individual needs (see Picht 1994: 119–121 and Weilgaard Christensen 2018: 21).

4.7   Competencies of general language consultants and terminologists

In 1998, the Nordic language councils and Nordterm organised a joint seminar which dealt with the different skills of general language consultants and terminologists. It was stressed that terminology work is concept-oriented, that it takes place within well-defined specialist areas with economic significance, and that it is based on a theory and method that is standardised and internationally recognised. On the other hand, general language consulting focuses on the linguistic expression, it is national, and it takes place in fields with more limited economic significance; in conclusion, it is carried out for the general good and the public interest (Lindgren, 1999b: 21–25). The seminar contributed to mutual understanding and professional respect.

4.8   Concept relations and concept systems

Concept relations and systems have been at the centre of the theory and practice of terminology since the beginning. In Finland, at the University of Vaasa, a contribution to research in these areas was made by Nuopponen in her PhD dissertation (1994) and her articles (e.g. 2005). She takes as her point of departure the dichotomy of logical vs. ontological concept relations introduced by Wüster (1971), and further reorganises and enhances the diverse types of ontological concept relations in particular, which, in addition to partitive relations, also covers those often referred to as 'associative'. In her typology, *ontological* relations are divided into those of *contiguity* (partitive, enhancement, locative, material, property, temporal, rank) and *influence* (causal, developmental, activity, origination, transmission, dependency, correlation, and representation) (Nuopponen 1994; 2005; 2022), and all these relations have subtypes. Several of these types were later included in the ISO 704 standard (2022). Since the existing graphical representations, i.e. tree and rake diagrams presented e.g. in textbooks and standards, were not sufficiently robust and flexible to cover more than the basic types of relations (generic, partitive), Nuopponen elaborated a mind-map-like satellite model that can represent any type of relations and concepts (Nuopponen 1994, 1998, 2011). Later developments of 21st century terminology management systems have proven that this approach works well (e.g., EcoLexicon, Coreon, TermWeb, and i-Term).

Around the turn of the century, Danish researchers carrying out the interdisciplinary OntoQuery project on ontology-based querying of text databases saw the need for a more extended relation typology. Building on the long terminology research tradition at CBS and the research experience in lexical semantics at Copenhagen University, the joint research team compared terminological concept relations with their equivalents in lexical semantics, and as a result built a unified hierarchical model. They found that although the focus (words vs. concepts) and purposes differ, these two traditions share many relation types (Madsen et al. 2002). As a result, they proposed a hierarchy of relations, which consists of the following relation types: hyponymy, location (dynamic/static), purpose, activity (activity-source, etc.), function, causal, role (agent/patient/instrument/result), measurement, partitive (subpart/partition/material/set-element), property-characteristic, and temporal (phase/development). The activity relations can be subdivided according to location relations (e.g., activity-static location relation). In the role relations, roles can be combined with other roles (e.g., activity-patient relation) (Madsen et al. 2002). Subsequently, the hierarchy has been modified to account for new materials and purposes.

4.9 Systematic concept analysis

Within her research and teaching activities, Nuopponen (1994, 1998, 2011) has further developed terminological analysis (see e.g. Picht and Draskau 1985b) in order to accommodate any type of conceptual clarification needs beyond those of terminology work. This systematic concept analysis method focuses on finding various types of relations between concepts and on analysing concepts step by step within the framework of the systems of concepts. At the core of the analysis is the previously mentioned satellite model which permits the use of a typology of concept relations. A description of the method can be found in Nuopponen (1994, 1998, 2011). The method has been applied in various research projects. Kristiansen (2000) has applied the satellite model method in her research to evaluate the autonomy status of a discipline, using the emerging field of organisational behaviour as a case study. Her study showed that, apart from offering the means to analyse the present content of a concept and its location in the concept system (just like traditional terminological analysis does), the method may also include concepts referring to "scientific constituents in parent disciplines" in the analysis. Additionally, it facilitates an "analysis of a discipline's historical development, and, consequently, the history of science in general." (Kristiansen 2000: 17).

4.10 Dynamic concepts

In her research, Pilke (2000) has enhanced the knowledge of field-specific concepts that are realised as actions or events, i.e., *dynamic concepts*. Earlier research and practical guidance have been applicable mainly to material objects, which is not adequate for dynamic concepts. According to her model, based on an empirical study analysing definitions in LSP glossaries in three different fields, action concepts and event concepts are distinct concepts, but have some overlapping characteristics. The typical (classes of) characteristics for the action concepts are those of intention, method, circumstances, location, and time. In addition to the two last ones, event concepts have influencing factor and manner of happening as typical characteristics. Later, Pilke also addressed non-verbal means (e.g., pictures) of expressing dynamic concepts in glossaries.

4.11 Terminological concept analysis vs. conceptual data modelling

Forming part of the computational linguistics environment, terminology researchers at CBS were also engaged in data modelling activities, both in teaching and in DANTERM Centre consultancy projects. This resulted in research into the differences between terminological concepts on the one hand, and classes in conceptual data modelling on the other. Madsen and Thomsen (2009b) showed that the characteristics of concepts do not correspond to attributes of classes, since the latter are used for describing differences between individuals, whereas characteristics describe similarities between the individuals in the class denoted by the concept.

4.12   Formalisation and automatisation of terminology work

Inspired by Copestake (1992) and her work on the Lexical Knowledge Base, in the late 1990s, three researchers at CBS started work on modelling the characteristics of terminological concepts as feature-value pairs (Thomsen 1997; Madsen 1998). The group adopted Carpenter's (1992) mathematically formal feature theory to develop 10 principles for terminological ontologies (Madsen et al. 2004), and experimented with an implementation of the principles in CAOS, a computer system for Computer Assisted Ontology Structuring. The principles include a formal mathematical treatment of inheritance of characteristics, subdivision criteria, delimiting characteristics and polyhierarchy in concept systems. The formal treatment makes it possible to automatically create ontologies.

The last version of CAOS was presented in Madsen and Thomsen (2009a). The principles and the application of feature-value pairs have proven useful in practical terminology projects carried out by the DANTERM Centre, and in teaching terminological methods at CBS.

In the DanTermBank project, between 2011 and 2015, a research group experimented with automatic methods to extract terminological knowledge in the form of terms, concept relations, and characteristics, and to automatically validate the resulting terminological ontologies, based on their earlier work on the formalisation of the treatment of characteristics (Lassen et al. 2013).

4.13   Development of terminology management tools

The DANTERM concept has informed the design of terminology management systems developed in Denmark:

1. the mainframe DANTERM database (based on the STATUS database system) (Engel and Madsen 1985).
2. DANTERM for Windows (Engel and Buhl 1999) aimed at translators.
3. DANTERM[CBS] (Hull et al. 1999) aimed at a broader audience including students.
4. Termbank Syd developed for students of the translation study programmes at SDU (Toft 2012).

5. i-Term (Madsen 2005), which has an integrated module for concept diagrams and includes fields for characteristics in accordance with the theoretical work on the mathematical formalisation of characteristics in Denmark. i-Term is currently operated and developed by DANTERM Technologies.

In Finland, Sanastokeskus has its own terminology management system developed specifically to meet its needs.

In Norway, from the 1980s, RTT developed a set of software tools and a simple database system tailored around the NTRF format (and its predecessor). The tools were used during terminology work as well as for the production of glossaries.

4.14 Domain loss and joint term groups

The position of the official languages in the Nordic countries and the threat of domain loss, i.e., the threat primarily posed by English to the domestic languages in many special fields, has been recognised and discussed quite intensely in the Nordic countries (see Laurén et al. 2002). A special focus area in the Nordic countries has been terminology planning both in practice and research. In their research collaboration, Christer Laurén, Johan Myking, Heribert Picht, and Sigurður Jónsson have focused on domain dynamics and domain loss from the point of view of terminology (Jónsson et al. 2013).

During the 1990s, joint term groups were started in Finland and Sweden within specialist areas in which the focus was on monitoring the influx of English terms and proposing equivalents in Swedish and Finnish as quickly as possible. In Sweden, the first group was the Joint Group for Swedish Computer Terminology (initiated in 1996) (Lindgren 1999a: 38–47). Within the framework of the EU's MLIS (Multilingual Information Society) programme, similar groups were formed in Finland and Norway.

In purely organisational terms, the term groups have been broad networks. Quite a few cooperative networks were formed among the Nordic countries. The groups consist of subject matter experts and terminologists, and sometimes also of journalists, language consultants, and translators. They have worked continuously as new concepts needed to be named in Swedish, Finnish, or Norwegian. Their work has been important in preventing domain loss within new, rapidly growing areas of expertise.

For some time, the issue of domain loss dominated the debate, but as a result of criticism being levelled against the usefulness of the concept as such, it grew less prominent (Myking, in press). In the early 2020s, domain loss re-emerged as an issue of concern and is once again the focus of debate and conferences (Thelen,

Wermuth, and Van Vaerenbergh, eds., in press). For some of the Nordic languages, such as Greenlandic and Sami, significant efforts have resulted in some domain gain and regain, partly as a result of the development of language technology tools (term banks, spell checkers, automatic translation tools, etc.).

An example of a joint Nordterm terminology vocabulary project was the development of the Terminology of Terminology in Nordic Languages 2001–2005, financed by the Nordplus Programme. The aim of the project was to update the vocabulary of terminology in five Nordic languages, which was originally compiled in 1989, and to harmonise this vocabulary with ISO 1087–1:2000 and ISO 704:2000. The vocabulary was published as an i-Term database (Nordterm term base) as described by Madsen et al. (2006), and comprises 92 terminological entries in Danish, English, French, Faroese, Finnish, Greenlandic, Icelandic, Northern Sami, Norwegian (Bokmål and Nynorsk), and Swedish, with concept diagrams and definitions in most of the languages.

5.   Nordic term banks

5.1   Denmark

Since the early 1980s, many attempts have been made to create a Danish national term bank, starting with the project DANish TERMbank, which resulted in the DANTERM Concept (see Section 4.4), and terminology collected through various projects, including master's theses at SDU and CBS, and the Danterm Centre Contract (DANTERMcentret 2001).

The Danish National Health Authority carried out the Sundterm Project, with the aim of developing a comprehensive Danish medical terminology (Toft 2009). Socialstyrelsen (the Danish National Board of Social Services) and Sundhedsdatastyrelsen (the Danish Health Data Authority) have developed term bases in collaboration with the Danterm Centre, both of which provide public access to their terms and concept systems.

Unfortunately, public funding has focused on shorter projects, allowing for the development of tools, but it has never been possible to achieve continuous funding for the production of terminological data or for running the organisation needed to maintain a national term bank in Denmark.

5.2   Finland: TEPA term bank

Three term banks are provided by the Terminology Centre: the TEPA Term Bank and the term banks on Finnish IT terminology and on finance terminology (Nykänen 1999).

In the 1970s, inspired by the term banks planned in the other Nordic countries, particularly the Swedish term bank TERMDOK, which had been available to the public since 1979, the Centre became interested in creating a Finnish term bank. The Centre began storing terminological data on a computer in the early 1980s. An agreement concerning the maintenance of the term bank in a TRIP database was signed in 1984 with the Helsinki University of Technology. The University provided computer resources for the storage, maintenance, and daily operation of the term bank. The Centre was responsible for compiling the data in a format suitable for computer storage (Suonuuti 1985: 13).

The Finnish term bank was named TEPA (an abbreviation of Tekniikan termipankki, 'term bank of technology,' as the Centre worked mainly with technical terminology at the time). TEPA was in internal use by the Centre's staff starting in 1985, and was opened to the public in 1987, first by paid subscription but since 1997 free of charge on the web. Since 2007, TEPA has been maintained using the MOT® dictionary software developed by Kielikone Ltd., a Finnish language service company. MOT® uses the Nordic Terminological Data Format (NTRF) to store data, see Section 4.3. With MOT®, it is also possible to publish concept diagrams and illustrations included in the glossaries. TEPA's user interface is available in Finnish, Swedish, and English (Ylisalmi 2007).

TEPA contains special language terms and their definitions displayed in multilingual terminological entries. The Centre's own publications form the core of TEPA, but the term bank also contains other special subject vocabularies, dictionaries, and terminological databases compiled by other specialists (Ylisalmi 2007). The most common languages in TEPA are Finnish, Swedish, English, German, French, and Danish. There are also some terms in Estonian, Norwegian, Russian, and Spanish, and occasional entries in Latin, Italian, Dutch, and Portuguese. At the end of 2023, TEPA held about 343,000 term records.

5.3   Iceland: The Icelandic term bank

After years of preparation, the Icelandic term bank, previously known as Orðabanki Íslenskrar málstöðvar (lit. the Word Bank of the Icelandic Language Institute) was opened online in 1997. Íslensk málstöð (the Icelandic Language Institute) was responsible for its operation until September 2006, when it merged with the Árni

Magnússon Institute for Icelandic Studies. Along with improvements made to the user interface in 2018, the term bank was renamed, Íðorðabankinn (the term bank).

Íðorðabankinn is by far the largest resource for terminology collections in Iceland. It provides access to Icelandic equivalents of foreign terms, and definitions in Icelandic and other languages. One of the key aims is to standardise terms used within specialised fields since confusion arises when many different terms are used for the same concept.

This term bank has grown significantly since it was established, from 13 terminology collections and 30,000 term records to now over 70 collections in different specialised fields totalling approximately 188,000 term records.

Some of the terminology is published in glossaries produced by the Árni Magnússon Institute, but most is compiled by experts from different fields. An agreement has been made with the contributing editors granting them free access to the editing interface of the term bank, and in return, the institute publishes the terminology. Nevertheless, editors still retain all rights to their data and can publish them elsewhere if and when they choose to.

The terminology publications vary in size from a few hundred terms to thousands. Bilingual terminology (Icelandic/English) comprise over half of the data in the term bank; of the remaining half, terminology from one glossary has only Icelandic terms and the rest are multilingual (ranging from three to eleven languages). Definitions are found in approximately half the glossaries, some comprise definitions in languages other than Icelandic, which indicates their origin, and some provide grammatical information, e.g. gender and word class (Þorbergsdóttir 2017b).

5.4   Norway

Based on the comprehensive Terminol Project on oil terminology described in Section 3.4, the Norwegian Term Bank centre at the University of Bergen developed an extensive terminology database, called NOT, on a semi-commercial basis. This database as well as the RTT vocabularies and other sources now form the building blocks of the Norwegian Terminology Portal, the Norwegian Terminology Portal (Termportalen), officially launched in 2021. The portal is hosted at the University of Bergen. The aim of the gateway is to co-operate actively with national terminology groups representing various institutions and professional organisations. The Norwegian organisation for standardisation, Standards Norway, runs a national term base, Termlex, for various subject fields.

Also, the Language Council of Norway (Språkrådet) offers a number of glossaries, many of them including the two official languages, Bokmål and Nynorsk.

5.5   Sweden: Rikstermbanken (Swedish national term bank)

At TNC, an interest in storing terminology using computers arose as mentioned mentioned in Section 4.14 in the late 1960s, and efforts to create an electronic system for managing terminology resulted in TERMDOK, which was published in different formats, including as the first commercial CD-ROM in Sweden. The effort put into a Nordic term bank (in the EU-funded project Nordterm-Net) and, in 2002, the TISS project in Sweden, combined to lay the foundation for work on a national term bank. Overall, TISS contributed substantially to TNC's ability to create an overview of terminological activities in Sweden; in particular, a survey of existing terminological resources showed that substantial resources existed at a national level which might be included in a term bank. In 2005, TNC's ideas, presented in the TISS programme, were taken into account by two Swedish parliamentary acts which stressed the need for and possible uses of a national term bank. TNC's success in achieving continued financial support from the state was realised thanks to intense lobbying about the importance of terminology work as well as of the value of a shared national repository for terminologies. Some of the arguments provided (Nilsson 2009) were that a national term bank would

–   provide simpler and quicker access to terminology from a large number of domains
–   facilitate faster dissemination of new terms
–   bring about enhanced terminological quality as the contents will be continuously checked, edited, and updated
–   make terminology work more efficient as a result of the easier re-use of existing terms and definitions.

After years of preparation, Rikstermbanken was inaugurated on March 19, 2009. The term bank is multilingual, takes a descriptive (rather than prescriptive) approach, and aims to gather as much Swedish terminology as possible. However, some priorities were put forward as described in Nilsson (2009): the accepted terminological material should be

–   extensive, considering the number of domains covered and the number of terms and concepts
–   representative, i.e. the most important domains should be covered
–   varied, i.e. the terminological material should preferably be of different kinds and originate from different organisations
–   reliable
–   of high terminological quality.

After many years in existence, Rikstermbanken has no real competitor at a national level, and it is still the largest collection of terminology in Sweden. It is used more and more as a reference source, and often it is referred to as an entity of its own, rather than as the collection of separate sources, which is what it actually is. At the closure of TNC in 2018, the responsibility for Rikstermbanken was transferred to the terminologists at Isof (the Institute for Language and Folklore), who continue to develop it (Nilsson 2009; Nilsson and Dobrina 2011; Dobrina et al. 2012).

6.   Terminology training and teaching

6.1   Overview

Although a long tradition of terminology work exists in the Nordic countries, the terminology profession is still relatively unknown. For a long time, university courses in terminology were offered only to a limited extent, initially in Finland and Denmark. It was not until the late 1980s and the 1990s that courses began to be taught also in Sweden, Norway, and Iceland, to varying degrees.

Not surprisingly, the fact that comprehensive terminology training at the university level did not exist meant that no strong professional identity existed among terminologists. Many of the terminologists employed in terminology centres have been hired on the basis of their general competencies in language, linguistics, technology, and the various domains. Good analytical skills and a systematic approach have been other desirable skills. Thus, the terminological craft itself has been taught according to the principle of learning by doing.

In most Nordic countries, terminology courses have been offered by the terminology centres (TNC, the Finnish Terminology Centre, the DANTERM Centre, the Language Council of Norway), some custom-made for project partners, others more general in nature. In Denmark, Greenland, and Finland, terminology courses have been offered as part of university programmes in translation or communication since the mid-1970s. Consequently, several master's theses and doctoral dissertations on terminology have been written in Denmark, Finland, and also Norway.

Picht (1985: 5–6, 1988: 17) describes the first decades of terminology training in Denmark. Initially, short introductory courses on fundamental principles of terminology were offered to staff members and language students at the business schools of Copenhagen (CBS) and Aarhus (ASB). From the 1980s onwards, terminology training became increasingly research-based. In the 1990s, LSP and terminology theory became an important part of the master's programmes in computational linguistics at CBS and SDU, and at CBS, term base development and computational terminology were included as well (Thomsen 2000). From 1990, SDU offered an online terminology course (Grue et al. 1994). Initially, most of the training was based on internal teaching material, but in 1999, the first Danish textbook on terminology was published by Bodil Nistrup Madsen (Madsen 1999).

In Finland, the University of Vaasa was the first to offer university level courses in terminology. Nuopponen (1996, 1997) describes terminology teaching in Vaasa, which started with a single introductory course as part of language studies in the late 1970s. Terminology studies were gradually developed into extended electives for translation and language students and were also offered to communication students from the beginning of the 1990s. Already during the 1990s, terminology courses were used as pilot courses for developing online teaching methodologies. Later, these experiences were utilised as the basis for developing an online terminology specialisation within the framework of the master's programme in technical communication. In addition to internal (online) teaching material, the Finnish textbooks by TSK (Tekniikan Sanastokeskus 1989), Haarala (1981) as well as Nuopponen and Pilke (2010) have been used as teaching material.

Since 2008, a separate terminology course has been an element of translation studies at the University of Iceland.

In Norway, plans were made to develop academic terminology courses. In a collaboration between the University of Bergen and the LSP Centre at the Norwegian School of Economics (Norges Handelshøyskole, NHH), a number of master theses and doctoral dissertations were completed from 1991, see Section 8. Nevertheless, attempts at establishing permanent university-level courses failed to attract students. Until now, no significant permanent training activities exist at Norwegian academic institutions, but in 2010, an international PhD course in terminology and resource harmonisation was offered at Norges Handelshøyskole (NHH).

As already mentioned, in Sweden terminology training at university level has been fairly limited in scope, including a few lectures and courses within university programmes for language consultants, text designers, translators, and interpreters. However, the TNC was a kind of pioneer within terminology training and terminology courses, and these training activities were further developed from the 1990s and onwards, with the offering of a series of courses open to anyone. Seminars on particular aspects of terminology work (such as concept analysis, definition writing and glossary making) were also organised to raise terminological awareness. In addition to the Swedish version of the *Guide to Terminology* (Suonuuti 2004), a plethora of teaching materials and real-life based exercises were developed for these courses and seminars. The TNC also offered a course at the Institute for Translation and Interpretation Studies at Stockholm University.

In a number of separate seminars, special focus was given to the terminological responsibility of lawyers and journalists.

Two courses deserve more detailed description at this point: TERMDIST as a Nordic collaborative initiative, and the Danish Master of Language Administration, which can be considered a special effort to allow language workers to move to management level.

6.2   TERMDIST — a joint Nordic training initiative

In 2005, a working group was formed with the aim of developing a web-based master's programme in terminology for students in the Nordic countries. The working group consisted of representatives from universities in Denmark, Finland, Norway, and Sweden. In addition, TNC and the Árni Magnússon Institute for Icelandic Studies participated. The initiators of the group believed that globalisation and the increased influence of English in trade, industry, and the scientific community risked impoverishing the Nordic languages in terms of special language communication. Teaching terminology and terminology management to a broad target group was therefore considered highly justified. A challenge was the fact that no Nordic country thought it possible to gather enough students to carry out a master's degree on its own. Developing and offering the course jointly was therefore considered a win-win situation. The target group of the programme included translators, interpreters, information specialists, technical writers, and experts in various domains. After a series of challenging preparations, including developing web-based lectures and selecting course literature, a pilot course was given in the autumn of 2009. The languages of instruction were Danish, Norwegian, and Swedish. The results were encouraging, and the course has since been given four more times to nearly 100 students (Kristiansen and Þorbergsdóttir 2016). Unfortunately, after 2011, for financial, organisational, and practical reasons, the course was discontinued (Nilsson 2011). The full master's programme was never realised, but the course itself was proof of successful Nordic cooperation across linguistic and educational borders. Indeed, responsibility for the various modules was divided among the participating countries, which also meant that students could submit assignments in any of the Scandinavian languages. Furthermore, the course resulted in the creation of multilingual Nordic pedagogical material in terminology, and it demonstrated how a joint course may be necessary in regions in which individual universities are unable to attract enough students. Finally, course evaluations showed how this type of course could be of interest to Nordic companies and their employees (Kristiansen and Þorbergsdóttir 2016).

6.3   Master of language administration (MLA)

From 1999 to 2008, a master's programme in language administration was offered jointly by CBS and SDU. The programme comprised four terms of part-time studies aimed at students with at least three years of relevant job experience, following a BA in foreign languages or similar. The overall focus of the programme was to give students competencies enabling them to move to management level within a language field. One term was dedicated to terminology and term bases, with a focus on methodology and data structure, and also included business aspects such as cost-benefit analysis (Grinsted and Thomsen 2008) and business process maturity (Thomsen 2006), which were applied to terminology work in this context. In 2002, the MLA programme was awarded the international Electronic Document Systems Foundation (EDSf) prize for Excellence in Education for Innovation in Continuing Education.

7.   Nordic contributions to the international terminology community

7.1   International terminology organisations

Following the POINTER project (POINTER 1995), it was recommended that a European association for terminology should be created, and in 1996, the European Association for Terminology, EAFT, was founded in Kolding, Denmark. Nordic terminologists played an important role in establishing and operating the organisation. Through the years, the chair position of the association has been held by Nordic representatives (Annelise Grinsted, Jan Hoel, Henrik Nilsson), and many more have participated in its activities and held positions on the Board, promoting the Nordic view and terminology in general to other European countries as well as exchanging experiences (Lervad and Nilsson 2008). Most of the Nordic terminology organisations and associations also continue to be members and to support its activities. The EAFT aims to:

- further plurilingualism in Europe through terminology
- provide a platform at the European level for the promotion and co-ordination of terminological activities and for the heightened awareness, improved recognition and continued professionalisation of the terminology sector
- create active liaisons with other organisations, associations and institutions in the terminology sector at all levels.

In addition to the biannual Terminology Summit, one of the association's most important achievements is the drafting and publishing of the Brussels Declaration for international co-operation on terminology (2002), to which Nordic terminologists contributed once more. In this document, a series of principles and possible actions to be taken in order to promote special language communication based on multilingualism are presented. The intention was to create a document which would show the importance of terminology in society, and which could be useful in different contexts. The declaration was signed by representatives of a large number of terminology organisations and has been used in official contexts, e.g., during efforts to stop the cancellation of terminology training in Hungary. Nordterm has a working agreement with EAFT.

Finally, over the years, Nordic terminologists have been active on the board of the two organisations the International Institute of Terminology Research (IITF) and Gesellschaft für Terminologie und Wissenstransfer (GTW), also known as the International Association for Terminology and Knowledge Transfer. IITF was dismantled in 2016 and is now integrated into the EAFT, which continues to publish the scientific journal Terminology Science and Research (TSR). Until its dissolution in 2022, an important activity of GTW was the organisation of the triannual TKE conferences on Terminology and Knowledge Engineering, several of which were organised by CBS researchers.

7.2   The Nordic terminology community and ISO/TC 37

Nordic participation in ISO/TC 37 Language and terminology, a technical committee of ISO (International Organization for Standardization), see also Chapter 17, undoubtedly deserves to be considered one of the most significant contributions made by the Nordic terminology institutions to international terminology activities. ISO/TC 37 was established in 1952, and the Nordic countries became involved in the committee at an early stage. Since terminology institutions in the Nordic countries (TNC in Sweden, RTT in Norway, TSK in Finland) were regarded as a primary resource of terminological competence in these countries, it was no wonder that, together with researchers from Vaasa and CBS, terminologists who belonged to their staff became involved in TC 37's work. Many Nordic representatives held (and still hold) some of the key positions in TC 37. Nordic representatives have served as TC 37 chairs, or as secretaries or chairs of subcommittees as well as conveners and project leaders of TC 37's working groups. And finally, many Nordic terminology experts have contributed to the development of international terminology standards.

One of the most telling examples of the Nordic contribution to international terminology standardisation might be the story of the development of two flagship standards: ISO 1087–1:2000 and ISO 704:2000 and ISO 704:2009. The work on these standards started in the early years of TC 37's existence, but it took many years before they were first published (ISO 704 in 1967 and ISO 1087–1 in 1990). Participants of the working groups came from differing professions and backgrounds —

technical writers, librarians, linguists, IT specialists, academics — which caused difficulties in reaching a consensus on a wide range of issues. Thanks to their practical experience in terminology work, their theoretical background, and common standpoint on many of these issues established during the years of a close Nordic collaboration, the Nordic participants often succeeded in presenting a common front which fostered acceptance of their well-founded solutions to terminology problems and challenges.

The engagement in TC 37 has also resulted in intensive Nordic collaboration in the field of terminology. One example is the joint Nordic project Terminology of Terminology mentioned in Section 4.14. Another is the publication of the *Guide to Terminology* by Heidi Suonuuti (2001) who chaired TC 37 from 1991 to 1997.

The engagement of Nordic terminology experts and researchers in international standardisation has been of mutual benefit: Nordic terminologists, with their vast experience and long-term tradition of Nordic co-operation, have helped increase the level of terminological awareness in the working groups of TC 37, and the gain for Nordic terminologists and researchers was new insights into terminology and standardisation issues acquired through collaboration with other international experts.

8.   Concluding remarks

In Norway, systematic terminology work started as early as the late 1890s, and in Iceland in 1919. As a result of the demand for technical terminology, terminology institutions were founded around 1940 in Norway, Sweden, and Denmark (the latter only for a short period) and in the mid-1970s in Finland. In Denmark and Finland in particular, research and formalised university education have been integrated, whereas most of the terminology activities at the University of Bergen are related to research. Most Icelandic terminology activities have been conducted by a large number of committees consisting of subject matter experts working on a voluntary basis. In 1991, the situation improved when the Icelandic Language Fund was established, the purpose of which is to support terminology projects. In Sweden, TNC has been the most important player in terminology activities. In general, however, Nordic researchers and practitioners have contributed to academic articles and presentations at international conferences and in publications on a wide range of topics, many at a meta-level (methodology of terminology, the terminologist profession, and terminology methods compared to those of concept modelling, informatics, enterprise architecture, and so forth.).

The Nordic terminology landscape has not resulted in a specific Nordic terminology school (Picht 2007: 35). Nordic terminology work is, however, characterised by a concept-oriented approach to terminology with solid theoretical foundations. At the same time, with the exception of Denmark, the Nordic countries, particularly Iceland and Norway, have invested much effort into language planning. In Iceland, early projects focused on language purism and policy, including a preference for native neologisms over borrowings. In Denmark, mathematical formalisation and automatisation of terminology work was in focus.

Altogether, in the Nordic countries, a clear consensus has existed on viewing terminology theory, practice, and training as a whole (Picht 2007: 36). This fact has had a supportive influence on terminology development in all the Nordic countries. Through Nordterm, the Nordic countries have had an important forum for discussion and for determining how the countries might complement each other.

The Nordic terminology landscape has changed during recent years. Denmark, Norway, and Sweden no longer have terminology centres. In Norway and Sweden, the language councils are now responsible for terminological activities. In Iceland, development went in the opposite direction: the first terminology activities started outside university settings, whereas today, activities are often conducted jointly between the Árni Magnússon Institute for Icelandic Studies and subject matter experts. In Denmark, this type of close co-operation with the national language council to create a term bank or terminology centre has not been possible; since the the Danish Language Council is only responsible for orthography, not semantic issues. Over the years, the terminology centres have played an extremely important role in collecting empirical data. In Sweden, for example, close co-operation with large private companies, such as Scania and Atlas Copco, has taken place. Also, the centres have created multiple LSP glossaries. Finally, the Finnish and Swedish term banks, TEPA and Rikstermbanken, must be highlighted as important achievements of the centres. Rather than having a separate terminology centre as in Finland, all Nordic countries, with the exception of Denmark, have now integrated their terminology activities into the government bodies responsible for overall national linguistic activities (general language, minority languages, sign language, language technology, etc.). This has placed terminology in a new context in which target groups other than subject matter experts have become stakeholders in terminology work, leading to a further exploration of the links between terminology and general language, of de-terminologisation and term formation, and also of language technology developments that are useful for terminology work. In this new reality, co-operation within Nordterm becomes even more important and significant.

Generally, most terminology research has taken place at universities in Denmark, Finland, and Norway. In Denmark, terminology research has benefitted from being part of the computational linguistics research environment, hence the focus on terminology management tools, data modelling, and formal methods for terminology work. In Finland, terminology research has focused on new methods related to concept analysis and typologies of concept relations. In Norway, terminology research at the University of Bergen and Norges Handelshøyskole (NHH) has been based on empirical data derived from terminology projects in various fields. Teaching and training activities have taken place in all countries. In Denmark and Finland, several universities have offered terminology courses, mainly as parts of study programmes in translation and communication. University courses in terminology have been offered to a lesser extent in Iceland and Norway. In addition, terminology teaching and training have been part of the activities of the centres, especially in Denmark, Finland, and Sweden. Extensive experience gained from terminology teaching and training resulted in TERMDIST, a joint Nordic web-based master's programme in terminology. Unfortunately, external factors caused the discontinuation of this otherwise successful study programme.

The number of language professionals holding the title of 'terminologist' has remained small. The healthcare sector stands out in this regard. It has brought terminology to the forefront via its activities aimed at classification and code sets (such as SnoMED CT and ICD). Other professional vocations have recently started to include terminological activities, such as concept modelling, as an important part of their work: enterprise architects, information architects, data architects, business analysts, informaticians, knowledge engineers, and others. Although their perception of terminology is often different from that of organisations with extensive experience in the field such as Nordterm, their recognition and interest has nonetheless helped to make the need for terminology work more visible in the Nordic countries.

Valuable personal contacts have developed over the years, not least through the Nordterm symposia with associated social events, graduate courses, seminars, and working groups. Many participants have been involved in Nordterm activities for several decades. Such important personal relationships are definitely a success factor for the efforts still being made. Also, undoubtedly, the formalisation of Nordterm co-operation in 1987 through statutes has strengthened co-operation and joint responsibility, while keeping Nordterm an open forum for anyone interested in terminology. Thus, one thing that has remained is the Nordic will to co-operate and achieve common goals, directly and indirectly, through mutual inspiration and sharing of new knowledge as well as through further development of terminology theory and tools. This demonstrates that the Nordterm network is also able to adapt to new conditions.

References

Andersen, Øivin, and Johan Myking. 2018a. "Norwegian LSPs." In *Language for Special Purposes. An International Handbook*, ed. by John Humbley, Gerhard Budin, and Christer Laurén. 234–254. Berlin/Boston: De Gruyter Mouton.

Andersen, Øivin, and Johan Myking. 2018b. "The Case of the Oil Industries." In *Language for Special Purposes. An International Handbook*, ed. by John Humbley, Gerhard Budin, and Christer Laurén. 535–548. Berlin/Boston: De Gruyter Mouton.

Ansteinson, John. 1948–1994, *Engelsk — norsk teknisk ordbok* (multiple editions). Trondheim: F. Bruns bokhandels forlag.

Ansteinson, John. 1954–1994, *Norsk — engelsk teknisk ordbok* (multiple editions). Trondheim: F. Bruns bokhandels forlag.

Bucher, Anna-Lena. 1994. "Nordterminitiativtagare." In *Festskrift til Gert Engel i anledning af hans 70 års fødselsdag*, ed. by Annelise Grinsted, and Bodil Nistrup Madsen, 115–126. Copenhagen: Samfundslitteratur.

Bucher, Anna-Lena. 2016. "National terminology centers — In the interest of the public good." In *Tänkta termer. Terminologihänsyn i nordiskt perspektiv*, ed. by Nina Pilke, and Niina Nissilä. 72–99. VAKKI Publications 5. Vaasa: Vasa universitet.

Budin, Gerhard. 1994. "Do we Need an Object Theory?" International IITF-Workshop Theoretical Issues of Terminology Science. Riga, 19–21 August 1992. *IITF-Series* 4: 203–208. Vienna: TermNet.

Carpenter, Bob. 1992. *The Logic of Typed Feature Structures*. Cambridge, MA: Cambridge University Press.

Chaffey, P. et al. (eds). 1984. *ADNOM. Norwegian — English Glossary. Names and terms from public and private activity*. Oslo: Universitetsforlaget.

CLARA. 2010. "Terminology and Resource Harmonisation." *Report on the CLARA researcher training course on integration of terminological language resources across domains and languages*. Bergen, Norway.

Copestake, Ann. 1992. *The Representation of Lexical Semantic Information*. University of Sussex at Brighton, Cognitive Science Research Papers, CSRP 280.

DANLEX Group (Ebba Hjorth, Jane R. Jacobsen, Bodil Nistrup Madsen, Ole Norling-Christensen, and Hanne Ruus). 1987. *Descriptive Tools for Electronic Processing of Dictionary Data. Studies in Computational Lexicography*. Lexicographica Series Maior 20. Tübingen: Max Niemeier Verlag.

DANTERMcentret. 2001. *Viden om viden, Del 1 — Udvikling, Slutrapport for projektet Udvikling af metoder og værktøjer til oprettelse og drift af virksomhedsinterne terminologibaser*. Copenhagen: DANTERMcentret.

DANTERMcentret. 2002. *Viden om viden, Del 2 — Forskning, Slutrapport for projektet Udvikling af metoder og værktøjer til oprettelse og drift af virksomhedsinterne terminologibaser*. Copenhagen: DANTERMcentret.

DANTERM-Klassifikationsudvalget (Bodil Nistrup Madsen, Heribert Picht, and Gert Engel). 1994. *Danterm-Klassifikation: Studieudgave for Syddansk Universitet og Handelshøjskolen i København*. Kolding: Institut for Erhvervsforskning.

Dobrina, Claudia, Henrik Nilsson, and Peter Svanberg. 2012. "Stadieväxling: utmaningar för en nationell terminologi(in)samling." In *Samarbetet ger resultat: från begreppskaos till överenskomna termer: Nordterm 2011, Vasa 7–10 juni 2011*. Vaasa: Vasa universitet.

de Beaugrande, Robert. 1996. "LSP and Terminology in a New Science of Text and Discourse." In *TKE'96; Terminology and Knowledge Engineering. Proceedings of the 3rd International Congress on Terminology and Knowledge Engineering, 26–28 august 1996, Vienna*, ed. by Christian Galinski, and Klaus-Dirk Schmitz, 12–26. Frankfurt: Indeks Verlag.

DS 2394–1. 1998. *Leksikalske datasamlinger. Indholds- og strukturbeskrivelse. Del 1: Taksonomi til klassifikation af oplysningstyper*. Copenhagen: Dansk Standard.

Engel, Gert, and Ole Buhl. 1999. "DANTERM for Windows." In *Terminology in Advanced Microcomputer Applications, Proceedings of the Fourth TermNet Symposium*, 67–84. Vienna: TermNet.

Engel, Gert, and Bodil Nistrup Madsen. 1985. "DANTERM." *TermNet News — Journal of the International Network for Terminology, 12*. Special Issue on the Nordic Countries, ed. by Heribert Picht, and Jennifer Draskau, 8–10. Vienna: Infoterm.

Grinsted, Annelise, and Hanne Erdman Thomsen. 2008. "Cost-Benefit Analysis of the Introduction and Implementation of a Terminology Management System." In *Managing Ontologies and Lexical Resources: 8th International Conference on Terminology and Knowledge Engineering. TKE 2008*, ed. by Bodil Nistrup Madsen, and Hanne Erdman Thomsen, 317–332. Copenhagen: Litera.

Grue, Frank, Ellen Christoffersen, Jette Olsen, Ole Buhl, and Lars Johnsen. 1994. "Vejen til en højre læreanstalt." In *Vækstårene*. Handelshøjskole Syd — Jubilæumsskrift Bind 1, ed. by Niels H. Assing. 73–95. Copenhagen: Samfundslitteratur.

Haarala, Risto. 1981. *Sanastotyön opas*. Kotimaisten kielten tutkimuskeskuksen julkaisuja 16. Helsinki: Kotimaisten kielten tutkimuskeskus.

Halldórsson, Halldór, and Baldur Jónsson. 1993. *Íslensk málnefnd 1964–1989. Afmælisrit*. Reykjavík: Íslensk málnefnd.

Hilmarsson-Dunn, Amanda, and Ari Páll Kristinsson. 2010. "The Language Situation in Iceland." *Current Issues in Language Planning*, 11:3, 207–276.

Hjulstad, Håvard, and Carol Eckmann. 1999. *Nordic Terminological Record Format (NTRF)*. Oslo: Rådet for teknisk terminologi.

Hull, Anthony, Bodil Nistrup Madsen, and Hanne Erdman Thomsen. 1999. "DANTERM[CBS] for everyone." In *Terminology in Advanced Microcomputer Applications, Proceedings of the Fourth TermNet Symposium*, 67–84. Vienna: TermNet.

ISO 1087–1: 2000. *Terminology work — Vocabulary — Part 1: Theory and applications*. Geneva: International Organization for Standardization.

ISO 704. 2000, 2009, 2022. *Terminology work — Principles and methods*. Geneva: International Organization for Standardization.

Jolkkonen, Lena. 2008. "Om Nordterms betydelse för terminologens identitet och kompetensutveckling" In *Med tydlig intension. En festskrift till Anna-Lena Bucher på 60-årsdagen*, ed. by Henrik Nilsson, 86–91. Solna: Terminologicentrum TNC.

Jónsson, Sigurður. 2007. *Det vilda tänkandet och det kultiverade. Isländsk fackspråklig språkvård med tyngdpunkt på första hälften av 1900-talet*. Acta Wasaensia. Vaasa: Vasa universitet.

Jónsson, Sigurður, Christer Laurén, Johan Myking, and Heribert Picht. 2013. *Parallellspråk og domene*. Oslo: Novus forlag.

Kristensen, Bente. 1994. "Terminologiarbejdets udvikling og organisation på Handelshøjskolen i København." In *Festskrift til Gert Engel i anledning af hans 70 års fødselsdag*, ed. by Annelise Grinsted, and Bodil Nistrup Madsen, 66–76. Copenhagen: Samfundslitteratur.

Kristensen, Johs. 1941. "Nordisk sprogligt samarbejde. Akademiet for de tekniske videnskaber opretter en terminologicentral." *Ingeniøren* 72: 201–202.

Kristiansen, Marita. 2000. "Emerging Disciplines in the Behavioural Sciences. Assessment of Disciplinary Autonomy by Terminological Conceptual Analysis." *Unesco Alsed-LSP Newsletter*, 23(2), 6–23.

Kristiansen, Marita, and Ágústa Þorbergsdóttir. 2016. "Termdist — a joint Nordic Terminology Training Initiative." In *Tänkta termer. Terminologihänsyn i nordiskt perspektiv*, ed. by Nina Pilke, and Niina Nissilä. VAKKI Publications 5. Vasa, 269–290. Vaasa: Vasa universitet.

Kulturdepartementet. 2009. *Svensk författningssamling (SFS)2009:600. Språklag*. Sverige: Sveriges Riksdag.

Lassen, Tine, Bodil Nistrup Madsen, and Hanne Erdman Thomsen. 2013. "Automatisk opbygning og validering af terminologiske ontologier." In *Från förarbete till förvaltning — terminologiarbete steg för steg — NORDTERM 18*, ed. by Henrik Nilsson, 140–163. NORDTERM.

Laurén, Christer, and Heribert Picht. 1993. "Vergleich der terminologischen Schulen." In *Ausgewählte Texte zur Terminologie*, ed. by Christer Laurén, and Heribert Picht, 493–539. Vienna: TermNet.

Laurén, Christer, Johan Myking, and Heribert Picht. 1998. *Terminologie unter der Lupe. Vom Grenzgebiet zum Wissenschaftszweig*. Vienna: TermNet.

Laurén, Christer, Johan Myking, and Heribert Picht. 2002. "Language and Domains: a Proposal for a Domain Dynamics Taxonomy." In *LSP & Professional Communication*, Vol. 2, No. 2, October 2002.

Laurén, Christer, and Heribert Picht. 2006. "Approaches to Terminological Theories. A Comparative Study of the State-of-the-Art." In *Modern Approaches to Terminological Theories and Applications*, ed. by Heribert Picht, 163–184. Bern: Peter Lang.

Lervad, Susanne, and Henrik Nilsson. 2008. "Galão och galej — om EAFT och terminologiskt samarbete i Europa." In *Kunnskap og fagkommunikasjon, Nordterm 15, Bergen 13.–16. juni 2007*, ed. by Jan Hoel, 152–156. Oslo: Språkrådet

Lindgren, Birgitta. 1999a. "Internationalisering och domänförlust " In *NORDTERM 10*, ed. by DANTERMcentret, 27–33. Copenhagen: DANTERMcentret.

Lindgren, Birgitta (ed). 1999b. *Terminologi och språkvård — rapport från en konferens den 24–26 april 1998 i Gentofte*. Oslo: Nordiska språkrådet.

Madsen, Bodil Nistrup. 1998. "Typed Feature Structures for Terminology Work — Part I." In *LSP — Identity and Interface — Research, Knowledge and Society. Proceedings of the 11th European Symposium on Language for Special Purposes*, ed. by Lita Lundquist, Heribert Picht, and Jacques Qvistgaard, 339–348. Copenhagen: Copenhagen Business School.

Madsen, Bodil Nistrup. 1999. *Terminologi 1 — Principper og metoder*. Copenhagen: Gad.

Madsen, Bodil Nistrup. 2005. "Implementation of Research Results in the Development of an Internet Terminology and Knowledge Management System." In *Proceedings from Terminology in Advanced Management Applications. 7th International Conference on Multilingual Knowledge and Technology Transfer — Terminology Science and Research, Vol.* 16, ed. by Nina Pilke, and Birthe Toft, 39–53. Bergen: International Institute for Terminology Research (IITF).

Madsen, Bodil Nistrup, Bolette Sandford Pedersen, and Hanne Erdman Thomsen. 2002. "Semantic Relations in Content-based Querying Systems: A Research Presentation from the OntoQuery Project." In *Proceedings from OntoLex '2000: Workshop on Ontologies and Lexical Knowledge Bases, Sept. 8–10 2000, Sozopol, Bulgaria*, ed. by K. Simov, and A. Kiryakov, 72–81.

Madsen, Bodil Nistrup, Hanne Erdman Thomsen, and Carl Vikner. 2004. "Principles of a system for terminological concept modelling." In *Proceedings of the Fourth International Conference on Language Resources and Evaluation*, ed. by Maria Teresa Lino, Maria Fransisca Xavier, Fátima Ferreira, Rute Costa, and Raquel Silva, 15–19. Paris: ELRA.

Madsen, Bodil Nistrup, Hanne Erdman Thomsen, and Annemette Wenzel. 2006. "i-Term for NORDTERM." In *Workshops Proceedings: W16 Terminology Design: Quality Criteria and Evaluation Methods (TermEval). (LREC 2006)*, ed. by Rute Costa, Fidélia Ibekwe-SanJuan, Marie-Claude L'Homme, Adeline Nazarenko, and Henrik Nilsson. 1–7. Genova.

Madsen, Bodil Nistrup, and Hanne Erdman Thomsen. 2009a. "CAOS — A tool for the Construction of Terminological Ontologies." In *Proceedings of the 17th Nordic Conference of Computational Linguistics NODALIDA 2009 — NEALT Proceedings Series, Vol.* 4, ed. by Kristiina Jokinen, and Eckhard Bick, 279–282. Northern European Association for Language Technology (NEALT). Tartu: Tartu University Library.

Madsen, Bodil Nistrup, and Hanne Erdman Thomsen. 2009b. "Terminological Concept Modelling and UML Diagrams." In *International Journal of Metadata, Semantics and Ontologies (IJMSO)*, 2009, Vol. 4 No. 4. 239–249.

Madsen, Bodil Nistrup, Hanne Erdman Thomsen, Tine Lassen, Louise Pram Nielsen, Anna Elisabeth Odgaard, and Pia Lyngby Hoffmann. 2012. "Consistency and Interoperability in a National Term Bank." In *Proceedings of the 10th Terminology and Knowledge Engineering Conference: New Frontiers in the Constructive Symbiosis of Terminology and Knowledge Engineering*, ed. by Guadalupe Aguado de Cea, Mari Carmen Suárez-Figueroa, Raúl García-Castro, and Elena Montiel-Ponsoda, 242–257. Madrid: Universidad Politécnica de Madrid.

Madsen, Bodil Nistrup, and Hanne Erdman Thomsen. 2016. "The DANTERM Model Revisited." In *Term Bases and Linguistic Linked Open Data: TKE 2016, 12th International Conference on Terminology and Knowledge Engineering*, ed. by Hanne Erdman Thomsen, Antonio Pareja-Lora, and Bodil Nistrup Madsen. 24–33. Copenhagen: Copenhagen Business School.

Myking, Johan. 1998. "The Concept of 'motivation' in Terminology: Some Reflections on its Definition and Applicability." In *LSP — Identity and Interface — Research, Knowledge and Society. Proceedings of the 11th European Symposium on Language for Special Purposes*, ed. by Lita Lundquist, Heribert Picht, and Jacques Qvistgaard, 339–348. Copenhagen: Copenhagen Business School.

Myking, Johan. 2001. "Against Prescriptivism? The 'socio-critical' challenge to terminology." *Terminology Science & Research*. Vol. 12 (2001) No.1–2, 49–64.

Myking, Johan. (In press). "Demise or staying alive? 'Domain loss' in terminology." In *Domain Loss and Gain in Contemporary Terminology Studies*, ed. by Thelen, Marcel, Maria-Cornelia Wermuth, and Leona Van Vaerenbergh. Amsterdam: Amsterdam University Press.

Myking, Johan, and Sylvi Dysvik, and Håvard Hjulstad 2018. "Fagspråksarbeid." In *Norsk Språkhistorie 2 — Praksis*, ed by Helge, Sandøy, and Agnete Nesse. 365–417. Oslo: Novus.

Nilsson, Henrik. 2009. "The Realisation of a National Term Bank — How and Why?" In *ELETO — 7th Conference "Hellenic Language and Terminology*. Attica: Hellenic Society for Terminology.

Nilsson, Henrik. 2010. "Towards a National Terminology Infrastructure." In *Terminology in Everyday Life*, ed. by Frida Steurs, and Hendrick Kockaert, 61–78. Amsterdam: John Benjamins.

Nilsson, Henrik. 2011. "TERMDIST: Teaching Terminology Multilingually at a Distance." In *La formation en terminologie: actes de la Conference internationale de Bucarest, 3–4 novembre 2011*, 147–161. Bucureşti: Editura ASE.

Nilsson, Henrik. 2022. "Terminologifrämjandet — om att fylla ett hål i Terminologi-Sverige." In *Nordterm 22: Begreppsarbete och informationshantering (Helsingfors, Finland den 1–2 juni 2021)*, 62–64. Helsinki: TSK.

Nilsson, Henrik, and Claudia Dobrina. 2011. "Två år med Rikstermbanken — vad händer nu?." *Språkbruk* 2011:2, 9–12.

Nilsson, Henrik, Antti Kanner, and Tiina Onikki-Rantajääskö. 2016. "Post och bank — om lagring av terminologi, den svenska Rikstermbanken och den finska Vetenskapstermbanken." In *Tänkta termer. Terminologihänsyn i nordiskt perspektiv*, VAKKI Publications 5, 100–136. Vaasa: Vasa universitet.

Nordterm Steering Committee. 1988. "Special Issue on Nordterm." *Nordisk Tidskrift for fackspråk och terminologi*, 2/1988.

Nordterm Steering Committee. 2021. NORDTERM Statutes.

Nuopponen, Anita. 1994. *Begreppssystem för terminologisk analys*. Acta Wasaensia. Vaasa: Vasa universitet.

Nuopponen, Anita. 1996. "Multiple Goals of Teaching the Methods and Theory of Terminology." In *Conference: In the beginning was the term*. Mons, Belgium.

Nuopponen, Anita. 1997. "Att integrera terminologiläran i olika utbildningsprogram." In *NORDTERM '97*, ed. by Håvard Hjulstad, 49–55. Oslo: Rådet for teknisk terminologi, NORDTERM.

Nuopponen, Anita. 1998. "A Model for Systematic Terminological Analysis." In *LSP — Identity and Interface Research, Knowledge and Society*, ed. by Lundquist, Lita, Heribert Picht, and Jacques Qvistgaard, 363–372. Copenhagen: Copenhagen Business School.

Nuopponen, Anita. 2005. "Concept Relations v2. An Update of a Concept Relation Classification." In *Terminology and Content Development*, ed. by Bodil Nistrup Madsen, and Hanne Erdman Thomsen, 127–138. Copenhagen: Association for Terminology and Knowledge Transfer.

Nuopponen, Anita. 2011. "Methods of Concept Analysis — Tools for Systematic Concept Analysis (Part 3 of 3)." *The LSP Journal — Language for Special Purposes, Professional Communication, Knowledge Management and Cognition* 2: 4–15.

Nuopponen, Anita. 2022. "Conceptual Relations. From the General Theory of Terminology to Knowledge Bases." In *Theoretical Perspectives on Terminology. Explaining Terms, Concepts and Specialized Knowledge*, ed. by Pamela Faber, and Marie-Claude L'Homme, 63–85. Amsterdam: John Benjamins.

Nuopponen, Anita, and Nina Pilke. 2010. *Ordning och reda. Terminologilära i teori och praktik.* Stockholm: Norstedts.

Nykänen, Olli. 1999. "TSK — 25 vuotta sanastotyön asiantuntemusta." In *Toimikunnista termitalkoisiin. 25 vuotta sanastotyön asiantuntemusta*, ed. by Kaisa Kuhmonen, 5–15. Helsinki: Tekniikan Sanastokeskus.

Picht, Heribert. 1985. "Terminology Research and Terminology Training." *TermNet News. Special Issue on the Nordic Countries* 12: 5–6. Vienna: TermNet.

Picht, Heribert. 1988. "Terminology Work in Denmark." *Nordisk tidskrift för fackspråk och terminologi 2/1988. Special Issue on Nordterm*: 13–20. Copenhagen: Copenhagen Business School.

Picht, Heribert. 1994. "Entstehung, Grundlage und Anwendung der DANTERM-Klassifikation." In *Festskrift til Gert Engel i anledning af hans 70 års fødselsdag*, ed. by Annelise Grinsted, and Bodil Nistrup Madsen, 115–126. Copenhagen: Samfundslitteratur.

Picht, Heribert. 1998. "Terminographie in Regionalen Organisationen I: NORDTERM." In *Fachsprachen*, ed. by Lothar Hoffmann, Hartwig Kalverkämper, Herbert Ernst Wiegand, Christian Galinski, and Werner Hüllen, Part 2, 2144–2150. Berlin: De Gruyter.

Picht, Heribert. 2007. "NORDTERM — et forum med tradition og fremtid" In *Nordterm 15. Kunnskap og fagkommunikasjon*, ed. by Jan Hoel, 35–47. Oslo: Språkrådet.

Picht, Heribert, and Jennifer Draskau (eds). 1985a. *TermNet News. Special Issue on the Nordic Countries.* Vienna: Infoterm.

Picht, Heribert, and Jennifer Draskau. 1985b. *Terminology: An Introduction.* Surrey: University of Surrey.

Pilke, Nina. 2000. *Dynamiska fackbegrepp. Att strukturera vetande om handlingar och händelser inom teknik, medicin och juridik.* Vaasa: Vasa universitet.

POINTER. 1995. *POINTER: proposals for an operational infrastructure for terminology in Europe.* European Commission.

Rangnes, Odd Kjetil. 1996. "Norske oljearbeideres holdninger til norsk oljeterminologi." In *Fackspråk i olika kontexter. Forskning i Norden*, ed. by Christer Laurén, and Marianne Nordman, 77–83. Vaasa: Vasa universitet.

Spang-Hanssen, Henning. 1972. "Teknisk terminologiarbejde i Danmark og Dansk Sprognævns rolle heri." *Språk i Norden* 1972: 73–78. Nämnden för svensk språkvård.

Suonuuti, Heidi. 1985. "Organisation of Terminology Work and Forms of Co-operation." *TermNet News — Journal of the International Network for Terminology*, 12. *Special Issue on the Nordic Countries*: 13. Vienna: TermNet.

Suonuuti, Heidi. 2001. *Guide to Terminology.* Nordterm 8. Helsinki: Tekniikan Sanastokeskus.

Suonuuti, Heidi. 2004. *Terminologiguiden: en guide till terminologiarbete i teori och praktik.* Solna: Terminologicentrum TNC.

Sæbøe, Randi. 1996. "Norsk språk i møte med en anglo-amerikansk kultur. En sosiologsk analyse av språksituasjonen i norsk petroleumsvirksomhet — prosjektpresentasjon." In *Fackspråk i olika kontexter. Forskning i Norden*, ed. by C. Laurén, and M. Nordman, 68–75. Vaasa: Vasa universitet.

Tekniikan Sanastokeskus. 1989. *Sanastotyön käsikirja. Soveltavan terminologian periaatteet ja työmenetelmät.* SFS-käsikirja 50. Helsinki: Suomen Standardisoimisliitto SFS.

Thelen, Marcel, Maria-Cornelia Wermuth, and Leona Van Vaerenbergh (eds) (in press). *Domain Loss and Gain in Contemporary Terminology Studies.* Amsterdam: Amsterdam University Press.

Thomsen, Hanne Erdman. 1997. "Feature Specifications Applied to the Field of Life Insurance." *Terminology Science and Research*, vol. 8, 21–35. Vienna: TermNet.

Thomsen, Hanne Erdman. 2000. "The Integration of Terminology Training in Danish Education Programmes." In *Conference on Cooperation in the Field of Terminology in Europe*, Paris, 17–18–19/05/1999, Palais des Congrès, 269–277. Paris: Union Latine.

Thomsen, Hanne Erdman. 2006. "Om at komme fra ord-arbejde til terminologiarbejde: Procesmodenhed på terminologiområdet." In *Ord og termer: Proceedings fra Nordterm 2005 (Nordterm, Vol. 14)*, ed. by Ágústa Þorbergsdóttir, 243–255. Reykjavik: Íslensk málstöð.

Toft, Birthe. 2002. "A Unified Metascientific Basis for Future Terminology Science?" In *Porta Scientia I, Lingua Specialis. Proceedings of the University of Vaasa 95*, ed by M. Koskela, C. Laurén, M. Nordman, and N. Pilke, 189–200. Vaasa: University of Vaasa.

Toft, Birthe. 2009. "Motivation of English and Danish Medical Terms: A Contrastive Analysis." In *Terminology Science & Research, Journal of the International Institute of Terminology Research* 2009, Vol. 20.

Toft, Birthe. 2012. *Introduktion til terminologi på ED.* Internal teaching material.

Toft, Birthe. 2013. "How to Create a Methodology of Conceptual Visualization Based on Experiential Cognitive Science and Diagrammatology." In *Multimodal Communication*, Vol. 2(1), 2013, 31–54.

Weilgaard Christensen, Lise Lotte. 2018. "Brugeraspekter ved emneklassifikationer til fagsproglige ressourcer." *Fackspråk i nordiska ordböcker, LexicoNordica 25 — 2018*, 17–34.

Wüster, Eugen. 1971. "Begriffs- und Themaklassifikationen. Unterschiede in ihren Wesen und in ihrer Anwendung." *Nachrichten für Dokumentation*, 22: 3, 98–104.

Ylisalmi, Anu. 2007. "TEPA-termipankki on uudistunut." *Terminfo* 3/2007: 12.

Ylisalmi, Anu. 2010. "Monistetusta vihkosesta verkkolehdeksi — Terminfo-lehti täytti 30 vuotta." *Terminfo* 4/2010.

Þorbergsdóttir, Ágústa. 2017a. *NORDTERM 19 Forvaltning af fagsprog i samfundet, Hvem har ansvaret? Hvem tager ansvaret?* Proceedings from Nordterm 2015. Reykjavík: Árni Magnússon Instituttet for Islandske Studier.

Þorbergsdóttir, Ágústa. 2017b. "Den islandske termbanks forskellige resurser." In *Nordiske Studier i Leksikografi 14*, ed. by Ásta Svavarsdóttir, Halldóra Jónsdóttir, Helga Hilmisdóttir, and Þórdís Úlfarsdóttir, 262–270. Reykjavík: Nordisk Forening for Leksikografi & Árni Magnússon Instituttet for Islandske Studier.

Þorbergsdóttir, Ágústa. 2020. "Tilblivelsen af fagordbøger og termsamlinger i Island." *Nordiska studier i lexikografi 15*, 337–346.

CHAPTER 16

Terminology in Lithuania
Theoretical foundations

Albina Auksoriūtė
Institute of the Lithuanian Language

The evolution of Lithuanian terminology is examined in three phases:
(1) the period of independent Lithuania (1918–1940), (2) the years of the
occupation of Lithuania (1940–1990), and (3) the years following the
restoration of Lithuania's independence (1990–2020). An analysis of
Lithuanian terminology management is presented, starting with a
discussion of the terminology commissions, followed by a brief presentation
of the resources available for the development of Lithuanian terminology.
The discussion of terminology research in Lithuania focuses on the
terminology theory published by the philosopher Stasys Šalkauskis and on
the work of other terminologists.

Keywords: Lithuanian terminology, terminology commissions, terminology
management, terminography, terminology research

1. Introduction

When introducing Lithuanian terminology, first the management of Lithuanian
terminology and terminology research should be discussed. Terminology management has been defined quite broadly as "any deliberate manipulation of terminological information" (Wright and Budin 1997:327). ISO Technical Committee
37 uses the terms *terminology work* and *terminology management* synonymously
and provides a specific definition: "work concerned with the systematic collection, description, processing and presentation of concepts and their designations"
(ISO 1087:2019, 3.5.1). This chapter follows the definition of terminology management as defined in the ISO standard and uses both terms synonymously. Similarly, *terminology science* is to be understood as: "science studying terminologies,
aspects of terminology work, the resulting terminology resources, and terminological data" (ISO 1087:2019, 3.1.12).

https://doi.org/10.1075/tlrp.24.16auk

The aim of this chapter is to introduce and discuss the evolution of the management of Lithuanian terminology and terminology research in the twentieth and the early 21st century. Taking into account the historical and cultural background of the evolution of Lithuanian terminology, three phases of this process are distinguished: (1) the period of independent Lithuania (1918–1940), (2) the years of the occupation of Lithuania (1940–1990), and (3) the years following the restoration of Lithuania's independence (1990–2020). The aim is to provide a detailed analysis of the management of Lithuanian terminology at each stage, a discussion of the organised management of terminology: the activities, principles, results, and significance of the various terminology commissions for further development of terminology, and an overview of terminology resources, such as dictionaries of terms and the Term Bank of the Republic of Lithuania. The discussion of terminology research in Lithuania will include a detailed introduction and evaluation of the terminology theory published by the philosopher Stasys Šalkaus-kis during the period of independent Lithuania and of the work of terminologists after the restoration of Lithuania's independence.

2.   The period of independent Lithuania (1918–1940)

After the restoration of the independent state of Lithuania in 1918, political and cultural circumstances were more favourable for the development of the Lithuanian language, it was used in all spheres of life of the Lithuanian nation, including those spheres where it was either not admitted at all during the tsarist occupation[1] (in the army, in government offices), or where it was restricted (in schools, in the press, and elsewhere). For the first time in the history of Lithuania, the *Constitution of the State of Lithuania of 1922* [*Lietuvos valstybės konstitucija*] officially declared Lithuanian as the state language. The development of science and education became a matter of concern, school textbooks were published, Lithuanian terminology in the relevant fields began to be created and the first collections of terms were prepared. The creation and management of terms was carried out solely on the initiative of individual linguists and specialists in various fields. As the demand for Lithuanian terminology was rising, it became necessary to create Lithuanian terms and to manage terminology in an organised way.

---

1. From 1795 to 1914.

2.1   Management of Lithuanian terminology

2.1.1   *Activities of the Terminology Commission*

Following the example of the Latvians, the linguist Jonas Jablonskis (1860–1930) proposed that the Ministry of Education establish a terminology commission, which would oversee terminology issues. Jablonskis believed that within the main Terminology Commission, smaller terminology commissions would be needed to focus on terminology in various fields.

In March 1921, the Terminology Commission (Terminologijos komisija, hereinafter referred to as the Commission) was set up under the Ministry of Education and consisted of ten members: linguists Kazimieras Būga, Jonas Jablonskis and Antanas Vireliūnas, literary scholars and theologians Aleksandras Dambrauskas-Adomas Jakštas and Juozas Tumas-Vaižgantas, the writer Pranas Mašiotas, the philosopher Pranas Dovydaitis, the lawyer and the first president of Lithuania Antanas Smetona, the lawyer Vladas Požela, and the artist Adomas Varnas. The first meeting of the Commission was held on 21 April 1921. According to the minutes of the meeting, "the first task assigned to the Commission was to unify the official language of the public bodies. It was also agreed that the terms of the various subject fields should be revised and corrected" (*Terminologijos komisijos protokolai* 1921: 1). The Commission decided that the representatives of the ministries concerned should submit draft terms to the Commission for consideration, with explanatory sentences accompanying each term. They were also invited to discuss the terms. The Commission resolved to establish sub-commissions for mathematical, scientific, geographic, literary and legal terms, each with three members, and to invite specialists from outside the Commission to participate.

Due to various disagreements among its members and the purist perspective held by some, the Commission's membership changed several times during its existence. The Commission considered terms in economics, physics, railways, geography, warfare, mathematics, medicine, land reclamation, literature, technology, law, education and other fields, which it published in periodicals. In 1924, Vireliūnas published terms approved by the Commission in the areas of excise, law, civil engineering telephony, geography, education, and political economics.

In 1926, the Ministry of Education decided to dissolve the Commission and entrusted Kaunas University with the task of forming a new commission. A new Terminology Commission was established at the university in 1926, and statutes were drafted, but it did not start its work.

In summary, the work of the Terminology Commission for the evolution of Lithuanian terminology was of immense significance during this period. Numerous terms in different fields that were necessary for public life were discussed, adopted, and published, the majority of which entered usage and continue to be used today. The Terminology Commission formed in 1921 was the first commission established on the initiative of the state. It was the activity of this commission that heralded the beginning of organised management of Lithuanian terminology.

2.1.2 *Lithuanian terminology resources*

Since the first dictionaries of Lithuanian terms were published before the restoration of the independent state of Lithuania, the year 1900 is considered to mark the beginning of the published resources of the now independent state of Lithuania.[2] Thirteen dictionaries of terms of various fields were published in Lithuania from 1900 to 1940 (Figure 1, the numbers in each subject field indicate the number of publications); most were short collections of Russian-Lithuanian and Lithuanian-Russian terms.

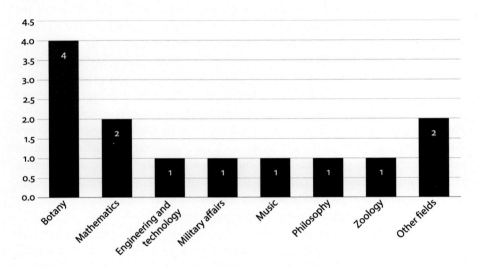

Figure 1. Distribution of the dictionaries of terms by fields from 1900–1940

---

2. The first printed glossary of Lithuanian terms — *Botanika arba Taislius auguminis* — a Lithuanian-Latin dictionary of botanical terms — was published in Shenandoah (Pennsylvania, USA) in 1900. In Lithuania, the first printed dictionary of terms was *Žolynas. Lietuvos augalų žodynas ir augalų taislas* (Verdure, a Lithuanian-Latin and Latin-Lithuanian dictionary of botanical names with Russian and Polish equivalents), published by Povilas Matulionis (1860–1932) in Vilnius in 1906.

The Lithuanian Dictionary of Botany [*Lietuviškas botanikos žodynas*], compiled by the Commission of the Botanical Dictionary in 1938, is considered the best dictionary of terms of its time (Keinys 1985: 190–191). It includes about 3,300 names of plants in Latin, Lithuanian, Russian, Polish, and Latvian, with synonyms and variants from spoken and written Lithuanian; it also includes a Lithuanian-Latin index of names, and a glossary of Latin adjectival names of taxa. In it, one can find not only systematically presented names of plant families, genera, and species, the synonyms and variants of which have references to written sources or locations, but also explanations of the origins of the Latin names and descriptions of plants. This dictionary is still in use both by botanists when preparing indices of Lithuanian names of plants and writing research reports and by terminologists in their research on Lithuanian names of plants.

2.2   Stasys Šalkauskis' theory of terminology

Stasys Šalkauskis (1886–1941) was an outstanding public figure, philosopher, and educator in independent Lithuania. He is the founder and one of the main creators of the philosophy of Lithuanian culture. The central idea of his philosophy was that the main objective of Lithuanian culture, which stood at the crossroads of the West and the East, was the synthesis of these two cultures.[3] His attitudes were influenced by the ideas of the Russian philosopher Vladimir Solovyov and Catholic Neotomist philosophy.

Šalkauskis' terminology legacy consists of three parts: (1) his research into terminology theory, (2) his publication, in 1937, of a dictionary of philosophical terms in four languages (Lithuanian, French, German, and Russian), complete with an appendix of explanations and examples of term usage,[4] and (3) his preparation of a dictionary on the general terminology of pedagogy [*Bendroji pedagogikos terminija*]. Part of Šalkauskis' most important work on terminology was included in volume 1 of his Selected Works [*Rinktiniai raštai*] published in Rome on the occasion of the centenary of his birth in 1986. Volume 2 of Šalkauskis' Works, published in Vilnius in 1991, contains almost all his major works in terminology, including the above-mentioned dictionary.

---

3. "Šalkauskis developed an original conception of the philosophy of culture, the uniqueness of which is defined by two factors. Firstly, Christianity is interpreted through the prism of the philosophy of culture, and this is what makes it applicable to democracy. Secondly, this discipline is transformed into an ideology, and is thus able to participate in the political life of interwar Lithuania. Šalkauskis perceived the nurturing of culture as the main goal of a nation state" (Jokubaitis and Jokubaitis 2020: 31–32).

4. with the German-Lithuanian part published at a later time.

Šalkauskis' theoretical work, which he published in 1925, 1927 and 1934 in four issues of the academic journal *Logos* of Kaunas University, is of immense importance for Lithuanian terminology. In this work, he defined the essence and characteristics of a term, the sources, categories, and usage features of terms, and formulated general rules for the formation of Lithuanian terms.

> In explaining the properties of a term and its relations to logical, grammatical, and philosophical categories, Stasys Šalkauskis relied mainly on the work of the medieval philosopher and scholastic theologian Duns Scotus' (1265–1308) *Grammatica speculativa* and research by French linguists, for example: *Essai de sémantique* by Michel Bréal (1832–1915), *Le Langage* by Joseph Vendryes (1875–1960) and others.   (Gaivenis 1983: 128–129)

Šalkauskis begins by pointing out that linguistics is very closely related to the discipline of philosophy and therefore it is philosophers, interested scholars, and linguists alone who are fully competent to deal with this field. "It is thus self-evident that only through the joint and coordinated effort of linguists, philosophers, or otherwise interested scholars that our scientific terminology can be purposefully determined". (Šalkauskis 1925: 2).

Šalkauskis did not consider terminology an independent branch of science but defined it as a special part of semantics and thus presented his theory of terminology by starting from the word and the term. In his analysis of the relationship between the two, he stressed that the word was related to the term and everything that was inherent in the word, i.e. its essence and properties, was also applicable to the term. Therefore, a good understanding of the word, and especially of the word signifying a concept, was indispensable for a good understanding of the concept itself. According to Šalkauskis, words were manifestative signs for concepts and suppositional signs for objects (*verba sunt signa manifestative conceptuum, suppositive rerum*) (6–9).

Understanding terminology in this way, he concluded that a term is inseparable from a sign and from the concept: "a term is always a verbal sign signifying a thing and expressing a concept corresponding to it, although not all such words are terms. To become a term, such a verbal sign must enter the sphere of some science and must be scientifically processed" (Šalkauskis 1925: 12). The philosopher gives the following definition of a term: "A term is a word that signifies a concept having a specialised meaning within a scientific discipline" (6).

Šalkauskis drew attention to the ambiguity of the word *terminology*; he split the concept of terminology and proposed two separate terms: he referred to "the totality of terms" as *terminija* (a terminology), while the word *terminology* designated the "science of terms."

> The new term *terminija*, which is a regular derivative from the class of collective nouns (derived from the noun *terminas* 'term' plus the collective suffix *-ija*) can be described as monosemantic, accurate, and intelligible. The term *terminologija* possesses the same qualities.   (Auksoriūtė et al. 1994: 51)

This usage has already become common in the current Lithuanian language.

Šalkauskis presents the main methods of term formation and describes the usage of terms. He distinguishes three main methods: (1) using living human language, (2) leveraging the power of word formation, in other words, coining new terms, and (3) borrowing from other languages.

Following August Leskien's work *Die Bildung der Nomina im Litauischen* [Word Formation in Lithuanian] (1891), Šalkauskis was the first to study the categories of terms and the ways of expressing them. He offers the following definition of a category of terms: "For us, a category of terms is nothing else than a group of terms, typical in their types of derivation, usually in their suffix, and corresponding to a group of concepts sharing a certain affinity" (1934: 6). He distinguished the categories of concepts that terms express (action, quality, relation, tools, places, etc.). He also analysed the way terms are derived and discussed their classification according to the above categories.

The acceptable conditions for borrowing terms from other languages, put forward by Šalkauskis, are important. In his view, borrowing foreign words is justified only when "the required term cannot be obtained either by the adaptation of a word of ordinary human language, or by the creation of a new term by means of compounding or by means of derivation" (1927 I: 24).

Šalkauskis divided the general rules of term formation into three groups: (1) ancient rules, (2) novelty rules, and (3) rules of evolution (1927 II: 172–174). The ancient rules include the principle of maximum utilisation (it is neither appropriate to borrow a foreign term nor to produce a new one of one's own if a word from human language can be satisfactorily adapted for scientific use) and the principle of traditional validity (no word established in a language may be removed from scientific use without a clearly justified reason). His novelty rules embracing the principles of typicality, maximum utility, and aesthetics are also important, because current terminology requires that a newly coined term should be of the typical derivation type and able to produce new derivatives. He proposed only two rules of evolution: categorical inflections[5] and the alteration of the sense and meaning of words.[6] At the time, the principles of term formation that he

---

5. For corresponding categories of concepts, their characteristic inflexional endings are used.

6. Where necessary, the sense and meaning of words are altered only in the ways justified by the laws of language and logic.

formulated were significant as they informed how most of the new Lithuanian terms were created.

Šalkauskis applied the theory of terminology in practice, in regulating the terms of philosophy. His dictionary of philosophical terms was published in 1937 in the second issue of the *Logos* magazine and as a separate book in 1938. The dictionary consisted of about 1,600 philosophical terms in Lithuanian with equivalents in French, German, and Russian, accompanied by an appendix of explanatory notes and examples of usage and a German-Lithuanian section.

Šalkauskis conducted theoretical work on terminology independently and at a similar time as the engineer Eugen Wüster, the pioneer of the General Theory of Terminology which took hold in Central Europe (see also Chapters 7 and 8).

> Unlike Wüster, Šalkauskis took the word as the starting point in his terminology and moved from form to content. His theory of terminology is philosophical. In originality and depth of thought, this theory was at the level of European science at that time.
> (Gaivenis 2002: 115)

Šalkauskis' theory of terminology was not known abroad as it was published only in Lithuanian, but in Lithuania, the principles of term formation formulated by him were followed by the majority of specialists and were supported by linguists.

During the Soviet period, Šalkauskis' scientific legacy was considered unscholarly due to ideology, and the publications in which his theory of terminology was published were kept in special library collections. Despite that, his works on terminology have always been known to Lithuanian philosophers and linguists, his theory of terminology has been used, and some of his principles of and requirements for term creation (typicality, constancy, ease of formation, aesthetics, etc.) are still followed.

In conclusion, Šalkauskis' research on terminology contributed significantly to the standardisation, systematisation, and creation of Lithuanian scientific terminology, and the dictionary of philosophical terms was significant not only for the development of the terminology of philosophy, but also for the evolution of the discipline of philosophy as such.

3.   The Soviet occupation

In the summer of 1940, the occupation by the Soviet Union ended the statehood of Lithuania. It marked the onset of systematic destruction in all spheres of life, including the education system, and rapid Sovietisation of political, social, economic, cultural, and spiritual life under the guise of "socio-economic transformation," "the realisation of social justice," and the like (Stašaitis 2008: 39). The

Lithuanian people immediately felt what the Soviet national policy and the result-ing language policy meant.

> The Lithuanian language ceased to be the national language and Russian began
> to be used alongside it; in some areas, especially in the army, it was soon com-
> pletely banished. Gradually, it was pushed or even excluded from many other
> areas of public life.   (Keinys 1994:64)

Research studies, with the exception of those pertaining to Lithuanian philology and the history of Lithuania, were published almost exclusively in Russian. The Lithuanian language was pushed out of culture, public information media, book publishing, and other spheres. All dissertations were required to be written in Russian, papers in research journals were also published only in Russian, with some journals providing only Lithuanian abstracts. During the Soviet period, the evolution of terminology in the fields of religion, warfare, communications, transport, numerous branches of science, industry, and energy was halted or sus-pended, although work on terminology did not cease outright.

3.1   Management of Lithuanian terminology

In spite of the severely restricted conditions imposed by Soviet occupation, work on Lithuanian terminology continued mainly through the efforts of linguists.

3.1.1   *Activities of the Terminology Commission and the Terminology Council*

In 1947, the Terminology Commission was established under the Presidium of the Academy of Sciences (Mokslų Akademijos Prezidiumas) to organise and coor-dinate the work on terminology; in 1951, it was transferred to the Institute of the Lithuanian Language (Lietuvių kalbos institutas). The Commission consisted entirely of linguists, who worked hard to create and further develop Lithuanian terminology in spite of efforts by the Soviet government to impose Russian. This Commission did considerable work in encouraging specialists in various fields to pay more attention to the management of Lithuanian terminology.

The Commission applied not only linguistic but also logical requirements to the terms under consideration and paid attention to their precision, systematic nature, and motivation. In its work, the Commission observed the principle of consistency: it did not change terms already in use without good reason.

In the period 1951–1971, the Commission considered a large number of terms in various fields, revised over ten dictionaries of terms, consulted with institutions and enterprises on a wide range of issues related to the use of terminology, and organised conferences and meetings with specialists on the creation, develop-ment, and dissemination of Lithuanian terms (Keinys 1985:179–196).

At the end of 1971, the Commission was replaced by the Terminology Council (Terminologijos taryba, hereinafter the Council) established under the Presidium of the Academy of Sciences of the Lithuanian SSR, in order to include specialists of various fields. The Council's main objectives were: (1) to coordinate and organise the work on Lithuanian terminology, (2) to approve the dictionaries of terms, and (3) to recommend scientific and technical terms.

The Council was composed of 23 eminent specialists in various scientific and technical fields and was headed by linguists: Vytautas Mažiulis was its chair, Jonas Kruopas (after his death, Stasys Keinys) the vice-chair, and Kazimieras Gaivenis the secretary. It functioned on a volunteer basis and relied on over twenty terminology commissions comprised of specialists from various fields. These commissions prepared and discussed dictionaries and sets of terms in their respective fields for later approval by the Council. The terminology commissions in botany, physics, zoology, mathematics, agronomy, and other fields were quite productive and regularly collaborated with terminologists-linguists.

In 1971, the Terminology Group (Terminologijos grupė), headed by Gaivenis, was established at the Institute of the Lithuanian Language and Literature (Lietuvių kalbos ir literatūros institutas). This group contributed to the work of the Council and organisation of its activities. At that time the practical terminological work was conducted by the Terminology Group. The Council operated until 1992, but it was not very active in the final few years. For the development of Lithuanian terminology during the Soviet period, the activities of the Council were important in that it approved a number of terminological dictionaries, continued to encourage specialists in various fields to manage their own terminology, and established the Terminology Group for practical terminology work. In 1991, Terminology Group evolved into the Terminology Department of the Institute of the Lithuanian Language (Lietuvių kalbos instituto Terminologijos skyrius) and undertook not only practical work but also terminology research.

3.1.2   Lithuanian terminology resources

During the Soviet period, the compilation of dictionaries of terms continued.

> Dictionaries of terms were usually compiled by the most eminent subject specialists and/or research teams. Although generations of researchers and linguists, institutions, ideologies, and other fundamental things changed during the upheavals in the life of the state and the nation, the structure of the development and approval of dictionaries of terms remained.   (Klimavičius 2003: 15)

It should be stressed that not only dictionaries but also encyclopaedias and fundamental academic works were prepared and published during this period, for example, *Lietuvos TSR fizinė geografija* [Physical Geography of the Lithuanian

SSR] (1958–1965, 2 volumes), *Lietuvos TSR flora* [Flora of the Lithuanian SSR] (1958–1980, 6 volumes).

> The terminology in some areas, particularly in economics, law, politics, philosophy, and public life, was developed and organised primarily on the basis of Russian terminology in the respective areas. Many of the dictionaries that were developed in other fields, too, were bilingual, initially with the Russian language as the first, and later on, in major dictionaries, more often with the Russian language as the second. (Keinys 2004: 224)

From 1941 to 1989, 168 dictionaries of terms from various fields were compiled and published (Figure 2). Translation dictionaries (Russian-Lithuanian or Lithuanian-Russian) account for 54% of all the dictionaries published in this period.

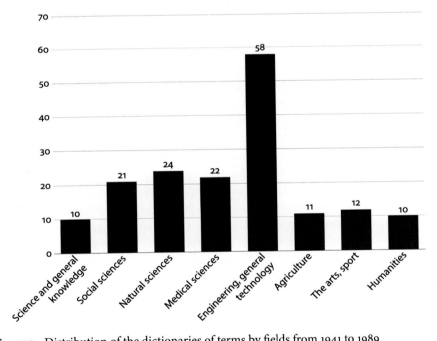

Figure 2. Distribution of the dictionaries of terms by fields from 1941 to 1989

Among the most important explanatory dictionaries (terminological dictionaries with definitions, vocabularies) are those on botany, chemistry, woodworking, land reclamation, scientific and technical information, music, textiles, and zoology. Most of these dictionaries are not only explanatory: they provide equivalents in Russian or other languages.

3.2   Research into Lithuanian terminology

During the Soviet period, research into Lithuanian terminology was mainly conducted at the Institute of the Lithuanian Language and Literature. There was little scientific and theoretical research, and terminologists were mostly involved in terminology management. The main line of theoretical research was carried out in the field of linguistics. Four doctoral dissertations in the field of terminology were defended.

During this period, research on Lithuanian terminology followed the theoretical work of the Soviet, mainly Russian, scholars. Western European literature was hard to access at the time, and some works by foreign authors were only available in Russian sources. In their articles written in the 1970s, Lithuanian terminologists mainly relied on the work of the Russian engineer and terminologist Dmitry Lotte (1898–1950) (see also Chapter 10). Angelė Kaulakienė translated *Kak rabotat nad terminologiyei* about terminology work that is based on the work of Lotte and the Committee for Scientific-Technical Terminology of the Academy of Sciences of the USSR (1973). Later, the works of Valeriya Danilenko (1977), Aleksandra Superanskaya (1989) and others were referred to. The terminology theory of the Russian scholar Danilenko was purely linguistic. She considered terms to be the most important and informative part of the lexicon of the scientific language and explained numerous topical issues in linguistics: the differences between the norms of terminology and the standard language, specialisation of the means of term formation, the importance of context for a term, the specificity of semantic processes in the language of science, and others (Gaivenis 2002: 121–128). The terminology theory of Superenskaya, Nataliya Podolskaya, and Nataliya Vasilyeva is significant in that it is perhaps the first time that the terminological views of the Russian and Viennese schools had been brought together (Gaivenis 2002: 128–131).

It should be noted that the works of Ernest Drezen (1892–1937) from Latvia are not mentioned in the works on Lithuanian terminology: for political reasons, his works were not published in the Soviet Union and no references to him were made (see also Chapter 10).

Research papers appeared only in research journals published in Lithuania and not in other republics of the Soviet Union: terminologists from the Institute of the Lithuanian Language prepared and published three volumes of the journal *Kalbos kultūra* [Language Culture: 1973, 1979, 1983] in which they discussed the usage of individual terms or the problems of the formation and usage of terms in particular fields. Four volumes of the journal *Lietuvių kalbotyros klausimai* [Issues in Lithuanian Linguistics; 1975, 1979, 1983, 1985] are devoted to terminology. In their articles, Lithuanian terminologists dealt with the formation of

Lithuanian terms, synonymy of foreign and Lithuanian terms, terminology of individual fields, and Šalkauskis' theory of terminology.

Relevant issues regarding the theory and practice of Lithuanian terminology were also addressed in articles published in Series A of *Lietuvos TSR Mokslų akademijos darbai* [Works of the Academy of Sciences of the Lithuanian SSR].

Gaivenis' (1979) article deserves a mention here. In it, he discusses the first attempts to formulate the principles of Lithuanian terminology in the nineteenth and the early twentieth centuries, identifies the international codes of nomenclature for the natural sciences, which had a marked impact on Lithuanian terminology, and analyses the principles informing the development and standardisation of Lithuanian terminology. He points out that these principles reflect the practice of terminological work at that time. Specifically, he explores ten principles of Lithuanian terminology (Gaivenis 1979: 77–86):

1. terminology norms are derived according to the norms of the standard language
2. interdisciplinary coordination of terms is necessary
3. the need for naming is determined by specialists, while linguists advise on the names themselves
4. the main source of terminology is the lexicon of the standard language and dialects, while secondary sources include international words or lexicons of other languages
5. only one term is needed for each concept
6. when naming a new concept, consideration must be given to how related concepts are named
7. new terms must be correct and convenient for the derivation of future neologisms
8. an established term must not be changed without valid reasons
9. when adopting a term among synonyms, preference should be given to the term that most accurately reflects the essential and distinctive features of the concept, is more systematic in its conceptual system, and respects word formation rules
10. each term must be accompanied by a definition.

In 1980, Keinys published *Terminologijos abėcėlė* [The Alphabet of Terminology], in which he discussed the concept of *term*, types of terms, requirements for terms, term formation methods, among other topics. It is the first Lithuanian terminology textbook, which for many years was used not only by scholars in Lithuanian studies but also by specialists in all fields of study working or preparing to work in terminology management. This book was the reference work on Lithuanian terminology right until the appearance of Gaivenis' monograph *Lietuvių termi-*

nologija: teorijos ir tvarkybos metmenys [Lithuanian Terminology: An Outline of Its Theory and Management] in 2002.

Between 1979 and 1990, six theoretical and methodological seminars on terminology were organised in the Baltic countries, in Vilnius, Tallinn, and Riga successively, at which papers were given not only by local terminologists, but also by scholars from Russia, Belarus, Ukraine, and other republics of the Soviet Union. Volume 24 of the journal *Lietuvių kalbotyros klausimai*, which appeared in 1985, contained articles based on the papers presented at the 1983 seminar. Written in Russian, they deal with the issues of the language of science, the theory and practice of terminology relevant at the time, and the culture of language, with considerable attention also paid to comparative research.

Analysing the motivated and unmotivated term in Estonian terminology, the Estonian terminologist Tiiu Erelt entered into a discussion with the Russian scholar Danilenko and pointed out that Danilenko holds the view that the most objective way to determine motivation is to distinguish between derivative-morphological, syntactic, and semantic types of motivation. In Erelt's opinion, this assessment is probably objective from the point of view of the Russian language; as for the Estonian language, there is no need to distinguish syntactic motivation. Morphemic motivation also applies to word phrases (Erelt 1985: 157).

Comparing Latvian and Lithuanian linguistic terms, the Latvian scholar Laimutė Balodė concludes that during 1980, a growing number of foreign linguistic terms appeared in both Latvian and Lithuanian, while there were much fewer new terms formed of elements of Latvian or Lithuanian itself, and that Lithuanian terminologists are considerably more active in the creation of these terms (1985: 16).

In her analysis of the semantic problems of terminology, the most prominent Latvian terminologist Valentīna Skujiņa refers to the works of Lotte, who she considers the founder of the Soviet school of terminology.[7] She argues that the correct solution to the semantic problems of terminology is to be found in Danilenko's works (Skujiņa 1985: 139) and concludes that the clarity of a term is the guarantor of the clarity of the idea and the guarantee of a higher level of culture of the language of science (145).

---

7. In the choice of the optimal scientific term, the requirements set out in Lotte's work, among which the requirement of systematicity has a special place, have not lost their relevance (Skujiņa 1985: 145).

4. After the restoration of Lithuania's independence (1990–2020)

The restoration of the independent state of Lithuania in 1990 had a significant impact on various areas of state activity.

> Since 1988, when Lithuania underwent various political, economic, and social changes, which fundamentally shaped the further development of the state, language issues have not been left behind. It was understood that language plays a very important role in the life of the state and society, and therefore when the Constitution of the Republic of Lithuania, the main law of the country, was adopted in a referendum on 25 October 1992, the Lithuanian language was once again given the status of the official language, which it had gained in interwar Lithuania, but which it had lost during the Soviet years.   (Vainiutė 2010: 37)

As the conditions for the development of the Lithuanian language in the public life of the state and in all its spheres were favourable, it was necessary to bring the Lithuanian language back to the spheres from which it had been banished during the Soviet period. On 31 January 1995, the Seimas of the Republic of Lithuania (Lietuvos Respublikos Seimas) adopted the Law on the State Language of the Republic of Lithuania (Lietuvos Respublikos valstybinės kalbos įstatymas), which establishes the most important areas of the use of the state language in public life, and regulates its protection, control, and the legal liability for non-compliance with this law.

4.1 Management of Lithuanian terminology

4.1.1 *Terminology work of the State Commission of the Lithuanian language*

Regarding terminology planning, Heribert Picht points out that

> One form of terminology planning at the national level is the creation or improvement of terminologies for relevant subject fields in a language which still lacks a given terminology or the existing terminology is underdeveloped and does not serve the purposes of knowledge in the language in question.
>
> (Picht 2009: 20)

After the re-establishment of independence, not only the policy and planning of the Lithuanian language, but also the planning of terminology gained in importance. Terminology was facing numerous challenges:

> First of all, the terms in the areas where our language was either not officially used at all or only partially used were dealt with. These areas included aviation, railway transport, maritime transport, warfare, communications, and others. Urgent

> work on the preparation of Lithuanian standards — a field of work previously
> neglected due to bureaucratic clumsiness — commenced.   (Keinys 2004:26)

On 20 June 1990, the Resolution of the Presidium of the Supreme Council of the Republic of Lithuania (Lietuvos Respublikos Aukščiausiosios Tarybos Prezidiumas) established the State Commission of the Lithuanian Language (Valstybinė lietuvių kalbos komisija, hereinafter the Language Commission). The Language Commission was authorised to make decisions on issues concerning language codification and standardisation and its implementation as the State language.

In addition to its other activities, the Language Commission is responsible for terminology management. It evaluates dictionaries and terminology standards and approves terms for legal acts and draft laws. It has implemented a number of state programmes fostering language standardisation, usage, development, and dissemination and has supported the compilation and publishing of dictionaries since 1996. It invites tenders for, and finances, the compilation of various specialised dictionaries.

Seven regular sub-commissions of the Language Commission were established. One is the Terminology Sub-Commission (Terminologijos pakomisė), which discusses and debates with specialists on terminological dictionaries, terminology standards, terminology of legal acts, recommendations of the Language Commission on terminology, terminological queries of the EU institutions, and other topics.

In 2003, the Seimas of the Republic of Lithuania approved the first *Guidelines for State Language Policy* 2003–2008 [*Valstybinės kalbos politikos gairės*], which had been drafted by the Language Commission. In 2018, the *Guidelines for State Language Policy 2018–2022* were approved. The objectives of state language policy include the following: to accelerate the management of Lithuanian terminology and to promote terminological activities in public, research, and higher education institutions. In 2019, the Government approved the *Plan of Measures for the Implementation of the Guidelines* 2019–2022 [*Valstybinės kalbos politikos 2019–2022 metų gairių įgyvendinimo priemonių planas*], which foresees the following measures: to ensure the development of the Term Bank of the Republic of Lithuania, compile dictionaries of terms, and prepare collections of articles on terms. These measures are implemented and funded by the Lithuanian Language Commission.

4.1.2   *Lithuanian terminology resources*

Terminological dictionaries. The most productive and efficient period of dictionary publishing was between 1990 and 2020, when over 465 terminological bilingual or multilingual dictionaries, glossaries, and special monolingual encyclopaedias in various fields were published. Almost half of the dictionaries are explanatory with or without equivalents in other languages. To a large extent, the recent explosion of terminographic work is due to state support.

It should be stressed that although 646 terminological dictionaries were published in Lithuania up to 2020, which is quite a large number (Figure 3), and some fields can boast of even several dictionaries, not all fields are covered by high-quality, appropriately-prepared explanatory dictionaries. Also, recently the number of dictionaries has been decreasing: while about 20 dictionaries were published annually between 2004 and 2007, the average number of dictionaries published from 2009 to 2012 was about ten, and from 2016 to 2020 it dropped to about five.

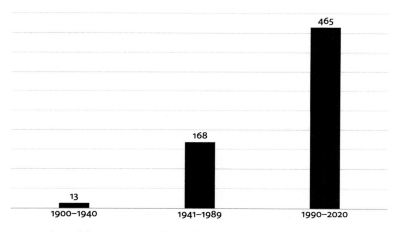

Figure 3. Number of dictionaries published between 1900 and 2020

The Term Bank of the Republic of Lithuania (Lietuvos Respublikos terminų bankas). Today, the key resource of Lithuanian terminology is the Term Bank of the Republic of Lithuania (hereinafter the Term Bank), which is administered by the Language Commission. The Term Bank is free and open to everyone online. It should be noted that the Term Bank is not integrated or linked to any EU databases, but the Lithuanian terminologists and translators working for EU institutions use it extensively.

In 2003, the Language Commission, together with the Office of the Seimas of the Republic of Lithuania, initiated the creation of this national Term Bank. The Parliament subsequently passed a law that regulates the creation, management, usage, and funding of the Term Bank as well as the duties, rights and responsibilities of the individuals and institutions providing, managing, and using the data it contains. The structure, data categories, rules of creation, ordering and usage, technical data, requirements and software functions are defined in the *Methodology of the Term Bank of the Republic of Lithuania* (2004) [*Lietuvos Respublikos terminų banko metodika*]. The purpose of the Term Bank is to ensure consistent usage of approved Lithuanian terms, particularly those used in legal acts, and to provide a common information system for various public authorities.

The Term Bank contains terms from dictionaries and terminology standards, legal terminology, terms published in the recommendations of the Language Commission, and other sets of terms. The legislative terms discussed by the Terminology Sub-Commission and approved by the Language Commission are added to the Term Bank and marked *aprobuotas* ('approved'). Dictionaries (mostly the explanatory type), terminological standards, and sets of terms that receive positive assessment of the Language Commission are added to the Term Bank and marked *teiktinas* ('recommended') (Umbrasas 2013: 96–122; Auksoriūtė 2016: 325–339). The status of a term also determines its further use. Some terms recommended by dictionaries, especially new terms, do not always catch on and are not used by specialists in the field; sometimes they remain only as dictionary suggestions. The situation is different with approved legislative terms: after publication in the Term Bank, they enter official usage, into other legal acts, so one can say that all approved terms are established in usage. As of June 2022, the Term Bank contained over 256,600 term entries and data from 50 dictionaries.

4.2   Research in Lithuanian terminology

4.2.1   *Works by Lithuanian terminologists*

After 1990, terminology research continued at the Institute of the Lithuanian Language, which is the only institution in Lithuania that has a separate terminology division. The mission of the department was linguistic research in Lithuanian terminology and the management and standardisation of scientific and production terms, which included two sub-missions: research into terminology issues and the standardisation of terms in various fields. In 2003, the department was reorganised and renamed the Terminology Centre (Terminologijos centras).

Initially, the Terminology Centre focused on diachronic linguistic research on terminology; since 2015, it has been publishing more synchronic research on terminology in various fields. Seven doctoral dissertations in the humanities in the field of historical terminology were defended at the Institute of the Lithuanian Language between 1990 and 2020. Terminologists at the Institute publish their research mostly as research papers, but several of their larger works should also be mentioned.

In 2002, Gaivenis published the only theoretical work on Lithuanian terminology *Lietuvių terminologija: teorijos ir tvarkybos metmenys* [*Lithuanian Terminology: An Outline of Its Theory and Management*]. The monograph deals with the standardisation of Lithuanian terminology, discusses key properties of terms and their requirements, describes term formation principles and methods, and analyses the methods of terminology management. It also reviews the theories by the best-known Lithuanian and foreign terminologists whose influence on Lithuanian terminology has been most pronounced.

With regard to the characteristics of terms, Gaivenis analyses the typology of terms, extension and intension in definitions, grammar, pragmatics, regularity, precision, the systematic aspect, stylistic neutrality, convenience of formation, and more. He attributes the precision of terms to their unambiguity, definiteness of meaning, and motivation and observes that in practice, these properties are not easily achieved and are not uniformly understood in the work of term standardisation. In dealing with motivation, he stresses that "it cannot be said that motivated terms are precise and unmotivated terms are imprecise. Only misleadingly motivated terms should be considered imprecise" (Gaivenis 2002: 39). He argues that the precision of terms is mainly related to their semantics, while the systematic aspect of terms is mostly related to their logical requirements (40). In his detailed analysis of term formation methods, Gaivenis agrees with Šalkauskis' view that "the most important source of terminology [...] is the lexicon of one's own language. Only when we cannot find the right word in it can we create a neologism or borrow a foreign term" (51). Gaivenis offers a thorough analysis of key theoretical aspects of Lithuanian terminology, and the book remains relevant and valuable twenty years after its publication.

In 2016, Palmira Zemlevičiūtė published a comprehensive monograph in which she examined the semantics and expression of the terminological medical lexicon in six manuscripts and in printed bilingual Lithuanian-German and German-Lithuanian 17th and 18th century dictionaries of Lithuania Minor. She also provided a detailed analysis of the meanings, structure, and origin of this lexicon and identified the following peculiarities: Lithuanian-ness (its popular character), polysemy, variation, and synonymy (Zemlevičiūtė 2016: 407–409).

In 2018, seven researchers at the Terminology Centre[8] published linguistic research on terms of informatics and computing that had been used in the Lithuanian language for over thirty years, and assessed the state and changes of this terminology. Their analysis of the borrowed terms in the two fields led to an unexpected conclusion:

> Most of the borrowed terminology of informatics and computer science consists of words derived from Ancient Greek and Latin, with a significant number of words from French and German. Although it is generally accepted that English is the language of computing and informatics, [...] it has been found that purely English borrowed terms were in a minority.   (Auksoriūtė et al. 2018: 401)

---

8. Albina Auksoriūtė, Jolanta Gaivenytė-Butler, Solvita Labanauskienė, Asta Mitkevičienė, Robertas Stunžinas, Alvydas Umbrasas, Palmira Zemlevičiūtė

Terminology research is conducted not only at the Institute of the Lithuanian Language, but also at universities. Six doctoral dissertations in the field of terminology were defended between 2001 and 2020, examining, for example, the contributions of corpus linguistics or presenting comparative studies of medical and legal terms.

It should be noted that there is a shortage of terminologists in Lithuania, not only of those engaged in terminology management, but also in research. More research is needed to identify patterns and trends in the formation and use of terms in various scientific fields, to reveal clear directions in how terminology is being developed, and to elaborate effective terminology management methods. Given the rapid technological development in natural language processing, the application of language technologies to the management of Lithuanian terminology also deserves increased attention. The significant contributions of Lithuanian researchers, in particular Šalkauskis, to terminology theory could form a springboard for more theoretical reflection.

4.2.2   The journal Terminologija

The Terminology Centre of the Institute of the Lithuanian Language prepares and publishes the annual research journal *Terminologija* [*Terminology*]. The first issue of the journal appeared in 1994, its executive editor was Keinys. The editor of the second issue was Gaivenis.

> Stasys Keinys, the first editor of Terminologija, favoured the concept of a half-scientific and half-popular science journal and sought to cover as many practical aspects of terminology as possible.   (Umbrasas 2020: 271)

Later, under Gaivenis's editorship, the journal began to focus more on research. Issues 1–12 of the journal were published only in Lithuanian, and the main sections were established early on. The section Terminology and the Present contained not only articles dealing with the practical issues of Lithuanian terminology at the time, but also some focusing on theoretical issues. In addition to terminologists, specialists in various fields published articles on terminology in physics, computing, radioelectronics, mining, mathematics, and other fields. The second section, The History of Terminology, contained articles on historical manuscripts and printed sources of Lithuanian terminology.

With issue 13, *Terminologija* became an international journal, with an international editorial board and articles published in Lithuanian, English and Russian. It continues to be focused on both theory and practice. It examines theoretical issues, principles and perspectives, best practices in the development and dissemination of terminology in Lithuania and other countries and presents linguistic and terminological resources.

The number of research publications by Lithuanian authors dealing with theoretical issues has not increased since *Terminologija* became an international journal. On the other hand, there has been a slight shift in the approach to some subjects, and new topics addressed that had not yet been analysed by Lithuanian scholars. In one article, Keinys notes that a fresh approach is being considered regarding the *unambiguity* of scientific terms:

> Scientific terms should not be confined to a narrow, mandatory for all framework of universal unambiguity, because terminology regulations are not like army regulations, and scientists are not blind in enforcing them. Were that the case, science would not be a creation [...] we probably do not always realise whether a term is really unambiguous, and especially whether it will have the same and only one meaning after a while. After all, the language of science, and thus its terms, changes with the evolution of science. (Keinys 2013: 53)

In another article, applying the semantic methodology of word phrase analysis, Mitkevičienė investigated the usage of the term *sąvoka* ('concept' in scientific and academic Lithuanian). She observed that in scientific language,

> The terms *sąvoka* and *terminas* are used [...] also as contextual synonyms. The use of the term *terminas* instead of *sąvoka* can be seen as metonymy. Contextual synonymy of terms can be justified only if it does not affect precision and clarity. (Mitkevičienė 2017: 126)

In their articles, foreign authors address more theoretical issues in this journal. Heribert Picht examines the main fields of knowledge covered by terminology as a theoretical and applied scientific discipline and identifies the seven pillars of terminology: knowledge, systematisation, transfer, terminological working methods, terminography, education and training in terminology, localisation and terminology planning. He stresses that "the aim of this overview has been to give an idea of the components in the field of terminology and to make the interdependence between them visible" (Picht 2009: 20). In another article, Picht analyses concepts as reflections of societal changes (2013: 21).

Johan Myking discusses theoretical problems of term formation with respect to both terminology research traditions and recent developments of terminology theory. He maintains that

> Theory development helps to promote a common discourse community, that theory is helpful to practitioners and, consequently, that any answer must take into account that terminology consists of two main aspects: it is a field of research and yet it never escapes the function of practice. (Myking 2020: 28)

By 2020, world-renowned terminologists from eighteen countries had published articles in *Terminologija*, which attests to the journal's global scope and reputation. As of 2020, the journal is also freely available online, where all issues can be found.

5.   Conclusion

The period of independent Lithuania (1918–1940) is of particular importance for Lithuanian terminology for two reasons. First, Lithuanian terminology began to be systematically managed by the first Terminology Commission, which approved and published Lithuanian terms in various fields, most of which became the core terminology of those fields. Also, the Commission established working procedures that persist to this day, whereby sets of terms were prepared by specialists in certain fields and then were discussed with the specialists and linguists. Second, the philosopher Stasys Šalkauskis developed an original theory of terminology, which had a great impact on the development of Lithuanian terminology.

During the Soviet occupation (1940–1990), terminology management in Lithuania was mainly carried out by the Terminology Commission, the Terminology Council, and the Terminology Group of the Institute of the Lithuanian Language and Literature. The characteristic feature of Lithuanian terminography of this period was that both explanatory and translation dictionaries (the dominant type) usually contained Russian equivalents. Research on Lithuanian terminology took a mainly linguistic orientation and was based exclusively on works by scholars from Russia and from other Soviet republics, as Western literature was not accessible at the time.

After the restoration of independence in 1990, the management of Lithuanian terminology intensified with the preparation of dictionaries of terms and the launch, in 2003, of the national Term Bank, the largest and most reliable source of standardised Lithuanian terms freely available on the internet and functioning as a common information system for public institutions. Since 1993, the State Commission of the Lithuanian Language has been overseeing the management of Lithuanian terminology and terminology planning and shaping terminology policy in Lithuania. Over 465 dictionaries of terms and encyclopaedias in a wide range of fields were published between 1990 and 2020, almost half of which are monolingual or multilingual explanatory dictionaries.

After 1990, terminology research was mainly conducted at the Institute of the Lithuanian Language. Since 1994, the institute has been publishing the international scientific journal *Terminologija*. Initially, articles mostly focused on historical research in Lithuanian terminology, but in the last decade more attention has been paid to synchronic research on terminology in various fields.

To summarise, terminology management and research in Lithuania have continuously evolved since the beginning of the 20th century; the theoretical principles of terminology and the ways of managing Lithuanian terminology have already been established.

Acknowledgements

The chapter and all quotations from Lithuanian sources cited were translated into English by Diana Barnard.

References

Auksoriūtė, Albina, Rosita Medišauskienė, Kazimieras Gaivenis, and Stasys Keinys. 1994. "The terminology work of S. Šalkauskis." In *IITF-series 4: International conference on Terminology Science and Terminology Planning: In commemoration of E. Drezen (1892–1938)*. Riga, 17–19 August 1992: 49–54.

Auksoriūtė, Albina. 2016. "Current State of Terminology in Lithuania: Scientific Research, Management and Education." *Acta Baltico-Slavica* 40: 325–339.

Auksoriūtė, Albina, Jolanta Gaivenytė-Butler, Solvita Labanauskienė, Asta Mitkevičienė, Robertas Stunžinas, Alvydas Umbrasas, and Palmira Zemlevičiūtė. 2018. *Lietuviškos informatikos ir kompiuterijos terminijos tyrimai*. Vilnius: Lietuvių kalbos institutas.

Balodė, Laimutė. 1985. "O latyshskoi i litovskoi lingvisticheskoi terminologii (skhodstvo i razlichiia)." *Mokslo kalbos kultūros ir terminologijos problemos. Lietuvių kalbotyros klausimai* 24:11–16.

Danilenko, Valeriya. 1977. *Russkaya terminologiya. Opyt lingvisticheskogo opisaniya*. Maskva: Nauka.

Erelt, Tiiu. 1985. "Motivirovannyi i arbitrarnyi termin v estonskoi terminologii." *Mokslo kalbos kultūros ir terminologijos problemos. Lietuvių kalbotyros klausimai* 24:156–160.

Gaivenis, Kazimieras. 1979. "Bendrieji lietuvių terminijos kūrimo ir norminimo principai." *Lietuvos TSR Mokslų akademijos darbai*. A serija 3 (68): 77–86.

Gaivenis, Kazimieras. 1983. "S. Šalkauskio terminologijos teorija." *Lietuvių kalbos specialioji leksika. Lietuvių kalbotyros klausimai* 22: 128–136.

Gaivenis, Kazimieras. 2002. *Lietuvių terminologija: teorijos ir tvarkybos metmenys*. Vilnius: Lietuvių kalbos instituto leidykla.

International Organization for Standardization. ISO 1087:2019. *Terminology Work and Terminology Science — Vocabulary*. Geneva: ISO.

Jokubaitis, Alvydas, and Linas Jokubaitis. 2020. "Politinė Stasio Šalkauskio kultūros filosofijos prasmė." *Politologija* 4 (100): 8–33.

Kaulakienė, Angelė (tr). 1973. *Terminologijos darbas*. Vilnius: Mintis.

Keinys, Stasys. 1980. *Terminologijos abėcėlė*. Vilnius: Mokslas.

Keinys, Stasys. 1985. "Mokslo ir technikos revoliucija ir lietuvių terminologijos raida." *Mokslo kalbos kultūros ir terminologijos problemos. Lietuvių kalbotyros klausimai* 24: 179–196.

Keinys, Stasys. 1994. "Lietuvos valstybė, tauta ir kalba." *Kalbos normalizacijos klausimai. Lietuvių kalbotyros klausimai* 31: 57–66.

Keinys, Stasys. 2004. "Terminologijos raida, būklė, vaidmuo ir uždaviniai į XXI amžių įžengus." In *Terminologijos istorijos ir dabarties problemos*, ed. by Stasys Keinys, 219–239. Vilnius: Lietuvių kalbos instituto leidykla.

Keinys, Stasys. 2013. "Dėl mokslo terminų vienareikšmiškumo supratimo." *Terminologija* 20: 47–55.

Klimavičius, Jonas. 2003. "Lietuvių terminografija: praeities bruožai, dabarties sunkumai ir uždaviniai." *Terminologija* 10: 9–32.

Mitkevičienė, Asta. 2017. "*Sąvoka* lietuvių mokslo kalboje." *Terminologija* 24: 94–126.

Myking, Johan. 2020. "Term Formation – Is There a State of the Art?" *Terminologija* 27: 6–30.

Parliament of the Republic of Lithuania. 2003. *Republic of Lithuania Law on Term Bank.*

Parliament of the Republic of Lithuania. 2018–2022. *Nutarimas dėl Valstybinės kalbos politikos 2018–2022 metų gairių.*

Picht, Heribert. 2009. "The Seven Pillars of Terminology." *Terminologija* 16: 8–22.

Picht, Heribert. 2013. "Concepts as Reflection of Societal Changes." *Terminologija* 20: 10–23.

Skujiņa, Valentīna. 1985. "O nekotorykh semanticheskikh problemakh nauchnoi terminologii." *Mokslo kalbos kultūros ir terminologijos problemos. Lietuvių kalbotyros klausimai* 24:138–145.

Stašaitis, Stanislovas. 2008. "Istorija Lietuvos mokykloje 1940–1941 metais: tautiškumo naikinimas ir sovietinės ideologijos diegimas." *Istorija. Lietuvos aukštųjų mokyklų mokslo darbai* 2: 39–52.

State Commission of the Lithuanian Language. 2004. *Methodology of the Term Bank of the Republic of Lithuania.*

Superenskaya, Aleksandra, Nataliya Podolskaya, and Nataliya Vasilyeva. 1989. *Obshchiaya terminologiya. Voprosy teorii.* Moskva: Nauka.

Šalkauskis, Stasys. 1925. 1927 I. 1927 II. 1934 I. "Terminologijos teorija ir lietuviškoji filosofijos terminija." *Logos*, 1925: 1–21. 1927 I: 1–32. 1927 II: 171–174. 1934 I: 1–58.

Šalkauskis, Stasys. 1937 II. "Bendroji filosofijos terminija." *Logos*, 1937 II: 113–209.

Šalkauskis, Stasys. 1938. *Bendroji filosofijos terminija.* Kaunas: Spindulys.

Šalkauskis, Stasys. 1986 I. *Rinktiniai raštai I. Filosofinės studijos.* Roma: Lietuvių katalikų mokslo akademija.

Šalkauskis, Stasys. 1991. *Raštai II. Filosofijos ir pedagogikos terminija.* Vilnius: Mintis.

Umbrasas, Alvydas. 2013. "Lietuvos Respublikos terminų bankas: 10 metų po įstatymo priėmimo." *Terminologija* 20: 96–122.

Umbrasas, Alvydas. 2020. "Lietuvių terminologija atkurtosios nepriklausomybės pradžioje." *Terminologija* 27: 258–280.

Vainiutė, Milda. 2010. "Lietuvių kalbos kaip valstybinės konstitucinis statusas: pagrindiniai aspektai." *Jurisprudencija* 4 (122): 25–41.

Wright, Sue Ellen, and Gerhard Budin (eds). 1997. *Handbook of Terminology Management 1: Basic Aspects of Terminology Management.* Amsterdam: John Benjamins.

Zemlevičiūtė, Palmira. 2016. *XVII–XVIII amžiaus Mažosios Lietuvos žodynų terminologinė medicinos leksika.* Vilnius: Lietuvių kalbos institutas.

CHAPTER 17

The evolution of terminology standardisation

Christian Galinski
Infoterm

The need for terminology unification and harmonisation grew significantly after the European Renaissance, and even more so during the industrial revolutions. Formal standardisation of terminologies began around 1900, efforts to standardise the methods of terminology standardisation in the mid-1930s. Today, there are standards for many aspects of terminology science and its manifold applications encompassing terminology theory and methodology, terminological activities and infrastructures, terminology management software and tools, terminological data, etc. After World War II, developments in the area of terminology standardisation accelerated with new facets and in a growing number of domains and subjects. Infoterm played a significant role in these developments with the result that standardisation has probably become the largest field of cooperation in terminology at international, regional, and national levels.

Keywords: unification, harmonisation, standardisation, terminology science, terminological data, terminological principles and methods, terminology work, terminology management, technical standardisation, standards developing organisation (SDO), Infoterm

1. Outline and basic concepts

This chapter provides an overview of the distinct aspects of terminology standardisation throughout history (Section 2), via the relation between technical and terminology standardisation (Section 3), and the harmonisation of the principles and methods of terminology standardisation (Section 4), down to the conclusions (Section 5).[1]

---

1. The preparation of this chapter was facilitated by access to the extensive information and material of the Infoterm Archive, as well as by the author's long-time engagement in collaborative activities in the field of terminology standardisation.

https://doi.org/10.1075/tlrp.24.17gal

Terminology standardisation is defined as "development of *terminological entries* in *terminology standards* and of terminology sections in other standards, and their approval by a *standardizing body*" (ISO 10241–2:2012 — *Terminological entries in standards — Part 2: Adoption of standardized terminological entries*, clause 2.3.1). This refers to, on the one hand, standards documents containing only terminological entries and, on the other, standards on various subjects containing terminological entries to clarify their technical or scientific concepts.

Technical standards today can cover any field of specialised knowledge, each having its specific "terminology" defined as a "set of *designations* and *concepts* belonging to one *domain* or *subject*" (ISO 1087:2019 *Terminology work and terminology science — Vocabulary*, clause 3.1.11). As "*designations* can be a *term* including *appellations*, a *proper name*, or a *symbol*" (ibidem, clause 3.4.1), terminology standardisation today involves the standardisation of terms as well as non-verbal designations, such as formulas, symbols, and coding systems, in a broad range of diverse types of standards documents.

The modern history of terminology standardisation is closely connected with the activities of the Austrian engineer Eugen Wüster (1898~1977), the establishment of technical committee TC 37 — Terminology (Principles and Coordination) of ISO after the Second World War (WWII), and the foundation of the International Information Centre for Terminology (Infoterm) in 1971.

2.   Standardisation from earliest roots till around 1900

According to Wang (2011:5), "historically, technical innovation and standardisation were interweaved together." The same applies to communication conventions in standardisation, starting with informal collaborative unification efforts up to the formal terminology standardisation activities of today.

2.1   Evolution of terminology and roots of terminology standardisation

An early form of terminology standardisation must have already existed more than 5,000 years ago in various parts of the world when large and highly structured societies came into being. Only after writing systems emerged with pictographic and proto-cuneiform characters about 5,600 years ago, do we have concrete evidence about how major languages and early terminology evolved (Galinski 2021).

Early Greek philosophers (flourishing in the Hellenistic period 323~246 BCE), in connection with their reflections on nature, the universe, and human language, were striving to clarify the meanings of words used for describing the objects of their intellectual interest. This could be seen as early ancient theoretical reflections about terminology. Chapter 1 describes major aspects of the impact of the Greek intellectual legacy on Latin from Roman times till today.

In Europe, early Greek philosophical literature — although translated into Latin — was mostly lost or forbidden for several centuries after the collapse of the Roman empire (Kintzinger 2003). Only a fraction of this literature was re-introduced — primarily via Arabic translations — in Western Europe with a profound impact on Europe's Renaissance period (15th~16th c.) (see also Chapter 2). It laid the basis for scientific and technological development over the next centuries, leading up to the first industrial revolution in Europe (1760~1820/1840) (Freely 2009, see also Chapter 3).

The development of scientific languages in the modern age started without established rules and principles in the 18th and 19th centuries.

> The consequence was chaos in the concept systems of almost all scientific disciplines at the dawn of the modern era. [...] In all subject fields, the natural systems of concepts start to proliferate with an unordered multitude of terms which can be reduced only later.   (Oeser 1994: 24–25)

As this situation was hampering scientific and technical development, experts started international cooperation to harmonise theoretical and methodological approaches. Some efforts were also geared towards terminology unification in various fields of science (supported by the emerging media as well as advances in printing technology, postal services, and later telecommunication) for instance in scientific nomenclatures and taxonomies, including the *Systema Naturae* (1735) and *Species Plantarum* (1753) of Carl Linnaeus (1707~1778) (Galinski 2021). However, rapidly evolving industrialisation in Europe needed harmonisation approaches going beyond these unification efforts in the sciences. Chapter 7 covers this need for unification under a broad perspective.

2.2 Terminology unification, standardisation, and harmonisation till 1945

Towards the end of the 19th century, industrialists like the English iron and steel dealer Harry J. Skelton complained — as reported by Wang (2011: 8) — about differences in (informal) standards between companies making trade increasingly difficult and strained:

> Architects and engineers generally specify such unnecessarily diverse types of sectional material or given work that anything like economical and continuous manufacture becomes impossible. In this country no two professional men are agreed upon the size and weight of a girder to employ for given work.

Thus, the Engineering Standards Committee was established in London in 1901 as the world's first national standardising body and predecessor of the British Standards Institution (BSI).

In several fields, terminology unification efforts took place, some of which resulted in or were later coordinated with standardisation activities, such as (Galinski 2020):

- In 1865, the International Telegraph Union (today: International Telecommunication Union, ITU) was created as the first organisation to set international standards in order to connect national telegraph networks.
- In 1875, the International Bureau of Weights and Measures (BIPM) was created in Paris.
- Discussions starting at the first International Electrical Congress in Paris in 1881 were continued at subsequent Congresses and led to the inaugural meeting on 26 June 1906 of the International Electrotechnical Commission (IEC), which started terminology standardisation efforts in 1908.
- In 1892, an international conference in the field of inorganic chemistry was convened, from which proposals for standardisation arose, finally resulting in the establishment of the International Union of Pure and Applied Chemistry in 1919 (IUPAC).
- In 1926, the International Federation of the National Standardizing Associations (ISA) was founded primarily focused on mechanical engineering. It was suspended in 1942 during World War II.

3.   Technical standardisation and terminology standardisation after 1945

After 1945, two (formal) SDOs continued or resumed their technical standardisation activities including the preparation of standardised terminological entries:

- ITU with its Telecommunication Standardisation Sector developed ITU-T Recommendations most of which include standardised terminological entries.
- IEC with its terminology committee: IEC/TC 1.

ISO joined IEC and ITU as the successor of ISA, when soon after the war, the newly formed United Nations Standards Coordinating Committee (UNSCC) approached ISA with a proposal to form a new global standards organisation. In 1946, delegates from 25 countries agreed on the establishment of ISO, which officially began operations in 1947.

ISO/TC 37 was one of ISO's first technical committees (French 1985). Contrary to other TCs, which standardise terminologies (or vocabularies) in their specific domains, ISO/TC 37 was assigned to develop methodological standards for terminology standardisation — in continuation of the pioneering work of ISA/TC 37 before the war (see Section 4.1).

With the intensification of terminology standardisation activities after 1945, the need for harmonised rules and procedures became urgent. Similar to the period between the wars, SDOs were faced with different approaches to terminology unification, while there was still a lack of a coherent theoretical basis to be applied to terminology standardisation. In addition, it was recognised that terminologies and related documentation languages, such as classification systems and documentation thesauri, are important for the management of standardisation activities, the production and archiving of standards documents, and for the exchange of bibliographic information on standards. Later, the introduction of computers and software was seen as a potential solution to existing problems, but it also led to new requirements.

Wüster's work in the 1950s to take stock of practical and theoretical approaches (and to test their results in practical terminology work) corresponded with the need for more information on standards at that time. Gradually it became understood that standards information as well as information and documentation (I&D) in terminology standardisation are closely related. Standards information refers to information *on* standards documents but it reveals only rudimentary information about their content. Wüster's stocktaking (Wüster 1955, 1959; later continued by Infoterm; see Krommer-Benz 1977, 1985, and Felber et al. 1979) turned out to be extremely laborious, comprising, amongst others, aspects of librarianship, I&D, classification studies, and the emerging computer science. However, as a result of the dissemination of the above information, the 1980s and 1990s became a period of intense cooperation and cross-fertilisation between the fields of terminology and I&D (Galinski 2019). For example, scholars of I&D and classification studies such as I. Dahlberg (1992) also distinguished themselves in terminology theory. Efforts from various sides contributed to the harmonisation of principles and methods of terminology standardisation in ISO/TC 37, on the one hand, and to the development of terminology science, on the other (see Section 4.1).

The above-mentioned stocktaking was considerably supported by UNESCO with the aim to foster the development of methodology standards in ISO/TC 37 and ISO/TC 46 — Information and Documentation, which were considered as closely related, if not complementary at that time. In the meantime, three European standards organisations (ESO) were established to develop European standards (EN) complying with the needs of the European Union (EU):

- The European Committee for Standardisation (CEN),[2] founded in 1961, develops European Standards (EN) in various sectors with the aim to support the emergence of a European internal market (also referred to as the single market) for goods and services (European Commission 2014). It closely cooperates with ISO based on formal agreements.
- The European Committee for Electrotechnical Standardisation (CENELEC), founded in 1973, develops ENs in the fields of electrical engineering. It closely cooperates with IEC based on formal agreements.
- The European Telecommunications Standards Institute (ETSI), established in 1988, supports the development and testing of ENs for ICT-enabled systems, applications, and services. It closely cooperates with ITU as well as IEC and ISO based on formal agreements.

As the standards of the ESOs are recognised by ITU, IEC and ISO as international standards, the ESOs too are considered international "formal" SDOs issuing de-jure standards. Hence, this acknowledgment also applies to the standardised terminological entries contained in their standards. Moreover, the above-mentioned agreements between ISO, IEC, and ITU, on the one hand, and the ESOs, on the other hand, provided the basis for gradually intensified cooperation, also covering the use of major management instruments like the (partially adopted) ISO/IEC Directives and the (fully adopted) International Classification of Standards (ICS), as well as the coordinated use of the ICT system to organise and manage standardisation activities. This cooperation also includes the application of the rules for terminology standardisation based on ISO/TC 37 standards and led to discussions about developing joint systems for the standardised terminology of the international "formal" SDOs, and possibly also including the data categories necessary for documenting standardised terminologies in a joint standardised metadata registry. These discussions and concomitant harmonisation efforts refer to:

- IEC's standardised terminologies of the International Electrotechnical Vocabulary (IEV) continuously developed today by 124 TCs and many subcommittees (SC) plus more than 10 other kinds of committees — and especially its IEC/TC 1 — Terminology
- ISO's standardised terminologies accessible online at the Online Browsing Platform (OBP) which comprises most of the standardised terminological entries developed by about 700 TCs or SCs.

Some of the above-mentioned terminologies are included in so-called terminology standards (or vocabulary standards), which sometimes comprise thousands

---

2. Here and elsewhere, the letter N refers to words for "standards" that start with N (e.g. *norme* and *normalisation*) in French and some other European languages.

of standardised terminological entries. However, most of the standardised terminological entries are produced as part of technical standards (see Section 1).

Thus, a global standardisation ecosystem emerged, in which terminology
standardisation increasingly plays an essential role.

4.   Harmonisation of principles and methods for terminology standardisation

Starting around 1900, several approaches for dealing with terminological information emerged. In the decades after WW II, Wüster's (1970: 11) statement that "[s]ub-
ject standardisation requires language standardisation" [Sachnormung erfordert
Sprachnormung] (in fact largely referring to terminology standardisation) proved
its relevance in practice. Increasingly, it was recognised that well-prepared standardised terminological entries enhance the quality of the respective technical standard, while standardised terminologies based on harmonised principles and
methods are equally indispensable. Wüster (1974) endeavoured to establish a comprehensive general theory of terminology as "border field between linguistics, logic,
ontology, information science and the subject fields" aiming at a solid scientific
foundation for terminology standardisation. Thus, the idea of the General Theory
of Terminology was born.

Oeser (1994) emphasised that terminology is one of the indispensable fundamentals of all sciences, as it is a major aspect of epistemology and logic:

> A short glance at the history of science tells us: wherever special terminologies
> developed in scientific disciplines such as physics, botany, zoology, etc., they are
> based on classical conceptual logic. [...] Prescriptive or normative terminology
> work thus becomes applied logic.   (Oeser 1994: 25–26)

Under this perspective, terminology science is closely related to the philosophy
of science, as that developed by the Vienna Circle in the 1920s and 1930s (Oeser
1998: 113). But most scholars reflecting on scientific and technical terminology in
the first half of the 20th century were far from considering the emerging need for
prescriptive approaches in terminology standardisation. In Chapter 8, Trojar provides a nuanced account of Wüster's pioneering ideas in various areas of contemporary science theory and beyond, duly assessing their impact on both scientific
theories and technical practices to the present day.

4.1 Pioneers of standardised terminological principles and methods before 1945

While applied linguistic and lexicographical approaches for publishing specialised dictionaries and the like were already thriving in the private sector in the 19th century, the SDOs that emerged after 1900 took a different direction. Between the two wars, terminology standards had already appeared in an increasing number of TCs at national and international levels. Thus, the question arose: which methodological approach should be taken for terminology standardisation and the publication of standardised terminologies? After WW II, the efficiency of terminology standardisation became a strategic methodology issue and standardising organisations again were confronted with the same question.

In this context, two people had a significant influence on the development of standardised terminological principles and methods: Eugen Wüster (1898~1977) and Alfred Schlomann (1878~1952). Wüster's starting point was conceptual logic. "For the Vienna Circle science was a propositional system, for Wüster a concept system." (Oeser 1998:113). The reactions of Wüster and Wittgenstein[3] to the basic positions of the Vienna Circle were similar insofar as both applied "language criticism." While Wittgenstein focused on criticism of general language, Wüster directed his criticism to special language. Wüster referred to the logician Freytag-Löringhoff (1955), who, according to Oeser (1994:30), "proved, more consistently than other defendants of classical logic, that conceptual logic contains formalized propositional logic as a special case." Wüster tried to understand the philosophical dimensions of terminology first, while Schlomann just tried to conceive a better design for collecting and managing terminological data in the form of a collaborative endeavour.

In 1899, the Association of German Engineers (VDI) embarked on the ambitious project to collect all technical terminology existing in the German language — estimated around 4,000,000 entries — in the *VDI-Technolexikon* (Wesolowski 2010:192). The association decided to follow the semasiological approach in contemporary mainstream linguistics (or lexicology), starting data collection with technical terms and recording their different meanings. In 1907, the first results were evaluated, leading to the conclusion that it would take another 40 years to complete this compilation if continued with an alphabetical ordering method characteristic of lexicography. But there was a theoretical and methodological alternative and Schlomann was given the chance to prove the practicality of his approach.

---

3. Ludwig Josef Johann Wittgenstein (1989~1951): Austrian-British philosopher famous for his philosophical contributions to logic, mathematics, language, and the mind.

Towards the end of the 19th century the onomasiological approach had emerged in linguistics, prominently in Romance language studies. "Onomasiology [...] received its name in 1902, when the Austrian linguist Adolf Zauner published his study on body-part terminology in Romance languages" (Grzega and Schöner 2007: 8). It was Schlomann (Lowe and Wright 2006), an engineer like Wüster, who adopted the onomasiological approach and developed a systematic and semi-structured method that involved the recording of the terminological entries by concepts, each represented by different terms, and ordering them according to their conceptual relations. With the discovery that Schlomann's method was more efficient than traditional alphabetical lexicographical methods (Felber and Budin 1989: 140), work on the VDI-Technolexikon was suspended. Between 1907 and 1932 Schlomann published 17 *Illustrierte Technische Wörterbücher* [Illustrated Technical Dictionaries] in six languages in different subject fields. Work was conducted with broad international cooperation based on guidelines devised by Schlomann (Felber and Budin 1989: 141). Wüster was obviously influenced by Schlomann, whom he frequently mentioned in his fundamental study *International standardisation of language in the field of electrical engineering* (Wüster 1931 and later editions).

Judging from his aforementioned study (actually Wüster's doctoral dissertation), his private book collection, and his correspondence, Wüster was highly knowledgeable in various fields of philosophy and linguistics, especially the branches of Austrian Philosophy dating from 1862 to 1930 (Budin 2016: 15). However, unlike traditional academic scholars, he was also a practitioner in lexicography, especially Esperanto lexicography, before he focused his efforts on terminology research and related fields like I&D and classification studies (Felber et al., 1979). Thus, the field of terminology, with its concept-orientation as distinct from lexicology, started to emerge in the first decades of the 20th century. Like the VDI, the IEC had started work on terminology in 1908 with a lexicographical approach but switched to a structured conceptual approach in 1927. In 1938, the IEC published the first edition of IEC's *International Electrotechnical Vocabulary (IEV)*, containing standardised terminological entries (Felber and Budin 1989: 140). Being a renowned Esperantist, Wüster contributed a considerable number of equivalents in Esperanto to this edition (Blanke 2003; see also Chapters 7 and 8). Therefore, it can be inferred that Wüster knew about the IEC rules for the preparation and layout of the terminological entries in the IEV.

In 1936, triggered by the 1931 publication of Wüster's dissertation, the International Federation of the National Standardizing Associations (ISA) established ISA/TC 37 — Terminology, to formulate general principles and rules for terminology standardisation. This committee planned four classes of future recommendations: (1) Naming principles, (2) International harmonisation of terms,

(3) Monolingual vocabularies, (4) Multilingual vocabularies. ISA's Secretariat was held by Germany, which shared the committee management with Wüster heading the Austrian sub-secretariat for international technical terms (Felber et al. 1979: 62).

4.2   The emergence of international standards on terminology methodology

The following sections summarise the development of standardised principles and methods at international levels which is closely related to the history of ISO/TC 37 and Infoterm. After 1970, the development phases largely coincide with the respective decades.

4.2.1   Foundation phases of ISO/TC 37 (after 1951) and infoterm (after 1971)

Work in ISA/TC 37, interrupted by World War II, was resumed in the framework of one of ISO's first technical committees, namely ISO/TC 37. In 1951, Wüster (with great efforts involving international organisations) intervened to prevent ISO/TC 37 from being disbanded due to inactivity. The committee became operational in 1952 and continued with an adapted ISA scheme of planned recommendations (ISO/R). Work in ISO/TC 37 advanced very slowly, but still focused on standards for terminology work in general under four categories adapted from pre-war ISA/TC 37: (1) Vocabulary of terminology, (2) Procedure for preparing national or international standardised vocabularies, (3) National and international standardisation of concepts, terms, and their definitions: principles for their establishment and criteria of value, (4) Layout of monolingual and multilingual vocabularies, including lexicographical symbols (French 1985: 249).

In parallel, Wüster undertook the preparation of his celebrated classified dictionary, *The Machine Tool*, under the auspices of the UNECE in a systematic and highly collaborative way. The dictionary entries were "classified" in Wüster's (1971) terms by concept classification as well as theme classification. In the published book Wüster (1968) meticulously documented the approach followed, even recording the hours spent by individual experts and helpers involved.

In 1969, ISO decided to start a collection of international standardised terms in classified order, namely the *ISO Technical Vocabulary (ITC)*. However, the project did not proceed due to the enormous human resources required and the lack of sufficiently detailed standardised principles and methods for terminology standardisation using the aforementioned classified approach (Wüster and Infoterm 1974: 12). Nonetheless, *The Machine Tool* did serve as a proof of concept for the future development of a concept-based terminology standardisation methodology.

Until 1971, Wüster managed the committee at his private terminology centre in Wieselburg (Lower Austria) on behalf of the Austrian Standards Institute (then called ON). When Infoterm was established in 1971, Helmut Felber became the first Director of Infoterm and took over Wüster's operational role in ISO/TC 37 by becoming the secretary of the committee. As did Wüster before him, Felber cooperated with the ISO Central Secretariat (ISO/CS), for instance in contributing to the early versions of the *Directives for the technical work of ISO* as well as to the *ISO Guide 2:1983 General terms and their definitions concerning standardisation, certification and testing laboratories* (4th edition). The section on terminology in the early Directives began with the statement:

> Terminology may appear as an independent vocabulary standard or as part of a standard dealing also with other aspects. When preparing terminology standards, the principles and methods related thereto as established by ISO/TC 37 shall be followed whenever applicable.   (French 1985: 251)

French (1985: 255), then Secretary of INFCO/ISONET,[4] concludes: "ISO/TC 37 has established the basis for terminological activities within ISO. This work can easily be under-estimated and insufficiently recognized since it is spread across the whole of the technical structure of ISO and so not immediately obvious."

Although Infoterm was entrusted with the secretariat of ISO/TC 37, Wüster remained the spiritus rector of developments in ISO/TC 37 and beyond in several fields related to terminology until his death in 1977. Being an avid reader and devoted lecturer as an honorary professor at Vienna University, Wüster continued working on ISO/TC 37 documents, also using them for the preparation of teaching material. Felber edited this material, which was published posthumously as Wüster's renowned *Introduction to the General Theory of Terminology and Terminological Lexicography* (Wüster 1979). Financed by the Austrian government and substantially supported by UNESCO, Infoterm continued Wüster's efforts.

It took more than 15 years before ISO/TC 37 finalised five ISO recommendations and one ISO standard. ISO/R 704:1968 became ISO 704:1987 *Principles and methods of terminology*, and the above-mentioned ISO/R 919 and ISO/R 1149 as well as ISO/DP 4466 *Layout of multilingual vocabularies* were discontinued by the committee and much later replaced by ISO 10241:1992. Also worthy of mention is ISO 6156:1987 *Magnetic tape exchange format for terminological / lexicographical records (MATER)*. Though soon after it was published it became outdated in terms of the technical state of the art, due to rapid developments in modern markup formats (SGML, XML), this standard was necessary for the existing large-scale terminology databases. It was the product of ISO/TC 37/WG 5 — Computer-assisted Terminology and Lexicography, which was established in 1974 to develop standards concerning the computerisation of terminological data (Galinski 2009; Felber et al. 1979).

---

4. ISO Information Network developed by the Information Committee of ISO.

4.2.2   *Consolidation phase of ISO/TC 37 and infoterm in the 1980s*

Terminology standardisation increasingly became an attractive topic, not least due to the international Terminology Summer School (TSS) organised by Infoterm in 1982 (and thereafter annually), the publication of Felber's (1984) *Terminology Manual*, and various projects undertaken for UNESCO and European institutions. The number of experts delegated from national SDOs to participate in ISO/TC 37 activities increased — and the evolving language, translation, localisation, and interpreting industries gradually became interested. This necessitated a restructuring of ISO/TC 37. So far, only one subcommittee existed, namely ISO/TC 37/SC 1, which was established in 1980.

ISO/TC 37/SC 2 was founded in 1983 to develop standards related to terminography and lexicography. After several modifications, today its scope reads: "Standardisation of terminological methods and applications for languages and linguistic content." One of its most important achievements is the development of the ISO 639 series[5] about language codes, which nowadays are used in almost every ICT application in the world. SC 3 was established in 1985 to develop standards concerning computerised terminography and other computer applications for terminology and related language resources. After some modifications, today its scope reads: "Standardisation of the specification, design and interoperability of terminology resources."

Towards the end of the 1980s, terminology started to become a topic of strategic interest, especially in Europe, where machine translation and multilingualism were high on the political agenda. This allowed Infoterm to establish the Association for Terminology and Knowledge Transfer (GTW) and to organise the first international conference on Terminology and Knowledge Engineering (TKE) in cooperation with the European Commission in 1987. In 1988, the International Network for Terminology (TermNet) was founded with the support of UNESCO, followed by the founding of the International Institute for Terminology Research (IITF) in 1989. Both GTW and IITF were engaged in activities related to terminology standardisation.

This period is characterised by a gradual shift of focus towards practical professional applications and computer applications. This shift of focus unexpectedly triggered work on new standards regulating principles and methods. Both of these areas of interest also became attractive outside Europe, such as in Japan, China, South Africa, and Latin America. Taking the opportunity, Infoterm initiated or participated in the foundation of several national or regional terminology associations and networks during the 1980s, thus also enlarging the membership of ISO/

---

5. Today: *Code for individual languages and language groups.* ISO 639:2023.

TC 37. Not least, due to its first annual meeting week outside of Europe, namely in Tunis in 1989, ISO/TC 37 became more aware of the need to take into consideration a broader range of linguistic and cultural traditions in its standards. At its plenary meeting in Tunis, ISO/TC 37 embarked on a major revision of its operational structure. The SCs were restructured in line with the new ISO/TC 37 *Strategic Policy Statement* (its first *Business Plan*) of 1988. This reform also led to a new working mode with well-defined responsibilities of working group convenors and project leaders. New working items clearly indicated a shift towards application-oriented approaches. Furthermore, after 1989, it became regular practice to hold these meetings alternatingly one year in Europe, and the other outside of Europe. This fostered the development of terminological activities and the establishment of national terminology associations or networks.

The above-mentioned development and activities offered ideal opportunities for recruiting new experts for standardisation in ISO/TC 37 — often through liaisons and cooperation activities with other technical committees of international as well as national SDOs. The success of these activities led to an extension phase for both Infoterm and ISO/TC 37, which did not remain unnoticed at ISO/CS.

4.2.3 *ISO/TC 37 and Infoterm in the 1990s: A new atmosphere of change*

Over the years, the number of SDOs requesting principles, rules, and guidelines for terminology standardisation had increased. In the 1960s, the British Standards Institution (BSI) had published BS 3669:1963 *Recommendations for the selection, formation, and definition of technical terms*. In 1981, the DIN technical committee "Machinery" developed a manual for the preparation and layout of terminology standards, *Regelheft für die Ausarbeitung und Gestaltung von Terminologienormen*. Individual TCs at international and national levels started to develop their own rules for the elaboration of terminology standards. Recognising the pressure, Infoterm submitted a *Draft ISO Guide: Layout of terminology standards* to ISO/CS for consideration in 1983.

Given the imminent development of parallel — potentially conflicting — rules and guidelines for terminology standardisation, Michael Leaman, then Director of Methodology and Editing of ISO/CS, concurred with Infoterm, represented by Christian Galinski, about the urgency of harmonised ISO rules concerning terminology standardisation. Consequently, Infoterm organised an ad hoc group that, in close collaboration with Leaman, started to devise normative rules for terminology standardisation from ISO 704:1987 and examples of standardised terminological entries selected from ISO standards. Given the urgency, the emerging standard was fast-tracked through the voting process and published as international standard 10241:1992 *International terminology standards — Preparation and layout*. The publication triggered the revision of ISO 704:1987 which finally resulted in the second edition in 2000 *Terminology work — Principles and methods*.

At European and international levels an atmosphere of change set in with shifts in policy discourse from the "information society" to "knowledge societies" with new foci including multilingualism and digital content that favoured standardisation in the ICTs as well as their manifold applications. Infoterm succeeded in rallying support for raising awareness about the importance of methodology standards and, in particular, terminology standardisation.

At the European level, Infoterm assisted government institutions during the planning and implementation of the *Multilingual Action Plan* (MLAP) and *Multilingual Information Society* (MLIS) up to the eContent Programmes, which paralleled the EU's Framework Programmes FP 4 (1944–1998) and FP 5 (1998–2002). Since that time, most EU projects must duly consider multilingualism, terminology, and standardisation aspects. Infoterm regularly informed ISO/TC 37 experts about these developments, some of whom became directly involved, which further stimulated standardisation activities in ISO/TC 37 and beyond.

At the international level, interest in terminology and related standardisation activities increased, for instance, in the organisations of the UN system in connection with major policy discussions. In collaboration with ISO/TC 37 experts, Infoterm endeavoured to firmly integrate the topics of terminology and methodology standardisation into multilingualism, ICT-related and other policies in the 1990s. This was in line with UNESCO policy, but also took into account existing large-scale multilingual terminology databases, for example in Canada (TERMIUM, see Chapter 12) and the European Commission (EURODICAUTOM, now IATE, see Chapter 20), whose hosts were closely monitoring the standardisation activities of ISO/TC 37. Organisations like the OECD, UNESCO, WHO, FAO, and others of the UN system started to modernise their approaches concerning terminological data and to upgrade their applications for several purposes, including data exchange and cooperation.

Awareness about the value of methodology standards in terminology standardisation was growing. Gradually, international organisations joined ISO/TC 37 activities as international liaisons, some of them even getting actively involved in the development of standards. The establishment in 1993 of the International Collaborating Centre for Terminology of the World Health Organization (WHO) opened new horizons for TC 37. At the same time, Infoterm encouraged terminology stakeholders to develop infrastructure and start projects in support of ISO/TC 37 standardisation activities, which led to the establishment of:

- China Terminology Network (China TermNet) in 1993
- European Language Resources Association (ELRA) in 1994
- Council for German-Language Terminology (RaDT) in 1994
- European Association for Terminology (EAFT) in 1996

- East Asia Forum on Terminology (EAFTerm) in 1997
- German Terminology Information and Documentation Centre (DEUTERM) in 2000.

When Infoterm became an independent international scientific association in 1996, it reorganised its promotion and publication strategy, which also greatly helped to promote ISO/TC 37 activities and terminology standardisation in general. A great variety of articles and books were published, most of them at least mentioning terminology standardisation. In addition to regular reports on ISO/TC 37 in *TermNet News* and *Infoterm Newsletters*, the periodicals *Terminology Standardization and Harmonization* (TSH) and *StandardTerm* (STT) regularly published information about terminology standardisation.

After initiating the EU project Proposals for an Operational Infrastructure for Terminology in Europe (POINTER) in close cooperation with TermNet within the MLAP framework, Infoterm organised the EU project European Network of Terminology Information and Documentation Centres (TDCnet) in the MLIS framework in 1998 (Schmitz 2002). The activities of the project consortium in terms of the preparation of deliverables, organisation of conferences and workshops, promotion of terminology and its manifold applications, etc., were ideal for promoting ISO/TC 37 standards and recruiting new experts for ISO/TC 37 activities.

The revised ISO/TC 37 *Business Plan* for 2001/2002 reflects the progress made with eight published international standards and twelve additional standardisation projects in progress. Thus, the activities in the 1990s paved the way for new dynamics in the new millennium.

4.2.4 *Further progress after 2000*

Not least due to the TDCnet project activities and the close cooperation with ELRA, the new ISO/TC 37/SC 4 — Language Resource Management was established in 2002, involving many experts from the fields of language technologies. Consequently, the title of ISO/TC 37 was adapted to Terminology and Other Language and Content Resources.

While ISO/TC 37/SC 1 was still working on the 3rd edition of ISO 704 *Terminology work — Principles and methods*, ISO 10241:1992 was revised to become the two-part ISO 10241–1:2011 *Terminological entries in standards — Part 1: General requirements and examples of presentation* and ISO 10241–2:2012 *Terminological entries in standards — Part 2: Adoption of standardized terminological entries*. Thanks to these and other standards, ISO/TC 37 gradually strengthened its recognition as one of the nine ISO TCs working on horizontal standards, meaning that their standards are adopted by other ISO TCs.

UNESCO encouraged Infoterm and ISO/TC 37 activities, e.g., by mentioning "terminology" and "methodology standards" in the *Recommendation concerning the Promotion and Use of Multilingualism and Universal Access to Cyberspace* in 2003 or by publishing the *Guidelines for terminology policies — Formulating and implementing terminology policy in language communities* (Infoterm 2005), on which the ISO/TC 37 standard ISO 29383:2010 — *Terminology policies — Development and implementation international* is based.

In 2005, ISO/TC 37 decided to establish a new SC 5 — Translation and Interpreting and Related Technology (transforming ISO/TC 37/SC 2/WG 6 — Translation and Interpretation Services into an SC of its own). This prompted ISO/TC 37 to change its title to Language and Terminology and to define its scope as "Standardisation of descriptions, resources, technologies and services related to terminology, translation, interpreting and other language-based activities in the multilingual information society" in 2017.

When Infoterm passed on the management of the ISO/TC 37 secretariat to China in 2009, it continued to support ISO/TC 37 by coordinating activities with other committees in ISO, IEC, and the ESOs, external liaison organisations, and EU project consortia. Thus, ISO/TC 37 became aware of the need to consider aspects of eAccessibility and eInclusion and included such aspects in standards related to interpreting technology, controlled language, language varieties, sign languages, plain language, etc. Based on a handful of interconnected CEN Workshop Agreements (CWA) of the CEN/WS "Multilingual eCataloguing and eClassification in eBusiness," ISO/TC 37/SC 3 embarked on developing ISO 22274:2013 *Systems to manage terminology, knowledge and content — Concept-related aspects for developing and internationalizing classification systems.* Following a request from the EU-project OASIS,[6] work on ISO 17347 *Ontology Integration and Interoperability (OntoIOp) — Part 1: The Distributed Ontology Language (DOL)* started in ISO/TC 37/SC 3 in 2016. The international Object Management Group (OMG) took over the respective working group from ISO and in 2018 released the document as *Distributed Ontology, Model, and Specification Language Version 1.0.*

The developments after 2000 indicate a major shift of standardisation topics in ISO/TC 37 towards applications of terminological approaches or data in other fields in collaboration with international liaisons and other standardising committees. By 2020, ISO/TC 37 had developed more than 60 international standards. Despite the annual meetings taking place online from 2020 to 2022 due to the world-wide COVID-pandemic, ISO/TC 37 continued its successful development. At the hybrid onsite and online annual meeting in Brussels in June 2023, proposals for standardisation activities in new application fields were discussed. By the end of 2023, 80 standards had been published, and 33 standards documents were under development.

---

6. OASIS — Open Architecture for Accessible Services Integration and Standardisation.

5.   Conclusions and outlook

This chapter has outlined the history of terminology standardisation in its broad sense as well as that of ISO/TC 37 and Infoterm and their impact on terminology science. When the need for the standardisation of terminologies arose around 1900 in the emerging field of technical and industrial standardisation, examples of practical concept-oriented terminology unification existed, for instance, in the form of the evolving scientific nomenclatures (see Section 2.2). There also existed early concept-oriented (onomasiological) theoretical approaches in branches of philosophy, linguistics, and lexicology towards the end of the 19th century. But these examples were not thought about in early terminology standardisation.

Two engineers, namely Eugen Wüster (1898~1977) and Alfred Schlomann (1878~1952), had a significant impact on the evolution of modern terminology standardisation both in terms of practical approaches as well as the development of an appropriate theory and methodology. Schlomann proved the practicability of the concept-oriented approach by organising with international collaboration the preparation of the 17 *Illustrated Technical Dictionaries* in six languages based on guidelines as a rudimentary form of scientific methodology between 1907 and 1932.

Wüster began as a scholar and practitioner of Esperanto lexicography before he committed himself to terminology in all its facets (see 4.2). His substantial impact on terminology standardisation and on the field of terminology at large began with his role in ISO/TC 37 after the committee's revitalisation in 1951 in cooperation with UNESCO. While he continued lexicographical work in Esperanto, he started to organise through international collaboration: (a) collecting information on existing specialised dictionaries and vocabularies for UNESCO; (b) compiling the data for his *Machine Tool* dictionary; and (c) drafting the scientific foundations for a comprehensive theory of terminology in ISO/TC 37.

The SCs 2, 3, 4, and 5 established in ISO/TC 37 from 1983 to 2005 developed many new standards on terminology principles and methods for standardisation purposes, as well as for various applications such as language services, language resource management, and natural language processing. ISO/TC 37 standards became extensively referred to in the ISO/IEC Directives and many vocabulary standards of various TCs.

The prescriptive terminology approach of ISO/TC 37 was also adopted by organisations and industry beyond the field of standardisation. As standardisation became increasingly formalised especially at the international level, terminology standardisation became integrated into the standardisation system, and terminology approaches — from theory to methodology — had to be standardised, too. The concept-oriented, i.e., language-independent, and thus multilingual, approach of ISO/TC 37, as well as its emphasis on cooperative work, have become widely acknowledged, especially in regulatory environments. Concomitant with the cooperation among SDOs, the collaboration network of ISO/TC 37 grew. Thus, ISO/TC 37 standards are an integral part of the Global Standardisation Ecosystem, which Conte (2019) aptly illustrated in Figure 1:

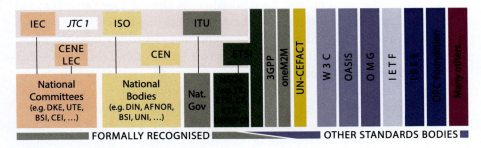

Figure 1. The Standardisation Ecosystem

The quantity of standardised, harmonised, or unified terminologies has grown exponentially over the last 50 years, not least due to new subjects, committees, and SDOs that emerged in the field of standardisation. The terminology approach, as developed and matured for standardisation purposes, has become acknowledged as one of the main methodological approaches in the field of terminology.

References

Blanke, Detlev. 2003. "Terminologiewissenschaft und Plansprachen." *Interlinguistische Informationen. Beiheft* 10: 9–24.

Budin, Gerhard. 2016. "Der Beitrag der österreichischen Philosophie zur Entwicklung der Theorie der Terminologie." *edition* 2: 5–16.

Conte, Antonio. 2019. "EU Standardisation Policy." *ETSI Technology Awareness Roadshow for SMEs. Turin, July* 4, 2019. PowerPoint presentation.

Dahlberg, Ingetraut. 1992. "Knowledge Organization and Terminology: Philosophical and Linguistic Bases." *International Classification* 19-2: 65–71

European Commission, Directorate-General for Communication. 2014. *Internal Market — From Crisis to Opportunity — Putting Citizens and Companies on the Path to Prosperity.* Publications Office.

Felber, Hemut, Friedrich Lang, and Gernot Wersig (eds.) 1979. *Terminologie als angewandte Sprachwissenschaft. Gedenkschrift für Univ.-Prof. Dr. Eugen Wüster.* München: K.G. Saur.

Felber, Helmut, Magdalena Krommer-Benz, and Adrian Manu (eds.) 1979. *International Bibliography of Standardized Vocabularies / Bibliographie de Vocabulaires normalisés / Bibliographie der Normwörterbücher.* Infoterm series, 2 [4. München: K.G. Saur.

Felber, Helmut. 1984. *Terminology Manual*. Vienna: Infoterm.

Felber, Helmut, and Gerhard Budin. 1989. *Terminologie in Theorie und Praxis*. Tübingen: Gunter Narr Verlag.

Freely, John. 2009. *Aladdin's Lamp: How Greek Science came to Europe through the Islamic World*. New York: Vintage Books.

French, E. J. 1985. "Terminological Activities in ISO and their Wider Significance." In *Terminologie und benachbarte Gebiete / Terminology and Related Fields / Terminologie et Disciplines connexes*, 247–258. Wien: Infoterm.

Galinski, Christian. 2009. "History of ISO/TC 37 and Infoterm." *edition* 2: 19–23.

Galinski, Christian. 2019. "Blütezeit der Zusammenarbeit zwischen Terminologie einerseits und Information und Dokumentation (IuD) andererseits: 1980–2000." In *Terminologie: Epochen, Schwerpunkte, Umsetzungen. Zum 25-jährigen Bestehen des Rats für Deutschsprachige Terminologie*, ed by Petra Drewer and Donatella Pulitano, 21–43. Berlin: Springer Vieweg.

Galinski, Christian. 2020. "The Emergence of Terminology Science and Terminological Activities." In *Actes de la conférence TOTh 2019*, ed. by Christoph Roche, 25–33. Charenton-le-Pont Cedex: Le Comptoir des presses d'universités.

Galinski, Christian. 2021. "The Evolution of Human Communication and Terminology." In *Tudományterületek találkozása. Köszöntő kötet Muráth Judit tiszteletére*, ed. by Ildikó Fata, and Márta Fischer, 232–251. Pécs: Faculty of Economics, University of Pécs.

Grzega, Joachim, and Marion Schöner. 2007. *English and General Historical Lexicology. Materials for Onomasiology Seminars*. Eichstätt-Ingolstadt: Katholische Universität Eichstätt-Ingolstadt (Onomasiology Online Monographs vol. 1).

Infoterm. 2005. *Guidelines for Terminology Policies: Formulating and Implementing Terminology Policy in Language Communities*. Paris: UNESCO (CI 2005/WS/4).

Infoterm. 2003–2023. *Infoterm Annual Reports*.

Kintzinger, Martin. 2003. *Wissen wird Macht: Bildung im Mittelalter*. Ostfildern: Jan Thorbecke.

Krommer-Benz, Magdalena. 1977. *World Guide to Terminological Activities: Organizations, Terminology banks, Committees*. Infoterm series 4. Munich: Verlag Dokumentation Saur.

Krommer-Benz, Magdalena. 1985. *World Guide to Terminological Activities: Organizations, Commissions, Terminology Banks*. Infoterm series 4. Munich: K.G. Saur.

Lowe, Elizabeth, and Sue Ellen Wright. 2006. "The Life and Works of Alfred Schlomann: Terminology Theory and Globalization." In *Modern Approaches to Terminological Theory and Applications*, ed by Herbert Picht, 153–161. Bern: Peter Lang.

Oeser, Erhard. 1994. "Terminology and Philosophy of Science." In *International IITF Workshop Theoretical Issues of Terminology Science Riga, 19~21 August 1992*, ed. by Jennifer Draskau, and Heribert Picht, 24–34. Vienna: TermNet.

Oeser, Erhard. 1998. "Wüster and his Impact on the Philosophy of Science." In *Eugen Wüster (1898–1977) Leben und Werk., ein österreichischer Pionier der Informationsgesellschaft / His Life and Work. An Austrian Pioneer of the Information Society*, ed. by Erhard Oeser, and Christian Galinski, 105–115. Vienna: TermNet.

Schmitz, Klaus-Dirk. 2002. "European Terminology Documentation Centre Network (TDCnet)." *LSP and Professional Communication*, 2-2: 113–116.

von Freytag-Löringhoff, Baron. 1955. *Logik. Ihr System und ihr Verhältnis zur Logistik.* Stuttgart.

Wang, Ping. 2011. "A Brief History of Standards and Standardization Organizations: A Chinese Perspective." *Economic Series*: 117. Honolulu: East-West Center.

Wesolowski, Tilmann. 2010. "Der wissenschaftspublizistische Wettlauf um die Standardisierung der technischen Terminologie: Ein Beitrag zur Geschichte der Verwissenschaftlichung der Technik." *Sudhoffs Archive*: 94-2: 183–194.

Wüster, Eugen. 1931. *Internationale Sprachnormung in der Technik, besonders in der Elektrotechnik.* Berlin: VDI-Verlag (1970. 3rd ext. ed. Berlin: Bouvier und Co.).

Wüster, Eugen. 1955. *Bibliography of Monolingual Scientific and Technical Glossaries: Volume I. National Standards / Bibliographie de Vocabulaires Scientifiques et Techniques Monolingues. Volume I Normes Nationales.* Paris: UNESCO.

Wüster, Eugen. 1959. *Bibliography of Monolingual Scientific and Technical Glossaries. Volume II: Miscellaneous Sources / Bibliographie de Vocabulaires Scientifiques et Techniques Monolingues. Volume II: Sources diverses.* Paris: UNESCO.

Wüster, Eugen. 1968. *The Machine Tool: An Interlingual Dictionary of Basic Concepts / Dictionnaire Multilingue de la Machine-Outil. Notions Fondamentales.* London: Technical Press.

Wüster, Eugen. 1970. "Sachnormung erfordert Sprachnormung." *O+B Organisation und Betrieb*, 25–11.

Wüster, Eugen. 1971. "Begriffs- und Themaklassifikationen. Unterschiede in ihrem Wesen und ihrer Anwendung." *Nachrichten für Dokumentation* 22-3: 98–104 and 33-4: 143–150.

Wüster, Eugen. 1974. "Die Allgemeine Terminologielehre — Ein Grenzgebiet zwischen Sprachwissenschaft, Logik, Ontologie, Informatik und den Sachwissenschaften." *Linguistics* 119: 61–106.

Wüster, Eugen. 1979. *Einführung in die Allgemeine Terminologielehre und Terminologische Lexikographie*, ed. by Helmut Felber. Wien: Springer-Verlag.

Wüster, Eugen and Infoterm. 1974. *The Road to Infoterm.* München: Verlag Dokumentation.

CHAPTER 18

Cultural terminology
An African contribution

Marcel Diki-Kidiri
African Academy of Languages (ACALAN)

Until the 1980s, African linguistics was dominated by descriptive and comparative linguistics. Linguists strongly refrained from intervening in African languages and modifying them in any way so as not to distort linguistic authenticity. However, when some languages attained national or official status and were used in adult literacy, applied linguistics were developed by dedicated institutions throughout Africa. Supported by international organisations and collaborative networks, these institutions produced thematic lexicons in African languages. Some Africanist linguists directed their research toward linguistics for development, paying special attention to speakers' needs. Finally, through workshops organised at the laboratory Langage, Langues et Cultures d'Afrique Noire (LLACAN) in the French Centre National de la Recherche Scientifique (CNRS) in Paris, Marcel Diki-Kidiri developed the theory of Cultural Terminology, various aspects of which have been presented and acknowledged in several international conferences.

Keywords: Cultural Terminology, appropriation of knowledge, African languages, percept, concept, signifier, terminological diversity

1. Introduction: What is Cultural Terminology?

Cultural Terminology is a dynamic approach to terminology as a discipline that is based on the cultural dimension of human beings in their synchronic relationship with their environment and in their diachronic evolution through their accumulation of knowledge and technical skills. Thus people, as individuals and as a community, are the raison d'être of terminological research, whose objective is to enrich the language of a community of speakers to make it a better tool for the appropriation of knowledge. This appropriation induces an evolution of the people's culture and knowledge. Finally, the process of appropriation itself is dynamic in the sense that each new reality is apprehended via a perception grid consisting

https://doi.org/10.1075/tlrp.24.18dik

of concepts already installed in the culture and qualified as archetypes. If the new reality cannot be aligned with any of the existing archetypes, it will itself become a new archetype and may in turn serve as an archetypical cue for the apprehension of future new realities.

Cultural Terminology is thus different from Wüsterian terminology,[1] long held to be the canon, on the one hand because it puts culture at the base of its approach, and on the other hand, because it aims at the appropriation of knowledge and not the harmonisation of terms from one language to another such as is practiced, e.g., in the International Organization for Standardization (ISO).

International cooperation bodies in the field of language planning (e.g. Office Québécois de la Langue Française (OQLF) in Québec, Office International de la Francophonie (OIF) in France) have played a crucial role in the development of specialised lexicons in African languages and thus, to some extent, in the genesis of Cultural Terminology.

2.   From description to language planning

Until the 1980s, African linguistics was dominated by descriptive and comparative linguistics. The purpose was to document the structure of each of the 1,500 to 2,000 African languages, their typologies and genealogies, as had been done for Indo-European languages. Throughout this period, linguists rightly refrained from intervening in the languages they described to avoid adapting them in any way so as not to distort their linguistic properties and thus the results of their analyses. In the meantime, in Europe and Canada, the need to adapt European languages to the expression of fast-growing technologies and new concepts was becoming more and more pressing, and important institutions were created to standardise, modernise, enrich and teach their terminology and phraseology on several levels, institutions such as, to speak only of the case of French, the Office Québécois de la Langue française (OQLF, see also Chapter 12), the Délégation Générale à la langue française et aux langues de France (DGLFLF), the Conseil international de la langue française (CILF), the Conseil supérieur de la langue française (CSLF), and the Organisation internationale de la francophonie (OIF) (see also Chapter 21). These organisations are non-academic institutions, some with ties to political power, and their activities clearly fall within the political will of states to ensure what is considered good language management. The normative

---

1. For a more in-depth presentation of Cultural Terminology compared to other terminology approaches, see Diki-Kidiri (2022).

dimension of their activities was not well suited to the descriptive ethics of linguistic research on African languages carried out in academic research centres. Even in France, until as late as 1990, based on this author's experience, terminology was still seen as a governmental policy to promote a language, not a scientific research field. But things started changing in the 1980s when French-language terminology networks integrated as partners in their organisation the African centres and institutes of applied linguistics.

3.   From thematic lexicons to sustainable development

Between 1981 and 1990, under the auspices of the ruling Socialist government in France, the French-speaking area[2] was transformed into a political space called *Francophonie* advocating for greater solidarity between its member states. Moreover, terminology was becoming fully accepted as an academic discipline in Francophone universities.

At the same time, more and more states in Africa officially granted national and/ or official language status to all or some of their native languages and encouraged their use in public services (communication, administration, courts, religion), adult literacy and school education (e.g., Mali (Bambara), Niger (Songay-Zarma, Hausa, Tamasheq), Burkina Faso (Moore), Central African Republic (Sängö), Burundi (Kirundi), Rwanda (Kinyarwanda), Madagascar (Malagasy) etc.). With the teaching of certain languages in schools, adult literacy and language applications multiplied and applied linguistics developed in dedicated institutions (often called "Institut/Centre de Linguistique Appliqué") established within universities throughout Africa. Supported by international organisations[3] these African institutions regularly sent their academic representatives (civil servants, academic assistants, teachers, translators, linguists and terminologists) to attend international conferences and present their work or discuss their concerns. One could no longer continue to further entrench the French language in these countries, most of which were former French colonies, while ignoring the languages that are more widely spoken there. As a result, the African languages of the French-speaking countries were redefined as "partner languages of French" (Rakotomalala 2005), which

---

2. This area covers all the French-speaking countries in the world and a few non-French-speaking countries which wanted to strengthen political links with France when the Francophonie was created.

3. e.g. Agence de Coopération Culturelle et Technique (ACCT), Association des Universités Partiellement et Entièrement de Langue Française-Université des Réseaux francophones (AUPELF-UREF), Summer Institute of Linguistics (SIL)

justified their involvement in the linguistic planning activities of the francophone agencies such as OIF, the Association des Universités Francophones (AUF) and networks as the Réseau international de néologie et terminologie (Rint), the Réseau international des Observatoires francophones de l'industrie de la langue (Riofil), and the network Linguistique, Terminologie Traduction (LTT).

By participating in the activities of the three networks of institutional collaboration (Rint, Riofil, Rifal,[4] LTT), African institutes and centres of applied linguistics began to produce thematic lexicons in African languages, notably within the framework of the Lexiques thématiques d'Afrique centrale (LETAC) program initiated and supported by the ACCT from 1981 to 1986. These lexicons (relative to, e.g., economics, agriculture, education, administration, finance, justice, medicine, mathematics, elections) were most often produced by institutional agents of the applied linguistics centres. They translated lists of vocabularies from French, without a prior theoretical reflection to determine an appropriate methodology or an efficient strategy to implement them. Since 1983, many thematic glossaries have been produced and published by the ACCT/OIF in the national languages of Central African countries. Unsurprisingly, almost all the works thus produced remained unused for any *development activity*, for lack of an effective implementation strategy. The term *development activity* refers to any activity that contributes to the development of the country and the improvement of the condition of life of its population, e.g., economic, health, culture, and education activities. This experience revealed the need to completely rethink the approach to terminology in African languages. It shows how important it is, before starting a terminology project in the field, to carefully determine the socio-professional framework that precisely delineates the sector of knowledge concerned, the scope of the terminology activity (local, national, international) and its target audience (e.g. specific user groups or the public in general). Involving a well-chosen relevant sample of the target audience directly in the research and terminology work of the concerned knowledge sector at an early stage ensures a smooth implementation of the terminologies produced.

4.   Towards a linguistics for development

The growing ideology of sustainable development spurred a need for an epistemological framework for work on language. Also, whenever one discusses the production of terminologies in African languages, the question of terminology

---

4. Réseau International Francophone d'Aménagement Linguistique (RIFAL) resulted from the merging of Rint and Riofil.

for development always comes to the heart of the discussion (Ntahomvukiye 1992: 9–13, Métangmo-Tatou 2019, Tourneux 2004, 2006, 2009, 2015). Some Africanist linguists began to direct their work towards taking into consideration the speakers' needs of the languages being described. These languages were no longer to be considered simply as raw products harvested in a field and processed in a laboratory to extract knowledge for the researcher and the scientific community. By considering the speakers' needs, linguists, because of their position as language specialists, assume the duty and the right to participate in the development of these languages so that their speakers appropriate the knowledge they need to develop and flourish in this modern, increasingly globalised world. This approach of directly involving speakers in language research to better satisfy their linguistic needs would later be called *linguistics for development* by Léonie Métangmo-Tatou (2019) and summed up by Henry Tourneux:

> The observation of the functioning of development projects (...) which take place in French-speaking Africa, shows in most cases that there is a communication gap between the promoters of the projects (generally originating from the countries of the North or trained in the countries of the North) and those who should be the happy beneficiaries. The former, armed with their technical knowledge, do not even consider the idea that a technique, however adapted and efficient it may be, cannot achieve the slightest result if those who must implement it have not appropriated it. What are the factors that can lead to reluctance? We will mention the most obvious ones: (1) lack of understanding of the technique itself and the processes of its application; (2) incompatibility of the technique with the local culture; (3) the fact that the technique is proposed/imposed from above or from outside, which, from this point of view, amounts to the same thing; (4) the absence of real consultation between project promoters and local populations, which means that the expectations of the latter may have little to do with what the promoters wish to develop; (5) the improvised and uncontrolled use of interpreters who establish a communicational filter between the project promoters and the recipients. (...) We therefore suggest that another linguistic specialty be opened, to be called "linguistics for development."   (Tourneux 2015: 41)[5]

In the African context, far from being just an academic intellectual exercise, any serious terminology project aims at improving the well-being of people. So, terminology must be part of a collection of linked development programs that, in many cases, include literacy. Henry Tourneux rightly pointed this out:

> [In contrast], hundreds of millions of Africans use African languages in 90 percent of everyday situations. From a development perspective, the only chance of acquiring the exogenous modern knowledge and skills that are essential for

---

5. All translations in this chapter are those of the author.

> improving the well-being of all is to express them in local languages. What are the conditions that need to be met to successfully pass on this knowledge to people who need it but cannot access it because of the language barrier?
>
> (Tourneux 2015:163)

To begin with, one of the urgent tasks is to stabilise the spelling of languages which have no fixed spelling[6] or whose spelling can be greatly improved[7] because it is impossible to develop and disseminate vocabularies of specialised knowledge in a language that does not have a standardised orthography or written form. Over a billion of people cannot learn, in a few years, specialised knowledge with its huge number of terms only by oral communication. Marcel Diki-Kidiri, Gérard Galtier, and Dave Roberts, as well as other researchers working at a grass-root levels in the ambit of SIL, go beyond the simple phonetic and phonological transcriptions and propose to endow each language studied with a reasoned, transdialectal spelling, built on the structural possibilities of the language, and technically manageable by speakers who are always closely associated with their research. It is obvious that African languages can develop and realise their full potential only by acquiring a widely practiced written form. This would make it possible to appropriate imported knowledge originating outside Africa as well as rediscover ancestral knowledge.

Henry Tourneux took an interest in the traditional knowledge of the Fula of Northern Cameroon, which he described in two publications (Tourneux 2004, 2006) that have become references in the linguistics for development approach. Later, through workshops organised at the LLACAN (CNRS) in Paris, Diki-Kidiri and Edema developed the foundational elements of what is referred to as *Cultural Terminology*. The first task was to deconstruct the axiomatic ideas of the Wüsterian terminology that are dominant in Europe, where this deconstruction was justified by empirical linguistic observation. Some examples are described in the following paragraphs.

1. The dichotomy between common language and language for special purpose is asserted as if there were an *impervious boundary* between the two, while many technical terms are nothing more than a specialised use of common words in the common language (e.g. 'string' in geometry, 'bug' in computer science, 'minute' in administration, 'pole' in physics, 'black hole' in astrophysics, and so forth) and conversely many technical terms have entered into the common language through media, such as advertising even though the average speaker does not know exactly what they mean (e.g., enzyme, gluten,

---

6. See Diki-Kidiri 1977, 1982.

7. See Galtier 1980; Roberts 2008.

paracetamol, coronavirus, covid, AIDS). Many people do not know the difference between the pathogen (coronavirus, HIV) and the resulting disease (COVID_19, AIDS). It is obvious that the boundary between a language for special purpose and common language is porous (see Chapter 13 regarding Cabré's Communicative Theory of Terminology). Also, language for special purposes always remains a particular variety of the common language. It may be said that a mathematics book is written in French, English, or Spanish. But it is never said that it is written in mathematical language because such a language does not exist independently of a natural language. It follows that what African speakers may need is to develop the special language component of their own common languages.

2. It is assumed in the General Theory of Terminology (GTT) that contrary to the words of common language, which are considered as potentially polysemic and dependent on a pictorial and poetic culture, or whose artistic use can make understanding difficult, technical or specialised terms are said to be clearly understandable because they are governed by their denotational meaning with which they have an unambiguous relationship. There are several examples which prove the contrary, but the case of the term *terminology* itself will suffice as it designates (a) the discipline dedicated to the study of terms, (b) all the terms used by an author or a company, and (c) all the terms of a specialty area. Biunivocity is therefore relative and should not be considered as a *sine qua non* condition to achieve the clarity of scientific discourse.

3. By using terms rather than common words to express specialised concepts, it is assumed that specialised discourse will be unambiguous and thus clearly understood. And yet, teachers are often forced to explain lessons with general words because they are not easily understood with technical terms. It was this experience that led Temmerman (2000: 59) to undertake and develop her Sociocognitive Approach to terminology in which she prefers defining *units of understanding* instead of *concepts*. Technical terms require specific learning to be assimilated, which is a basic condition for accurately and easily communicating in a language for special purposes (see Chapter 8). Indeed, in an exchange between experts of the same field, there is no communication breakdown as the experts are already trained in that specialty and are familiar with all the technical terms of their specialty. But for the public at large, watching a discussion among experts on TV is just boring as they are unlikely to understand what the discussion is about.

4. In the GTT, culture, poetry, synonymy, homonymy, and metaphor (reduced to a stylistic embellishment) are to be excluded from terminology as they disturb the clarity of specialised communication. However, in particle physics, terms such as 'flavor,' 'strange,' 'charm,' 'color,' and 'truth' are used even in

Western languages. In computer science, terms like "mouse, chips, bug, memory, screen, cursor, upload, download, paste, key, keyboard, password, shell" etc, are all metaphors. Are there not therefore metaphor and poetry, and hence culture, in special language? As it can be seen from above, a quick scratch of some "exact sciences" easily shows several metaphors.

Based on this observation, it can be assumed that metaphor, poetry, and culture abound among technical terms in several areas of specialisation. In fact, the role of metaphor, poetry and culture in forming technical terms has been previously acknowledged in the scholarly literature (Terral 2004, Lakoff and Johnson 1980, Ramavonirina 2000: 43–45, Temmerman 2022: 21). This observation led the initiators of Cultural Terminology to conduct a thorough reflection on metaphor which, far from being a mere literary device, turns out to be a powerful mental process of conceptualisation. Diki-Kidiri, Mbodj, and Edema published the first article (1997) that describes the conceptual approach and precise method of Cultural Terminology.

> Addressing the vocabulary needed to work with a computer (e.g. keyboard, screen, memory, drive, cursor, click, upload, etc.) the authors are interested in the expression of the same concept in different languages and cultures, by carefully analysing the conceptualisation processes implemented in the language of each culture. This allows them to address (a) technical issues related to Terminography in African languages; (b) the requirements of the user in relation to neology and language for special purpose; (c) the question of medium: hypermedia lexicon versus paper lexicon.   (Diki-Kidiri et al. 1997: 94)

Cultural Terminology researchers have observed that the denomination (the linguistic signifier) itself seems motivated by the perception that people have of the things they observe; this led researchers to question the arbitrary relation between the signifier and the signified as theorised by Ferdinand de Saussure (1916, reissue 1971: 183). The proponents of Cultural Terminology have come to consider that if the object 'tree' as perceived is a contextual instance of the concept 'tree,' and if its name (the signifier 'tree') is motivated by the perception of the speaker (the *percept*), then the spectrum of the linguistic sign must include three elements: signifier, percept (the observer's perception), and concept. While the relationship between the signifier and the concept is undeniably arbitrary, the relationship between the signifier and the percept is culturally motivated. Marcel Diki-Kidiri, Edema Atibakwa Baboya, Henry Tourneux, and Maria Teresa Cabré have contributed through discussions to the theory and methods of Cultural Terminology (Diki-Kidiri 1998, 2000: 27–31, Diki-Kidiri et al. 2008).

5. Cultural Terminology and socially oriented terminologies

While the researchers were developing Cultural Terminology as a distinct approach at the LLACAN in Paris, they were visited by François Gaudin of the
University of Rouen, who shared with them his views on Socioterminology,[8] an
approach that shares many common points, particularly the need to adapt specialised discourse and technical vocabulary to the target audience, and consider
the role of parallel specialised discourses involving different social groups, such
as workers and engineers, operating in the same field (see Chapter 11). However,
socioterminology does not deal with the question of the appropriation of new
knowledge by a linguistic community of a culture quite different from that of the
source community such as between the peoples in Africa and Western cultures.
The specificity and usefulness of each of the two approaches became apparent
after this exchange. At an international conference on terminology held in Paris
in 2000, Diki-Kidiri and Edema presented a poster comparing the European
and African approaches to terminology, showing points of convergence and divergence (Edema 2000: 31–38). For Europe as for Africa, terminological activity
aims at the enrichment of languages which are the subject of linguistic adaptation. But in Europe, this activity mainly concerns advanced industrial technologies while in Africa it is much more about documenting basic techniques and
basic knowledge useful for development. Also, the context and supportive infrastructures, such as a technical literature, qualified human resources, dedicated
institutions, and so forth are far more numerous in Europe than in Africa. As
a result, African terminology aims more at the appropriation in a language of
the basic knowledge and technologies necessary for development in the general
sense, while in Europe, local and international standardisation of terminology is
more focused on linguistic and semantic appropriateness. However, the necessity and the methods of the implementation and diffusion of neologisms remains
the same in Europe as in Africa. Several elements of this comparison, such as
the impact that the availability of human resources or dedicated institutions may
have, are not due to differences in theoretical approaches, furthermore, they are
likely to evolve over time.

   In 2001, at the invitation of Maria Teresa Cabré, Diki-Kidiri taught Cultural
Terminology in Barcelona, and supervised doctoral research that would later
appear in a reference work on Cultural Terminology (Diki-Kidiri (dir), Edema,
Mbodj, Suarez de la Torre, Rull 2008). Cabré's communicative approach to terminology (1998) shares with Cultural Terminology the notion of terminological
variation (both conceptual and denominational) based on the polyhedral nature

---

8. To learn more about Socioterminology, see Gaudin, 2003.

of the term (Cabré 2000: 10–15) and the role of cultural diversity in the perception of reality. Rita Temmerman, as noted an advocate of Sociocognitive terminology,[9] and Danièle Dubois, a psycholinguist specialising in sensory perceptions and cognition, also shared insights that are relevant for Cultural Terminology. It became clear from these exchanges that Cultural Terminology should diverge from the fundamental paradigm of Wüsterian theory and focus on the questions relating to the perception of reality (between subjectivity and objectivity), to categorisation (prototypicality, relativity) and to conceptualisation (between universality and cultural motivation). It also became increasingly recognised that a cultural approach to terminology would be suitable for languages that, like African languages, need rapid development without loss of their identity (Welsh for example, see Chapter 31).

6.   Cultural Terminology since 2010

Between 2007 and 2009, at the request of the International Criminal Court (ICC), Diki-Kidiri translated several documents on the Court's activities, structures and prerogatives into Sängö. These documents were intended to prepare people from the Central African Republic to cooperate in a major forthcoming trial concerning that country. People who do not speak French were to testify at this trial. The Court therefore needed Sängö interpreters. However, qualified interpreters who were proficient in Sängö and French did not exist anywhere in the world. The Court would therefore need to train some people who speak Sängö and French, possibly having their training validated by professors from European schools of interpretation. It was in this context that Diki-Kidiri was recruited to be part of the training team. He applied the method advocated in Cultural Terminology to build up not only legal vocabulary in Sängö but also the legal discourse reflecting practices specific to the ICC (Diki-Kidiri 2014: 90–110). As demonstrated by Florence Terral (2004), legal terminology is particularly impacted by the culture of the language community in which it was forged, resulting in increased difficulties in cross-cultural translation.[10] The examples described in the following paragraphs illustrate this assertion.

The word *right* in the term *human rights* does not have an equivalent in Sängö. However, in the tradition of group hunting, a net is spread on one side of the hunting area, and the hunters form a line on the opposite side. They set fire

---

9. See Temmerman (2000: 54–68) for a presentation of Sociocognitive Terminology.

10. Consider the differences between Common Law and Civil Law, both western systems (See Chapter 12). Differences between a western legal system and a non-western one are likely to be even greater.

to the bush to drive the animals into the nets. The animals that are caught in the nets are speared to death. In sharing the remains of an animal, specific parts of the animal's body are reserved for the owner of the fire, the net, and the spear. But the head of the animal is always reserved for the village chief, even if he does not participate in the hunt. This share of the animal's body that automatically goes to someone is called *ngura* in Sängö. With the decline of this method of hunting, the use of the word *ngura* has also declined, so that it no longer comes to mind when speaking of what is rightfully one's own in general. It is therefore through research in cultural knowledge that this word has been recovered to take on the general meaning of someone's right.

The International Criminal Court does not have a prison but rather a detention centre. Similarly, it does not have prisoners but detainees. Indeed, people convicted by the ICC serve their sentence in a prison of an ICC member state and not at the ICC itself. There, they become prisoners. Before that, they are just detainees waiting to be tried. In Sängö, people do not make this subtle distinction between detainee and prisoner, nor between detention centre and prison. The verb *kânga* means to tie up, to imprison, and the words *dakânga* and *wakânga* mean prison and prisoner respectively. To render *to detain* as distinct from *to imprison*, it was therefore necessary to use another verb, *gbânzi*, meaning to hold back, to prevent, and likewise to propose the neologisms *dagbânzi* and *wagbânzi* for detention centre and detainee. These neologisms, being formed on the model of *dakânga* and *wakânga*, are easily understood. Yet, only through intensive use will they assume their specific meaning as different from *dakânga* and *wakânga*. The legal vocabulary in Sängö that resulted from this work is only a starting point for the further development, using the Cultural Terminology approach, of the legal discourse and vocabulary in Sängö based on legal practice in the Central African Republic.

The reference book that presents the theory, working methods, and applications of Cultural Terminology remains that on the scientific vocabularies in African languages, by Diki-Kidiri et al in 2008. Since then, number of theses (e.g. Manifi Abouh 2023) have been defended which have served to further develop those theories and methodologies. Cultural Terminology has also been presented at several conferences both in Africa and in Europe.

7.   Conclusion

The Vienna school of terminology aimed to make the Wüsterian approach a general theory that would be worthy and valid in all circumstances and exempt from all contingencies and variations. It has achieved its objective regarding terminology standardisation as practiced by ISO and other standardisation bodies. In this sense, the Wüsterian theory remains an invaluable reference point. But this vision focused on standardisation is by no means the only way to perceive and deal with terminology, and therefore cannot constitute a general theory of this discipline. The Wüsterian theory has not withstood the test of empirical observation in specific real-life contexts that any theory must pass. When objective data from the field do not comply with a theory, it is not the data but the theory that need be reconsidered.

The socially oriented theoretical approaches to terminology that emerged in the 1990s provide ample evidence of the opinion that a general theory of terminology applicable to the discipline in all its facets cannot be reduced to the Wüsterian conception inherited from the past. Cultural Terminology has always been seen by its advocates as one part of a building that would include other terminology theories. Only such a building would then have the scope necessary to be considered a general theory of terminology. Meanwhile, Cultural Terminology, like other approaches, continues to serve people's real needs.

References

Cabré, Maria Teresa. 1998. *Terminology: Theory, Methods and Applications*. Amsterdam: John Benjamins.

Cabré, Maria Teresa. 2000. "Terminologie et linguistique: la théorie des portes." *Terminologies Nouvelles* 21:10–15.

de Saussure, Ferdinand. 1916. reprint 1971. *Cours de linguistique générale*. Paris: Payot.

Diki-Kidiri, Marcel. 1977. "Le sango s'écrit aussi..., esquisse linguistique du sango, langue nationale de l'empire centrafricain." *L'homme* 19-2: 94–95.

Diki-Kidiri, Marcel. 1982. *Kua tî ködörö. Introduction à l'instruction civique*. Paris : SELAF.

Diki-Kidiri, Marcel, Chérif Mbodj, and Atbakwa Baboya Edema. 1997. "Des lexiques en langues africaines (sängö, wolof, lingála) pour l'utilisateur de l'ordinateur." *Meta* 42(1): 94–109.

Diki-Kidiri, Marcel. 1998. "Question de méthode en terminologie en langues africaines." *Revue française de linguistique appliquée. Terminologie : nouvelles orientations*. Vol III:15–28.

Diki-Kidiri, Marcel. 2000. "Une approche culturelle de la terminologie." *Terminologies nouvelles* 21: 27–31.

Diki-Kidiri (dir). 2008. *Le vocabulaire scientifique dans les langues africaines, Pour une approche culturelle de la terminologie*. Paris: Éditions Karthala.

Diki-Kidiri, Marcel. 2014. "Le vocabulaire juridique en sängö, une application de la terminologie culturelle." In *Dynamics and Terminology*, ed. by Rita Temmerman, and Marc Van Campenhoudt, 90–110. Amsterdam: John Benjamins.

Diki-Kidiri, Marcel. 2022. "Cultural Terminology: An Introduction to Theory and Method." In *Theoretical Perspectives on Terminology: Explaining Terms, Concepts, and Specialized Knowledge*, ed. by Pamela Faber and Marie-Claude L'Homme. Amsterdam: John Benjamins. 197–216. .

Edema, Atibakwa Baboya. 2000. "Terminologie européenne et terminologie africaine: éléments de comparaison." *Terminologies nouvelles* 21: 32–38.

Galtier, Gérard. 1980. *Problèmes dialectologiques et phonographématiques des parlers mandingues.* (Doctoral thesis). Paris: Université Paris VII.

Gaudin, François. 2003. *Socioterminologie, une approche sociolinguistique de la terminologie.* Bruxelles: Duculot de Boeck.

Lakoff, George, and Mark Johnson. 1980. *Metaphors We Live By.* Chicago: University of Chicago Press.

Manifi Abouh, Maxime Yves Julien. 2023. *La « linguistique pour le développement » par la terminologie et la traduction. Avec une expérience heuristique dans le domaine agricole en yambeta.* Paris: Poclande.

Métangmo-Tatou, Léonie. 2019. *Pour une linguistique du développement. Essai d'épistémologie sur l'émergence d'un nouveau paradigme en sciences du langage.* Québec: Editions science et bien commun.

Ntahomvukiye, Hilaire. 1992. "Quelle terminologie pour quel développement?" *Terminologies Nouvelles* 9: 9–13.

Rakotomalala, Dorothée. 2005. *Le partenariat des langues dans l'espace francophone: description, analyse, gestion.* Paris: L'Harmattan.

Ramavonirina, Oliva Rahantamalala. 2000. "Symbolisme végétal et terminologie dans la culture malgache." *Terminologies Nouvelles* 21: 43–45.

Roberts, Dave. 2008. *L'orthographe du ton en kabyè au banc d'essai.* PhD thesis. INALCO.

Temmerman, Rita. 2000. "Une théorie réaliste de la terminologie: le sociocognitivisme." *Terminologies Nouvelles* 21: 58–64

Temmerman, Rita. 2022. "Terminological Metaphors: Framing for Better and for Worse." In *Researching Metaphors — Towards a Comprehensive Account*, ed. by Michele Prandi, and Micaela Rossi, 111–131. Oxfordshire: Routledge.

Terral, Florence. 2004. "L'empreinte culturelle des termes juridiques." *Meta*, 49(4): 876–890.

Tourneux, Henry. 2004. "Comment parler de la résistance des insectes aux insecticides avec les paysans cultivateurs de coton." In *Mécanismes et stratégies de gestion de la résistance des insectes d'intérêt agricole aux insecticides en Afrique et en Asie.* Ouagadougou, Burkina Faso: CIRAD.

Tourneux, Henry. 2006. *La communication technique en langues africaines: lutte contre les ravageurs du cotonnier (Burkina Faso — Cameroun).* Paris: Karthala.

Tourneux, Henry. 2009. "Linguistique et développement. Et si, pour sortir du malentendu, le dialogue interculturel avait besoin d'un nouvel outil?" *La Grande Oreille* 39: 39–41.

Tourneux Henry. 2015. "Pour une linguistique du développement." In *Selected Proceedings of the Symposium on West African Languages*, ed. by S. Baldi, and G.C. Batic, 163–176. Naples: Università degli studi di Napoli.

PART 3

Terminology the world over

CHAPTER 19

Terminology in the Arab world
Dynamics and developments

Andree Affeich & Rima Baraké
Lebanese American University | Lebanese University

This chapter traces the history of modern Arabic terminology. It begins with the 19th century, when translation contributed to the creation of terminology in different fields. Two countries emerged as the main catalysts: Egypt and Syria. Moving on to the 20th century and onwards, the chapter focuses on activities related to terminology within several organisations and academies. These activities were the fruit of promising projects of Arabisation and contributed to the creation and dissemination of terms. Nevertheless, each academy and institution had its own terminology, which resulted in a proliferation of synonyms. This factor, coupled with others highlighted in this chapter, is likely to have negatively affected the status of modern Arabic terminology.

Keywords: Arabic, Arabisation, translation, sciences, technologies

1. Introduction

The modern history of Arabic terminology begins in the 19th century, when Arabs, especially in Egypt and Syria, translated and/or created terms in different fields of knowledge, mainly in the sciences, and used these terms for teaching sciences in their native language. It is mainly through translation that Arabs created new terms for concepts that originated from Western cultures, either in the first centuries of Hegira, when Arabs translated philosophical and scientific texts from Greek into Syriac and then into Arabic, or in the 19th century, particularly under the rule of Muhammad Ali in Egypt, who sought reform on a large scale that went beyond modernising the state. The use of the Arabic language and translation into Arabic was an effective means of enabling this modernisation; courses in medicine were given in Arabic at the School of Abu Zaᶜbal and in Qasr al-Ayni

https://doi.org/10.1075/tlrp.24.19aff

in Egypt from 1830 until 1887.[1] Therefore, a plethora of terms pertaining to various fields of sciences was introduced into the Arabic lexicon. In Syria, after the collapse of the Ottoman Empire in 1922, Arabic became the official language in the country, and science courses, for instance, were taught in Arabic at the School of Medicine in Damascus.

Many activities related to the creation of a new modern Arabic scientific terminology took place during the 19th century. The present study also attempts to show the role of Arabisation in the 20th century onward in creating new Arabic terms for new concepts.

2.   Terminological activities from the 19th and 20th centuries onward

In the 19th century, at the beginning of the /Nahḍa/[2] ('Renaissance'), foreign terms had to be rendered into Arabic at the discretion of political authorities, and the process of rendering them was very fast-paced. Arabic scientific terminology had to depict in a very short time — a few decades — an essentially French terminology that had itself taken at least two centuries to develop.

There were two places where Arabic scientific terminology was systematically developed in this period: Egypt and Syria.

Between 1805 and 1848, Egypt was under the rule of Muhammad Ali, who pursued military and economic objectives and promoted teaching the sciences in Arabic.

Ali carried out major works and reforms in Egypt. In the first phase, he called upon European scientists, the first cohort of whom were Italian, and then, at a later stage, the French (Al-Zourgan 1998). Western scientists who taught in Egypt were assisted by translators who translated the content of their courses into Arabic. In the School of Medicine, for instance, translators and proofreaders formed a translation academy. They produced, within five years, a dictionary of medical vocabulary, which included upwards of 6,000 entries (Sawaie 1999).

The methods translators followed to create modern Arabic scientific terms can be presented, according to Sawaie (1999), as follows:

---

1. After this date, and with the establishment of the English mandate, the language of teaching was changed to English, and it has remained so until today.

2. Words, terms, or expressions put in the text between two slashes are transcribed according to a system used to transcribe Arabic words and called 'Times Beyrut Roman', and are then translated into English by the authors.

a. They used Arabic terms whenever possible. These terms were mainly extracted from ancient Arabic books.
b. They resorted to the Arabisation of European terms that refer to modern inventions or names previously unknown in the Arabic language. By Arabisation was meant the process of using foreign terms, with some modification and adaptation that took into account the phonological system of the Arabic language.
c. They translated European terms literally.

In the second phase, Ali sent Egyptian students on a mission to Europe, the first group in 1813 to Italian cities such as Rome, Milan, and Florence, to learn the military arts and various professions, such as shipbuilding and engineering. The second group, which comprised 42 students, was sent to France in 1826. Between 1813 and 1848, over 300 students were sent on missions to Europe (Sawaie 1999; Al-Zourgan 1998; Al-Chayyal 1951).

Upon their return to Egypt, students were asked to write reports in Arabic in which they had to translate new scientific concepts, using linguistic means for generating new terms, mainly neologisms and borrowings.

One of the most famous scholars of the 19th century was Rifa'a Rafi' al-Tahtawi, who contributed to the search for the most appropriate Arabic terms to render technical concepts and ideas from the West that he had become familiar with during his stay in Paris in the years 1826–1831. Al-Tahtawi's interest in terminology and its development continued after his return to Egypt and through his practice of translating books and working in /Madrasat al-'Alsun/ ('School of Languages') founded by Ali, where the instructors and students were entrusted with translating scientific, intellectual, literary, and legal books into Arabic.

Al-Tahtawi resorted mainly to two techniques to create Arabic terms expressing Western ideas and concepts: the first technique consisted of making use of terms that existed in classical and colloquial Arabic language (Al-Zourgan 1998). He gave new meanings to these terms so that they could refer to new ideas and innovations. This process is referred to as *semantic borrowing* or sometimes *transdisciplinary borrowing*. The second technique involved the Arabisation of French terms (Sawaie 1999).

Additionally, an official printing press was established in Egypt in 1821, called /al-Maṭbaʿa al-'Ahliyya/ (National Printing Press), and works by European authors were translated into Arabic. Schools and academic institutions were also founded such as /Madrasat al-'Alsun/ (School of Languages) in 1835, which provided training in translation and interpreting.

Primary education was also widely developed. Various scientific, literary and schoolbooks were printed. Arabic was the official language in Egypt and was also used in education. Modern scientific and technical terminology, therefore, emerged in the first half of the 19th century and included a certain number of loan terms.

It is worth noting that the press that appeared under Ali's rule played a major role in the development of modern Arabic and formed the linguistic framework wherein Arabic scientific and technical vocabularies developed naturally (Lelubre 1992). This was also clearly mentioned by Hardane (1994: 486):

> [...] The Arabic press, which was particularly prosperous in Egypt and Lebanon, played for a long time the role of an academy and a standardisation body, by 'imposing' hundreds of new terms covering different scientific and technical fields, which appeared in daily newspapers and specialised journals (our translation).

In general, the translation movement in the 19th century left its mark on the transfer of terms, especially from French. During the reign of Khedive Ismail (1863–1879), the passion for European development was at its zenith. The translation movement and the acquisition of sciences and arts from Europe encouraged the use of new Arabic terms to refer to European concepts, such as /jâmiᶜa/ ('university'), /mustašfa/ ('hospital'), /ᶜajala/ ('wheel'), /sikkat ḥadîd/ ('railway'), and /an-naẓẓârât al-muᶜaẓẓima/ ('magnifying glasses'). In addition, many foreign terms were borrowed, especially from French, due to the difficulty of finding and/ or creating Arabic equivalents at that time. We can mention some examples, such as *électricité* ('electricity'), *institut* ('institute'), *opéra* ('opera'), and *piano* ('piano'), which were respectively borrowed into Arabic.

In Syria, the second region of major developments, a literary renaissance took shape in the mid-19th century. Religious missions played an important role in the emergence of this renaissance, in the sense that they founded many institutions where teaching was done in Arabic. Scientific books were published in Arabic, and the terms used in those books were selected on the basis of the terminology already used in Egypt.

In 1919, the Faculty of Medicine in Damascus was founded, where teaching is done to this day in Arabic. When it was inaugurated, King Faisal I of the Arab Kingdom of Syria or Greater Syria[3] decided that teaching should be done in Arabic, and his decision was endorsed by faculty members, who were the pioneers of Arabisation in their time, notably the physicians Jamil al-Khani, Ahmad Hamdi al-Khayyat, and Murshid Khater, as well as the pharmacist Abd al-Wahab al-Qanawati, and the chemist Salah al-Din al-Kawakibi, all of whom made great efforts to develop the Arabic language, adapt it to scientific writing and enrich it with terminology (Khasara 2003, Badinjki 1994).

---

3. A region that included present-day Syria, as well as Lebanon, Palestine and Jordan.

Modern Arabic scientific terminology thus dates back to this period. It is worth noting that these terminological activities resulted in the compilation of the first Arabic specialised dictionary by the Egyptian linguist Mohamed Bin Omar Al-Tunisi. This dictionary, covering terms used in the medical field and titled /Aš-šuḏûr aḏ-ḏahabiyya fi l-alfâẓ aṭ-ṭobiyya/ [Golden Nuggets in Medical Terminology], was the fruit of collaboration among many Egyptian physicians who took it upon themselves to create new medical terms in Arabic.

Nevertheless, not all of the terms created in the 19th century have survived. Many loan terms, for instance, have been discarded and replaced by newly-created Arabic terms; for example, *étamine* ('stamen') and *pistil* ('pistil'), two French terms from the field of botany which refer to parts of a flower, were first borrowed and expressed in Arabic as follows: أستام /astâm/ and بستيل /pistîl/. However, by the second half of the 19th century, these were replaced by Arabic terms مِدَقّة /miḍaqqa/ and سداة /sadât/, which are still used today (Al-Shihabi 1965).

In conclusion, the Arabic terms developed in Egypt and Syria have clearly played an important role in shaping the terminological landscape for two main reasons mentioned by Lelubre (2005): first, the presence and dominance of the scientific literature in Arabic in these two countries, and second, for political reasons, among other things, the presence of Syrian or Egyptian workers in certain Arab countries, as has been the case in Algeria since independence.

From the 20th century onward, with the huge number of new concepts that had to be named in Arabic in fields such as medicine, engineering, telecommunication, and computing, a more methodical and controlled approach had to be put in place to accelerate the creation of terms and consequently the development of a modern scientific and technical Arabic language. Activities related precisely to terminology have been, to a certain extent, institutionalised and practised within several organisations, academies, centres of research, and universities in the Arab world since the beginning of the 20th century. Nevertheless, decisions taken by the academies of languages in the Arab world concerning precisely rules of term formation and dissemination have come to be "dead letters," to quote Hamzaoui (1975).

The 20th century was also characterised by a terminological instability or proliferation of terms which were not standardised and unified by one official body in the Arab world. This major problem, with its causes and consequences, is discussed in Section 4. However, Arabisation remains the main key to accessing terms in sciences and technologies. Its role and contribution to the creation and dissemination of terminology in the Arab world are discussed in the following section.

3.   The role of Arabisation in the dissemination of terms

To raise the question of modern terminological activity in the Arab world is above all to evoke a problem concerning Arabisation. Since the /Nahḍa/ ('Renaissance'), Arabisation has been a subject of great interest to the Arab world. It is a multidimensional question that lies at the intersection of politics, culture, language, etc. Nevertheless, only the linguistic aspect of the question concerns us in this study. What does the term *Arabisation* actually mean?

This term has at least two interconnected meanings: the first refers to the use of the Arabic language in areas where a foreign language is used, as is the case with the Arabisation of administration or education, especially concerning scientific subjects such as mathematics, physics, chemistry, and biology, which continue to be taught nowadays in different Arab countries in a foreign language, mainly French and English. This is what Kloss (1969) named "status planning," an aspect of language planning which consists, among other things, of expanding the domains in which a language is used and of declaring this language as official. The second meaning refers to the development of Arabic terminology in different fields of knowledge; in other words, it refers to the process of creating and finding Arabic equivalents for foreign terms (Affeich 2010). In Kloss's (1969) terminology, this is called "corpus planning," another aspect of language planning which consists, among other things, of developing a language (its grammar, lexicon, etc.) and creating new words or terms in this language (see Chapter 12). In what follows, we consider this second meaning, which is related to the process of creating and developing new terms that refer to concepts created in another part of the world. At this level specifically, several questions arise. What bodies or entities are in charge of undertaking the Arabisation task? What is their authority in the Arab world? Are their decisions and recommendations considered? Is Arabisation taking place at the level of the entire Arab world or country by country? By what means are the created terms disseminated? These are the questions we will try to answer in the following paragraphs.

Several bodies are in charge of Arabisation tasks or projects. These are, successively, producers, disseminators, users, and finally standardisers.

3.1   The producers

Producers of terminological work in the Arab world are the national academies on the one hand, and the institutes, universities, and research centres on the other.

3.1.1 *The academies*

The idea of establishing an Arab language academy began to take shape towards the end of the 19th century. The aim was to found an institution similar to the French Academy, the role of which would be to restore to the Arabic language the possibilities of expression that would enable it to reflect a modern and authentic culture; a culture that is new but that would somehow be a continuation of the history of Arab-Muslim science and culture in its golden age.[4] Several Arab academies were established over the years, with the most important ones in Egypt, Iraq, Jordan, Algeria, and Syria. Their activities are diverse and not limited to linguistic or terminological issues. Four have played a determining role in relation to terminology and are listed below in chronological order:

a.   The Arab Academy of Damascus (formerly the Arab Scientific Academy) was founded in 1919. This Academy's terminological work was accomplished in collaboration with universities, such as the Faculty of Sciences and the Faculty of Medicine of Damascus where the language of instruction is Arabic. Since 1922, the Academy has published a journal titled /Al-mažmaᶜ al-ᶜilmi l-ᶜarabi/ [The Arab Scientific Academy] (Affeich 2010).

b.   The Arab Academy of Cairo (formerly the Royal Academy of Cairo) was founded in 1932, and its influence in the Arab world is indisputable. This and other academies were created to provide an institutional structure that would focus on linguistic problems and the adaptation of the Arabic language to the needs of the modern world (Baraké 2008). Indeed, there was an urgent need to reform the Arabic language to make it capable of rapidly creating new terms to respond to the significant globalisation and the dramatic advancement of science and technology. This Academy has a rich history of debates and opposing views and opinions on many questions relating to the Arabic language. Broadly speaking, its main objective consists of developing the Arabic language, including but not limited to morphology and syntax (Hamzaoui 1975). In 1963, it published a book that details major decisions related to terminology creation and development, titled /Mažmûʾat al-qararât al-ᶜilmiyya wa l-fanniyya/ [Set of Scientific and Technical Decisions].

---

4. The Arabic Golden Age refers to the Abbasid period from the 8th to the 14th centuries. This period was marked by economic, political, cultural, and scientific flourishing in the history of Arabs and Muslims. In the 8th century in Baghdad, the Abbasid caliph Al-Ma'moun founded /Bayt al-Ḥikma/ [The House of Wisdom], which brought together astronomers, physicians, geographers, philosophers, and men of letters. During this period, one of the biggest projects in the Arab world saw the light of day. It consisted of translating different scientific works from Greek into Syriac and then into Arabic.

c. The Iraqi Academy of Sciences was founded in 1947 to encourage scientific research and publications in the Arabic language, the production of dictionaries, and the revival of Arabic scientific and literary tradition (Affeich 2010).

d. The Jordan Academy of Arabic was founded in 1976. Among the many objectives set out by this academy are the standardisation of terminology in the Arab world and the translation into Arabic of academic scientific works to Arabise higher education in Jordan. This Academy collaborates with other Arab academies, as well as with /Maktab Tansîq at-Taᶜrîb/ (Arabisation Coordination Bureau) of the Arab League Educational, Cultural and Scientific Organisation (ALECSO). It has translated 20 scientific books in the fields of mathematics, physics, and chemistry, among others, which were meant to support the Arabisation of higher education in Jordan (Khasara 2001).

3.1.2 *Institutes, universities and research centres*

Institutes that have played a major role in creating and promoting Arabic terms and producing research papers on terminology include the following:

a. The Institute of Studies and Research on Arabisation was founded in 1962 in Rabat, Morocco. Its activities cover various tasks, namely the creation of terminological databases, terminological research, and the development of specialised lexicons.

b. The Arabisation Coordination Bureau in Rabat, which is connected to ALECSO, was founded in 1961 to enrich the Arabic language and modernise it so that it could adapt to the needs of modern life and keep pace with the evolution of knowledge and the continuous development of science and technology.

Research centres have been most active in terms of publishing works and organising national and international conferences on terminology.

a. The Arabic Lexicology, Terminology, Lexicography, and Translation Bureau is based at Lumière University Lyon 2, France.

b. The Centre for Study and Research in Arabic Terminology is based in the School of Translators and Interpreters of Beirut at Saint-Joseph University (Lebanon).

c. The Arab Centre for Arabisation, Translation, Authorship, and Publication was founded in 1989 in Damascus (Syria). This Centre operates under the umbrella of ALECSO. Its objective is to Arabise higher education in the Arab world and translate technical and scientific works into Arabic. It also publishes a bi-annual journal titled /At-taᶜrîb/ [Arabisation].

d. The Association of Arabic Lexicology in Tunisia publishes a journal titled /Mažallat al-mucžamiyya/ [Journal of Lexicology].

e. The Moroccan Association for Lexicographic Studies publishes a journal titled /Ad-dirâsât al- mucžamiyya/ [Lexicographic Studies]. The first issue appeared in May 2002.

f. The Scientific and Technical Research Centre for the Development of the Arabic Language, based in Algiers, publishes the journal /al-Lisâniyyât/ [Linguistics]. Its mission is to implement research projects in the field of language sciences applied to the Arabic language in order to develop this language on both the didactic and technological levels.

g. The Kuwait Foundation for the Advancement of Sciences was established in 1976 and is chaired by His Highness the Emir of Kuwait. By 1994 it had published 91 books; some were written in Arabic while others were translated from foreign languages into Arabic. The institution also publishes /Mažallat al-culûm/ [Journal of Sciences], which is an Arabic translation of the journal *Scientific American* (Khasara 2003).

h. The Translation and Arabisation Centre was founded in 2006 at King Abdulaziz University in Saudi Arabia. Its objective is to encourage faculty members to translate books into Arabic and support the Arabisation movement.

The role of individuals in the development and creation of terms is also worth mentioning. They could be scientists, researchers, linguists, terminologists, or translators, who contribute significantly to enriching the Arabic lexicon. However, their role in this regard is not as simple as one might imagine. They were, and still are, confronted with two somewhat conflicting attitudes: the first is a purist attitude and is mainly advocated by the academies that consider the Arabic language sacred since it is the language of the Holy Quran, and therefore, proscribe the use of lexical borrowing, and instead encourage internal borrowing based on lexical units that already exist in Arabic. The second attitude is user-oriented and consists of adapting the language to the needs of Arabs and opting for frequently used terms.

3.2   The disseminators

The disseminators include compilers, publishers, government-led projects, termbases, and some multilingual corporations.

3.2.1   *Compilers*

The compilers of lexicons, dictionaries, and encyclopedias obviously play a key role in Arabic terminology. A few remarks should be made about modern Arabic technical and scientific dictionaries. Almost all of these dictionaries are bilingual or multilingual and are widely available on the market for different users. They are important vehicles for promoting terms. However, as Lelubre (2000: 3) notes:

> [...] their role is much more important than that of French or English lexicographers, who in general mention only terms in usage, or eventually mention the use of competing terms: in Arabic, authors of lexicographic works must choose among the many synonyms offered, and when they cannot find Arabic equivalents — or those available do not please them — they create some, without even indicating that this is their own creation; very often the sources are not indicated, much less the criteria of the choices made (our translation).

The lexicographic presentation also sometimes leaves much to be desired. While Arabs have had a solid lexicographic tradition for centuries, we can note that no lexicographic standards are respected in the entry list: nouns are sometimes put in plural form for no reason, adjectives in feminine, certain entries are lemmatised, others not, the Arabic part is often not at all vocalised, etc. However, a dictionary is supposed to be a reference book, and as such, certain vowels should be indicated, especially when it comes to two homographic terms. For instance, when not vocalised, a trilateral root such as 'k t b' كتب could be read and understood in different ways: /kataba/ كَتَبَ ('he wrote'), /kutiba/ كُتِبَ ('it is written'), /kutub/ كُتُب ('books'), /katb/ كَتْب ('the act of writing'), /kattaba/ كَتَّبَ ('he made someone write'), etc. This is the central problem of contemporary Arabic lexicography. Moreover, there are few lexicons or dictionaries that contain definitions of terms. In general — and even if they are major works — Arabic dictionaries are simple multilingual vocabularies which only give a list of equivalents without any definitions.

3.2.2 *Publishers*

Publishing houses publish lexicons, dictionaries, and encyclopedias, as well as journals, and technical and scientific works. They often have editorial committees that may intervene in the choice of terms.

One of the leading publishers in the Arab world, known for publishing dictionaries and encyclopedias, is Librairie du Liban. Founded in 1944 and based in Lebanon, Librairie du Liban produces specialised monolingual and multilingual dictionaries covering various fields, such as business, law, science, technology, and more. Its database, *mu3jam.com,* offers full access to up to 80 general and specialised dictionaries, available through monthly or annual subscription.

3.2.3   Government-led projects

Numerous projects aiming to develop Arabic terminology have been led by governments in the Arab world; some of the major ones are described in the next paragraphs.

Launched in 2007 by His Highness Sheikh Mohamed bin Zayed Al Nahyan, now President of the United Arab Emirates and ruler of Abu Dhabi, the project known as /Kalima/ ('A Word') aimed at:

> reviving the translation movement in the Arab world and supporting the vibrant cultural activity in Abu Dhabi to boost its contributions to the regional and international cultural landscape. It also seeks to establish an Arab cultural renaissance that incorporates various branches of human knowledge with books as its pillars, in addition to organising translation-related events and activities.
>
> (Kalima website)

With a target of translating 100 titles per year, by December 2016, /Kalima/ had translated 900 books into Arabic from more than 13 languages in different fields of knowledge. Clearly these translations dealt with significant amounts of terminology.

The Arab Centre for Authorship and Translation of Health Science was established in 1983 in Kuwait by the Arab Ministers of Finance. By 2003, the centre had published 84 books related to health and sciences, some of which were written in Arabic and others translated into Arabic. Among its several achievements were (1) the creation of the Arab Medical Information Network, which encompasses a database of specialised medical dictionaries, a bibliographic database covering medical literature written by Arab medical authors in Arabic and other languages, and a directory of health education and research institutions in the Arab world, and (2) the publication of an Arabic quarterly periodical titled /Taᶜrîb aṭ-tib/ [Arabisation of Medicine], the first issue of which was published in 1997 (Khasara 2003).

3.2.4   Terminology banks

Many terminology banks and databases, whose role is to facilitate access to information for writers, scientists and translators, have been created in different parts of the Arab world, the most important of which is the online terminology database of the Arabisation Coordination Bureau in Rabat. In fact, since its inception in 1961, this Bureau has established partnerships with international terminology databases and has mainly worked on collecting foreign terms and finding equivalents for them in Arabic. Thus, the Bureau's efforts culminated in the launch of a quadrilingual online terminology database (Arabic, French, English, and German), freely accessible on its website, and the publication by 2016 of more than 58 trilingual dictionaries covering different technical and scientific fields. Moreover, since 2008, ALECSO and the German Federal Ministry for Economic Cooperation and Development have been collaborating on a joint project called Arabterm, through the Arabisation Coordination Bureau and the German Agency for International Cooperation. This online, freely accessible database includes equivalents as well as definitions in Arabic for terms in English, French, and German belonging to technical fields and different industrial sectors. This project has brought together experts in different fields as well as senior translators and editors. As example, for the term *active solar system*, Arabterm provides the following equivalents in French, German and Arabic: *système solaire actif, aktives solarsystem*, and *niẓâm šamsiʿîžâbi*. Arabterm allows users to search for terms in any of the four languages, but with its user base being primarily Arabic, it provides definitions only in Arabic.[5]

Germany has also tried to reinforce its relations with the Arab world through collaborative terminology initiatives. To that effect, in 1979, Siemens in Munich began to include Arabic terms in its terminology database thanks to an agreement with the Arabisation Coordination Bureau. This was mainly for commercial reasons since the company wanted to enrich its database with Arabic terms to facilitate the translation of products and related materials destined for the Arabic market. According to this agreement, Siemens provided the Bureau with terminology in German, French, and English, in exchange for their equivalents in Arabic (see Chapter 22).

In addition to the organisations and institutions that created databases of Arabic terminology, others also contributed to the dissemination of terms by encouraging translators to publish bilingual glossaries on their websites. This is the case of the Arab Organisation for Translation which was established in 1999,

> in response to a long-time aspiration of Arab intellectuals considering translation a necessary means for Arab renaissance that supports development through the transfer of knowledge, dissemination of scholarly thought, and enhances the development of the Arab language itself.   (organisation website)

An initiative was announced in December 2021 by the Dubai Future Foundation in the United Arab Emirates on the occasion of the celebration of International Arabic Day. The foundation launched the online, freely accessible *Arabic Glossary for Future Terminologies*,

---

5. For 'active solar system', for example, the definition is: /'Niẓâm šamsi yastacmil tažhîzât musâcida (midakka maṭalan) linaql al-ḥarâra min al-mustaqbil ila l-mustacmil'/ ('A solar system that uses auxiliary equipment -a pump for example- to transfer heat from the receiver to the user').

to build on its efforts of sharing scientific and future knowledge in the Arab region. The glossary is also designed to grow over time by providing the public an opportunity to suggest new terms to be added to the platform.

(Arabic Glossary website)

3.2.5 *Multinational corporations*

Multinational corporations such as Microsoft contribute largely to the dissemination of technical terms in many languages, including Arabic. Their objectives are to market and sell their products in Arabic-speaking countries. Through its language portal and terminology collection called Microsoft Terminology Collection (MTC), the company established a set of standard terms used with its products.

> The Search Terminology box [...] allows users to perform quick searches in different languages. MTC (English-Arabic) can be saved in TBX file format. A Microsoft terminology file contains the following data: concept ID, definition, source term, source language identifier, target term, and target language identifier. It can integrate with Microsoft products and computer-assisted translation (CAT) tools.
>
> (Hassan 2017: 72–73)

Moreover, Microsoft created a multilingual online database of computing terms, the Language Portal, which was made public in 2009. This database shows the terms with their definitions in English as they appear in the Microsoft Terminology Collection, as well as in localised Microsoft products. In the latter, we can interestingly find some collocations; for instance: browse the Internet, connect to the Internet, request Internet access, and others. This clearly shows the role that companies like Microsoft are playing in the creation and dissemination of terms.

3.3 The users

Users of Arabic terminology include translators, writers, instructors, researchers and scientists in different fields. It should be noted in this context that technical and scientific translation is a fundamental element in the process of Arabisation:

> [...] Indeed, Arabisation is only conceivable — that is to say realistic — if Arabic-speaking students, technicians, and engineers can have access in Arabic to the most recent knowledge, and therefore to the world's scientific and technical literature in a broad way: which supposes an important and constant effort in terms of translation, which itself supposes the use of an adequate terminology... which only can be justified if it is widely used... [...] Hence the vicious circle: no Arabisation without terminology or translation, no translation without terminology. Terminology is meaningless without Arabisation, Arabisation is meaningless without translation.   (Lelubre 2000: 3) (our translation)

Unlike the 19th century where translation of books into Arabic played an instrumental role in the creation of terminology and the transmission of scientific knowledge from abroad, and where this activity flourished as a result of the large number of books translated into Arabic, the 20th and 21st centuries are both characterised by a decline in this activity. In fact, the number of technical and scientific books translated into Arabic remains modest, and the share of technical and scientific translation in the overall volume of translation into Arabic is low. What is this phenomenon due to, and how could it be understood and explained? In his book on the current state of translation in the Arab world, Shawqi Jalal (2004) mentions the statistics drawn up by UNESCO in 1992, which show that only one book is translated into Arabic every year for every one million Arabic speakers, whereas for comparison purposes, in Spain, and for the same number of people, 240 books are translated per year. The freely accessible UNESCO database of the world's translated books, Index Translationum,[6] places Egypt as the leading country in the Arab world for publishing books translated into Arabic, with a total number of 5,399 books published by 2009. For comparison purposes, Spain, for instance, was ranked as the leading country for publishing books translated into Spanish, with a total number of 196,090 books published by 2008. This highlights that the number of books translated into Arabic is still, in the 20th and 21st centuries, significantly lower compared to translations into languages such as Spanish (see Chapter 13) or other European languages.

How should these figures be interpreted? Being aware of the great difficulty of analysing and explaining this fact, Hamzé (2015) cites a reason which, according to him, could be fundamental in explaining the scarcity of works translated into Arabic. This reason is related to the teaching programmes in the Arab world and to the place occupied by the Arabic language within these programmes, and the relationship that this language maintains with foreign languages nowadays considered the languages of science. As we have pointed out, teaching across the Arab world is mostly done in foreign languages, that is, English and French. As a result, these two languages are very important in the lives of students, sometimes even from an early age, and become for them the only languages of learning and culture. This could lead, as Hamzé (2015) notes, to co-existing communicative situations: in the first, the mother tongue, i.e. Arabic, is used in daily activities and in the second, English and French are used in learning and teaching instances. Thus, with instruction delivered in English or French, there is little need to translate books that would be used in these environments into Arabic. This is how one could understand why the number of translated books into Arabic decreased in the 20th and 21st centuries.

---

6. Data collected from different countries by the Index team stretch from 1982 to 2014.

3.4   The standardisers

Countries in the Arab world maintain standardisation bodies to establish national standards and to contribute to international standards developed by the International Organization for Standardization (ISO). These include Algeria, Tunisia, Morocco, Saudi Arabia, Egypt, Sudan, Iraq, Syria, Lebanon, and Jordan. Four of them are taking part in the ISO technical committee TC37, whose role is to establish standards related to terminological principles and methods, terminology work and documentation, language codes, translation and interpreting, as well as language resource management (see Chapter 17).

Furthermore, the Arabisation Coordination Bureau is in charge of coordinating the various terminological standardisation activities in the Arab world. Hamzaoui (1986) describes the Bureau as the first legal and linguistic initiative, and its creation as an important historical initiative in Arabic scientific and cultural life. From its inception in 1961 until 1983, it has standardised nearly 70,000 terms in approximately 23 fields of knowledge. The Bureau dealt with the issue of terminology standardisation in two ways.

1.   Extracting Arabic terms related to a certain field of knowledge and submitting them to experts who choose what they consider to be the correct and accurate ones. At a later stage, the work of the experts is submitted to a general Arabisation conference consisting of specialised committees, and during a public session, terms that best reflect the concepts are adopted.
2.   Using methodologies that allow the creation of terms in modern scientific Arabic, such as metaphor, derivation, Arabisation, and blending when necessary, preferring standard Arabic over colloquial, choosing terms that allow derivation, and preferring monolexical terminological units over complex ones. These methodologies were formalised during a special seminar held in Rabat in 1981 (Hamzaoui 1986). To disseminate its work, the Bureau publishes /al-Lisân al-ᶜarabi/ [The Arabic Language], a journal with various articles related to terminology.

As mentioned, many people and institutions are involved in the creation of terms in the Arab world. For primarily political reasons, their decisions and recommendations are often not taken into consideration, and all their efforts related to Arabisation have often not extended beyond the boundaries of the countries in which they were initiated. However, while their work shows that there is interest in creating Arabic terms, the reverse side of this somewhat ad-hoc production is undoubtedly a level of terminological anarchy. If it is true that terminological inflation (use of two or more terms referring to the same concept) is not specific to Arabic, it must, however, be acknowledged that the Arab world presents certain conditions that are favourable to this terminological inflation:

- political divisions between Arab states
- the use of foreign languages (either English or French)
- variations due to the existence of many regional dialects.

(Lelubre 2000: 4, our translation)

4.   Terminological instability and proliferation of terms

The status of Arabic terminology today can be summarised by the words of Rousseau (2007: 115) who said: "Everyone makes their terminology in their corner, on their stove" (our translation). While there are several academies and institutions whose mission is to monitor the proper use, proper functioning and modernisation of the Arabic language, each has its own distinct terminology, a silo situation that leads to a proliferation of synonyms, quasi-synonyms, and geographical variants (Baraké 2008). Indeed, "this proliferation of institutions reflected a major problem in terminology creation in the Arab world — duplication of effort and a consequent lack of uniformity" (Emery 1983: 84–85). When Wüster put in place the basis of terminology work, he was motivated by the need to create terms that would allow unambiguous communication between engineers and industrialists. If we look at modern Arabic terminology, we cannot help but notice that communication in Arabic specialised language between the different regions and countries in the Arab world is significantly impeded due to terminological instability and an abundance of terms, in addition to other factors, such as diglossia — the multiplicity of dialects — and the richness of the Arabic language itself, which abounds in synonyms (Darir et al. 2019).

The Arab academies have produced and published vast numbers of technical and scientific terms in almost all fields of knowledge. However, what is regrettable is the fact that these academies were unable to ensure that the terms created would gain acceptance among Arab speakers and, therefore, would become actively used.

Other factors have contributed to this proliferation of terms: as mentioned in Section 3, the languages of teaching used nowadays at schools and universities across the vast majority of the Arab world are foreign, mainly English and French. Furthermore, much of the development and advancement in science and technology take place in Western countries, which has resulted in the creation of terms to refer to new concepts in the languages of these countries, and which has consequently made the Arab world a recipient and importer of this foreign terminology.

All these factors are likely to have negatively impacted the status of terminology in Arabic during the 20th century onwards with respect to the naming of new concepts in the fields of science and technology.

5.   Conclusion

It could be said that all the efforts made by the aforementioned institutions, organisations and individuals remain insufficient for many reasons.

There is a general lack of awareness among Arabs of *terminology* as an independent discipline. The title of *terminologist* as a profession or vocation is virtually unknown in the Arab world, and training in terminology is limited to introductory modules in BA and MA curricula. Hence, the teaching of terminology as an independent subject in Arab countries is practically nonexistent, and the discipline remains largely dependent on translation and linguistics.

The inability of the Arabic language to keep pace with new foreign discoveries is a concern. The standardisation of terms is far from being the only problem that modern Arabic terminology is facing. The number of terms for new concepts in English and/or European languages is very large, and the Arabic language is behind in finding and proposing equivalents for so many terms. It was estimated as long as 20 years ago that for every 7,300 terms created per year, only 2,500 have equivalents in Arabic and this gap is expected to increase (Al-Khoury 2004).

There is also the Arabic diglossia mentioned in Section 4, where colloquial forms of Arabic manifested in regional and local dialects, literary Arabic used in literary works, and modern standard Arabic used for example in administration, exist side by side in the 22 countries that form the Arab world. While one could point to this diglossia as evidence of the richness of the Arabic language, these linguistic *varieties* can lead to ambiguity and lack of precision and homogeneity in Arabic scientific and technical terms.

Arabic is a language spoken over a vast territory that stretches from the Arabian-Persian Gulf to the Atlantic Ocean, with no central linguistic authority to standardise its terminology. Although the Arabisation Coordination Bureau seems to have been playing this role in the past few years, there is still a great deal of work to be done for the Arabic language to have standardised terminology and to ensure that this terminology is used by different speakers throughout the Arab world. The academies, universities, and other competent authorities in the Arab world have attempted to set regulations for the creation of terms in Arabic, but it was clear that their job was a real challenge since they were operating more or less in silos. The lack of coordination between these institutions on the one hand, and, on the other, the fact that some of their projects were never finished (Al-Khatib

2002) have added to this problem. Cooperation among the different Arab countries and entities in the field of terminology is of utmost necessity today if we want to establish a terminological activity, similar to the one occurring in the Nordic countries, based on theory, practice, and training (see Chapter 15). Also, the challenge of disseminating terminology across the Arab world has to be addressed by all relevant entities and authorities if we want to ensure that Arabic terms created in various fields are reaching Arabic language speakers. The only country that has, until now, succeeded in standardising and unifying terms is Syria. This is because of the synergy that existed between different parties, clear political decision-making, and a national campaign that led to cooperation between the educated classes and the general public. However, there are two sides to every coin; regardless of our position on the work achieved by all parties, we cannot but acknowledge that this lexical, terminological and linguistic activity, in addition to all the effort that was made within the framework of unifying methodologies for the creation and standardisation of terms, have had a great impact on the Arabisation movement, and their results have significantly contributed to the linguistic development of the Arabic language.

References

Affeich, Andrée. 2010. *Rupture et continuité dans le discours technique arabe d'Internet*. PhD thesis. Lumière University Lyon 2.

Al-Chayyal, Jamal-Eddine. 1951. *Târiḵ at-taržama wa l-ḥaraka l-ṯaqâfiyya fi ᶜašr Muḥammad ᶜali*. Cairo: Dar al-Fikr al-Arabi.

Al-Khatib, Houssam. 2002. "Aṯar at-taržama wat-taᶜrîb 'iġnâ' al-ᶜarabiyya." *At-taᶜrîb* 24: 11–30.

Al-Khoury, Shehade. 2004. *Naḥwa manhažiyya muwaḥḥada liwaḍiᶜ al-musṭalaḥ*. Arab Academy of Damascus website.

Al-Shihabi, Mustapha. 1965. *Al-musṭalaḥât al-ᶜilmiyya fi l-luġa l-ᶜarabiyya fi l-qâdîm wa l-hadît*. Damascus: Arab Academy of Damascus.

Al-Zourgan, Muhammad Ali. 1998. *Al-žuhûd al-luġawiyya fi l-muštalah al-ᶜilmi l-ḥadît*. Damascus: Ittihad al-Kouttab al-Arab.

Badinjki, Taher. 1994. *The Challenge of Arabisation in Syria*. Al-Zaytoonah University of Jordan website.

Baraké, Rima. 2008. *La terminologie de la spatiologie: étude diachronique et descriptive de l'évolution d'un domaine et de sa structuration conceptuelle dans les trois langues français, anglais et arabe*. PhD thesis. Sorbonne Nouvelle University.

Darir, Hassane, Abdelhamid Zahid, and Khalid Elyaboudi. 2019. "Terminology Standardization in the Arab world. The Quest for a Model of Term Evaluation." In *Handbook of Terminology: Volume 2 Terminology in the Arab World*, ed. by Abied Alsulaiman, and Ahmed Allaithy, 31–58. Amsterdam: John Benjamins.

Emery, Peter G. 1983. *Towards the Creation of a Unified Scientific Terminology in Arabic*. ACL Anthology website.

Hamzaoui, Mohamed Rached. 1975. *L'Académie de langue arabe du Caire. Histoire et œuvre.* Tunis: University of Tunis.

Hamzaoui, Mohamed Rached. 1986. *Al-manhažiyya l-ᶜâmma li-taržamat al-muṣtalaḥât wa tawḥidiha wa tanmîṭiha (al-mîdân l-ᶜarabi).* Beirut: Dar Al-Gharb Al-Islami.

Hamzé, Hassan. 2015. "At-taržama wa mužtamaᶜ al-maᶜrifa." *Al-mažalla l-ᶜarabiyya liṭ-ṭaqâfa* 61: 147–179.

Hardane, Jarjoura. 1994. "Rôle du français dans l'élaboration terminologique arabe." In *Une francophonie différentielle*, ed. by Sélim Abou, and Katia Haddad, 481–499. Paris: L'Harmattan.

Hassan, Sameh Saad. 2017. "Translating Technical Terms into Arabic: Microsoft Terminology Collection (English-Arabic) as an Example." *Translation & Interpreting* online journal Vol 9 No 2: 67–86.

Jalal, Shawqi. 2004. *At-taržama fi l-ᶜâlam al-ᶜarabi. Al-wâqiᶜ wat-taḥaddi.* Cairo: Al-Mažlis al-'Acla lil-Buḥût.

Khasara, Mamdouh. 2001. "Aṭar at-taᶜrîb fi t-tanmiya l-luġawiyya." *At-taᶜrîb* 22: 65–84.

Khasara, Mamdouh. 2003. "Tažribat al-Kuwayt fi taᶜrîb at-taᶜlîm al-žâmiᶜi wa taᶜrîb al-ᶜulûm." *At-taᶜrîb* 26: 69–86.

Kloss, Heinz. 1969. *Research Possibilities on Group Bilingualism: A Report.* Quebec: International Centre for Research on Bilingualism.

Lelubre, Xavier. 1992. *La terminologie arabe contemporaine de l'optique: faits — théories — évaluation.* PhD thesis. Lumière University Lyon 2.

Lelubre, Xavier. 2000. *Introduction à la terminologie arabe.* Lecture notes. Lumière University Lyon 2.

Lelubre, Xavier. 2005. *La langue arabe de spécialité dans le domaine de la physique.* HDR Thesis. Lumière University Lyon 2.

Rousseau, Louis-Jean. 2007. *La médiation linguistique : vers l'adaptation des principes méthodologiques et des pratiques terminographiques.* Realiter website.

Sawaie, Mohammed. 1999. *'Azmat al-muṣtalaḥ al-ᶜarabi fi l-qarn at-tâsiᶜ ᶜašar.* Beirut: Dar Al-Gharb Al-Islami.

CHAPTER 20

Terminology cooperation in the EU — IATE

Annamaria Fotos, John Kirby & Riitta Majaniemi
European Commission

This chapter describes the history and development of IATE, the EU's
terminology database, from 1998 to the present day, listing some of the
challenges faced in both its creation and its constant improvement, and the
solutions found. It takes us from its conception, through its complete
redevelopment, to today's state-of-the-art terminology database. As a
database owned by the European institutions and driven by the needs of
translators working on EU documents and legislation, IATE has benefitted
from extensive interinstitutional cooperation, and its development has been
aided by considerable input from translators and other end users.

Keywords: European Union, terminology database, terminology
management, translation support, interinstitutional cooperation, public
sector information, multilingual communication, standardisation

1. Background and start of the IATE project

The European Union (EU) is an international organisation with 27 member states
and 24 official languages. The basis of its language regimen is Council Regulation
1/1958, which gives equal status to all official languages: legislation is published in
all official languages, and citizens can use any of the official languages to communicate with the EU institutions and bodies. Therefore, translation has a key role in
how the EU works. As all language versions have the same legal effect, the resulting texts need to be accurate, consistent and clear. An important element in this is
the correct use of terminology.

Before IATE, the EU institutions and bodies had approached terminology work
in various ways, and effective terminology cooperation did not exist (Rummel and
Ball 2001). The largest institutions had created their own on-line terminology databases: the European Commission (EC) had Eurodicautom, the Council of the
European Union had TIS (Terminological Information System), and the European
Parliament had Euterpe. These were available for users within and outside the institutions. In addition, many institutions and bodies used internal databases or

https://doi.org/10.1075/tlrp.24.20fot

glossaries (Rummel and Ball 2001, Johnson and Macphail 2000). Consequently, there was no single point of access for users; translators needed to search for terms in three different interfaces, in addition to their own local sources. Furthermore, as there was only a minimum of cooperation and standardisation in the terminology work carried out, terminological inconsistencies arose between the institutions and efforts were duplicated (Rummel and Ball 2001).

Since 1995, the EU institutions and bodies had discussed translation-related cooperation within the Interinstitutional Committee for Translation (ICT, later the Interinstitutional Committee for Translation and Interpretation, ICTI). However, the first concrete steps were taken only in 1998, when the Translation Centre for the Bodies of the European Union, a small EU agency, started a project to create a terminology database to standardise and manage the terminology of the Centre and of all its clients, called IATE (InterAgency Terminology Exchange).

This ambitious project was launched by Alastair Macphail, the Head of the Language Technology Section of the Translation Centre. The funding was provided through the EU's IDA (interchange of data between administrations) programme (Palos Caravina 2000). Meanwhile, the project had aroused great interest amongst the other institutions, so the Translation Centre was requested to launch a feasibility study on the creation of an interinstitutional terminology database. The study was delivered in April 1999. After a thorough analysis of the situation, the selected IT consultancy company, ATOS, recommended the merging of all data into a single, fully-interactive interinstitutional terminology database, with a common data model (Johnson and Macphail 2000).

In September 1999, after the Translation Centre had launched its own development stage for the IATE database, the other institutions decided to join the project and create a single central terminology database for all the institutions, bodies and agencies of the EU (Rummel and Ball 2001). The initial project name was then changed to InterActive Terminology for Europe (IATE), to reflect the project's interinstitutional nature.

The technical development was carried out by a Greek company, Quality and Reliability (Q & R), and the linguistic engineering by the Danish government research institute Center for Sprogteknologi (Johnson and Macphail 2000, Rummel and Ball 2001).

Various interinstitutional groups handled the project management, as there were several important elements requiring careful consideration and thorough discussion.

A key starting point was determining the structure of the terminological record (called 'entry' in IATE). The project partners chose a concept-oriented approach, based on ISO standard 12620:1999 — *Computer applications in terminology — Data categories*. The original proposal of the entry structure included four levels: (1) the language-independent level (corresponding to entry level, top level or concept level in other systems) contained the domain, origin, and other language-independent metadata; (2) the language level recorded the definition and language-related comments. The definition was placed at the language level due to the multilingual regimen of the EU, in order to ensure equality across languages; (3) the term level contained all term-related data; (4) the word level was intended for part-of-speech data, but in the end was not implemented.

One major decision concerned the choice of the domain classification system. Eurodicautom had used a very detailed but complex Lenoch classification, which was not considered suitable for ordinary users. Preference was given to the EuroVoc Thesaurus,[1] for several reasons: it was based on EU texts and therefore covered the relevant domains, it already existed in all official languages, and it already had a proper maintenance mechanism, operated by the Publications Office (Rummel and Ball 2001).

Another important aspect to be discussed was the ownership of IATE content: whether all content should be under interinstitutional ownership, and therefore modifiable by all IATE partners, or whether each institution should be clearly marked as the owner of their data, allowing only users of that institution to make changes to the content owned by them. It was finally decided to opt for the latter (Rummel and Ball 2001).

As for validation, a few project partners preferred to have control of their own content in IATE (Palos Caravina 2000), and therefore an institution-specific validation cycle was chosen instead of an interinstitutional one. Each institution was responsible for monitoring entries created by its users, and could freely decide how the validation was organised.

In addition, it was crucial to integrate the new database in the terminology and translation workflow (Rummel and Ball 2001). Except for the Translation Centre, translators did not have direct write access to the terminology databases, and terms researched and documented by them were not necessarily shared with colleagues. Therefore the new database needed to have a quick and easy way for translators to share their terminology work, making sure at the same time that the quality of the entered data was verified (Rummel and Ball 2001).

The project partners had high hopes for the future database, and expected IATE to contribute to faster access to terminology, elimination of duplication, higher quality of data and, of course, better use of human and financial resources (Johnson and Macphail 2000). They paid special attention to IATE's user-friendliness, so that

---

1. The Eurovoc thesaurus is updated regularly. The current version of IATE uses the 2018 build of Eurovoc for stability purposes.

it would be suitable for different user groups, like translators, terminologists and EU citizens (Rummel and Ball 2001).

The development of the IATE project started in January 2000, and during the first phase, the detailed specifications of the system were drafted (Palos Caravina 2000). The first prototype was ready for testing in summer 2001, and after that several test rounds were run. The following legacy databases were imported into IATE:

– Eurodicautom (European Commission – DG Translation)
– TIS (Council of the European Union)
– Euterpe (European Parliament)
– Euroterms (Translation Centre for the Bodies of the EU)
– CDCTERM (European Court of Auditors).

What made this exercise challenging was the large amount of content to be merged: in July 1999, the largest database, Eurodicautom, contained over 1.24 million entries, TIS had 200,000 entries, Euterpe had 171,000 entries (Johnson and Macphail 2000), and Euroterms had 180,000 entries. In addition, every institution had their own approach to terminology work, and all terminology databases had a different structure and different set of metadata. Therefore mapping rules needed to be defined between the old databases and the new one (Rummel and Ball 2001).

In 2003, full-scale user tests with the final version were run, and a user survey was conducted to gather feedback. IATE was finally operational and available for internal use in summer 2004. It was then gradually adopted as the main terminology tool by the project partners.

2.   Early years of IATE

The first IATE system (IATE 1) was based on Oracle, and data was stored in UTF8 format. The web-based user interface was programmed in Java (Fontenelle and Rummel 2014). The database was hosted by the EC's Data Centre, and it was — and still is — managed by the IATE Support and Development Team based at the Translation Centre.

Various interinstitutional groups assumed responsibility for the management and further technical development of IATE. In addition, users were able to provide feedback and development proposals. The first on-line survey on the operational database was run in spring 2005, giving valuable information on how IATE was used and perceived in practice.

In the beginning, IATE contained more than 8 million terms in over a million entries. EU translators found it very useful: during 2005, which was its first full year of operation, between 10,000 and 12,000 queries were made per day. The option of on-line data editing also proved fruitful: around 250 new terms were added and around 300 existing terms were modified or validated per day.

Right from the start, it was clear to the IATE partners that the database contained a large amount of poor, obsolete and duplicate data. The duplication was mainly due to the merging of the previous separate databases, which often contained entries on the same concepts (Fontenelle and Rummel 2014). Various consolidation efforts were made within the institutions and at interinstitutional level to tackle the issue. Interinstitutional consolidation proved to be an extremely complex undertaking, requiring a great deal of work and human resources. Moreover, resources were also needed for other tasks: in addition to the "noise" created by duplication, there was "silence" in IATE: content needed to be added in languages that had gained official EU status in 2004.

The project partners were aware that proper terminology work and the maintenance of a terminology database required a good deal of human resources. In practice, the available resources were not sufficient: in many translation services, terminology was considered a supplementary task to be carried out if and when the translation workload allowed it. Therefore the project partners proposed as early as 2007 that at least the European Commission, the European Parliament and the Council of the European Union should assign a set percentage of their staff to IATE-related work. This would be beneficial for the translators' productivity and for the overall quality of translations. This was implemented, but only to the extent allowed by the availability of resources in each institution.

Great efforts were made to ensure consistency and quality in the content. It was important that all users having the right to add and update records would do so correctly, because in IATE, the result was immediately visible to all internal users. Therefore, in addition to IATE *Writing Rules*, another document, called *Best Practice*, was distributed to all users with editing rights, in order to explain the general principles of using IATE and to guarantee harmonised working methods. A more concrete way of guaranteeing quality was the validation cycle, triggered automatically by the tool for every change made. Validation was carried out by native-speaker terminologists in each language section in accordance with a set of established rules.

Communication was a key aspect in running a common database. Depending on the case at hand, it took the form of e-mail or a commenting feature called 'marks,' which could be attached to individual IATE entries. In addition, central coordination teams started to regularly discuss common topics and decide on uniform practices. The first meeting of the Coordination Cell for Terminology took place at the Translation Centre in December 2005, where the mandate and the work programme for 2006 were defined. Formal cooperation was enacted within the Interinstitutional Committee for Translation and Interpretation and its sub-groups.

In addition to the obvious gains in the field of terminology, the development and the launch of IATE brought the language services of the EU institutions and bodies closer to each other, and created a concrete framework for linguistic cooperation between translators and terminologists within and between the institutions (Fontenelle and Rummel 2014). For example, in 2005, the IATE Data Management Group started to organise interinstitutional meetings for terminologists of the same language. These were the beginning of a very fruitful communication within the language communities.

3.   Public IATE

Eurodicautom, TIS and Euterpe had all been open to and widely used by the general public, and the IATE partners acknowledged the need to have a public version of IATE as well. The related administrative questions and technical conditions were discussed at various levels: the IATE working groups, ICTI and the Secretaries General. ICTI approved the principle of external access on 22 September 2005.

The IATE Support and Development Team worked on a separate IATE dissemination database and its search interface, which was adapted and further improved based on feedback from internal testers. Finally, in April 2007, the Eurodicautom site was shut down, and public users were redirected to the IATE database. The following few months were considered the last test phase, to demonstrate the application's performance and stability and to further improve the user interface.

IATE was officially opened to the public on 28 June 2007, giving access to over 8 million terms in 23 official EU languages. It quickly became very popular; during the first few years the average number of queries per day was around 200,000. Based on substantial feedback received in the IATE public mailbox, it was clear that users appreciated the richness of IATE as a terminological source, and the user-friendly interface. The estimated user community was around 220,000 people. IATE was accessed from around the world, with queries arriving from more than 170 different countries.

4.   Interinstitutional cooperation

Once IATE was up and running in both its internal and public forms, the importance of continued cooperation between the European institutions in the field of terminology did not diminish. The IATE Management Group was created in 2009 and continues to meet to this day. Its aim is to deal with IATE development issues, ensure content coordination, oversee cooperation with third parties, and perform administrative and reporting tasks. For other, more specific, mandates, various other groups and task forces have been created over the years.

The terminology coordinators of the central terminology services have also met several times a year since 2008 to discuss current issues in terminology work, projects, IATE consolidation, best practices, and to reach agreements on proceedings in IATE and on methodology.

The information flow between the institutions has remained healthy. Outside the official meetings, daily contact continues with regard to specific issues (a particular IATE entry, for example), using conventional communication channels. In 2014 a further means of communication was created in the shape of EurTerm, the in-house European Union Terminology Portal. This web platform provides a wide variety of information on IATE, training materials, EU terminology projects, other terminology resources, the various IATE coordination groups, news and blog posts, and is also used internally as a wiki to post comments on technical issues.

5.   External cooperation and the Irish terminology project

IATE has regularly attracted interest from universities and other institutions working in the field of terminology, and many projects have been carried out with universities from all over Europe. These have often involved students working on IATE content as part of an academic study. Some have been more successful than others and problems have occasionally been encountered with the quality of the work delivered. Although cooperation with universities was considered an excellent way of extending and improving the terminology in IATE at a rather low cost for the institutions, and cooperation with external experts was, in principle, desirable, it has also required, however, a considerable involvement of internal staff and has by no means been a no-cost solution.

One highly beneficial and long-term undertaking has been what is generally referred to as the 'Irish terminology project'. The GA IATE project is an initiative established by the EU institutions in 2007, in collaboration with the Irish government, to ensure a sufficient supply of terminology in the Irish language for translation requirements arising from the language gaining official status in the EU. Work commenced in 2008 and by 2013 around 55,000 terminological entries had been processed and returned to IATE (Bhreathnach, Cloke and Nic Pháidín 2013).

For the EU institutions, the parameters of this project have been ideal: the project has been fully financed by the Irish authorities; the contributors have been among the most highly qualified terminologists of the language; and the Irish terminologists have benefited from first-rate IT support. Despite these excellent conditions, one full-time EC terminologist has nevertheless been required to handle this project and deal not only with technical problems, but also content-related issues.

6.   Consolidation of the database

Concerns about the quality of the data in IATE persisted, not only in terms of their internal usefulness, but also the image they presented via IATE Public. It was felt that, whilst modifications to the IATE data structure may be needed, the underlying problem remained the poor quality of some IATE data and the number of duplicates. Only systematic consolidation could, in the long run, ensure the quality and usefulness of IATE. To this end, an interinstitutional CleanUp Task Force was created in 2014, tasked with a structured approach to cleaning up the database. By 2016, the Task Force had deleted over 16,000 entries, but had also realised that, compared with the high number of entries in IATE, such an achievement was relatively insignificant. In any case, the shift in working methods had also led to a slight change in the Task Force's goals. The objective now was mainly to facilitate the integration of IATE data into CAT (Computer-Aided Translation) tools. The institutions were therefore encouraged to agree on a completion indicator at language and entry level that reflects the metadata richness of an entry. This indicator would contribute to excluding low-quality content from data being exported to CAT tools and, in particular, SDL Trados (now Trados Studio).

A further challenge to consolidation of IATE had been the cumbersome method of merging entries, which relied on a manual comparison of two data entries. If there were several duplicate entries of the same concept, the merging process had to be carried out several times. To accelerate the merging process, the central terminology coordinators of the European institutions requested a new feature: the multimerge. In 2016, a new menu item was made available to administrators, allowing the merging of one primary and several secondary entries into a single new entry with a new ID. The data at language-independent level and language level were concatenated, whilst data at term level were inserted.

7.   Technical developments

In the years between the launching of IATE and the appearance in 2018 of IATE 2, many technical changes and developments were made to the database, mainly at the instigation of the IATE Management Group. These included, for example, the creation of an Undelete option, allowing unwanted or mistaken deletions to be reversed; the removal of ownership restrictions for deletions; the harmonisation of user roles and rights across the EU institutions; and harmonisation of the attribution of reliability values[2] for entries.

Perhaps the most important changes in this period were ones reflecting the evolution of working methods within the translation departments of the institutions. As more and more translation work was completed using the Trados Studio CAT tool and translators became increasingly interested in consulting terminology from within Studio, the IATE development team also addressed the issue of integrating IATE and SDL Trados. The aim was to provide users with two methods of accessing IATE: directly, one term at a time by querying the IATE database, and indirectly, by importing a document-specific glossary, sourced and compiled automatically from IATE, into the CAT tool.

In parallel, to enable terminologists to create termbases for a specific translation or subject area, IATE developers worked on a term recognition module (TRM), to be incorporated into the interface. A proof of concept was implemented in 2013 but the project was not without difficulties. Algorithms needed to be created for the morphological analysis and term detection, a converter needed to be installed so that users could submit various formats (Excel, XML, HTML, Word, PDF, and PowerPoint), and an appropriate list of exclusions needed to be established in order to reduce the amount of data retrieved from IATE that had no value for translators (including, for example, 2-letter terms, or upper case letters). It was therefore not until January 2017 that the TRM was made available in production for IATE administrators. It is now also open to many other categories of user.

8.   IATE's public image

Following the IATE opening ceremony in 2007, little attention was initially paid to the public version of IATE. No marketing or publicity was carried out, and the tool was made available for public use, with a regularly updated content, but little concern for how it was received. The original intention, after all, had been to

---

2. The reliability value is a five-star rating system indicating the trustworthiness of a term.

create a tool for translators and other staff of the EU institutions; its availability to the general public was just a generous by-product.

In 2011, this view begin to change within the institutions, and there was a growing feeling that the visibility and usage of IATE Public should be enhanced. It was thought that the public version of IATE should be aimed at language professionals (including freelancers), and not framed as a sort of online dictionary.

One technical obstacle to this was that the public and internal versions were housed in separate databases and systems. Not only did this separation pose a risk that the data could diverge, but it also required additional maintenance work. This issue was solved in 2013 with the migration of IATE Public from Hummingbird/Fulcrum to Oracle Intermedia, thus ensuring that IATE Public was now a full subset of 'internal' IATE. Only confidential and non-validated terms would now be excluded from the public interface. The migration chiefly concerned the web server (where an Oracle Application server was replaced by WebLogic) and the indexing tool (where Oracle Intermedia was substituted for Hummingbird-Fulcrum). The main advantage of the use of Oracle Intermedia was that IATE Public could now be updated automatically; in other words, new terms were visible in IATE Public as soon as they had been validated.

Interest in IATE Public grew, with many users making use of the option of exporting IATE content. In 2013, the Executive Committee on Translation had approved a new legal notice for IATE Public. This new text had permitted the re-use of a subset of IATE data without restriction, the only obligation being that IATE was to be acknowledged as the source of the data. Subsequently, between July and October 2014, over 5,000 downloads of the IATE export in TBX were recorded.

In late 2014, in response to user feedback about the difficulties in managing the large export file (which contained all EU languages), an extraction tool was developed in Java, allowing users to select their preferred language(s), domain(s) and evaluation value(s) from the complete export file and obtain a subset of data, which could then be managed easily in third-party tools. By April 2015, 12,371 downloads had been carried out. A new version of the TBX file for download was then made available in May 2015, with further improvements and corrections following user feedback. The TBX file was subsequently updated on a quarterly basis in order to provide users with the latest IATE data.

Other improvements made to the IATE Public interface included the display of entry-to-entry links and cross-references as active hyperlinks, the inclusion of image files, and the addition of a list of Frequently Asked Questions that had been prepared in 2013.

9.   Language coverage

It is only to be expected that a terminology database created and run by the institutions of the EU should have a fairly extensive language coverage. Indeed, not only is the interface available in all 24 official languages of the EU; terms in all those languages, plus Latin and 'Multilingual' (a label to cover language-independent terms, such as chemical formulae, ISO codes, etc.) are also included in Public IATE. In internal IATE, there are also some entries in non-EU languages, inserted as dictated by political necessity for reasons of international cooperation.

In 1999, the initial specifications for IATE had already included extensive coverage of languages, and, technically, the subsequent accession of Member States with different languages to those already present (Bulgarian, Croatian, Czech, Estonian, Hungarian, Latvian, Lithuanian, Maltese, Polish, Romanian, Slovak and Slovene) and the elevation of Irish to full language status have required little or no technical adaptation. The challenge has been the addition of content. Whereas existing languages boasted thousands, if not hundreds of thousands of terms, the new languages needed, effectively, to start from scratch.

More often than not, the impetus for the addition of terminology in these languages was provided by the translation of the *acquis* (established EU law), which national translators undertook as the countries prepared to join the EU. The work on catching up has continued ever since, sometimes posing challenges for translators and terminologists alike. How, for example, should Maltese terminologists produce an extensive set of railway terminology when the island of Malta has no railway system? How should Hungarian terminologists approach terminology on seafaring or marine life, when the landlocked status of Hungary has bridled technical or political interest in these areas in the past? The answers to these challenges are perhaps too complex to detail here; suffice it to say that sometimes terminologists have had to show a certain level of inventiveness.

10.   IATE 2.0

While IATE received new and improved features based on the requests of its users, the underlying technologies could not keep pace with the changing technological environment and needs of translators working in the EU institutions. By 2015, it became clear to the IATE Management Group that a complete redevelopment would be needed to replace the system's obsolete or ageing technologies, rigid architecture and data structure, "in order to prepare it for future challenges, including interoperability, modularity, scalability and data exchange" (Zorrilla-Agut and Fontenelle 2019). In contrast to the evolution of IATE 1, where technological issues predominated, with IATE 2, much of the impetus for development stemmed from the requirements of end users.

10.1   Defining and designing the new database (2015–2018)

The Data Entry Task Force (later renamed the IATE 2 Task Force) of the IATE Management Group was entrusted with defining the requirements for IATE 2 (Dechandon 2016) that would satisfy user needs in all participating institutions. The Task Force comprised managers, terminology coordinators, terminologists and translators of the EU institutions.

Chaired by the IATE Tool Manager, the group kept in close contact with the IATE Support and Development team. The development work was based on the 'agile approach,' and was carried out in sprints and tracked via milestones. User stories were drafted to describe every feature in a non-technical way, so that end users could give feedback without possessing technical expertise. The Task Force reviewed and validated the user stories, taking into account several differ-ent points of view (e.g. public users, internal and external translators querying the database, terminologists and terminology coordinators).

The requirements described in the user stories centred on content manage-ment, reusability of data and user-friendliness. To be able to adapt IATE to the requirements, technologies had to be identified, an architecture had to be designed and an infrastructure had to be built. The new IATE had to be user-friendly, effi-cient and accessible; at the same time, it needed to offer fast and automated (or semi-automated) ways of exporting data for review and management offline and for use in computer-assisted environments. In addition, it had to allow the exploita-tion of terminology data for other tools via web services and application program-ming interfaces (APIs).

10.1.1   *Modified data structure*

The data structure of the previous version was retained for the most part, as it was largely based on the data categories of ISO 12620 and covered the needs of its users. However, new metadata fields and values had been included or made mandatory for users, to account for the specific circumstances that arise from IATE being the terminology management tool of an international institution where legislation is multilingual, while the main working languages are limited to English, French and German.

As adopting legislation in the EU is based on a decision-making process that involves the EC submitting proposals to the Council and the European Parlia-ment, which can adopt them at first reading or second reading, a lifecycle field was added at the language-independent level to indicate whether the record cov-ers a concept that appears in a text that has not yet been adopted (lifecycle value 'proposed'), This field can also indicate terms that refer to concepts that are no longer in use or in existence (lifecycle value 'historical'), or to concepts that appeared solely in a Commission proposal that was not adopted (lifecycle value 'abandoned').

In addition, a direct link was established to EUR-Lex, the European Union Law database. In IATE 1, whenever reference was made to a legislative act of the EU, terminologists had to insert and sometimes revise the title of the act from EUR-Lex, and had to construct a link by using the CELEX number.[3] For IATE 2, the user community wanted a simpler method, preferably without the need to switch between applications. The resulting EUR-Lex module was one of the improvements most praised by terminologists after IATE 2 was officially launched.

The EC drafts legislation in one of the working languages (usually English or French). The texts are then translated into all official languages (with each language version having equal status, including at the drafting stage). To achieve consistency across the languages, the concept to be recorded in the terminology database is usually defined in the language of the draft, which then 'anchors' the concept, all other language equivalents having to contain terms that denote the same concept. This is a very important point that needed to be underpinned by requiring users to specify an 'anchoring' language whenever a new record is created.

Source reference fields were also made mandatory, with the added option of including multiple reference fields, e.g. to indicate both an external reference and an EU-specific reference, in order to support translators of documents drafted in the EU institutions.

As IATE is not only a tool to record and query terminological data, but also to manage terminology work in the EU institutions, additional management fields at language and term level were also requested.

Furthermore, some metadata fields were expanded, e.g. the cross-references at the language-independent level to indicate conceptual relations beyond the previously very limited 'related, broader/narrower and antonym' scope of this field. The cross-reference field in IATE 2 displays the first term in the anchor language of the cross-referenced entry, an improvement over IATE 1 where only the ID number appeared. The subject-field taxonomy was also expanded with the addition of two more levels of the Eurovoc classification system.

10.1.2 New technologies, infrastructure and architecture

The IATE 2 system is built as RESTful APIs and based on Docker technology, which ensures openness and interoperability with other systems as needed. The IATE 2 graphical user interface (GUI) is based on the Angular web application framework. After thorough analysis of available technologies that would support

---

3. The CELEX number is a unique identifier for a document in EUR-Lex. For more information, please see the EUR-Lex help page on CELEX numbers.

the needs expressed, particularly a near real-time search, full text search capabilities and open source analysers allowing customisations, it was decided to switch to the search engine technology provided by Elastic (Elasticsearch, based on the Lucene library, and Kibana, a data visualisation dashboard, among other components). Elasticsearch is also used as the main database to store IATE content.

The initial architecture was preserved with a view to eventually migrating both the database and the application to the Cloud.

> Along with the improvements in infrastructure and architecture, the front-end also received significant update. The graphical user interface was completely overhauled to present a clean, modern 'façade'. The interface was made to be responsive on different devices (PCs, mobile phones and other mobile devices). Web Content Accessibility Guidelines (WCAG) 2.0 were followed for the most used screens (search, results, data entry). A screen reader support was also implemented for the main IATE pages, following WAI-ARIA recommendations, which make it easier for the visually-impaired, for example, to use Text-To-Speech (TTS) engines to translate on-screen information into speech.   (Zorrilla, 2019)

The three-level (language-independent, language level and term level) data model allows the use of an internal unique identifier and a URI per level that can be exploited by the system and other systems as well (Zorrilla 2019).

Exploitation of the data and metadata contained in IATE 2 was enhanced by the possibility of connecting to it via APIs, and also by making the manual export of data more user-friendly. The 'Advanced search' module was a successor of a rather intimidating pseudo-SQL querying functionality in IATE 1. Instead of using a specific query language that can be difficult for the uninitiated, the new interface offers a simpler query-building feature, using metadata labels that users see in the database every day, and familiar Boolean operators.

Using the Term Recognition Module (TRM), in-house translators were already able to send documents to IATE 1 for analysis; however, this module was redeveloped to offer more targeted results with the help of Elasticsearch's in-built stemmers and tokenizers.

10.2   Launching the new IATE (2018–2019)

IATE 2 (in consultation-only mode) was released to the public in November 2018. It was followed by an official launch event, in Luxembourg, where 300 participants and other interested parties via web streaming could view presentations on the new features given by representatives of the IATE partner institutions.

In February 2019, the new system, complete with advanced data management features, was launched for in-house translators and terminologists. While the terminology records had been transferred by that date, transferring the history of previous operations took some time. The IATE 1 system was kept operational for two more years to ensure that there was no data loss. It was finally decommissioned in February 2021.

10.3 Continuous development and maintenance (February 2019–present)

With the new system officially launched, the IATE 2 Task Force continued to meet monthly to discuss further developments and approve the changes made to the terminology database. Members of the group monitored the new IATE and reported bugs and users' further requests for improvement to the development team. For that purpose, a feedback page was created on the interinstitutional wiki, EurTerm, which was accessible to all the IATE partner institutions, so that they would be apprised of the change requests made and the bugs reported.

During the initial development phase, the Cloud had already been proposed as the best hosting solution, in order to accommodate such a large user community querying and updating IATE concurrently. During the first year after the launch, Cloud solutions had been scrutinised for suitability and security. The IATE Management Group then decided that a switch to Cloud technology would also be beneficial to users, for speed and reliability of access is of the essence as the workload continues to grow for all translators. In 2021, the initial on-premises infrastructure was migrated to the Cloud for scalability, higher performance and security, and affordability.

Several features were also redeveloped, as users requested additional functions and as members of the IATE 2 Task Force gained more experience with the new system. It is now for example possible to share an entry in a bilingual display with a simple mouse click, which either copies the URL for pasting into a document or CAT tool, or opens an e-mail application for forwarding. It is also possible to share an 'Advanced search' query by either copying, downloading, or forwarding the query. The filter 'field completion score' (previously 'completion indicator', see Zorrilla 2019) also underwent several development stages.

By the end of 2021, the new IATE was stable and established, and the development team could concentrate on two supporting features, the Terminology Projects Module (TPM) and the Term Extraction Module (TEM).

As previously mentioned, one of the basic requirements defined by the IATE 2 Task Force centred on the improvement of content management. A natural evolution from that requirement was the wish that projects coordinated in the institutions could be fully drafted, prepared, monitored and followed-up in IATE itself, without using additional external tools such as Excel tables, e-mails, wikis or other collaborative sites. The TPM was developed with the cooperation of several IATE user groups. It enables the coordinator of a project to manage the project from the initial stages to its completion within one system. It allows the creation of a list of candidate terms, which can be then used to create draft records (labelled 'raw') for later completion. It also facilitates the detection of possible duplicates and other related records. Once the project is finalised for the anchor language, it can be assigned to the terminologists or translators in the language units of the institutions who add or revise their language entries. A forum-like platform ensures that users can share feedback and comments in the application itself. TPM also facilitates cooperation with external collaborators, such as universities, student trainees or experts.

In 2022, development was focussed mainly on collaborative features, including the TPM, but also on the Term Extraction Module (TEM). A proof of concept for monolingual extraction in the main working languages had already been released with the launch of IATE 2. Following layout changes and improved rendering of results, the module is being further developed to support bilingual term extraction.

Developments under consideration also include "strategies for guiding the users to select the right domain (for example, by exploiting metadata in the EU legal references from Cellar/EUR-Lex used to document a concept, term or context in an entry), identifying and correcting wrong domains in IATE (with the help of machine learning to disambiguate concepts following analysis of the text fields populated in an entry: definition, context, note, etc.), as well as direct consumption of EuroVoc data" (Zorrilla 2019).

11.   Outlook

IATE's past is interlinked with the growth and development of the European Union. Consequently, there is more data available for languages spoken in the member states before the 2004 EU enlargement than for the languages spoken in countries that joined the EU after 2004. The challenge is still to strike the necessary balance between the need to consolidate obsolete and duplicated data and to add new records.

Various features already in place facilitate the cleaning and consolidation of IATE data. Further developments will also focus on this aspect. The continued development of the TEM, APIs and CAT tool plugins will ensure that due attention is also paid to enriching the database.

Technological progress in computational linguistics and other related areas continues to be monitored, and IATE will be adapted accordingly. And, of course, fine-tuning remains an ongoing process: new ideas spring up continually and are implemented when feasible.

IATE is perceived within the EU institutions as one of the most successful products of interinstitutional cooperation. The future looks bright as the fruitful cooperation of the various EU translation services continues.

References

Bhreathnach, Úna, Fionnuala Cloke, and Caoilfhionn Nic Pháidín. 2013. "Terminology for the European Union. The Irish Experience: The GA IATE Project." Galway: Cló Iar-Chonnacht.

Dechandon, D. 2016. "From IATE to IATE 2 or when Technologies are Agents of Change and Means to Improve Users' Satisfaction." In *Proceedings of the 38th Conference of Translating and the Computer*, 19–32. London: Asling.

Fontenelle, Thierry, and Dieter Rummel. 2014. "Term Banks." In *International Handbook of Modern Lexis and Lexicography*, ed. by Patrick Hanks, and Gilles-Maurice de Schryver, 1–12. Heidelberg: Springer.

International Organization for Standardization. 2009. *ISO 12620:2009: Terminology and other Language and Content Resources — Specification of Data Categories and Management of a Data Category Registry for Language Resources.*

Johnson, Ian, and Alastair Macphail. 2000. "IATE — Inter-Agency Terminology Exchange: Development of a Single Central Terminology Database for the Institutions and Agencies of the European Union." *LREC Workshop on Terminology Resources and Computation*, Athens.

Palos Caravina, Maria-José. 2000. "Validation and Quality Control Issues in a New Web-Based, Interactive Terminoloy Database for the Institutions and Agencies of the European Union." *Translating and the Computer* 22. London: Aslib.

Regulation No 1 determining the languages to be used by the European Economic Community, Consolidated text, Document 01958R0001–20130701.

Rummel, Dieter, and Sylvia Ball. 2001. "The IATE Project — Towards a Single Terminology Database for the European Union." *Translating and the Computer* 23. London: Aslib.

Zorrilla-Agut, Paula, and Thierry Fontenelle. 2019. "IATE 2: Modernising the EU's IATE terminological database to respond to the challenges of today's translation world and beyond." *Terminology. International Journal of Theoretical and Applied Issues in Specialized Communication* 25, no. 2: 146–174.

CHAPTER 21

Terminology in France
Evolution of its official framework

Danielle Candel
Université Paris-Cité

This chapter deals with the history, theories and practices of official terminology in France. The establishment of official French terminology, including neology, was initiated in the 19th century in France but was formalised and intensified in recent decades. Terminological activity in France, which also makes use of work done in other areas of the Francophonie, such as Quebec, carefully organised for over fifty years, involves about twenty committees. They operate on the basis of accumulated experience in a wide range of domains (science, technology, industry, economy, culture). The aim is to show how terminology work fits in with lexicographical activities, establishes links with the official terminology framework and to describe its historical evolution.

Keywords: terminology, lexicography, neologism, definitions, domains, official terminology, enrichment process, prescription, description

1.   Introduction

This chapter is concerned with the official terminology process that has been set up in France and has operated in contemporary periods. This process embodies the will of the State to defend its language through its continuous enrichment. The analysis of the official terminology process in France described here is substantiated by references to documents and also reflects the experience of the author who has been directly involved in official French lexicography and terminography. We begin by sketching the development and contributions of institutions engaged in terminology. These aspects are treated in Section 2 (where the influence of Eugen Wüster, an early promoter of terminology, is also mentioned). Some of the premises of French prescriptivism will be considered in that section, first with the foundational ordinance of Villers-Cotterêts and then with the creation of the *Académie Française*. The more recent institutions and committees

https://doi.org/10.1075/tlrp.24.21can
© 2025 John Benjamins Publishing Company

that were involved in setting up the present official terminology process will then be covered together with the role of individuals who had a significant influence. Section 3 gives a brief account of the current situation and describes the committees engaged in the official terminology framework, while Section 4 gathers examples originating from this framework and discusses their impact on dictionaries and other media. The historical evolution of this framework is presented in the final section.

2.   Official institutions and international links

The history of official terminology in France is intimately linked to that of organisations involved in the terminological endeavour such as the International Society of Automation, ISA (founded in 1945), the International Organization for Standardization, ISO (set up in 1947), and the International Electrotechnical Commission, IEC (founded in 1906). Eugen Wüster, currently portrayed as the founder of the discipline of terminology, was himself active in ISO and in IEC (concerning Wüster, see also Chapter 8). He was also invested in Infoterm, the International Information Centre for Terminology at Unesco, and in Termnet (International Network for Terminology).[1] In 1952, Technical Committee 37 was established in ISO (see also Galinski in this volume, Chapter 17) to develop standards governing terminology work (see for instance Cabré 2005: 192; Candel, Samain and Savatovsky 2023). Terminological work carried out in France is in some ways linked to — and even derived from — these activities.

Having summarised some international activities in terminology, we can now examine French initiatives in this field, discuss connections between prescriptivism and terminological issues, and show results of terminological organisation in France.

---

1. Wüster was not only active in the international organisation of terminology but also was a practicing terminologist and this explains why his name is encountered in contemporary terminology data. For example, in the termbase of the Government of Québec (Le Grand dictionnaire terminologique), the entries for *flow-regulating valve*, *throttle valve* and *throttle* are attributed to Wüster himself (1968). This example illustrates that Wüster was involved in the practice of terminology in addition to developing his influential General Theory of Terminology. The French equivalent *ajustabilité de la poussée* for 'throttability' was finally published in the official French terminological database FranceTerme (10/01/2023).

3.   History of French prescriptivism: Some elements and issues

One often distinguishes the description of language from prescriptive actions, which indicate how one should use language, both spoken and written. The development of official terminology is in this sense aligned with prescriptive approaches, and the idea of prescribing language rules has a long history in France.

3.1   French, an officially recommended language

French has been the official language in France since the *Ordinance of Villers-Cotterêts* (1539) promulgated by King François the first. The Ordinance established that the French language was to be used in all courts and administrative services, replacing Latin. About a hundred years later the French Academy (Académie française) was founded by Richelieu in 1635 with the mission of providing "certain rules to our language and make it pure, eloquent and capable of dealing with the arts and sciences"[2] (our translation). This is but one manifestation of France's engagement in the defence of its language by establishing prescriptive institutions. This prescriptivism is reflected in the Academy's dictionary, the *Dictionnaire de l'Académie française*, as of its first edition in 1694. The Academy has always considered that its specific mission was to provide rules for the French language. And, as explained in article 24 of the Academy's statutes, it also set as its goal to ensure that French as a language could adequately convey knowledge in the arts and sciences. It is interesting to examine the successive editions of this dictionary and note that the eighth edition (1932–1935) contains about twice as many words as the seventh. This growth is essentially due to the integration of a large volume of specialised vocabulary. Similarly, the ninth edition which is, in 2023, in its final stages of completion, includes a further amount of scientific and technical terms, that to some extent reflect the enrichment of the French language as a result of official terminological activities.

In addition to the well-established Académie française, a number of other councils, committees and structures successively concerned themselves with the French language. Bernard Quemada played a key role in these various institutions and understood early on the dynamic nature of language and the need for international terminological efforts (Quemada 1978). He engaged in a range of activities in this direction while heading the CNRS dictionary project *Trésor de la langue française*.

The second part of the 20th century saw the creation of committees aimed at "defending" the French language. In 1993, the Prime Minister, advised by the

---

2. Bylaws of the Académie française, 1635, article 24.

Conseil supérieur de la langue française (1989–2006), requested that the Comité consultatif de la langue française be focussed on French language usage in sciences and technology, and that its actions be aimed at the enrichment of French in the context of the rapid development of information and communication technologies.

3.2   Terminological development as a policy

The aim of terminological development (*aménagement terminologique*) was pursued by the Haut Comité pour la défense et l'expansion de la langue française, created under President de Gaulle (1966) and by its successor the Haut Comité de la langue française (1973). The same period also saw the foundation of the Association française de terminologie (AFTERM, 1975).

In that period, the Haut Comité promoted legislative action in defence of the French language which resulted in the decree establishing the first generation of ministerial terminology committees (1972). A further step was taken with the Bas-Lauriol law passed by the government in 1975 to prevent direct borrowing and to promote new words, with their definitions and usage recommendations. This law was followed, in 1994, by the *Loi Toubon*.[3]

A useful synthesis explaining sources and diverse elements contributing to the development of the official terminological process can be found in *La Terminologie en France* (Union Latine 1995, edited by Daniel Prado). It describes French institutions such as the Haut Conseil de la francophonie (1984), the Conseil supérieur de la langue française (1989–2006), the Délégation générale à la langue française DGLF (1989-), the INaLF (1977-, which became the ATiLF), the CTN (Centre de terminologie et de néologie, see Humbley 1995), Terminology at the Ministry for Higher Education and Research (see Guyon 1995), and the Conseil international de la langue française (CILF, 1967-).

In France, terminology is recognised as an element of language planning. Linguists such as Loïc Depecker, Jean-Michel Eloy, and John Humbley (see Humbley 1995, 1997, 2000, 2018), and others like Samy Boutayeb and François Gaudin, have been quite active in this landscape. The development of terminology in France is also linked internationally, through the Rint network (Réseau international de néologie et de terminologie, 1986-) and the Realiter pan-Latin network (1993-). These organisations help in adapting the French language to scientific and technological areas.

---

3. Law protecting French in official government publications, advertisements, workplaces, commercial contracts etc.

In this general landscape the Comité d'étude des termes techniques français, which was created in 1954 and operated until about 1970, is worth mentioning. In an essay published in 1972 about creating technical terms, Combet, Agron and their colleagues indicate that they approve of the French laws requiring authors of patents to use French terms. They also raise the question of steering the evolution of language in a specific direction:

> In what follows, it is not a question of a general translation. Each of the foreign terms is studied only within its domain and meanings given to it by the French when it is used as such. These meanings often differ from those of the word in its original language (our translation)
>
> (Comité d'étude des termes techniques français 1972:1)

The aim of the process is to propose a French word to replace an English one, and not to "translate" the English term literally but rather to adopt a term that complies with the inherent properties of French as a language. Let us recall the case of "horizon scanning" (domain: Santé et Médecine, Health), which produced "prospective sanitaire" (expanded form: "surveillance prospective sanitaire," as published in the *Journal official de la République française*, June 19, 2024). This perspective is to be contrasted with the current misconception that officially recommended terms are "translations" of English terms: this may of course happen (i.e.: "virtual circuit" for "circuit virtuel" (Telecommunications, September 22, 2000, initially October 3, 1984), but it is mostly not the case. Combet, Agron and their coauthors differentiate between (1) a word-for-word translation and (2) the use of an English term, or of a French equivalent for the English term as it is used by native speakers. This underlines the difference between "translating" and elaborating official terminology.

3.3   Elaborating official terminology: The official terminology committees, and the role of the Académie française

Recognising the need to enrich the French language as well as the duty of the state in this regard, to guide the enrichment process and disseminate its results, in 1997 the Prime Minister launched the Commission Générale de terminologie et de néologie. To demonstrate the government's support of language enrichment, government administrations committed to using the official vocabularies (Juppé 1997). In his response to the Prime Minister, Maurice Druon, Perpetual Secretary of the French Academy, insisted on the role of the Academy as a "guardian of the language." The common goal was to combat the "invasion" of terms of Anglo-Saxon origin, not only in the field of science and technology but also in everyday life. In 1997, it was decreed that the Academy approve terms (and their definitions) before their publication in the *Journal officiel de la République française (JO)*. These terms could only be made public if they had been approved by the Academy. In the ninth edition of its Dictionary, the Academy made recommendations which are included within the official terminology process, specifically aimed at avoiding the use of English terms, which can affect the clarity of discourse in policy. The *Dictionnaire de l'Académie* was made accessible online in 2022 thanks to Laurent Catach, to help disseminate the terminology to the wider public. The Dictionary website also includes the FranceTerme terminology database.

It is worth noting at this stage that terminological development did not always go smoothly as evidenced for example by the dismay expressed by Maurice Druon, editor of the Academy's dictionary, when the word *dangerosité* was proposed as an equivalent of 'dangerousness.' The natural way to express this concept in French would be with the phrase *qui a un caractère dangereux* or *qui présente un danger*. For him, accepting *dangerosité* into the French language would be worse than accepting pure anglicisms such as *corner* or *football*, even though *dangerosité* does not violate any French morphological rules (Druon 1998: 460–461). This opinion was not shared by other linguists on the committee, who voiced their opposition to his proposal. However, Druon and his colleagues were fighting a losing battle since the term *dangerosité* was already in the French language as far back as 1963 according to the *Petit Robert* dictionary, 2011 edition.[4]

In many cases a neologism is already in use before it is officially recommended. This is because of the large number of scientific and technical concepts — between 4,000 and 10,000 (Union Latine 1995: 3) — that are being studied every year. As new terms for new concepts usually first appear in English, new French terms are officially created, and institutions and organisations may follow suit and start using these terms. This is generally how neologisms emerge in a natural way, before their eventual integration through the official enrichment process into the official lists of terms.

4.   Official French institutional framework

As official terminology has already been actively used in France over several decades, it may be interesting to examine the corresponding institutional framework and observe its evolution, methods and results. While giving a general view of French technical and scientific language, Rostislav Kocourek (1991, Chapter 5) already recognises the role of some of these official Committees.

---

4. On the relation between the *Dictionnaire de l'Académie* and the official French language enrichment process, see Candel 2017a.

In 2023, several institutional partners became involved in the official terminology framework, such as the Académie française, the French Academy of sciences, the Association française de normalisation (AFNOR — the French national standardisation body, which is a member of the International Organization for Standardization (ISO)), and various ministries.

Today, the official terminology framework comprises about twenty committees, each responsible for a specific domain or subject area. This structure reflects the primary importance of domains in terminology (as indicated by, among others, de Bessé 2000, Lerat 1995: 164, 175, 183, Lerat 2016).

4.1   A ministerial decree

The system described in the ministerial decree, published in 1986, concerns once more the enrichment of the French language. Its sixteen articles, signed by the Prime Minister as well as by fourteen ministers of the French government, establish the mandate of the Commission générale de terminologie et de néologie and the committees pertaining to specific domains. With support from other institutions, the committees are to identify areas where terms are lacking, propose or revise terms and neologisms, and disseminate the results of their work. Decisions are published in the *Journal officiel de la République française*.

These official terms are to be used in all documents issued by the government, administration, public services and institutions (decrees, circulars, instructions, directives, letters or any written material). This rule applies to radio or television programs as well. Official terms also must be used in texts defining contracts involving the State or public establishments. The decree finally indicates that this requirement extends to education, training and research activities in public establishments or organisations.[5]

4.2   The current situation

As of 2023, the official terminology framework comprises nineteen committees operating in various fields (see Commission d'enrichissement de la langue

---

5. If officially recommended terms are not used in place of other terms (mostly Anglo-American ones), sanctions may follow. Professionals are required to use the French language for the designation, offer or presentation of goods, products and services for the proper information of consumers. The DGCCRF (Direction Générale de la concurrence, de la consommation et de la répression des fraudes), Directorate General for Consumer Affairs and Fraud Control — Ministry of Economy, opened in 2022 about 3000 criminal proceedings, including 32 cases for failure to use the French language.

française 2023). These committees, managed by the Délégation générale à la langue française et aux langues de France, propose practical solutions to terminology issues, recommend French terms for new concepts, formulate definitions, monitor new concepts, and support the French terminology needs of their hosting ministries (see also Delavigne and Gaudin 1994, Depecker 1997 and 2001, Candel 2017b). Two university research teams prepare data for the terms being considered.

In 2023, a document entitled *1972-2022 – 50 termes clés du dispositif d'enrichissement de la langue française* was released to mark the fiftieth anniversary of the French language enrichment process, clearly showing that language enrichment is mainly driven by innovations in technical vocabulary. In 2015, the Commission Générale de terminologie et de néologie became the Commission d'enrichissement de la langue française, reflecting the idea that terminology enrichment is in fact language enrichment taken as a whole. Within the framework of this committee, specialists continue to closely work with terminologists and linguists, thus keeping the scientific and technical standards in the working groups at a high level. The committees collectively prepare definitions for specialised concepts in a manner that describes the concept precisely but at the same time aims to be easily understood by the general public (see also Candel 2017c, 2017d).

French terminology resources have also benefitted from the considerable activities in terminology development carried out in Quebec, particularly at the Office québécois de la langue française (OQLF), which was established in 1961 (concerning the development of terminology in Canada, see Francœur, Chapter 12). This public institution, which has a mandate to protect and promote the French language, defines Quebec's policy on French as the official language and considers terminological issues. Its databank, the Grand Dictionnaire terminologique or GDT, is regularly interrogated by terminology researchers. TERMIUM Plus, the terminology database of Canada's Government, is another frequently-used resource. French terminological data is also provided by the European IATE database (Interactive Terminology for Europe).

5.   Evolution of official French terminology

To demonstrate how official French terminology evolved, we begin by comparing official recommendations that were published in the *Journal Officiel de la République française* with others published more recently. We then examine the *Trésor de la langue française* dictionary (CNRS, 1971–1994; the sixteen volume paper version followed by the on-line version *TLFi*), particularly as it refers to the official enrichment process. Finally, we look at how the well-known commercial dictionary *Petit Robert de la langue française* deals with recent terminological evolutions.

5.1   The official journal of the French Republic

The example discussed in Table 1 was taken from the official governmental publication *Journal officiel de la République française,* announcing the enrichment of Health and Medicine Vocabulary (decree signed by the French Minister of Health). This corpus includes two publications separated by 25 years: 2/01/1975 and 22/09/2000. The terminological activity of approving recommendations between these two periods was constantly evolving and the 2000 version includes entries that are generally better structured. Thirty terms were published in 1975. Eighteen of them remained in the 2000 version (*axénique, cardial, cabrade, clairance, claquade, corbeillage, déconnexion, délétion, enjambement, éveinage, festonnement, inducteur, lissage, moniteur, monitorage, stimulateur, translocation, trappage*).

Table 1. The evolution of official French terminological activity from 1975 to 2000, for thirty terms from the medical domain, as observed in the *Journal officiel de la langue française*

Data type	1975 30 terms	2000 18 terms remaining, out of the 30 terms
(a) Headword	*lissage, ou remodelage*	*lissage*
(b) Domain	The domain is indicated for only five terms:	The domain is indicated for eleven more terms:
	Anesthesiology: *absorbeur* *cabrade* *déconnexion* *inducteur*	Health and Medicine: *axénique* *cardial* *clairance* *claquade* *corbeillage* *éveinage* *festonnement* *lissage* *moniteur* *stimulateur*
	Genetics: *délétion*	
		Biology/Genetics: *enjambement*

Table 1. *(continued)*

Data type	1975 **30 terms**	2000 **18 terms remaining, out of the 30 terms**
(c) Definition	Two definitions are proposed for: *clairance*	One of the two definitions was removed for: *clairance*
(d) English original term	No English equivalent is given for thirteen terms: *cardial, chiropraxie, coloscope, coloscopie, corbeillage, délétion, éveinage, mastologie, mastologue, nucal, préventologie, préventologue, translocation*	English equivalents provided for all remaining terms except one: *corbeillage*
(e) Elimination of French terms that seem of lesser importance for medical terminology	The following terms are included: *absorbeur, battade, chiropraxie, coloscope, coloscopie, dopage, mastologie, mastologue, -nucal, préventologie, préventologue, tire-veine*	All these terms have been removed.

An improved version of these results is provided in the 2000 edition, where, for instance, the domain is always given. While the terms *monitorage, stimulateur* and *trappage* are fine in both editions, the presentation of *moniteur* is enhanced in the second one.

Terminology work is mostly assumed to stabilise terms and their definitions. However terminologists may also be actors of change and innovation, as in their social approach of term's usages (see for instance Condamines, Delavigne, Gaudin & Picton in the present book, although the point of view may seem quite different). Experts in official terminology mostly remain aware of different ways of understanding notions or using terms, as well as of evolving notions or usages. A terminological definition should be given, in order to make sure the specialists of the field understand the messages they get.

Another interesting point lies in the changes that can be observed in the FranceTerme database. Table 2 shows how terms evolved in examples originating from four committees: Space Science, International Relations, Informatics, and Telecommunications.

Table 2. Evolution of official French terms (*Journal officiel de la langue française*):
new French entries for the same English terms

Committee	English term	Current official French term	Previous official French term
Space Science	*hosted payload*	charge utile hébergée (28/06/2017)	bouche-trou (31/12/2005)
International Relations	*snap-back, snapback*	clause de rétroaction (01/07/2022)	règle de caducité (13/12/2017)
Informatics	*Web, World Wide Web*	toile (09/12/2018)	toile d'araignée mondiale (16/03/1999)
Telecommunications	*ultra wideband, UWB*	à bande ultralarge (22/01/2020)	ultralarge bande (26/03/2006)

We will now examine the *Trésor de la langue française* and a recent edition of the *Petit Robert de la langue française*, as well as the current edition of the *Dictionnaire de l'Académie française*.

5.2 Official terminology in the *Trésor de la langue française* and in contemporary lexicography

The *Trésor de la langue française* (*TLF*, 1971–1994), in both its paper and online (*TLFi*) versions, conveys information about official decisions. This can be seen in the list of twelve examples given by the French official terminology committees (found in ten entries). The prescriptive statements are underlined in Table 3.

It appears that most of these recommendations are rather prescriptive. For example, we see verbal expressions such as *recommends, rejects, calls for, proposes, given by,* and *advocates*, as well as adverbs such as *preferably*, and so forth. Such prescriptive language is used throughout the recommendations in the *TLF*.

There is no standardised way to refer to official recommendations, to prescriptions available in this otherwise descriptive dictionary edited between 1971 and 1994. Other recommendations are given in a note (*Remarque*) referring to the official source. Several kinds of introductory formulations are also used. Some look more descriptive, simply proposing a French equivalent term to render an English one (such as *assurance multirisque* for 'comprehensive insurance,' or *épreuve de tournage* for 'rush').

The *TLF* dictionary includes some official terms known at the time of publication. The purpose of including these terms is to inform the public, and they in no way stand as a prescriptive form but simply quote some specific official terms.

Table 3. Prescriptive statements from the French official terminology committees in the *TLF* dictionary (our translation; emphasis added)

Year	Term	Release of the official decision[a]
1983	jet	A decree of 12 August 1976, from the Terminology Committee for Enrichment of National Defence Vocabulary, <u>rejects</u> this borrowing and <u>recommends</u> *avion à reaction*.
	jet-stream	The French equivalent term <u>recommended</u> by the Terminology Committee for Enrichment of National Defense Vocabulary is *courant-jet*, noun, masculine.
	liner	The Terminology Committee of Ministry of Defense <u>recommends</u>, in the decree of August 12 1976, to use <u>preferably</u> *avion de ligne*.
1985	assurance multirisque	Term <u>given</u> by the Terminology Committee of Ministry for Economy and Finance <u>in order to translate</u> Engl. *comprehensive insurance*
1986	off	The Terminology Committee for Audiovisual (*Journal Officiel* of 18 janv. 1973) <u>calls for</u> the replacement of *off* by *hors champ*.
1990	rush	An <u>official recommendation proposes to</u> replace *rush* by the term *épreuve de tournage* (Decree of 12 Jan. 1973, J.O., 18 Jan. [...])
1992	script(-)girl [...] ; scripte	The form <u>officially recommended</u> by the decree of 12 Jan 1973 and 24 Jan 1983 is [...] *scripte* [...].
	tansad, tan-sad	Synon. <u>recommended</u> by the Terminology Committee for Automobile in 1973: *selle biplace*.
1994	télédétéction	Term <u>officially recommended</u> in order to translate the Engl. *remote sensing* 22/09/2000
	téléécriture, télé-écriture	Term <u>officially recommended</u> in order to translate Engl. *telewriting* 27/04/1982
	télémaintenance	Term <u>officially recommended</u> in order to translate Engl. *housekeeping*. 22/09/2000
	téléprompteur	*TELEV.* The Ministerial Committee for Terminology <u>advocates</u> *télésouffleur*

a. Our translation.

Finally, we can acknowledge the contributions of general lexicography by recalling how the *Dictionnaire de l'Académie* in its current version, and the *Petit Robert de la langue française* dictionary in its 2020 electronic version, manage evolving terminological units.

Over time, the *Dictionnaire de l'Académie* became increasingly concerned with contemporary terminology. It recommends using a French term as an equivalent when an English term has made its way into French usage, but in so doing, the English borrowed term that is not recommended is nevertheless still cited. For example, for the English term *digital*, the term *numérique* is certainly correct and the only one having the Academy's approval; nevertheless, the dictionary also includes the English borrowed term *digital* which is widely used in French. The same approach can be found for *mémoire vive* instead of *Random Access Memory* or *RAM*, *listage* instead of *listing*, *fioul* instead of *fuel*, *jeune pousse* (included under the entry *pousse* !) rather than *start-up*, or *fac-similé* rather than *reprint*, with the sentence *doit être préféré à l'anglais [...]* being repeated in the updated version of the dictionary. That said, one notices that both *listing* and *listage* were analysed and defined in the *TLF* (volume 10, 1983). Similarly, the term *courriel* which found an early usage in Quebec was supported by the Academy in an attempt to replace the English term *e-mail*. While on the one hand proscribing the English terms, the Academy nonetheless cites them.

The *Petit Robert* dictionary is generally more descriptive than prescriptive. In an analysis of the 2020 electronic version, Niklas-Salminen (2021) examined terms registered between 1980 and 2020. She counted 422 words borrowed from British English and 51 words from US English, terms recommended by the Commission générale de terminologie et de néologie (or Commission d'enrichissement de la langue française). It appears that official French recommendations cannot completely avoid English or American words.

Among these borrowings, 11% are acronyms (such as *ADSL, MOOC, wifi*), and 35% are comprised of a single word which has assumed a new meaning (*booster, box, broker*). The anglicisms mostly belong to the domains of Information technology (*cloud, crackeur/euse, darknet, e-learning, hackeur/euse* or *hacker*), Multimedia (*biopic, stand-up, teasing*), Sports, Automotive or Economics (*benchmark*). Niklas-Salminen (2021) notes that 38% of the anglicisms are compound nouns (*airbag, benchmark, blockchain, hashtag, joystick, snowboard; beach-volley, flashball, story-board*); among the derived forms she notes nouns with a verbal base (*booster, morphing, spoiler, tuning*); and she finally cites simple forms (*chat, deal, fitness, hub, tag*).

Concerning *beach-volley*, an official recommendation (2008) proposes a French version with "sur sable": *volley sur sable*. One more thing worth mentioning. In 2003, the Commission générale de terminologie et de néologie was asked to respond to a request from the French Presidency for a French equivalent of the English term *flashball*, which refers to a military or law enforcement concept. That was no easy task because at the same time the relationship to law enforcement terminology needs to be taken into account. As explained in FranceTerme (2003), both *Flash-ball* (French trademark) and *flashball* are used in French, but neither should be. The Commission's response was *arme de défense à balles souples,* which is clearly a much longer term but nevertheless fully respectful of French syntax and morphology.

6.   Concluding remarks

This chapter has focused on the development of official terminology in France. It describes the system which has progressively evolved in which the stakeholders and more specifically domain specialists and official experts are gathered in committees missioned to enrich the French language. This network operates in a structured manner, collecting and studying new concepts in areas of innovation, defining these concepts, and determining what they consider to be proper French equivalents. Their coordinated work is then passed on to another committee for approval before publication and dissemination. Sometimes, these committees practice a form of pure prescriptivism. This is normal, as the official enrichment process for the French language operates in a prescriptive way. At other times, the approach becomes descriptive. The work of the committees constitutes a solid basis for the emergence of official terms which are then published in the *Journal officiel de la République française,* and their use becomes mandatory in government publications.

One may conclude that the enrichment process relies on a prescriptive approach with, nevertheless, a rich touch of descriptive elements. Regardless of the approach taken, the importance of the specialist's point of view is without question. The process in general has evolved in a positive direction, in its operation, its capacity to integrate different viewpoints, in the spirit of cooperation between the committee members.

This official enrichment process has certainly improved since 1979 when Alain Rey wrote "The Terminology committees in the various ministries, working without examining the terminological systems as a whole, have only been able to give very partial and often questionable results" (Rey 1979: 114, our translation). One cannot be as critical today, as these committees are well organised and managed. Although they initially work independently of each other, they collaborate when necessary. Their work is generally of high quality. And today it is available online where it can be easily accessed by the general public and, when necessary, updated.

Official terminology has improved. Interestingly, and perhaps this is a reflection of changing perceptions, in the names of some committees, the terms *terminologie* and *néologie* have been replaced by *enrichissement de la langue,* thus, for example, in 2015, the Commission générale de terminologie et de néologie became the Commission d'enrichissement de la langue française. In a similar vein, the Banque de terminologie du Québec is now included in a broader Vitrine linguistique.

Even if it remains difficult to precisely evaluate how all this work helps to improve the development of French terminology, the enrichment process continues to feature impressive and fruitful collaboration between domain experts and linguists (in 2022, 235 terms were added to FranceTerme; and over nine thousand entries were officially published at the end of 2023). There is considerable value in the sharing of ideas between experts, terminologists and linguists. Their collaboration is a primary asset of the enrichment process which determines the nature and quality of the work done.

Acknowledgments

The author gratefully thanks the editors, as well as the reviewers of this chapter, for their helpful comments and suggestions.

References

Béjoint, Henri, and Philippe Thoiron. 2000. *Le sens en terminologie*. Lyon: Presses universitaires de Lyon.

Cabré, Maria Teresa. 2005. "Lexicographie versus terminographie: comment les technologies déplacent leur affrontement." In *De la mesure dans les termes, Hommage à Philippe Thoiron*, ed. by Henri Béjoint, and François Maniez, 189–210. Lyon: Presses universitaires de Lyon.

Candel, Danielle. 2017a. "Prescription and Tradition: From the French *Dictionnaire de l'Académie* to the Official French Language Enrichment Process (1996–2014)." In *Prescription and Tradition in Language, Establishing Standards across Time and Space*, ed. by Carol Percy, and I. Tieken-Boon van Ostade, 273–287. Bristol: Multilingual Matters.

Candel, Danielle. 2017b. "Normes en terminologie officielle (France, 1996–2014)." *Cahiers de Lexicologie* 110(1): 29–43.

Candel, Danielle. 2017c. "Note sur la néologie en terminologie officielle en France. Le rôle des experts des domaines (1997–2017)." *Neologica* 11: 139–152.

Candel, Danielle. 2017d. "Expert, profane: quels rôles en terminologie officielle?" In *Ceci n'est pas une festschrift, Texte zur Angwandten und Romanistischen Sprachwissenschaft für Martin Stegu*, ed. by Peter Handler, Klaus Kaindl, and Holger Wochele, 161–172. Berlin: Logos.

Candel, Danielle, Didier Samain, and Dan Savatovsky. 2023. *Eugen Wüster et la terminologie de l'école de Vienne*. HEL Livres, 2. Paris: SHESL.

Comité d'étude des termes techniques français. 1972. *Termes techniques français — Essai d'orientation de la terminologie*. Paris : Hermann.

Commission d'enrichissement de la langue française. 2023. *1972-2022 – 50 termes clés du dispositif d'enrichissement de la langue française*. Paris: DGLFLF.

de Bessé, Bruno. 2000. "Le domaine." In *Le sens en terminologie*, ed. by Henri Béjoint, and Philipe Thoiron, 182–195. Lyon: Presses universitaires de Lyon.

Delavigne, Valérie, and François Gaudin (eds). 1994. *Implantation des termes officiels. Terminologies nouvelles.* ACCT/Communauté française de Belgique.

Depecker, Loïc. 1997. *La mesure des mots: cinq études d'implantation terminologique.* Mont-Saint-Aignan: Publications de l'université de Rouen.

Depecker, Loïc. 2001. *L'invention de la langue.* Paris: Larousse — Armand Colin.

Dictionnaire de l'Académie française. 1992. Neuvième édition (de "A" à "sommairement").

Druon, Maurice. 1998. "La neuvième édition du Dictionnaire de l'Académie Française." In *Le Dictionnaire de l'Académie française et la lexicographie institutionnelle européenne*, Actes du colloque international, 17, 18 et 19 novembre 1994, ed. by Bernard Quemada, 455–461. Paris: Honoré Champion.

Guyon, Anne. 1995. "La terminologie au sein du ministère de l'enseignement supérieur et de la recherche." *Terminometro. La terminologie en France*, Hors-série no.1, 21–23. Paris: Union Latine.

Humbley, John. 1995. "Création et buts du Centre de terminologie et néologie (CTN)." *Terminometro. La terminologie en France*, Hors-série no.1: 18–20. Paris: Union Latine.

Humbley, John. 1997. "Language Planning and Terminology Planning — The Francophone Experience." In *Handbook of Terminology Management, Vol. I*, ed. by Sue Ellen Wright, and Gerhard Budin, 261–277. Amsterdam: John Benjamins.

Humbley, John. 2000. "La terminologie." In *Histoire de la langue française 1945–2000*, ed. by Gérald Antoine, and Bernard Cerquiglini, 315–338. Paris: CNRS Editions.

Humbley, John. 2018. *La néologie terminologique.* Limoges: Lambert-Lucas.

Juppé, Alain. 1997. *Discours d'Installation de la Commission générale de Terminologie et de néologie.* Paris, 11 février 1997.

Kocourek, Rostislav. 1991. *La langue française de la technique et de la science.* 2nd ed. Wiesbaden: Brandstetter.

Lerat, Pierre. 1995. *Les langues spécialisées.* Paris: Presses universitaires de France.

Lerat, Pierre. 2016. *Langue et technique.* Paris: Hermann.

Niklas-Salminen, Aïno. 2021. "Les recommandations officielles proposées pour remplacer les anglicismes dans le *Petit Robert de la langue française.*" *Kalbotyra*, 74: 141–159.

Quemada, Bernard. 1978. "Technique et langage." In *Histoire des techniques*, ed. by Bertrand Gilles: 1146–1240. Encyclopédie de la Pléiade. Paris: Gallimard.

Quemada, Bernard. 1998. *Le Dictionnaire de l'Académie française et la lexicographie institutionnelle européenne.* Actes du colloque international, 17, 18 et 19 novembre 1994 (avec la collaboration de Jean Pruvost). Paris : Honoré Champion.

Rey, Alain. 1979. *La terminologie: noms et notions.* Paris: Presses universitaires de France.

Tieken-Boon van Ostade, Ingrid, and Carol Percy (eds). 2017. *Prescription and Tradition in Language. Establishing Standards across Time and Space.* Bristol: Multilanguage Matters.

Trésor de la langue française (TLF), Dictionnaire de la langue du XIXe et du XXe siècle. 16 vol. 1971–1994. Paris: Klincksieck — CNRS.

Trésor de la langue Française informatisé (TLFi). ATILF — CNRS & Université de Lorraine.

Union Latine. 1995. *La terminologie en France.* Terminometro Hors-série n°1.

CHAPTER 22

Terminology in Germany
Theory, research, education and application

Klaus-Dirk Schmitz
University of Applied Sciences, Cologne

Germany has a long tradition in terminology science and terminology
management, influenced by researchers from Austria and the Nordic
countries. This article starts with the beginnings of this historical evolution,
shows the influence of Eugen Wüster, and gives insights about the
beginnings of terminology standardisation. Furthermore, scientific and
professional activities in the field of terminological research, teaching,
projects and tools development are described, from the very active 1980s
until today.

Keywords: terminology science, terminology standardisation, terminology-
related associations, terminology projects, termbases

1.   Introduction

Efforts to clarify the technical terms and expressions belonging to specific disciplines have a centuries-old tradition. For the German speaking area, noteworthy
is Albrecht Dürer (1471–1528), the famous painter, printmaker and mathematician
who endeavored to create a German-language terminology of mathematics.

However, we can only speak of systematic terminology work in the true sense
since the second half of the 19th century. The technological revolution of this
period led to great progress, but in many cases also to disorderly and rather ad-
hoc technical developments and their resulting designations. The first standardisation activities were launched to address this situation. Initially, the focus was
on the development of substantive standards, i.e. the standardisation of objects
and procedures. These standardisation efforts were often hampered by communication problems, for example, when several competing terms were used for the
same concept. The standardisation of terminology became urgent, since objects
and procedures can only be standardised in a binding and unambiguous manner if there is also agreement on the terminology used to communicate about

https://doi.org/10.1075/tlrp.24.22sch

them. Immediately after its foundation in 1906, the International Electrotechnical Commission (IEC) began to standardise electrotechnical terminology. During the more than 30 years it took to complete this work, valuable insight, which is still valid today, was gained into terminology work. Terminology work in Germany led to similar reflections. As early as 1917, the technical committees of the German Standards Committee (Deutscher Normenausschuss, DNA) established their own terminology subcommittees.

2. Eugen Wüster and the standardisation of terminological principles

Initially, the focus was on defining individual concepts and their terms; very soon, however, it was recognised that standardisation of individual terms can only lead to useful results if uniform principles apply to all those involved in the work. Therefore, members of these terminology committees began to look for regularities in the structure of existing terminologies in order to establish rules for the formation of new designations. These efforts formed the starting point for the development of basic terminological standards and thus also for the establishment of the standards committee for terminological principles and methods (Normenausschuss Terminologie, NAT) at the German Standards Institute (Deutsches Institut für Normung, DIN).

The work of Eugen Wüster (1898–1977) (see also Chapter 8) was of great importance for the aforementioned endeavors. In 1931, Wüster published his dissertation entitled *Internationale Sprachnormung in der Technik, besonders in der Elektrotechnik*, in which he developed his concept of a scientifically-based terminology theory and showed methodical ways to solve terminological problems. This and other works by Wüster published in scientific and professional journals in Germany (see Picht and Schmitz 2001) shaped the emerging areas of terminological research as well as practical terminology work, both for standardisation purposes and other applications or environments.

In 1950, the German Standards Committee (DNA) established a subcommittee called Terminology, which submitted its first draft standard, DIN 2330 *Normungstechnik; Begriffsbildung; Regeln* [*Standardisation technology, Formation of concepts, Rules*], in 1953. In 1957, after taking into account the feedback from experts, the standard was published under the title *Begriffe und Benennungen — Allgemeine Grundsätze* [*Concepts and terms — General principles*]. DIN 2330 with the current title *Terminologiearbeit — Grundsätze und Methoden* [*Terminology work — Principles and methods*] is still today the main standard for terminology theory and practice in Germany.

3.   The "Roaring 80s" in Germany

After the publication of DIN 2330, several terminology related articles in scientific and professional journals, mainly authored by Eugen Wüster (see Picht and Schmitz 2001), and notably the 1979 publication of Wüster's lectures at the University of Vienna (*Einführung in die Allgemeine Terminologielehre und Terminologische Lexikographie*, edited by Helmut Felber) prepared the ground for terminological activities in other communities as well as in organisations and industry.

In the framework of the German Association of Interpreters and Translators (Bundesverband der Dolmetscher und Übersetzer, BDÜ), professionals and leaders from the translation industry, who recognised the importance of terminology work for translation, came together in the early 1980s. In May 1985, in Cologne, the BDÜ hosted a gathering of professionals to discuss terminology where Ingo Hohnhold of Siemens AG Munich gave a keynote speech entitled *Was ist, was soll, was kann Terminologiearbeit — nicht nur für Übersetzer? [What is, what should, what can terminology work do — not only for translators?* (our translation)] At this event, a permanent working group was created to study terminology methodologies, and a framework resolution with objectives for translation-oriented terminology work was formulated.

To avoid limiting the focus of activities to translation-related terminology work, and to gain further independence from the BDÜ, the organisers of that event, joined by other interested experts, met in May 1987. This would become known as the first German Terminology Day, and was followed soon after by the founding of the German Association for Terminology (Deutscher Terminologie-Tag e.V., DTT). DTT is still very active today with some 300 individual and institutional members mainly, but not only, from German speaking countries.

During the 1980s, the first university courses on terminology work were offered. Reiner Arntz, lecturer at the University of Saarbrücken, and later professor at the University of Hildesheim, integrated terminology lessons and seminars in curricula for translators and interpreters at both universities. Together with Heribert Picht, professor at Copenhagen Business School, he published in 1982 the *Einführung in die übersetzungsbezogene Terminologiearbeit* (Arntz and Picht 1982). Over the years, this book was updated and complemented to account for modern information technology aspects by Felix Mayer and later Klaus-Dirk Schmitz, and still appears in the eighth edition the main handbook for terminology work in German (Arntz, Picht and Schmitz 2021).

Three other important publications in German, focusing on different perspectives of terminology work, should be mentioned. In 1989 Helmut Felber and Gerhard Budin, both professors at the University of Vienna, published the monograph *Terminologie in Theorie und Praxis* (Felber and Budin 1989). Ingo Hohnhold, terminology coordinator at Siemens Munich, contributed several articles about practical terminology work to *Übersetzungsorientierte Terminologiearbeit* (Hohnhold 1990). And in 1990 KÜWES (Konferenz der Übersetzungsdienste west-europäischer Staaten), a conference later known as KÜDES, published *Empfehlungen für die Terminologiearbeit* in German and five other languages with a focus on terminology work in public organisations.

At around this time, attention was drawn to the relations between terminology and knowledge engineering. In 1986, the Association for Terminology and Knowledge Transfer (GTW) was founded in Trier, with support from Infoterm (the International Information Centre for Terminology, Vienna), with Christian Galinski and Gerhard Budin playing a leading role. The first conference on Terminology and Knowledge Engineering (TKE), which took place in 1987 in Trier (see Czap and Galinski 1987), attracted several hundred experts from various related disciplines such as terminology, knowledge organisation, classification, and computer science. Afterwards, TKE conferences were held every three years in in Trier (Czap and Nedobity 1990), Cologne (Schmitz 1993), Vienna (Galinski and Schmitz 1996), and Innsbruck (Sandrini 1999). After further events in Nancy, Dublin and Madrid, TKE and GTW were moved in 2005 to Copenhagen, where GTW was dissolved in 2022.

The 80s also saw the rapid development of computational aids for terminology management. Mainframe computers were used in large organisations and companies in Germany from the end of the 60s (e.g. LEXIS at the Bundessprachenamt in Cologne, TEAM at Siemens AG in Munich). Mini computers with the first software for computer-aided translation (e.g. Ericsson CAT) spread widely in translation departments of ministries and companies throughout Germany. However, the rise of microcomputer technology, starting with the first IBM-PC in 1981, changed the world of computer use for terminology management dramatically. Karl-Heinz Freigang, Felix Mayer and Klaus-Dirk Schmitz installed and tested almost 20 PC tools for terminology management at the University of Saarbrücken, and published the results in *TermNet Report 1* (Freigang, Mayer and Schmitz 1991). Two thirds of the tools had been developed and marketed in Germany. One of these tools was MultiTerm, developed by Trados in Stuttgart and launched in 1990, at that time running under MS-DOS with a freely-definable entry structure, but lacking real concept orientation. In the years that followed, MultiTerm was further developed and optimised and remains the market leader for terminology management systems world-wide.

4.   Terminology activities in the last thirty years

4.1   Deutscher Terminologie-Tag e.V. (DTT)

The Deutscher Terminologie-Tag e.V. (DTT) began life in 1987 as a legal entity in its own right. The scope of the organisation was specifically widened to approach terminology from a neutral point of view and to allow the participation of specialists and translators in the related fields of information and documentation science, technical writing, and communication in special languages. It aims to support individuals and organisations in the preparation, clarification and storage of monolingual and multilingual terminologies and in the utilisation of existing terminologies. DTT has nominated several terminology experts to an advisory council, the Deutsches Institut für Terminologie (DIT) e.V. Starting in 1989, the DTT has been holding biennial conferences, which have enjoyed great success.

In addition to its conferences, DTT organises seminars and webinars, publishes a peer-reviewed bi-annual terminology journal, and awards the DTT sponsorship every two years. Its handbook, *Best Practices 2.0*, available in German and English, provides practical guidelines for terminology work, with modules for principles and methods, tools and technologies, project management, economic aspects and copyright, among others.

4.2   Rat für Deutschsprachige Terminologie (RaDT)

During the 3rd International Congress on Terminology and Knowledge Engineering — TKE'93 in Cologne, experts in the field of terminology met to establish a German-language terminology initiative. In 1994, the Council for German-language Terminology (Rat für Deutschsprachige Terminologie, RaDT) was established at the inaugural meeting on the premises of the German Commission for UNESCO in Bonn.

An initiative of the German, Austrian and Swiss UNESCO Commissions, the RaDT is an expert group (approximately 25 members) comprising German language organisations, associations, government agencies, business and educational groups which deal with terminological issues, applications and curricula. The group's goal is to represent all organisations concerned with terminology from all German language regions including Luxembourg, South Tyrol and Belgium. Its objectives include the following:

- to increase awareness of terminology in German language countries
- to promote co-operation and collaboration in the field of terminology
- to co-ordinate and support terminological activities
- to create, disseminate and help implement guidelines for terminology policy and strategy.

Since 1994, RaDT has been meeting twice a year at various locations in German speaking areas to exchange information and produce publications. It has issued guidelines on a range of terminology-related topics including the professional profile of terminologists, introductory material for subject matter experts, and domain loss in the German language (RaDT 2005). Some papers are also available in languages other than German.

4.3 Terminology teaching and training

There is a long tradition of teaching terminology science, practical terminology work and computer applications for terminology management at German universities. Terminology modules are integrated into curricula for translation and interpretation studies as well as for technical writing. Notable professors include Reiner Arntz at Hildesheim, Petra Drewer at Karlsruhe, Felix Mayer at Munich, Christoph Rösener at Flensburg and Germersheim, Peter A. Schmitt at Leipzig, Hans Schwarz at Magdeburg, and Klaus-Dirk Schmitz at Cologne, all of whom have also published terminology-related scientific papers and monographs.

In 2006, a Masters degree in Terminology and Language Technology was created at Technische Hochschule Köln (TH Köln). Graduates of this program find employment in industry or organisations as terminologists, terminology managers or language technology specialists.

4.4 Terminology research projects at TH Köln

From 1995 to 2015, several terminology related research projects were carried out at the department for information management and the department of multilingual communication at TH Köln, initiated and led by Klaus-Dirk Schmitz. The projects were co-financed by national and European research funds.

The TDCnet project (European Terminology Information and Documentation Network), which was completed between 1998 and 2000, aimed to establish a virtual terminology directory in the form of a logical and physical network of information and documentation centres for terminology in Europe. The project was initiated and co-financed by the EU Commission within the framework of the MLIS (Multilingual Information Society) action plan.

Recommendations and technical specifications were developed on the basis of analyses and user surveys, which precisely define the holdings to be managed and service tasks to be carried out within a national or regional documentation center for terminology. Additionally, a markup language for terminology-related bibliographic and factual data, TeDIF (Terminology Documentation Interchange Format) was developed by the German member of the network, DEUTERM (in Köln), and later tested and implemented. This interchange format enabled the consolidation of data from individual centers into a common unified database. Most of this data was made available to the general public free of charge via ETIS, the European Terminology Information Server. More than 10 partners from all parts of the EU collaborated in building the prototype of the network under the coordination of Infoterm.

In 2000 and 2001, the SALT project (Standards-based Access to multilingual Lexicons and Terminologies) was co-funded by the EU Commission under the Fifth Framework Programme (Information Society — Human Language Technologies). This project extended its scope beyond Europe through the participation of American scientists and companies. It aimed to develop formalisms, tools and programs to convert data from differently-structured terminology collections, terminological exchange formats and dictionaries for machine translation systems into a uniform format that allows data to be exchanged between different repositories. The XLT format developed in the SALT project used XML as a basis, taking into account current developments and specifications of the World Wide Web Consortium and working closely with ISO (ISO/TC37/SC3) in this area. The SALT project essentially used two formats, namely OLIF (Open Lexicon Interchange Format), which allows exchange between lexical resources of machine translation systems, and MARTIF (MAchine-Readable Terminology Interchange Format), which had been standardised as an exchange format for terminological data within the ISO framework (ISO 12200:1999). The SALT project consortium was also involved in an ambitious EU project, IATE (Interactive Terminology for Europe) (see also Chapter 20), which aimed to create a terminology database common to all institutions of the EU. Within the framework of the SALT project, the Institute for Information Management at TH Köln played a leading role, e.g. by describing the different formats and database structures and defining the specifications for the development of the conversion programs.

From 2000 to 2002, the WebTerm project, co-financed by a German national program for the Promotion of Application-Oriented Research and Development at Universities of Applied Sciences, aimed to structurally consolidate the results of terminology research carried out in the framework of diploma theses into a publicly-available uniform database. The terminology developed through this student research was typically confined to a particular subject area and systematically and conceptually elaborated in two or three languages. A concept system was created, and the terminology was thoughly documemented with designations, definitions, contexts, sources, grammatical information, illustrations and a concept system position indicator (notation). Since 1995, MultiTerm has been used to manage this terminology data. In 1997, a separate MultiTerm database was created to store detailed bibliographical information. WebTerm offered direct access to the terminological data of more than 220 systematic terminology collections via the web, not only alphabetically via the term, but also systematically via the concept systems. Unfortunately, WebTerm is no longer available, since funding was lacking to update the source code for current internet browser versions.

Figure 1. List of systematic terminological data collections in WebTerm

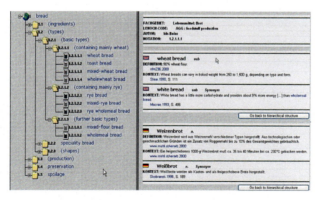

Figure 2. Systematic representation and a terminological entry in WebTerm

The objective of the research and development project Deutsches Terminologie-Portal was to develop a web-based terminology information portal that would serve as a contact point for terminological questions, both from small and medium-sized enterprises that lack terminology competence, and larger enterprises, authorities and organisations that do already maintain terminology units. The project was co-financed by the regional funding program TRAFO (Promotion of Transfer-Oriented Research at Universities of Applied Sciences) from 2001 to 2003. The portal was primarily intended to provide a subject-oriented inventory of terminology resources available on the internet that contain German terminology. In addition, it was intended to offer guidelines about how to manage terminology resources efficiently, and how to set up a computer-aided terminology management solution in a commercial setting. Information on organisations, associations, information centers, events, education and training courses, publications, standards and software tools in the field of terminology also were provided.

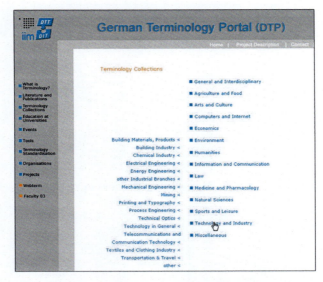

Figure 3. Terminology collections at the German Terminology Portal

Between 2011 and 2014, the DTP website was redesigned through the TIPPS project (Terminology Information Policy, Portal and Service).

The aim of the EU co-funded Eurotermbank project (2005–2006) was to create a central online terminology database for the languages of the new EU members: the Baltic States, Poland and Hungary. To permit the exchange of terminological data among existing national and European terminology databases, exchange formats and procedures were developed and implemented in compliance with international standards. EuroTermBank collected, harmonised and made accessible a large number of existing terminology and lexicographical resources. In addition to the TH Köln Institute of Information Management, the TILDE company (Latvia), the Latvian Academy of Sciences, the University of Copenhagen, the Institute of Lithuanian Language, the MorphoLogic company (Hungary), the University of Tartu and the Information Processing Centre OPI (Poland) were partners in the project. Access to Eurotermbank is still maintained by Tilde.

From 2005 to 2007, the DANDELION project (Data Modeling and Data Exchange for Software Localisation) aimed to optimise tools used in the localisation of software products by improving their recognition and management of the types of linguistic data typically found in software environments. These types of linguistic data were classified and described and an overall procedure for managing localisation units was developed. The different types of localisation units were assigned to specifically-developed terminological data categories in order to provide localisation-aware information, such as the location of the unit on a software interface. Existing data exchange formats, such as TBX-Basic, were also adapted in order to achieve adequate integration into software localisation tools. As a result, among other additions, the data category /termLocation/ was included in the DaCatInfo data category repository and in TBX Basic.

Within the framework of the nationally co-funded ELCAT project (2008–2010), an innovative web-based e-learning platform for terminology training was developed. This platform was intended to help domain experts and new terminologists understand the principles and methods of terminology work. The project was carried out in cooperation with representatives from the automotive industry, whose employees now have access to an effective online continuing education course.

Co-financed by the EU Commission from 2012 to 2014, the TaaS project (Terminology as a Service) aimed to provide a cloud-based platform for terminology work, including extraction, management, maintenance, exchange and reuse. The services included the identification of monolingual and multilingual text corpora, terminology extraction with equivalence search, the collection of terminological information, and the cleaning and maintenance of terminology inventories, all available in different forms adapted to the modern working environment of language service providers and technical writers. The platform also adhered to international standards and best practices of terminology theory (in terms of the data model and other features) and included support for file formats that can be recognised by various content systems (machine translation, authoring/editing, and translation memory). Project partners included the Institute for Information Management of TH Köln, the companies TILDE (Latvia) and Kilgray (Hungary), the University of Sheffield (UK) and the Translation Automation User Society (TAUS), based in the Netherlands.

5.   Summary

Germany has a long tradition in terminology science and terminology management, influenced by Austrian scientists and institutions like Infoterm and TermNet, but also by researchers from the Nordic countries such as Heribert Picht, Gert Engel, Christer Laurén and Johan Myking. Many scientific papers and monographs have been published in German (e.g. Drewer and Schmitz 2017). For the past few decades, terminology teaching and training have become very popular in curricula for translators, technical writers and, of course, terminologists; in addition, professional associations provide courses, seminars and conferences on terminology topics. Terminology management applications and termbases are now widespread in industry and organisations, where they are used not only to support translation, localisation and technical communication, but also for marketing, catalog production, and search engine optimisation, where they play an essential role in supporting consistent and clear corporate language (see Schmitz and Straub 2018). Finally, standardisation of terminology principles and methods has a long tradition in Germany; although several ISO standards were translated and adapted for Germany and for the German language, the more fundamental standards actually originated in Germany (see Schmitz 2022).

References

Arntz, Reiner, and Heribert Picht. 1982. *Einführung in die übersetzungsbezogene Terminologiearbeit.* Hildesheim: Olms.

Arntz, Reiner, Heribert Picht, and Klaus-Dirk Schmitz. 2021. *Einführung in die übersetzungsbezogene Terminologiearbeit.* 8. Auflage. Hildesheim: Olms.

Czap, Hans, and Christian Galinski (eds). 1987. *Terminology and Knowledge Engineering.* Frankfurt: Indeks Verlag.

Czap, Hans, and Wolfgang Nedobity (eds). 1990. *TKE '90: Terminology and Knowledge Engineering.* Vol. 1 and Vol. 2. Frankfurt: Indeks Verlag.

Drewer, Petra, and Klaus-Dirk Schmitz. 2017. *Terminologiemanagement.* Berlin/Heidelberg: Springer.

Felber, Helmut, and Gerhard Budin. 1989. *Terminologie in Theorie und Praxis.* Tübingen: Narr.

Freigang, Karl-Heinz, Felix Mayer, and Klaus-Dirk Schmitz. 1991. *Micro- and Minicomputer-based Terminology Data Bases in Europe.* TermNet Report 1. Vienna: TermNet.

Galinski, Christian, and Schmitz, Klaus-Dirk (eds). 1996. *TKE '96: Terminology and Knowledge Engineering.* Frankfurt: Indeks Verlag.

Hohnhold, Ingo. 1990. *Übersetzungsorientierte Terminologiearbeit.* Stuttgart: Intra.

KÜWES (Konferenz der Übersetzungsdienste westeuropäischer Staaten). 1990. Empfehlungen für die Terminologiearbeit. Bern: Schweizer Bundeskanzlei.

Picht, Heribert, and Klaus-Dirk Schmitz (eds). 2001. *Terminologie und Wissensordnung — Ausgewählte Schriften aus dem Gesamtwerk von Eugen Wüster*. Vienna: TermNet.

RaDT (Rat für Deutschsprachige Terminologie). 2005. *Domänenverlust im Deutschen — Stirbt Deutsch als Fachsprache?* Bern: RaDT.

Sandrini, Peter (ed). 1999. *TKE '99: Terminology and Knowledge Engineering*. Vienna: TermNet.

Schmitz, Klaus-Dirk (ed). 1993. *TKE '93: Terminology and Knowledge Engineering*. Frankfurt: Indeks Verlag.

Schmitz, Klaus-Dirk (ed). 2022. *Normen für Terminologiearbeit, Technische Redaktion und Übersetzen*. 2. Berlin: Beuth-Verlag.

Schmitz, Klaus-Dirk, and Daniela Straub. 2018. *Successful Terminology Management in Companies — Practical Tips and Guidelines*. Stuttgart: TC and more.

Wüster, Eugen. 1979. *Einführung in die Allgemeine Terminologielehre und Terminologische Lexikographie*. Schriftenreihe der Technischen Universität Wien. Vienna: Springer.

CHAPTER 23

Terminology in Greece
Bodies, works and activities

Kostas Valeontis[1], Panagiotis G. Krimpas[2], Katerina Toraki[1],
Marianna Katsoyannou[3], Mavina Pantazara[4],
George Tsiamas[1], Afroditi Giovani[1]
& Anna Anastassiadis-Symeonidis[5]
[1] Hellenic Society for Terminology | [2] Democritus University of Thrace |
[3] University of Cyprus | [4] National and Kapodistrian University of
Athens | [5] Aristotle University of Thessaloniki

Greek contributions to terminology date back to Plato and Aristotle. In the
20th century, various initiatives were undertaken to collect, record and
describe the concepts of different subject fields in the sciences and the
humanities. The chapter presents selected aspects of the systematic
development of terminology science and terminology work in Greece,
especially during the last five decades. Standardisation activities by
terminology-relevant bodies and working groups are presented, as well as
examples of relevant academic and research activities. Finally, a brief
overview of the main theoretical considerations and methodological issues
is also provided.

Keywords: Greek terminology bodies, terminology conferences,
terminology standardisation, terminology work

1. Roots of terminology in Ancient Greece

Terminology is an essential part of the scientific register (Taavitsainen 2001) of
a language. Greek contributions to terminology date back to the distant past. Of
course, concepts and concept relations have existed since the beginning of human
activity, but the study of concepts, their relations and their 'names', i.e. terms and
appellations, goes back to Plato and Aristotle (see also Chapter 2). Classical (Attic)
Greek, besides Latin, is a traditional and well-established source of neoclassical
terms and term elements used in most European and other languages to denote
concepts of science (Nybakken 1959, Ayers 1986, Kanarakis 2017). Greek has the

https://doi.org/10.1075/tlrp.24.23val

oldest written tradition among European languages and its influence on other languages goes back to Ancient Greek colonisation and/or trade. The prolonged Greek-Latin co-existence in the Italian Peninsula lent Latin many religious, philosophical, physical, medical and artistic terms. During the Post-Classical times and Late Antiquity Greek became the source-language for the translation of classical and Christian texts into Latin, while other languages terminologically influenced by Greek in that time were Demotic and Coptic (both descendants of Egyptian), Hebrew, and Aramaic (including Syriac). In the Early Middle Ages Arabic, Armenian, Ge'ez, Gothic and Old Church Slavonic adopted many Greek religious and cultural terms. Some five or more centuries later West Germanic languages borrowed some Greek religious terms, mostly via Church Latin, Gothic and, later, learned Latin and Romance languages, especially French. During the Renaissance Greek influence especially on Italian and French became stronger via translations of classical Greek texts. From the 17th century CE to date the Greek-inspired scientific terminology has been flourishing in major European languages.[1]

Medicine and chemistry are renowned for such internationalisms: it has long been reported that almost three-quarters of English medical terminology is of Greek origin, which is attributed to the fact that rational medicine was founded in the 5th century BCE, i.e. the golden age of Greek civilisation (Banay 1948: 1–2). Loyson (2009: 1195) writes that "[i]n chemistry there are hundreds of terms used commonly that are derived from the ancient Greek language and, generally, academics make use of these terms without often realising the exact meaning of the underlying words." Greek has diachronically been a cultural language for European and European-influenced language communities (Krimpas 2016). Banay (1948: 1–2) summarised the reasons why Greek-based terminology became so popular e.g. with medical scientists (but the same holds true for numerous fields): Greeks were the first to describe phenomena based on observation; the Greek language lends itself easily to word-building using components of already established terms; Greek terminology is easily understandable by experts of various ethnic backgrounds. If one knows e.g. the Hippocratic terms *neûron*[2] 'nerve' and *pathos* 'disease', they will easily guess the meaning of *neuropathy* and, by extension, of any other term beginning with the combining form *neuro-* or ending in the combining form *-pathy*.[3]

---

1. On the various aspects of Greek influence on other languages see, e.g., Kanarakis (2017), Ralli (2019), Krimpas (2024).

2. Transliteration of Greek words is here based on an accented version of ALA-LC (2010) for Ancient Greek and on ELOT743, 2nd ed. (2001) for Modern Greek.

3. cf. Haspelmath (2009: 37–38).

Whenever Classical Greek already had a term in a given subject area (e.g. philosophy), borrowing took place either via Latin or directly from Greek with the relevant graphic, phonological and morphological adaptations current in the recipient language.[4] But Greek-based neologisms for new concepts were (and are) coined in languages other than Greek by means of new combinations between Greek-based (or between Greek- and Latin-based) combining forms and/or affixes, sometimes in morphologically unexpected ways (e.g. *psychedelia* instead of the less current but morphologically correct *psychodelia*) (Krimpas and Chaika 2022). Greek-based words, combining forms and scientific affixes are to be found mostly in European languages (Anastassiadis-Symeonidis 2022), which is why they are considered part of Europeanisms (Kirkness 1984: 109). Moreover, since many of them have also made their way into languages outside Europe that have been under the influence of one or more European languages (e.g. Japanese, Malay, Swahili or Tagalog), they can be included in the broader concept of internationalisms (Wexler 1969: 77).

2. Terminology in Greece in the modern period

While Greek provided material for the creation of terms in other languages, the very word *terminology*, which apparently was first created in German (*Terminologie*) (Rey 1995: 15), was introduced as a French calque into Modern Greek in 1846 in the form *orologia*.[5] Although this term has been used for decades by scientific and professional communities, it has been until recently absent from Modern Greek dictionaries, along with *orologos* 'terminologist' and *orografia* 'terminography'. In addition to the international, at the time, interest in naming new concepts in the context of rapid scientific and technological progress, in Greece the use of language in science was inevitably linked to the Greek language question (hereinafter GLQ) and to the concomitant ideological dispute resulting from diglossia: during the 20th century, until 1976, in Greece two different varieties of Greek were used in parallel, namely *katharevousa* ('purist (variety)') and *dīmotikī* ('colloquial (variety)'); the first served as the higher register prescriptively imposed on public administration, education and other domains of public life despite being largely artificial and insufficiently mastered by speakers (Ferguson 1959), and the second serving as the lower variant used in everyday conversation despite being largely a

---

4. On the reverse scenario, e.g. Latinate terminology borrowed into Greek and relevant issues see Krimpas (2023).

5. see e.g. Koumanoudis (1900).

descendant of Ancient Greek (through Koine and Medieval Greek).[6] Apart from the social conflicts it gave rise to, that situation also conditioned the development of scientific terminology by imposing forms that made use and understanding of terms more difficult than in other languages (Toraki 2011).

Like in the rest of Europe, in the first decades of the 20th century engineers and technically educated people in general were increasingly showing a special interest in terminology[7] — probably also because they were affected by differing preferences of scientists and professionals and realised the importance of terminological harmonisation for a more effective communication (Toraki 2007). This fact is documented even before the establishment (in 1923) of the Technical Chamber of Greece (Techniko Epimelītīrio Elladas, TEE) through articles, letters and the like, published in technical magazines such as *Archimīdīs* and *Erga* as well as later in the TEE-published *Technika Chronika* and *Enīmerōtiko Deltio*. The magazines themselves embraced such views, as suggested e.g. by a note under the title "We need a Greek vocabulary of technical terms" published in 1927 in the Editorial column of *Erga*; through examples from the textile industry, the note pointed out the need to gather existing technical terms, to create original Greek terminology and carry out systematic terminology work rather than just calquing foreign terms.

Since its establishment, TEE has been interested in terminology at all levels: creation and recording of terms, publication of special dictionaries, as well as standardisation and support of terminology work. In 1928, a committee was set up to compile a quadrilingual technical glossary, whose individual thematic sections were progressively published in *Technika Chronika*. At the same time, TEE systematically supported the publication of independent works, mainly multilingual dictionaries, in various scientific and technical fields. G. Chalkiopoulos' quadrilingual (Greek ~ English ~ French ~ German) technical dictionary (1951) greatly contributed to the development of Modern Greek engineering terminology, with successive editions of multilingual glossaries. M. Kolaitis' two-volume bilingual (English > Greek) dictionary of pure and applied mathematics (1976) was also an innovative work, particularly due to linguistic issues explicitly taken into account as described in his extensive preface (1976: ix–ci) (see more in Section 5).

The contribution of TEE to standardisation is also of particular importance for terminological research, especially in relation to Eurocodes, standards and other normative technical texts. TEE was the first Greek body to deal with such issues

---

6. More information about the multiple learned varieties of Greek see e.g. in Krimpas (2019: 59–61).

7. On Greek scientists' terminology practices during the 19th to early 20th century see Tampakis (2015).

by founding, in 1933, the Hellenic Standardisation Committee (Ellīnikī Epitropī Protypopoiīseōs, ENO standing for ENOpoiīsī 'unification'), as well as by issuing the ENO *Bulletin de Normalisation* [Deltion Protypopoiīseōs ENO]. Aside from an interruption during World War II, ENO operated for more than three decades as the national organisation for standardisation, while the Hellenic Organisation for Standardisation (Ellīnikos Organismos Typopoiīsīs, ELOT) was established in 1976 (see more in 3.1).

The efforts to develop terminology focused on many other fields of specialised knowledge such as chemistry and medicine. In the field of chemistry, the nomenclature of chemical compounds was examined; such terminology presents difficulties due to the mixing and competition among neoclassical elements of Greek and Latin origin. The first book in which Modern Greek chemistry terms were proposed was A. Gazis' translation of B. Martin's *The Philosophical Grammar*, published in 1799, followed by a Modern Greek nomenclature published in 1842 by X. Landerer (Mavropoulos 2021a, 2021b). Nowadays, one of the most notable works in this field is the bilingual, bidirectional (English <> Greek) *Dictionary of chemical terms* (Efstathiou 1998), now available also online, with more than 10,000 entries covering more than 20,000 concepts.

Despite such efforts, chemical nomenclature and terminology in Modern Greek has not yet been systematised, nor has it been fully harmonised with the internationally established International Union of Pure and Applied Chemistry (IUPAC) nomenclature and terminology (Siskos and Filopoulos 1997). Names and terms are variously adapted to Greek, while at other times the relevant international conventions are applied, which results in inconsistency and variation in the rendering and use of basic terms, a situation comparable to other fields as well (Krimpas 2023); moreover, each university department of chemistry in Greece has its own terminological tradition (Efstathiou 2014). In 2014, the first Panhellenic Conference on Chemical Nomenclature and Terminology was held by the Association of Greek Chemists (AGC), followed by the second Conference with the cooperation of the Pancyprian Union of Chemists (PUC) in 2018, while similar activities are regularly held for the purpose of addressing such issues.

In medicine, as early as the 18th century, scientists, often multilingual and having knowledge of other fields as well (mathematics, philosophy, etc.), produced original and/or translated scientific books and dictionaries, thus contributing to the development and establishment of Modern Greek medical terminology (Karamperopoulos 2008, Toraki 2019). The peculiarity of this field is that, while its concepts are largely imported, their names in the various European languages often contain formative elements of Classical Greek origin and thus the terms are generally treated as back-loanwords in Greek etymological dictionaries despite actually being internationalisms (Krimpas 2023: 3).

In the context of the GLQ, important initiatives were taken to support the spoken variety of the language. As early as 1902, the Brotherhood for the National Language (Adelfato tīs ethnikīs glōssas) was founded in Constantinople, while in the 1940s academics began to teach and write medical books in vernacular Greek. In 1943, the debate about diglossia and the GLQ was fuelled by the publication of various articles on language and medical terminology in the journal *Akadīmaïkī Iatrikī*. Currently, efforts continue thanks to actions taken by the Centre for Greek Medical Information, Terminology and Documentation (Kentro Ellīnikīs Iatrikīs Plīroforīsīs, Orologias kai Tekmīriōsīs, IATROTEK), which was established by the Society of Medical Studies in the mid-1980s.

Following the at least nominal[8] legal settling of the GLQ in 1976, new initiatives were undertaken to develop terminology in all fields, the first being a series of lectures in 1977 by the Moraïtis School (Athens), a private educational institution, in collaboration with the most prominent scientists of the time, who were interested in the study of terms and the compilation of specialised glossaries (Anastassiadis et al. 1977).

3.   Organisations involved in terminology

3.1   Hellenic Organization for Standardization

A landmark in the history of terminology in Greece is 1976 when the Hellenic Organization for Standardization (Ellīnikos Organismos Typopoiīsīs, ELOT) was established, thereby institutionalising the national standardisation of terminology. A prerequisite of this activity is the development of common special languages and commonly accepted terminology in all domains.

Each ELOT Technical Committee deals with the special language of its subject field, in particular the relevant terminology. The terms resulting from the adoption of European and International Standards as ELOT Hellenic Standards are added to the ELOT termbase, which contains tens of thousands of terminological entries (not yet publicly available).

---

8. cf. Krimpas (2019) for an extensive discussion about the continuing effects of the GLQ into Standard Modern Greek.

3.1.1   *Terminology and language resources*

Technical Committee ELOT/TC 21 Terminology — Language resources was established in 1978 under the name Technical Terminology at the initiative of the TEE (Valeontis 1988, Katsoyannou and Toraki 2010 and 2011, Pantazara 2021). This committee, being the Greek national mirror committee of ISO/TC 37 Language and Terminology, participates in its work, attends its annual meetings, and contributes constructive comments to the international standards it produces. The members of the committee are delegates from relevant standardisation, research, educational, academic and language professional bodies.

ELOT/TC 21 prepares Hellenic Terminology Standards implementing various International Recommendations and presents ELOT Standards in special publications (Valeontis 1988) in order to contribute to the consistent application of ISO principles for term formation. The major part of the terms in the standards prepared by ELOT/TC 21 are finally included in the freely accessible multilingual terminological database with the terminology of terminology (TermTerm).

3.1.2   *Information and documentation*

The field of information science relies on the field of terminology for developing the tools used to organise and manage information resources, such as thesauri and other controlled vocabularies. ELOT/TC 22 actively participates in the development of documentation and information science by cultivating and establishing relevant Greek terminology. All the Greek terms and definitions contained in the ELOT/TC 22 Standards, along with equivalent terms in English and French, have been entered in a terminology database (DOCUTERM) freely accessible on the ELETO website (see 3.3).

3.2   Other working groups

Three important working groups (WGs) which adopted and applied the ISO principles and whose activity and production have contributed to terminology research and coordination are the Permanent Group for Telecommunication Terminology (MOTO), the ELOT/TC 48/WG1 Information Technology Terminology, and the ELOT/TC 2/WG5 Sound Insulation. Greek terms produced by such groups are included, respectively, in the TELETERM, INFORTERM, and ACOUTERM termbases freely accessible on the ELETO website (see 3.3).

3.3   Hellenic Society for Terminology

The Hellenic Society for Terminology (Ellīnikī Etaireia Orologias, ELETO) is the only Greek association exclusively active in terminology (Valeontis and Filopoulos 2001). It was established in 1992 by the members of the following founding bodies: ELOT/TC 21, MOTO, ELOT/TC 48/WG1, ELOT/TC 2/WG5, the Terminology Group of the Panhellenic Association of Mechanical-Electrical Engineers, the National Centre for Public Administration, and IATROTEK, as well as several other contributors. However, it is worth mentioning that two years earlier, two significant initiatives had taken place that basically led to its foundation.

In 1990, at the initiative of the General Secretariat for Research and Technology (GSRT), a Working Group, named Terminology Rendering, was established to study the state of terminology in Greece and to plan a coordinated research programme on creating and establishing Greek terminology on a national scale. The WG completed its work and submitted its final report; however, no progress has been recorded afterwards.

In the same year, at MOTO's initiative, ELOT/TC 21, MOTO, ELOT/TC 48/WG1, and ELOT/TC 2/WG5, as well as the Terminology Group of the Panhellenic Association of Mechanical-Electrical Engineers, signed an agreement aiming for the inter-committee and inter-field harmonisation of Greek terms (Valeontis 2004: 137–138).

ELETO is a member of, and/or cooperates with, a number of international organisations including the International Information Centre for Terminology (Infoterm) (see also Chapter 17), the European Association for Terminology (EAFT), the International Network for Terminology (TermNet), and, formerly, of the now inactive International Institute for Terminology Research (IITF).

Additionally, ELETO has developed fruitful national and international cooperation with bodies having similar purposes such as universities, public authorities and professional associations. For example, it contributed to the syllabus of a Master's programme at the Ionian University (lectures on terminology standardisation, 2001–2002) and offered courses on the principles of terminology and terminography (2003–2013) for the Technoglossia Interdisciplinary Master's Programme, offered by the Institute for Language and Speech Processing (ILSP), the National Technical University of Athens (NTUA), and the National and Kapodistrian University of Athens (NKUA).

ELETO undertakes, and/or participates in, actions to promote open access to and consensus on terminology. For example, in 2000, ELETO actively participated, among other institutions, in the Coordination Committee of the National Programme for Terminological Coordination (EPOS). In 2006, ELETO organised, in Athens, a conference to examine the French Commission d'enrichissement de la langue française (see Chapter 21) and investigate the possibility of establishing an analogous system in Greece. Following the conference, ELETO and the Ministry of Education jointly drafted a bill on the establishment of a terminology coordinating body in Greece, to be called National Body of Terminology; however, the bill was not submitted to Parliament at that time.

Today, the ELETO website offers free online access to: (a) all the papers presented in the biennial terminology conference Hellenic Language and Terminology organised by ELETO (14 conferences, 439 papers), (b) more than 200,000 terminological entries by means of 15 termbases, including those above-mentioned in 3.1 and 3.2, and (c) many glossaries and dictionaries. Since 1993, ELETO has been reporting its activities in the bimonthly bulletin *Orogramma*.

3.4   Hellenic Network for Terminology

In 2015, at the initiative of the Greek Language Department of the Directorate General for Translation (DGT) of the European Commission, the Hellenic Network for Terminology (Ellīniko Diktyo Orologias, EDO) was established, in which ELETO actively participated. EDO was a communication network for scientific, legal and technical terminology and translation issues in the Greek language. It brought into contact the language services of EU institutions with public administration in Greece and Cyprus, with scientific and professional foundations and bodies, as well as with translation and interpreting professionals. Urgent terminological issues were discussed in EDO's domain wikis, and Greek equivalents of non-Greek terms were prescribed for the Greek translations of official European documents (Doudoulakaki 2017). The terms were imported into IATE (see Chapter 20). EDO terminated its activities in December 2023.

4.   Education and research

University scholars and researchers, working especially on language and translation, promote terminology in Greece by developing research projects, courses, terminology resources, as well as by organising scientific and other academic events and publishing relevant works.

4.1   Research institutions

The Research Centre for Scientific Terms and Neologisms (KEEON), established in 1966, is one the 14 research centres of the Academy of Athens. Its main mission is to collect and study Modern Greek neologisms and propose Greek equivalents for recent scientific terminology. Since 1986 it has published 15 issues of the *Bulletin of Scientific Terminology and Neologisms*, containing terms from various domains.

The Institute for Language and Speech Processing (ILSP) was established in 1991, but its history goes back to 1985 when a small team of linguists and information technologists worked on the EUROTRA machine translation project. Progressively, the team has expanded and is currently one of the leading R&D organisations in Greece in the fields of language, knowledge and content technologies. The ILSP brings together experts from computational linguistics, machine learning, signal processing, computer science, statistics, psycholinguistics, cognitive sciences, humanities and physics. Its activities include the development of terminology and language resources for Greek, such as specialised lexica and corpora for various domains, term extraction tools, thesauri as application ontologies, and tools for the conceptual organisation of verb-centred multiword expressions (see 4.4 and 4.5).

4.2   Education

Only in a few cases is terminology taught as an independent module in academic institutions. The latter focus almost exclusively on translation-oriented terminology rather than theory-oriented terminology[9] and their pedagogical orientation is descriptive rather than language planning-relevant. A review of the curricula of Greek higher education institutions (Pantazara 2019) suggests that only one of the university courses examined explicitly includes terminology theory as a module (taught at the Democritus University of Thrace). There is also a limited number of courses aimed at developing skills in terminological methodology (regardless of language and subject field), usually offered in the curricula of postgraduate translation programmes. Terminology is mostly approached through courses that aim at developing language skills in specialised domains. Seminars and courses in specific languages, terminology and/or translation aimed at a wider audience (and not only at students) are offered by higher education language centres and specialised private or public institutions.

---

9. The term was coined by Thelen (2015: 348–349) and denotes "the type of terminology work done by terminologists who are essentially concerned with the relation between terms and concepts, concept formation, term formation and standardisation" as against translation-oriented terminology, which is "carried out by translators for use in translations."

4.3   Terminology events

The first conference on standardisation of terminology was organised in 1992, by TEE and ELOT/TC 21 with support from ELETO. Since 1997, ELETO has been organising the biennial conference Hellenic Language and Terminology with particular reference to Greek terminology. This conference is supported by a large number of terminology scholars and co-organisers. In 2013, in conjunction with the ninth Conference Hellenic Language and Terminology, a Symposium on National Languages and Terminology in Higher Education, Science and Technology was co-organised by ELETO, EAFT, NKUA, and the University of Cyprus. Various relevant seminars and training workshops have been held by ELETO members since 2007.

4.4   Terminology resources

An interesting series of bilingual, bidirectional legal terminology dictionaries with tens of thousands of entries, all edited and/or compiled by academics, magistrates and/or doctors of law have been published by Nomiki Vivliothiki publishing house, specialised in legal literature: English <> Greek (Dakoronia 2021), French <> Greek (Fortsakis and Gardounis 2020), German <> Greek (Vathiotis 2013), Italian <> Greek (Valmantonis and Vidali 2014), Spanish <> Greek with Portuguese Annex (Livas 2014), and Greek <> Latin (Kontaxis and Kitsakis 2014). All those dictionaries are rich in examples from real life legal practice.

Linguistic terminology glossaries can be found in Greek translations of books. During the same period, Prof. M. Setatos urged the linguists of the Philology Department of the Aristotle University of Thessaloniki (AUTh) to start translating internationally important books on synchronic linguistics into Greek. Thus, A. Martinet's 1960 book *Éléments de linguistique générale* was translated by A. Charalampopoulos (Martinet 1976), and G. Mounin's *Clefs pour la linguistique* was translated by A. Anastassiadis-Symeonidis (Mounin 1984). Each is supplemented by a bilingual glossary (Greek to French).

Later, several major dictionaries of linguistics were published in Greek: (a) Dimitriou's *Dictionary of communication and semiotic analysis terms* (1980), *Dictionary of linguistic terms* (1983) and *Dictionary of semantic terms* (1986) and (b) Crystal's *Dictionary of Linguistics and Phonetics*, which was translated into Greek by Prof. of Linguistics G. Xydopoulos (2003).

In the domain of translation, the book *Translation Terminology*, edited by J. Delisle, H. Lee-Jahnke and M. C. Cormier (1999), was translated into Greek by G. Floros, a professor of translation studies, in 2008 (Delisle et al. 2008[1999]). For translation students, the link between professional translation and terminology work has been created through projects with TermCoord (the Terminology Coordination Unit of the European Parliament, operational until 2022). As part of the collaboration with TermCoord, MA students at Greek Universities (namely, AUTh and the Ionian University) have created glossaries in various domains.

In the area of thesauri construction, activities have been pursued based on international terminology and documentation standards and practice. Initially they were developed to cover mainly the needs of scientific libraries (Giannibas 2005, Toraki et al. 2008), while research institutions are also involved, such as the National Centre for Social Research (EKKE), the National Research Foundation (EIE) and the ILSP, which has developed application ontologies for cultural objects, gastronomy, and other areas (Markantonatou et al. 2021). The Institute of Computer Science (ICS-Forth) also has a long and pioneering experience in the development of terminological tools and thesauri, especially in the cultural and humanities areas, through its Centre for Cultural Informatics (CCI). Its projects include the multilingual thesaurus for the humanities DYAS, which is being developed as a collaborative effort by the Academy of Athens, the NKUA and the Athens School of Fine Arts (DARIAH GR/DYAS and APOLLONIS projects).

In the domain of information science, Liblex has been published, which is an online Greek-English Dictionary of Information Science created within the framework of the Kallipos project for Open Academic Electronic Editions (Kapidakis et al. 2024). In the domain of sciences, the comprehensive, quadrilingual (English, French, German, Greek) dictionary of scientific and technical terms (Vasileiadou-Zachou et al. 2004) is worth mentioning, as it includes about 49,000 terms taught in AUTh technical and scientific faculties.

Finally, a large number of terminology resources, such as glossaries and corpora developed by various bodies described here, are collected in the national repository CLARIN:EL (the Greek part of the CLARIN ERIC European Infrastructure for Language Resources and Technologies), which provides open access to a distributed network of institutional repositories.

4.5   Terminology projects in academia

Various terminological projects have been undertaken by academic staff and students at Greek universities, such as those in linguistics and translation.

A recent ILSP-hosted lexicographic project, IDION, which was based on the PARSEME EU project (IC1207 — COST Action), dealt with verb-centred Modern Greek multiword expressions (VMWEs). They were documented according to syntactic flexibility, semantics and semantic relations with other expressions, which, along with synonymy, revealed the conceptual organisation of VMWEs. The project aimed at developing a full network of semantic relations among VMWEs that define a concept, using the web to identify usage tendencies (Markantonatou et al. 2019).

In the domain of linguistics, a collaborative project to create a multilingual *Linguistic Terminology Dictionary* was undertaken by AUTh (Anastassiadis-Syméonidis 1994). This project was initiated in the 1970s by M. Setatos, a Professor of Linguistics at the Department of Philology of the AUTh. Under the supervision of Setatos, linguists catalogued important English, French, German and Russian-language books on linguistics, rendered linguistic terms into Greek and created terminological entries on index cards.

5.   Theory and methodology

Greek literature is not rich in works on theoretical or applied terminology, and this despite the marked interest shown by translators and other language professionals as well as other experts in specific domains who seek support for the often ad hoc choices they have to make in order to complete their tasks.

The lexicographer Kolaitis (1976), who talked about language with well-known personalities of Greek letters such as P. Vlastos and K. Cavafy, describes his efforts to find adequate Greek renderings to designate concepts originally expressed in English, to adopt a term or a variant form of a term in use or an ancient word with a new meaning or newly-coined terms. As for choosing between the two written language idioms, *katharevousa* 'purist (variety)' and *dīmotikī* 'vernacular (variety)', he gave preference to the form more easily assimilated by both — and it is noteworthy that he was very much aware of terminological concepts such as description and prescription, monosemy and polysemy, or between simple and learned vernacular. What is interesting are his findings about the then current state of Greek terminology, e.g. (a) that a systematic recording of vernacular terms was lacking, even though many of them had their exact equivalent in English; (b) that a gap existed between oral and written language; (c) that vernacular terms matched their English equivalents better than purist ones, which were largely calqued on French multiword terms; (d) that the Modern Greek vocabulary (of average speakers) did not include new terms, mostly scientific and technical ones, to name new concepts; (e) that new terms were not in any way correlated with existing ones; and (f) that neither did clear definitions exist (he invented such terms as *orismologia* and *orismologīsī* based on English 'orismology'), nor was terminological scrutiny applied. In other words, he identified a serious failure of systematic terminological work. He took a position on issues of polysemy, synonymy, and translation from French, German and English into Greek, he placed particular emphasis on the role of context for choosing a term to denote a concept, and he proposed criteria for new term formation. His selected case studies of English terms and the strategies he used to render them into Greek are also interesting. All this suggests that Kolaitis' work deserves to be counted among the first terminography works based on a theoretical reflection extending well beyond empirical term use.[10]

Greek participation in Terminology-related international activity via ELETO, ELOT/TC 21 or cooperating bodies in the framework of the biennial ELETO-organised conferences Hellenic Language and Terminology contributes to the promotion of terminology theory and practice at interlingual level as e.g. in the case of the so-called *analogue rule* (Valeontis 2005).

The principles of the General Theory of Terminology (see also Chapter 8) were first published in Greek in the national ELOT standards in 1981, which are mostly based on various versions of ISO standards related to concept systems, characteristics, definitions, designations, terms, and term formation principles.

Work done in theoretical or applied terminology is mostly illustrated in the proceedings of the conferences Hellenic Language and Terminology, as well as in the increasing number of articles and monographs published in the last decade. Some hallmark Greek-language books on terminology are Katsoyannou and Efthimiou (2004), Krimpas (2009), Valeontis and Krimpas (2014), Keramidas (2015), and Krimpas et al. (2023), while the number of doctoral theses prepared in relevant fields is also constantly increasing.

Greek terminology organisations such as ELETO and ELOT/TC 21 mainly based their research on Wüster's theory. Currently, modern terminological approaches do also exist, such as those oriented towards either the Communicative Theory of Terminology (see Chapter 13) or Textual Terminology (see Chapter 11) using corpora and relating to, e.g., terminology didactics, IT research (mostly language applications and AI), printed and electronic lexicography, and translation. Koutsivitis (1986) completed one of the first studies on translation and terminology, followed by linguists — especially Katsoyannou and Efthimiou (2004) — representing the academic field that has so far offered the greatest contribution to terminology theory in the Greek language. Another valuable contribution to terminology theory is the work of Anastasiadis-Symeonidis discussing, on the one hand, linguistic issues posed by the transition from *katharevousa* to *dīmotikī* with examples from various fields, ranging from geology to public administration and, on the other hand, specific morphological issues of the Greek language that can be part of a proposed terminological grammar.

Anastassiadis-Symeonidis' research (2022) is based on Corbin's (1987, and forthcoming) theoretical framework, focusing on the concept of scientific suffix.

---

10. Interestingly, Kolaitis' (1964) article in *Technika Chronika* includes Modern Greek renderings of the terms *engineer* and *engineering*.

Scientific terminological suffixes can be specific to a language register and/or a domain, following different rules when they appear in a terminological, non-colloquial linguistic context. In Modern Greek such suffixes have in fact been borrowed from western European languages (English, French, German; cf. Anastassiadis-Symeonidis 1997), which had already borrowed and re-analysed Ancient Greek suffixed terms. For example, the deverbative suffix *-sis* is used in Ancient Greek to form terms such as *psōríāsis* 'the state of having *psōr(a)*, i.e. scabies' via the verb *psōriô* (deriving from < *psōriáō*) 'to have *psōr(a)*'; in major western languages the suffix has been re-analysed as *-iasis* (*psor-iasis*) and used to form denominal medical terms denoting non-inflammatory conditions. In later times, *-íasis* has been borrowed by Modern Greek to coin new terms such as *echinokokkíasī* 'echinococcose' (Tsiakmakis 2017). Similarly, Ancient Greek *diásta-sis* 'separation, detachment, distance', passed into French as *diastase* 'luxation, enzyme', and gave rise to the suffix *-ase*, used in denominal biochemical terms to denote enzymes: *amylase, cellulase, lipase* etc. Modern Greek has, in its turn, borrowed the suffix *-ase* and integrated it as *-asī*, e.g. in *kyttarin-asī* 'cellulase' (Anastassiadis-Symeonidis and Fliatouras 2015). In all those cases, similar inherited Modern Greek suffixes facilitated the integration of the borrowed, Ancient Greek-based ones.

6.   Conclusion

This chapter has summarised Modern Greek terminology research and its state-of-the-art. Further research is needed in this respect, involving such pivotal thematic areas as ICT, robotics, banking, renewable resources, and environmental and human rights.

References

Anastassiadis, Anna, Christos Christidis, Spyros Doxiadis, Theodosios Tasios, Christos Giannaras, Adamantios Pepelasis, and Nikos Kyriazidis. 1977. *Provlīmata metaglōttismou stī neoellīnikī glōssa.* Series of lectures. Moraïtis School, 161.

Anastassiadis-Syméonidis, Anna. 1994. "Un dictionnaire multilingue de linguistique." *Meta* 39 (4): 598–614.

Anastassiadis-Symeonidis, Anna. 1997. "Glōssikes diadikasies kata tī dīmiourgia tōn orōn." In *Ellīnikī Glōssa kai Orologia: Anakoinōseis 1ou Synedriou,* ed. by Vasileios A. Filopoulos and Tota Anagnostopoulou, 77–87. Athens: ELETO.

Anastassiadis-Symeonidis, Anna. 2022. "Lexikografia kai epistīmonika epithīmata." In *Lexikografia kai morfologia: Ī thesī tīs morfologias sta lexika tīs neas ellīnikīs,* ed. by Marianna Katsoyannou and Anna Anastassiadis-Symeonidis, 95–108. Athens: Patakī.

Anastassiadis-Symeonidis, Anna, and Asimakis Fliatouras. 2015. "To epithīma -*as(ī)* stī vio-chīmeia." In *Ellīnikī Glōssa kai Orologia: Anakoinōseis 10ou Synedriou*, ed. by Kostas Valeontis, 76–86. Athens: ELETO.

Ayers, Donald M. 1986. *English words from Latin and Greek Elements* (2nd ed.). Tucson: University of Arizona Press.

Banay, George L. 1948. "An Introduction to Medical Terminology I. Greek and Latin Derivations." *Bulletin of the Medical Library Association* 36 (1): 1–27.

Chalkiopoulos, Georgios. 1951. *Lexikon technikōn orōn eis tessaras glōssas*. Athens: Techniko Epimelītīrio Elladas.

Corbin, Danielle. 1987. *Morphologie dérivationnelle et structuration du lexique* (tomes I et II). Villeneuve d'Ascq: Presses Universitaires de Lille.

Corbin, Danielle. forthcoming. *Le lexique construit. Méthodologie d'analyse*. Villeneuve d'Ascq: Presses Universitaires du Septentrion.

Crystal, David. 2003 [1980]. *Lexiko glōssologias kai fōnītikīs*. Athens: Patakī.

Dacoronia, Eugenia (ed). 2021. *English-Greek Greek-English Dictionary of Legal Terms (4th edition)*. Athens: Nomikī Vivliothīkī.

Delisle, Jean, Hannelore Lee-Jahnke, and Monique C. Cormier (eds). 2008 [1999]. *Orologia tīs metafrasīs*. (*Translation Terminology*, translated by Georgios Floros). Athens: Mesogeios.

Dimitriou, Sotiris. 1980. *Lexiko orōn epikoinōnias kai sīmeiōtikīs analysīs 2*. Athens: Kastaniotī.

Dimitriou, Sotiris. 1983. *Lexiko orōn glōssologias (A+B)*. Athens: Kastaniotī.

Dimitriou, Sotiris. 1986. *Lexiko orōn sīmantikīs*. Athens: Kastaniotī.

Doudoulakaki, Chrysoula. 2017. "Ellīniko Diktyo Orologias kai leitourgia tīs Ypīresias Epeigousas Apodosīs Orōn." In *Ellīnikī Glōssa kai Orologia: Anakoinōseis 11ou Synedriou*, ed. by Kostas Valeontis, 403–421. Athens: ELETO.

ELOT 402: 2010 *Terminology Work — Principles and Methods*. ELOT.

ELOT 561–1: 2006 *Terminology Work — Vocabulary*. ELOT.

Efstathiou, Constantinos. 1998. *Aggloellīniko Ellīnoaggliko lexiko chīmikōn kai syggenōn me tī chīmeia orōn*. Athens: n.p.

Efstathiou, Constantinos. 2014. "Katataxī provlīmatōn ta opoia synantōntai stīn Ellīnikī Chīmikī Onomatologia kai Orologia." Paper presented at the 1st Panhellenic Conference on Chemistry Nomenclature and Terminology, Athens, Greece, 22 February 2014.

Ferguson, Charles. 1959. "Diglossia." *Word* 15 (2), 325–340.

Fortsakis, Théodore, and Emmanuel Gardounis (eds). 2020. *Français-grec grec-français: dictionnaire juridique*. Athens: Nomikī Vivliothīkī.

Giannibas, Dionyssios. 2005. "O Thīsauros Ellīnikōn Orōn: ena ergaleio gia tī thematikī organosī tou periechomenou." In *Ellīnikī Glōssa kai Orologia: Anakoinōseis 5ou Synedriou*, ed. by Kostas Valeontis and Giōta Kazazī, 182–193. Athens: Techniko Epimelītīrio Elladas.

Haspelmath, Martin. 2009. "Loanwords in the World's Languages II: Lexical Borrowing: Concepts and Issues." In *Loanwords in the World's Languages: A Comparative Handbook*, ed. by Martin Haspelmath and Uri Tadmor, 35–54. Berlin: Mouton De Gruyter.

ISO 1087–1: 2000 — *Terminology Work — Vocabulary*. Geneva: International Organization for Standardization.

ISO 704: 2000 — *Terminology Work — Principles and Methods*. Geneva: International Organization for Standardization.

ISO/R 704: 1968 — *Naming Principles*. Geneva: International Organization for Standardization.

ISO/R1087: 1969 — *Vocabulary of Terminology*. Geneva: International Organization for Standardization.

Kanarakis, Georgios (ed). 2017. *The Legacy of the Greek Language*. New York/Boston: Peridot.

Kapidakis, Sarantos, Katerina Toraki, Stella Chatzimari, Kostas Valeontis, and Ypapanti Kytta. 2024. *Dictionary of Information Science: Greek-English Terminological Dictionary*. Online: Kallipos.

Karamperopoulos, Dimitrios. 2008. "Ellīnikī iatrikī orologia: oi aparches tīs kata ton Neoellīniko Diafōtismo." *Archeia Istorias Epistīmōn Ygeias* 25 (2), 244–247.

Katsoyannou, Marianna, and Eleni Efthimiou (eds). 2004. *Ellīnikī orologia: erevna kai efarmoges*. Athens: Kastaniōtī.

Katsoyannou, Marianna, and Katerina Toraki. 2010. "The Greek Technical Committee of Standardization on Terminology TE21." Paper presented at the 5th Terminology Summit: Quality matters, Budapest, Hungary.

Katsoyannou, Marianna, and Katerina Toraki. 2011. "Zītīmata typopoiīsīs stīn orologia: O rolos kai oi draseis tīs Epitropīs Orologias TE21 tou ELOT." In *Ellīnikī Glōssa kai Orologia: Anakoinōseis 8ou Synedriou*, ed. by Kostas Valeontis, 415–424. Athens: ELETO.

Keramidas, Sotirios G. 2015. *Zītīmata orologias stīn technikī metafrasī*. Athens: Diaulos.

Kirkness, Alan. 1984. "The etymology of Europeanisms, or: Lexicographers' Difficulties with 'lexicographer'." In *LEXeter '83 PROCEEDINGS: Papers from the International Conference on Lexicography at Exeter, 9–12 September 1983*, ed. by Reinhard R. K. Hartmann, 109–116. Tübingen: Niemeyer.

Kolaitis, Memas. 1964. "Engineer — Engineering: Themata tīs Ellīnikīs Orologias." *Technika Chronika, Genikī Ekdosis* 245, 55–58.

Kolaitis, Memas. 1976. *English-Greek Dictionary of Pure and Applied Mathematics (with Greek-English Appendices), in two volumes*. Athens: Techniko Epimelītīrio Elladas.

Kontaxis, Thrasyvoulos Th., and Stauros Kitsakis. 2014. *Latiniko lexiko nomikōn orōn kai ekfraseōn*. Athens: Nomikī Vivliothīkī.

Koumanoudis, Stefanos. 1900. *Synagōgī neōn lexeōn ypo tōn logiōn plastheisōn: Apo tīs alōseōs mechri tōn kath' īmas chronōn*. En Athīnais: Typois P. D. Sakellariou.

Koutsivitis, Vasilis. 1986. "Orologikes kai metafrastikes paratīrīseis me aformī to ellīniko keimeno tīs Synthīkīs EOK." *Terminologie et Traduction* 3: 15–27.

Krimpas, Panagiotis G. 2009. *Ī metafrasī nomikōn orōn stis diethneis symvaseis: Ī periptōsī tīs Symvasīs tou Schengen*. Athens: Sakkoulas.

Krimpas, Panagiotis G. 2016. "Aspects diachroniques et synchroniques du grec en tant que langue culturelle: terminologie, néologie, purisme." In *Plurilinguisme et créativité scientifique*, ed. by Pierre Frath and José Carlos Herreras (Plurilinguisme 2), 90–100. Vincennes: L'Observatoire européen du plurilinguisme.

Krimpas, Panagiotis G. 2019. "Pseudologioi typoi kai yperdiorthōsī stī Neoellīnikī Koinī me vasī ta epipeda glōssikīs analysīs." In *To logio epipedo stī sygchronī Nea Elltīnikī: Theōria, istoria, efarmogī: Apo ton oiko sto spiti kai tanapalin...*, ed. by Asimakis Fliatouras, and Anna Anastassiadis-Symeonidis, 57–126. Athens: Patakī.

Krimpas, Panagiotis G. 2023. "Latinate Terminology in Modern Greek: An 'intruder' or an 'asset'?" *Open Linguistics* 9 (1): 1–16.

Krimpas, Panagiotis G. 2024. "Greek Background of Modern Scientific Terminology." In *Encyclopedia of Greek Language and Linguistics Online*, ed. by Georgios K. Giannakis. Online: Brill.

Krimpas, Panagiotis G., and Oksana Chaika. 2022. "Some Desiderata in Teaching Scientific and Legal LSP in Modern Greek: The Case of Loanwords." *International Philological Journal* 13 (3): 102–111.

Krimpas, Panagiotis G., Elpida Loupaki, Mavina Pantazara, and Eleni Tziafa. 2023. *Zītīmata orologias stī sygchroni metafrastikī praktikī: Diepistīmonikes proseggiseis.* Online: Kallipos.

Livas, Sotirios (ed). 2014. *Español-griego griego-español: diccionario jurídico.* Athens: Nomikī Vivliothīkī.

Loyson, Peter. 2009. "Influences of Ancient Greek on Chemical Terminology." *Journal of Chemical Education* 86 (10): 1195–1199.

Markantonatou, Stella, Panagiotis Minos, George Zakis, Vassiliki Moutzouri, and Maria Chantou. 2019. "IDION: A database for Modern Greek multiword expressions." In *Proceedings of the Joint Workshop on Multiword Expressions and WordNet (MWE-WN 2019)*, ed. by Agata Savary, Carla Parra Escartín, Francis Bond, Jelena Mitrović, and Verginica Barbu Mititelu, 130–134. Florence: Association for Computational Linguistics.

Markantonatou, Stella, Katerina Toraki, Panagiotis Minos, Anna Vacalopoulou, Vivian Stamou, and George Pavlidis. 2021. "AMALTHEIA: A Dish-Driven Ontology in the Food Domain." *Data* 6 (4): 41.

Martinet, André. 1976 [1960]. *Stoicheia Genikīs Glōssologias (Éléments de Linguistique Générale*, translated by A. Charalampopoulos). Thessaloniki: Aristotle University of Thessaloniki, Institute of Modern Greek Studies.

Mavropoulos, Avraam. 2021a. "Ī onomatologia tōn Anorganōn Enōseōn stīn Ellada, kata tīn periodo 1800–2000." *Chīmika Chronika* 83 (1): 11–18.

Mavropoulos, Avraam. 2021b. "Ī onomatologia tōn Organikōn Enōseōn stīn Ellada, kata tīn periodo 1837–2000." *Chīmika Chronika* 83 (2): 14–20.

Mounin, Georges. 1984 [1973]. *Kleidia gia tī Glōssologia (Clefs pour la linguistique*, translated by Anna Anastassiadis-Symeonidis). Athens: Morfōtiko Idryma Ethnikīs Trapezīs.

Nybakken, Oscar E. 1959. *Greek and Latin in Scientific Terminology.* Ames: Iowa State College Press.

Pantazara, Mavina. 2019. "Schediasmos enos ellīnofōnou programmatos katartisīs stīn Orologia." In *Ellīnikī Glōssa kai Orologia: Anakoinōseis 12ou Synedriou*, ed. by Kostas Valeontis, Panagiotis G. Krimpas, Mavina Pantazara, Katerina Toraki, and Giorgos Tsiamas, 85–97. Athens: ELETO.

Pantazara, Mavina. 2021. "Metafrasī kai Typopoiīsī: to ergo tīs epitropīs ELOT/TE21." Paper presented at the 7th Meeting of Greek-speaking Translation Studies Scholars, Thessaloniki, Greece.

Ralli, Angela. 2019. "Greek in Contact with Romance." In *The Oxford Encyclopedia of Romance Languages*, ed. by Mario Loporcaro, and Francesco Gardani. Online: Oxford University Press.

Rey, Alain. 1995. *Essays on Terminology.* Amsterdam: John Benjamins.

Siskos, Panagiotis A., and Vasileios A. Filopoulos. 1997. "Prosarmogī tīs Ellīnikīs Chīmikīs Onomatologias stīn agglikī tīs Diethnous Enōseōs Katharas kai Efarmosmenīs Chīmeias." In *Ellīnikī Glōssa kai Orologia: Anakoinōseis 1ou Synedriou*, ed. by Vasileios A. Filopoulos, and Tota Anagnostopoulou, 389–402. Athens: ELETO.

Taavitsainen, Irma. 2001. "Language History and the Scientific Register." In *Towards a History of English as a History of Genres*, ed. by Hans-Jürgen Diller, and Manfred Görlach, 185–202. Heidelberg: Winter.

Tampakis, Kostas. 2015. "The Once and Future Language: Communication, Terminology and the Practice of Science in Nineteenth and Early Twentieth Century Greece." *History of Science* 53 (4), 438–455.

Thelen, Marcel. 2015. "The Interaction Between Terminology and Translation: Or Where Terminology and Translation Meet." *trans-kom* 8 (2): 347–381.

Toraki, Katerina. 2007. "Chrīseis tīs glōssas kai glōssikes nootropies stous mīchanikous: ī typopoiīmenī kai ī koinī neoellīnikī glōssa stous chōrus drasīs." In *Ellīnikī Glōssa kai Orologia: Anakoinōseis 6ou Synedriou*, ed. by Kostas Valeontis, 224–235. Athens: Techniko Epimelītīrio Elladas.

Toraki, Katerina. 2011. "Glōssiko zītīma kai epistīmonikī orologia: mia dierevnīsī diadromōn kai synantīseōn." In *Ellīnikī Glōssa kai Orologia: Anakoinōseis 8ou Synedriou*, ed. by Kōstas Valeontis, 369–381. Athens: ELETO.

Toraki, Katerina. 2019. "Iatrikī kai technikī orologia: omoiotītes kai diafores kai mia anaphora ston Vyrōna Samio." Presented at the 12th Conference Hellenic Language and Terminology, Athens: ELETO.

Toraki, Katerina, Stella Chadjimari, Danae Georgaki, and Stamatina Tsafou. 2008. "Development of a Greek Thesaurus of Scientific Terms." In *17th Greek Academic Libraries Conference.* Ioannina: University of Ioannina.

Tsiakmakis, Euripidis. 2017. "To morfīma -iasī sto lexilogio tīs pathologias tīs Neas Ellīnikīs." In *Ellīnikī Glōssa kai Orologia: Anakoinōseis 11ou Synedriou*, ed. by Kostas Valeontis, 41–51. Athens: ELETO.

Valeontis, Kostas. 1988. *Analysī tōn vasikōn archōn tīs technikīs orologias.* Athens: ELOT.

Valeontis, Kostas. 2004. "Typopoiīsī orologias: To paradeigma tīs Monimīs Omadas Tīlepikoinōniakīs Orologias (MOTO)." In *Ellīnikī orologia: erevna kai efarmoges*, ed. by Marianna Katsoyannou and Elenī Efthimiou. Athens: Kastaniōtī.

Valeontis, Kostas. 2005. "The 'Analogue Rule': a Useful Terminological Tool in Interlingual Transfer of Knowledge." Paper presented at the 2nd Terminology Summit. *Infoterm Newsletter* 117, 2–9.

Valeontis, Kostas, and Vasilis A. Filopoulos. 2001. "Prosfates allages gia tī dīmiourgia ellīnikōn orōn kai ī Ellīnikī Etaireia Orologias." In *Ellīnikī Glōssa kai Orologia: Anakoinōseis 3ou Synedriou*, ed. by Kostas Valeontis, 305–323. Athens: ELETO.

Valeontis, Kostas E., and Panagiotis G. Krimpas. 2014. *Nomikī glōssa, nomikī orologia: theōria kai praxī.* Athens: Nomikī Vivliothīkī.

Valmantonis, Ioannis, and Sofia Vidali (eds). 2014. *Italiano-greco greco-italiano: dizionario giuridico*. Athens: Nomiki Vivliothiki.

Vasileiadou-Zachou, Afroditi, Freideriki Dimeli-Konstantinou, Berts Stepanian, and Euthalia Finoglou-Charsouli. 2004. *Lexicon: Tetraglōsso lexiko epistīmonikōn kai technikōn orōn (agglika, gallika, germanika, ellīnika)*. Thessaloniki: University Studio Press.

Vathiotis, Konstantinos (ed). 2013. *Deutsch-griechisches griechish-deutsches Rechtswörterbuch*. Athens: Nomikī Vivliothīkī.

Wexler, P. 1969. "Towards a Structural Definition of 'internationalisms'." *Linguistics* 7 (48): 77–92.

CHAPTER 24

Terminology in Hungary

From standard Hungarian to terms and scientific names

Ágota Fóris
Károli Gáspár University of the Reformed Church in Hungary

This chapter describes historical events and figures that impacted the evolution of terminology in 20th century Hungary. There have been several periods in Hungary when terminological activities were intertwined with linguistics, and the study of specialised vocabulary and the formation of terminology in the Hungarian language were treated as a prominent professional and scientific field. One such period was during the Hungarian Language Reform in the 18th and 19th centuries, when the renewal of terminology was successfully achieved; I briefly outline the most important historical, political, social and linguistic milestones of this period. The central part of the chapter covers the history of Hungarian terminology in the 20th century and is divided into four parts: the first two decades of the 20th century (1900–1920), the period after the First World War (1920–1945), the period after the Second World War (1945–1989), and the decade after the regime change (1989–2000). The chapter ends with a discussion of trends in 21st century Hungary.

Keywords: Hungarian terminology, language reform, specialised terminology, principles of terminology, language standardisation and codification

1. A brief history of Hungarian terminology

In the literature on the history of the Hungarian language, the period from 1772 to 1920 is referred to as the Era of Modern Hungarian (Újmagyar kor). The subsequent period, beginning in 1920 and continuing to the present day, is referred to as the Era of Contemporary Hungarian (Legújabb magyar kor) (Dömötör 2015). Books on the history of the Hungarian language discuss Modern Hungarian, i.e., the period up to the 1920s, in great detail and depth. One particular period of early

https://doi.org/10.1075/tlrp.24.24for

Modern Hungarian, that of language reform, is studied more extensively, proba-bly because the codification[1] and standardisation[2] of the Hungarian language took place largely during this period. These two periods — modern and contemporary — were separated by the *Treaty of Trianon* of 1920. Following the implementation of this Treaty, Hungary lost the majority of its territory, and consequently one third of Hungarian native speakers found themselves under the influence of a different state language. As a result, the Hungarian language evolved differently among its native speakers, both within Hungary, and in neighbouring countries as a minority lan-guage. Also, Hungary went from a multilingual state to a monolingual state, while the Hungarian language became a pluricentric language (Vančo et al. 2020). Since 1920, Hungary has undergone several ideological and systemic changes, as well as radical social transformations, which all have had an impact on the Hungarian lan-guage and its terminology (Laczkó 2015).

2. Hungarian language and terminology up to the end of the 19th century

Since the settlement of the Hungarian tribes in the Carpathian Basin in CE 896, the common language spoken was Hungarian. And since the establishment of the kingdom in 1000, the official language (i.e. the language of legislation and public administration) was Latin, but the use of Hungarian was also partly pre-served; in the private sphere, Hungarian and other languages were used. The Kingdom of Hungary was a multi-lingual, multi-cultural, multi-ethnic state whose inhabitants (citizens) identified as *Hungarus*. Latin mostly remained the official language until the mid-19th century, with Hungarian recognised as the official lan-guage in some areas (e.g., in Transylvania) and at certain times; in the 19th cen-tury, German was also introduced briefly twice. The language of education also varied depending on several factors, including the level of education (primary, secondary, tertiary), the mother tongue spoken by the inhabitants of the region, and the prevalent religion (Lajtai 2004, Andrássy 2017, Szarka 2017).

It was the period of the Enlightenment and Romanticism in the 18th and 19th centuries when national consciousness, and with it nationalism, was strengthened. As part of this, the nationalities of the empire (Hungarians, Slovaks, Romanians,

---

1. *Codification* in linguistics is the process of selecting, developing and prescribing a model for standard language usage.

2. *Language standardisation* is the process by which conventional forms of a language are established and maintained, whereas *technical standardisation* is the process of developing and implementing technical standards based on the consensus of different parties.

and others) considered the importance of having a mother tongue in their journey towards nationhood (Magocsi 1993: 78, Sugar 1990: 254, Sauvageot 1971). Thus,
Hungarian became the official language in the Kingdom of Hungary (in the Hungarian part of the Austrian Empire) in the eyes of the law in 1844, replacing Latin,
and gradually it was introduced as the language of public administration, education and science. However, the 19th century national ideal attempted to combine
conflicting ideologies. On the one hand, the political concept of the nation which
consisted of many different peoples (thus it was multilingual and multicultural),
was based on territorial unity and multilingualism, i.e., all citizens of the unitary
Hungarian nation were equal members of the nation, regardless of their ethnicity.
On the other hand, the concept of the nation-state also emerged, and it considered
the Hungarian ethnic group and language primary to be a state concept. As a result
of the Austro-Hungarian Compromise of 1867 that created the Austro-Hungarian
Monarchy, a multinational state, where Hungarians, Romanians, Serbs, Slovaks,
Russians and Germans were all recognised as equal nations in Hungary, with linguistic and political equality, and equality of all was guaranteed in the constitution. From a linguistic point of view, the *Law on Nationalities* (Act XLIV of 1868)
regulated the official use of the various languages; but people were free to use the
language of their choice in private. This law declared Hungarian the state language, but at the same time legal regulations also had to be published in the main
languages used by the other nationalities, and compulsory education had to be
provided for everyone in their mother tongue (Andrássy 2017: 69). In daily practice, however, the Hungarian understanding of the nation-state, i.e. that the nation
equals the state, was constantly gaining strength, and as a result there was a trend
towards "magyarisation" (Szarka 2017). This was facilitated both by state support
for the Hungarian language and culture and the use of assimilation tools, as well
as by dynamic social and economic modernisation processes. The benefits of economic and industrial development, and the possibility for economic, political and
social advancement all demanded the integration of individuals into Hungarian
society and the ability to speak Hungarian. Hungarian was gradually adopted as
the language of education, the number of lessons taught in Hungarian increased,
and Hungarian-language schools became more widespread. Magyarisation efforts
were also strongly reflected in the use of language and terminology, and language
reformers often enforced this policy to the extreme. The aim was to replace every
foreign word with a Hungarian word, often leading to the creation of neologisms
that did not conform to the rules of Hungarian word formation, or to the creation
of a huge number of neologisms which proved to be impossible to adopt at that
rate, for example in the case of scientific nomenclatures.

   A particularly important period in the standardisation and codification of the
Hungarian language was that of the Language Reform (Nyelvújítás) in the 18th

and 19th centuries, which saw the development of the independent nomenclature and terminology of various disciplines (Tolnai 1929, Kovalovszky 1955, Fábián 1955, 1984, Pais 1955, Tolcsvai Nagy 2022). Language Reform started with a linguistic renewal, aiming at the creation of scientific terminology in Hungarian. Earlier, the language of science was Latin. The development of scientific language (primarily nomenclature and terminology) varied from discipline to discipline, and only that of the natural sciences (e.g., physics, chemistry, earth science) followed similar principles because natural sciences were closely connected (Kovalovszky 1955). Hungarian terminology in fields such as medicine, mathematics, physics, botany, and literature, emerged in the 18th and 19th centuries, and was recorded in specialised dictionaries produced with the collaboration of specialists in the field. From the beginning of the 19th century, a large number of law dictionaries and auxiliary materials were published, then the individual counties gradually switched to the use of the Hungarian language in legislation. These initiatives supported the dissemination and institutionalisation of uniform terminology (Tolnai 1929).

Following the renewal of scientific language, focus shifted to the languages of economy and industry. In the 19th century, the period of Hungarian Language Reform coincided with the development of Hungarian capitalism. On this period, Fábián claimed that the creation of Hungarian terminology in industrial and economic sectors was a conscious process of magyarisation that aimed to overthrow the privileged position of the upper classes in education (who used mostly Latin and German). Industrial development and agricultural mechanisation required both the employment of Hungarian workers and the creation of a Hungarian terminology that was easy to understand and use. According to Fábián, the creation of technical terminology and of words in the general language followed the same uniform morphological rules, but initially many different word forms coexisted. It was only in the second half of the 19th century that a greater number of specialised dictionaries and periodicals appeared, which helped create a more uniform terminology (Fábián 1955).

The aim of the language reform was to facilitate the creation of common-sense Hungarian words. New words should be of internal origin whenever possible, while respecting the grammatical and morphological rules of the Hungarian language. Calques should be avoided, and the adopted word or expression should reflect the attributes of the underlying concept so that it fits into the terminological system of related terms and concepts. This activity was referred to as *word formation* or *coining of new words*, not translation. Since most scientific concepts had names in the languages of the European nations, the main task for Hungarians was not to create, define and classify concepts, but to find Hungarian names for existing ones. Accordingly, systematising concepts and terms, developing a terminological system, and assigning meaning were less significant tasks. Conscious terminological systematisation happened only later, in the 1900s, under the influence of the fields of science (Fóris 2005, Fóris 2010a).

The need to distinguish between *terminology* and *nomenclature* arose at the time of the Language Reform. According to Kovalovszky (1955), the most significant distinguishing feature is that terms denote general concepts and names denote individual concepts. From a historical linguistic point of view, the establishment of Hungarian scientific terminology and nomenclature dates to the period of the Language Reform. This was the process of forced *magyarisation* of terms. Nevertheless, most of the terms developed in the nomenclature or terminology of chemistry at this time remained isolated and intermittently used designations. They did not become widely used (Szabadvári and Szőkefalvi-Nagy 1972, Szentgyörgyi 2014).

Several plans to establish a Hungarian scientific society, by bringing together Hungarian-speaking scholars of science and literature were made at the end of the 18th century. In 1825, the initiative was undertaken to establish the *Tudós Társaság* ('scientific society'), which was enacted into law by the Hungarian Parliament in 1827. This group began its work in 1830, and from 1845 it was officially named the Hungarian Academy of Sciences (Magyar Tudományos Akadémia). The new institution aimed to promote the Hungarian language in general, and to support the development of its scientific language. (These goals remain stated in the Academy's mission statement.) Among its first achievements were the standardisation of Hungarian spelling and the codification of grammar (word formation and syntax). The Academy published the first spelling dictionary[3] in 1832, a descriptive grammar in 1846 and an explanatory dictionary in 1862, and also edited various LSP dictionaries (Tolnai 1929).

At the end of the 19th century, the results of the Language Reform were reviewed, and two key factors played a significant role in this process: the journal *Magyar Nyelvőr*, established in 1872, and the codification activities of the Academy.

In the 18th and 19th centuries, standard Hungarian was thus established and codified, and some of the specialised languages (LSPs in Hungarian) were standardised and codified. According to Tolcsvai Nagy (2017), other important factors leading to modernisation and the shift towards capitalism were industrialisation, urbanisation, and, closely related to these, improved mobility and the development of transportation and communication networks. There was a need for a homogeneous, skilled workforce whose members could effectively communicate with each other, and so mass education was prioritised. In the field of specialised

---

3. A spelling dictionary is a special type of linguistic dictionary that can be used to check the correct spelling of words (e.g. word stems, conjugated forms, compounds, names, dates).

languages, the need to ensure clear and effective communication became particularly important.

3.   Terminology in the 20th century

3.1   The first two decades of the 20th century

After the turn of the century, efforts to actively use the Hungarian language more continued, as did the collection, organisation and revision of terminology created in the previous decades. Numerous works summarising the results of the period of the Language Reform and the decades that followed were produced, including the significant work by Kálmán Szily titled *A magyar nyelvújítás szótára* [Dictionary of the Hungarian Language Reform] (Szily 1902–1908). The dictionary of the language of crafts was also completed during this period: after forty years of persistent work, the specialised vocabulary collected under the leadership of János Frecskay was published in the *Mesterségek szótára* [Dictionary of Crafts and Trades] (Frecskay 1912). This work consists of two parts: the first contains descriptions of fifty trades (e.g. carpenter, joiner, tinker, tinsmith, blacksmith, mason) in Hungarian, and the second is a corresponding Hungarian — German and German — Hungarian dictionary whose terms directly relate to those descriptions (containing about 9,000–10,000 headwords). German terminology was initially used in industry, as craftsmen were either of German origin or had learned their trade in German-speaking areas. The translation of the terminology of the crafts is attributed to Frecskay's persistent work under the auspices of the Academy.

The first two decades of the 20th century were characterised by urbanisation, with capitalism and linguistic innovation playing major roles. The ideal of improving the language by purifying it culminated in the activities and publications of linguistic groups, who sought to combat foreign words and other foreign expressions.

3.2   The period after the First World War

The Austro-Hungarian Monarchy (see Section 2) came to an end with the First World War and subsequent peace treaties. The Dual Monarchy was dissolved and, as noted above, as a result of the Treaty of Trianon of 1920, Hungary transformed from a multicultural, multilingual country to a monolingual, monocultural nation-state. At the same time, a significant number of Hungarian-speaking people found themselves as minorities in the newly created neighbouring nation-states (e.g. Romania, Czechoslovakia). Each of the nation-states that emerged in Central Europe at this time sought to strengthen their own culture and language, and it was during this period that efforts to standardise national languages and create national terminologies were intensified (Szarka 2017).

The new territorial arrangements also included an international system for the protection of minorities, which obliged both Hungary and the other successor states to apply uniform criteria. Thus, language law remained basically unified, but the legal status of languages changed. Hungarian remained the official language in Hungary, while it became a minority language in all neighbouring countries (Andrássy 2017: 71).

According to Tolcsvai Nagy (2017), "the survival of the Hungarian language" was the main issue in this period, which was reflected in the strengthening of the official status of standard Hungarian. The role of popular language education was strengthened by books and journals that were dedicated to "preserving" the language, published by well-known authors and journalists.

Terms in various fields continued to be collected and classified in published dictionaries and glossaries. For example, one such work of this time covered the history of Hungarian mathematical language, including a glossary of mathematical terms (Keresztesy 1935). Since numerous dictionaries were published, a dictionary bibliography was also compiled, which included details on specialised dictionaries (Sági 1922). Vilmos Tolnai's summarising analysis of the period of the Language Reform was published during this period (Tolnai 1929).

By the 1920s, the basic vocabulary of sports in Hungarian was consolidated, the rules of competition and the rules of all sports in the country were published in Hungarian, and the most important technical terms were collected. Sports magazines and sports journals still used many foreign words, and the style of wording (e.g., the word choice, sentence fluency) was also foreign (Germanisms and Latinisms).[4] Some sports (football, cycling) became massively popular at this time, and thus the terminology of sport was in need of renewal. The period that followed is referred to as the Era of Sports Language Reform. It began as a movement to make the language of sports more Hungarian, partly as it appeared in sports daily newspapers such as *Nemzeti Sport* as well as a journal aiming to cultivate a more polished Hungarian language, titled *Magyarosan*. Regular competitions were organised to create new Hungarian sports terms, which were then implemented consistently and accurately by newspapers, official bodies, and individuals in the fields of education and sport until eventually their usage was widespread (Bárczi 1935, Bánhidi 1971).

---

4. For example, the use of the definite article before a personal name (*a János* — 'the John'), the use of the indefinite article in a non-essential context (*ez egy jó könyv* — 'it's a good book'), and the use of passive constructions (*be van zárva* — 'it's closed') are regarded as Germanisms. The use of Latin words in Hungarian texts (e.g. numerus, spectaculum), which seems somewhat archaic, and the use of Latin text structure are considered Latinisms.

Nevertheless, the first manifestations of Hungarian standards emerged in the latter half of the 19th century, as evidenced by the construction plans for the Fiume railway line. However, the formal and official institutionalisation of technical standardisation in Hungary did not occur until 1921, when the Hungarian Industrial Standardisation Committee (Magyar Ipari Szabványosító Bizottság) was established. From 1933 it was known as the Hungarian Standards Institute (Magyar Szabványügyi Intézet), until it was restructured in 1941 to operate under the supervision of the Minister of Industry as the Hungarian Standards Institute Association (Magyar Szabványügyi Intézet Egyesület), which continued until 1945. By this time, the Institute had issued approximately 900 Hungarian National Standards (MOSZ) (Pónyai 2010).

3.3 The post Second World War era

Under the Paris Peace Treaty of 1947, for the second time Hungary lost the territories it had regained in the 1930s and 1940s, and a large number of Hungarian speakers were again forced to live outside its borders. Hungary came under Soviet influence, and in 1948 former private companies were nationalised, and there was widespread centralisation. Large-scale industrialisation began in Hungary, which had a significant impact on the revival of Hungarian terminology work. The formerly strong ties with Western countries in the areas of science, economy, and industry were severed or weakened. However, new bonds were formed with the Soviet Union in those same areas. These changes required the translation of Russian-language books, service and user manuals, and other publications into Hungarian in addition to continual terminological work. The official language remained Hungarian, while the former influence of German, English, and other languages was drastically reduced and replaced by the need for Russian language skills and Russian-speaking specialists and translators.

Historically, the Moscow School[5] of terminology had the most direct influence on the research and development of Hungarian terminology, but the Vienna School[6] and Prague School[7] also left their impressions. Additionally, some major events left their mark on standardisation in Hungary during this period: the translation of Wüster's (1931) dissertation into Russian and its publication; the Soviet support for Wüster's international standardisation efforts in terminology; and the establishment of the ISO committee on terminology (TC37).

---

5. On Russian terminology works see Shelov et al. 2004; and refer to Chapter 10 of this book.
6. On Wüster's terminological work refer to Chapter 8, Chapter 17, and Chapter 22.
7. About the Prague School, refer to Chapter 9.

Interdisciplinary cooperation between linguistics and the branches of science, combined with the publication of new LSP dictionaries, enhanced the development of terminological research. This was the time when János Klár and Miklós Kovalovszky published their summary of technical scientific terminology, which discussed terminology in detail and combined the results of the Hungarian Language Reform and the Moscow terminology school (Klár and Kovalovszky 1955). Their monograph consisted of three chapters. The first chapter summarises the history and initial phase of terminology, with a focus on the Hungarian Language Reform. The second chapter reviews the theoretical issues of terminology and their practical implications, drawing on the principles of the Moscow school of terminology. Chapter three presents the contemporary issues of terminology and technical language use in the light of the previous two chapters. In my opinion, the second chapter of the work is the most interesting and the most relevant. The authors describe the principles of terminology, including the onomasiological approach (where the concept is the starting point of enquiry), the relationship between the concept and the term, and the importance of the terminological system. Drawing on the principles of logic and philosophy, they explain that a concept is defined by its attributes, and that the most important requirement for defining a concept is to include all the necessary and sufficient features of that concept, a process that requires abstraction (Klár and Kovalovszky 1955: 22). The concept can be named, and terms identified, only through this process. In all cases, the terms assigned to concepts are accepted based on the tacit or conscious consensus among native speakers who work in the field in question. Klár and Kovalovszky then discuss classification, i.e. the rules for establishing a terminological system. The first task is to collect and define the key concepts of the discipline (or industry). This is followed by comparing these concepts, identifying their semantic relations with other concepts and thereby also determining their place in the terminological system (Klár and Kovalovszky 1955: 31).

When developing a terminological classification or system, there are several objectives: (a) that the terminological system accurately reflects the conceptual system of the discipline, (b) that the position of the concepts in the terminological system and their designations are determined based on the features of the concept and on the overall conceptual system in which they are members, and (c) that the classification proceeds from general concepts to specific concepts. In other words, classification involves organising the concepts that have emerged through the process of cognition, establishing a corresponding system of terms, arranging the concepts from general to specific, and defining the relationship between concepts (and their designations). Aspects of term creation are analysed in great detail, and eight the principles of term creation are described, all supported by abundant examples (Klár and Kovalovszky 1955: 41–43; see Fóris 2005 for a description of the principles).

The codification of standard Hungarian (the language of educated people) and of some Hungarian terminologies had already commenced in the 16th and 17th centuries, but a conscious effort to codify and standardise the language was undertaken during the Language Reform in the 18th and 19th centuries. Grammars, spelling rules, and dictionaries were the tools of codification, while newspapers, popular science and specialised journals were the means of creating and disseminating terms. We still lack sufficient data on the impact of standardisation on different language varieties, including Hungarian terminologies (Laczkó 2015). As observed by Kovalovszky in 1955, there was no prior study tracing the history of the vocabulary of most disciplines, or of Hungarian scientific language in general (Kovalovszky 1955: 240). Although a monograph was published on Hungarian dictionary literature during the Age of Enlightenment and the Hungarian Reform Era (Gáldi 1967), and representatives of the individual disciplines — primarily within the framework of professional organisations and the Hungarian Academy of Sciences — carried out considerable terminological work, the origins and results of this work were seldom processed and documented. One of the few exceptions was the monograph on the history of chemistry, including its terminology and nomenclature, published in 1972 (Szőkefalvi-Nagy 1972). However, it was not until the 21st century that the history of terminology was thoroughly documented (such as the history of Hungarian medical language: Bősze et al. 2021; PhD dissertations on languages of economics and engineering, law, music, mathematics, sports). During this period, the field of physics saw significant research and development into laser technologies in Hungary. This historical period is discussed by Fóris (2022: 134):

> At international forums, research findings were published in English and Russian; in Hungary, laboratory work, education, dissemination and popularization, and preparation for application were (and still are) carried out in Hungarian. Public presentation of scientific results and the discussion of terminological suggestions and recommendations were provided by the relevant professional and working committees of the Hungarian Academy of Sciences (MTA) and the professional forums and journals [...] of the member associations of the MTESZ (Association of Technical and Natural Science Organizations). This enabled the development of a common approach in the scientific and application areas related to terminology in Hungarian.

Standard Hungarian was significantly further codified in the mid-20th century. In this prescriptive regulating process, the codification of Hungarian spelling rules and the publication of spelling dictionaries had and still have a very important role (Laczkó 2015), including for LSPs. While the spelling code remains applicable to both for general language and LSPs, the rules for creating scientific nomenclature were (and still are) determined by each discipline (such as chemistry, biology, and earth science). International organisations have standardised nomenclature (scientific names), resulting in a standardised terminology that was published internationally in sector standards. At the national level the Hungarian Academy of Sciences was responsible for scientific names (units of nomenclature) and the development of auxiliary materials (such as rules and dictionaries). For example, the Nomenclature Committee of its Section of Chemical Sciences, which was established in 1960 under the leadership of Tibor Erdey-Grúz, published the first nomenclature and spelling rules in the field of chemistry (Fodorné-Csányi et al. 2016). The spelling rules for Hungarian plant names were first proposed by Szaniszló Priszter, discussed by the Academy's Botanical Committee in 1982 and approved by the Spelling Committee in 1983 (Ludányi 2021).[8]

The distinction between *terminology* and *nomenclature*[9] has been a topic of discussion since at least the 19th century. One key point of differentiation is that terms are used to designate general concepts (terminology), whereas names designate objects or individual concepts (nomenclatures) (Kovalovszky 1955, Bessé et al. 1997, ISO 1087: 2019). The creation of terms is governed by general language grammar (word formation rules), while the rules for the creation of scientific names (nomenclature) are specific to the given science. In the case of disciplines with both nomenclature and terminology, such as chemistry, biological taxonomy and geography, establishing both a grammar (rules for forming scientific names) and a dictionary of scientific names is required, while in the case of disciplines that feature only terminology, the creation of dictionaries is sufficient (terms, explanation of their meaning, and equivalents). Terminology and nomenclatures were published in various types of dictionaries, glossaries and databases, as the meaning of terms (in definitions or contexts) is important in addition to questions of form. In the Hungarian language, new scientific names were created in the nomenclatures of chemistry and biology based on their own formation rules. In the case of anatomy, however, Latin terms (not nomenclatures) were largely adopted. Similarly, in the absence of grammatical rules of their own, what other disciplines and scientific fields developed tends to be *terminology*, rather than nomenclature, and indeed specialists often use the words *terminology, nomenclature,* and *taxonomy* as synonyms (Bölcskei and Fóris 2022).

---

8. For more information on Hungarian specialised spelling codes and dictionaries see Ludányi (2021).

9. Refer also to point 2 in relation to the 19th-century works. A *nomenclature* is a "terminology resource structured systematically according to pre-established naming rules. Example: International Code of Virus Classification and Nomenclature. Nomenclatures have been elaborated in various domains, such as biology, medicine, physics and chemistry." (ISO 1087: 2019)

The codification of general language and LSPs, with its high social prestige, favoured a prescriptive approach to language cultivation.[10] Linguists of the language cultivation movement wrote language guides and gave educational lectures, and there were TV and radio programs instructing the Hungarian people on correct ways of speaking and writing. The main purpose of language cultivation was to teach Hungarian grammar rules to non-linguists, including domain specialists in scientific fields, who were creating terms in LSPs. The creation of new terms requires knowledge of both the attributes of concepts and the rules of word formation. Thus it became important to produce guides for domain experts on the rules of spelling, grammar (especially syntax), and above all word formation (Klár and Kovalovszky 1955, Grétsy 1964). Linguists assisted these experts in creating and using correct words, phrases, and sentences that complied with the rules of standard Hungarian. The objectives of language cultivation did not include direct research on LSPs. Instead, its purpose was to disseminate the established rules and norms of standard Hungarian (Fóris 2010b).

Until the middle of the 20th century, technical texts were mainly produced, read and used by experts, teachers and students of the discipline, and technical texts were usually translated into other languages by those individuals. In the 1950s, due to a surge in technological advancements, and the resulting mass production of technical goods (such as household appliances, cars), the number of texts (such as instruction manuals) needing to be translated increased considerably. In this context, domain professionals could no longer continue to assume the role of translators. Technical writers and translators, for their part, had to ensure their texts could be understood by customers and users of all backgrounds (Zabóné-Varga 2015). Consequently, difficulties in the use of terminology became more frequent. In response to these challenges, LSP translation emerged as an independent field within translation studies (Klaudy 2007: 26–28). In the 1970s, translators specialising in LSPs formed groups at Hungarian universities, and with this came the teaching of LSPs. These developments provided fertile ground for the development of both a theoretical foundation and practical methodologies for terminology work.

---

10. *Language cultivation* (or *popular language education*) is the prescriptive dissemination and enforcement of the rules of the standard language, promotion of "nice" and "correct" language use, the dissemination of the current linguistic norm. It is rooted in the "ideal language" of Romanticism. This movement often combats foreign words and other foreign expressions and styles. Based on Nekvapil (2008), the objective of language cultivation is to implement minor alterations to a language, primarily affecting its orthography, lexicon, or stylistic conventions, with the aim of maintaining it in good condition ("taking care of language"). He traces the origin of language cultivation back to the Prague School of Linguistics.

In the 1950s, in response to the issues of terminological shortcomings and difficulties in translation, the Akadémiai Kiadó publishing house published a series of technical dictionaries. These were followed in the next decades by bilingual dictionaries in technical fields and natural sciences and a series of explanatory dictionaries in technical fields, titled the *Műszaki értelmező szótár* (Zabóné-Varga 2015). Another significant development in the dissemination of Hungarian terminology was the establishment, in 1955, of Műszaki Könyvkiadó, a publishing house specialising in technical fields. The related literature focused on Hungarian terminology and jargon; it was only in the late 1960s that a guide on translating technical books was published, providing guidance on Hungarian grammar, term formation and writing.

Like everything else, standardisation was placed under the direct control of the state in 1948, and by 1951, the Hungarian Standards Office (Magyar Szabványügyi Hivatal) was established. Hungarian standards (including terminological standards) were issued in Hungarian and had a binding effect. Until 1995, the Office was responsible for standardisation at the national level (Pónyai 2010).

In the Hungarian literature, the Vienna school of terminology and its Wüsterian principles were first described in István Pusztai's paper (Pusztai 1980). At the same time, research on the sociolinguistic aspects of specialised languages also began in the 1970s and 1980s. Notable is Mihály Hajdú's summary of sociolects (Hajdú 1980) and the proceedings of the presentations given at the Hungarian linguists' conference on the stratification of the Hungarian language, which contains a large number of papers on specialised languages (Kiss and Szűts 1988).

The language of sports in Hungarian and its codification were also important at this time and continued to be closely linked to the history of sport. Compared to the 1930s, which focused on the language used in newspapers, the late 1940s and onward saw a massive increase in the publication of Hungarian textbooks, rulebooks and manuals. This publication period laid the foundations for sports science and were valuable from a linguistic and sports history point of view. The most important works dealing with the history of sports language are related to both the history of sports (e.g. Bánhidi 1971), and to language cultivation in this field (e.g. Fábián 1963). In general, linguistic studies on sports language concentrated on the language used by press and sports fans, while sports manuals, lexicons, and other publications addressed the sports language used by sports professionals. During this period, specific terminology was created for officially registered sports. This terminology can be found in rulebooks, and in some cases in bilingual or multilingual dictionaries. Sporting directors played a major and decisive role in creating the rulebooks, and the new terms proved to be professionally and linguistically appropriate (Fóris and Bérces 2005).

To summarise, the 1950s to the 1990s in Hungary were characterised by the publication of technical dictionaries, binding standardisation, codification of scientific nomenclature and terminology, and consistent use of terms. The codification of both the general language and specialised languages was consolidated, and the codification of scientific nomenclature and specialised terminology, was carried out within the framework of the Academy. The prescriptive approach to codification was in line with the ideal language approach to developing Hungarian. The instruments of codification, i.e., grammars, spelling rules and dictionaries were compiled from a prescriptive viewpoint, and the standardisation of terminology followed suit. For geopolitical reasons, among the international schools and trends in the field of terminology, the principles and practice of Wüsterian terminological standardisation were partly transmitted to Hungarian professionals through Soviet mediation, and these too were largely in the form of standards, translation guidelines and specifications; in the linguistic and translation-related literature, however, there were only a few publications on this subject.

3.4   The decade after the regime change of 1989

More changes in Hungarian industry, economy and society began to occur in the 1980s, and were facilitated and accelerated by the political regime change of 1989, the technological developments of the 1990s (mainly in the field of information technology, internet, telecommunications) and Hungary's accession to the EU in 2004. Hungarian terminology experienced a huge boom following the turn of the millennium.

> Let us examine an example from economics. The transformation of the Hungarian economy began in the 1980s (with, amongst others, the introduction of a new system of taxation in harmony with the market; the formation of a dual-level banking system, that is, a central bank and commercial banks; conversion to a fixed [currency] price regime, etc). Still, only at the end of that decade were the legal and political conditions crucial to privatisation and the multi-party system created, which made a peaceful transition possible. The two most important steps in the substantial changes in the terminology of economics were the change of political system in 1989, and accession to the European Union in 2004.
>
> (Fóris 2010a: 39)

Decentralisation and privatisation replaced the centralised, state-led management of previous decades. New enterprises, publishing houses, and translation offices were established, multinational companies appeared, and the terminology of economics and trade had to be adapted to Western (mainly English, German, French) concepts. Many foreign words were adopted, mostly of international and English origin, while new Hungarian terms were also created. Bilingual and multilingual glossaries were published, primarily to assist technical translation.

Since the 1990s legislation in the former socialist countries and their successor states in the Carpathian Basin allowed for the adoption of new standards (Bölcskei 2019). The Hungarian Standards Office was transformed into an independent public organisation in 1995, and the Hungarian Standards Institution (Magyar Szabványügyi Testület) was established. Its primary task was to introduce EU standards in Hungary — and, where possible, provide for their translation into Hungarian — and also oversee certification. Active engagement in standardisation was one of the preparatory steps and conditions for Hungary's accession to the European Union in 2004. National standardisation is always carried out in Hungarian as the country's official language. However, the involvement in international and European standardisation processes means that English also plays an important role, particularly in technical fields, and, for financial reasons, some European standards have been introduced in Hungary in their English versions. In fact, more than two thirds of Hungarian standards — and with them their terminology — are only available in English.[11] The international standards on terminological processes (from ISO TC37) are not available in Hungarian, either.

It is also worthwhile to mention changes during this period in sports terminology. The significance and function of sport changed radically at the end of the 20th century. Recreational and grassroots sports (e.g. cycling, rowing), which encouraged healthy lifestyles, were overshadowed by personalised sports services (e.g. fitness, wellness). Competitive sport became a profession and a livelihood for both athletes and their team, and the language of sport transformed into a popularised specialised language. Sport also became a means of mass entertainment, a global business, which had an impact on the terminology. Between the second half of the 1980s and first half-decade of the 2000s, dozens of new sports and sports federations were registered in Hungary; nearly half of all sports practiced today were established in this period. This growth trend continues as new sports emerge on a regular basis. Some of these new sports retained their original terminology (such as Far Eastern martial arts), while others, such as rugby, adopted Hungarian terms. The terminology of new sports has been included in dictionaries, manuals and rulebooks, and studies on sports terminology have been published (Fóris and Bérces 2005, 2006).

---

11. The introduction of EU standards in Hungary represents an important step, comprising the translation of the English standards into Hungarian and the subsequent review of the Hungarian text. However, only a limited number of standards are translated in practice. This trend has persisted since the 2000s, with two-thirds of Hungarian standards currently in English. Only the title page is translated into Hungarian; a legal requirement for the document to be distributed.

During this period, the normative and codifying role of the Hungarian Academy of Sciences in the use of Hungarian scientific language, and thus in terminology, declined significantly for several reasons. On the one hand, the system of scientific qualification was restructured, and postgraduate education shifted to universities (PhD level, introduction of the Bologna system). On the other hand, the language of publication, primarily in natural and medical sciences and mathematics, shifted towards foreign languages, mainly English. Scientific publishing in Hungarian declined — a trend that continues today. Fortunately, higher education programs in Hungarian helped to preserve scientific terminology. While in many European countries English has become the main language of tertiary education (especially at Master's and PhD level), the language of higher education in Hungarian universities has remained primarily Hungarian (Fóris 2010c).

The prestige of language cultivation has declined. In addition to normative grammars and dictionaries, descriptive grammars, and more recently corpus-based grammars, dictionaries and databases have emerged. In linguistics, descriptive, data-based, empirical research has strengthened, while in terminology, the standardising and prescriptive trend gave way to the descriptive approach aimed at harmonisation in support of diversity (e.g. translation-oriented and language planning-oriented approaches) (Fóris and Bölcskei 2019).

4.   The 21st century: An outlook[12]

By the turn of the millennium, the countries in the Carpathian Basin had completely overhauled their legal systems, and as part of this process, they also created new language laws. In Hungary, the amended constitution still did not proclaim the official language of the country, but it did state that minorities were building blocks of the state, and that it would ensure the use of their mother tongue, education in their mother tongue and the use of names in their own language.[13] The new *Constitution* (called the Fundamental Law of Hungary) was adopted in 2011. It proclaimed that the official language of the country is Hungarian (Andrássy 2017: 74–75). The terminology used by Hungarians of the former historical Hungary, who later found themselves living outside of its new borders, diverged and

---

12. For further information regarding the history and trends of Hungarian terminology in the 21st century, refer to Fóris (2024).

13. "National minorities living in Hungary shall have the right to use their mother tongue, to use names in their own languages individually and collectively, to nurture their own cultures, and to receive education in their mother tongues." Article XXIX (1), THE FUNDAMENTAL LAW OF HUNGARY (as in force on 1 January 2023).

then reconnected with Hungary's terminology after the regime change and the country's accession to the European Union in 2004. The events of the 20th century had led to the diversification and separation of Hungarian terminology (since Hungarian is a pluricentric language, see Section 1), and to terminological gaps in LSPs. Fortunately, the 21st century brought effective changes in public and higher education, vocational training, scientific qualification and publication between the different Hungarian-speaking communities (Benő and Péntek 2019). However, Hungarian terminology has not yet been harmonised or unified. Today, the main recommendation for a Hungarian terminology strategy is to create a national terminology database (Fóris and Bölcskei 2019).

In the last decade, Hungarian higher education has shifted towards English-language programmes, especially at Master's and PhD levels, partially due to the government sponsored Stipendium Hungaricum scholarship programme for international students, which since 2013 aims to support the internationalisation of Hungarian higher education.

Since the first half of the 20th century, the coordination and standardisation of international nomenclature, including symbols, units and scientific names, have been the responsibility of international professional organisations.

Whereas previously the different Sections of the Hungarian Academy of Sciences were responsible for the creation of Hungarian nomenclature (rules and dictionaries alike, see Section 3.3), currently an Intersectional Committee (the Hungarian Intersectional Standing Committee on the Hungarian Language) is responsible for adapting nomenclature rules, regulating spelling in LSPs and producing rules and language manuals. The work of this Committee is focused on spelling issues, and not on terminological work in the modern sense, which means that it is not responsible for creating terminological databases. The key reference works of the Hungarian spelling system are the spelling rules and spelling dictionaries of LSPs. Spelling regulation in LSPs is a complex process that can be achieved through the cooperation of linguists and domain specialists.[14]

Another notable example is medical, and particularly anatomical, terminology. Latin terms are used for anatomical structures (e.g., Latin and Hungarian: *ramus interventricularis anterior, ramus circumflexus;* English: *anterior interventricular branch, circumflex branch*), whereas English terms are increasingly used for clinical concepts (e.g., *left anterior descendent coronary artery, LAD*). In particular, English terms are common in the context of newly discovered diseases and therapeutic procedures (e.g., *bypass, AIDS, COVID*), as in these cases there is no established Latin terminology (Varga 2014, Bölcskei and Fóris 2022).

---

14. See Ludányi 2021 for an overview of the spelling regulation and spelling dictionaries of Hungarian LSPs.

In the Hungarian literature on terminology, the 2000s saw the rediscovery of Wüster's principles, with an increasing number of publications discussing the terminological schools of the 1930s. Additionally, German terminological principles were introduced into Hungarian terminological literature, particularly through standardisation activities facilitated by Christian Galinski's active networking efforts.[15] At the same time, there has been increased interest in other approaches to terminology, particularly the communicative theory of terminology, following the work of the Catalan linguist Maria Teresa Cabré (1999),[16] and the sociocognitive approach advocated by Rita Temmerman (2000) (see for example translation-oriented terminology in Fóris 2022; or conceptual metaphors and metonymies in LSPs by Sólyom 2020, 2021).

Terminology work in 21st century Hungary has also been closely intertwined with the field of translation (Fóris 2022). Academic research on terminology, especially in terminology theory and applications, and training was strengthened. Many publications and PhD dissertations were produced in these areas. Terminology as a discipline has been introduced into higher education (BA, MA and PhD levels) and a Master's in Terminology was established at the Károli Gáspár University (2011–2018); further training in terminology has been launched. The demand for terminology work has increased, resulting in the creation of translation-oriented termbases. Examples include the Hungarian part of IATE,[17] the creation of Termin (under the Ministry of Justice) and the creation of terminology databases in companies. Unfortunately, however, neither a national terminology portal nor a national terminology database have yet been launched (Fóris and B. Papp 2020). Terminology organisations and research groups have been established, some of which are members of international terminology organisations. These include the Council of Hungarian Terminology (MaTT) in 2005; TERMDOK and TERMIK in 2006; the Terminology Section of MANYE in 2018, and the Hungarian Language in Sciences Presidential Committee of the Hungarian Academy of Sciences in 2017. Most recently, a Terminology Research Group was established in 2021 within the Institute for Lexicology of the Hungarian Research Centre for Linguistics (see Fóris 2022: 115–119).

---

15. For standardisation refer to Chapter 17 and for the terminology works in Germany refer to Chapter 22.

16. About the terminology in Spain and the Communicative Theory of terminology, refer to Chapter 13.

17. For a detailed account of the history of IATE, refer to Chapter 20.

5.   Conclusion

The codification and standardisation of Hungarian terminology and nomenclature began during the Language Reform in the 18th and 19th centuries. In the 20th century, Hungarian terminological work — which was primarily influenced by Russian terminology and Wüsterian principles — was linked to and aligned with international normative standardisation efforts. During this period, the most important tasks were terminology standardisation and the publication of LSP dictionaries.

In the 21st century, the publication of LSP dictionaries has so far been only moderately complemented by the compilation of terminological databases: although terminology databases comprising Hungarian terms are beginning to emerge, few are publicly available. There is a pressing need for a publicly accessible, national terminology database.

Terminology as a discipline has been introduced in higher education in the humanities and in translation courses.

Current trends now favour descriptive, communication-oriented approaches in terminology, especially those that emphasise sociological and translation-oriented needs. Studies focussed on cognitive processes, such as the role of metaphor in LSPs, are also increasing in number.

Funding

This research was supported by the project titled Studies of Specialized Languages: The theory and applications of terminology by the Faculty of Humanities and Social Sciences at Károli Gáspár University of the Reformed Church in Hungary.

Acknowledgements

I would like to thank the reviewers and editors of this book for their thoughtful questions and valuable suggestions.

References

Andrássy, György. 2017. "A magyar nyelv és a magyar nyelvközösség jogi helyzete." In *A magyar nyelv jelene és jövője*, ed. by Gábor Tolcsvai Nagy, 64–90. Budapest: Gondolat.
Bánhidi, Zoltán. 1971. *A magyar sportnyelv története és jelene. Sportnyelvtörténeti szótárral.* Budapest: Akadémiai Kiadó.

Bárczi, Géza. 1935. "Sportnyelvújítás." *Magyarosan* IV (7–8): 157–160.

Benő, Attila, and János Péntek. 2019. "A terminológiastratégia szintjei és feltételei Erdélyben." In *Terminológiastratégiai kihívások a magyar nyelvterületen*, ed. by Ágota Fóris, and Andrea Bölcskei, 59–72. Budapest: L'Harmattan — OFFI Zrt.

Bölcskei, Andrea. 2019. "A szabványosítás online forrásai a Kárpát-medencében." In *A szabványosítás fordítási és terminológiai vonatkozásai*, ed. by Ágota Fóris, and Andrea Bölcskei, 137–148. Budapest: KRE — L'Harmattan.

Bölcskei, Andrea, and Ágota Fóris. 2022. "A névtudomány, a nevezéktan és a terminológia viszonya, érintkezési pontjai." *Névtani Értesítő* (44): 59–78.

Bősze, Péter, Katalin Kapronczai, and Borbála Keszler (eds). 2021. *A magyar orvosi nyelv története*. Budapest: Medicina Kiadó.

Cabré, Maria T. 1999. *Terminology. Theory, Methods and Applications*. Amsterdam: John Benjamins.

de Bessé, Bruno, Blaise Nkwenti-Azeh, and Juan C. Sager. 1997. "Glossary of Terms Used in Terminology." *Terminology* 4 (1): 117–156.

Dömötör, Adrienne. 2015. "A nyelvújítás." In *A magyar nyelv*, ed. by Ferenc Kiefer. Budapest: Akadémiai Kiadó.

Fábián, Pál. 1955. "A gazdasági élet nyelve." In *Nyelvünk a reformkorban*, ed. by Dezső Pais. Budapest: Akadémiai Kiadó.

Fábián, Pál. 1963. *Sportsajtónk nyelvéről. Tanulmányok a magyar nyelv életrajza köréből*. Budapest: Nyelvtudományi Közlemények 40.

Fábián, Pál. 1984. *Nyelvművelésünk évszázadai*. Budapest: Gondolat.

Fodorné-Csányi, Piroska, György Horányi, Tamás Kiss, and László Simándi. 2016. *Szervetlen kémiai nevezéktan*. Budapest: Akadémiai Kiadó.

Fóris, Ágota, and Edit Bérces. 2005. "Sport, gazdaság, terminológia." *Tudásmenedzsment* 2: 117–127.

Fóris, Ágota. 2005. *Hat terminológia lecke*. Pécs: Lexikográfia.

Fóris, Ágota, and Edit Bérces. 2006. "A wellness terminológiája." *Magyar Nyelvőr* 130 (4): 399–413.

Fóris, Ágota. 2010a. "The Situation and Problems of Hungarian Terminology." In *Terminology in Everyday Life*, ed. by Marcel Thelen, and Frieda Steurs, 35–46. Amsterdam: John Benjamins.

Fóris, Ágota. 2010b. "A szaknyelvkutatás modelljei és módszerei: szociolingvisztikai megközelítés." *Magyar Nyelv* 106 (4): 424–438.

Fóris, Ágota. 2010c. "Hungarian, as the Language of Education in the Universities of the Carphatian Basin." In *Nacionalni jeziki v visokem šolstvu. National Languages in Higher Education*, ed. by Marjeta Humar, and Mojca Žagar Karer, 71–78. Ljubljana: ZRC Publishing, Scientific Research Centre SASA.

Fóris, Ágota, and Andrea Bölcskei. 2019. "Ajánlások a magyar terminológiastratégiához." In *Terminológiastratégiai kihívások a magyar nyelvterületen*, ed. by Ágota Fóris, and Andrea Bölcskei, 140–164. Budapest: L'Harmattan — OFFI Zrt.

Fóris, Ágota, and Eszter B. Papp. 2020. "A Preliminary Study for the Information Structure of the Terminology Entry in the Hungarian (national) Terminology Database." In *Svijet od riječi. Terminološki i leksikografski ogledi*, ed. by Ivana Brač, and Ana Ostroški Anić, 325–342. Zagreb: Institut za hrvatski jezik i jezikoslovlje.

Fóris, Ágota. 2022. *Translation and Terminology. Theory and Practice in Hungary*. Budapest — Paris: Károli Gáspár Református Egyetem — L'Harmattan.

Fóris, Ágota. 2024. "The History and Recent Trends of Terminology in Hungary in the 21st Century." *Terminologija* 31: 53–74.

Frecskay, János. 1912. *Mesterségek szótára*. Budapest: Hornyánszky Viktor.

Gáldi, László. 1967. *A magyar szótárirodalom a felvilágosodás korában és a reformkorban*. Budapest: Akadémiai Kiadó.

Grétsy, László. 1964. *Szaknyelvi kalauz*. Budapest: Közgazdasági és Jogi Könyvkiadó.

Hajdú, Mihály. 1980. *A csoportnyelvekről*. Budapest: ELTE-MTA.

ISO 1087: 2019. *Terminology Work and Terminology Science — Vocabulary*. Geneva: International Organization for Standardization.

Keresztesy, Mária. 1935. *A magyar matematikai műnyelv története*. Debrecen: Harmathy Nyomdavállalat.

Kiss, Jenő, and László Szűts (eds). 1988. *A magyar nyelv rétegződése*. 1–2. Budapest: Akadémiai Kiadó.

Klár, János, and Miklós Kovalovszky. 1955. *Műszaki tudományos terminológiánk alakulása és fejlesztésének főbb kérdései*. Budapest: MTESZ.

Klaudy, Kinga. 2007. *Languages in Translation*. Budapest: Sholastica.

Kovalovszky, Miklós. 1955. "Tudományos nyelvünk alakulása." In *Nyelvünk a reformkorban*, ed. by Dezső Pais, 227–312. Budapest: Akadémiai Kiadó.

Laczkó, Krisztina. 2015. "Az újmagyar és az újabb magyar kor." In *A magyar nyelv*, ed. by Ferenc Kiefer. Budapest: Akadémiai Kiadó.

Lajtai, L. László. 2004. *Nemzetkép az iskolai történelemoktatásban 1777–1848*. Pécs — Budapest: Iskolakultúra — Országos Széchenyi Könyvtár — Országos Pedagógiai Könytár és Múzeum.

Ludányi, Zsófia. 2021. "A szaknyelvek helyesírásának szabályozásáról. Elmélet, gyakorlat, dilemmák." In *Tartalomfejlesztés és dokumentáció. Nyelvészeti kutatások*, ed. by Ágota Fóris, and Andrea Bölcskei, 147–174. Budapest: KRE — L'Harmattan.

Magocsi, Paul Robert. 1993. *Historical Atlas of East Central Europe*. Seattle and London: University of Washington Press.

Nekvapil, Jiří. 2008. "Language Cultivation in Developed Context." In *The Handbook of Educational Linguistics*, ed. by Bernard Spolsky, and Francis M. Hult. Malden (MA): Wiley-Blackwell.

Pónyai, György. 2010. "Szabványosítás és terminológia." *Magyar Terminológia* 3 (1): 3–7.

Pais, Dezső (ed). 1955. *Nyelvünk a reformkorban*. Budapest: Akadémiai Kiadó.

Pusztai, István. 1980. "A bécsi terminológiai iskola elmélete és módszertana." *Magyar Nyelvőr* CIV (1): 3–16.

Sági, István. 1922. *A magyar szótárak és nyelvtanok könyvészete*. Budapest: Magyar Nyelvtudományi Társaság.

Sauvageot, Aurélien. 1971. *L'Édification de la langue hongroise*. Paris: Klincksieck.

Shelov, S. D., V. M. Leichik, Heribert Picht, and Christian Galinski (eds). 2004. *Russian Terminology Science (1992–2002)*. IITF-Infoterm-Series 12. Vienna: Nomos Verlagsgesellschaft.

Sólyom, Réka. 2020. *Szaknyelvi szemantika. Funkcionális kognitív elemzések.* Budapest: KRE —
L'Harmattan.

Sólyom, Réka. 2021. "Conceptual Metaphors and Metonymies in a Technical Text on Quality
Management Systems." In *Linguistic Research in the Fields of Content Development and
Documentation*, ed. by Ágota Fóris, and Andrea Bölcskei, 353–373. Budapest/Paris: KRE
— L'Harmattan.

Sugar, Peter (ed). 1990. *A History of Hungary.* Indianapolis: Indiana University Press.

Szabadvári, Ferenc, and Zoltán Szőkefalvi-Nagy (eds). 1972. *A kémia története
Magyarországon.* Budapest: Akadémiai Kiadó.

Szarka, László (ed). 2017. *A modern szlovák nacionalizmus évszázada 1780–1918. Párhuzamos
nemzetépítés a multietnikus Magyar Királyságban.* Budapest: Akadémiai Kiadó.

Szentgyörgyi, Rudolf. 2014. "Terminológia és (nyelv)politika. A magyar kémiai nómenklatúra
születése, tündöklése és bukása." In *Tudomány, technolektus, terminológia. A tudományok,
szakmák nyelve*, ed. by Ágnes Veszelszki, and Klára Lengyel, 291–298. Budapest: Éghajlat
Könyvkiadó.

Szőkefalvi-Nagy, Zoltán. 1972. "A magyar kémiai szaknyelv kialakulása." In *A kémia története
Magyarországon*, ed. by Ferenc Szabadváry, and Zoltán Szőkefalvi-Nagy. Budapest:
Akadémiai Kiadó.

Temmerman, Rita. 2000. *Towards New Ways of Terminology Description. The Sociocognitive
Approach.* Amsterdam: John Benjamins.

Tolcsvai Nagy, Gábor. 2022. *Alkotás és befogadás a magyar nyelv 18. század utáni történetében.*
Budapest: Akadémiai Kiadó.

Tolcsvai Nagy, Gábor. 2017. "A magyar standard helyzete." In *A magyar nyelv jelene és jövője*,
ed. by Gábor Tolcsvai Nagy, 222–238. Budapest: Gondolat.

Tolnai, Vilmos. 1929. *A nyelvújítás.* Budapest: Magyar Tudományos Akadémia.

Vančo, Ildikó, Rudolf Muhr, István Kozmács, and Máté Huber (eds). 2020. *Hungarian as a
Pluricentric Language in Language and Literature.* Frankfurt am Main: Peter Lang D.

Varga, Éva Katalin. 2014. "Anatómiai nevek régen és ma. Latin helyett angol?" *Modern
Nyelvoktatás* 20 (1–2): 35–42.

Wüster, Eugen. 1931. *Internationale Sprachnormung in der Technik, besonders in der
Elektrotechnik.* Berlin: Verein Deutscher Ingenieure.

Zabóné-Varga, Irén. 2015. *Műszaki szövegek fordításának terminológiai problémái német —
magyar nyelvpárban járműipari szövegek alapján.* PhD thesis. Budapest: ELTE BTK.

CHAPTER 25

Terminology in Indonesia
Appropriating or conveying modernity

Jérôme Samuel
Institut National des Langues et Civilisations Orientales

This chapter examines terminology in standard Indonesian — a variant of Malay which is Indonesia's national language. After an introduction on the early developments of terminology in the Malay-speaking world before and during the colonial era, it delves into the terminological policies, including cooperation between Indonesia and Malaysia, whose national languages are closely related. It examines the principles and methods adopted by the Indonesian language agencies, and then presents a selection of terms and their formation processes, which reveal an essentially translational terminology. It then attempts to evaluate the outcomes in implementing official terminologies, and in reducing terminology dispersion. The last part focuses on the terminological resources produced in Indonesia.

Keywords: Indonesia, Indonesian, Malay, language policy, neology, dictionaries

1.   Introduction

To talk about the history of terminology in Indonesia is a misleading strategy, especially if trying to isolate the argument solely to Indonesian. On the one hand, terminological concerns, with their denominational, normative and dictionary implications appeared in Indonesia long before a language — Malay — was called "Indonesian" at the end of the 1920s. On the other hand, it is difficult to extract Indonesian from the dialectal complex of which it is one of two standardised national languages (the other being Malay, or Malaysian), or from the larger multilingual ensemble of languages of the region (Javanese, Sundanese, Balinese, Buginese, etc.) having both ancient written translations and terminologies in different specialised domains.

The first aspect that will be discussed in this chapter can lead to questioning the continuities and ruptures of Malay, and then Indonesian terminology, in

https://doi.org/10.1075/tlrp.24.25sam
© 2025 John Benjamins Publishing Company

terms of practices, terminological policies, and principles of neology, during and after the colonial period. The second directly questions the relationship between Indonesian in Indonesia and Malay in Malaysia: can they be reconciled, and to what extent? The third investigates the influence of multilingualism, and especially of Javanese as one of the languages involved, on the whole terminological endeavour in Indonesia.

These three aspects of the question of terminology in Indonesia run through the whole chapter, where we shall, in turn, explore the terminology developments in Malay before the "birth" of Indonesian. We also examine the frameworks, policies and achievements of various language agencies in developing terminology from the mid-20th century to the beginning of the 21st century, before comparing this terminology with terminology that arose spontaneously, in terms of implantation and regulation. We shall conclude with a brief description of the terminological resources developed over the considered period.

2.   The first terminological developments in the Malay world

2.1   Precolonial terminology

Texts in languages for specific purposes (administration, religion, law) were recorded in ancient and now-extinct forms of Malay (Old-Malay) and Javanese (Old-Javanese), starting respectively from the end of the 7th and 8th centuries. Languages for specific purposes are also attested for more recent periods and linguistic forms (Classical Malay, Modern Javanese) which appeared after the 14th century in a larger scope of domains. While in the domain of religion, and to a lesser extent law, there were considerable numbers of loanwords (from Sanskrit and Arabic), in the other domains recorded in written sources in different local languages, most terms were of vernacular origin — this includes several "traditional" domains, which can be highly technical. The production of specialised manuscripts, with their terminologies (sometimes simply nomenclatures), presented in forms characteristic of local cultures, continued during the colonial period.[1]

Although these terminological domains did not undergo systematic developments, it must be noted that as of the 8th century, some specialised dictionary forms did exist, for Javanese and later Balinese, called *kṛtabhāṣā* (< skt. *saṃskṛtabhāṣā*, 'Sanskrit language'), from the Indian *kośa* tradition. These *kṛtabhāṣā*, written on *Borassus flabellifer* palm leaves, were bilingual lists, some with annotations

---

1. For the Javanese and Balinese manuscripts, see Pigeaud vol. I, 1967: "IV. Sciences, Arts, Humanities, Law; Folklore, Customs and Miscellanea". For Malay, see Piah 2002: 478–479.

allowing for the comprehension of Sanskrit or Old-Javanese texts (Sanskrit > Old-Javanese, Old-Javanese > Modern Javanese or Balinese) either grouped themati-cally or, later, simply following the text they glossed. While most *kṛtabhāṣā* are ancient, the production of this type of glossary continued sporadically until the 18th century in Java and the early 20th century in Bali (Pigeaud 1967: 294–295; Schoterman 1981; Behrend 1999).

2.2   Terminology as a colonial enterprise

The situation radically changed during the colonial period (1818–1942),[2] with the establishment of administrative, military, educational, and medical structures. For the colonial power, this necessitated the regulated use of common languages for communication — Dutch and Malay — , and the production of texts and language resources for those domains where Malay was the vehicular language.

In administration, it was normative texts (treaties, regulations, procedures), starting with the *Inlandschreglement* (Native Regulations, 1848), which were translated and regularly updated in Malay. The introduction of primary school teaching to local populations, in the mid-19th century, led to the publishing of textbooks, mostly in Malay. Although these texts and the terms they use are not very specialised, it is clear that there was a concern at the time about how to deal with new concepts and neology.

Starting in the 1900s, more attention was given to orthographical, lexical and grammatical standards (van Ophuysen 1901, 1910), contrasting with the dialectal fragmentation of previous periods. In the following decades, the number of Malay publications addressing technical topics grew, whether to respond to the needs of technical secondary education or the demands of a larger public and the increas-ingly specialised vernacular press. The state-owned publisher Balai Poestaka ('Bureau of Literature'), created in 1907, produced many technical works, mostly translated from Dutch by young Indonesian scholars (Samuel 2005: 130–159; Samuel 2009b).

However, the use of Malay for communicating in different subject fields ran into the same difficulties with the terminology of higher learning as that experienced by the Native Doctors' School, created in Batavia in 1864, which in 1875 changed its language of instruction from Malay to Dutch, a policy that continued until 1942. At the time of Indonesian independence (1945), the entire elite class — intellectual,

---

2. European presence, first Portuguese and then Dutch, dates back to the beginning of the 16th and 17th centuries, but it was very localised, imperialist and mercantile without being colonial-ist. It did not have any effect on terminologies until the 19th century. The invasion of the Dutch Indies by the Japanese army in March 1942 ended this period.

technical, administrative and political, with the exception of religious — were Dutch-speaking.

Lastly, the production of terminological resources (dictionaries, specialised bilingual lists, nomenclatures) was not neglected in domains such as marine, administration, health, and especially natural sciences. Also remarkable is the appearance of "modernising dictionaries" (Zgusta 1990), entirely compiled by Indonesian authors. These works, conceived in the 1920s and 1930s for a Malay-speaking readership with a knowledge of Dutch, covered the essential domains of political and social life, offering the conceptual and lexical keys to a purely exogenous colonial modernity; they are therefore loanword dictionaries. Their production continued throughout the 20th century, but their vocation changed: while the earlier versions were destined for a learned readership, the most recent, produced at the end of the 20th century, addressed an audience of pupils and a broader public.

3. Structures and principles of Indonesian institutional terminology

The first outlines of an institutional terminology — i.e. terminology developed by government language agencies — projected into a yet-to-be independent Indonesia were drawn just before the end of the colonial period, during the First Indonesian Language Congress (June 1938; Samuel 2005: 179–194), with the stated aim of creating a language agency. Terminology was not neglected on this occasion, with a paper entitled "Adapting foreign words [read: terms] and ideas to Indonesian" (ibid 187, author's translation).

The author Amir Sjarifuddin, who was also an Indonesian nationalist, raised the issue of modernising the Indonesian scientific lexicon, following the example of Western languages. He argued in favour of enrichment through loanwords, drawing from the stock of the international scientific lexicon based on Greco-Latin roots: it was a matter of providing Indonesian with a certain terminological transparency and of liberating it from Dutch "tutelage." However, he recognised the need to adapt the phonetic form of the loanwords to the characteristics of the Indonesian language and to limit foreign influence to the lexicon only (Samuel 2005: 187–188).

These were good intentions but heralded the emergence of Indonesian institutional terminology for the decades to come, in particular its translational orientation.

3.1   Indonesian national level

Starting in 1942, institutional terminological activities were part of the larger context of the spread of Indonesian, the success of which was immediately visible. A minority language which had in the past been vehicular, Indonesian was adopted as the language of modernity and of the newly independent state. The advances in literacy, all through the second half of the century, and the development of mass media, sealed the unanimously recognised success.

3.1.1   *The institutional framework*

The first institutional structure for terminology emerged during the Japanese occupation and the first works were published during the War of Independence (Komisi Bahasa Indonesia 1946 and 1947). Shortly thereafter, a Terminological Commission was formed (Komisi Istilah, KI, 1950–1966), initially within the University of Indonesia (Jakarta) and later under the authority of the Prime Minister.

The KI had an extensive hierarchical structure, bringing together specialists of different domains from the country's best universities, whose sole objective was to create as many terms as possible, starting from a common linguistic source familiar to the intellectuals of the time: Dutch. From 1951 to 1964, between 130,000 (our estimate as in Samuel 2005) and 320,000 terms (Indonesian language agencies' estimate) were created and published in bilingual terminological lists in a supplement to the University of Indonesia's journal, *Medan Bahasa* (Samuel 2005: 256). The ambition to equip Indonesian with an exhaustive terminology was based on the belief that a command of the lexicon would pave the way to mastering the sciences and techniques. This turned out to be an illusion as those who had access to neologisms were also fluent in Dutch.

After a long transition period caused by the political situation (1966–1975), culminating in the dramatic end of Soekarno's rule and violent imposition of a military regime under General Suharto, institutional terminological activities gained new impetus based on renewed methodological-conceptual bases and with a renewed structure and staff, partly within the framework of Indonesian-Malaysian linguistic cooperation. However, the aim remained the terminological enrichment of the national language, without theoretical considerations.

Institutional terminological activities were undertaken within a new language agency (National Centre for Language Development and Cultivation, Pusat Pembinaan dan Pengembangan Bahasa, now Pusat Bahasa, Language Centre), which marked the beginning of terminological planning (Moeliono 1985). In 1982, in cooperation with the Malaysian language agency, the Indonesian agency launched an impressive project to create key dictionaries in physics, chemistry, mathematics and biology, which continued for 15 years (Samuel 2005: 397 sqq).

3.1.2 *Terminological procedures*

The issue of word formation, addressed first in 1938, reappeared several times in normative texts aiming at regulating the influx of new terms (Pandji 1942, Kementrian 1950, Pusat 2007). The most complete among these texts was, and still remains, the *Pedoman Umum Pembentukan Istilah,* PUPI [General guidelines for the formation of terms], a concise guidebook issued in 1975 by the Indonesian language agency and aimed at the general public. It briefly defines key concepts in lexicography and terminology in a Wüsterian way (see Chapter 8), indicates the preferred sources of new terms (first Indonesian, then local languages, followed by English, and lastly other foreign languages), explains morphosyntactic processes for Indonesian, and addresses issues of semantics, orthography and transliteration, focusing on the rules for the integration of loanwords. Indeed, the PUPI does not reject loanwords at all, but did reject unintegrated borrowings.

The importance given to the issue of loanwords in this guidebook should be highlighted. Through its recommendations, the lexical stock of Indonesian is prioritised for the formation of new words, followed by that of regional languages of Indonesia, while the use of borrowed terms from foreign languages is considered a last resort; foreign languages are ranked according to political, cultural and religious imperatives and choices. There is never any mention of Dutch — throughout the 20th century, the lists and dictionaries produced by the language agencies and by private editors designated all non-Indonesian source terms, whatever language they come from, as "foreign" (Indon. *asing*), according to the practice established during the Japanese occupation. These priorities may seem to create barriers, but they were generally applied with flexibility, rather than purism.

3.2 Indonesian-Malaysian terminological cooperation

Indonesian and Malaysian are the standard forms of two variants of the same language, Malay, but social, demographic, and linguistic contexts, and the national linguistic narratives, differ completely (Samuel 2005:385 seq.). Whereas Indonesian, in a minority as a mother tongue, is largely accepted in a highly multi-ethnic and multilingual country, in Malaysia, Malay or Malaysian is foremost an identity marker, the language of the majority and political power-holding Malay community, as distinguished from the Chinese and Indian communities formed through immigration. The name of the national language, called Malay or Malaysian[3] depending on the period, highlights the linguistic tension between community

---

3. The terms "Malay/Malaysian" in Malaysia, and "Malay" in Singapore and Brunei Darussalam, refer to the same standard language, distinct from that in Indonesia. In Indonesia, "Malay" refers to different, non-standardised dialectal variants.

(Malay) and nation (Malaysian), and English serves as the inter-communitarian language of communication in urban and educated spheres (Gill 2014, chap. 2). Moreover, in Malaysia, English is the language of the old colonial power, and that of integration into the contemporary world, following the Singaporean example. On the institutional level, the first language agency (Balai Pustaka, 1956) was created before independence in 1957, and in 1959 it became the Dewan Bahasa dan Pustaka (Institute of Language and Literature, DBP), which continues to operate to this day.

Linguistic cooperation between the two countries started at the end of the 1960s, resulting in the adoption in 1972 of a common orthographic standard. That same year Indonesia and Malaysia created a joint structure, which Brunei joined in 1984, the Majelis Bahasa Brunei-Indonesia-Malaysia (MABBIM, Language Council of Brunei Darussalam, Indonesia and Malaysia).

The main axis of MABBIM's works concerns the harmonisation of languages in the terminological domain. It became a planned enterprise in 1982, conceived as a complementary part to Indonesian and Malaysian institutional terminology activities. This harmonisation plan was based, in terms of neology, on a common methodological tool (PUPI) and on the strategy of translating individual terms from English into the national standards. This seemed perfectly feasible, as it was a matter of exploring the new project on key dictionaries mentioned above. Indonesian-Malaysian terminological harmonisation prospered until the end of the 1990s, before petering out.

Nonetheless, between 1976 and 1995 the MABBIM produced around 160,000 terms based on English source word lists, both loan translations and borrowings, with the Indonesian and Malaysian versions proposed by both parties being then discussed in common to facilitate "terminological harmonisation" (Indon., Mal. *penyelarasan istilah*).

The terminology of electromagnetism, for which the language agencies published several dictionaries (Malaysian: Ismail 1990; Indonesian: Prawirosumartono et al. 1993, Wilardjo 1993, Yohannes et al. 1996) is a telling example of the very mitigated success of the harmonisation process. It shows that the plans carried out by the MABBIM were based on political considerations rather than concrete needs. These dictionaries bring together 712 concepts named by as many terms in each of the two languages, of which 34.3% are identical, 55.0% are wholly or partly different, and 10.7% ambiguous.

3.2.1 *Realities and effects of the harmonisation*

It must be highlighted that the neological approach of the two countries differs substantially. With respect to the use of affixes, for example, Malaysian terminologists opted for more conservative neologisms than their Indonesian counterparts. They notably refused Dutch-derived nominal suffixes, *-itas* (<*-iteit*), *-isasi*

(<-*isatie*) and -*asi* (<-*atie*), completely assimilated and productive in Indonesian since the 1950s, and rejected it in favour of Malay constructions.

Similarly, Indonesians prefer to adopt loanwords (internal or external) rather than giving new senses to words from the common lexicon, in order to preserve monosemy as much as possible: Indon. *efek* (< Ang. *effect*) vs Mal. *kesan*, 'effect', Indon. *ajek* (< Jav. *ajeg*) vs Mal. *mantap*, 'constant'. Thus, the DBP's institutional neology contains fewer loanwords (contrary to common usage in Malaysia) and is morphologically less innovative.

Concerning the effects of harmonisation, they can be assessed by considering the mutual intelligibility of the two standard forms among a particular population, type of text and register, i.e. techno-scientific literature and its users.

The degree of mutual intelligibility between Indonesian and Malaysian has not been clearly determined, other than the empirical observation that the essential part of communication is understood, which is evidently not enough when it comes to languages for specific purposes. Despite the lack of in-depth studies,[4] some recent unpublished preliminary works on terminology highlight that the main obstacles to mutual intelligibility between the two languages are related to the following factors:

1. the lexicon originating from regional languages and dialects
2. the homonyms and polysemic forms whose activated meanings are not the same in the two languages: base *imbas* > Indon. **imbasan** *magnetik* / 'magnetic **induction**' and Mal. *frekuensi* **imbas** / '**scanning** frequency'
3. certain morpho-semantic constructions (complex affixation)
4. other morphological constructions or multiword terms, where the status of one of the components can lead to confusion, such as *nyah*, understood as a component with privative meaning in Malaysian (**penyahmodulasian** / '<u>de</u>modulation') and as a verbal interjection in Indonesian ('go away!').

Other aspects do not present obstacles to mutual intelligibility of terms among learned scientific speakers, such as the lexical variations in non-specialised standard Malay (for example Mal. *rintang* vs Indon. *hambat*, 'to obstruct'), or the variations linked with loanwords (English, Arabic, Sanskrit), as the source term is generally known, despite some differences in levels of integration. Similarly, the different choices of common affixes, such as Mal. *kapasitor laluan sampingan* vs Indon. *kapasitor <u>lalu</u> sampingan*, 'by-<u>pass</u> capacitor', do not impede mutual intelligibility of terms in the two languages.

All in all, approximately two-thirds of the 712 terms subject to the harmonisation process examined here are immediately intelligible or require little effort

---

4. See Omar 2002.

to be understood by both linguistic communities, which is probably sufficient for specialists to read a text written in a variant of Malay that is different from their own. Nonetheless, it appears that one still needs to resort to the use of English, to ensure complete and unambiguous understanding.

3.2.2   *What aims?*

These only partially successful attempts at harmonisation were further compromised by the institutions involved working independently of each other especially in the form results were presented, since the essential question of the definition of concepts was neglected, so that harmonising forms did not guarantee harmonising concepts. Formal convergence does not (necessarily) imply conceptual convergence, unlike translational terminology.

However, the reasons for overlooking definitions can be understood: harmonising definitions would have imposed the use of common definitional terms and formulas, in order to achieve the harmonisation of the terms of the two languages. This was unthinkable for the Malaysian language authorities (DBP), which consider themselves guardians of Malayness through a specifically national form of Malay (Malaysian), but regarded Indonesian as foreign and less worthy of esteem: as Blommaert and Verschueren explain, "language creates identity and discontinuity. It unifies and it divides." (1998: 202). Also, since the 1990s, the growing anglicisation of higher scientific and technical education in Malaysia has impeded efforts towards the creation of Malay terms, conducted in Malaysia alone or together with Indonesia. The aim of harmonisation is thus called into question, and note that it has never been clearly defined. The absence of joint Indonesian-Malaysian publications leads us to believe it was less a matter of favouring mutual terminological intelligibility than of unifying the terminologies based on a rather abstract goal, following the success of the 1972 common orthographic reform, but essentially bureaucratic and distant from real terminological needs.

3.3   The evolution of neological procedures

Looking back on the neological procedures in place over the last 150 years, it can be observed that over time terminologists and translators have not employed the same solutions to resolve their denominational difficulties. We shall distinguish four phases.

3.3.1   *Pre-independence neology*

In older texts and up until the 1920s, few new terms were coined, as the texts involved were not particularly specialised compared to later periods. The translators of these texts, who had to render many Dutch compounds, preferred compounding to derivation and loanwords (for examples from medicine, see Samuel 2005: 149–150).

In contrast, the technical texts translated from Dutch in the 1920s and 1930s, more specialised than the previous ones, made greater use of Dutch loanwords, with little or no adaptation, making their origin apparent. It is these partially assimilated borrowings from Dutch, especially the less assimilated, that the Indonesian linguists of the 1950s seized upon to justify the work of the KI. However, these texts contain some perfect Malay derivatives, and the multiword terms are often blends, as the authors prefer to use components taken from the general lexicon to coin new words, thus the multiword term *inductie jang diam* (*statische inductie* / 'static induction', literally 'induction that stays') or the compound *telepon kepala* (Du. *koptelefoon* / 'headphone', Indon. *kepala*, 'head'; Kostyurin 1937). Other than the subordinate position of Malay to Dutch due to the colonial context, the neological choices reflect the degree of specialisation, the skill of the translator, and the practice in the classroom (many of these works were technical textbooks) or the workshop.

Moreover, in the translated technical texts, to assist readers in understanding the neologisms and foreign words, paraphrasing, definitions and autonyms are largely used, as are parentheses, which allow the authors and translators to associate the known with the unknown. The abundance of equivalents and annotations reveals the discomfort of the translators, who are constantly obliged to employ neology, under pressure to avoid loanwords, and let the reader choose which equivalent to use.

3.3.2 *Komisi Istilah neology*

After 1942, the degree of specialisation in scientific and technical texts remained for a time similar to that of the end of the colonial period. Higher education and research were still using Dutch as the intellectual elites had not yet changed, so the needs concerned mainly popularising literature and scientific and technical education in secondary schools. The Indonesian government publisher Balai Pustaka republished works that were previously published by its colonial predecessor (Balai Poestaka), re-editing the same texts, updating the spelling, applying the Suwandi reform (1947), sometimes adding a bilingual technical glossary (cf. de Vos 1937 and 1951).

Nonetheless, the term formation methods were changing. A study of the KI's terminological resources shows a decrease in the number of loanwords which were systematically adapted, phonetically and orthographically: *kapasitet* < *capaciteit* ('capacity'), *akustik* < *accoustiek* ('acoustic'), etc. The process of composition, using a hyphen, was considered particularly useful in translating Dutch compounds (hereafter, the underlining and bold distinguish compounding and derivation elements): *cepat-baur* < *diffusiesnelheid* ('diffusion rate'), etc. More-over, greater use was made of derivation: **pemancaran** < *uitstraling* (base *pancar*; 'radiation'), also through the combination of affixes: *kesejajaran* < *evenwijdigheid* (base *jajar*; 'parallelism'), etc., all the while respecting the principle of concision (PUPI 2007:10).

In the early 1970s, a new team of terminologists reviewed many of the neolo-gisms that had been created by the KI, but today, many of those older neologisms remain in use. They have been used by contemporary editors and translators, and they formed the basis of several scientific and technical dictionaries, including the first monolingual Indonesian technical dictionary (Anwir et al., 1953). Often revised and re-edited, unreliable but very comprehensive these affordable dictio-naries have circulated widely over several decades, more so than the works of the KI and the Pusat Bahasa (Samuel 2001, 822 and 1126–1133).

3.3.3   *Pusat Bahasa neology*

Since the 1970s, the issue of techno-scientific literature (whether translation, adaptation or the original texts) and its terminology have greatly evolved.

Firstly, the source language of the texts and terms to be translated has changed, as Dutch has disappeared to the benefit of English. This process, which started in the mid-1950s (aeronautics), was accelerated by the break in relations between Indonesia and its former colonial power (1957). But the causes of this phenomenon are fundamentally the international dominance of English and the growth of non-Dutch-speaking Indonesian elites. This change in source language had consequences for translation and terminology. Indonesian translators and terminologists willingly employed calques, they started taking inspiration from English forms and found new terminological solutions.

Secondly, the terminologies and texts are no longer the same as they had been. There were greater needs for terminology, as illustrated by the extensive vocabu-lary of Pusat Bahasa's "basic" scientific dictionaries, or in the medical dictionaries, some privately published. But the Indonesian intellectual elite's command of Eng-lish, including the student population, long remained mediocre. Contrary to what happens in Malaysia, and despite the huge presence of English in techno-scientific domains, Indonesian higher education is essentially taught in Indonesian, which explains the existence today of university-level Indonesian techno-scientific liter-ature, which was non-existent until the 1970s.

Concerning neological procedures, at least the ones in use in official ter-minological circles, some new trends should be highlighted. While the higher frequency of longer multiword terms can be associated with a greater specialisa-tion of source terms, the development of other procedures was the result of linguistic and extra-linguistic choices. Three procedures are representative of those promoted by the Pusat Bahasa, although they emerged during the KI era.

Borrowing from the regional lexical stock was a long-standing recommendation, which led terminologists to turn to the major regional languages, for example, *pencacah* (< prefixed Jav. base *cacah*) / 'counter.' This is more an ideological choice than a linguistic or socio-linguistic one, even in the case of Javanese, which is spoken by 40% of Indonesians. This use of regional languages aims at making Indonesian Malay even more Indonesian by incorporating regionalisms, following the country's motto "Unity in diversity." The difficulty involved in this choice comes from the fact that it is limited by the linguistic skills of the terminologists on one hand, and of the terminology's users on the other. Thus, a pan-regional choice does not guarantee the efficiency of communication among nationals.

The second procedure, neo-classical word formation, uses free or bound lexical morphemes, and components of different origins (*alih* 'trans-', *eka-* 'uni-, mono-', etc.), which can be attached to an unaffixed base: *lewat jenuh* / 'supersaturated,' or derived: *pengawagasan* (*-awa-*) / 'degassing.' This procedure corresponds to A. Sjarifuddin's 1938 proposal to take inspiration from the Greco-Latin constructions of the international scientific lexicon.

The third procedure is combined affixation, taking one of two forms.

1. Simple combined affixation, i.e. affixation added to a construction which already is affixed: *keberserian* / 'luminosity' (first affix *ber-*, second affixes *ke-/-an*), is used increasingly including in everyday language, and independently of official linguistic institutions. It is a basic trend in contemporary Indonesian.
2. Complex affixation (Samuel 2009c), unknown until the 1980s, is very different. It combines two affixes and other components at the same time and produces calques of English: *keterkutuban* / polarizability or *keTAKterbedaan* / INdistinguishability.

Complex affixation is much rarer, but noteworthy, as Pusat Bahasa's experts systematised its use to translate into Indonesian English terms suffixed with '-ability,' '-ibility.' It is "complex" because it counter-intuitively plays on the polysemy of the prefix *ter-*, whose three distinct potential meanings are accidental (the oldest), stative-resultative (the most frequent) and abilitative (the rarest). Only abilitative is activated in the derived forms mentioned here, often through morphological and semantic neology, and systematically associated with a nominal affix (*ke-/-an*). This produces terms which are affixed *keter-/-an*, unlikely in words spontaneously created and which are constructed as morphological calques. These neologisms are found alongside simple combined affixation, of the same form but where the value of the prefix *ter-* does not correspond to neologisms produced through complex affixation. The productivity of this series of terms, the general dynamics of contemporary Indonesian, the transparency of the calque all go towards suggesting that this terminological matrix could be accepted in the long run.

All in all, the morphological models are few in number but very productive. They correspond to the language's potential, purposely put to use by official terminologists at the expense of other models, as can be seen in the diachronic study of Indonesian neologisms between the 1950s and the 1980s, or in the synchronic and contrastive study of MABBIM's Indonesian and Malaysian neologisms. In a situation of terminological dependency, relying on translation from a dominant language, coining new terms usually takes the form of the calque. The switch from one source-language to another (Dutch to English) and from one type of morphological procedure to another can be illustrated in Table 1.

Table 1. Evolution of neological choices, 1960s–1980s (Samuel 2009b: 607)

Dutch vs English	Komisi Istilah (1950–1966)	Pusat Bahasa (from 1975)
Zelfinductie	*induksi (sen)diri*	
Auto-induction, self-induction		*swainduksi*
geleidingsvermogen	*daya-antar*	
Conductivity		*keterhantaran*

The two generations of Indonesian terminologists responsible for these neologisms used a common procedure, formal calque, but having applied it to different languages, the results also differ. Dutch, a Germanic language, has considerable facility in forming long compounds; this model was in favour during the Dutch Indies period and the KI period, whose members were all Dutch-speaking. On the other hand, English has incorporated in its lexicon a large number of Greco-Latin roots and affixes. However, the shift from a Dutch compound-based model to the English neo-classical one is not radical, as none of these procedures is or has been exclusively employed and several intermediary forms exist; moreover, the Dutch model is still used today.

4.   Institutional terminology and spontaneous terminology

As a counterpoint to the above approach, exclusively focused on official terminological activities, we shall here highlight the effects they produce on usage, through terminological planning and the implantation of standardised terms.

4.1 Implantation of official terminologies

One way of evaluating the success of officially produced versus spontaneous terminology is to observe the uptake in a corpus of strictly representative texts (school textbooks in this case, generally written directly in Indonesian). The example of the terminology of thermodynamics in secondary school textbooks published in the 1990s shows the extent of divergence between the Pusat Bahasa creations and the choices of the authors (themselves physics teachers) and independently authored dictionaries (Samuel 2005, Chapter 12).

The comparison of terms referring to 61 basic concepts in the domain is revealing, even, for example, in relation to the most fundamental concepts, 'conductivity,' 'convection,' and 'heat.' The official terminologists failed to foresee how their choices in terminology would lead them into a dead end.

1. For 'conductivity,' their choice was that of a morphologically complex term, *terterhantaran* (*hantar*, 'to conduct'), avoiding the loanword *konduktivitas* and rejecting the older procedure (compounding) which had given *daya hantar* (*daya*, 'force'). The rejection of *konduktivitas* is even more surprising given that the suffix *-itas*, introduced in the 1950s to Indonesianise the Dutch *-iteit* (Eng. *-ity*) has become productive in Indonesian

2. For 'convection,' the loanword *konveksi*, potentially polysemic,[5] was rejected in favour of a Javanese loanword, *ilian*. This is semantically questionable: although it suggests a flow (*ilian* < Jav. *ili* 'to flow' and Indon. suffix *-an*), it is a downward flow, that of a liquid, while convection is an upward movement

3. For 'heat,' the choice was a semantic neologism derived from a poorly attested Malay form, *bahang* ('incandescence'), the rejection of the Dutch loanword *kalor*, despite it being in use and integrated into Indonesian at the morphophonemic level, and of the common term, *panas*. The rejection of *panas* can be understood, given its categorial ambiguity as a noun-verb.

Generally speaking, the school textbooks seem to pay little attention to the Pusat Bahasa's official terms, what they judge to be effective communication, implying the use of oral exchanges in the classroom and elsewhere, combined with a form of neological conservatism: the schoolbooks and the term lists of the 1950s (and the dictionaries derived from these lists) are closer to each other with regards their use of terms than to the Pusat Bahasa dictionaries.

It must however be remembered that the acceptability of a neologism and its uptake by language users can take time and follow unexpected paths. Such is the

---

5. *Konveksi* is often phonetically assimilated as /kɔnfɛksi/, like *konfeksi* (< Dutch *confectie* / "garment").

case with the term *bahang*, which appears nowadays as a specialised neologism *pulau bahang (perkotaan)* / '(urban) heat island,' while the construction *pulau kalor* / 'heat island' is not found. The synonymy involved is acceptable to all, speakers and language planners alike, as it concerns clearly distinct sub-domains (thermodynamics vs. town-planning) and registers (scientific vs. school).

4.2   Terminological variation and dispersion

A second way of assessing institutional terminological activities consists of examining how a terminological domain with a high percentage of synonyms was treated by official terminologists: did their choices help reduce or regulate terminological variance? And how? For this, we shall take as an example the heat treatment of metals, whose terminology has been compiled from textbooks, university lecture notes, technical articles and standards, for the most part translated from English (US and UK), German (Germany and Austria) and Dutch between 1977 and 1995 (Samuel 2009a and unpublished). This terminology comprises 357 concepts — physical phenomena, industrial processes, parameters, technical materials, etc., expressed in the form of 1,081 terms of which 780 occur only once in the corpus. This latter figure in itself indicates the poverty and fragility of the terminology chosen, which is not surprising given that the terminology is still barely stabilised. Among the terms, we will focus on those using or built on the base *sepuh* ('dark; old'), whose frequency must be highlighted: 78 terms in the corpus, referring to 54 different concepts, of which 48 are heat treatment processes, often very different or even contradictory.

Sepuh is, in fact, an old technical term, found in several Indonesian languages, including Malay and Javanese, and in different sub-domains of traditional metalworking:

1. in steel metalwork to indicate a process known as 'quench hardening'
2. in gold smithing to indicate a surface treatment aimed at improving the metal's appearance by giving it a darker colour (via plating or colouring)
3. a Javanese homonym, semantically linked to the meaning of *sepuh* in gold smithery, meaning 'dark,' but also 'old.'

The polysemy of the term and how it is used in related technical domains should have led language planners (translators and terminologists) to be extremely cautious, but the attractiveness of its technical roots, the practical belief that the term would be more accessible to users and the prospect of successfully creating terms from an autochthonous lexical stock put those concerns aside.

The language planners took different approaches concurrently, each accompanied by a widening of the meaning of *sepuh*:

1. via generalisation, to indicate other mass treatments (as opposed to surface treatments), sometimes even for metal softening, contrary to common and workshop use
2. via transfer from one technical domain (gold smithing) to another (steel metalwork), to indicate surface treatments (chemical enrichment, followed by hardening or not)
3. via semantic borrowing, to indicate ageing treatments, which aim at hardening the mass of metal through delayed physical phenomena (hence the name), with no relationship to the treatments mentioned above.

In addition to the fact that translators often pick words from different semantic fields without any systematic approach, they all developed their own terms, so that the derivative *penyepuhan* alone (practice or execution of *sepuh*) corresponds to six different concepts: heat treatment (the domain itself), quench hardening, age hardening, ageing (mass treatments), ageing (phenomenon), and carburizing (surface treatment).

Affixation is not much help in making the terms less ambiguous: the circumfix[6] *peN-/-an* (*penyepuhan*) can indicate any process, the prefix *peN-* and the suffix *-an* any agent (bath or medium). The other elements of the multiword term are determinant only if they describe the specific characteristics of the process, solving the ambiguity of the polysemous head word. Finally, context is essential, but context is there to help the readers' comprehension only in certain texts (handbooks, lecture notes, articles, standards), while professional technical documents do not typically include them. Moreover, bilingual terminological lists aimed at helping with technical translation do not help users who are not bilingual, and many Indonesian users have only a very limited command of languages other than Indonesian and one regional language.

Finally, the Pusat Bahasa opted for a comprehensive autochthonous paradigmatic logic, making *sepuh* the basic name of the domain — heat treatment —, thus its use to indicate all sorts of treatments in the form of consistent multiple-word terms. This approach makes sense, but has not contributed to diminishing terminological confusion, as it runs contrary to the actual use made by domain specialists, engineers, technicians, and specialised translators. The rejection of well-formed, transparent/motivated loanwords in actual usage, in particular, is hard to understand (Samuel 2009a).

During the initial phase when a terminology is under construction, a certain degree of synonymy is inevitable. In this case, the linguistic diversity of translated publications and the lack of appropriate skills on the part of certain actors, in

---

6. Combination of a prefix and a suffix on the same base with a single function.

particular text producers and editors, have made the situation worse: exactly the type of situation typical of a country which is terminologically and technically dependent. While the semantic richness and age of the base *sepuh* made it crucial in the workshop, far from all ambiguity, the Pusat Bahasa, indulging in the temptation of terminological indigenousness, did not achieve its aim, as regulator, to create a healthy degree of terminological variation.

5.   Terminological resources: Diversity and linguistic dependency

In this section we discuss terminological resources, highlighting the relationship between specialists (scientists, terminologists, linguists), other users, and the term or resource itself, as well as the relationship between spontaneous production and the regularised production of the terminological agencies.

Only the terminological resources elaborated between the end of the colonial period and the end of the 20th century, 1942–1995,[7] will be considered here. In the post-1995 period, growth in production and digitalisation of both the resources and their diffusion, make it more difficult to identify and count the number of resources produced. During this half-century period, 1,076 documents (dictionaries, lists of terms, vocabularies, etc.) were found, of which 750 have been described (Samuel 2000 and 2001). The study of these publications highlights an initial dynamic phase (1946–1955), which corresponds to private editorial activity and that of KI, followed by a slowing down until the mid-1970s, and a very strong and sustained increase until 1995. Private publishing accounts for most publications (66.3%), with official language planning institutes lagging far behind (30.6%).

Classifying the documents following an internal typology (i.e. according to their content and structure) reveals that the usual categories concerning interlinguistic contact between foreign language(s) and Indonesian are only applicable to some of them (47%). These documents, called here "classic," are mono- or plurilingual dictionaries and bilingual terminologies. Of this group, 34% are "multisource" with entries from different languages, generally European, and simply described as "foreign" (*asing*), with their Indonesian equivalent. Only 3.3% of these resources are strictly bilingual and bidirectional, the others being unidirectional (foreign language > Indonesian), sometimes with a reversed index.

The main finding of this classification is the high proportion of typologically "hybrid" dictionaries (53%), which, in their design, do not place the languages on the same level, with often a range of foreign languages (rarely regional languages)

---

7. The total number of enumerated terminological resources is 1,286, published between 1741 and 1995 (Samuel 2001).

on the one side, Indonesian on the other. This hybrid production is difficult to classify into subsets, given the entries' heterogeneity (multiple languages) and the nature of the articles (equivalents, definitions or annotations), even within one single dictionary. We shall nonetheless distinguish several types and sub-types.

In the "unbalanced dictionaries" (31.5%), Indonesian is somehow minoritised; these dictionaries are mostly passive with respect to treatment of Indonesian (entries in foreign languages, with annotations in Indonesian, but no Indonesian equivalents). The "mixed" types contain entries in both Indonesian and foreign languages, with annotations and/or Indonesian equivalents. Finally, loanword dictionaries include entries with assimilated loanwords accompanied by Indonesian annotations. The heterogeneity of entries means the user is never sure of finding a term in a given language, or its Indonesian equivalent.

The learners' dictionaries (21%) are more reliable resources with a more complex design: multilingual with definitions (foreign entries, with equivalents and annotations in Indonesian) or bilingualised monolingual (Indonesian entries, with equivalents and annotations in English). They are mostly published by language, academic and ministerial entities.

The mere existence of these dictionaries, and their quantity, reflect Indonesian's dependency on foreign languages on lexical and terminological levels. The result is resources that one could say belong to the genre "dictionary," but whose objective is different. Thus, many among them offer a general presentation of modern knowledge through the terms they bring together, but their aim is not to be used as an aid to translation. Their aim is to give access to knowledge, not exclusively lexicographic or encyclopaedic, and they materialise a form of appropriation of this knowledge; their readership is not made up of language experts, or experts in specialist domains, but rather anyone wishing to learn.

More than half a century after independence, this knowledge remains globally "foreign" in its origin and not wholly Indonesian linguistically, as is shown by the entries. These "unbalanced" hybrid dictionaries reflect an indifferent attitude towards neological and lexical sources and highlight the authors' lack of concern for drafting and editorial quality (questionable spelling of foreign terms, approximative alphabetical order, etc.). This means that some multilingual terminological resources mix entries taken from a range of languages, with no distinction (unbalanced mixed dictionaries, which place an undifferentiated set of foreign languages in opposition to Indonesian), while others mix, in their entries, Indonesian and foreign terms. These are potential loanwords, and therefore the stereotypical example of these dictionaries is the loanword dictionary, where only the annotations are in Indonesian, and equivalents are not offered even when they exist. Thus, these hybrid dictionaries shed light on the progressive assimilation of foreign forms and legitimise borrowing as the main source of language enrichment. They express a linguistic relativism explained by the prestige accorded to foreign languages since well before the colonial and contemporary periods, the attractiveness of what foreign languages convey and the secondary position of Indonesian for the majority of its speakers.

6.   Conclusion

In societies familiar with both written sources and technology, the massive introduction of European knowledge and techniques, starting in the mid-19th century, led to a remarkable appetite for modernisation. The language of Indonesia that benefited the most from this ambition was Indonesian, the Malay of Indonesia, the main vehicular language of the region, the language of colonial modernity and of the independence movement that emerged from it.

In this context, the spread of terminologies and their written forms played an important role, based on the idea that the command of the terms would lead to the command of the knowledge they conveyed. Between 1942 and 1966 this was the idea that motivated the creation of hundreds of thousands of terms, with no real objective other than to produce new terms. Then, the illusion of exhaustiveness was abandoned, with the more modest ambition of developing inter-translatability between Indonesian and the foreign languages that conveyed modern knowledge (Ferguson 1968:28; Moeliono 1985:114). This ambition was behind the formulation of terminological policies, placed under the double focus of language planning and Indonesia-Malaysia cooperation. However, there was little change in the way new terms were formed, testifying to the powerful attractiveness of loanwords — direct or not —, which remain a constant source of new terms in Indonesian.

The study of these terminological policies highlights some failures which might not be failures after all. While implantation, in Indonesia as elsewhere, has been the weak link of terminological policy due to its frequent failures, it must be remembered that it is a long process. In fact, some terms created in the 1950s are in common use forty years later, while others created in the 1990s are taking root today. Indonesia-Malaysia cooperation has struggled with some limitations not only because of the different sociolinguistic environments and linguistic narratives of the two countries, but also because of their two very different situations. While in Malaysia, Malaysian did not resist the lure of technical and scientific English, especially in higher education, the position of Indonesian remains far more solid.

References

Anwir, B.S., B. Latif, B. Sjarif, R. Sumarto, and M. Pamenan. 1953. *Tafsiran Kamus Tehnik*, Djakarta: Stam.

Behrend, T.E. 1999. "The Writings of K.P.H. Suryanagara. Shifting Paradigms in Nineteenth-Century Javanese Thought and Letters." In *Bijdragen Tot de Taal-, Land- en Volkenkunde. Encompassing Knowledge. Indigenous Encyclopedias from Ninth-Century Java to Twentieth-Century Riau*, ed. by T. Day and W. Derks, 155–3, 309–341.

Blommaert, J., and J. Verschueren. 1998. "The Role of Language in European Nationalist Ideologies." In *Language Ideologies. Practice and Theory*, ed. by B.B. Schieffelin, K.A. Woolard and P.V. Kroskrity, 189–210. Oxford: Oxford University Press.

De Vos J. 1937. *Pemimpin soepir dan montir kendaraan motor*. 1st ed. Batavia: Balai Poestaka.

De Vos J. 1951. *Pemimpin supir dan montir kendaraan motor*. 5th ed. Batavia: Balai Pustaka.

Ferguson, Ch. 1968. "Language development." In *Language Problems of Developing Nations*, ed. by J. Fishman, Ch. Ferguson, and J.Das Gupta, 27–35. New York: John Wiley and Sons.

Gill S.K. 2014. *Language Policy Challenges in Multi-Ethnic Malaysia*. Dordrecht: Springer.

Ismail, Othman and Rogayah Hussin (eds). 1990. *Kamus Fizik. Elektromagnet, Kelektrikan dan Kemagnetan*. Kuala Lumpur: Dewan Bahasa dan Pustaka.

Kementrian Pengadjaran, Pendidikan dan Kebudajaan. 1950. *Bentuk Istilah*. Djakarta.

Komisi Bahasa Indonesia. 1946–47. *Kamoes Istilah*. 2 vols. Djakarta: Poestaka Rakjat.

Kostyurin, S. 1937. *Jang haroes diketahoei orang tentang hal radio*. Batavia-Centrum: Balai Poestaka.

Moeliono, A.M. 1985. *Pengembangan dan Pembinaan bahasa. Ancangan Alternatif di dalam Perencanaan Bahasa*. Jakarta: Penerbit Djambatan.

Omar, A.H. 2002. "Wujudkah tembok bahasa antara bahasa Malaysia dan Indonesia?" In *Setia dan Santun Bahasa*, 115–135. Tanjong Malim: Universiti Pendidikan Sultan Idris.

Pandji, Poestaka. 2602 [1942]. "Mempersatukan bahasa." In *Pandji Poestaka*, 29 August 2602, 730–731.

Piah, H.M. 2002. *Traditional Malay Literature*. Kuala Lumpur: Dewan Bahasa dan Pustaka.

Pigeaud, Th.G.Th. 1967. *Literature of Java. Vol. I Synopsis of Javanese Literature 900–1900 AD*. Leiden: KITLV.

Prawirosumartono, W., L. Wilardjo, and H.C. Yohannes. 1993 (1988). *Kamus Fisika. Elektromagnetika*. Jakarta: Pusat Pembinaan dan Pengembangan Bahasa.

Pusat Pembinaan dan Pengembangan Bahasa. 2007. *Pedoman Umum Pembentukan Istilah*. 3rd ed. (1st ed. 1975). Jakarta: Departemen Pendidikan dan Kebudayaan.

Samuel, J. 2000. *Politique Terminologique et Modernisation Lexicale: le Cas de l'Indonésien*. PhD Dissertation. Paris: Institut des Langues et Civilisations Orientales.

Samuel, J. 2001. *Katalog beranotasi ensiklopedia, kamus dan daftar istilah bahasa Indonesia (1741–1995)*. Jakarta: Pusat Bahasa-Forum Jakarta Paris-Yayasan Obor Indonesia.

Samuel, J. 2005. *Politique Terminologique et Modernisation Lexicale: le cas de l'Indonésien*. Paris-Louvain: Institut des Langues et Civilisations Orientales-Peeters.

Samuel, J. 2009a. "Mengindonesiakan Istilah-Istilah 'Perlakuan Panas' atau Bagaimana Menyadur Kata Lama Menjadi Istilah Baru." In *Sadur: Sejarah Terjemahan di Indonesia dan Malaysia*, ed. by H. Chambert-Loir. Jakarta-Bandung: KPG-EFEO-Forum Jakarta Paris-Pusat Bahasa-Universitas Padjadjaran.

Samuel, J. 2009b. "Penerjemahan ilmu dan teknologi di Indonesia." In *Sadur: Sejarah Terjemahan di Indonesia dan Malaysia*, ed. by H. Chambert-Loir, 593–611. Jakarta-Bandung: KPG-EFEO-Forum Jakarta Paris-Pusat Bahasa-Universitas Padjadjaran.

Samuel, J. 2009c. "Potensialitas dan keterbatasan inovasi morfologis dalam bahasa Indonesia. Contoh kombinasi afiks *keter-/-an*." *Wacana* 11–2 (October), 294–318.

Samuel, J. Unpublished. *Terminologie indonésienne du traitement thermique des métaux (présentation du domaine, terminologie et analyse des termes).*

Schoterman, J. 1981. "An Introduction to old Javanese Sanskrit Dictionaries and Grammars." *Bijdragen tot de Taal-, Land- en Volkenkunde* 137, no. 4, 419–442.

Van Ophuysen, C.A. 1901. *Kitab logat Melajoe. Woordenlijst voor de spelling der Maleische taal.* Batavia: Landsdrukkrij.

Van Ophuysen, C.A. 1910. *Maleische spraakkunst.* Leiden: Van Doesburgh.

Wilardjo, L. 1993. *Glosarium Fisika.* Jakarta: Pusat Pembinaan dan Pengembangan Bahasa.

Yohannes, H.C., A. Susanto, and D. Murniah. 1996. *Kamus Elektronika-Optoelektronika.* Jakarta: Pusat Pembinaan dan Pengembangan Bahasa.

Zgusta, L. 1990. "The Role of Dictionaries in the Genesis and Development of the Standard." In *Wörterbücher, Dictionaries, Dictionnaires. Ein Internazionales Handbuch zur Lexikographie. An International Encyclopedia of Lexicography. Encyclopédie internationale de lexicographie*, ed. by F.J. Haussman, O. Reichmann, H.E. Wiegand, and L. Zgusta, vol. 1, 70–79. Berlin: Walter de Gruyter.

CHAPTER 26

Terminology in Italy
A rising field of research

Claudio Grimaldi
Parthenope University of Naples

This contribution aims to trace a profile of the recent history of Italian research on terminology, taking into consideration the most relevant studies on the subject conducted in the field of Italian linguistics. In the first part, we will frame the most important works in LSPs in this area. The second part focuses on the role of the Italian Association for Terminology (Ass.I.Term) and other research institutions in recognising Italy's need for a systematic reflection on terminology, from both a theoretical and practical point of view.

Keywords: specialised languages, LSPs, Italy, Italian linguistics, Italian Association for Terminology

1. The study of specialised languages

Italian research on terminology was for a long time characterised by numerous studies and publications concerned mainly with defining the concept of "specialised languages" (*linguaggi specialistici*). Between the end of the 1980s and the early 1990s in particular, research and analysis methods were outlined and expanded on, leading to numerous specific studies in the field of terminology during the first two decades of the 21st century. This dynamic would result in terminology studies gaining recognition in Italy not only in the field of Italian linguistics, but in foreign linguistics as well. In fact, for a long time, Italian studies had focused almost exclusively on the broad study of languages for specific purposes (LSPs), neglecting analyses of a more specifically terminological and ontological nature. The period leading up to the 1990s witnessed an increase in the number of studies concerned with the field of lexicography, which had undergone a profound renewal in response to major social changes and the demands of linguistic policy. This allowed for the role of Italian on the national and international level to be defined regardless of specialised and domain-specific language, and

https://doi.org/10.1075/tlrp.24.26gri

despite the massive use of English in communication. From this perspective, from the 1980s to the late 1990s terminology research in Italy has been marginalised due to a lack of institutional and academic recognition, insufficient funding, and disagreement regarding the separation between applied linguistics, language pedagogy, linguistics and foreign languages.

In various academic studies published in Italy since the 1960s, the main focus of the academic community concerned with Italian linguistics was the definition and characterisation of LSP. In the studies that have dealt with LSPs (Berruto, Berretta 1977) — at least until the early 1990s —, the concept of LSP has taken on different and divergent names, which are not always treated as synonymous, for example, *lingue speciali, linguaggi speciali,*[1] *sottocodice* (Dardano 1973; Berruto 1974, 1987), *linguaggio settoriale, linguaggio specialistico-settoriale* (Beccaria 1973), *tecnoletto* and *microlingua* (Balboni 1982). However, as Cortelazzo points out (1994:7), this terminological distinction is almost never accompanied by an apparent differentiation in meaning or definition. This is because, with a few exceptions, there is a lack of explicit definitions of the categories used in studies on sectorial language varieties. From this point of view, it is always Cortelazzo (1994) who precisely delimits the boundaries of research in this field and provides more and more opportunities for the development of studies in terminology, and in the relationship between different codes in specialist communication. Gualdo (2016:371) outlines the strengths of Cortelazzo's (1994) work in clearly sketching the Italian linguistic situation, which was characterised by weakness and a lack of systematicity applied to developing lexicons of crafts and industries, a long-standing and enduring distrust of lexicography for technical, scientific and specialised vocabulary, and the failure of national institutions and scholars to address demands for terminological standardisation and normalisation (see Chapter 17). Considering these peculiarities of the Italian academic and linguistic landscape, it is clear that the studies conducted in the field of linguistics were initially only oriented towards defining the concept of specialised languages (*linguaggi specialistici*) and, subsequently, what to include within this concept. Many definitions oscillated from one variant to another and have only been partially harmonised in recent years.

From this perspective, it is useful to trace back the history of the previously mentioned studies, which also allow us to define the boundaries of terminological research conducted in Italy. In fact, in the last fifty years terminology research in

---

1. If in Italian *lingua* is typically understood as the verbal communicative code exclusive to the human species, *linguaggi* can also include the expression of concepts through non-verbal means: symbolic means, such as formulae, and iconic means, such as diagrams and graphs, or even illustrations, animations, films and others.

Italy was carried out under the umbrella or within the context of LSP research, with an interest primarily on the lexicon, and subsequently on the syntactic, rhetorical, and textual levels. It is only in the last two decades that Italy's interest in the theory and practice of terminology as a discipline has emerged thanks to increased attention to the study of the relationship between terms and concepts, as well as the development of terminographic activities in academic and institutional contexts. From our point of view, the analyses of the evolution and variety of Italian designations for the concept of LSP by Gualdo and Telve (2011), Gualdo (2016), and Ondelli (2019) are particularly valuable references in order to accurately determine when terminology studies in a strict sense began in Italy.

In the 1990s it was Cortelazzo (1994: 8) who proposed an exhaustive definition of *special language*: a functional variety of a natural language, dependent on a sector of knowledge or a sphere of specialised activity. According to Cortelazzo, a special language is constituted at the lexical level by the use of specialised terms that are specific to a particular field or discipline, often with precise definitions, and at the morphosyntactic level by a set of regularly recurring selections within the inventory of forms available in the language. Cortelazzo also justifies the choice of choosing the term *special languages* (*lingue speciali*) as opposed to the more recurrent term *domain-specific languages* (*linguaggi settoriali*), where *speciali* brings the Italian denomination closer to those used in other languages, such as *special languages* in English or *langues de spécialité* in French. Moreover, according to Cortelazzo, *special languages* is more restrictive than *domain-specific languages*. As in previous studies, Cortelazzo's work identifies and defines the lexicon as the founding element of special language. However, the novelty of his work within the panorama of Italian research of that time is linked to the acknowledgement that special languages can express themselves also on a communicative level that is realised (in partially different forms) in the contact between experts and non-experts, in popularisation through the mass media, and in didactics.

During the 1990s, the debate persisted regarding the study of LSP and its designations within the larger context of Italian academia. Dardano (1994: 497) proposes to use the designation *scientific languages* (*linguaggi scientifici*). From this point of view, Dardano emphasises how the history of scientific vocabularies is not so much a history of words, but rather the history of the functioning of such vocabularies, for example the interrelationships of words and concepts.

Also during the first half of the 1990s, Sobrero (1993) frames the definition of LSP research under the denomination of *special languages* (*lingue speciali*), i.e. an umbrella term to cover both *specialised languages* (*lingue specialistiche*), when referring to the hard sciences, and *domain-specific languages* (*lingue settoriali*). Serianni (2012), as for him, continues to emphasise the importance of referentiality, and among the various designations to denote LSP he prefers *domain-specific languages* (*linguaggi settoriali*).

Some studies show that the uncertainty regarding the usage and the synonymy of these various denominations is still widely present (Rovere 2010; Serianni 2019). Many of these studies have also proposed an overview of the uses of the Italian language in the history of some disciplines. This is true for Serianni and Trifone (1994), whose work includes a section on domain-specific languages containing several essays devoted to various scientific languages. This is also the case in the work by Antonelli, Motolese and Tomasin (2014: 13–14), in which there is no reference to the term *specialised languages* (*lingue di specialità*) or its alternatives.

Denominative and definitional uncertainty still persists around the name to be attributed to LSP studies. In the wake of De Mauro's argument (2014: 227–250), Gualdo (2016) considers that *specialised languages* (*linguaggi specialistici*) is by now the most appropriate denomination to identify the *domain-specific languages* (*linguaggi settoriali*). His reasoning states that the latter, as a result of diaphasic variation (didactic dissemination and communication between expert and non-specialists) and more pronounced conditioning by the mass media, are characterised, in contrast to *specialised languages* (*linguaggi specialistici*), by a weakening of the typical traits of *domain-specific languages*, such as the regularity in the processes of term formation, the high rate of specific technicalities, and the rigid univocity of both terms and the concepts they designate (Gualdo, Telve 2011: 17–21).

The study of specialised languages and terminologies has finally been recognised through the publication of a number of reference works such as Gualdo (2009a), Gualdo and Telve (2011), Nesi and De Martino (2012), and Grimaldi and Zanola (2021), which allow, many years after the work of Gotti (1991), to clearly and more easily define diversified methodologies of investigation, with a focus on reflections of a synchronic, diachronic and comparative nature.

On the one hand, the studies mentioned so far have made it possible to frame the field of research on LSPs, in which the study of terms and concepts is also included, and define the boundaries of investigation with respect to other fields of research, such as linguistics, applied linguistics, and language pedagogy, and works of common language. On the other hand, they have made it possible to identify the specific features of these languages, among which lexicon certainly ranks highly. Revisiting the first aspect, it is important to emphasise here the intervention of Beccaria (2006: 55–56), who noted that the distinctions between everyday language and technical-scientific language are becoming increasingly blurred, and that the sciences are introducing more and more neologisms into everyday language. As a result, while the average educated person once knew few scientific words, today they know many. In fact, from this point of view, the presence of specialised terminology in the common language is especially noticeable in those disciplines or fields of knowledge that have a more intense relationship with everyday life.

Traditionally, Italian researchers of specialised languages have paid particular attention to the core characteristics of these languages, namely the lexicon and word formation, with reference to the difference between general language and specialised language. At least until the 1990s, studies on LSPs focused on lexical aspects, without including in-depth reflections on ontological aspects and lacking a linguistic policy perspective. However, in recent years, LSP investigations have also included reflections of a termino-ontological nature, broadening the perspective on other aspects related to the relationship between terms, discourse, and text; morphosyntax and textual organisation have increasingly been recognised (Zanola 2008). Nonetheless, as Arcangeli (2012: 281) notes, it is clearly the words that truly convey fundamental meaning in specialised communication. Thus, the fact remains that the lexicon is what provides distinctive elements to identify a special language with respect to other special languages, as well as to the common language.

According to Dardano (1994: 498), until at least the 1990s, the lexical perspective remained the focus for many Italian researchers of LSPs, which are studied for their specific characteristics, such as reference to a particular field of knowledge, definiteness, systematicity, precision, univocity, and referentiality. Referring to the research conducted in Italy on LSPs during the 1970s and 1980s, Dardano (1994: 502–503) observes that the study of scientific languages, and more generally of domain-specific languages, was highly developed in Germany (see also Chapter 22), in Anglo-Saxon countries and in France (see also Chapter 21), by way of novel experiences that led to new methods and the refinement of research objectives. According to Dardano, it was clear that univocity, the procedure of designation, referential specificity, and stability of meaning — traits that were considered particular to scientific languages — were rather representations of tendencies. Dardano notes how research concerning Italian morphology, syntax, textual organisation and pragmatic features lagged behind that of European counterparts, such as Germany, the United Kingdom, and France. Until the 1990s, the interest of Italian researchers was more oriented toward diatopic varieties of Italian than terminology. Methods concerning the analysis of scientific language were therefore not well developed. Dardano (1994: 503) wanted to see an increase in Italian research so that scientific discourse could be considered dynamic, processual and flexible according to different contexts and situations.

2.   The Italian Association for Terminology

The creation in 1991 of the Italian Association for Terminology (Ass.I.Term) on the initiative of a group of Italian scholars, researchers, translators and documentalists marked a turning point in the development and recognition of terminology in Italy. Through this Association, the need for greater clarity in scientific language was realised, in hopes that, with improved clarity, Italian scientific language would support national industriousness, and achieve full parity with the scientific languages of other nations.

The need to conduct research in the 1990s to support the further development of LSPs in Italian was progressively met by the publication of various works. Some of these works emphasised other peculiarities (in addition to vocabulary and word formation) of LSPs. These would include syntax and textual texture, and also the effects of channels and contexts of use (such as how language adapts to the intentions of communication and the relationship between transmitter and receiver). There has been no shortage, however, of publications that framed terminology studies in both theoretical and applied perspectives.

The growth of perspectives on the investigation of LSPs has made certain expressions such as *specialised communication* (*comunicazione specialistica*) (Cavagnoli 2007) and *specialised discourse* (*discorso specialistico*) (Gotti 2005) commonplace (see also Chapter 7). It is also important to point out the works that, even before the 1990s (Altieri Biagi 1965, 1990) but especially from the 1990s onwards (Librandi, Piro 2006; Nesi, De Martino 2012; Sergio 2010; Biffi 2008), have allowed Italian research on LSPs to proceed with the study of specialised terminology. Some of these works took a diachronic perspective, framed within the specific field of knowledge to which it belongs, but others tackled scientific discourse as a whole. In this sense, recent studies of particular relevance and critical depth are also reported from the research conducted in the field of foreign languages both in relation to scientific writing (Zanola 2014b; Grimaldi 2017; Grimaldi, Humbley 2021) and terminology and terminography (Raus 2013; Faini 2018; Prandi et al 2013; Altmanova et al 2018; Zollo 2020).

Within the Italian tradition of research related to LSPs, the absence of reference works and a disciplinary tradition in the fields of terminology and terminography, which appear to be much more mature in other European and non-European countries than they are in Italy, has often been underlined. Gualdo (2016: 379) points out that the lack of terminology research in Italy was partly due to the absence of institutional and academic recognition, a lack of funding, and uncertainty and conflict in the delimitation between applied linguistics, language pedagogy, linguistics, and the study of foreign languages. Certainly the creation of Ass.I.Term and the activities carried out and promoted in a number of university contexts that are now benchmarks for research in the field of terminology, to which we will return later, have allowed for increased interest from the national and international academic community. This recognition of research in the field of terminology has been progressively consolidated thanks to Zanola's numerous publications on the subject (2012, 2014a, 2015, 2018) and various collections of articles in proceedings of conferences of national and international importance (Collesi et al 2013; Zanola et al 2016; Conceição, Zanola 2020; Grimaldi, Zanola 2021; Grimaldi et al 2022). Nevertheless, from a theoretical point of view, the study of terminology in Italy has followed the emergence of the main theories of the discipline internationally (the General Theory of Terminology, the Communicative Theory of Terminology, Textual Terminology and Socioterminology, and Frame-based Terminology — see also Chapters 8, 11, and 13), without so far the creation of a theory of identification and management of terms derived from scholars in the national territory. Therefore, Italian scholars have used the main terminology theories according to their specific research needs, adapting terminological inquiry tools to the purpose of their investigative activities and resorting to the most useful computer tools for terminological analysis according to their current research projects.

It is useful to emphasise that, alongside the studies on LSPs mentioned so far, a large part of the reflection conducted within the Italian academic community has been directed to the study and analysis of loanwords — mainly of English origin — and neologisms, from a perspective that is often linked to the research field of terminology (in particular, Adamo, Della Valle 2017, 2018). In the 1990s, the debate on the volume of loanwords in both technical-scientific communication and common language led to numerous publications and purist positions. In this sense, Dardano (1994: 551) emphasises that the dominance of English as the vehicular language of science and technology provoked intense reactions that in Italy, unlike in France, were hardly ever translated into language policy directives. Giovanni Nencioni (1984, 1987), the driving force behind the founding of Ass.I.Term and its first President, emphasised as early as the 1980s that alongside the process of terminological reorganisation, a process of technification of the Italian language was underway. Words that were in current and popular use were giving way to learned synonyms or words formed with Latin and Greek roots. Nencioni highlighted the positive aspect of this trend, namely the adaptation of Italian to the European lexicon, which at that time united the western languages of Europe in the technical and intellectual fields, on the basis of Latin and Greek. The sore point for Nencioni remained that of loanwords: after the Second World War, Italy was overwhelmed by Anglo-Saxon culture and the English language, which led to a great interest in translations and direct contact with the Anglo-Saxon world in both social sciences and scientific disciplines. Consequently, students turned to English as a second language of study to the detriment of French or German. A few years later, Nencioni (1994, 1997) pointed out that the omnipresence of technology in daily life dominated national cultures and made linguistic purism impossible to impose as a language policy. In other words, a surge in the production of new concepts and inventions was accompanied by an urgent need for new technical terms that the limited stock of the traditional lexicon could not provide. New terms were therefore formed, violating the natural structures and rules (morphology, syntax, etc.) of national languages, unlike the terms formed by scientists in the Renaissance who combined Latin and Greek roots to denote new meanings. Nencioni highlighted that those roots were further adapted in English, which also created acronyms, further complicating the typology and clouding the transparency of the terms. In the 1980s, Nencioni noted that, unlike in Italy, countries like France placed a strong emphasis on technical neology, focusing on the correct use and precise meanings of English-derived prefixes, roots, and suffixes, as well as on the proper ways to combine them. It was this kind of orientation that led Nencioni and other researchers working in the field of documentation and classification to establish Ass.I.Term with a goal to direct research and action towards the development and maintenance of national terminology. The primary intent was to form connections between initiatives and activities in various scientific fields, inviting them to exchange information and experiences. According to Nencioni (1994: 11), the aim was to foster, among linguists, the creation of a methodological approach to terminology so that the Italian scientific language would acquire, in all its branches, the precision needed to support national productivity and achieve full parity with the scientific language systems of other nations.

The gradual recognition, strengthening and consolidation of Italian terminology research has therefore been possible thanks to the activities and actions of a series of players who had been promoting research and training in terminology since the 1990s. A key role continues to be played by Ass.I.Term. After meetings and discussions on the occasion of its foundation, in particular the discussion for the creation of an information association on terminology in Italy, which took place in Rome on June 24 1991, Ass.I.Term held a second conference in November 1991 to encourage the cooperation of scientists and other professionals towards the common goal of creating appropriate channels of communication and dissemination. Nencioni, who at that time was also the President of the Accademia della Crusca, hoped that the Association would be a forum for establishing a linguistic policy attentive to the evolution of the lexicon. The aims and fields of activity that the Association still proposes today are summarised in article 3 of its founding statutes (our translation):

1. to promote scientific and technical information in the Italian language through the valorisation of the terminology of special or domain-specific languages
2. to promote scientific and professional relations between users of Italian terminology by participating in, sponsoring or organising seminars, meetings, and conferences in Italy and abroad

3. to promote the enrichment of scientific and technical terminology in the Italian language and the collection of related information and knowledge

4. to promote the dissemination and coordination of activities in the field of scientific and technical terminology

5. to encourage training in the various disciplines and professions related to the production and management of terminology, also by providing subsidies or scholarships

6. to contribute, with other national and international institutions, to the achievement of the aims of Ass.I.Term.

Ass.I.Term, whose main areas of interest are neology, documentation and institutional communication, encourages the enrichment of scientific and technical terminology in the Italian language by promoting monolingual and multilingual products for translators and specialists in technical and scientific communication. It also creates opportunities for theoretical debates and exchange, and encourages reflection on themes of naming and conceptualisation. Ass.I.Term also provides a terminology consulting service in diachronic and synchronic dimensions for national and international institutions and organisations. It is also actively involved in the preparation and analysis of terminology products, corpora processing, data quality validation and translator and terminology training (Gualdo 2009b). Each year, it holds an annual conference to enable dialogue on terminology-related research carried out within Ass.I.Term and the broader Italian academic research community.

Ass.I.Term also collaborates with other national and international institutions and scientific entities, such as the Accademia della Crusca, the Pan-Latin Terminology Network REALITER, Eurac Research, the Italian Standards Authority-UNI and the International Information Centre for Terminology-Infoterm, as well as with Italian associations of interpreters and translators. In addition, it has actively participated in initiatives promoted by the Network for Excellence in Institutional Italian-REI, a network of professionals created by the Italian Department of the Directorate-General for Translation of the European Commission, active between 2005 and 2018. The aim of this Network was to promote an 'institutional' Italian that was clear, comprehensible and accessible to all. In this regard, REI has promoted the harmonisation of terminology and the sharing of existing databases, and identified criteria for the validation of terms including neologisms.

Several initiatives that Ass.I.Term started continue on an on-going basis, such as the organisation of and participation in terminology seminars in various Italian and international locations, as well as support for terminology training programmes in universities.

Research centres in Italy have collaborated with Ass.I.Term to raise awareness of research and study in the field of terminology in Italy. These centres include the Centro di Ricerca in Terminologia Multilingue-Ce.R.Te.M. at the University of Genoa and mainly the Osservatorio di Terminologie e Politiche Linguistiche-OTPL at the Università Cattolica del Sacro Cuore of Milan. Created on the initiative of the Faculty of Foreign Languages and Literatures of the University of Genoa, Ce.R.Te.M. is an inter-university research centre whose members include academics and researchers, both local and international. As a promoter of numerous research initiatives and as a partner in national and international events in the field of terminology, the OTPL (Università Cattolica del Sacro Cuore) works in a diachronic and synchronic perspective and intends to deepen the knowledge of specialised terminologies in Euro-American languages through scientific, theoretical and applied research. The OTPL also offers a post-graduate course in Terminology and Translation Services.

Other notable developments in terminology research are the activities promoted by laboratories, research centres, university departments and particularly PhD courses. These include: the Laboratorio di Terminologia e Traduzione Assistita-LabTerm at the University of Bologna, which includes terminology management among other research interests; the Laboratorio di Documentazione of the University of Calabria-Labdoc; the Department of Legal Sciences, Language, Interpretation and Translation-IUSLIT of the University of Trieste, where the study of terminology is aimed at the training of translators and interpreters, and research projects relating to terminology and terminography are emphasised; and a PhD course covering terminology in Linguistic, Terminological and Intercultural Studies, offered since 2008 at the Parthenope University of Naples. Through these various educational programmes, the study of terminology can offer new research paths for advancing national and international scientific reflection.

While translators and linguists have been gaining knowledge of the value of terminology through training, its relevance in every social, professional, humanistic, scientific, and technological sphere is not as well known. In addition to spreading awareness, showing a passion for rigour and precision in the use of terminology remains a primary objective of Ass.I.Term, which, thanks to the active contribution of its members, who include university professors and researchers, PhD students, members of national research centres, translators, school teachers and freelancers, continues to carry out targeted training, dissemination and awareness-raising actions in the field of terminology. These actions, in synergy with those carried out in Italy by research centres, laboratories, academic faculties and PhD courses, have led to a broader recognition of the field of terminology research in the academic and extra-academic spheres. Although there is still a lack of funding available for some activities in the field of terminology and terminography, and thus the realisation of ambitious, wide-ranging projects cannot be guaranteed, the field of terminology studies in Italy continues to be enriched by works that are contributing to the consolidation of reference materials and a disciplinary tradition in the fields of terminology and terminography that is at least equal to those of other European countries, many of whose study programmes are more established and reference works more historically consolidated.

References

Adamo, Giovanni, and Valeria Della Valle. 2017. *Che cos'è un neologismo*. Roma: Carocci.

Adamo, Giovanni, and Valeria Della Valle (eds). 2018. *Il Vocabolario Treccani. Neologismi. Parole nuove dai giornali* 2008–2018. Roma: Istituto della Enciclopedia Italiana.

Altieri Biagi, Maria Luisa. 1965. *Galileo e la terminologia tecnico-scientifica*. Firenze: Olschki.

Altieri Biagi, Maria Luisa. 1990. *L'avventura della mente. Studi sulla lingua scientifica dal Due al Settecento*. Napoli: Morano.

Altmanova, Jana, Maria Centrella, and Katherine E. Russo (eds). 2018. *Terminology & Discourse/Terminologie et discours*. Bern: Peter Lang.

Antonelli, Giuseppe, Matteo Motolese, and Lorenzo Tomasin (eds). 2014. *Storia dell'italiano scritto. III: Italiano dell'uso*. Roma: Carocci.

Arcangeli, Massimo. 2012. "Tra alti e bassi: l'italiano in borsa nell'era della globalizzazione." In *Lingua italiana e scienze. Atti del Convegno internazionale (Firenze, Villa Medicea di Castello, 6–8 febbraio 2003)*, ed. by Annalisa Nesi, and Domenico De Martino, 281–298. Firenze: Accademia della Crusca.

Balboni, Paolo E. 1982. "Le microlingue: considerazioni teoriche." *Scuola e lingue moderne* 20: 107–111.

Beccaria, Gian Luigi (ed). 1973. *I linguaggi settoriali in Italia*. Milano: Bompiani.

Beccaria, Gian Luigi. 2006. *Per difesa e per amore. La lingua italiana oggi*. Milano: Garzanti.

Berruto, Gaetano. 1974. *La sociolinguistica*. Bologna: Zanichelli.

Berruto, Gaetano. 1987. *Sociolinguistica dell'italiano contemporaneo*. Roma: La Nuova Italia Scientifica.

Berruto, Gaetano, and Monica Berretta (eds). 1977. *Lezioni di sociolinguistica e di linguistica applicata*. Napoli: Liguori.

Biffi, Marco. 2008. "La lingua tecnico-scientifica di Leonardo da Vinci." In *Prospettive nello studio del lessico italiano. Atti del IX Congresso SILFI (Firenze, 14–17 giugno 2006)*, ed. by Emanuela Cresti, 129–136. Firenze: Florence University Press.

Cavagnoli, Stefania. 2007. *La comunicazione specialistica*. Roma: Carocci.

Collesi, Patrizia, Anna Serpente, and Maria Teresa Zanola (eds). 2013. *Terminologie e ontologie. Definizioni e comunicazione fra norma e uso*. Milano: EDUCatt.

Conceição, Manuel Célio, and Maria Teresa Zanola (eds). 2020. *Terminologia e mediação linguística: métodos, práticas e atividades*. Faro: Universidade do Algarve.

Cortelazzo, Michele A. 1994. *Lingue speciali: la dimensione verticale*. Padova: Unipress.

Dardano, Maurizio. 1973. *Il linguaggio dei giornali italiani*. Bari: Laterza.

Dardano, Maurizio. 1994. "I linguaggi scientifici." In *Storia della lingua italiana*, ed. by Luca Serianni, and Pietro Trifone, 497–551. Torino: Einaudi.

De Mauro, Tullio. 2014. *Storia linguistica dell'Italia repubblicana*. Bari: Laterza.

Faini, Paola (ed). 2018. *Terminologia, linguaggi specialistici, traduzione. Prospettive teoriche e pratiche*. Trento: Tangram.

Gotti, Maurizio. 1991. *I linguaggi specialistici. Caratteristiche linguistiche e criteri pragmatici*. Firenze: La Nuova Italia.

Gotti, Maurizio. 2005. *Investigating Specialized Discourse*. Bern: Peter Lang.

Grimaldi, Claudio. 2017. *Discours et terminologie dans la presse scientifique française (1699–1740). La construction des lexiques de la botanique et de la chimie*. Oxford: Peter Lang.

Grimaldi, Claudio, and John Humbley. 2021. "How Metaphor Shaped Eighteenth Century Botanical Terminology in French." In *Variations on Metaphor*, ed. by Ilaria Rizzato, Francesca Strik Lievers, and Elisabetta Zurru, 128–142. Cambridge: Cambridge Scholars Publishing.

Grimaldi, Claudio, and Maria Teresa Zanola (eds). 2021. *Terminologie e vocabolari. Lessici specialistici e tesauri, glossari e dizionari*. Firenze: Florence University Press.

Grimaldi, Claudio, Eleonora Marzi, Paola Puccini, Maria Teresa Zanola, and Silvia Domenica Zollo (eds). 2022. *Terminologia e interculturalità. Problematiche e prospettive*. Città di Castello: I libri di Emil.

Gualdo, Riccardo. 2009a. "Linguaggi specialistici." In *XXI Secolo, vol. 2: Comunicare e rappresentare*, ed. by Tullio Gregory, 395–405. Roma: Istituto della Enciclopedia Italiana.

Gualdo, Riccardo. 2009b. "L'Ass.I.Term per la formazione in terminologia." *Publif@rum* 9.

Gualdo, Riccardo. 2016. "Linguaggi specialistici e settoriali." In *Manuale di linguistica italiana*, ed. by Sergio Lubello, 371–395. Berlin/Boston: de Gruyter.

Gualdo, Riccardo, and Stefano Telve. 2011. *Linguaggi specialistici dell'italiano*. Roma: Carocci.

Librandi, Rita, and Rosa Piro (eds). 2006. *Lo scaffale della biblioteca scientifica in volgare (secc. XIII–XVI). Atti del Convegno (Matera, 14–15 ottobre 2004)*. Firenze: SISMEL/Edizioni del Galluzzo.

Nencioni, Giovanni. 1984. "La lingua italiana oggi." *Pagine della Dante* LVIII–4: 1–6.

Nencioni, Giovanni. 1987. "Lessico tecnico e difesa della lingua." *Studi di lessicografia italiana* 9: 5–20.

Nencioni, Giovanni. 1994. "Linguistica e terminologia tecnico-scientifica." *Lexicon Philosophicum. Quaderni di terminologia filosofica e storia delle idee* 7: 5–12.

Nencioni, Giovanni. 1997. "Evoluzione storica della lingua nazionale." *Comunicazioni sociali* XIX: 116–119.

Nesi, Annalisa, and Domenico De Martino (eds). 2012. *Lingua italiana e scienze. Atti del Convegno internazionale (Firenze, Villa Medicea di Castello, 6–8 febbraio 2003)*. Firenze: Accademia della Crusca.

Ondelli, Stefano. 2019. "Che cosa intendiamo per 'linguaggi settoriali e specialistici'? Evoluzione terminologica e prospettive di ricerca." In *Parole nostre: le diverse voci dell'italiano specialistico e settoriale. Atti del XV Congresso della Società internazionale di Linguistica e Filologia italiana*, ed. by Jacqueline Visconti, 77–95. Bologna: il Mulino.

Prandi, Michele, Anna Giaufret, and Micaela Rossi (eds). 2013. *Il ruolo della metafora nella creazione di terminologie*. Genova: Genoa University Press.

Raus, Rachele. 2013. *La terminologie multilingue*. Bruxelles: De Boeck.

Rovere, Giovanni. 2010. "Linguaggi settoriali." In *Enciclopedia dell'Italiano*, ed. by Raffaele Simone, 804–806. Roma: Istituto della Enciclopedia Italiana 2010–2011.

Sergio, Giuseppe. 2010. *Parole di moda. Il "Corriere delle Dame" e il lessico della moda nell'Ottocento*. Milano: FrancoAngeli.

Serianni, Luca. 2012. *Italiani scritti*. Bologna: il Mulino.

Serianni, Luca. 2019. "I linguaggi specialistici nell'italiano di oggi: un territorio impoverito." In *Parole nostre: le diverse voci dell'italiano specialistico e settoriale. Atti del XV Congresso della Società internazionale di Linguistica e Filologia italiana*, ed. by Jacqueline Visconti, 21–36. Bologna: il Mulino.

Serianni, Luca, and Pietro Trifone (eds). 1994. *Storia della lingua italiana*. Torino: Einaudi.

Sobrero, Alberto A. 1993. "Lingue speciali." In *Introduzione all'italiano contemporaneo II: La variazione e gli usi*, ed. by Alberto A. Sobrero, 237–277. Bari/Roma: Laterza.

Zanola, Maria Teresa (ed). 2008. *Terminologie specialistiche e tipologie testuali*. Milano: EDUCatt.

Zanola, Maria Teresa (ed). 2012. *Costruire un glossario: la terminologia dei sistemi fotovoltaici*. Brescia: Vita e Pensiero.

Zanola, Maria Teresa. 2014a. "Attività terminologica e fonti di documentazione ieri e oggi: problemi e metodi." *Mediazioni* 16: 1–16.

Zanola, Maria Teresa. 2014b. *Arts et métiers au XVIIIe siècle. Essais de terminologie diachronique*. Paris: L'Harmattan.

Zanola, Maria Teresa. 2015. "La terminologia, una galleria della lingua: arti, mestieri e saperi per la trasmissione della conoscenza." *La Crusca per voi* 51(II): 2–8.

Zanola, Maria Teresa. 2018. *Che cos'è la terminologia*. Roma: Carocci.

Zanola, Maria Teresa, Carolina Diglio, and Claudio Grimaldi (eds). 2016. *Terminologie specialistiche e diffusione dei saperi*. Milano: EDUCatt.

Zollo, Silvia Domenica. 2020. *Origine et histoire du vocabulaire des arts de la table. Analyse lexicale et exploitation de corpus textuels*. Bern: Peter Lang.

CHAPTER 27

Terminology in North Macedonia
An evolutionary journey

Nikolche Mickoski
Macedonian Academy of Sciences and Arts

This chapter provides an overview of the development of Macedonian
terminology after the codification of the Macedonian language and the
initial efforts for drafting specialised terminology. It sheds light on the
participation of Macedonian linguists in collaborative terminology projects
in the former Yugoslavia and the International Committee of Slavists. It
elaborates on the importance of the *Dictionary of Macedonian Language,*
which laid the groundwork for future lexicographic and terminographic
projects. The chapter provides a detailed overview of the theoretical
foundations of the Macedonian Scientific and Professional Terminology
project which led to the publication of draft terminology in terminological
bulletins and terminological dictionaries. Blazhe Koneski is the most
significant scholar who contributed both theoretically and practically to the
development of Macedonian terminology.

Keywords: Macedonian, Koneski, Macedonian terminology, Macedonian
lexicon, Dictionary of Macedonian language, temporary terminology,
terminological bulletins, terminological dictionaries

1.   Beginnings of Macedonian terminology

Lexicography and terminology, although too often overlooked, have always played
an important role in the history of the Macedonian people. The history of Macedonian lexicography and terminology starts with the dictionary of four Balkan
languages by Daniel Moscopolites in 1794, which is the first printed text employing
Macedonian dialects, and continues with the dictionary of four languages and
the dictionary of three languages by Georgi Pulevski (Pulevski 1875). Macedonian
reformer Misirkov was the first to suggest that the Macedonian lexicon should be
sourced from all Macedonian dialects (Misirkov 1903: 145).

https://doi.org/10.1075/tlrp.24.27mic

1.1   Foundations of the Macedonian lexicon

Blazhe Koneski (1921–1993) is the most prominent Macedonian linguist. He built on the work of Macedonian reformers and cultural workers. Koneski was deeply involved in the activities regarding the codification of a standardised Macedonian language. He was a member of the Commission for Language and Orthography (Комисија за јазик и правопис), which proposed the Macedonian alphabet, later adopted by the People's Government of Federal Macedonia in 1945, and he also worked on the proposal for Macedonian orthography which was adopted by the Ministry of Education in 1945. He was very interested in and devoted to the lexical enrichment and terminology modelling of the Macedonian language and he greatly contributed to the establishment and development of modern Macedonian lexicography and terminology.

Following the codification of the modern Macedonian language, Koneski tried to raise awareness among Macedonian scholars about the task that they would be confronted with in the future. He predicted that adopting abstract terms in the language would be very important.

> Once a language is formed as a standard language, first and foremost, it will be confronted with the need to enrich the vocabulary with many abstract words. [...] Vernacular language gives us just enough to express the phenomena of everyday life. On the other hand, the standard language should express all the complexity of contemporary artistic and scientific thought. It should independently satisfy the need it is confronted with — being still unelaborated, unarmed — that it is faced with the immediate need, with all the persistence, to adopt a large number of terms from scientific, social, public, political, and cultural life. Actually, this is one of the most important and most specific efforts employed on the young standard language.   (Koneski 1946: 35)[1]

There were two different considerations and suggestions regarding abstract terms. The first Commission for the Macedonian language, alphabet, and spelling, established by the Presidium of ASNOM (Anti-fascist Assembly for the National Liberation of Macedonia), prepared a Study (State Archive of the Republic of North Macedonia: 1944) recommending that abstract words in the standard Macedonian language be borrowed from Russian because, in their view, the latter was rich in abstract terms. The second Commission did not accept this recommendation. Koneski, as a member of the second Commission, argued that Macedonian folklore had a very long and rich tradition and that it had sufficient expressions that could be used as terms denoting abstract concepts. The second Commission reached the final decision that the Macedonian lexicon should be enriched with

---

1. All translations in this chapter have been done by the author.

words originating from all Macedonian dialects; new words should be formed using productive suffixes; foreign words should be borrowed also, but only as necessary (Koneski 1952: 56).

Koneski was aware that terminology would be a paramount challenge awaiting Macedonian linguists.

> The young standard language was confronted with the challenge posed by modern means of communication, as well as by all forms of cultural and social life it was meant to serve. Therefore, there were calls to start lexicographic work as soon as possible. (Koneski 1981: 130)

Following the codification of the Macedonian language, Koneski declared that drafting the Macedonian general-language dictionary as well as terminological dictionaries was the most pressing linguistic task. He accepted both challenges, and took a leading role in the implementation of the projects.

1.2   Macedonian terminology after the Second World War

The need for scientific and professional terminology in Macedonian was recognised immediately after the Second World War, when the language started to be taught in schools. Both teachers and students needed harmonised Macedonian terms from various subject fields.

1.2.1   *Temporary terminology*

In response to the need for standardised terminology, the Macedonian Ministry of Education established a commission tasked to draft a list of terms for the subjects taught in schools such as grammar, geography, nature, pedagogy, psychology, mathematics, physics, and chemistry. In 1947, the Ministry of Education published the *Времена терминологија* (*Vremena terminologija*) [Temporary Terminology] as a word list of about 5,500 terms in alphabetical order without definitions for use in schools as well as for translations from various languages into Macedonian. The document was called Temporary Terminology because it was meant to provide terms that were to be used for a limited period of time until standard terms could be defined. Most of the terms introduced by the Temporary Terminology were accepted by users and are still used today. Examples of these terms are *дропка* (*dropka*) ('fraction'), *именител* (*imenitel*) ('denominator'), *броител* (*broitel*) ('numerator'), *потсвест* (*potsvest*) ('subconsciousness'), and *образование* (*obrazovanie*) ('education'). Other terms were not accepted by the users and were replaced with new and more suitable terms. Examples of these terms are *вадење* (*vadenje*) ('deduction') replaced by *одземање* (*odzemanje*), *нараснување* (*narasnuvanje*) ('increase') replaced by *зголемување* (*zgolemuvanje*), *тек број* (*tek broj*) ('odd number') replaced by *непарен број* (*neparen broj*), and *чифт број* (*chift broj*) ('even number') replaced by *парен број* (*neparen broj*). In the word list of geographic terminology, some toponyms, predominantly country names, were incorrect. Such examples are *Данија* (*Danija*) for Denmark instead of the correct *Данска* (*Danska*), *Ејре/ирланд* (*Ejre/irland*) for Ireland instead of *Ирска* (*Irska*), and *Китај* (*Kitaj*) for China instead of *Кина* (*Kina*). The importance of this work is that it provided teachers and students with important and frequent terms and prevented the use of different terms for denoting the same concept.

1.2.2 *Efforts for standardisation of specialised terminology*

Professionals recognised the need for drafting appropriate Macedonian terms in order to denote the concepts they used in their work. In journals, they paid special attention to the challenges they encountered when trying to find the most suitable term for a concept. For example, Bojanovski (1951: 88–92) provided a list of terms with definitions from political economy originating from his translation of all three volumes of Marx's *Das Capital* from German into Macedonian. Gjorgjeski (1952: 185–188) analysed a number of legal and economic terms used in Macedonian laws and regulations and suggested more suitable ones for some concepts. Koneski (1952: 90–92) observed that professional terminology was created in this context on an ad hoc basis and that this could be to the detriment of the Macedonian language. He favoured public discussion regarding terminology because it provides a platform for coordination between professionals and linguists. Koneski appealed to professionals to learn the grammatical rules governing Macedonian, and apply those rules when creating new terms, which they were frequently required to do without the advice of qualified linguists.

2.   Macedonian terminology in a broader context

North Macedonia was part of the Socialist Federal Republic of Yugoslavia, initially as the People's Republic of Macedonia (1944–1963) and then as the Socialist Republic of Macedonia (1963–1991), until its declaration of independence in 1991, when it became the Republic of Macedonia under its constitutional name. Macedonian scholars followed the initiatives for the unification of national terminologies and the publishing of terminological dictionaries in all fields of knowledge. Macedonian representatives actively participated in the working groups and commissions for terminological dictionaries established in the former Yugoslavia and within the International Committee of Slavists.

2.1   Macedonian terminology in the Yugoslavian context

Specialists from various scientific and professional areas in the former Yugoslavia identified the need to use harmonised and specialised terminologies in various areas. Thus, numerous working groups were formed, featuring representatives and linguists from all official languages in the former Yugoslavia, including Macedonian. Specialists from various scientific and professional areas also participated. The work of the working groups resulted in terminological dictionaries being published in various domains including pure sciences (Михайлов et al. 1969), metallurgy (Gaković et al. 1971), archival science (Androić 1972), and the military (Avramović et al. 1982). The geodetic dictionary (Stefanović 1980) contains equivalents in eight languages. Macedonian translation equivalents were prepared and published beforehand as a geodetic dictionary (Lazarov 1978).

2.2   Macedonian terminology and the International Committee of Slavists

Macedonian scholars contributed to the terminological dictionaries prepared by the working groups within the International Committee of Slavists. In 1977, the first volume of the *Slovník slovanské lingvistické terminologie* [Dictionary of Slavonic Linguistic Terminology] (Jedlička 1977) was published in Prague. It included 2,226 systematically organised terms and their equivalents in eleven Slavonic languages (Czech, Slovakian, Polish, Lusatian Sorbian, Russian, Ukrainian, Belorussian, Bulgarian, Macedonian, Serbo-Croatian, Slovenian) and in three western languages (English, French, German). The second volume of the Dictionary (Jedlička 1979) included alphabetical indexes of terms in all 14 languages. Macedonian translation equivalents were provided by Vidoevski, Ugrinova-Skalovska, Koneski, and Toshev and were taken up by Macedonian scholars and authors. Nevertheless, some Macedonian translation equivalents were deemed obsolete and improved translation equivalents were provided and used. For example, *еднозначен збор* (*ednoznachen zbor*) replaced the term *моносемантичен збор* (*moonsemantichen zbor*) for 'monosemantic word,' *основен елемент* (*osnoven element*) replaced the term *базисен елемент* (*bazisen element*) for 'basic element,' the spelling of the word for 'slang' changed from the transliterated *сланг* (*slang*) to transcribed *сленг* (*sleng*). This dictionary is the only dictionary of linguistic terminology containing terms in Macedonian. The Lexicographic centre at the Macedonian Academy of Sciences and Arts has been working on a dictionary of linguistic terms, which will be published in the near future.

In 1983, the Macedonian Academy of Sciences and Arts published a joint work of Slavic scholars titled "*Основен систем и терминологија на словенската ономастика*" [Basic system and terminology of Slavic onomastics] (Vidoevski

1983) describing a system for Slavic onomastics, including the related terminology. This terminological dictionary was an attempt to unify onomastic terms in eleven Slavic languages and in German, with definitions provided in Macedonian, Russian, and German. It also focussed on harmonising linguistic and geographical terminology. The aim of the publication was to encourage the use of harmonised terminology and to employ the principle of concept orientation for synonymous words. Vidoevski published a bulletin on onomastic terminology (1984), which adopted the same terminology as defined in the previous publication, thus reinforcing harmonised Macedonian terminology in the field of onomastics.

3.   Dictionary of the Macedonian language

After the second world war, Koneski was the most prominent scholar who recognised the pressing need of drafting a Macedonian dictionary. He published several papers about the Macedonian lexicon (1945, 1946, 1950) where he called for the collection and arrangement of lexicon-related material. According to Koneski, "The Macedonian standard language should be truly Macedonian" (1946: 38) with its unique structure derived from the vernacular language. He noted that the Macedonian language is by no means lacking in words, and that Macedonians should use each and every word rooted in the lexical richness of folk songs and folk tales, as well as various dialects (see also Chapter 18).

The task of drafting a dictionary of the Macedonian language and elaborating unified terminology was also recognised as high priority in the Prologue of the journal *Makedonski jazik* (Editorial board 1950: 1–2), which stated that Macedonian linguists should work to create terminology in all areas.

3.1   Preparatory work

The watershed moment for creating a dictionary of the Macedonian language occurred in 1951, when the Ministry of Education of the People's Republic of Macedonia established a three-member commission, presided over by Koneski, with a mandate to produce the dictionary. For some terms, especially for terms denoting tools, a visual representation was included. According to the guidelines (Editorial 1951: 27) the dictionary would play a major role in the development of standard Macedonian because it would enrich the lexicon, it would introduce folk words to replace the flood of foreign words that were infiltrating written texts, it would create the necessary terminologies, and it would present the rich Macedonian lexicon to the public.

People from all over the country submitted terms from different subject areas. For instance, more than one hundred terms were provided by Radoslav Petkovski, subsequently presented in six editions of *Makedonski jazik*. Most of these terms belonged to ornithology and botany. Markov (1953: 11–17) analysed the material submitted by the public and provided additional guidelines, explaining the necessity for common terms that were used regularly to be submitted instead of terms known only by few, and that definitions should be provided whenever possible. The dictionary was published in three volumes between 1961 and 1966 and laid the groundwork for future lexicographic and terminology projects.

4.   Macedonian scientific and professional terminology

The Macedonian Academy of Sciences and Arts (MASA — Македонска академија на науките и уметностите) was established in 1967, under the presidency of the academician Blazhe Koneski. MASA immediately recognised the need to draft a national terminology, and its first long-term project, led by Koneski, focussed on Macedonian scientific and professional terminology (MSPT). In order to lay the grounds for the project, two bodies were established: the Macedonian Terminology Board and Linguistic Commission, with Koneski acting as president of both.

4.1   Theoretical foundations of Macedonian terminology

The main responsibilities of the Linguistic Commission were to provide language-related guidelines for the MSPT project, offer advice to the expert commissions, revise drafts and approve final versions of the terminology dictionaries prior to their publication. In 1971, it published a methodology for the terminology work. The Commission recognised the need for suitable terms to represent new or emerging concepts and stressed that advancements in science go hand in hand with advancements in language.

> Terms, those language signs, represent facts and notions that are an integral part of every science. This means that science cannot progress without language, just as language cannot develop without improving the science and that no matter how sufficient facts are, no matter how correct hypotheses based on facts are, they will only produce an incorrect impression if we do not have correct terms to denote them. (Theses 1971: 3)

The Linguistic Commission determined that new terms in the Macedonian language appeared *ad hoc*, usually when a specialist needed to designate a new concept. These specialists were experts in their respective fields, not in linguistics. Therefore, to denote new concepts, they often opted to use terms originating in a foreign language, sometimes adapting them through transliteration or transcription. Occasionally they created their own terms, some of which violated language rules (morphology). Another challenge occurred when specialists introduced different terms for the same concept, leading to synonyms and other inconsistencies. On the other hand, an even bigger problem arose when the same term was used to denote different concepts. The Commission concluded that terminological dictionaries would address these problems. Since the ultimate goal of the MSPT project was to draft terminological dictionaries from various fields, it was decided that the material would be presented in the form of thematic terminological bulletins so that people working in the field could provide feedback.

Since the process of creating a rational terminology is conducted in several phases, the Linguistic Commission provided guidelines for each phase of work of the expert terminological commissions (Theses 1971: 5–7). The first phase involves identifying and manually extracting the key terms in a given subject field and providing precise definitions by the terminologists. The terms should be extracted from representative works, such as textbooks and manuals, papers, debates, journals, with a focus on the fields in which there is a constant influx of new terms. Gaps in the resulting lists should be filled with terms obtained from foreign books or foreign terminological dictionaries. The terms from these sources should be translated into Macedonian or adapted to Macedonian language norms.

The second phase involves classifying the terms through a systematisation and classification of the underlying concepts. The Linguistic Commission (Theses 1971: 6) proposed two manners of presentation: in alphabetical order and in "clusters." It noted that dictionaries in alphabetical order were shorter and cheaper to produce than dictionaries with clustered terms, but one cannot get adequate insight into the overall terminology to determine, for example, which concepts are not represented by a term or which concepts are expressed by more than one term (resulting in unwanted synonymy). As an alternative to alphabetical order, the Commission recommended clustering terms in groups according to their meanings (concept orientation) because this manner of presentation provides a clearer picture of concepts and the range of terms that denote them, and permits relations between the concepts to be established. In addition, clustering terms semantically enables the position of the term, in relation to similar terms, to be identified. According to Lotte (1961: 72–73), scientific terminology should not be a simple collection of words, but a system of words or phrases connected in a certain way with each other. The Commission opted for the theoretical approach defined by the Russian school of terminology (see also Chapter 10) and recommended that terminology work should follow the basic principles for creating a terminological system and the requirements for the terms included in the terminological system as defined by Lotte (1961: 18–36): monosemy, correctness, consistency, linguistic economy, and derivability. Moreover, it provided explanations for some of the basic principles mentioned above (Theses 1971: 11–13). It also provided additional guidelines for reasonable elimination of terminological synonymy (14–15), stating that the term should be free from undesirable associations, harmonised with established terms, linguistically correct, frequently used, and, if it is a strictly scientific term, it should follow the international terminology. This means that striving to use Macedonian terms in spite of everything can result in creating impossible, artificial, and incomprehensible constructions. For example, instead of inventing Macedonian terms for 'vector' and 'scalar,' the transliterated terms *вектор* (*vektor*) and *скалар* (*skalar*) should be used.

Regarding the use of foreign terms for denoting concepts, the Linguistic Commission stated that overburdening terminology with foreign terms should be avoided, but it recognised that there is not a single language in the world that is able to use only domestic/native terms. While linguistic borrowing is inevitable and a common process, if there is a domestic term for a given concept, it should be preferred over the foreign one. Nevertheless, the insistence on using domestic terms at all costs (purism) can lead to creating improbable and artificial constructions that are barely understandable (Theses 1971: 15). Additionally, if there are synonymous terms denoting the same concept, and each term meets some of the criteria, it might be reasonable to retain both albeit with a functional distinction (16). Functional distinction in this context means that a context should be provided for each of the terms so that the user can reach an informed decision about which term is suitable for use. For example, *идно време* (*idno vreme*) ('future tense') should be used in primary school textbooks, while the term *футур* (*futur*) ('future tense') should be used in research papers.

In the terminology bulletins, a template was provided for each of the two manners of presentation: alphabetical and semantically clustered (Theses 1971: 19–20) (Figure 1 and Figure 2).

АГЕНС ЗА ЖЕЛИРАЊЕ
Сх. агенс за желирање
E.   gelling agent
D.   Gelatiniermittel
F.   gélatinisant
P.   желатинирующий агент

Средство што овозможува желирање
(желатинирање).

АГЕНС ЗА ЛАДЕЊЕ
Сх. Агенс за хладење
E.   cooling agent
D.   Kälteträger, Kühlmittel
F.   Agent de refroidissement
P.   охлаждающий агент

Средство (средина) за ладење -
за одземање на топлина.

АГЛОМЕРАЦИЈА
Сх. агломерација
E.   agglomeration
D.   Agglomerierung
F.   agglomération
P.   агломерация; спекание

Собирање или натрупување на честички
од супстанца.

АГРЕГАТ
Сх. агрегат
E.   aggregate
D.   Aggregat
F.   agrégat
P.   агрегат

Маса со различни (по големина)
составни делови.

АГРЕСИВНИ ОТПАДНИ ВОДИ
Сх. агресивне отпадне воде
E.   corrosive waster-water
D.   agressive Abwässer
F.   eaux résiduaires aggrésives
P.   агрессивные сточные воды

Отпадни води што вршат агресија
на околината (корозија).

АГРЕСИВНОСТ
Сх. агресивност
E.   aggressiveness
D.   Aggressivität
F.   agressivité
P.   агрессивность

Напаѓање, Нагризување или нарушу-
вање на некоја материја од хемика-
лии(киселини, бази и сл.).

АГРОХЕМИЈА
Сх. агрохемија
E.   agricultural chemistry
D.   Agrikulturchemie
F.   chimie agricole
P.   агрохимия

Хемија која се занимава со испи-
тување на влијанието на земјата
врз исхраната и составот на кул-
турните растенија.

Figure 1. Terms presented in alphabetical order

```
05-15-075
МОЖНОСТ НА ИЗОЛАЦИЈАТА           Општ израз што се употребува
Сх -                            за означување на способноста
Sl. izolacijska zmožnost,       и употребливоста на некоја
    izolacijska zmogljivost      материја како изолатор.
Е.  insulating propriety
F.  pouvoir isolant
D.  Isoliervermögen
P.  -
```

```
05-15-080
ИЗОЛИРА (ДА СЕ ИЗОЛИРА)          Да се спречи спроводникот да
Сх. изолирати                   дојде до контакт меѓу него и
Sl. izolirati                   и соседниот спроводник, а со
Е.  to insulate                 употреба на соодветна матери-
F.  isoler                      ја за изолирање.
D.  Isolieren
P.  изолировать
```

```
05-15-085
ИЗОЛАЦИЈА                       1. Сите изолатори кои се упо-
Сх. изолација                      требуваат во конструкциите
Sl. izolacija                      на машините или апаратите.
Е.  insulation                  2. Со овој термин се означува
F.  isolation                      исто така условот да се
D.  Isolation                      биде изолиран.
P.  изоляция
```

```
05-15-090
ИЗОЛИРАН                        Квалитет, односно својство
Сх. изолиран                    постигнато со материјалите за
Sl. izoliranost, izolacijsko    изолација.
    stanje
Е.  insulated
F.  isolement
D.  Isolation (szustand),
    Isolierung, isoliert
P.  изолированный
```

```
05-15-095
ДИЕЛЕКТРИК                      Средина (медиум на материја)
Сх. диелектрик                  во која лесно стационарно оп-
Sl. dielektrik                  станува електрично поле.
Е.  dielectric
F.  diélectrique
D.  Dielektrikum
P.  диэлектрик
```

Figure 2. Clustered terms

4.2   Terminological bulletins and terminological dictionaries

In the early days of the MSPT project, the activities undertaken led to the creation of terminological bulletins and terminological dictionaries. Terminological bulletins are collections of terms from various subject fields. For each field, a separate terminological commission was established consisting of university professors, linguists, and professionals working in the relevant field. Over 25 specialised terminology commissions with more than 160 members were established with the task of preparing draft terminologies from different subject fields. Each commission prepared a set of terms in Macedonian with definitions and translation equivalents and published them in a terminological bulletin. The bulletins were distributed to universities, state institutions, libraries etc. and were reviewed by professionals as well as the general public. The commissions updated the terms and definitions according to feedback received. When there were enough acceptable and approved terms, a terminological dictionary was published. An example of this workflow can be found in the early published bulletins. The first terminological bulletin, published in 1971, contained a list of about 6,000 terms in Macedonian in the field of architectural construction. The two terminological bulletins published the following year were updated according to remarks, comments, and suggestions from the relevant stakeholders. University professors (Kardelev, Trajkovski, and Organdziev 1972: 18–31) provided remarks, comments, and suggestions which were systematically grouped as language-related comments, comments on the vagueness of some terms (due to the missing definitions), incorrect and unsuitable terms with supporting explanations and suggestions for more suitable replacements, as well as suggestions for improving awkward terms. In addition, there were comments and suggestions from language professionals, as well as architects, and comments from the Institute for architectural studies and design of the largest Macedonian construction company, Beton.

The first dictionary published in the MSPT project was about the terminology of sociology (Chokrevski et al. 1995), 20 years after the publication of the first terminological bulletin on sociology.

Even though the Linguistic Commission favoured the clustered arrangement in the Theses, for unknown reasons, the alphabetical order was used almost exclusively in its terminological bulletins. Only two bulletins — for electrotechnics and botany/zoology — adopted the clustered arrangement.

The Commission predicted that it would take at least 10 years to complete the implementation of the MSPT project, yet, the MSPT project has been part of the long-term programme of MASA since it was established and new terminological dictionaries are published regularly. A detailed overview of the MSPT project is provided by Mitevski (2015: 19–31) and Mickoski (2020: 55–61). The Commission provided a list of 29 subject areas that should be prioritised (Theses 1971: 16–17). Since the beginning of the project over 50 years ago, 114 terminological bulletins and 6 terminological dictionaries have been published, a significant terminological resource that contributes to the standardisation and proper use of harmonised terminology in the Macedonian language.

5.   Conclusion

Macedonian terminology has shown rapid growth and development since the codification of the standard Macedonian language. The progress achieved proves that the decision to develop terminology by using words from Macedonian folklore was a wise one. As Koneski stated, when standardising the language, Macedonian linguists did not need to create anything new, rather they adapted, codified, reframed and contextualised language that already existed. Just as the foundations of the language existed, so too did the elements of terminology, and the challenge was to connect the terms that already existed in folklore with the concepts that they can denote. The Macedonian Scientific and Professional Terminology project continues to define and harmonise scientific and professional terminology through its dictionaries in many subject fields, and Macedonian scholars continue to follow the footpath of their predecessors by taking inspiration from the rich treasure trove of Macedonian folklore when developing domain-specific terminology.

References

Androić, Mirko (ed). 1972. *Rječnik arhivske terminologije Jugoslavije: hrvatsko, srpsko, slovensko, makedonski, englesko, francusko, njemačko, rusko, talijanski*. Zagreb: Savez Drustava Arhivskih Radnika Jugoslavije.

Avramović, Dušan, and Petar Petrović (eds). 1982. *Uporedni rečnik vojnih pojmova, srpskohrvatski, makedonski, slovenački, albanski, mađarski*. Beograd: Vojnoizdavački zavod.

Bojanovski, Dime. 1951. "За некои термини од политичката економија." *Преглед* No. 1: 88–92.

Chokrevski, Tomislav et al.. 1995. *Социолошки терминолошки речник*. Skopje: Faculty of Philosophy and Macedonian Academy of Sciences and Arts.

Editorial board. 1950. "Уводна реч." *Македонски јазик* I, No. 1: 1–2.

Editorial. 1951. "За речникот на македонскиот јазик." *Македонски јазик* II, No. 2: 25–28.

Gaković, Nikola (ed). 1971. *Metalurški rečnik: iz oblasti crne metalurgije: sa odgovarajućim izrazima na srpskohrvatskom, slovenačkom, makedonskom, engleskom, francuskom, nemačkom i ruskom jeziku*. Beograd: Udruženje jugoslovenskih železara.

Gjorgjeski, Boshko. 1952. "За некои нерасчистени прашања на нашата правна и економска терминологија." *Македонски јазик* No. 8–9: 185–188.

Jedlička, Alois (ed). 1977. *Slovník slovanské lingvistické terminologie I*. Praha: Academia Praha.

Jedlička, Alois (ed). 1979. *Slovník slovanské lingvistické terminologie II*. Praha: Academia Praha.

Kardelev, Petar, Strezo Trajkovski, and Angel Organdziev. 1972. "Забелешки кон објавените термини од областа на архитектонските конструкции." *Билтен на одборот за изработување на македонска терминологија*, year II, No. 1: 18–31. Macedonian Academy of Sciences and Arts.

Koneski, Blazhe. 1945. "Одживените речнички елементи во нашиот јазик." *Нов ден* I, No. 3: 3–8.

Koneski, Blazhe. 1946. "Белешки за речникот на нашиот јазик." *Нов ден* II, No. 7–8: 35–50.

Koneski, Blazhe. 1950. "Македонскиот јазик денеска." *Социјалистичка зора* II, No. 1: 1–22.

Koneski, Blazhe. 1952. "За правната и економската терминологија." *Македонски јазик* No. 4: 90–92.

Koneski, Blazhe. 1952. *Граматика на македонскиот литературен јазик. Дел* 1. Skopje: State Publishing House of PR Macedonia.

Koneski, Blazhe. 1981. "Македонскиот речник." In *Јазични теми* 128–140. Misla.

Lazarov, Dime. 1978. *Многујазичен геодетски речник на FIG*. Skopje: Сојуз на геодетските инженери и техничари на Македонија.

Linguistic commission of Macedonian Academy of Sciences and Arts. 1971. "Тези за работата врз македонската терминологија." *Билтен на Одборот за изработување на македонска терминологија* 1: 3–17.

Lotte, Dmitrij Semenovich [Лотте, Дмитрий Семенович]. 1961. *Основы построения научно-технической терминологии. Вопросы теории и методики*. Москва: Издательство академии наук СССР.

Markov, Boris. 1953. "Забелешки за лексичкиот материјал во Билтенот". *Македонски јазик* No. IV: 11–17.

Mickoski, Nikolche. 2020. "Макропроектот Македонска научна и стручна терминологија — тековна состојба и идни активности." *Bulletin of the Terminology Commission under the International Committee of Slavonic Scholars*: 55–61.

Mihailov, Alexandr Ivanovich [Михайлов, Александр Иванович] (ed). 1969. *Терминологический словарь по научной информации (на русском, сербохорватском, словенском и македонском языках)*. Beograd: Institut za naučno-tehničku dokumentaciju i informacije.

Misirkov, Krste. 1903. *За македонцките работи*. Sofia: Printing House of the Liberal Club.

Mitevski, Vitomir. 2015. "Македонската стручна и научна терминологија. Достигнувања, состојби, перспективи." In *Македонската апстрактна терминологија и нејзиното наследство*, 19–31. Skopje: Matica Makedonska.

Pulevski, Georgi. 1875. *Речник от три језика*. Belgrade: State Printing House.

State Archive of the Republic of North Macedonia. 1944. *Елаборат на Комисијата за установуене на македонски литературен јазик, азбука и правопис*. Фонд Президиум на АСНОМ К — 8. Skopje.

Stefanović, Milutin (ed). 1980. *Višejezični geodetski rečnik*. Beograd: Savez geodetskih inženjera i geometara Jugoslavije.

Vidoevski, Bozhidar (ed). 1983. "*Основен систем и терминологија на словенската ономастика*." Skopje: Macedonian Academy of Sciences and Arts.

Vidoevski, Bozhidar. 1984. *Ономастичка терминологија*. Skopje: Macedonian Academy of Sciences and Arts.

CHAPTER 28

Terminology in Slovakia
A path towards autonomy

Jana Levická & Miroslav Zumrík
Slovak Academy of Sciences

This chapter aims to portray the development of Slovak terminology in the 20th century with respect to the long historical coexistence of the Slovak and Czech nations, their culture and languages. Throughout the century, the Slovak and Czech languages were in a dynamic relationship where more than one tendency as well as several historical and paradigmatic shifts occurred. This fact raises the question of what factors are at play and what strategies are at hand when terminologies of different languages are being unified in a common state. The chapter seeks to answer at least some of these questions by drawing a historical picture, presenting terminological case studies and introducing several philosophical concepts.

Keywords: Slovak language, Czech language, Czechoslovakia, lesser used languages, principles of terminological work, standard language, codification, philosophy of language, language contacts

1.   Introduction

This chapter describes, analyses and interprets the historical and developmental directions that Slovak terminology took in the 20th century. Research into lesser used languages and their terminologies could provide new knowledge about the mechanisms and dynamics that lie behind the development of a language and terminology and what can be learned about the possible transnational application of this dynamic.

The 20th century provides enough material over a relatively long enough period of time for observing developmental tendencies. But even more important, it was during this century that the very existence and usefulness of autonomous Slovak terminology was successfully defended and its most rapid growth took place in both its quality and usage. It was also a period of substantial political and ideological changes, volatility, revisions and reconfiguration of both Slovak

https://doi.org/10.1075/tlrp.24.28lev

and Czech terminology. By the same token, the 20th century represents a recent past, resonating into the present day. From the historical point of view, this means the desire to treat the topic through the prism of the long-lasting relationship between the culture and languages of Slovaks and Czechs,[1] in particular over the years they lived and interacted together in the single country that *de facto* existed between 1918 and 1939 and again from 1945 to 1993, but also prior to these periods. Presented and reflected here is the claim by Eugen Pauliny that the Slovak language throughout its history has been in a constant dialectical relationship with the Czech language and terminology (1964:5). Naturally, this relationship will be analysed here from the Slovak perspective.

Three main issues are discussed, the first of which is how Slovak language and terminology developed over time. Here, the objective is to describe the changing coexistence between the Slovak and the Czech language. The second addresses terminological principles and practices for building terminologies, which have continued since Slovak was first codified. The final interpretative and conclusive part presents some concepts and models that are being applied to the relationship between both languages.

Methodologically speaking, terminology in any given language represents a specific lexical domain and it cannot be reduced to just one of the functional styles (see Chapter 9), given that terminology is a scientific discipline that takes into account the relationship between the term and the concept that the term designates (Horecký 1974:129). Terminology dynamics can thus underlie principles that need not be identical with those governing other sub-disciplines of linguistics.

2.   Slovak and Czech prior to the first codification of Slovak

Czech historian Jan Rychlík (2015:14) notes that the history of present-day Czech Republic and of Slovakia are asynchronous. The asynchronicity of the development of standard language/terminology in Czech and Slovak might even have contributed to the fact that historical linguistics and terminology in these two languages accentuate different main points of research interest. While Slovak linguists and terminologists aimed at establishing a genuine, autonomous Slovak terminology via both cooperation with and delimitation from their Czech counterparts, Czech terminologists, who were already more advanced, focussed on the development of structuralist ideas (which, nevertheless, were also present in

---

1. For a thorough treatment of the topic, see Pauliny (1966).

Slovak linguistics, see Ľubomír Novák (1935)). The outlined difference in the Slovak and Czech linguistic and terminological perspectives is reflected in Chapter 9.

The different "starting lines" (Lipowski 2005:9) for both nations result from the fact that except for the short period of Great Moravia (833–907), which united parts of present-day Slovakia and the Czech Republic, both Czechs and Slovaks experienced separate development throughout the centuries within different political entities. Their distinct development remained unchanged when the crowns of Bohemia (territory of the present-day Czech Republic) and Hungary (which included present-day Slovakia until the end of 12th century) were unified in 1490 under two Jagellonian kings and both kingdoms were incorporated into the Habsburg monarchy in 1526. The Kingdom of Hungary managed to retain special status within the monarchy with its own specific administration, legal system, culture (including the status of Protestant denominations) and economy, which contributed to the perception of the Slovaks as both similar to and different from Czechs.

In the early medieval period prior to the coronation of St. Stephen in 1000, when present-day Slovakia (then called Upper Hungary) came under the control of Árpád's tribal confederation, Latin was the dominant or lone language of state administration, education and culture, as well as of the church. However, in the 14th and 15th centuries, dialects and regional variants of Slovak started to penetrate into administrative communication and law, which is attested from court documents, such as rulings conveyed to disputing sides (Pauliny 1966:17). Therefore, the beginning of legal and administrative terminology in Slovak can be traced to the High Middle Ages.

In the 15th century, Czech started to be used in Upper Hungary in written, formal communication as a "cultural language,"[2] since it was close to Slovak, intelligible and already standardised. It met the local population's need for a written form of a "common means of communication"[3] (Pauliny 1966:30). The presence of Czech was further strengthened with the onset of the Reformation, the religious struggles in Bohemia and the migration of Czech Protestants in the 17th century to Upper Hungary, where Protestants adopted the Czech of 1613 Kralice Bible as their liturgical language. Slowly but steadily Slovak lexical and grammatical elements infiltrated the written Czech language used in Slovak-speaking areas,

---

2. Language used for "higher form" of communication, in contrast to folk language. In terms of the history of Slovak language, cultural language includes all "higher," more cultured or cultivated means of communications used in writing for cultural communication.

3. All translations of terms and citations from Slovak or Czech into English in this chapter were provided by the authors.

while the process of "Slovakisation," at the same time, gradually led to a language that "no longer could be considered Slovak Czech" (Pauliny 1966: 78).

National integration advanced as people migrated within Upper Hungary and communication intensified between the two languages, and because Slovaks had no significant economic, political or cultural centre, several supra-regional forms of Slovak evolved into West, Central and East supraregional, supradialectal prestige varieties.

The impetus for the first attempt to standardise Slovak emerged in Bratislava and was based upon the "cultural language" of Trnava, a lively centre of culture and learning as well as of an archdiocese. The language was codified by Anton Bernolák in 1787 from Western dialects combined with some structural elements taken from the Central supraregional variety of Slovak.

Progress by Bernolák in standardising the language was eventually halted because of factors like the response to the Enlightenment, resistance by the Catholic Church hierarchy, and the decreasing prestige of Western Slovakia toward the turn of the 19th century (Pauliny 1966: 100).

Bernolák's contribution to Slovak terminology development can be deduced from his works. The lexicographical section of his *Etymologia vocum Slavicarum* [Etymology of Slovak words] (1791) facilitated the consolidation of contemporary terminology (Habovštiaková 1962) especially in the field of grammar. Even though his major scholarly works (the *Dissertatio philologico-critica de literis Slavorum* [Philological and critical Dissertation of Slovak Letters] published in 1787 and *Gramatica Slavica* [Slovak Grammar] in 1790) were written in Latin, each and every grammatical term is followed by the Slovak equivalent in brackets. While these equivalents are almost exclusively adapted Czech borrowings, they are the outcome of an informed and carefully considered decision from among several existing terms. Further development of Slovak and its terminology have since proved him correct in his choices. Viera Dujčíková stressed that Bernolák's significance to the development of Slovak terminology lay in his ability to gather extensive terminological material, and his provision of a method for borrowing from Czech without hampering Slovak's own phonetic and morphological system (Dujčíková 1957: 683). Furthermore, he included many contemporary terminological units from zoology, botany and agriculture alongside terms related to housing, food and clothing in his 1825 extensive six-volume dictionary *Slowár Slowenskí, Česko-Latinsko-Ňemecko-Uherskí* [Slovak and Czech-Latin-German-Hungarian Dictionary].

In the 1840s, a second effort to standardise Slovak was undertaken by Ľudovít Štúr who — influenced by the ideas of German classical philosophers such as Johann Gottfried von Herder and Georg Wilhelm Friedrich Hegel — argued for the metaphysical necessity of using and developing the Slovak language, through which the spirit of the Slovak nation, its substance, could manifest and materialise itself (Dolník 2010a: 256). Štúr chose the northern part of the Central Slovak dialect area as the foundation, which differs more from Czech than Western Slovakian dialects. However, Štúr's attempt to standardise Slovak was not a radical parting of the ways between Slovak and Czech. While he wished to delimit Slovak orthography, phonetics, phonology and morphology from Czech as strictly as possible, he did not apply the same principle to Slovak lexis and terminology. As a result, a large part of the new Slovak lexis and vocabulary, such as terms and abstract nouns of general language, was in fact borrowed from the Czech language (Pauliny 1966: 111). The rationale for this attitude was again expressed in philosophical terms: Štúr considered grammar to be the spirit of language, while vocabulary was a mere material (Ďurovič 2007: 29). The freshly standardised Slovak then underwent numerous revisions, notably the revision of 1852 by Martin Hattala, approved by both Slovak Catholics and Protestants.

There were also attempts to collect and coin different terminologies as the standardised language slowly penetrated among increasingly more users and gained new social functions (Blanár 1963). Yet its knowledge was restricted to Slovak intellectuals, writers and people exposed to the cultural milieu in the town of Turčiansky svätý Martin. Individual authors and scholars put much effort into creating and consolidating terminology in specific domains, taking different approaches, with conflicting attitudes and varying results. Naturally, the resulting terminology was likewise varied and unstable, with written sources testifying to the proliferation of synonymy that resulted from parallel coining and usage of German, Latin and Czech loan words.

The beginnings of organised terminology work in Slovak can be found in the era of Matica slovenská, a nation-wide institution founded in 1863 that only survived for a dozen years. It was an authoritative body striving to consolidate the usage of terminology through expert commissions. Because of the absence of a scholarly linguistic journal, terminological glossaries and theoretical articles would appear instead in either Matica slovenská's journal *Letopis MS* or in literary journals and anthologies. These theoretical articles, as well as terminology collections themselves, indicated the differing attitudes on how to develop terminology, which can be summarised below:

1. More conservative — leaning on tradition and Czech terminological models with the aim of creating Slovak terminology based on term-formation procedures and roots understandable nation-wide
2. Seeking to create new terms according to Hungarian models and traditions while advocating purist tendencies.

The key element for systematic development of terminology in standard Slovak was the preparation and publication of textbooks for three newly established grammar schools where Slovak was the language of instruction (e.g. Ivan Branislav Zoch's 1868 dictionary of Slovak scientific terminology *Slovár vedeckého slovenského názvoslovia*).

In summary, Slovak terminology of this period developed to a great extent autonomously, which is reflected in contemporary scholarly articles. It is worth mentioning that, in this period, a specific definition was provided for many commonly used words (e.g. *voda* 'water', *železo* 'iron', *hlava* 'head', *ruka* 'hand', *koza* 'goat') to restrict their meaning to a specific domain, as several disciplines related to the humanities or natural sciences had only just started to use Slovak (Blanár 1963).

The Austro-Hungarian Compromise of 1867 intensified pressure on all non-Magyar ethnic groups in the Kingdom of Hungary to assimilate (see Chapter 24). Although the 1868 Nationality Act passed by the Hungarian Diet the next year declared all citizens of Hungary to be equal, it also defined them as forming a single nation in the political sense and Hungarian was to be its official language. In 1874–1875 Matica slovenská and all grammar schools that provided instruction in Slovak were closed by the government.

For the sake of comparison, in the second half of the 19th century, Czechs enjoyed relatively favourable conditions for their ethnic development, where in a short time they were able to build a complete system of education up to the university level along with a system of political parties, societies and cultural institutions. In 1880, Minister-President Karl Ritter von Stremayr decreed that Czech and German would become equal for communication between the state administration and citizens (Rychlík 2015: 35).

However, in compliance with the Hungarian legislation that obliged the Ministry of Interior to publish new acts immediately after their approval also in common languages of the lands of the Crown, the *Collection of Provincial Laws*, established in 1868, started to be translated also into Slovak. And it was the translation of Hungarian legislation and directives that significantly shaped the emerging Slovak legal terminology. The most remarkable and influential efforts in translation and terminology were accomplished by Samuel Czambel, whose almost three-decade tenure as an official translator lasted from 1881 until his death in 1909 (Valkovičová 1981: 29). In his articles on administrative and legal terminology, Czambel described the terminological chaos caused by the proliferation of terms for one and the same concept. He also sought to initiate a commission consisting of both linguists and lawyers that would contribute to the unification of Slovak legal terminology.

Czambel's terminology work can be summarised into the principles below, which cover both the conceptual and linguistic aspects:

- Finding inspiration in legal tradition
- Coining unambiguous and precise terms
- Preferring terms that enable further derivation
- Strictly adhering to linguistic consistency and productive term formation processes
- Respecting language usage and principles of standard Slovak
- Considering the needs of legal practice.

As the 20th century dawned, standard Slovak was evolving successfully even under the difficult conditions of the era (Kačala 2001: 11). Despite obstacles in the development of an academic style, a certain progress was being made thanks to specialised journals such as *Právny obzor* [Law Review], established in 1917.

3.   Slovak and Czech after the creation of a common state (1918)

The creation of Czechoslovakia brought together two territorial units whose legal system, political and economic situation, number of inhabitants, religion and education level were vastly different. Prior to its establishment, the idea of a new Czechoslovak or Czech-Slovak state was presented to the Allied Powers as the aspiration of the Czech and Slovak people to become independent from the Austro-Hungarian Empire. That is why the concept of a single political but not ethnic nation was developed, which should have been used as a pragmatic political tool or idea and abandoned later (Rychlík 2015). However, this concept of a single nation both in political as well as ethnic terms became the official ideology of the new state and was recognised by many Czechs and Slovaks.

In addition, the concept of one nation was mirrored in the concept of the "Czechoslovak language" as the official language of Czechoslovakia, governed by the Constitutional Act of 29 February 1920. Article 129 (1) stipulates that "the Czechoslovak language is the official language of the Republic" (Novák 1935: 186). Yet the definition of such a language is missing and the nature of the Czechoslovak language is explained only additionally, in a rather vaguely worded Article 4, which avoids using the terms Czech and Slovak languages. While Czech authorities would employ Czech "as a rule," Slovak officials would use Slovak. Thus, the Act opened up a wide scope for linguistic reflections and discussions regarding the concept "Czechoslovak language" (Lipowski 2005: 26–27) and also furnished the perfect environment for the Slovak language to be politicised.

Enacting the unified Czechoslovak nation with a virtually non-existent Czechoslovak language in two "versions" would cause instability within the state that was already apparent in the 1920s (Kačala 2001: 25). Elements in the Slovak side's political representation continuously aimed for some type of autonomy within the common state, while many in Slovakia perceived expressions of Czechoslovak ideology as a threat to their national identity and indeed its very symbol — the Slovak language. Regardless of some negative impacts, especially on the Slovak economy, the common state did enable the Slovak nation to mature and establish its own cultural, educational, social and political organisations at all levels. Rychlík claims this boom in Slovakia to have been unparalleled (2015: 67).

The reality of the new state allowed Slovak to finally be used in all walks of life, but it nonetheless represented an enormous challenge. In the first years of Czechoslovakia, Slovakia lacked qualified workers, clerks, teachers and experts with a sufficient command of Slovak, as well as textbooks and specialised literature in Slovak. In this respect, the arrival of thousands of Czechs to fill the vacancies were an invaluable help and both nations and languages found themselves in an intermediate contact which represented a new phenomenon (Kačala 2001: 26). However, close contact between Czech and Slovak speakers considerably eroded Slovak language usage and codification, even where it had once been stable (ibid: 27). Therefore, the 1920s saw indiscriminate borrowing of entire terminology sets from Czech into Slovak with only minor adjustments. The Slovak language was thus experiencing both rapid development (for it had to serve as an official language in a state for the first time in history), and intense penetration of Czech elements.

4.   Emancipation of the Slovak language in the 1930s

As the 1930s unfolded, a new generation of young Slovak intellectuals, and scientists in particular, stepped in to demand the right to engage in the problems of Slovakia and Slovak science independently. This became spectacularly apparent in the controversy unleashed by the publication of *Pravidlá slovenského pravopisu* [Rules of Slovak orthography], the first officially approved rules of Slovak orthography (Vážný 1931). Prepared by a commission led by Czech linguist Václav Vážný, who chaired the linguistic department of a renewed Matica slovenská, it legitimised many Czech words as variants in Slovak, thus mirroring the Slovak language destabilization of that time (Jarošová 2012: 257), as well as practically paving the way toward a unified Czechoslovak language (Kačala 2001: 34).

The Rules publication triggered an immense negative response from Slovak writers, scientists, publicists and the general assembly of Matica slovenská (Múcsková 2017), and even became a political issue (Rychlík 2015: 129). Furthermore, this provoked a wave of defensive reactions from the upcoming generation of Slovak linguists, which sparked the establishment of *Slovenská reč*, a scholarly monthly journal edited by Henrich Bartek which adhered to a strict and preoccupied concern about the purity of the language. The journal focused on the issues of Slovak language, the development of linguistic research and the creation and consolidation of Slovak terminology.

Linguistic evaluation of both old and new terminology in *Slovenská reč* was usually based on a retrospective comparison with Bernolák's comprehensive dictionary and, if possible, other smaller specialised dictionaries. The journal represented an effort to find linguistic arguments for accepting, keeping or refusing a form of a specific term or the term itself (either a new term or a borrowing, especially from Czech) or even reviving an older term (e.g. *čuv* and not *nerv* 'nerve', Slovenská reč 1935–36: 88). Neologisms were to be evaluated primarily from the perspective of linguistic correctness and functionality: (1) they had to comply with the inherent system of the Slovak language and (2) they had to be essential. This attitude was in line with the principles of language cultivation advocated by the Prague Linguistic Circle professing functionality and stability in language: unessential new coinages "destabilise standard Czech" (Mathesius 1932: 19).

Bartek claimed that Slovak literature had employed Slovak words as much as possible ever since Bernolák's attempted codification in the late 18th century (Bartek 1936–37: 296), and this principle of maximum use was equally applied to terminology. The rationale for this 150-year-long tradition was nation-wide understandability of terminology and therefore foreign words considered to be *unnecessary* were to be substituted by Slovak terms. For this reason, the editors of Slovenská reč recommended *vývoz* instead of *export* (Slovenská reč 1936–37: 308), for example. However, words and terms of foreign origin that had become a part of the Slovak lexicon were not to be discarded without due cause. Even terms from Austria-Hungary that were still functional and transparent should be preserved, especially legal terms, including those of Latin origin (Slovenská reč 1933–34: 261). Finally, there were occasions when it was found acceptable to coin or calque terms by means of non-productive or non-Slovak term-formation procedures where such terms proved to be needed for specialised communication — here principles of transparency and derivability prevailed over preference of productive and genuine Slovak procedures and word forms. Specific borrowings from Czech were also acceptable and essential, especially when they filled lexical gaps (e.g. Czech *vlajka* 'flag' or *tepna* 'artery', *tepnový* 'arterial').

Articles on Slovak terminology that appeared in *Slovenská reč* also advocated the requirement of conceptual accuracy, linguistic systematicity, derivability and the need to avoid false motivation, that is, refusal of mechanical calques, especially from Czech, that expressed false distinguishing features (e.g. Czech *liehovar* instead of Slovak *pálenica* for distillery since the Czech root incorrectly indicated that alcohol is boiled). The principle of conceptual accuracy of terms was usually dealt with in expert discussions among lawyers. As for the definition, an accurate term had to exactly "cover" the content of the notion, that is, it should express neither more nor less information than that included in the notion (Fundárek 1935/1936: 110).

One eloquent example is the consolidation of the Slovak nomenclature of anatomy. Though specialised medical literature in Slovak was no longer scarce and Halaša's medical and pharmaceutical dictionary, *Návrh lekársko-lekárnického názvoslovia*, had been published in 1926, Slovak medical terminology was still described as rather chaotic, which was why the 1935 publication of *Nomina anatomica* in Slovak by university professor and doctor Július Ledényi was essential and was considered a historical achievement both as a significant step towards the systematic consolidation of Slovak terminology (not just in medicine) and secondly because it sparked wider discussion (Horecký 1956: 27–28).

Yet this proposed Slovak anatomical nomenclature aroused opposition and even hostility among researchers and professors at Comenius University and it risked turning into a political issue for it was labelled as an anti-Czech activity. Subsequent discussions and a special commission, which sought to evaluate Ledényi's proposal, led to the formulation of eight principles inspired by the principles of Bohuslav Havránek, leading figure of the Prague Linguistic Circle (see Chapter 9):

1. approval of established words regardless of their word-formation
2. disapproval of words from an informal register, especially those whose connotation is vulgar or emotional
3. creation of terms that are different from general words
4. promotion of term formation by derivation
5. promotion of internationally recognised concepts
6. general preference for international terms or their calques
7. preservation of relationships with scientific terminologies of other domains
8. preservation of terms developed and used at Comenius University over the past 17 years.

However, the application of several of these principles was problematic or even disputable (such as the last one since the medical terminology at Comenius University was strongly influenced by the ideology of Czechoslovakism). Finally, as a *sine qua non* condition, the commission stressed that Slovak terminology should not differ unnecessarily from Czech terminology (ibid: 30).

In terms of language and its cultivation, Ledényi cooperated with Henrich Bartek and followed the criteria in Slovenská reč for linguistic correctness and consolidation of terminology. It should be emphasised that Ledényi's proposal was based on the international Latin nomenclature that had been published in Basel in 1895 and was thus valid and internationally compatible. Therefore, Ľudovít Novák (1935:149) recommended the adaptation of Czech nomenclature according to its Slovak counterpart in the process of terminological coordination. In spite of preliminary criticism, the new Slovak nomenclature of anatomy was adopted in everyday use of doctors and lay public and for 27 years remained a reliable reference source and the foundation for further revisions.

5.   Weakening of the Czech influence

The 1930s ended in a sequence of cardinal events. Slovak autonomy was declared on 6 October 1938, followed by the (first) split of Czechoslovakia, the establishment of the quasi-independent First Slovak Republic on 14 March 1939 and the outbreak of World War Two. The tragic war years, however, contributed toward strengthening the Slovak language as it became the official language of the wartime Slovak Republic. Matica slovenská likewise helped stabilise the standard language, offering — for instance — the general public practical language counselling.

The first half of the 1940s can be characterised by growing qualifications of Slovak professionals and progress in natural sciences and technology, leading to the creation of new terminologies and the free development of an academic and popularisation style with no influence from other languages (Kačala 2001:44). During World War Two, the Slovak language's previous convergence toward Czech experienced significant weakening, while divergent tendencies and a purist approach peaked (Lipowski 2005:67). This tendency toward purism would change over time. While in the 1930s linguists had been predominantly occupied with defending Slovak and removing Czech phonetic, morphological, lexical or syntactic sediments, the focus in the following decade shifted more toward accentuating those features of the Slovak language that differed from the Czech (ibid:74). In doing this, however, even some distorted and biased arguments were made, such as an unsubstantiated accentuation of Slovak euphony in comparison to Czech (ibid:75). Systematic development of terminology started in several fields, but it would remain unfinished (see Section 7 on military terminology).

6.   The Slovak language in the re-established Czechoslovakia after World War Two

The relationship between Czech and Slovak after the Second World War resumed under different circumstances. While Slovak had experienced a significant functional differentiation and growth of its lexis during wartime, and it had evolved into a language that could fully satisfy various social functions, the influence of Czech on the Slovak language continued with the restoration of the common state in 1945, but became more disguised (Lipowski 2005: 88).

One of the channels that influenced the linguistic "perception" of both Slovaks and Czechs was common radio and later television broadcasting, as well as the centralised administration of the state that underwent the Communist coup in 1948. In addition to restored contacts with the Czech language, Slovak saw increased internationalisation as the language was enriched especially with words from Russian and English. Their acceptance into the Slovak lexicon was even easier if they were coined from Latin and Greek roots as the Slovak wordstock even now comprises a relatively higher proportion of internationalisms than Czech (Horecký 1999: 81). Moreover, in the effort to achieve a clear and detailed delimitation of Slovak, internationalisms have often been preferred to prevent excessive borrowing from Czech (Habovštiaková 1993: 210).

Terminology was a chapter of its own with the most intense quantitative and qualitative growth (Kačala 2001: 64). At the initiative of Ján Horecký, one of the most important and influential Slovak linguists in the second half of the 20th century, a small department of terminology was created at the Ústav slovenského jazyka Slovenskej akadémie vied a umení (Slovak Language Institute of the Slovak Academy of Sciences and Arts). The department, which he led, existed for eight years and its members laboured intensively (see Levická – Zumrík 2019) and efficiently in cooperation with experts from dozens of various fields to create new terms and compile more than 30 terminographic works. For many fields of study, this was the first time terminology had ever been published in Slovak.

Ján Horecký initiated the creation of the *Slovenské odborné názvoslovie* [Slovak Professional Terminology], a monthly journal focused solely on terminology. In 1956 his dissertation was released as a monograph entitled *Základy slovenskej terminológie* [The Fundamentals of Slovak Terminology]. In what has since become a classic work of Slovak linguistics, Horecký presented the first theoretical underpinning for the creation and consolidation of Slovak terminology. The core of his book deals with analysing and defining characteristics of terms, both conceptual and linguistic (transparency, systematicity, well-established usage, unambiguity, accuracy, and derivability), as well as with the linguistic structure of terminological units. As Horecký's starting point was that of a linguist –

considering terminology an integral part of any standard language — he also required that a term should meet all phonological and word-formation criteria of this standard language in order to ensure its nation-wide understandability and usage. Though he emphasised linguistic criteria, at the same time he advocated that a term must comply with the requirements of transparency, systematicity, unambiguity and accuracy. With an extensive analysis of naming types in different fields, Horecký affirmed the linguistic focus terminological thinking was taking in Slovakia in accordance with the Prague School of Terminology (see Chapter 9) and its structural and functional approach. What makes Horecký's monograph important is his contribution to the effort to capture the comprehensiveness of terminological studies, starting with their historical roots, development, and social context and subsequently producing a differentiation in individual fields of study and disciplines.

The 1960s witnessed the trend toward a proclaimed coordination and unification of Slovak and Czech terminology, dictated largely by a rise in politically motivated efforts to regulate the relationship between Czechoslovakia's two official languages while driven by the strategy of developing and converging nations and nationalities that was embraced in late October 1961 at the 22nd Congress of the Communist Party of the Soviet Union. While Slovak politicians made the development of both nations their priority, the Czechs focused on their convergence, although they interpreted it as the merging of the two nations (and languages).

Both of these contradictory trends were also evident in Czechoslovak linguistics, most notably at conferences in Liblice (1960), Bratislava (1962) and Smolenice (1965 and 1966), which played a crucial role in the post-war history of Slovak and in the development of Slovak terminology in particular. The 1960 conference was dominated by criticism of the Slovak terminological work carried out in the 1950s as an expression of linguistic purism and downright anti-Czech attitudes. Conference participants also stressed the need for the convergence of Slovak towards Czech and the creation of a unified terminology. Two practical consequences of the Liblice conference emerged: a common Central Czechoslovak Committee of Terminology[4] was established and *Slovenské odborné názvoslovie* [Slovak Nomenclature] was replaced with a new bi-monthly journal of terminology, *Československý terminologický časopis*, first published in 1962. Its mission was to promote contacts between Czech and Slovak and to unify their terminologies in line with politically declared goals. The two conferences in Smolenice were held after months of discussion among the general public and Slovak cultural community in response to the

---

4. The committee only met three times, indicating that it primarily played a symbolic role. This interpretation is confirmed by Horecký's words that it was a "stillborn central committee of terminology" (Horecký 1990: 261).

publication of a new six-volume *Slovník slovenského jazyka* [Dictionary of the Slovak Language] in 1959–1968, which was criticised for including many Czech words (Múcsková 2017). At the conferences, new criteria were drafted and approved for classifying the standard language and for language cultivation including terminology. These reforms appeared in *Tézy o slovenčine* [Theses on Slovak], which can be viewed as a retrospective approval of the terminological work and criteria that had been presented by Horecký's department (Ružička 1967).

Naturally, unification efforts and tendencies in Czechoslovakia prioritised (mutual) intelligibility of terms. Sometimes, variability was acceptable as can be seen with the abbreviations used in both languages for "cooperative collective farm" — JZD in Czech and JRD in Slovak. In other cases, strictly linguistic rules were overshadowed by usage, such as in the controversy involving the pair *točovka — sústruh* for 'lathe'. Even ideological and political influences appeared in the unification of Czecho-Slovak terminologies, as shown in the next sections.

6.1   The case of *točovka* vs *sústruh*

Ján Horecký believed it necessary to "analyse contact phenomena between Czech and Slovak objectively, especially as a purely linguistic problem (though it affects social and political sphere)" (1967: 43). In 1965, he reacted to the nation-wide debate of the previous year on the borrowing of Czech words by emphasising, specifically in regard to terminology, that the Slovak terminology used in various disciplines had borrowed many terms from Czech without detriment to "Slovakness," but there had also been many new terms different from Czech (1965: 196).

One example of his arguments in favour of using and promoting words and terms of Slovak origin instead of unnecessary borrowings from Czech is his defence of the Slovak neologism *točovka* ('lathe') for which he became a target of strong criticism at the Liblice conference. The situation involves the parallel use of Slovak *točovka*, proposed in the interwar period, and the Czech borrowing *sústruh*. Horecký pointed out that these terms were variably and inconsistently used even within a single publishing house or by one and the same author (1951–52: 110). The general hesitance about which of them was "correct" lasted until the end of the 1950s (1957: 53). Though the Czech borrowing seemed to be used more often, Horecký argued that the frequency of usage could never be a reliable criterion of correct language (1957: 53).

Horecký's priority was to identify which term is justified in standard Slovak from the historical perspective and subsequently "to evaluate which one of them is more fit for the emerging Slovak terminology of metalworking" (1951–52: 110). Therefore, on the basis of an extensive analysis of older linguistic sources and

word-formation analysis, he concluded that the Czech borrowing was unnecessary, while the proposed Slovak term was functional and highly motivated. Moreover, he pointed out that the motivation of *točovka* is analogous with equivalents
in other languages, both Slavic and non-Slavic.

On the other hand, Horecký included counter arguments in favour of keeping
the Czech borrowing:

1. Absence of the derived verb from the proposed Slovak term (need to coin verbs
   točovkovať, podtočovkovať), while *sústružiť* was already being commonly used
2. Frequent usage of *sústruh* by several companies in Slovakia
3. Need for a unified terminology within Czechoslovak industry and the economy.

However, the length of usage of the Czech borrowing by Slovak speakers (mentioned already by Bernolák) from as early as the 18th century, its increased frequency in the common state and the centralised economy finally helped to
promote the term *sústruh* in Slovak terminology in spite of the linguistic arguments. The latest, fourth edition of the authoritative Slovak dictionary *Krátky
slovník slovenského jazyka* (KaČala - PisárČiková - Považaj 2003) labelled it as a
word from standard Slovak.

6.2   The case of *autostráda* vs. *diaľnica*

Two terms were introduced into Slovak in the interwar period to denote the concept of 'motorway,' the adapted Italian borrowing *autostráda* and the Czech word
dálnice. According to linguists, the term *autostráda* was already well-established
in the 1950s (Meliš-Čuga 1952: 123). In the 1970s and 1980s, the use of *autostráda*
was more frequent than *diaľnica* in standard Slovak, while in Czech the frequency
order was just the opposite (Ružička 1975: 99). Therefore, Slovak linguist Jozef
Ružička recommended promoting international terms in both languages in order
to resolve the framework for coordinating Czech and Slovak terminology, arguing
that a term of international origin links both languages with other languages.

From the very beginning, the Czech borrowing was greeted with strong
objections by linguists who were focusing on the cultivation of Slovak (Mlacek
1999) and their recommendations remained consistent throughout the second
half of the 20th century.

In the 1930s, Slovenská reč mentioned several arguments in favour of the
Italian borrowing over the proposed form *diaľnica*, including the non-systemic
root of the Czech word and its false, even problematic motivation (Slovenská
reč 1938–39: 121). Moreover, they argued that promotion and usage of the Czech
borrowing instead of the Italian one is not possible as it would also require

the substitution of all other compound words starting with the prefixoid *auto-*. Therefore, only the words *autostráda* and *autostrádový* were recommended to be used as terms.

While the first volume of the comprehensive Slovak monolingual dictionary *Slovník slovenského jazyka* (Peciar et al. (eds.) 1959) did not include the Czech borrowing, the sixth volume (Peciar et al. (eds.) 1968) labelled it as a word borrowed from Czech, but not quite suitable for standard language practice. This attitude remained in recommendations of Slovak linguists for two more decades (Mlacek 1999:91). Nonetheless, both competing synonyms remained in everyday usage among Slovak speakers and were used to coin derived words and multi-word terms. Jozef Mlacek believed (1999:93) that communication standards favoured *dial'nica* and saw it as a more transparent term than the Italian borrowing, which Slovak speakers perceived as more "foreign" and far less understandable.

Present-day Slovak corpus data (version prim-10.0-public-all) provide insight into the usage of these two competing terms in processed texts from 1955 onwards. Overall statistics indicate that the Czech borrowing *dial'nica* has been used at least 20 times more often than the Italian borrowing *autostráda* (*dial'nica* 37.24 per million | ARF:[5] 22,274.55 vs *autostráda* 1.40 per million | ARF: 939.08). However, specialised texts such as motoring magazines have only been using the term of Italian origin, which reflects the consistent recommendations provided by Slovak linguists. Interestingly, the corpus data also roughly reflect the change in the usage of both terms (see Figure 1 and 2).

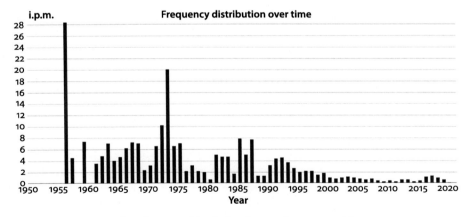

Figure 1. Frequency distribution of the Italian borrowing *autostráda*

---

5. Average reduced frequency is one of many adjusted frequencies that can be obtained from a corpus, it "discounts" multiple occurrences of a word that occur close to each other, e.g. in the same document.

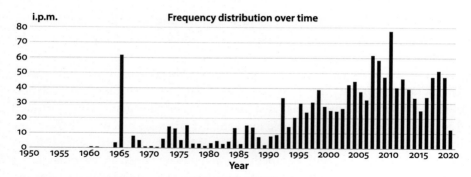

Figure 2. Frequency distribution of the Czech borrowing *diaľnica*

In sociolinguistic terms, it seems that alongside the centralised Czechoslovak economy and common mass media, it was the political and ideological pressure to keep Slovak as close to Czech as possible that played a decisive role in reversing the usage of the two analysed competing terms. As prominent Slovak linguist Ján Kačala wrote (1992: 87), Lubomír Štrougal had intervened personally at the end of the 1960s in the standardisation of Slovak just prior to his appointment as prime minister of Czechoslovakia. He demanded that the Slovak branch of the nation-wide company that was building motorways in Czechoslovakia use the same name as the Prague-based headquarters and for Slovak linguists to stop discouraging people from using the Czech borrowing. Kačala claims that the term *diaľnica* had to be treated as an accepted and correct standard Slovak term, so consequently this Czech borrowing ultimately prevailed in usage.

7.   An example of effective terminology coordination

The beginnings of Slovak military terminology can be traced back to the mid-19th century when Slovak was proclaimed an official language of military command by Emperor Franz Joseph, and Ján Francisci, a Slovak poet and captain of volunteer Slovak military units, drafted a glossary of basic Slovak military terms (Oktavec 1948–49). Although Slovak would be subsequently used as a language of communication in some Hungarian regiments, this fact had no impact on the further development of Slovak military terminology.

In the 19th century, however, Slovak was employed as a language for commanding fire brigades. Manuals comprising military terms were published in Slovak in the 1880s–1890s, drawing a great deal of inspiration from established Czech terminology that had been systematically created in the "spirit" of standard Czech

(Lipowski 2005: 116). Therefore, Czech influence on Slovak terminology occurred prior to the establishment of the common state.[6]

The development of military terminology in Czechoslovakia in the interwar period was limited strictly to Czech. Terminology work that was carried out by a special commission established by the Ministry of Defence in Prague was adopted by the Czechoslovak army. Because Slovak terminology had been poorly developed, Czech terms were used and Slovak officers issued their commands in Czech, even inside Slovakia (Chorvát 2011: 42). The Czech language's dominant position within the Czechoslovak army was criticised in Slovakia as early as the 1920s and the criticism only increased in the following decade (Novák 1935: 196).

Change came with the establishment of Slovak autonomy in 1939, when the autonomous Slovak government announced that Slovak would be the commanding and official language in Slovakia (Chorvát 2011: 45). Naturally, even greater emphasis was put on developing Slovak military terminology during the wartime Slovak Republic. Two terminological documents were published in 1941 and 1942 in compliance with the principles of language cultivation advocated by *Slovenská reč*. They show that Czech terminology was still used as a model, but when there were new terms and commands created, they tended to diverge from Czech as much as the nature of the two languages would allow. As far as the political context is concerned, Slovak war-time terminology also bore witness to what was regarded as indiscriminate borrowing from German (Chorvát 2011: 47).

After World War Two, the Košice programme of the new Czechoslovak government introduced equal legal status and usage of Slovak and Czech in the Czechoslovak Army. However, this change was based on the assumption that it was possible to arrive at total uniformity of terminology in both languages.

Coordinated efforts to develop military terminologies in both languages were initiated by a committee of the Ministry of Defence cooperating with the Slovak Language Institute represented by Ján Horecký. The priority was to codify commands in Czech and Slovak. The outcome from this endeavour was the publication of the *Vojenský terminologický slovník* [Dictionary of Military Terminology] (1966), and prior thereto the *Česko-slovenský vojenský slovník* [Czech-Slovak Military Dictionary] (1962) with some 27,000 entries.

Naturally, the pursuit of matching Slovak and Czech terminology would eventually be limited especially due to the phonological and word-formation differences between the two languages. These differences were reflected in non-transparent

---

6. There was a very short period of Czech and Slovak *terminological coexistence* in the Czechoslovak legions fighting during the First World War in Soviet Russia when the official language was either Czech or Slovak. Moreover, daily reports show signs of elementary terminology work and coordination (Chorvát 2011: 39).

terms and especially in the non-equivalence of Czech and Slovak homonyms (Lipowski 2005: 121). Unification principles included giving preference to variants, synonyms or obsolete words that are close or identical to counterparts in other languages and even employing words coined with non-systematic affixes. It can be argued that such a solution could only be possible in a restricted field of communication that employs a controlled language.

8.   "Normalisation" of the relationship between the languages

The 1970s and 1980s were characterised by a certain normalisation of the relationship between Czech and Slovak, in other words, stabilisation or "parallel development within the limits of law" (Lipowski 2005: 136). There were at least two trends present in society: one convergent and aimed at reducing language differences and the other a parallel trend where concurrent development of the languages was promoted and strengthened. It was the latter trend that gradually won out thanks to positive conditions. This approach was characterised by using concurrent Czech and Slovak expressions and creating concurrent neologisms. The parallelism took different shapes (derivational, formal, functional), while the objective was mutual compatibility or "predictability" of the languages (ibid: 142).

The mutual influence resulting from everyday contact of the two languages in Czechoslovakia gradually evolved into a quasi-bilingual state, although this was truer for Slovaks than Czechs. The term *bilinguality* (dvojjazykovosť) was defined by Viera Budovičová (1974) and Ján Horecký (1987) as a form of translingual contact when an utterance is issued in somebody's mother tongue, and he or she receives the answer in another language without any problems comprehending it (Lipowski 2005: 143). In the case of Slovak and Czech, however, a revised definition of the term bilinguality would be needed, because language users not only have to be in command of their mother tongue (Slovak or Czech), but they also need a certain form of passive bilingualism (ibid). In this way, a distinct "to a certain degree abstract" language emerges, which could be labelled Czechoslovak (ibid: 144).

The split of former Czechoslovakia into two independent countries in 1993 naturally ended a certain phase in the contact of the two languages, and followed with the next chapter of a "continuing story," as suggested by the title of the book by Mira Nábělková (2008). It could, however, be debated whether this was an event where the Slovak language had now turned from a transcendental object into an autonomous, self-governing entity (Lipowski 2005: 161). The division into two separate countries could accordingly be seen more like a fluid transition into something brand new rather than a rupture (Kačala 2005).

9.   Conclusion

Any coexistence of languages within social structures spanning from micro- to macro levels takes on different forms, always dependent on given historical, geographical, political and cultural conditions. The sometimes intense mutual entanglement of Czech and Slovak, or more precisely, the centuries long usage of Czech in Slovakia, can be perceived in connection with any of the historical debates in Czech and Slovak linguistics, specifically whether these two languages are even separate, autonomous languages, or rather two forms of a common language (Lipowski 2005:13).

That is why a metaphor of a historical and cultural tangle-like relationship between the Czech and Slovak nations could be used, with reference to the concept of phenomenological "tangle," coined by the Czech philosopher Martin Nitsche. The philosopher points to the "methodological precedence" of the "tangle," taken as a primordial epistemological situation and characterised by phenomenological complexity where there is no possibility at all to even "orient" oneself, that is, to localise and discern the subject and object in their relationship (Nitsche 2016:12).

In a similar figurative way, Jarošová (2012) likened the codification process model to the movement of a clock pendulum; one turning point is Slovak coming relatively close to Czech and the other is Slovak being as autonomous and as "relatively free from Czech" as possible. The first movement can be exemplified with Bernolák's and the second with Štúr's codification, while Jarošová argues that both points are not to be taken as exact conceptual opposites (2012:256). The pendulum's back-and-forth swing is rather an ongoing series of "drifting between extreme points" and a "chaotic movement" that temporarily resulted in "hybrid-like" forms of the Slovak language (ibid:257).

In addition, Dolník proposed several concepts to model the Czech and Slovak historical relationship. In *Teória spisovného jazyka* [Theory of the Standard Language] (2010a), he introduces two options for solving the question of codification in which there are two related, contact languages. The first option would be for the neighbouring communities to see their standard languages as two variants of a single one, the so-called "variant model," while the other option would be of two coexisting autonomous languages — the "coexistence model." In the case of Czech and Slovak, both options were considered but, no later than with the 1852 revision by Hattala, it became clear that the choice had been made in favour of the coexistence model (2010a:76).

Dolník further suggests that the Czech language had for Slovaks a so-called "identificatory function" (ibid). Since it could potentially and temporarily function as their standard language, it provided linguistic means perceived to a lesser extent as being borrowed or foreign, and, at the same time, it served, together with Hungarian, as a framework for the self-delimitation of evolving standard Slovak (ibid: 93).

It should also be stressed that Slovak terminology demonstrated its ability to evolve in a relatively short period of time and to meet the need of functional stylistic and lexical differentiation. Slovak society, while propelled by its long coexistence with the Czech nation, has thus proven its vitality, in that the Slovak language (including terminology) has, to use the words of J. Dolník, been able to both accommodate itself and assimilate impulses from surrounding environments (see e.g. 2010b: 22). Moreover, the role of individuals ought not to be underestimated, as the aforementioned objectives of terminological work had in Slovak settings been brought to full bloom to a great degree since the 1950s, thanks to Ján Horecký, as mentioned earlier. The Slovak language also showed openness towards internationalisation, and was able to draw from and make use of various sources of terminology enrichment.

Both individual and collective contributions to terminology development were therefore critical, such as the achievements of scientists, cultural activists, scientific and cultural institutions, editors and journals. Such a development of a functional language is described by Dolník (2021) as having stemmed from both "horizontal language needs" and "vertical language needs" (2021: 70–86). These two kinds of needs reflect two fundamental anthropological axes. In this respect, the horizontal development of language represents the variety of functional styles a language user can learn to apply in order to achieve given communicative goals, while the vertical development seeks an authentic, genuine, perhaps ideal language, and is thus also occupied with language improvement, standardisation and "effectivisation," or, as Dolník put it, "the idea of positive separation" (2017: 75–86). An argument could be made that both Slovak society and individuals over time have managed to develop the Slovak language in at least two such directions.

Finally, the language and its terminologies may also be viewed in dynamic interaction with their surroundings, where a spontaneous urge exists to find the most efficient ways for nations and languages to coexist, while not preventing them from developing their own specificity.

References

Bartek, Henrich. 1936–193. "Budúcnosť slovenčiny." *Slovenská reč* 5 (9–10): 295–301.

Blanár, Vincent. 1963. "K terminológii v matičných rokoch." *Československý terminologický časopis* 2 (5): 257–274.

Budovičová, Viera. 1974. Spisovné jazyky v kontakte. Sociolingvistický pohľad na dnešný vzťah slovenčiny a češtiny. *Slovo a slovesnost* 35 (3): 171–181.

Chorvát, Peter. 2011. "Dejiny slovenskej vojenskej terminológie." *Vojenská história* 15 (1): 33–54.

Dolník, Juraj. 2010a. *Teória spisovného jazyka so zreteľom na spisovnú slovenčinu.* Bratislava: Veda, vydavateľstvo Slovenskej akadémie vied.

Dolník, Juraj. 2010b. *Jazyk — človek — kultúra.* Bratislava: Kalligram.

Dolník, Juraj. 2017. *Jazyk v sociálnej kultúre.* Bratislava: Veda, vydavateľstvo Slovenskej akadémie vied.

Dolník, Juraj. 2021. *Jazyk v sociálnej praxi.* Bratislava: Veda, vydavateľstvo Slovenskej akadémie vied.

Dujčíková, Viera. 1957. "Pramene bernolákovskej gramatickej terminológie." *Slovenské odborné názvoslovie* 5 (3): 65–68.

Ďurovič, Ľubomír. 2007. "Kodifikácia novej spisovnej slovenčiny — predpoklady a kompromisy." In *Ľudovít Štúr a reč slovenská. Prednášky z konferencie konanej 13. — 14. júna 2006 v Bratislave,* ed. by Slavomír Ondrejovič, 24–34. Bratislava: Veda, vydavateľstvo Slovenskej akadémie vied.

Fundárek, Jozef. 1935–1936. "Predložky *do* a *za* v právnickej terminológii." *Slovenská reč* 4 (4–5): 109–111.

Habovštiaková, Katarína. 1962. "K charakteristike slovnej zásoby a terminológie u Bernoláka." *Československý terminologický časopis* 1 (6): 321–331.

Habovštiaková, Katarína. 1993. "Charakteristika slovnej zásoby štúrovčiny v širšom vývinovom kontexte." *Slovenská reč* 58 (4): 207–215.

Horecký, Ján. 1951–1952. "Točovka alebo sústruh." *Slovenská reč* 17 (4): 110–114.

Horecký, Ján. 1956. *Základy slovenskej terminológie.* Bratislava: Vydavateľstvo SAV.

Horecký, Ján. 1957. "Točovka." In *Jazyková poradňa,* ed. by G. Horák, and J. Ružička, 53–54. Bratislava: Slovenské pedagogické nakladateľstvo.

Horecký, Ján. 1965. "Kritériá terminológie." *Československý terminologický časopis* 4 (4): 193–200.

Horecký, Ján, Karel Richter, and František Švarc. 1962. *Česko-slovenský vojenský slovník.*

Horecký, Ján. 1967. "O zásadách pri tvorení názvoslovia." *Kultúra slova* 1 (1): 129–133.

Horecký, Ján. 1974. "Základné problémy terminológie." *Kultúra slova* 8 (5): 129–132.

Horecký, Ján. 1987. *Vzťahy medzi češtinou a slovenčinou.* In *Acta Universitatis Carolinae. Philologica 4–5. Slavica Pragensia XXX,* ed. by Viera Budovičová, 49–53. Praha: Univerzita Karlova.

Horecký, Ján. 1990. "Jazyková politika v r. 1948–1988." *Kultúra slova* 24 (8): 259–265.

Horecký, Ján. 1999. "Internacionalizácia a europeizácia slovenčiny." In *Internacionalizácia v súčasných slovanských jazykoch: za a proti,* ed. by Ján Bosák, 80–82. Bratislava: Veda.

Jarošová, Alexandra. 2012. "Bohemizmy a kodifikačné „kyvadlo"." In *Jazykoveda v pohybe*, ed. by Alena Bohunická, 255–263. Bratislava: Univerzita Komenského Bratislava.

Kačala, Ján. 1992. "Jazykoveda v minulých desaťročiach." *Kultúra slova* 26 (1): 7–12.

Kačala, Ján. 2001. *Spisovná slovenčina v 20. storočí*. Bratislava: Veda, vydavateľstvo Slovenskej akadémie vied.

Kačala, Ján. 2005. "O slovenčine a češtine staronovo." *Literárny (dvoj)týždenník* 18 (43–44): 15.

Kačala, Ján, Mária Pisárčiková, and Matej Považaj. 2003. *Krátky slovník slovenského jazyka*. Bratislava: Veda.

Levická, Jana, and Miroslav Zumrík (eds). 2019. *Človek a jeho jazyk IV. Terminologické inšpirácie Jána Horeckého./Man and His Language 4. Selected Terminological Papers of J. Horecký*. Bratislava: Veda, vydavateľstvo Slovenskej akadémie vied.

Lipowski, Jaroslav. 2005. *Konvergence a divergence češtiny a slovenštiny v československém státě*. Wrocław: Wydawnictwo Uniwersytetu Wrocławskiego.

Mathesius, Vilém. 1932. "O požadavku stability ve spisovném jazyce." In *Spisovná čeština a jazyková kultura*, ed. by B. Havránek, and M. Weingart, 14–31. Praha: Melantrich.

Meliš-Čuga, Ľudovít. 1952–1953. "K návrhu nových pravidiel slovenského pravopisu." *Slovenská reč* 18 (4): 116–124.

Mlacek, Jozef. 1999. "Diaľnica a superdiaľnica." *Slovenská reč* 64 (2): 91–96.

Múcsková, Gabriela. 2017. "O slovenskom purizme a anti-purizme v kontexte jazykových ideológií." In *Jazyky a jazykové ideológie v kontexte viacjazyčnosti na Slovensku*, ed. by I. Lanstyák, G. Múcsková, and J. Tancer, 39–79. Bratislava: Univerzita Komenského.

Nábělková, Mira. 2008. *Čeština a slovenčina v kontakte. Pokračovanie príbehu*. Bratislava — Praha: Veda — Jazykovedný ústav Ľ. Štúra SAV — Filozofická fakulta Univerzity Karlovy.

Nitsche, Martin. 2016. *Metodická přednost spleti. Tranzitivně-topologický model fenomenologie*. Praha: Togga.

Novák, Ľudovít. 1935. *Jazykovedné glosy k československej otázke*. Turčiansky sv. Martin: Matica slovenská.

Oktavec, František. 1948–1949. "Vojenská slovenčina okolo povstania z r. 1848–49." *Slovenská reč* 14 (3–4): 65–73.

Pauliny, Eugen. 1964. "Pri zelenom stole: naša reč." *Kultúrny život* 19 (46): 5.

Pauliny, Eugen. 1966. *Dejiny spisovnej slovenčiny I. Od začiatkov až po Ľudovíta Štúra*. Bratislava: Slovenské pedagogické nakladateľstvo.

Peciar, Štefan et al. (eds.). 1959. *Slovník slovenského jazyka I*. Bratislava: Vydavateľstvo SAV.

Ružička, Jozef. 1967. "Tézy o slovenčine." *Kultúra slova* 1 (2): 33–41.

Ružička, Jozef. 1975. "O jazyku celoštátnych učebníc." *Kultúra slova* 9 (4): 97–101.

Rychlík, Jan. 2015. *Češi a Slováci ve 20. století : spolupráce a konflikty 1914–1992*. Praha: Vyšehrad.

Slovak National Corpus — prim-10.0-public-all. Bratislava: Jazykovedný ústav Ľ. Štúra SAV 2022.

Peciar, Štefan et al. (eds.). 1968. *Slovník slovenského jazyka VI. Doplnky - dodatky*. Bratislava: Vydavateľstvo SAV.

[s.n.]: "Živé striebro- rťuť-orťuť." 1932–1933, *Slovenská reč* 1 (7): 159; "Z právnickej terminológie." 1933–1934, 2 (9–10): 261–262; "Rozličnosti." 1935–1936, 4 (2–3): 77–88; 1936–1937, 5 (9–10): 301–320; 1938–1939, 7 (3–4): 120–128.

[s.n.]. 1966. *Vojenský terminologický slovník*. Praha: Naše vojsko.

Valkovičová, Gizela. 1981. Kodifikačné snahy S. Czambela pri ustaľovaní slovenskej právnej terminológie." *Slovenská reč* 46 (1): 28–36.

Vážný, Václav. 1931. *Pravidlá slovenského pravopisu*. Praha: Státní nakladatelství.

Zoch, I. Branislav. 1868. "Slovár vedeckého slovenského názvoslovia." *Letopis Matice slovenskej* 5 (1): 14–24.

CHAPTER 29

Terminology in South Africa

A unique multilingual context

Mariëtta Alberts
Pan-South African Language Board

South Africa has twelve official languages: Afrikaans, English, the nine Sintu languages and South African Sign Language. Terminology plays a pivotal role in functional language development and the promotion of multilingualism in South Africa. The focus in this chapter is on the institutional dimension of terminology development in all official languages. This chapter also gives attention to language policies and consequential terminology policies in terms of subject-oriented terminography, translation-oriented terminography, language planning-oriented terminography, and finally linguistic community-oriented terminography. Various collaborating bodies assist the national terminology office with terminology development. Also discussed are approaches to training on terminological practices and principles, as well as the influence of human language technologies on terminology development.

Keywords: community-oriented terminography, human language technologies, language planning-oriented terminography, language policy, standardisation, subject-oriented terminography, terminology development, terminology management, terminology policy, translation-oriented terminography

1. Introduction

South Africa is a country with 12 official languages (i.e. Afrikaans, English, isiNdebele, isiXhosa, isiZulu, Sesotho, Sesotho sa Leboa, Setswana, Siswati, Tshivenda and Xitsonga (the last nine of these languages are collectively known as Sintu languages), and South African Sign Language (SASL). The *Constitution of the Republic of South Africa* Act 108 of 1996 (now *Constitution*, 1996) specified 11 official languages, but in 2023 South African Sign Language (SASL) was added as the twelfth official language. The Sintu languages were previously called African languages but the designation was changed to distinguish the African languages

https://doi.org/10.1075/tlrp.24.29alb

spoken in South Africa from those other African languages spoken in the rest of the African continent.

The country is faced with an extremely complex situation of institutional terminology management and a considerable need to develop resources to support each language's status. This poses an extraordinary challenge for language planning and terminology development.

In South Africa, specialised communication has a central hub in terminology, and thus terminology plays a vital role in language development and the promotion of multilingualism. The notion that information is most effectively acquired (decoding process) and conveyed (encoding process) through the first language (L1) or mother tongue of the speaker or reader, and that precise and standardised terminology is the means by which unambiguous communication is achieved in specialised fields, supports the assertion that each of these official languages requires the vocabulary or terminology needed to fulfil all of the necessary functions of life in the nation. When it comes to specialist communication, it is often the language of habitual use (i.e. English) for the relevant subject areas (e.g. chemistry, physics, psychology, zoology) or domains (e.g. art, music), and not necessarily the L1, that becomes the natural medium of communication. In the context of South Africa, the concern is to ensure the functionality of the official South African languages and the rights of their L1 speakers. The hegemony of English, however, hampers terminology development in the other official languages.

The supplying of appropriate polythematic terms (i.e. the terms of various subject areas or domains) is a national priority, especially in a multilingual dispensation. The official languages can develop into functional languages in all spheres of life through the efforts of language offices, tertiary institutions, private initiatives, and publishers.

There is, however, a stark contrast between the ideal of multilingualism and the unfortunate limitations on available funding and human resources to produce terminological data and products in the multiple official languages. There is unfortunately a general lack of coordination and cooperation among terminology agencies in South Africa which leads to duplication of projects, which in turn leads to a proliferation of terms for the same concept in the same subject area and/or language and therefore miscommunication and a lack of standardisation. It is important to document, retrieve, revise, and update the terminology of various subject areas and domains in all registers to enable subject-related communication.

Standardised terminology can contribute to exact communication and reduce misinterpretation and misunderstanding. It contributes to the quality of translations, editing, interpreting services, dictionary compilation and specialised or subject related communication. It is therefore important to develop South Africa's official languages into functional languages in all spheres of human endeavours.

Terminology in South Africa has an interesting, albeit difficult history. All the indigenous languages (Afrikaans and the Sintu languages that later became official languages) were committed to writing. They were standardised in the process, and their orthographies and word-formation principles developed before any terminology development could begin.

Terminology practices in South Africa are governed by the language policy of the reigning government, e.g. bilingual or multilingual:

–   previous political dispensation (e.g. prior to 1994, predominantly the Apartheid era): bilingual technical dictionaries were compiled (English and Afrikaans);
–   present political dispensation (e.g. after 1994, the Post-Apartheid era): multilingual term lists are compiled in the official languages of the country (Afrikaans, English, isiNdebele, isiXhosa, isiZulu, Sesotho, Sesotho sa Leboa, Setswana, Siswati, Tshivenda and Xitsonga, and since 2024 also video clips in South African Sign Language).

The previous bilingual policy favoured the development of Afrikaans terminology. Government policy on language promotion prior to 1994 furthermore stipulated that the promotion of the Sintu languages was the task of the former national states and self-governing regions, and not of the South African government. Since 1995 structural considerations and policy have had an important effect on the practice of terminology in South Africa, and it was widely accepted to be the responsibility of government to develop and promote the Sintu languages. Terminologists working in a multilingual society such as South Africa are faced with conflicting situations: the Afrikaans, Sintu terminologies, and SASL video clips are developed to enhance the multilingual heritage of the country; however, the large number of languages makes this impractical and not economically viable. Additionally, there are very few trained terminologists, and available positions in terminology are scarce.

This chapter places particular emphasis on the various management strategies of institutionalised terminology practised during the different political dispensations prevailing at a particular time (i.e. the political systems such as Apartheid and Post-Apartheid that have authority during a particular era). It provides an overview of other nongovernment-related terminology projects in South Africa, and discusses terminology training issues in relation to the integrated terminology development model.

2.   Historical overview

The history of Afrikaans terminology in South Africa starts with the recognition of Afrikaans as an official language in 1925 (cf. 2.1). The history of Sintu language terminology in South Africa starts with structures similar to the erstwhile Language Boards that began in 1928 with the formation of language committees (cf. Mayevu 1996:30; Alberts 2000b). These have been changing over the decades both in formation and focus (cf. Mtintsilana and Morris 1988).

Since 1948 (the start of the Apartheid era) the construction of the Language Boards has taken a fundamentally political outlook both in its composition, function, and relation. These Boards were linked to 'independent homelands' and similar political formations. Their political role was to present a picture of separate development, primarily the homeland structures. Some of these Boards were accountable to the Chief Ministers and their Cabinets, some were accountable to the Department of Education and Training and some to both structures. These Boards were mainly funded by the homeland governments and had representatives of those governments as members (cf. Mtintsilana and Morris 1988). There were Language Boards for every Sintu language, though some would be duplicated for political purposes as in the case of isiXhosa in the Transkei and Ciskei and Setswana in South Africa and Bophuthatswana (cf. Ntshangase 1996).

2.1   The era of bilingualism (pre-1994)

The language situation in South Africa is unique. Several indigenous languages already existed when the first European Settlers landed at the Cape of Good Hope in 1652. Various Dutch dialects were influenced by the Khoe and San languages spoken by the local inhabitants. The influences of Portuguese, isiXhosa, Malayan, East Indian Languages, Arabic, German, French and English could also be seen in the *lingua franca* of the colonists at the time. Afrikaans, the only European language indigenous to South Africa, originates from these different languages coming into contact with one another. Previously known as Dutch Afrikaans, and originally as Cape Dutch, it is a language with unique characteristics that differs from contemporary Dutch. Originally Dutch was one of the official languages of South Africa. In 1925 Afrikaans became one of the official languages of South Africa. Dutch was replaced by Afrikaans in 1961 and removed as official language in 1984. Afrikaans and English enjoy equal status since 1925 (Alberts 2017:140–141).

With the recognition of Afrikaans as one of South Africa's official languages, language practitioners and subject-field specialists were made aware of the need to create and document Afrikaans term equivalents for existing English terms (Kapp

2009: 125). The first Afrikaans — English technical dictionary was published in 1918. Prior to that no technical dictionaries were published. Several terminology lists or technical dictionaries were compiled by individuals such as translators who started to collect terms from their own work and compile bilingual term lists for personal use. Later language bureaux started to collect terms to help translators with their translation work and to ensure the subsequent use of the documented terms — thereby initiating a standardisation process.

In 1928 the government established a Language Bureau at the Department of Education, Arts and Science. Similar bureaux were also established at the South African Railways and Harbours and at the South African Defence Force.

In the early 1940s, a need arose at the South African Academy for Science and the Arts (SAAWK) for Afrikaans to be developed into a fully-functioning language in various subject areas. In 1950 the government agreed to establish and finance a Terminology Bureau at the SAAWK. The Terminology Bureau started compiling bilingual term lists in a wide variety of disciplines (Kapp 2009: 126–127, Alberts 2015).

With the new political dispensation of 1948 (the start of the Apartheid era), interest in the Afrikaans language surged and an urgent need to develop Afrikaans terminology arose: suddenly, Afrikaans was required to take its proper place alongside English, a global language with a more established terminology in certain subject fields. Afrikaans terminology and its practises officially emerged as early as 1950, and adhered to the then bilingual policy of the country at the time.

Translators of the Language Bureau started documenting English and Afrikaans terms on index cards. Other language bureaux situated at government departments followed this practice. Soon thereafter several language bureaus at institutions such as the South African Iron and Steel Corporation, South African Bureau of Standards, South African Broadcasting Corporation, municipalities, etc. that employed translators also had a few terminologists to harvest the terminology of the relevant institution. They all started to compile bilingual terminology lists to standardise the terminology use within these organisations.

The government reorganised its language services in 1954 and moved both the Language Bureau of the Department of Education, Arts and Science and the Terminology Bureau of the SAAWK to the Department of Culture (later the Department of National Education). A new Language Bureau was created at the Department of Culture. The Terminology Bureau remained at the SAAWK and was financed by the Department of Culture (Kapp 2009: 127).

From 1956, a Terminology Division developed within the Language Bureau. Terminologists were appointed to extract terms from documents and to systematise and standardise the terminology of various subject fields. The terminologists received in-service training on the principles and practice of terminology work and novice terminologists worked under the supervision of a mentor. The terminologists worked in close collaboration with subject-field specialists. A variety of bilingual term lists and technical dictionaries were compiled and published. The terminology process was carried out according to the terminology practice which aligned with the principle of concept orientation (cf. Oeser 1998: 105–115; Alberts 2017: 60–63, 277): the concept was denoted (named) by a source language (SL) term (usually English) and a target language (TL) (Afrikaans) term equivalent was either added if it existed or was coined. Subject committees were established to work in collaboration with the terminologists and to verify and authenticate the polythematic terminology (Alberts 2003: 135).

The development of Afrikaans words and terms dominated the lexicography and terminology practices of the previous century (Alberts 2003: 134–135, Alberts 2015). Several bilingual (English — Afrikaans) and bidirectional technical dictionaries and term lists were published, aiming to supply Afrikaans with term equivalents to existing English terms, to enable subject-related communication in Afrikaans. Essentially, Afrikaans was developed to become a functional language capable of processing scientific and technological information on a par with English (Jordaan-Weiss 1996: 374).

The standardisation of terminological data is a process — by frequent use of source language (SL) and their related target language (TL) terms, the provided SL and TL terms penetrate the subject field and language and become standardised (Alberts 2017: 71–89; 274). There was (and unfortunately still is) a lack of coordination of efforts which leads to a duplication of projects by different institutions.

In 1958 a Technical Language Commission was established to assist with the coordination, production, and dissemination of Afrikaans terminology. It was replaced in 1966 by the Technical Language Liaison Committee (Cluver 1996).

The Coordinating Terminology Board (COTERM)] was formed in 1971 and replaced all the previous coordinating bodies. Its purpose was to oversee any terminology ventures undertaken by the various language offices, and to avoid duplication. At the time, the managers heading the language bureaux were members of COTERM (Alberts 2003: 136, Kapp 2009: 129).

COTERM developed criteria that would assist in the standardisation of terminographical methods and principles, and initiated efforts to computerise South Africa's terminology practice (Alberts 2003: 137). To ensure term penetration and the standardisation of terms in the various subject areas (e.g. botany, physics, psychology, zoology) and domains (e.g. music, art), COTERM stipulated that each terminology-related institution had to identify core terms related to their area of competence and supply these to the Bureau of the Dictionary for Afrikaans

(WAT) for inclusion in the general dictionary for Afrikaans. Copies of all technical dictionaries and term lists had to be supplied to the WAT and South African
libraries. COTERM, however, did not properly fulfil its coordinating role and the
various language bureaux continued with their own activities.

The Terminology Bureau of SAAWK published several technical dictionaries
related to the higher echelons of science (Alberts 2003:135, Alberts 2015, Kapp
2009). The Terminology Division of the Department of National Education compiled and published bilingual, bidirectional translation dictionaries (Alberts
2003:135, Alberts 2015). There was an urgent need for polythematic terminology,
and although published dictionaries were in high demand, many concepts were
left undefined, since adding definitions would cause further delays. The terminologists worked in collaboration with subject-field specialists who assisted with term
creation. The Afrikaans terms are usually self-explanatory: *koppelvlak*: 'interface'
(computer science); *sukkelveld*: 'rough' (golf); *pynpolisie*: 'first-aid staff' (rugby);
stofsuier: 'vacuum cleaner' (home economics).

In 1976 the Terminology Division amalgamated with the Terminology Bureau
of the SAAWK to form a new Terminology Bureau under the auspices of the
Department of National Education (Alberts 2003:137, Alberts 2015). At the time
there were 30 terminologists employed at the new Terminology Bureau plus three
data typists. Term lists and technical dictionaries were still compiled in English
and Afrikaans only.

In 1984, the Human Sciences Research Council determined that the government's Terminology Bureau had to become the official national terminology office
responsible for the documentation and coordination of terminology in South
Africa (Cluver and Scheffer 1984). Since 1984 this office has been known as the
National Terminology Services (NTS). It was furthermore recommended that
COTERM be dissolved and replaced as the coordinating body by the government's NTS. This national terminology office henceforth acted as the national
management unit for terminology, according to the terminology model of 1984
(Scheffer 1987:33). Accordingly, the NTS later became the official national ter-
minology office of the Department of Arts, Culture, Science and Technology
(DACST), and functioned under the Science and Technology Branch of DACST
since it developed terminology for both subjects. During this period, the NTS
compiled and published a wide variety of technical dictionaries (Alberts 2003:137,
Alberts 2015).

Terminology development in South Africa experienced a fruitful period from
1950 to 1994, with special attention being paid to the development of Afrikaans
terminology.

2.2   The era of multilingualism (post-1994)

Although in the past the NTS and its predecessors, as institutions of government, primarily compiled bilingual, bidirectional English — Afrikaans technical dictionaries, the pressing need was soon acknowledged to develop terminology in the various Sintu languages. The NTS started research into word-formation principles in the Sintu languages and contacted the various Language Boards regarding the development of terminology in these languages. It was decided that multilingual technical dictionaries would henceforth also be compiled in the Sintu languages, with the addition of definitions and explanations (Alberts 2003:138).

In 1994 South Africa introduced a multilingual policy, and ever since national terminology projects have been officially undertaken in the eleven official South African languages. A budget was allocated by DACST to enable the appointment of Sintu-language terminologists and in 1995, the first Sintu-language terminologists — all L1 speakers of the various official languages — were appointed to document Sintu-language terminology in a variety of subject fields. The newly-appointed terminologists immediately received in-service training on the principles and methods used in terminology work. At that time, the office was comprised of 18 terminologists — seven English-Afrikaans terminologists, eleven Sintu-language terminologists, a Deputy Director as office manager, and a receptionist cum typist.

Those terminologists working primarily in the remaining nine official South African languages (i.e. the Sintu languages) began adding term equivalents to English terms in their first languages. Definitions and descriptions were added to the English — Afrikaans term lists. The Sintu-language terminologists rely on especially the Afrikaans term equivalents and definitions to assist them with the task of term creation (Jordaan-Weiss 1996:374, Alberts 2015).

In the past, the NTS published a regular catalogue that showcased existing scientific and technical dictionaries, as well as a *Catalogue of Language Resources.* The NTS used to publish a newsletter, *Termbroker*, at regular intervals with the aim to distribute and coordinate terminology information in respect of all official languages.

As the result of the Language Plan and Task Group (LANGTAG) report (1996), the NTS and the State Language Services of DACST amalgamated on 1 April 1998 to form the National Language Service (NLS). This new office was created under the Arts and Culture branch of DACST (Kapp 2009:130). The NTS was renamed the Terminology and Place Names Division (T&PN) of the NLS. In August 2001 the DACST was split to form two departments, the Department of Arts and Culture (DAC) and the Department of Science and Technology (DST). The translation and terminology sections were placed under the NLS, DAC.

Some aspects of the management of terminology and terminography have changed: prior to 2002, under the Science and Technology Branch of DACST, the NTS worked according to subject fields. But when the T&PN Division was placed under the NLS of the Arts and Culture Branch of the Department in 2002, the terminologists henceforth worked according to the language-specific needs of the previously marginalised Sintu languages spoken by minority groups, and placed emphasis on expanding their terminologies.

The name of the T&PN Division was later changed to the Terminology Coordination Section (TCS) of the NLS. Since 2009 the TCS has been a Directorate residing under the Chief Directorate: NLS. Currently there are only 11 terminologists employed at the TCS — one assigned to each official language. Officially, the TCS is the national office with the responsibility to assist the government, by providing terminology information in all official South African languages, coordinating terminology endeavours, and documenting and disseminating terminology.

A post for a South African Sign Language (SASL) terminologist had been approved in 2024 since SASL became an official language in 2023. SASL signs are captured as video clips, standardised, and disseminated to the deaf, hearing-impaired, interpreters, and the hearing society to allow communication between these groups.

Extensive research was done on copyright issues affecting terminology to determine the legal position of the TCS regarding the products created by this office. It was found that the dictionaries and term lists produced by the TCS are of an original nature if definitions are created by the office itself, and the publication of these will therefore not constitute copyright infringement of the sources consulted (Alberts and Jooste 1998).

Terminological information was originally documented on index cards and dictionaries were published by the Government Printer. When the TCS was later computerised, the MultiTerm Plus database system of TRADOS (now RWS Group) was used to form the basis of the national term bank, which enabled the office to disseminate terminological information both in printed and electronic formats.

Currently the Authumato Terminology Management System, developed by the Centre for Text Technology (CTexT), North-West University, serves as the national term bank of the TCS of the Department of Sport, Arts and Culture (DSAC). The system is web-based, and the terminological information is disseminated in various ways, i.e. as draft terminology lists, and as printed and online publications (Mnisi 2021). Copyright remains with DSAC but the multilingual term lists can be downloaded for personal use from the department website. The TCS has the infrastructure, but unfortunately lacks the personnel to produce some required terminology products.

3.   Terminology dimensions

Sager (1990) associates three basic terminology dimensions with a theory of terminology: cognitive, linguistic, and communicative. Newly appointed terminologists do not have applicable tertiary training nor any previous experience in terminology-related work, and they need to learn the basic principles governing terminography. These dimensions are the basis for developing principles of best practice in terminology work in South Africa.

3.1   Cognitive dimension

The aim of terminology work is to standardise a concept and its related term to ensure subject-related communication. The *cognitive dimension* relates the linguistic forms (terms) to their conceptual content (i.e. the referents in the real world). Terminology work is concept-oriented and the aim is to have a one-to-one relationship between concept (i.e. unit of thought) and term (i.e. linguistic unit). Each concept should preferably be denoted by a specific term in a specific subject area and language and the concept should be defined. This practice leads to the standardisation of concepts and terms. (Alberts 2017: 71–89). Different types of definition can be distinguished, e.g. intensional, extensional, contextual, partitive, and more (Alberts 2017: 76–79).

3.2   Linguistic dimension

The *linguistic dimension* examines the existing and potential forms in which terminology may be presented (i.e. specialised domains as well as orthographies of the languages). The first language in which a term is coined is the SL. This process is monolingual, and is called *primary term creation. Secondary term creation* can be bilingual or multilingual, and occurs with the transfer of knowledge to another target community (Alberts 2017: 89–104).

SL terms denote concepts, and term equivalents are supplied in various TLs, which may be an exact relationship (full equivalence) or only a partial one:

–   Full equivalence or congruence: (en) *water* (af) *water* (de) *Wasser* (xh) *amanzi* (zu) *amanzi*
–   Partial equivalence: (en) *blue* (tn) -*tala,* (en) *green* (tn) -*tala*[1]
–   Zero equivalence: (af) *veld* (en-ZA) *veld* (soil and vegetation), (af) *padkos* (en-ZA) *padkos* (food for the road), (zu) *lobola* (en-ZA) *lobola* (bride price)

---

1. The colours blue and green are both denoted with -tala in Setswana (tn).

Terms are representations of concepts, and are either linguistic, or non-linguistic (i.e. *formula, barcode, mnemonic sign*). They are formed by using a range of word-formation principles such as transliteration, borrowing, embedding, semantic transfer, neologisms, and more (Alberts 2017: 93–104).

3.3   Communicative dimension

The *communicative dimension* focuses on the use of terminologies, especially on standardisation and harmonisation processes, language development, information retrieval, cultural differences, consultation, collaboration, and dissemination (Alberts 2017: 104–114).

These principles form the basis for the development of best practice for the government-employed terminologists.

4.   Terminology harvesting approaches

In 2015 a survey of technical dictionaries revealed 368 English — Afrikaans bidirectional dictionaries and term lists in a variety of subject areas (Alberts 2015). A recent survey (Alberts 2024) indicates 550 bilingual technical dictionaries. This, however, is not the case for the nine official Sintu languages. Owing to the great backlog concerning the terminological development of these languages, various methods are being used to harvest terminology, e.g. subject-oriented terminography, translation-oriented terminography, linguistic community-oriented terminography, and language planning-oriented terminography (Alberts 2017: 173–220).

4.1   Subject-oriented terminography

The Terminology Coordination Section (TCS) (and its predecessors) usually begins with a specific SL, typically English, and then supplies translation equivalents in the ten other official languages. The national terminology office uses various terminology harvesting methods but usually works according to the subject-oriented methodology for term extraction (Alberts 2017: 177–179).

In subject-oriented terminography, the process is concept-based (concept-oriented). Terminologists consult subject-field specialists when determining the meaning of the concept to supply definitions, and linguists when supplying or coining translation equivalents in the various TLs for the SL terms. The TCS consult the National Language Bodies (NLBs) established by the Pan-South African Language Board (PanSALB) regarding verification and authentication issues.

4.2   Translation-oriented terminography

The NLS employs translators and therefore also takes part in translation-oriented terminography (TOT) (Alberts 2017:179–180). Terms in the SL text and term equivalents in the TL are aligned and harvested. These terms and related information are then submitted to the TCS to be documented and processed.

4.3   Linguistic community-oriented terminography

Language-specific terminologists are required to visit rural areas to document the local terminology related to bird and animal names, customs and beliefs, traditional medicines, and other social or cultural concepts. These terms can be obtained from the members of the linguistic community by way of oral communication. In the case of declining languages (i.e. languages/dialects that are not official languages), outreach to older members of the community is essential to preserve these languages/dialects, as when these people die, the knowledge of terms and related information (e.g. indigenous knowledge systems, oral traditions) dies with them (Alberts 2017:180–181). This field-based approach is referred to as *linguistic community-oriented terminography*.

Terminology is indeed harvested from rural and urban speech communities for documentation in the central national terminology bank. But because this process entails field-work and is costly, it is seldom undertaken. Consequently, many terms existing in smaller language communities are not documented, contributing to the general stereotype that the Sintu languages are incapable of naming abstract concepts. This is a fallacy. Numerous domains already contain a vast array of terms in the Sintu languages. The various rural dialects also contain a wealth of terms which could be harvested and utilised in the standard languages. In instances when multiple terms exist for the same concept in the same language, the proliferation of term equivalents leads to duplication, confusion, and poor communication. A further problem is that these terms are not documented using a systematic format, and are therefore not standardised.

Language-specific terminologists are required to do field-work relating to the official languages in urban areas — especially at language offices (cf. 6.2) and tertiary institutions (cf. 7.5; Figure 1) where the terminologists can extract terms and related information from translated documents, textbooks, curricula, master's dissertations, and doctoral theses at various tertiary departments. These terms are new, and if they are not documented (and translated into the relevant official languages where needed), they risk not being standardised and disseminated to target users.

4.4   Language planning-oriented approach to terminography

The language planning-oriented approach focusses on any official intervention to enhance the status of minority or disadvantaged languages. The underlying principle is that the function of an unstable or undeveloped language can change when official bodies intervene strategically. In such instances terminology imported from languages spoken in technologically advanced and dominant countries is replaced with local or native/indigenous equivalents (see also Chapter 12 Section 4.4).

In South Africa this kind of language planning is the task of official bodies such as PanSALB and the NLS. The aim of the Constitution (1996) is also to develop previously marginalised languages such as the Khoe and San and the South African Sign Language (SASL). In the case of SASL, the SASL NLB has created signs for various concepts. In efforts to standardise these signs, the SASL NLB of PanSALB had them captured in video clips and disseminated to relevant users, such as the deaf community, hearing-impaired people, and interpreters.

It should be noted that the different approaches of harvesting terminology are not mutually exclusive (Alberts 2017: 181–182).

5.   Terminology policy

The national terminology policy (NTP) for South Africa (cf. Layton, Alberts and Sanker 2024) was drafted in compliance with the Constitution (1996) relevant pieces of legislation, known structures, and prescripts of UNESCO and standardising bodies such as ISO/TC 37 and SABS/TC 37. The process of drafting a national terminology policy started in August 2023 and a final draft was submitted to the Department of Sport, Arts and Culture in June 2024 for implementation by the end of 2024.

The main objective of the national terminology policy for South Africa is to provide policy makers in government and other institutions with guidelines to support the development of terminology and the implementation of practices and methods in terminology management and terminology work (i.e. terminography) by the national terminology office, i.e. the Terminology Coordination Section (TCS) (cf. Layton, Alberts and Sanker 2024).

This policy is regarded as a strategy in coordination with, and supporting, the general development of such policy for South Africa, including all stakeholders from government (national, provincial, regional, local), organisational, educational (primary, secondary, and tertiary levels), publishing houses or private terminological enterprises. The NTP is evidence based and has a visionary approach. Various steps were recommended to realize the objectives by the implementation thereof (cf. Layton, Alberts and Sanker 2024).

The NTP was drafted after an extensive literature study, consultation with stakeholders (also with the SASL community), and the gathering of information from various sources. Its aim is to provide government, administration, tertiary institutions, publishers, non-profit and profit organisations, and private enterprises with guidelines for the development and implementation of a comprehensive approach to the planning and management of terminology in South Africa. It further aims to stress the importance of a functional national terminology service that comply to the prescripts of the multilingual policy as prescribed by the Constitution (1996) (cf. Layton, Alberts and Sanker 2024). The aim of the NTP is furthermore to provide the TCS with guidelines and implementation plans to improve its services, its coordination role, and its support to language units, various stakeholders, education (primary, secondary, tertiary), subject specialists, language practitioners, publishers, etc. (Alberts 2024).

6.   Collaborative terminography

Terminologists never work in isolation. They consult subject-field specialists when dealing with the concepts and terms of a specific subject field, and with linguists, first-language speakers, and language committees when supplying translation equivalents or when coining terms. An audit on terminology projects in South Africa was conducted by the TCS in June/July 2000 with a view to coordinate and facilitate terminology projects to ensure the documentation and dissemination of standardised multilingual terminologies (Alberts 2000a). It was decided to develop a national register for all terminology-related projects. This would avoid duplication of effort, and encourage collaboration. It was envisaged that all relevant terminology created by various bodies would in future be collected in the central national term bank of TCS.

6.1   Provincial collaboration

Language-specific collaborators situated in the various provinces were trained in 2000 by senior TCS staff members on the principles and practice of terminology work (Alberts et al 2000). The intention was to form a core group of these collaborators, largely linguists or language practitioners, to assist the language-specific terminologists employed at TCS.

6.2 Dedicated terminology offices

Other national, provincial, and local government departments, as well as semi-government and non-governmental organisations also compile term lists dedicated to vocation-specific domains. Between 2002 and 2010 translators at these offices received training on terminological principles and practice presented by the Director: Terminology Development and Standardisation, PanSALB.

The centralisation of terminological services in South Africa and related bureaucratic demands have created problems for terminology development, one of the most pronounced and concerning of which is this: since most language offices have downsized, subject-field specialists and academics are no longer interested in compiling technical dictionaries. Consequently, trained terminologists are increasingly scarce (Kapp 2009: 130–131).

6.3 Tertiary institutions

The political shift in 1994 provided a legislative context for transformation in all phases of education and a redress of imbalances resultant from the previous bilingual political dispensation. Language, among other issues, is seen as critical in fostering transformation in higher education. The development of all official languages to address imbalances of the past is a legislative imperative and is reflected in the legislative context of the Constitution of the Republic of South Africa (1996), various related acts, language policies, plans, and reports (Maseko 2012: 3–5, 34–36).

Section 27(2) of the Higher Education Act 101 of 1997 requires the Minister of Higher Education to determine language policy for tertiary education. Subject to the policy, councils of public institutions of higher education, along with their senates, must determine an institution's language policy, publish it, and ensure its availability on request. The main objective of the *Language Policy for Higher Education* is to promote multilingualism in institutional policies and practices at tertiary level.

Currently most South African tertiary institutions primarily use English as the language of teaching and learning. This is to the detriment of the other official languages. Afrikaans is not currently used as a language of instruction at tertiary institutions, even though Afrikaans terminology in all tertiary subject areas is readily available (Alberts 2015). Sintu languages are taught largely as subjects in their own right through the medium of English (Maseko 2012: 3). Several arguments underpin the value of instruction through the L1 of both trainer and trainee, but L1 education is currently not offered during the tertiary phase of education in South Africa — mainly because of poor policy decisions by tertiary institutions.

Students at tertiary institutions are confronted by course subjects that contain subject matter that is difficult to comprehend. This is in part caused by a lack of terminology available in the other official languages, especially in specific subject areas, and because the same concept is often denoted by different terms (e.g. digestive tract, gastrointestinal tract, alimentary canal). The proliferation of terms often leads to misunderstanding and confusion (Alberts 2017: 313–316, Maseko 2012: 5). The subjects are furthermore taught in English — many lecturers' and students' second (L2) or third (L3) language. Lecturers and students need to use English in the classroom to communicate but they do not understand the English terminology. Although there could be advantages to the lecturer and students to communicate in a shared language (e.g. English), the classes are linguistically mixed and English seems to be the *lingua franca* (see also Chapter 19 and 25) According to census statistics (2022) only 8.7 percent of South Africans are proficient in English (cf. Table 1). The 2022 census data (cf. Statistics South Africa. 2022) regarding language use in South Africa is presented in Table 1:

Table 1. South African census data 2022 on language use

Language	Percentage of speakers
Afrikaans	10.6
English	8.7
isiNdebele	1.7
isiXhosa	16.3
isiZulu	24.4
Sepedi/Sesotho sa Leboa	10
Sesotho	7.8
Setswana	8.3
SASL	0.02
Siswati	2.89
Tshivenda	2.6
Xitsonga	4.7
Khoi, Nama, San	0.01

By developing subject-specific terminology in the official languages and compiling multilingual, polythematic term lists, dictionaries, and other supporting teaching resources (e.g. multilingual study material), the process of transitioning the official languages into functional scientific and technical languages will be facilitated and, along with it, academic proficiency in the language of teaching and learning (Alberts 2017: 314, 324).

6.3.1   Dedicated terminology centres

Dedicated terminology centres at tertiary institutions could be of great value for language as well as subject-related departments (Alberts 2012). Various South African universities have embarked on the process of documenting terminology relevant to the various subject areas taught at these universities, which are made available to students on a blog (Alberts 2017: 320–328).

6.3.2   The Department of Higher Education

In 2014 ample funds were made available by the Department of Higher Education for the development of terminology at tertiary institutions. The aim was to develop a multilingual open-source term bank for Higher Education. The primary beneficiaries of this endeavour are first-year university students with a Sintu language as their first language. Afrikaans was not excluded but is not the main focus. The tertiary institutions were requested to collaborate to avoid duplication, but a 2015 audit on terminological activities in South Africa by Alberts (2015: 56–66) indicated that there were at the time several overlapping projects.

An online terminology service for tertiary institutions was intended to make effective terminological data available online for teaching and learning needs. Systems for recording comments on terminological data and to enable revision and easy data updates are unfortunately not available (Alberts 2015).

An online multilingual open-source term bank (OERTB) was created to co-ordinate terminology development endeavours by tertiary institutions and to develop the Sintu languages into languages of academic discourse, specifically to provide access to core concepts through the medium of the students' first languages. Unfortunately funding for this project was stopped.

6.4   Primary and secondary education

According to South Africa's official language policies, schools must choose a language (or languages) of teaching and learning. Most schools choose English or Afrikaans as opposed to the Sintu languages spoken in the geolinguistic area. The Sintu languages are thus only taught as subjects and are seldom used as medium of instruction. Teachers, however, use code switching as well as a trans-language process, alternating and blending languages to help learners understand concepts. It is proven by several research studies that learners conceptualise and learn best in their first language (Mahlalela-Thusi 2002, Mesthrie 2008, Maseko 2012), but due to its dominance, English is usually the chosen language of instruction. This is not ideal in a country with twelve official languages that each enjoy constitutional protection. It is important that learners do not lose their fluency in their mother tongue in favour of other, more convenient languages, as their first language is part of their identity.

It is therefore of critical importance to provide multilingual terminology for various learning areas in primary and secondary education. The TCS aims to develop these terminologies specifically to serve as support aids in primary and secondary education and facilitate processes of both teaching and learning.

6.5   PanSALB and its structures

Terminology endeavours by various language-specific compilers of technical dictionaries are coordinated by TCS and PanSALB and its structures.

6.5.1   *National Language Bodies*

PanSALB's National Language Bodies (NLBs) are in a good position to assist with terminology development in South Africa. All terminology and terminology products created in the country, not only those compiled by the TCS, must be submitted to the NLBs to be verified, and authenticated. The process, however, only relates to the linguistic value of the specific project since the NLB members are not subject-field specialists themselves.

The NLBs are also in a favourable position to assist with the process of standardising the terminologies, since they are well-versed in word-formation principles governing the creation of new terms, as well as with spelling and orthography rules.

6.5.2   *National Lexicography Units*

The trained lexicographers at the eleven National Lexicography Units (NLUs) of PanSALB, established in 2001, are mostly situated at tertiary institutions where they can harvest terminology. They are already situated in the geographical area (i.e. their geolinguistic area) housing the largest population of individuals speaking one of the official languages as their mother tongue, and are positioned to do field-work as suggested. They are also able to contribute multilingual polythematic terms to the Human Language Technologies (HLT) virtual network.

The NLUs are ideally placed to consult with linguists, academics, and subject-field specialists at the tertiary institutions. They have already compiled several dictionaries, which have been either self-published, or published by an established publishing house. An NLU for SASL is currently (2024) in the process of being established.

6.6   Independent terminology centres and other bodies

Several individuals and private institutions provide terminology to target users that cannot compile terminology lists themselves, e.g. projects by the SAAWK, the Centre for Political and Related Terminology in Southern Africa (CEPTSA), the Centre for Legal Terminology in African languages (CLTAL), Prolingua, and the Virtual Institute for Afrikaans (VivA). These bodies each collaborate with the TCS, PanSALB and publishing houses.

6.7   Publishers

Publishing houses also invest in terminology-related products. Publishers determine their own need for technical dictionaries in specific subject fields, and ask specialists to compile these dictionaries on their behalf. Subject-field specialists will also request publishing houses to print and publish their terminology-related manuscripts. Publishers have contributed to terminology development by printing various subject-related dictionaries (Alberts 2003: 137, Alberts 2015).

6.8   Terminology-related institutions in Africa

South Africa is the only country in Africa where terminology is officially practised separately from lexicography. The South African model functions well in cases where national terminology projects need to be undertaken (see also Chapter 18).

The models of the Institute for Kiswahili Research at the University of Dar es Salaam, the African Languages Research Institute in Tanzania, and the University of Zimbabwe in the country's capital Harare, could each respectively serve as examples where both lexicography and terminography work are done at the same institution.

In April 2005 a very successful Southern Africa Terminologists' Workshop was held in Pretoria. Various delegates from the Southern African Development Community (SADC) region attended the workshop and it was discovered that the terminologists in the region shared the same challenges. The workshop was intended to initiate a process of cooperative terminology development in the SADC region. The aims were to determine the latest developments in the fields of terminology and translation in the region, to determine whether a common terminological database could be established, to explore language development activities in the region, and to seek cooperation with other countries in Africa (Alberts 2010).

In 2009 an African Academy of Languages conference was held in Johannesburg to discuss various language-related issues, *inter alia* that Setswana (a language spoken in South Africa and in various other parts of Africa) had to be developed as one of the regional languages of Africa. Unfortunately, no substantial action was taken to follow-up on any of these initiatives.

6.9   International terminology-related institutions

South Africa aims to collaborate with international terminology bodies, and over the years South African delegates attended various international conferences. Several international guests also visited the TCS, where they shared valuable information.

South Africa liaises with various terminology-related international organisations, including the Organisation for Unification of Terminological Neologisms (which manages a World Bank of International Terms) (Stoberski 1998), the European Union, and UNESCO. South Africa also had a role in the development of the *Guidelines for terminology policies* (UNESCO 2005).

TCS is a member of international terminology institutions such as Infoterm and TermNet (see also Chapter 17). South Africa associates with other terminology-related and standardising bodies such as ISO/TC 37 through the national SABS/TC 37, the Danish Centre for Terminology, the Austrian Standards Institute, the Deutches Institut für Normung, the China National Institute of Standardisation and the Dublin Institute of Technology.

6.10   The Human Language Technologies initiative

The South African Government has approved the development of a national Human Language Technologies (HLT) virtual network. HLT include text-based language processing, speech recognition and processing, as well as research into language practice (e.g. lexicography and terminology), culture and technology.

On 5 October 2016, the Department of Science and Technology and the European Union jointly announced the establishment of a national centre for digital research, called the South African Centre for Digital Language Resources (SADiLaR). The aim of SADiLaR is to form a national cooperative network. The North-West University (NWU) functions as the core of this endeavour and it cooperates with the other participants — a hub and spoke model (a metaphor for the wheels of the ox wagons traditionally used for transport in South Africa). SADiLaR is housed at NWU but it functions as a separate entity and is financed by the Department of Science and Innovation (Alberts 2017: 386–399).

Several nodes form part of the spokes of the hub. The nodes conduct different projects, based on their experience, expertise and fields of knowledge — some projects deal with corpus development, others focus on speech recognition, and some concentrate on language technology and digitising (Calteaux 2021).

SADiLaR aims to reuse data as much as possible, and discourages duplication and proliferation of data and projects. Unfortunately, there is still a great deal of ignorance relating to HLT and people are reluctant to share data. They are unaware of the value of shared information, which is a valuable commodity in the context of language research and development. This is especially true in a multilingual country like South Africa, where several languages must be developed to the benefit of all collaborators, and where there are limited financial resources, and insufficient trained and skilled individuals for the many language-related tasks at hand (Alberts 2014, 2017: 324–400, 2022: 16–18).

The value added by SADiLar to any collaborating project is the availability of a disseminating platform, and its expertise in universal standards and accessibility. SADiLaR is the perfect platform for national and international dissemination of terminological data. It is imperative that terminology is shared for it to be utilised. There are currently no terminology-related projects at SADiLaR, however, there are hopes for a future collaboration with TCS.

7.   Terminology training

Terminology training encompasses numerous activities that enhance the knowledge and skills of specialist practitioners working in terminological environments; it is also the process of bringing a person (terminologist or collaborator) to an agreed standard of proficiency through instruction and practice.

The South African government requested national, provincial, and local government departments to establish language units to assist with language development and language-related work (such as translation work, interpreting, editing, journalism, publishing, and terminology development). These units are expected to meet certain criteria. For instance, they must adhere to current legislation, are required to develop at least three of the dominant language(s) spoken in their jurisdictions, and develop the terminology of the subjects related to their fields of expertise and vocation. The language practitioners (i.e. translators, editors, journalists, and interpreters) sometimes document institutionalised terms but they are not formally employed, nor trained, as terminologists.

Terminologists require special training (tertiary as well as in-service) to conduct terminology work according to specific terminographical principles and procedures (Alberts 2017: 301–328). Terminology training make a substantial contribution in developing the official languages into functional languages, and enhancing multilingual communication. The following levels of terminology training can be distinguished:

- Training of potential terminologists
- In-service training
- Reskilling of language practitioners
- Training of collaborators
- Tertiary training in theory and principles of terminology

7.1 Training of potential terminologists

The language practitioners at language bureaux create new terms regularly. But they remain uninformed on many useful word-formation principles, spelling, and orthography rules, as well as terminology harvesting and term creation, terminology management, and standardisation. The multilingual dispensation requires skilled language workers, and terminology training is aimed at enabling language workers to manage terminology in all aspects thereof.

Potential terminologists are given the opportunity to receive appropriate training before entering the profession. Between 2004 and 2010, such training was provided by the former Director of Terminology Development and Standardisation, PanSALB to interested parties. This included individuals, language bodies, language-related institutions, private institutions, government departments (local, provincial, and national), national parliament, NLBs, TCS, Language and Research Development Centres, and to students and academics at universities. The trainees were empowered to develop terminologies in their respective languages, subject areas, and vocations (Alberts 2017). This type of terminology training is crucial but, due to the Director's early retirement from PanSALB, has not continued.

7.2 In-service training

The TCS provides in-service training to all its terminologists. The terminologist/terminographer is trained in theoretical as well as practical principles that equip them to carry a project through all stages of the terminographical process.

From 1950 to 1994 junior terminologists worked under the supervision of senior terminologists who acted as their mentors. In 1995 the newly appointed Sintu-language terminologists received in-depth training in the theory and principles of terminology and the practices relating to terminography work. Unfortunately, there is currently only one terminologist per official language employed at TCS (Mnisi 2021). Together, these terminologists face challenges to confront the many subject-related communication problems, since they cannot cope with the demand to supply multilingual terminology in the diversity of subjects that require it.

7.3   Reskilling of language practitioners

In 2003 PanSALB started training unemployed language workers to assist with terminology development initiatives. This process also entailed the reskilling of language workers who were employed in related areas such as translation, editing, interpreting and journalism.

The recent decline in language-based studies at the post-secondary level has resulted in academics such as lecturers and teachers losing their jobs. Some of these academics were able to be retrained to become terminologists who could assist with supplying term equivalents and the translations of definitions (Alberts 2017: 304–305).

7.4   Training of collaborators

It is important to train collaborators who show a desire to know how to document and systematise the terminology they encounter daily. Relevant training enables collaborators to work according to fixed terminological procedures and supply the central national term bank with terminology related to their various specialist fields and domains (Alberts 2017: 305–309).

7.5   Tertiary training

The only tertiary facility offering a proper terminology course is the Department of African Languages, University of Pretoria. There are at present a few tertiary institutions in South Africa that offer courses in lexicography theory and principles. Aspects relating to terminology are dealt with as modules in courses in linguistics, translation, or lexicography studies. Terminology training as such receives too little attention in these modules (Alberts 2017: 309–313).

All the official languages are developed for use in higher education, which could encourage universities to offer terminology training as fully-fledged undergraduate and postgraduate courses. Students value terms and definitions supplied in their L1 allowing them to internalise the conceptual content of subjects. Furthermore, lecturers who are not proficient in the official languages, except perhaps English and Afrikaans, could enhance the usage of the other official languages by using bi- and multilingual technical dictionaries and online terminology products.

Another reason for offering terminology training is the need for the online dissemination of multilingual terms through SADiLar (Alberts 2017: 309–328, Sibula nd: 3; Maseko 2012: 32) .

In the future, schools for languages and tertiary language centres will need to offer terminology training, conduct terminology and terminography-related research and assist subject-related faculties with the compilation and dissemination of subject-related term lists. The aim must be to train terminologists to develop multilingual, polythematic terminology to help with developing the twelve official languages into functional languages for teaching and learning (Alberts 2014).

The process illustrated in the integrated terminology model developed by Alberts (2005) (cf. Figure 1) is designed to train under- and postgraduate students at tertiary institutions in the theory, principles, and practice of terminology and to provide language offices with trained terminologists. This process also includes the various role-players in the terminology creation and dissemination process. This process has significantly enhanced terminology development at tertiary institutions since 2005 (Alberts 2017: 322–328).

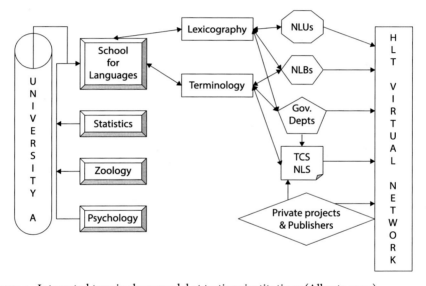

Figure 1. Integrated terminology model at tertiary institutions (Alberts 2005)

The integrated terminology training and development model entails the following procedures:

1. Term extraction in the SL from textbooks, tutorials, study guides, dissertations, doctoral theses, e.g. high frequency terms considered critical for students to grasp, core terms relating to the subject, and difficult terms at a specific tertiary instituition (e.g. University A)
2. Creation of definitions in the SL by language students, with the assistance of students majoring in a given subject field.
3. Verification of definitions by both language and subject-field lecturers.

4. Translation of SL terms and definitions into the TL(s) by students of different language departments. Experts in Greek and Latin at the specific university could assist with the etymology of terms originating from Greek or Latin and the transliteration process.
5. Database creation, maintenance, and dissemination by the IT department.
6. Verification of language-related principles (word-formation principles and orthographic conventions) by the relevant National Language Bodies (NLBs).
7. Inclusion of term lists in tutorials, study guides and textbooks.
8. Dissemination to other tertiary institutions, the TCS, language units, National Lexicography Units (NLUs) and publishing houses via SADiLaR (HLT virtual network) to promote the penetration of terms in subject fields and in the official languages, aiming at the standardisation of these terms (Alberts, 2017, pp. 323–328).

The integrated model was created to ensure collaboration between language centres/schools and other faculties, but also to facilitate national collaboration and interaction between tertiary institutions through the sharing of terminological data. The model has been implemented at various tertiary institutions and various term lists were since created and disseminated online. The process also establishes a better understanding for the value of standardised terminology in the conveying/encoding and retrieving/decoding of information.

8.   Conclusion

The terminology practice in South Africa has a long and interesting history. There were and still are several factors influencing the development of polythematic terminology in the South African languages. In the past, terminology development in South Africa was hampered by ideological, historical, educational, and sociolinguistic factors, the most fundamental of which were the language policies adopted in South Africa. With English and Afrikaans being the official languages up to 1994, the government actively supported terminology development in Afrikaans in efforts to ensure its parity with English. Several individuals, academics and institutions compiled technical dictionaries and ultimately terminology development moved to government bodies. The structures of the official bodies experienced many changes over the years, arising from especially political decisions.

Since 1995 factors relating to structure and policy have had an effect on the practice of terminology in South Africa. Terminologists with fluency in the Sintu languages were employed at the national terminology office. Several previously existing language bureaux have either been dissolved or downsized to perform minimal terminology-related functions. It has furthermore been accepted that the government is responsible for developing and promoting the Sintu languages and SASL. Since specialised communication has a central hub in terminology, it is a strategic resource and has an important role in a country's development — especially that of a multilingual country. Effective economic, scientific, and technical communication skills of the citizens of a country are developed through the use of correct and standardised terminology.

Terminology work officially continues on a national basis at the TCS, but various individuals and institutions collaborate in the process of documenting terminology relating to various subject areas in the different official languages.

The terminologists working in a multilingual society such as South Africa deal with conflicting situations. The Afrikaans, Sintu and SASL terminologies must be developed to enhance the multilingual heritage of the country, but there are too many languages to make this practicable and economically viable. There remains, however, a dire need for the documentation of the terminology of rural communities for language preservation, urban jargon, and academic fields. These factors stress the importance of the TCS working on a national basis, and according to a national terminology policy, to modernise and document the various technical vocabularies used in South Africa by means of multilingual technical dictionaries and an online term bank. It is furthermore important to provide in-service and tertiary training to various contributors in the field of terminology. An integrated terminology training model which includes the HLT initiative of the Government was developed and implemented for South African tertiary institutions.

It can be concluded that it is certainly a necessary objective in the South African context to encourage collaborative efforts in order to enhance terminology practice in South Africa so as to improve communication in various domains and to develop the official languages into fully-functional languages in all spheres of human endeavour.

References

Alberts, M. 2000a. "Audit on South African Terminology Projects." Unpublished document. Pretoria: National Terminology Service and the DACST.

Alberts. M. 2000b. "Overview of Current Initiatives in Terminology in South Africa." *NEOTERM — World Specialized Terminology 37–38* (Warszawa), 47–58.

Alberts, M. 2003. "Vaktaalontwikkeling en -opleiding in Suid-Afrika." In *ʼn Man wat beur. Huldigingsbundel vir Dirk van Schalkwyk*, ed by W. Botha, 127–161. Stellenbosch: WAT.

Alberts, M. 2005. "Envisaged Lexicography and Terminology Training Centre." Department of African Languages, University of Pretoria. Unpublished document. PanSALB.

doi   Alberts, M. 2010. "National Language and Terminology Policies — a South African
          Perspective." *Lexikos* 20(20): 599–620.

Alberts, M. 2012. "Terminology as an Aid in Teaching and Learning." Unpublished paper. The
          Closed Workshop on Verification of Scientific Terminology & International Translation
          Day, 28 September 2012. Bellville: Cape Peninsula University of Technology.

doi   Alberts, M. 2014. "Terminology Development at Tertiary Institutions: A South African
          Perspective." *Lexikos* 24(24): 1–26.

Alberts, M. 2015. "'n Oorsig van vaktaalontwikkeling and -opleiding in Suid-Afrika, met spesiale
          verwysing na Afrikaans." Unpublished report. Dagbreek Trust and SAAWK.

Alberts, M. 2017. *Terminology and Terminography Principles and Practice. A South African
          Perspective*. Milnerton: McGillivray Linnegar Associates.

doi   Alberts, M. 2022. "The South African National Lexicography Units — Two Decades Later."
          Lexikos 32(3): 1–24.

Alberts, M. 2024. *Terminology Development in South Africa*. Afrilex preconference SADiLaR
          Workshop, 1 July 2024. University of Pretoria, Pretoria.

Alberts, M., and M. Jooste. 1998. "Lexicography, Terminography and Copyright." *Lexikos* 8(8):
          122–139.

Alberts, M., S. Roets, and J. M. De Beer. 2000. *Terminology Training: Translation vs.
          Terminology*. Unpublished document. Terminology Coordination Section, Department
          of Arts and Culture.

Calteaux, K. 2021. *Information on SADiLaR*. Private email, 22 February 2021. Pretoria: CSIR.

Cluver, A.D. de V. 1996. "Language Development in South Africa. Final Report of the
          Language Plan Task Group (LANGTAG): Towards a National Language Plan for South
          Africa." In *Towards a National Language Plan for South Africa. The final LANGTAG
          Report*. Pretoria: DACST.

Cluver, A.D. de V., and C. J. Scheffer (eds). 1984. *HSRC Research on Terminological Issues in
          Southern Africa: Report on the Research Regarding Organisational Issues in Terminology*.
          (Term-1). Pretoria: HSRC.

Jordaan-Weiss, M. 1996. "Practical Terminology Work in South Africa: Problems, Solutions
          and Challenges." In *TKE '96: Terminology and Knowledge Engineering*, ed. by C. Galinski,
          and K-D. Schmitz, 373–380. Frankfurt am Main: Indeks Verlag.

Kapp, P. H. 2009. *Draer van 'n droom. Die geskiedenis van die Suid-Afrikaanse Akademie vir
          Wetenskap en Kuns, 1909–2009*. Hermanus: Hemel-en-See Boeke.

Layton, R., M. Alberts, and S. Sanker. 2024. *National Terminology Policy*. Pretoria:
          Terminology Coordination Section, National Language Service, Department of Sport,
          Arts and Culture.

Mahlalela-Thusi, B., and K. Heugh. 2002. "Unravelling Some of the Historical Threads of
          Mother-tongue Development and Use During the First Period of Bantu Education
          (1955–1975): New Developments and Research." *Perspectives in Education* 20(1): 241–257.

Maseko, P. 2012. "Advancing the Use of African Languages in SA Higher Education: Strategies,
          Challenges and Opportunities." Closed Workshop on Verification of Scientific
          Terminology and International Translation Day, 28 September 2012. CPUT, Bellville
          Main Campus.

Mayevu, G. S. 1996. "Development of the South African Literatures with Special Reference to Xitsonga. Department of Arts, Culture, Science and Technology." In *Proceedings of a LANGTAG Workshop on Issues in Language Development*. Pretoria: State Language Services, DACST.

Mesthrie, R. 2008. "Necessary Versus Sufficient Conditions for Using New Languages in South African Higher Education: A Linguistic Appraisal." *Journal of Multilingual and Multicultural Development* 29: 325–340.

Mnisi, S. 2021. "Catalogue of Term Lists or Technical Dictionaries." Private email, 12 December 2021. Terminology Coordination Section, National Language Service, DSAC.

Mtintsilana, P. N., and R. Morris. 1988. "Terminography in African Languages in South Africa." *South African Journal of African Languages* 8(4): 109–113.

Ntshangase, D. 1996. *Working Document: Future of the Present Language Boards*. LANGTAG Subcommittee on the Development of (South) African Languages, 20 February 1996. Unpublished document, Pretoria: DAC.

Oeser, E. 1998. "Wüster and his impact in the philosophy of science." In E. Oeser & C. Galinski (eds). *Eugen Wüster (1898–1977). Proceedings of the International Conference on Professional Communication and Knowledge Transfer Vienna, 24–26 August 1998*. Vienna: Infoterm, 105–115,

Oeser, E., and C. Galinski (eds). *Eugen Wüster (1898–1977). Proceedings of the International Conference on Professional Communication and Knowledge Transfer Vienna, 24–26 August 1998*. Vienna: Infoterm,

Republic of South Africa. 1996. *Constitution of the Republic of South Africa*. 1996. Act 108 of 1996.

Sager, J. C. 1990. *A Practical Course in Terminology Processing*. Amsterdam: John Benjamins.

Scheffer, C. J. 1987. "Promoting and Merging Terminological Activities in South Africa." *Logos* 7(2): 31–34.

Sibula, P. M. n.d. "Terminology Development: Challenges, Skills, Strategies and Stakeholders' Role." Unpublished paper. Unit for IsiXhosa, Stellenbosch University Language Centre.

Statistics South Africa. 2022. *South African National Census of 2022*.

Stoberski, Z. 1998. *Multilingual Dictionary of International Terms*. Warszawa: World Bank of International Terms (WBIT) within International Organization for Unification of Terminological Neologisms (IOUTN).

United Nations Educational, Scientific and Cultural Organisation (UNESCO). 2005. *Guidelines for Terminology Policies*. Vienna: Infoterm.

CHAPTER 30

Terminology in Switzerland
From practice to theory and back

Bruno de Bessé, Aurélie Picton & Donatella Pulitano
University of Geneva

This chapter presents the history of terminology in Switzerland, from the early 1980s to present day. It recounts the birth of the profession in this context and the simultaneous creation of the Terminology programme at the University of Geneva: indeed, the history of terminology in Switzerland goes hand in hand with the history of the Faculty of Translation and Interpretation of the University of Geneva, thus allowing for a symbiotic and privileged relationship with Swiss institutions. Reflections are also shared about the profession, its ties with training, and developments in research.

Keywords: Switzerland, pedagogy, terminology professionals, terminography, terminology research, academic and professional interactions

1.   Introduction

In this chapter, the history of terminology in Switzerland[1] is presented in four sections. We begin with a retrospective look at how terminology activities were introduced in the country and deployed in institutions. In Switzerland, the birth, development and evolution of terminology as a discipline can only be fully appreciated by examining the close links established between the University of Geneva's Faculty of Translation and Interpretation (FTI, formerly École de Traduction et d'Interprétation/ETI) and Swiss institutions. We therefore retrace the birth of the discipline in this context, starting in 1984 (de Bessé, 1988). We then outline the

---

1. The four official languages of Switzerland are German, French, Italian, and Romansh. Of the 26 cantons, one is trilingual (Graubünden/Grisons), three are bilingual (Bern, Fribourg, Valais), one is monolingual Italian (Ticino), four are monolingual French (Geneva, Jura, Neuchâtel, Vaud) and 17 are monolingual German.

https://doi.org/10.1075/tlrp.24.30de

different phases of terminology training at the University of Geneva and observe how they have been transferred to the professional sphere, for example in the Canton of Bern and the Swiss Confederation. This section is accompanied by a reflection on the key elements of this vision, which have enabled the development of terminology in Switzerland. After discussing the changes and uncertainties surrounding the training of terminologists in the country, as well as the influence of the professional world in safeguarding it, the third section offers a portrait of the country's terminology activities today, with a focus on the evolution of the profession in the Swiss context. We then discuss the role of terminologists, and put forward a proposal to suggest how the FTI can continue to train students and collaborate with those in the field, in order to innovate, strengthen and enhance both research activities and the profession in Switzerland.

Our study contributes to understanding the history of terminology in Switzerland and highlights the bridges between the academic and professional worlds. We thus hope to contribute to reflections on the future of the profession, its ties with research and training, and the privileged contact between the FTI and institutions in Switzerland.

2.   Birth of a discipline and start of its professionalisation: Little acorns

2.1   Beginnings and early growth

The history of terminology activities in Swiss companies and public administration is quite similar to that of other countries and institutions with multilingual backgrounds, such as Canada (see Chapter 12), Belgium, and the European Commission (see Chapter 20). Up until the 1980s, terminology work was mainly translation-oriented, facilitating the drafting of multilingual legislation (in federal and cantonal administrations) and product documentation (in companies operating throughout Switzerland and around the world).

In Switzerland, and particularly in the Swiss Confederation and the Canton of Bern, the 1980s marked the beginning of projects to set up terminology databases that were inspired by Eurodicautom, Termium and the Banque de terminologie du Québec. To this end, in 1984, the Canton of Bern sent a delegation to Canada headed by the Vice-Chancellor and head of the Office of Linguistic Services, Jacqueline Etter, to learn first-hand how to professionalise the work of translators and make it more efficient (the delegation was hosted by Alain Landry of the Canadian government's Secretary of State, who was in charge of the Translation Bureau at the time, see Chapter 12). Following this visit, a Canadian terminologist was sent on a temporary assignment to the Canton of Bern for several years to help implement institutional terminology activities.[2]

As terminology work intensified and terminology databases were created, it became evident that there was a need to train specialists. Stakeholders in Switzerland were galvanised by reflections from the world of translation and language industries (among others Boulanger et al. 1988, Newton 1992, Kay 1997, Bourigault et al. 2001) on the potential contribution of information technology to the profession. From the end of the 1970s to the beginning of the 1980s, several universities around the world began introducing terminology into their programmes, in order to offer their students new professional prospects.

It was at this time that ETI management had the idea of revolutionising the original terminology courses, which had consisted, until then, of copying and memorising long lists of terms related to economics, law and international institutions; thus, a true academic terminology programme was born. With the assistance of ETI, the Swiss Confederation and the Canton of Bern organised intensive terminology courses for the staff of their language services. These activities led to the creation of the Terminology Section at the Swiss Confederation and the Central Terminology Service at the Canton of Bern in the late 1980s, which were and still are responsible for coordinating and managing terminology activities in their respective institutions.

2.2   A key year: 1984

One key year in the development of terminology activities and training in Switzerland was 1984, as it was the year in which Bruno de Bessé was hired by ETI as a lecturer. Drawing upon his experience and contacts in Canada, France and the European institutions, he set up the first terminology course in Switzerland. From that year onward, all first-year ETI translation students took a compulsory course in terminology. The curriculum was developed with the help of advice from Juan Carlos Sager and Alain Rey.

The main objective of this initial course was to enable students to create their own terminology tools and resources, as well as use computers in their daily work. They learned how to use the methodology that had been devised to create multilingual records, which were fundamental to developing terminology databases that were beginning to appear not only in Switzerland, but also elsewhere in Europe and overseas. In addition to two written exams, the students had to hand in seminar papers and a glossary of 50 terminology records. Translation students

---

2. Ms. Françoise Parc then went on to work for the Terminology section at the Swiss Confederation.

also had to acquire skills in the field of specialised languages, morphology and neology. Up until then, the curriculum had not included a great deal of linguistics or lexicography. These key elements of linguistic work therefore had to be integrated, in addition to introducing students to a discipline that was not entirely new, but had expanded significantly between the end of the 1970s and the beginning of the 1980s.

2.3   Early achievements (until 2005)

2.3.1   *Supporting the birth of a profession*

Once basic training was in place, ETI management quickly saw the need to add terminology as a specialisation, first, to give all former ETI graduates who had not been able to benefit from this course the opportunity to learn about the discipline, and second, to train specialists who were now increasingly confronted with terminology issues and wanted to fill the many positions that were opening up in the field. This new specialisation made it possible to train professional terminologists who were not only capable of creating terminology records, but also had the skills to think about methodological and IT-related issues, as well as promote terminology activities within a company or organisation.

In 1986, the ETI therefore introduced a certificate of specialisation in terminology, the first of its kind in Europe. It was a one-year post-graduate programme, and during the course students were required to attend classes, complete an internship and write a thesis. Overall, the time devoted to this programme (620 h/year) corresponded to an average of 12 hours perweek for one year, including the compulsory internship and the writing of the thesis. In order to allow professionals to attend the programme in parallel with their main activities, the courses were grouped into one afternoon per week over the academic year (semester courses were only introduced with the transition to the *licence*). Finally, for those who were interested in the certificate course but could not attend, de Bessé and the terminology group organised continuing education days, which consisted of a programme in several modules that was intended for a limited number of participants from the private sector. This tradition continues up to this day.

Under the new terminology specialisation, students were required to complete an internship of 8 to 12 weeks duration in order to master their skills and put them into practice in a professional environment. Although students had always been encouraged to complete internships, this was the first time that they were mandatory. In addition to their exams, students now had to prepare a dissertation consisting of 100 bilingual (or trilingual) records in a specialised field that was generally proposed by the organisation hosting the internship, with the aim of enriching its terminology bank. The dissertation also included a theoretical study of a problem encountered in practice.

The certificate was an immediate success. Between 1986 and 2010, ETI awarded over 200 specialist certificates in terminology and their "successors", i.e., complementary certificates in terminology and Master's degrees in translation with a specialisation in terminology. Aspiring language services strengthened their ranks with many future terminology certificate holders. In some cases, translation departments that did not have terminologists made use of the knowledge acquired by the trainees to set up terminology processes. The ties with these early adopters are strong and still exist today.

Translators working for the administration of the Canton of Bern and the Swiss Confederation enrolled in the programme *en masse* early on. Many other institutions sent their employees to learn how to do what they were already doing intuitively, but without any fixed methodology. Among the first certificate holders were employees of the Swiss Confederation and companies such as ASCOM, UBS and Zurich. Furthermore, the certificate became a model for other Swiss educational institutions, such as the Zürcher Hochschule für Angewandte Wissenschaften (ZHAW)[3] — which has developed in a similar way to the FTI — and, internationally, the Universitat Pompeu Fabra (Cabré 2018 for example).

Although the terminology research and symposium landscape were modest at the time, the terminology group was at its forefront and actively participated in many initiatives. For example, in 1988, ETI organised the second international meeting on teaching, following the 1978 meeting at the Université Laval. This event was an opportunity to situate ETI's teaching within the educational landscape in Europe and around the world, and to inspire other institutions (de Bessé 1988). In 1991, ETI organised the Phraseology and Terminology in Translation and Interpreting conference, at the suggestion of Prof. de Bessé. Members of the terminology group gave multiple presentations in Switzerland and abroad at this time (such as "équivalences" 2001[4], JIAMCATT regularly, Madrid, capital de la terminología europea 1988). In addition, from 1990–95, the terminology group participated in a Swiss National Fund project entitled Construction of Multilingual and Computerised Encyclopaedic Dictionaries of Concepts (de Bessé 1992), in collaboration with Michel Léonard's team from the Centre universitaire informatique of the University of Geneva.

---

3. Until recently, the ZHAW delivered basic terminology training courses in the BA in Applied Languages and the MA in Applied Linguistics, as well as within the continuing education programmes.

4. "équivalences" is the yearly conference of the Swiss Association for Translation, Terminology and Interpretation.

2.3.2 *Growing ties between training and professionals*

In the meantime, de Bessé was hired by the State Chancellery of the Canton of Bern as a part-time terminology delegate. He was responsible for initiating the canton's terminology activities (including programming the terminology management software LINGUA-PC) (de Bessé and Pulitano 1996) and training all translators in the Canton of Bern in terminology. This training programme was co-organised by the Canton of Bern and the University of Geneva, thereby enabling cantonal employees to earn the title of translator-terminologist. This title is now included in the staff rules and regulations. Once again, this is an illustration of how professional terminology activities and key players are clearly and consistently linked with the teaching of terminology, as the latter is called upon to meet economic needs and be part of a social practice.

It was in this context that the Compu*term* interest group was created in 1989, once again upon the initiative of de Bessé, who was appointed Professor in October 1996. The aim of this group was to bring together all the key players in the discipline — which, at the time, was still very much a niche area — by organising a working day. The group decided to hold it as part of BÜFA, the office automation trade fair in Basel, as the issue of terminology was clearly relevant to the event. Among the guests were several organisations that already had terminology services and hosted ETI terminology trainees, as well as institutions that had language services or non-official terminology activities. The programme included presentations on working methods (best practices of the time), tools and challenges for terminology activities. These were followed by on-site presentations of various software packages available on the market. This successful initiative led to the creation of the Compu*term* meeting in 1992, which has been held every year since. The aim of the Compu*term* meetings is to take stock of terminology activities in Switzerland and provide a forum for key players in organisations that are particularly active in the field to exchange ideas. The subjects discussed at Compu*term* meetings have evolved in parallel with technical and methodological aspects. Participants at these meetings play a major role in maintaining and updating the training of terminologists in Switzerland. Many of the participating organisations contribute to the terminology assignments that have been carried out by students of terminography since 2012 by proposing topics that are useful for their terminology banks (see Section 4).

Finally, it should be noted that in the early 1990s, the Swiss Association of Translators and Interpreters (ASTI) changed its name to the Swiss Association of Translators, Terminologists and Interpreters (ASTTI). This move once again reflects the importance and recognition of this emerging profession in Switzerland.

3.   Evolution of a training programme: Sowing the acorns

3.1   Contextual changes and hazards

Following these years of growth and until 2011, various reforms and developments were introduced, leading to profound changes to the institutions, programmes and training methods in Switzerland, similarly to what happened in other countries in the last decades. Among the significant changes for terminology training in Geneva was the transition from the translation diploma to the translation *licence* in the 1990s. This led to annual courses being converted to semester-based courses, followed by the introduction of a doctoral degree. From the 2000s onwards, ETI developed a postgraduate diploma (DESS) in terminology (de Bessé 2002), which trained professionals in terminology data management and IT tools, and replaced the Certificate of Specialisation. In addition, a Diplôme d'études approfondies (DEA) in multilingual computational processing was introduced, thereby familiarising students with the multilingual dimension involved in the automatic processing of natural languages. This allowed students to access studies that could lead to a doctorate.

The transformation of diplomas into degrees at the Bachelor, Master, and Doctorate levels subsequently led to the cancellation of the DESS, but saw the birth of the Master's degree in translation with a major in terminology, which existed for several years. This was replaced in the early 2010s by the Faculty's current Master's degrees, leading to the obtainment of the title of Translator in Switzerland. At the same time, following Professor de Bessé's retirement, the necessity of terminology training at the University of Geneva was strongly challenged and there was even talk of abolishing the Terminology chair, and limiting the programme to a strict minimum. The professional community, which needed this training, along with representatives of Comp*u*term, voiced their opposition. Ultimately, the Terminology chair in the Department of Multilingual Computer Processing was retained. Terminology training and research in Geneva (and even Switzerland) was therefore preserved, thanks to its history and association with the broader community of language professionals.

3.2   Continuing a renaissance

In 2011, Aurélie Picton took up the position of Professor of Terminology at the Faculty. This nomination led to a number of changes, in terms of teaching style, pedagogical skill set and theoretical vision. Picton is an advocate of the principles and methods of Textual terminology (Condamines and Picton 2022, also Chapter 11 in this volume), which differs from the original Geneva tradition. The Geneva tradition is more distinctly conceptual and thus closer to Wüster's General Theory of Terminology (GTT) (see Chapter 8). After de Bessé's retirement, it has been carried forward by Donatella Pulitano, a lecturer who is member of the German speaking community. Far from feeding a theoretical boundary, this new constellation enables the Geneva terminology group to form a real bridge between two theoretical strands and two languages. Thus, the terminology group benefits from being at the intersection of theoretical visions and experiences, which complement each other and offer a unique perspective on terminology, in terms of its theories and practice: a terminology tradition that is oriented towards the concept and the organisation of knowledge (influenced by the GTT, see Chapter 8), and a textual tradition that is oriented towards corpora and the linguistic sign in discourse (Textual terminology and Socioterminology, see Chapter 11). This synergy is based on constant dialogue to clarify, particularly in each teacher's course curriculum, the differences and connections between concepts and perspectives. This is made possible only through good teamwork and mutual respect for each individual's theoretical views, which, when combined, are valued as a strength for Geneva's training program rather than as an obstacle. The terminology group has worked since on new research and projects that describe and mutually enrich each other, thus creating a unique environment to train terminologists, trigger reflections and anticipate future developments.

From a pedagogical point of view, the FTI programme combines theory and practice, promotes adaptability, is technology-oriented and, above all, fosters close collaboration between the key players from the Swiss professional context and the academic world. The terminology group therefore continues to be comprised of teachers from both the research and professional realms. Since the School of Translation and Interpreting (ETI) became a Faculty, its programmes have been revised (Prégent et al. 2009) and a doctoral degree has been introduced. Under the Bologna process, courses were distributed between the Bachelor's and Master's programmes. Students are now introduced to the concepts and theories of specialised languages at the Bachelor's level. Terminology skills are therefore mainly developed at the Master's level (and the doctoral level).[5] While fewer hours of terminology are being taught overall, the subject has nevertheless been maintained and reinforced through the creation of a Terminology specialisation in 2018, which was integrated into the Master's degree in translation and technologies.[6] This specialisation was designed to enhance and garner recognition for the students' skills as terminologists in the eyes of employers, as well as restore the visibility of the programme after the many changes that had occurred earlier

---

5. At FTI, the title of translator is also obtained at the Master's level only.

6. The terminology courses are available for all Master's degrees and can be taken individually.

(Gouadec 2002, Nilsson 2009, Pulitano 2018, RaDT 2020, Pulitano and Picton 2024). The Terminology specialisation at the Master's level is comprised of five courses, namely Terminology, Terminography, Terminotics, Corpus for Translation and XML and Multilingual Documents. For the Master's degree, students are also required to complete an internship, and to write a Master thesis.

From a research point of view, the terminology group continues to participate in numerous national and international projects. FTI maintains a strong network, both on a scientific level (e.g., with the universities of Toulouse, Paris 3 — Sorbonne Nouvelle, Grenoble, Lyon, Montreal, to name a few) and in the field (e.g., with the Comput*erm* professionals, with the French Space Agency, or, more recently, with the Swiss helicopter rescue company Air Zermatt), or as members of terminology associations such as the European Association for Terminology/EAFT and the Rat für Deutschsprachige Terminologie/RaDT, see Chapter 22). Within this framework, and in line with our theoretical approach, the members of the terminology group are currently focusing their research on dialectal variation (and esp. diachrony and diastraty) by examining the question of how terms circulate among and between groups of speakers and over time (as a process). The terminology group is also interested in analysing the linguistic, communicational and social roles of terms in professional contexts, as well as developing methodologies for corpus analysis, which now lie at the crossroads of Textual terminology and Socioterminology approaches. Furthermore, the group also works on best practices for terminology work, e.g., by contributing to standardisation work (DIN) and education of users of terminology (DTT, RaDT).

This historical overview has allowed us to highlight the circumstances surrounding the development of the terminology profession in the Swiss context and its special links with academic training in Geneva. In particular, we have emphasised the efforts of the terminology group in Geneva to turn the professional and academic changes it has experienced into a strength. In the next section, we examine how the profession has evolved in Switzerland since the 1980s.

4.   Terminology in Switzerland today: A sprouting oak

4.1   Professional context

As mentioned earlier, terminology work has developed in response to the unique translation needs of Switzerland as a multilingual country. Almost 40 years after terminology training and the first large-scale institutional terminology databases were implemented, many companies and institutions in Switzerland are still involved in terminology initiatives. Nevertheless, some have given up their terminology activities, some have limited them for a time only to return to them later, and others are faced with the task of justifying the need for terminology management due to a perceived lack of immediate return on investment.

In recent years, the Compu*term* Group has observed the coexistence of two diametrically opposed trends: on the one hand, some companies are reducing the size of their language departments, and in particular their terminology departments, going so far as to eliminate positions or outsource them. On the other hand, other companies have become aware of the benefits of terminology work and are actively hiring terminologists. Terminology therefore continues to play a very important, if not indispensable, role in the professional world.

Clearly, there remains a great need for terminology databases today, but terminologists are also increasingly called upon to work in language technologies and thus supply other areas of the language chain. Terminologists continue to create records for terminology banks, thereby preserving the knowledge of institutions and building on the work of the past four decades since terminology became a university subject and a certified profession in Switzerland. But now, they also work to integrate terminology into other applications and technologies, from translation memories to machine translation and LLMs, authoring systems, speech recognition, ontologies and ERP (Enterprise Resource Planning) or CRM (Customer Relationship Management) systems.

As Pulitano (2018) and the Council for German Terminology (RaDT) note in their Professional Profile (2020), job offers over the past ten years highlight a real diversification in terminology profiles and needs. In addition to fundamental skills (developing resources, creating terminology records, making linguistic recommendations, etc.), terminologists are increasingly involved in cross-functional projects that affect an organisation beyond its language services, towards knowledge management itself. They are responsible for training users of terminology and the technologies that are available to them. These tasks used to be performed by other specialists, but nowadays terminologists are increasingly expected to master a wider range of skills in technology, media, file formats, etc. They deal with increasingly numerous and eclectic domains that evolve rapidly. Specifically, the management of Web content (in particular, social media) represents a real challenge. The use of visualisation and knowledge modelling techniques are also more prevalent. Terminologist positions can be either very practice-oriented or very research-oriented, with technology watch or process implementation tasks. A high degree of adaptability and versatility is therefore expected.

It is also important to note that today, in Switzerland, terminologists are often no longer hired as translators or even translator-terminologists but as terminologists in their own right, with specific hiring procedures for this role. This reflects a true recognition (and even legitimisation) of the profession in Switzerland.

At the same time, although translation remains the primary environment in which terminologists work, terminology skills are needed in diverse communication and knowledge management contexts, but under different names: knowledge manager, linguistic engineer, ontologist, etc. The links between these roles and that of a terminologist are not always explicit and may not be identified by employers. There is therefore an urgent need to have terminology skills recognised under these different titles and contexts. University terminology training necessarily bears some responsibility for this recognition. If the skills and expertise of terminologists are to be recognised, regardless of the title attributed to the position, training courses must provide students with the cutting-edge skills they are expected to have, as well as enrich the links between the professional world and the academic world. This global reflection on how training has evolved and how the pedagogical programmes that are now available in higher education can be exploited is essential.

4.2   Academic context

The terminology group at the University of Geneva maintains close links with industry (terminology practice) in Switzerland and internationally, recognising the importance of passing on practical skills in the terminology courses, in terms of programme development, selecting which tools are to be taught, and when planning meetings and seminars with professionals in the field who can share with students their experiences and visions for the profession. The FTI continues for instance to attend meetings of the Compu*term* group, which, in fact, celebrated its 25th anniversary at the University of Geneva in 2017. It also remains attentive to professional developments and experiences in Switzerland. This is a reason why the terminology group uses project-based and active learning strategies (see Weimer 2017; Poumay 2014), particularly in Terminography and Terminology courses: these strategies encourage a closer collaboration with language professionals, while enabling (and even improving) the development of expected skills. We give here two examples of these pedagogic strategies, and emphasise how they can contribute to the bolstering of terminologists in Switzerland.

First, the Terminography course is a practical course that aims to teach students how to create terminographic resources. As it was the case in the past (see above), students are required to validate a glossary containing bilingual records, which are nowadays entered into a proprietary tool that was developed by the terminology group. However, since 2012, students have been provided with authentic assignments by key players in Swiss terminology, who are a constant presence in our faculty and are led by the members of Compu*term*. This terminology assignment is proposed by a company or institution that then acts as the "client" and collaborates with the assigned student throughout the semester, within the framework of a professional relationship. This scenario is a win-win model, since it allows students to better understand the concrete needs of the company or institution and how to address them. In addition, students learn to interact with subject-matter experts in the field, who are indispensable for terminology work. Knowing that they are doing real work for a real company encourages students to be more involved and invested than if they were only exposed to simulated situations. At the same time, partner companies and institutions can have direct contact with the next generation of professionals and benefit from the addition to their terminology resources, however modest that contribution may be (Pulitano and Picton 2018).

Second, the Terminology course focuses on theory and aims to have students reflect on the role of terminology in language policy management. In this course, students are given a terminology assignment based on an authentic scenario, developed in collaboration with authentic key players and designed as an opportunity to apply and appropriate advanced theoretical notions in terminology. The assignment is one that was recently dealt with or is currently being handled by the participating key players, and can involve, for example, the search for equivalents or denominations. It integrates various notions of terminology planning and language planning, which allow students to develop theoretical reflections while responding to a practical case. The authentic dimension of the assignment exposes students to the challenges of the professional world (Picton and Haeberli, 2023). Students collaborate with a professional who is experienced in this type of project, and the aim is to generate discussion and feedback, and promote the relevance of this type of work in a future career. Furthermore, each year, a terminologist is invited to meet with students to discuss the profession (Pulitano and Picton 2018). This direct involvement of professionals is particularly rich in pedagogical value and welcomed by the FTI's students. It also allows the teachers to better align their training with developments in the profession and provide a balance between theory and practice. In return, professionals have the opportunity to meet the next generation and share their thoughts on the demands and evolution of the profession, as well as on their expectation regarding the competences to be taught. Moreover, they can benefit from the students' reflections on their assignments to advance their own work.

In addition to these courses, developments in research and the training of doctoral students in terminology are also an asset in strengthening the training of future terminologists.

A number of PhD graduates have taken on strategic roles in companies that are making significant contributions to terminology work in Switzerland (as heads of department, in charge of implementing machine translation, etc.).

Others have taken up positions in the international academic research. The FTI's research must therefore remain close to the needs for innovation in the fields of terminology and translation in Swiss and international contexts. As stated before (Section 3.2), the development of projects that account for professional needs remains a priority for the terminology group, in line with Textual terminology and Socioterminology propositions.

5.   Concluding remarks: Towards the great oak of tomorrow

In this chapter, we have retraced the central milestones in the history of terminology in Switzerland and examined its existing form. We have reflected on the evolution of the profession in the Swiss context. In particular, we have highlighted the strong, privileged and necessary relationship between the University of Geneva and professional key players in the local field. We have thus shown how the FTI's training programme was born out of the needs of real professionals in the field, and has been developed with a practical orientation. These same professionals were there to defend the programme when it was at risk of cancellation. In a field such as terminology, teaching (and, to a certain extent, research) can only fulfil its role if it remains rooted in the constantly evolving needs of the companies and institutions that are stakeholders in that field.

Today, we are continuing our journey and working to nurture this relationship. As the academic and theoretical context changes and the profession evolves, we have learned to enrich our collaboration, for instance, by making use of new approaches proposed for university pedagogy and by developing applied research projects. Since the beginnings of terminology in Switzerland, key players in both the academic world and the professional field have worked together to navigate changes and turn them into strengths so that terminology will continue to thrive in the best possible way. Switzerland, as a multilingual country, and Geneva, as the host of many international organisations, are a true crossroads of languages. The FTI must remain at the forefront of research and education in the language industries in general, and in terminology specifically. We remain committed to meeting this challenge, and working hand in hand with the professionals in our field.

References

Boulanger, Jean-Claude, Pierre Auger, Conrad Ouellon, and Marie-Claude L'Homme (eds). 1988. *Origine et développement des industries de la langue.* Québec: Centre international de recherche sur le bilinguisme.

doi Bourigault, Didier, Christian Jacquemin, and Marie-Claude L'Homme (eds). 2001. *Recent Advances in Computational Terminology.* Amsterdam: John Benjamins.

Cabré, Maria Teresa. 2018. "Where is Terminology Today?" Public lecture of the Faculty of Translation and Interpretation, University of Geneva, 23 November.

de Bessé, Bruno. 1988. "L'enseignement de la terminologie à l'École de Traduction et d'Interprétation de l'Université de Genève." *Parallèles* 10: 63–67.

de Bessé, Bruno. 1992. "Des fichiers terminologiques aux bases de connaissances." In *L'environnement traductionnel : La station de travail du traducteur de l'an 2001*, ed. by André Clas, and Hayssam Safar, 1st ed., 283–300. Québec: Presses de l'Université du Québec.

de Bessé, Bruno. 2002. "École de traduction et d'interprétation de l'Université de Genève." *Traduire* 192: 53–67.

doi de Bessé, Bruno, and Donatella Pulitano. 1996. "Which Terms Should Firms or Organisations Include in their Terminology Banks? The Case of the Canton of Berne." In *Terminology, LSP and Translation: Studies in Language Engineering in Honour of Juan C. Sager*, ed. by Harold Somers, 35–46. Amsterdam: John Benjamins.

doi Kay Martin. 1997. "The Proper Place of Men and Machines in Language Translation." *Machine Translation* 12(1–2): 3–23.

doi Newton, John (ed). 1992. *Computers in Translation: A Practical Appraisal* (1st ed.). Oxfordshire: Routledge.

Picton, Aurélie, and Philippe Haeberli. (2023). "Du cours *ex cathedra* à la pédagogie par projet, en classe inversée. Un partage d'expérience pour la terminologie." *Recherche et pratiques pédagogiques en langues* 42(2)

doi Poumay, Marianne. 2014. "Six leviers pour améliorer l'apprentissage des étudiants du supérieur." *Revue internationale de pédagogie de l'enseignement supérieur* 30(1).

Prégent, Richard, Huguette Bernard, and Anastassis Kozanitis. 2009. *Enseigner à l'université dans une approche-programme.* Montréal: Presses internationales Polytechnique.

Pulitano, Donatella. 2018. "Le profil du terminologue — reloaded." In *Proceedings of the VIII ACT Terminology Summit*, 123–126. Luxembourg.

Pulitano, Donatella, and Aurélie Picton. 2018. "Les technologies au service de l'enseignement de la terminologie aujourd'hui : à la recherche d'un équilibre entre théorie et pratique." In *Proceedings of the 86th ACFAS Congress.* Chicoutimi.

Pulitano, Donatella, and Aurélie Picton. 2024. "L'enseignement de la terminologie à la Faculté de traduction et d'interprétation de l'Université de Genève." Oral communication, In *La didactique de la terminologie dans l'espace universitaire francophone : approches innovantes et outillées.* Thessalonique.

Rat für Deutschsprachige Terminologie. 2020. *Berufsprofil 2.0 Terminologin — Terminologe.* Köln, RaDT.

Weimer, Maryellen. 2017. *Active Learning: a Practical Guide for College Faculty.* Madison, WI: Magna Publications.

CHAPTER 31

Terminology in Wales

A journey towards standardisation

Delyth Prys, Tegau Andrews & Gruffudd Prys
Bangor University

The Welsh experience deals with developing terminology standards and guidelines in a minoritised language environment. Attempts to provide modern technical terminology for the Welsh language began as a voluntary, amateur activity without official backing, as part of an ambitious plan of domain gain, preparing for increased use of Welsh in education, public administration, law, health, etc. These domain gains have been increasingly realised, especially since the publication of various Welsh language acts and the establishment of the Welsh devolved government in 1998. The expansion of Welsh-medium education has been central to the development of Welsh terminology. The particular challenges of the Welsh language are explored, as are concept-based methodologies to develop Welsh more generally as a modern, flexible language for the 21st century.

Keywords: Wales, Welsh language, domain expansion, terminology standardisation, educational use, bilingual policies, endangered languages

1. The Welsh language context

Today Welsh is classed as a minoritised and endangered language. It is also one of 34 European languages reported on in the 2022 European Language Equality project for the European Commission (Prys et al 2022). According to the 2021 UK Government census it is spoken by 538,300 people in Wales over the age of three, or 17.8% of the population (Welsh Government 2022). This shows a decrease of 23,700 or 1.2% in the number of Welsh speakers in Wales since the 2011 census, which was not anticipated. Analysis of the results is on-going, but anecdotally, outward migration of young people from Wales in search of better job prospects and the detrimental effects of the COVID-19 pandemic are amongst the reasons cited.

Welsh belongs to the insular Celtic group of languages, all of which are now endangered. It is most closely related to the other Brittonic Celtic languages,

https://doi.org/10.1075/tlrp.24.31pry

namely Breton and Cornish. The other Celtic sub-group, the Goidelic languages, contains Irish, Scottish Gaelic and Manx, which are more distantly related to Welsh (Russell 1995). All modern Celtic languages share a common history as minoritised languages existing in the shadow of another dominant language, namely French in the case of Breton, and English in the case of the other five. Welsh has a long history as a language of high literature, with the earliest surviving texts dating back to around 900 AD (Williams 1972).

During the latter part of the 16th century, a group of Renaissance scholars in Wales were instrumental in establishing Welsh as a modern, scholarly language, producing the first printed Welsh books, and counteracting to some extent the negative effects of the Laws in Wales Acts, commonly known as the *Acts of Union*, of 1535 and 1542. These laws stipulated that henceforth English was to be the language of justice and administration in Wales, leading to the steady decline of Welsh during the following centuries. The language clauses of these acts were definitively repealed by the *Welsh Language Act* of 1993 (see Section 3).

The Renaissance in Wales went hand in hand with the Protestant Reformation, with great emphasis placed on translating the Bible into the vernacular. The first Welsh language version of the Bible was completed in 1588, and hailed as a masterpiece, setting the standard for an all-Wales common standard language for the next four hundred years (Currie 2022). An English-Welsh dictionary, *A Dictionary in Englyshe and Welshe*, was one of the first Welsh books printed (Salesbury 1547), followed by an influential Welsh–Latin/ Latin–Welsh dictionary, *Antiquae linguae Britannicae ... et linguae Latinae dictionarium duplex* (Davies 1632).

In the 18th and 19th centuries, anglicisation continued apace in Wales, driven both by the growth of the British state and the Industrial Revolution, of which Wales was an early centre with its abundance of iron and coal. Wales was one of the first countries in Europe to achieve mass literacy, doing so through the medium of the Welsh language (Davies 2007). Key to the achievement of mass literacy was the establishment of Circulating Schools by Griffith Jones of Llanddowror in the 18th century, later followed by the Sunday Schools set up in conjunction with Protestant chapels and churches throughout Wales. These were voluntary, bottom-up ventures, inspired by the belief that everyone should be able to read the Bible for themselves in their native language, and that many poor children, who were monoglot Welsh speakers, would die before they mastered English, if reading were taught to them in that language (James 2012). This drove the demand for religious and other books in Welsh, leading in the 19th century to the establishment of a Welsh popular press.

Despite increasing anglicisation therefore, it was also a period of great vitality in Welsh-language culture, bolstered by a new industrial working class who, although not rich, had enough money to pay for modest Welsh publications.

These included periodicals in the 1860s that had a reported circulation of 120,000 and a collection of poems entitled *Oriau'r Hwyr* of which 30,000 copies were sold between 1860 and 1872 (Davies 2007: 404–5). In fact, Welsh-language publishing at the time was such a commercial success that Scottish publishers considered moving into the market (ibid: 404). The Welsh public also had a great thirst for education and self-improvement, as evidenced in the sales of *Y Gwyddoniadur Cymreig*, a Welsh-language encyclopaedia of ten volumes and nearly 9,000 pages, published in instalments between 1854 and 1879 (Parry 1854–1879). Its publisher, Thomas Gee, spent £20,000 on this venture, and the sales were such that he was able recoup that outlay (Davies 2007: 404–405). This period saw a great expansion in the vocabulary of the Welsh language in order to deal with new concepts of the industrial age and increasing administrative bureaucracy. This included the words for 'railway' *rheilffordd* (earliest known use 1846), 'gas' *nwy* (earliest known use 1828), and 'committee' *pwyllgor* (earliest known use 1835) which are now well-embedded in the language (GPC Online 2014: s.nn.). Not all neologisms from this period withstood the test of time, however. The influential report *Welsh in Education and Life,* which examined the position of Welsh in education in the 1920s, noted that in the mid-nineteenth century, "people thought that there *must* be a native Welsh word to denote every object, and therefore supplemented the supposed deficiency of the common spoken language by invention" (Great Britain 1927: 259), even when perfectly adequate borrowings were already in use. So while the borrowing *het*, 'hat', was used in Welsh as early as the fourteenth century, in 1795 the native Welsh word *diddosben* was coined (GPC Online 2014: s.nn.). This, along with several other native words, such as *cerbydres*, 'train' (earliest known use 1848), and *perdoneg* 'piano' (earliest known use 1850), did not become accepted and English borrowings prevailed, in the aforementioned examples, namely *het, trên* (earliest known use 1851) and *piano* (earliest known use 1841) (GPC Online 2014: s.nn.). Neologisms filled lexical gaps in everyday language, and where some seem to have been readily accepted, others were ignored, or indeed condemned in the popular press of the day (Morgan 2002). Attempts at coining new scientific terms from native roots were particularly condemned, especially as they often showed ignorance of scientific concepts (Hughes 1990).

The new, expanded vocabulary of Welsh was disseminated through an increasing number of published dictionaries, produced mostly by amateur lexicographers (Hawke 2018). Foremost amongst them was John Walters, whose 1770–1794 *English to Welsh Dictionary* contained many useful new coinings, and William Owen Pughe whose strange but influential ideas about etymology and word formation "disrupted the academic study of Welsh for many generations" (Hawke ibid).

Figures such as Pughe were able to have a disproportionate influence on linguistic studies of Welsh as Wales had no centre of university education until the establishment of a university at Aberystwyth in 1872, paid for by public subscription. Other Welsh universities soon followed, leading to the establishment of a federal University of Wales in 1893 with three constituent colleges: Aberystwyth, Bangor and Cardiff (Jenkins 1993). Welsh religious nonconformists, who were the majority of the population of Wales by the mid 19th century, had effectively been barred from access to the old English universities until the *Universities Tests Act* 1871 because of their refusal to conform to the established Anglican church. Welsh could be studied as part of Celtic Studies at Oxford University, but it was the introduction of Welsh as a subject in its own right in the new Welsh university colleges that enabled scholarship and research on the Welsh language to grow as a professional discipline.

However, the legacy of an amateur tradition of lexicography, and a popular interest in vocabulary and the language in general, continued side by side with the new academic rigour. Despite an influx of new English borrowings to Welsh at a colloquial level, there was a general desire for the formal, written language at least to use correct terminology. Today this tension is portrayed as a difference in language register, with higher registers being more careful in their use of native words and phrases, and lower registers being more accepting of borrowings, code switching and other denoters of informal speech.[1]

2.   Welsh in education

A major development for the academic study of Welsh was the establishment of the Board of Celtic Studies in 1921 (on the pattern of the School of Irish Learning, founded in Dublin in 1903), consisting mainly of scholars from the University of Wales. It originally had three committees, one of which was the Language and Literature Committee, which soon began to publish Welsh/English bilingual lexicons in various specialist fields. By 1971 it had published nearly thirty lexicons in a range of subjects including biology, geography, history and physics (Andrews and Prys 2016). However, the language of instruction at university level in Wales, apart from a few exceptions, was English, and the terminologies were produced mainly to facilitate writing on these subjects in the Welsh-language popular press and to demonstrate that Welsh was a modern, living language in which one could discuss such matters. This cannot be described as an attempt to stop domain loss, as there had not been academic discourse in Welsh on these subjects previously, but rather as the expression of a desire to achieve domain gain, where

---

1. For more information about language registers in general, see ISO/TR 20694: 2018, *A Typology of Language Registers*.

a new generation would be able to discuss these matters fully in Welsh. Meanwhile, Welsh-medium schools began to be established from the mid 20th century onwards, creating demand for educational resources in Welsh (Andrews 2010). The first official Welsh-medium state-run primary school, educating children between the ages of 4 and 11, opened in Llanelli, south Wales, in 1947, while the first Welsh-medium secondary school, educating children between the ages of 11 and 18, was opened in north-east Wales in 1956. The number of Welsh-medium schools increased throughout the 20th century (Williams 2003). This trend has continued, and indeed accelerated, into the 21st century, and an increasing proportion of the pupils are now drawn from non-Welsh speaking homes (Welsh Government 2022).

Teachers in the early years struggled with the lack of suitable teaching resources for Welsh-medium education, including the lack of developed terminology. From the 1960s onwards small booklets of terminology for specific subjects were published, mainly by the WJEC (Welsh Joint Education Committee), an examination board which also provides educational resources for schools, and the Board of Celtic Studies which continued to be active in the field. These were usually English to Welsh wordlists, with no Welsh to English sections, showing clearly that the need was perceived as searching for Welsh equivalents of English terms already in circulation. These booklets were produced by committees of teachers and lecturers involved in the different subject areas, and were usually developed on a voluntary basis with contributors and editors working on them in addition to their everyday jobs. Teachers often depended on their own experience when elaborating these terminologies, and there were sometimes inconsistencies in how a single concept was referred to in different school subjects. For example, one problematic term was 'shear force,' where the Geography term list contained one Welsh equivalent while the Mathematics and Physics term list contained another. Upon examination, it was found that both Welsh terms denoted the same concept. The introductory pages of the early term lists often give interesting insights into the principles and guidelines used by their editing committees, with terms from scientific subjects often reflecting systematic organisation of the field (such as chemical concepts or genus-species in biology). This has been described as the *heroic* period of Welsh terminology research, when pioneers such as Dafydd Kirkman and R. Elwyn Hughes guided various projects, giving generously of their time and expertise (Prys 2003).

The first comprehensive Welsh terminological dictionary, *Geiriadur Termau* was a major step forward, reflecting "the effort of many people engaged in education in Wales to produce lists of terms required for the teaching of a number of school subjects through the medium of Welsh" (Williams 1973:xxx). This dictionary was bi-directional, containing a Welsh to English as well as an English to

Welsh section, and included information such as grammatical gender (Andrews and Prys 2016).

Not all terminology resources developed at this time were for the education sector. Word lists and terminological dictionaries were published for example for Local Government (University of Wales 1971) and Law (Lewis 1972). These resources fulfilled a valuable role at a time of rapidly expanding use of Welsh in the public sector and in education. A bibliography of 137 items was compiled in 1995 detailing these word lists and terminological dictionaries as well as other useful resources for Welsh-medium education (Prys et al 1995).

A major new development occurred in 1988 when the UK government introduced for the first time a standardised National Curriculum for all state schools in England and Wales, set out in the *Education Reform Act* (UK Government 1988). This was seen in Wales as an opportunity to overhaul terminology across all subject areas taught through the medium of Welsh, and also to establish a more rigorous basis for the development of Welsh school terminology, which would adhere to a set of principles and guidelines. Further developments since then, especially since the establishment in 1998 of a new devolved Government for Wales with responsibility for Education, have led to the National Curriculum in Wales developing separately from the one in England, with 2022 seeing the establishment of a new Welsh Curriculum (Welsh Government 2022). Changes in the curriculum, as well as advances in human knowledge, necessitate constant revision and expansion of Welsh terminology, making it a dynamic field of study.

In 1998 the first edition of the terminological dictionary for schools, *Y Termiadur Ysgol*, was published, having been commissioned by the School Curriculum and Assessment Authority in 1993 and developed by Bangor University (Prys and Jones 1998). A revised and enlarged edition was published as *Y Termiadur Addysg* in 2006 (Prys et al 2006). Since then the terminological dictionary has been continuously enlarged and updated, but has moved entirely to the digital sphere. Funded by the Welsh Government, its remit has expanded to include terminology from further education courses and domains, in addition to those found in primary and secondary education.

The publication of *Y Termiadur Addysg* was followed by new terminological dictionaries for Welsh-medium university education. In 2009, a new terminology project was funded to standardise terms for universities, in preparation for the establishment of a new virtual university college which now operates across almost all the institutions of higher education in Wales, the Coleg Cymraeg Cenedlaethol. All higher education terminological dictionaries were then brought together into one comprehensive volume, *Geiriadur Termau'r Coleg Cymraeg Cenedlaethol* (Andrews et al. 2009), which is only published electronically, and which also continues to be enlarged and updated.

Y Termiadur Addysg and *Geiriadur Termau'r Coleg Cymraeg Cenedlaethol* are companion works, enabling pupils and students studying through the medium of Welsh to use the same terminologies seamlessly from primary school through to university education and beyond. They use the same methodologies, principles, templates and IT platforms, and since these were established on broad standards, they have also been used to standardise terminologies in other technical fields.

3.   Terminology for language planning and translation

Subjects outside the field of education became more important at the end of the 20th century. One crucial development with long-term repercussions for terminology work and the status of Welsh in general was the UK Government's *Welsh Language Act* 1993, which stated that Welsh should not be treated less favourably than English. In the years following the establishment of devolved government for Wales in 1998, this was extensively built upon by successive laws, strategies, guidelines and action plans, published by the Welsh Government. These include the *Welsh Language (Wales) Measure* (2011), which made Welsh for the first time an official language in Wales alongside English; *Cymraeg 2050: A million Welsh speakers* (Welsh Government 2017), which laid out the ambition to nearly double the number of Welsh speakers by the middle of the century, and the *Welsh Language Technology Action Plan* (Welsh Government 2018), which laid a clear pathway to using technology to achieve these aims.

The Cymraeg 2050 strategy detailed corpora, dictionaries and terminology as vital components of its linguistic infrastructure, stating that "it is vitally important to have high-quality sources of terminology that facilitate the use of Welsh in all aspects of everyday life, including expert areas such as technology, law, and education" (Welsh Government 2017:72). The *Welsh Language Technology Action Plan* named Welsh-language speech technology, computer-assisted translation, and conversational AI as three areas it wanted to address (Welsh Government 2018:4), and also emphasised that in order to support Welsh-language content creation it would "support terminology, lexicography and corpora resources and other elements of Welsh language infrastructure" (ibid:6).

This led to an increasing demand for terminological resources for aspects of public life, such as the Welsh Courts system (Justice Wales Network 2011), Food Standards (Fidler et al 2018) and Social Services and Social Care (Prys et al 2015a). It was fortunate, therefore, that terminology for Welsh-medium education had laid the groundwork for more general principles and methods for developing and standardising technical terminology in Welsh. Education as a field encompasses a broad range of academic and occupational subjects, including scientific, legal and administrative areas. Many of these overlap with the responsibilities of the new Welsh government and thus provided a sound basis for developing new terminologies, whilst greater use of Welsh now outside the field of education allowed the newly standardised terms to gain wider acceptance and use.

In addition to the general impact of official bilingualism in the public sphere, in local government and other public agencies, the establishment of bilingual practice within the devolved government itself led to Welsh being used in domains where it was previously absent. This necessitated the establishment of a dedicated translation service, as well as appropriate terminological resources. Francoeur in Chapter 12 talks about the perception of "two distinct terminology schools or approaches — one grounded in translation, the other, in language planning" noting that both evolved hand in hand in Canada as a response to the growing demand for French terms. The same can be said of the Welsh experience, with terminology planning forming part of language planning policies, but the needs of translators also being present. More and more translators began to be needed in central and local government from the 1960s onwards, and the demand for terminology in this quarter grew with the establishment of devolved government in Wales in 1998 (Andrews 2010). In common with translation services throughout Europe at the time, which were faced with ever increasing demands on scarce resources, the Welsh Government's Translation Service adopted technological aids to translation, including translation memory systems to increase productivity (Screen 2017). Terminology management is usually an important part of such systems, allowing a team of translators to share glossaries and termbases, ensuring accuracy and consistency in their work. These terminological activities belong to the terminology approach grounded in translation, and the Welsh Government's own translation service has has made an important made an important contribution to Welsh terminological resources.

Since 2004, the Welsh Government's Translation Service has shared *TermCymru,* the termbase derived from its translation memory system, openly online. It covers those fields that have been devolved to the Welsh Government, such as Agriculture, Education, Housing, Health and Social Care, and the Environment. It also contains other useful information such as the names and titles of schemes, organisations and other entities. It indicates by means of a colour-coded system whether terms have been fully standardised (Status A), partially standardised (Status B) or are at the first stage of the standardisation process (Status C). Despite being geared primarily towards its own internal translation service and the needs of translators in general, it is widely used by all those who seek reliable terminology in Welsh for concepts used in government and administration.

In areas that have been traditionally discussed through the medium of Welsh, such as agriculture, the challenge can be to find standardised terms suitable for the whole of Wales from a number of regional and local words and phrases. An example is the word 'hedge' which has at least four Welsh equivalents (*perth, gwrych, clawdd, sietin*). Three of these (the exception is *sietin*) are used in TermCymru in different multi-word terms, with different levels of standardisation, and sometimes two are used together, acknowledging the problem of choosing one form over all others. More often, however, the problem is the lack of a native Welsh equivalent, especially in fields not previously encountered in Welsh. A unique European Union concept such as 'subsidiarity' has no equivalent Welsh concept, and necessitated the coining of a neologism *sybsidiaredd,* keeping the original lemma, and adding a Welsh suffix.

4.   The development of terminology science in Wales

Standardisation activities in Wales began in earnest in 1993, with the commission to create *Y Termiadur Ysgol*, the terminological dictionary for schools. One of the first tasks laid down by the project's steering committee was to research and produce coherent guidelines to inform the work. At the beginning, the project had been framed in terms of trying to ensure consistency between competing Welsh terms, given that the old WJEC terminology booklets tended to be confined to individual subject areas and inconsistencies appeared where concepts were relevant to more than one subject area. However, following the submission of the first report on *Cysoni Termau* ('making terms consistent') it was decided that the emphasis should be changed to *Safoni Termau* ('standardising terms') since it was argued that mere consistency would not be enough if the chosen term were of poor quality. Standardisation, on the other hand, implied a further level of care for the quality of the recommended terms, and the introduction of objective principles and guidelines in their elaboration.

Prior to this project, terminology development in Wales had been regarded mainly as a Welsh problem, with no reference to what was happening in other countries. This changed in 1993 when research for the Cysoni Termau report discovered the ISO family of standards, especially those that referred specifically to the standardisation of terms. Core standards such as *ISO 704 Terminology Work — Principles and methods* and *ISO 860 Terminology Work — Harmonization of concepts and terms* were found to be relevant and adaptable to the Welsh context, giving a framework and methodology for developing the science of terminology in Wales (Prys 2006). These ISO principles were summarised and adapted for Welsh in the *Guidelines for the Standardization of Welsh Terminology* written for the Welsh Assembly Government Translation Service and the Welsh Language Board (Prys and Jones 2007) and published both in English and in Welsh.

One of the new insights gained at this time was that the approach to perceiving and structuring terminology is concept-based, rather than being based on the word or lexical unit, and differs therefore from the compilation of traditional dictionaries.[2] This helped clarify the difference in approach between lexicography as descriptive, emphasising etymology, cognates, synonyms and other linguistic features, and terminology as prescriptive, intended to provide guidance on what terms should be used in technical domains, emphasising conceptual clarity and precision, avoiding polysemy and synonymy and, where necessary, coining and promoting neologisms. Translators in particular tended to treat all dictionary resources as being equal, sometimes favouring a general-purpose comprehensive dictionary over more specialised technical terminological dictionaries. Some public bodies have dealt with this by specifying the terminological dictionaries that should be used by teachers, lecturers, authors and translators. Education for translators has also attempted to correct this, for example the chapter on *Geiriaduron, termiaduron ac adnoddau defnyddiol eraill* ('dictionaries, terminological dictionaries and other useful resources') in Prys and Trefor (2015). New methods of disseminating terminological resources have also increasingly become a key part of terminology work since the 1990s. Moves away from paper-based products to various easy-to-use digital channels, such as online terminological dictionaries and databases, dictionary apps, and terminology lists in translation memory systems, have helped popularise standardised Welsh terms, and whilst terminologists tend to focus on the quality of the terminologies being elaborated, the wider distribution and ready availability of these digital resources has played an important part in ensuring that these terms are accessible to a wider audience (Prys et al 2015).

Another significant development which has become a field of scientific enquiry in its own right is the creation of digital tools, platforms and standards to store, develop and disseminate terminological resources. Initial guidance was obtained from *ISO/TR 12618 Computational aids in terminology — Creation and use of terminological databases and text corpora* (1994). This technical report has since been withdrawn, but at the time it enabled the creation of robust terminological databases which were built upon and ported over the years to other newer and more sophisticated systems, thus future-proofing the work and simultaneously keeping down costs. Keeping terminological data in one master database also enabled the production of terminologies in various different digital formats, without creating unintentional inconsistencies and errors. Given that research funded by the Welsh Government or its agencies is also usually disseminated free

---

2. See Chapter 17 for further discussion of the ISO standards and concept-based terminology principles.

of charge, the resultant dictionaries and apps are now accessible to a wide range of different stakeholders.

Terminological dictionaries usually have their own websites, in line with the desire of organisations to promote their own brand, for example the *Geiriadur Termau'r Coleg Cymraeg Cenedlaethol* (Andrews et al. 2009) can be accessed through the Coleg Cymraeg Cenedlaethol's own Resource Portal (Coleg Cymraeg Cenedlaethol n.d.), but all those that have been developed on the Bangor University template and system can also be accessed through the Welsh National Terminology Portal (Prys and Jones 2018) thus cutting down on search time and negating the need to visit several different websites.

The *Ap Geiriaduron* (Robertson et al 2014) phone and tablet app is the most recent method for accessing these terminological dictionaries. This app is available for both iOS and Android platforms and had been downloaded more than 390,000 times by May 2023 (Prys 2023). Given a Welsh-speaking population of under 600,000, this would suggest that it is used by a majority of Welsh-speakers. Of course it may also be used by people outside of Wales, and by Welsh learners, who form a large and important group in Welsh language revitalisation efforts. The significant uptake of this app has proved to be another positive result of dissemination through electronic means. Use of the online versions of the terminological dictionaries is also encouraging, totalling 14,081,901 searches by October 2022, of which 1,173,905 occurred in the previous six months (Prys 2022). Peaks and troughs in the usage figures confirm that it is used mainly in educational and work settings.

One interesting and unforeseen consequence of storing all the terminological data in master databases has been the ability to create the popular Vocab plug-in, which can be overlain on Welsh language websites and provides word by word translation from the linked dictionaries, enabling the user to look up difficult or unfamiliar words (Jones et al 2016).

Developments in terminology management systems have been as important as publishing and disseminating the standardised terms. These systems can automate and speed up the standardisation process, while at the same time keeping a record of decisions and archiving content as needed. Each entry in the system corresponds to a different concept and all related grammar and linguistic information is stored with that entry. Concept-based and cloud-based systems to allow dispersed teams of terminologists and subject specialists to collaborate at a distance were another important development, and the Maes T system used for the terminological dictionaries of the National Terminology Portal was an early example of this (Andrews and Prys 2011). Later advances included incorporating the issue-tracking software GitLab into the workflow, which allows terminologists across all projects to discuss, document and share information.

5.   Linguistic challenges encountered

Borrowing lexical items from other languages and adapting them to Welsh morphology is a common method of naming concepts in the Welsh language. This process relies on a certain amount of agreement amongst users of a language in order for the new lexical items to gain a wide currency. Welsh speakers can be reluctant to accept borrowings which sound too similar to English, even when those borrowings are actually from Latin or Greek bases. Obvious English borrowings also tend to be avoided in higher registers of Welsh (Rottet and Morris 2018: 341, 355, 421).

In fields like medicine, many terms created using Welsh bases are long established, however, in recent years, it has become more obvious that in very technical contexts, using international borrowings is often the better approach, as it is likely to avoid certain types of problems. For example, the native term for 'scapula,' used in schools, is *padell yr ysgwydd* (literally, 'pan of the shoulder'), however this presented problems when related terms were needed for university education, such as the adjective 'subscapular.' Attaching a prefix and an adjectival ending to a phrase such as this would have resulted in an unnatural and verbose structure such as *isbadell yr ysgwydd-aidd* (literally, 'under-pan of the shoulder-ish'). The twentieth century borrowing, *sgapwla,* is much better suited to coining adjectives, such as *isgapwlar*. Therefore, while the Welsh-based term *padell yr ysgwydd* is still acceptable in school terminology and less technical contexts, the Latin-based *sgapwla* is preferred in higher education and technical writing. In other cases of medical terminology, the established Welsh-based term was inexact, such as the term *llid yr ymenydd* (literally 'inflammation of the brain') used as equivalent for 'meningitis,' which was later changed to *meningitis.*

The conflict between choosing Welsh-based terms or international ones can also be seen in other fields such as mathematics, where the terms *uchafbwynt* ('highest point') and *uchafswm* ('highest sum') have historically been used for 'maximum.' In 2022, in an email discussion with Welsh-speaking mathematics lecturers, it became clear that while some still preferred the well-established Welsh-based terms, others were in favour of using the borrowing *macsimwm,* and creating other terms such as *minimacs* ('minimax') and *macsimeddio* ('maximize') from this borrowing (personal correspondence, Andrews 2022). Reasons in favour of using the borrowing were that in the context of bilingual teaching, it would be useful to have English and Welsh terms that are similar, and that it could be advantageous to have a slightly more vague Latin-based term which did not specify what thing (sum or point) was highest. Reasons against using it were that vagueness is not necessarily a good thing in mathematics, and that the Latin-based term sounds too similar to English, especially given that the stress on Welsh words falls, as a rule, on the penultimate syllable, whereas with the term *macsimwm* the stress would be on the first syllable.

English borrowings become part of the Welsh language when they undergo morphological developments and become naturalised, such as nouns mutating, acquiring a Welsh spelling and a Welsh plural ending (Hawke 2016). In some cases, it can be difficult to adapt English and international borrowings to Welsh in this way. Linguistic mutation is one difficult case.

Linguistic mutation in Welsh is a process whereby certain consonants are replaced by others, or removed, according to fixed rules. It is triggered by different grammatical factors and affects nine consonants. Mutation happens at the beginning of words (initial consonant mutation) and elsewhere. An example of initial consonant mutation is seen in *fy nghi* 'my dog.' Here, the masculine noun *ci* 'dog,' is preceded by the personal pronoun *fy* 'my' and this triggers the mutation of *ci* to *nghi*. The rules which govern this type of mutation are numerous, but unambigous. It is the mutations which take place elsewhere that can be problematic in term formation. For example, whereas certain native Welsh prefixes such as *ad-*, *dad-* and *rhyng-* (which could be translated to English as re-, un-, inter-) trigger mutation, international prefixes borrowed into Welsh, such as haemo-, bio- and micro- create a mutation conundrum.

6.   The welsh-termau-cymraeg discussion forum

After a century and a half of voluntary and bottom-up efforts to provide modern technical terminology for Welsh, the contribution of academic research and involvement of statutory bodies has been much appreciated and has enabled a more coherent development of terminology based on scientific principles. However, previous voluntary efforts have left a strong legacy of interest in terminological and linguistic matters amongst the general public. Welsh speakers in general are aware of the effort needed to maintain their language in the face of the encroaching power of English, and there is often lively debate about the acceptability or not of code-switching or loan words. Dedicated groups on social media enjoy discussing linguistic issues, and there are often news items on various terminological matters.

One long-running discussion forum, active since 1998, is the website welsh-termau-cymraeg. Hosted by the Jiscmail communication platform that is available at all UK universities, this email group was originally conceived of as a discussion forum for academics, but is now widely used outside academia, especially by translators, writers and anyone needing advice on Welsh terms. One of its strengths, in contrast to some other popular discussion platforms, is that it archives all discussions by month and message heading and enables quick searches for relevant terms. It does not offer *official* answers to terminological problems but depends on discussions and answers by others in the community. It thus presents an alternative voice to official methods of elaborating terminology and allows for a free exchange of ideas. It also helps in educating less experienced users in some basic terminology principles.

Members of this discussion group often are the first to identify new or difficult terms that need to be rendered in Welsh, and other list members are generous in their replies to such queries, either supplying Welsh equivalent terms that they themselves have used, or debating possible candidate terms and solutions. Due to intense interest, questions often trigger lively debates. In addition to technical terms, named entities, especially local geographical features and street names, idioms, and expressions are often asked about. For example, an enquiry about *pinch punch* as part of the phrase chanted in the children's traditional prank 'pinch punch first of the month' generated 14 messages about potential Welsh equivalents, including a reference to an old custom of carrying an ivy leaf to stop being pinched by other children. This type of bottom-up support on terminological and related matters shows a rich and balanced environment for what is still, despite all advancements made to date, a minoritised language community, living next door to one of the most influential world languages of the present day.

7.   Conclusion

The growth of Welsh in the public sphere in recent years would not have been possible without the provision and ready accessibility of suitable linguistic resources and terminology. Current popular discourse on linguistic matters in Wales seems to centre on questions of language register, or in other words, how formal or informal the language used for public communication should be, with less focus on terminological problems. There might be tension between the desire of some purists to uphold high conservative registers, and the pressure from more popular quarters to use more liberal registers in public communication. Lack of appropriate terminology is no longer used as an excuse to deny support for Welsh-medium education. Instead, there is great interest in terminology, with the heavy use of online terminological resources an indication of their success and popularity.

However, despite progress made, the continuing development of Welsh terminological resources and their effective provision to the masses remains fragile. Further progress in matters of policy and funding is at the mercy of changing political fortunes, and current global instability may yet pose a threat to many vulnerable languages, including Welsh.

In a fast-moving world, technological advances can be important aids in researching and disseminating terminology. Adopting digital, online approaches to building and disseminating terminologies has succeeded in cutting costs and improving accessibility. Future trends include making better use of corpora for terminology research and incorporating NLP (Natural Language Processing) tools to automate and improve the terminology standardisation process.

It may be argued that both public interest in terminological and linguistic issues on the one hand, and policy and funded standardisation activities on the other, stem from a national consensus in Wales that the Welsh language is worth safeguarding, not as a backward-looking museum piece, but as a flexible and comprehensive medium for all aspects of contemporary human communication. In that respect, the vision of Welsh Renaissance scholars such as William Salesbury has been vindicated, and despite its minoritised and endangered status, Welsh has been able produce, adapt, standardise and disseminate modern, technical terminology for its current needs.

The contribution of the international community, and the example of terminological activities in other languages, should be acknowledged. Engaging with the European Association for Terminology (EAFT) has helped Welsh terminologists learn about problems and solutions in other linguistic communities and play their part on the wider stage. The ISO language and terminology standards have also been instrumental over many years in providing Welsh terminology science with methodologies and guidelines that it could adapt to its own environment, enabling it to follow international best practice.

In conclusion, therefore, many different strands have contributed to allowing terminology science in Welsh to flourish and succeed. A long held popular conviction that Welsh can be made flexible and malleable enough to express any concept has helped, as have various policies and funding streams from the Welsh Government and its agencies in recent years. Finally, the support and encouragement of the international community has also played its role, and enabled the science of terminology in Welsh to achieve its current successes.

References

Andrews, T. 2010. *Current Practice in Website Localization and its Application to Welsh.* Unpublished doctoral thesis, Bangor University.

Andrews, T., and G. Prys. 2011. "The Maes T System and its use in the Welsh-Medium Higher Education Terminology Project." In *Proceedings of CHAT 2011: Creation, Harmonization and Application of Terminology Resources*, ed by T. Gornostay, and A. Vasiljevs, 49–50. Tartu, Estonia: NEALT.

Andrews, T., and G. Prys. 2016. "Terminology Standardization in Education and the Construction of Resources: The Welsh Experience." *Educational Sciences* Vol 6, Issue 1: 29–35.

Andrews, Tegau et al. 2009. *Geiriadur Termau'r Coleg Cymraeg Cenedlaethol.* Carmarthen: Coleg Cymraeg Cenedlaethol.

Andrews, Tegau. 2022. Personal correspondence. Email sent to Welsh-speaking mathematicians based in Wales and elsewhere, entitled "termau mathemateg Cymraeg am maximum, minimum, maximize a minimize" and their replies.

Coleg Cymraeg Cenedlaethol. n.d. *Coleg Cymraeg Cenedlaethol Resource Portal.* Carmarthen.

Currie, Oliver. 2022. "The Role of the Bible in Language Standardization Processes: The Case of Welsh." *Jezik in Slovstvo* 67(1–2): 27–47.

Davies, John. 1632. *Antiquae linguae Britannicae … et linguae Latinae dictionarium duplex.* London.

Davies, John. 2007. *A History of Wales.* Revised Edition. London: Penguin Books.

Fidler, Sioned, Siwan Jones, Rhys Hughes, and Delyth Prys. 2018. *Food Standards Agency Terms in Welsh.* Bangor and Cardiff: Bangor University and the Foods Standards Agency.

GPC Online. 2014. University of Wales Centre for Advanced Welsh & Celtic Studies.

Great Britain. 1927. *Welsh in Education and Life.* London: Her Majesty's Stationery Office.

Hawke, Andrew. 2016. *Geiriadur Prifysgol Cymru: Continuity, Compromise, and Change.* The XVIth International Congress of Celtic Studies. Bangor: Bangor University.

Hawke, Andrew. 2018. "Coping with an Expanding Dictionary: the Lexicographical Contribution to Welsh." *International Journal of Lexicography* 31, no. 2: 229–248.

Hughes, R. Elwyn. 1990. *Nid Am Un Harddwch Iaith: Rhyddiaith Gwyddoniaeth y Bedwaredd Ganrif ar Bymtheg.* Cardiff: University of Wales Press.

ISO/TR 20694: 2018. *A Typology of Language Registers.* Geneva: ISO.

James, E. Wyn. 2012. "Griffith Jones (1684–1761) of Llanddowror and His 'Striking Experiment in Mass Religious Education' in Wales in the Eighteenth Century." In *Volksbildung durch Lesestoffe im 18. und 19. Jahrhundert/Educating the People through Reading Material in the 18th and 19th Centuries*, ed. by Reinhart Siegert, Peter Hoare, and Peter Vodosek, 275–92. Bremen, Germany: Edition Lumière.

Jenkins, Geraint H. 1993. *The University of Wales: An Illustrated History*, Cardiff: University of Wales Press.

Jones, D. B., G. Prys, and D. Prys. 2016. "Vocab: a Dictionary Plugin for Websites." In *Proceedings of the Second Celtic Language Technology Workshop*, 93–99. Paris: TALN.

Justice Wales Network. 2011. *Terms for the Administration of Justice.* Caernarfon: Welsh Language Services HM's Courts and Tribunal Service.

Lewis, Robyn. 1972. *Termau Cyfraith — Welsh Legal Terms.* Llandysul: Gwasg Gomer.

Morgan, Menna. 2002. *Hanes Geiriaduraeth yng Nghymru o 1547 hyd 1914: gyda sylw arbennig i ddylanwad John Walters a William Owen Pughe ar eiriadurwyr 1805–1850.* Unpublished PhD thesis. Bangor: University of Wales.

Parry, John (ed). 1854–1879. *Y Gwyddoniadur Cymreig*. Denbigh: Gwasg Gee.

Prys, Delyth. 2003. "Providing the Terms: Standardizing Terms for Education in Wales." In *Speaking in Tongues: Languages of Lifelong Learning: Proceedings of the 33rd Annual Conference of SCUTREA*, 192–197. Bangor: University of Wales.

Prys, Delyth. 2006. "Setting the Standards: Ten Years of Welsh Terminology Work." In *Terminology, Computing and Translation*, ed. by Pius ten Hacken, 41–57. Tübingen: Gunter Narr Verlag.

Prys, Delyth, and Dewi Bryn Jones. 2007. *Guidelines for the Standardization of Terminology for the Welsh Assembly Government and the Welsh Language Board*. Cardiff: Welsh Language Board.

Prys, Delyth, Gruffudd Prys and Dewi Bryn Jones. 2015. "Quantifying the Use of Digital Welsh-language Language Resources." In *Language Technologies in Support of Less-Resourced Languages* (LRL 2015), 28 November, Poznan, Poland.

Prys, Delyth, and Dewi Bryn Jones. 2018. "National Language Technologies Portals for LRLs: a Case Study." In *Human Language Technology. Challenges for Computer Science and Linguistics*, ed. by Z. Vetulani, J. Mariani, and M. Kubis, 420–429. Springer.

Prys, Delyth, and J. M. Jones. 1998. *Y Termiadur Ysgol: Termau wedi'u safoni ar gyfer ysgolion Cymru / Standardized Terminology for the Schools of Wales*. Cardiff: ACCAC.

Prys, Delyth, and Robat Trefor. 2015. *Ysgrifau a Chanllawiau Cyfieithu*. Carmarthen: Coleg Cymraeg Cenedlaethol.

Prys, Delyth, J. P. M. Jones, and Hedd ap Emlyn. 1995. *Llyfryddiaeth Geiriaduron Termau*. Bangor: University of Wales Bangor.

Prys, Delyth et al. 2006. *Y Termiadur: Termau wedi'u Safoni / Standardized Terminology*. Cardiff: ACCAC.

Prys, Delyth, Gareth Watkins, and Stefano Ghazzali. 2022. *European Language Equality Report on the Welsh Language*. Dublin: ELE Consortium, Adapt Centre.

Prys, Delyth (with Care Council subject specialists). 2015a. *Care Council for Wales Terminology*. Cardiff: Care Council for Wales.

Prys, Gruffudd. 2022. *Adroddiad Y Termiadur Addysg — Hydref 2022*. Unpublished report sent to the Welsh Government.

Prys, Gruffudd. 2023. *Adroddiad Y Termiadur Addysg — Hydref 2023*. Unpublished report sent to the Welsh Government.

Robertson, Patrick, David Chan, Gruffudd Prys, and Dewi Bryn Jones. 2014. *Ap Geiriaduron*. Bangor: Bangor University.

Rottet, Kevin, and Steve Morris. 2018. *Comparative Stylistics of Welsh and English: arddulleg y Gymraeg*. Cardiff: University of Wales Press.

Russell, Paul. 1995. *An Introduction to the Celtic Languages*. Harlow, UK: Longman.

Salesbury, William. 1547. *A Dictionary in Englyshe and Welshe*. London.

Screen, Ben. 2017. "Effaith defnyddio Cofion Cyfieithu ar y broses Gyfieithu: Ymdrech a chynhyrchiant wrth Gyfieithu i'r Gymraeg." *Gwerddon* 23: 10–35.

University of Wales. 1971. *Termau Llywodraeth Leol — Iechyd Cyhoeddus*. Cardiff: University of Wales Press.

UK Government. 1988. *Education Reform Act 1988*.

UK Government. 1993. *Welsh Language Act 1993*.

Williams, Jac L. 1973. *Dictionary of Terms/ Geiriadur Termau*. University of Wales Press.

Welsh Government. *TermCymru* (n.d.).

Welsh Government. 2011. *Welsh Language (Wales) Measure 2011*.

Welsh Government. 2017. *Cymraeg 2050: A Million Welsh Speakers*.

Welsh Government. 2018. *Welsh Language Technology Action Plan*.

Welsh Government. 2022. *Curriculum for Wales: Planning and Priorities Guide*.

Welsh Government. 2022. *Welsh in the Home and in Education (Welsh Language Use Survey): July 2019 to March 2020*.

Welsh Government. 2022. *Welsh Language in Wales (Census 2021)*.

Williams, Ifor, Sir. 1972. *The Beginnings of Welsh Poetry: Studies*. Cardiff: University of Wales Press.

Williams, Iolo Wyn. 2003. *Our Children's Language: The Welsh-medium Schools of Wales 1939–2000*. Talybont: Y Lolfa.

About the authors

Mariëtta Alberts

Mariëtta Alberts started her career as a terminologist. She served on the Coordinating Terminology Board and the Language Task Group, did research on lexicography, terminology and computational linguistics, and is an accredited terminologist of the SA Translators' Institute. She retired as Director: Terminology and Standardisation (PanSALB). She received honorary membership from Infoterm, Afrilex and Prolingua. She received several awards for terminology-related projects. She published two books on terminology principles and practice (2017 and 2019).

Andree Affeich

Andree Affeich is Assistant Professor of Translation at the Lebanese American University (LAU-Beirut). She holds a Ph.D. in Multilingual Lexicology, Terminology and Translation from the University of Lyon 2. Between 2022 and 2023, she coordinated two programs at LAU: the BA in Translation and the BA in English. She is the recipient of a Fulbright grant, and was awarded a certificate of pride and honor by the Arab Translators Association in recognition of her achievements in the translation field and the academic field. She has authored and co-authored papers and book chapters on terminology and translation, and is member of the Pan-Latin Terminology Network (REALITER), of the Lexicology, Terminology, Translation network (LTT), and of the Arab Translators Union.

Amparo Alcina

Amparo Alcina is a Professor at the Universitat Jaume I of Castellón (Spain), where she teaches Translation Technology and Terminology and coordinates the research team TecnoLeTTra, which focuses on language, terminology and translation technology. She leads the ONTODIC series of research projects, which is creating onomasiological and combinatory dictionaries. She has designed an ontological model to represent and formalise lexical and terminological data in knowledge databases using descriptive logic and ontologies.

Anna Anastassiadis-Symeonidis
Anna Anastassiadis-Symeonidis is Professor Emerita of Linguistics at Aristotle University of Thessaloniki. She is interested in compilation of printed and electronic dictionaries, in neology, borrowing, word formation, multiword units and terminology. She is the author of 10 books and of over 200 papers published in journals and proceedings worldwide.

Tegau Andrews
Tegau Andrews is a terminologist at Bangor University's Language Technologies Unit and she is editor of the English-Welsh dictionary of terms for higher education, *Geiriadur Termau'r Coleg Cymraeg Cenedlaethol*. She is a member of BSI TS/1 and ISO/TC 37, Language and Terminology, and Project Leader of ISO 20539: 2023 Translation, interpreting and related technology — Vocabulary.

Albina Auksoriūtė
Albina Auksoriūtė is a senior researcher at the Terminology Centre of the Institute of the Lithuanian Language. She is the chief editor of the scientific journal *Terminologija* and of three scholarly collections, and one of the authors of the monograph "Research into Lithuanian terminology of informatics and computing." She has conducted research and published extensively on the history of Lithuanian terminology, the terminology of the natural sciences, and terminography.

Rima Baraké
Rima Baraké, Ph.D., is a university professor specialising in Language Sciences, Terminology, and Translation. She is a published author and regularly participates in global conferences on translation and terminology. She is a member of the Arab Translators Union and has translated various books across French, English, and Arabic.

Bruno de Bessé
Bruno de Bessé is an Honorary professor at the Faculty of Translation and Interpreting, and formerly professor at the School of Translation and Interpreting (University of Geneva), terminology delegate at the State Chancellery of the Canton of Bern, contributor to the editorial staff of *Le Robert Dictionaries* and member of the Associate Editorial Board of the *Terminology* journal.

Anna-Lena Bucher
Anna-Lena Bucher worked at the Swedish Centre for Terminology (TNC) from 1973 to 2014, first as a terminologist and from 2000 to 2014 as CEO. She has been actively involved in the Nordterm cooperation from the beginning.

Danielle Candel

Danielle Candel is Honorary Research Scientist, associate member of the laboratory "History of linguistic theories", CNRS, University Paris Cité. Her main research areas include prescriptive linguistics, terminology (through linguistic expertise and support for official Terminology and neology), and descriptive lexicography (as one of the writers of the CNRS dictionary *Trésor de la langue française*). Her publications focus on scientific and technical vocabularies, and lexicographical and terminological theories and practices, specifically in the French institutional framework.

Lise Lotte Weilgaard Christensen

Lise Lotte Weilgaard Christensen is associate professor emerita at the University of Southern Denmark. She has been developing and teaching terminology courses for four decades and has participated in a number of research projects on terminology and language-technology tools.

Anne Condamines

Anne Condamines is a senior researcher at CNRS (French Scientific Research National Center) in Toulouse. She is interested in specialised languages and has studied the variation of terminology and relationship markers depending on the domain and textual genre, by defining tooled corpus analysis methods. For several years she has also been working on the design and evaluation of Controlled Natural Languages. She maintains collaborations with researchers in AI and ergonomics.

Valérie Delavigne

Valérie Delavigne lectures in language sciences at Sorbonne Nouvelle University, and is a member of the Clesthia (EA 7345) research group. She has worked extensively with the French Institut National du Cancer, establishing an online dictionary for patients. As a sociolinguist she focuses on linguistic aspects of popularisation and is preparing a critical dictionary of ecology.

Marcel Diki-Kidiri

Marcel Diki-Kidiri is a university Professor, a former Senior Researcher at the French National Center for Scientific Research, a linguist specialising in Sanngo language, standardisation and language planning, and languages for special purposes. He initiated the Cultural Approach to Terminology, one of the current trends in the discipline. Academician of the African Academy of Languages (ACALAN), Medalist of the Academic Palms of the Central African Republic, he also holds a CNRS Labor Medal (France).

Claudia Dobrina
Claudia Dobrina, PhD, is an international expert in ISO/TC 37. She was secretary of ISO/TC 37/SC 1 from 1997 to 2007. She worked as a terminologist at the Swedish Centre for Terminology (TNC) from 1992 to 2014. She has published a number of papers on terminology work and terminological projects.

Joëlle Ducos
Joëlle Ducos is full professor of French medieval linguistics at Sorbonne University and at the Ecole Pratique des Hautes Etudes (France). Her research interests lie in scientific vulgarisation and French translations during the Middle Ages, and the beginnings of French terminology from the 12th century.

Ágota Fóris
Ágota Fóris is a full professor at the Department of Hungarian Linguistics of the Károli Gáspár University (Budapest, Hungary), and Head of the Terminology and Communication Research Group (TERMIK). She founded the Masters' in Terminology in Hungary in 2011 and led the program for the following 7 years. From 2008 to 2013 she was Editor-in-Chief of the *Magyar Terminológia* (Journal of Hungarian Terminology). She has been President of the Council of Hungarian Terminology (MaTT) since 2013, and President of the Working Committee on Applied Linguistics of the Hungarian Academy of Sciences since 2024. From 2010 to 2014 she held the position of Vice President of EAFT (European Association for Terminology). Her research and publication topics cover the field of terminology, LSP lexicography, semantics, translation, and applied linguistics.

Annamaria Fotos
Annamaria Fotos obtained her Master's degree in German philology at the University of Szeged, Hungary. After working as a school teacher, then university teaching assistant, she joined the Translation DG of the European Commission in 2009, and since 2016 she has been a terminology coordinator with responsibilities for project coordination and language technologies.

Inge Fourneau
Inge Fourneau is full professor of Medicine at KU Leuven (Belgium) and in charge of teaching the history of medicine. Although she covers the entire timeline, she is particularly interested in the development of medicine during the Middle Ages and the Early Modern Age.

Aline Francoeur

Aline Francoeur is Full Professor at the Université Laval, where she teaches Terminology at both the undergraduate and graduate levels. She has published in various leading journals among which are the *International Journal of Lexicography*, *Études de linguistique appliquée*, *Cahiers de lexicologie*, and *Lexicographica*. She has also edited or coedited several books, including *Multiple Perspectives on Terminological Variation* (John Benjamins, 2017). From 2015 to 2020, she was the editor-in-chief of TTR (*Traduction, Terminologie, Rédaction*), the journal of the Canadian Association for Translation Studies.

Michèle Fruyt

Michèle Fruyt is Professor Emeritus at Sorbonne-Université. Her work deals with all aspects of Latin linguistics, in particular word formation in Latin, suffixation and composition, as well as grammaticalization and the mechanisms of linguistic change from Archaic Latin to Late Latin.

Christian Galinski

Christian Galinski is the Director of the International Information Centre for Terminology (Infoterm), which he joined in 1980. From 1986 to 2009, he was Secretary of the Technical Committee ISO/TC 37 Language and Terminology. Many organisations benefitted from his engagement in projects with UNESCO, the EU, WHO, etc. focusing on interhuman communication, structured content, technical documentation and localisation, language and terminology policies, as well as copyright, eAccessibility and eInclusion issues related to terminology. He is consultant to non-governmental, governmental and intergovernmental organisations.

François Gaudin

François Gaudin is professor of linguistics at the University of Rouen, PhD in history and member of the laboratory LT2D (Lexicons, Texts, Discourses, Dictionaries). His research focused initially on socioterminology then on the cultural history of dictionaries. He lectures in lexicology, the history of dictionaries, linguistic and terminological policies, epistemology and ethics.

Michèle Goyens

Michèle Goyens is full professor of French linguistics at KU Leuven (Belgium). Her research interests lie in text editing and French diachronic linguistics. Her research focuses on the development of the French scientific, viz. medical terminology in the middle ages.

Afroditi Giovani

Afroditi Giovani is currently working in the field of AI for a global tech leader. She is a Board Member of the Hellenic Society for Terminology, and an independent researcher focusing on language and technology.

Claudio Grimaldi

Claudio Grimaldi (Chevalier de l'Ordre des Arts et des Lettres) is Professor in French Language at the University of Naples "Parthenope" since 2021. At the same University, he obtained an international PhD with a thesis which in 2016 was awarded the prize of the European Association of Terminology as the best PhD thesis in the field of terminology. Grimaldi's research fields concern diachronic terminology and the evolution of textual genres in scientific communication. Currently she is Secretary General of REALITER (2024–2027).

Håvard Hjulstad

Håvard Hjulstad was project manager at Standards Norway from 2003 until his retirement in 2019. He was employed at the Norwegian Council for Technical Terminology from 1982 to 2001, as director from 1990. He was chair of ISO/TC 37 from 1998 to 2009.

Åsa Holmér

Åsa Holmér is a language expert in LSP and terminology at the Swedish Language Council. She worked as a terminologist at the Swedish Centre for Terminology (TNC) from 1982 to 2018.

Marianna Katsoyannou

Marianna Katsoyannou is Associate Professor of General Linguistics at the University of Cyprus. She is a former Board member of SILF (Société Internationale de Linguistique Fonctionnelle, 2006–07), former president of EAFT (European Association for Terminology, 2008–10) and a Board member of Infoterm (International Information Centre for Terminology) since 2018.

John Kirby

John Kirby holds degrees from the University of Leeds and the University of Kent (UK). Before joining the European Commission in 1999, he worked as a translator, reviser, interpreter and technical writer in the private sector, and was also involved in the Metal and Langenscheidt T1 machine translation systems. Since 2015 he has been a terminology coordinator at the European Commission, with responsibilities for training and communication.

Dominika Kováříková

Dominika Kováříková is a corpus linguist at the Czech National Corpus, Charles University in Prague. Her research focuses on terminology, lexicology, and lexicography. She specialises in analysing extensive text corpora to uncover lexical, terminology, and morphology patterns in texts. She has authored a monograph *Quantitative Characteristics of Terms* published in Czech.

Panagiotis G. Krimpas

Panagiotis G. Krimpas is Full Professor of terminology, translation and legal texts at the Democritus University of Thrace (Greece) and BoD member of the Hellenic Society for Terminology. His research fields include terminology, translation, dialectology, and historical linguistics.

Natascia Leonardi

Natascia Leonardi is a researcher in Linguistics and teaches courses in Terminology, Terminography, and Computational Linguistics at the University of Macerata. Her main research interests centre on specialised communication, in particular, terminology theory and practice in their correlation with the organisation and management of knowledge. Her research and publications are also focused on the history of linguistic thought, artificial languages, computational linguistics, and humanities computing.

Jana Levická

Jana Levická is a researcher at the Ľudovít Štúr Institute of Sciences (Slovak Academy of Sciences) and chief investigator of the Slovak Terminology Database project and Slovak National Corpus project. She is interested in terminology, corpus linguistics, translation and translatology.

Bodil Nistrup Madsen

Bodil Nistrup Madsen, former professor emerita at Copenhagen Business School, covered multiple research areas: terminological knowledge modelling and knowledge management, ontologies versus classification systems, concept modelling versus data modelling. She was for many years chairman of ISO/TC 37/SC 3 and from 1998 to 2015 head of the DANTERM Centre. Bodil passed away in 2022.

Riitta Majaniemi

Riitta Majaniemi obtained her Master's degree in English and French from the University of Turku, Finland. Before joining the Translation DG of the European Commission in 1997, she worked as a translator in the public sector in Finland. Since 2006 she has been a terminology coordinator, with responsibilities for terminology outsourcing, interinstitutional cooperation and IATE data management.

Nikolche Mickoski

Nikolche Mickoski is a scholar in the fields of terminology, lexicography, and corpus linguistics. He works as the lead terminologist for the Macedonian Scientific and Professional Terminology project at the Lexicographic Centre of the Macedonian Academy of Sciences and Arts and teaches several specialised terminology courses at the Faculty of Philology at Ss. Cyril and Methodius University in Skopje.

Johan Myking

Johan Myking is professor emeritus at the University of Bergen, author or co-author of several publications and books on terminology and president of the IITF from 2009 to 2016.

Henrik Nilsson

Henrik Nilsson is an ECQA-certified terminologist and terminology teacher who works as a terminology consultant. He is a member of the Swedish terminology committee SIS/TK 115 and the current president of EAFT. He worked as a terminologist at the Swedish Centre for Terminology (TNC) from 1997 to 2018.

Anita Nuopponen

Anita Nuopponen is professor emerita of Technical Communication, University of Vaasa, Finland. She has been teaching and developing terminology courses for four decades. She has written and co-authored over eighty articles on terminology and related fields. She is active in ISO/TC 37/SC 1.

Tatiana Orel

Tatiana Orel holds a Ph.D. in Linguistics with specialisation in Terminology Studies from Moscow State Pedagogical University, Russia. She is a research fellow at Cogniva Information Science Research Institute (CISRI), Canada, where she contributes to architecting information systems and developing semantic models to improve the performance of AI for more effecient information management. Tatiana also works for the Government of Canada, where she researches and designs government strategies in information management. Her research interests include information management, AI, knowledge engineering, ontologies, and terminologies.

Mavina Pantazara

Mavina Pantazara is Associate Professor at the National and Kapodistrian University of Athens. She is Vice-President of the Hellenic Society for Terminology and head of the Greek standardisation committee ELOT/TC 21 (Terminology — Language Resources). Her research interests include translation, linguistic and cross-linguistic analysis, lexicography, terminology, and language technology.

Aurélie Picton

Aurélie Picton has been an associate professor at the Faculty of Translation and Interpreting at the University of Geneva since 2011. She teaches courses on terminology, language resources, languages for specific purposes and corpus linguistics. Her main research interests include term variation, term circulation, the use of language technologies, and corpus linguistics.

Ágústa Þorbergsdóttir

Ágústa Þorbergsdóttir has been actively involved in terminological management in Iceland for more than two decades. She is the editor of the Icelandic Term Bank.

Maria Pozzi

María Pozzi is a research professor at El Colegio de México working in terminology, terminology standardisation, children's terminography, and neology. She obtained her PhD in Computational Linguistics from the University of Manchester Institute of Science and Technology (UMIST). Since 1994, she has represented Mexico at ISO/TC 37. In 2006 she was awarded the Wüster Special Prize.

Delyth Prys

Delyth Prys is professor emerita at Bangor University, Wales. She was until recently Head of the Language Technologies Unit there and has authored and co-authored many terminology dictionaries and papers on terminology science.

Gruffudd Prys

Gruffudd Prys is the Head of the Language Technologies Unit at Bangor University where he oversees the development of speech and natural language processing technologies. He is also the senior editor of *Y Termiadur Addysg*, the dictionary standardising Welsh-language terminology for school-age education in Wales.

Donatella Pulitano

Donatella Pulitano is Head of the Central Service for Terminology of the State Chancellery of the Canton of Bern since 1994 and of the Central Language Services since 2021. Since 1995, she has been a lecturer in terminology at the Faculty of Translation and Interpreting of the University of Geneva, and gives continuing education courses in Switzerland and abroad. She is member of EAFT, Ass.I.Term, CompuTerm, DIT, DTT, and RaDT.

Beatrice Ragazzini

Beatrice Ragazzini holds an MA in Specialised Translation and is currently a Ph.D. candidate in Translation, Interpreting and Intercultural Studies, both at the University of Bologna. Her past research focussed on terminology theory applied to the periodisation of English medieval architecture. She is currently investigating how classifying and naming specialised concepts contributes to knowledge advancement in several scientific domains mainly in the 19th century.

Jérôme Samuel

Jérôme Samuel is a French researcher, full professor (Indonesian and Malaysian studies) at Institut National des Langues et Civilisations Orientales (INALCO, Paris), and Director of the Research Institute on Contemporary Southeast Asia (IRASEC, Bangkok). He was also the editor-in-chief of the journal *Archipel. Études interdisciplinaires sur le monde insulindien* (2021–2024). His work focuses on Indonesian Malay, its language policies, terminologies, specialised dictionaries, didactics and mutual intelligibility with Malaysian Malay. For the past 20 years, he has been conducting research on reverse glass painting in Indonesia (Java and Bali).

Klaus-Dirk Schmitz

Klaus-Dirk Schmitz was professor of terminology science at the Technical University of Cologne from 1992 to 2017. He was also co-founder and chair of the Council for German-Language Terminology (RaDT), president of Infoterm and chair of the DIN Standards Committee on Terminology (NAT). Currently vice-chair of the German Terminology Association (DTT), he sits on the advisory boards of various organisations, and is editor, author or co-author of numerous scientific publications. He was awarded the Eugen Wüster Prize in 2010 and the Beuth Denkmünze (DIN) in 2023.

Claudia Stancati

Claudia Stancati was professor of Philosophy of Language at the University of Calabria from 2001 to 2022. Her research interests focus on the relations between language and law, the history of linguistic ideas, the epistemology of the science of language, the specialised lexicon of philosophy and sciences and the classification of science in the early Twentieth century.

Sirpa Suhonen

Sirpa Suhonen is a terminologist at the Finnish Terminology Centre. She has worked there since 1997 doing terminology work in various subject fields.

Hanne Erdman Thomsen

Hanne Erdman Thomsen, former associate professor at Copenhagen Business School, has done research in formalisation and automisation of terminology work, and concept modelling versus data modelling. From 2004 to 2017 she was active in ISO/TC 37/SC 1.

Katerina Toraki

Katerina Toraki is chemical engineer and information scientist, member of Standardization Committees ELOT/TC 21 (Terminology — Language Resources) and ELOT/TC 22 (Information and Documentation) and Secretary of ELETO GESY. Her interests include terminology, information and knowledge organisation, ontologies, thesauri and other subject analysis and access tools.

Mitja Trojar

Mitja Trojar is a researcher at the Research Centre of the Slovenian Academy of Sciences and Arts (Ljubljana, Slovenia). His research interests include the history of linguistics (Slovenian linguistic terminology) and terminology (Eugen Wüster and his legacy), terminography (co-editor of the *Terminological Dictionary of Concrete Structures*) and historical linguistics (compiling entries for the *Dictionary of the 16th-Century Slovenian Literary Language*, Vol. II).

George Tsiamas

George Tsiamas is an engineer (MSc) of N.T.U. of Athens, M.A. of C.I.C.A of Nice, France, ELETO's founding member and currently Secretary General, member of GESY and other terminology bodies, ex-lecturer of Piraeus University and Strasbourg University, and a writer and researcher.

Kostas Valeontis

Kostas Valeontis is electronic physicist, chairman of MOTO (Permanent Group of Telecommunications Terminology), of ELOT/TC 48/WG1 (Information Technology Terminology), and of ELOT/TC 2/WG5 (Sound Insulation). Since 2006, he has been President of the Hellenic Society for Terminology (ELETO) and Chairman of its Scientific Council (GESY).

Marc Van Campenhoudt

A Romance languages philologist and linguist, Prof. Dr. Marc Van Campenhoudt taught in the Department of Translation and Interpreting (formerly ISTI) at the Université libre de Bruxelles. He founded the TERMISTI (now TRADITAL) research centre, where he conducted extensive research into terminology data modelling, specialised vocabularies and Language for specific purposes, with a particular focus on the maritime domain. For many years he chaired the Lexicologie, Terminologie, Traduction Network (LTT).

Fleur Vigneron

Fleur Vigneron is full professor of medieval French and history of French at Grenoble Alpes University (France). Her work focuses on agronomy and botany in scientific treatises during the Middle Ages, particularly by studying the specialised French lexicon.

Anu Ylisalmi

Anu Ylisalmi is a terminologist at the Finnish Terminology Centre. Her work involves terminology and ontology work, editing the centre's newsletter Terminfo, and maintaining the TEPA Term Bank.

Maria Teresa Zanola

Maria Teresa Zanola is Professor of French linguistics at the Catholic University of Milan. where she heads the observatory for terminology and language policy. As corresponding member of the Accademia della Crusca, she specialises in diachronic and arts and crafts terminology. She was Secretary General of REALITER (2012–2023), where she furthered the development of multilingual lexicons. Currently the President of the European Language Council, she studies language policy and plurilingualism in Higher Education.

Miroslav Zumrík

Miroslav Zumrík is a researcher at the Ľudovít Štúr Institute of Sciences (Slovak Academy of Sciences) and teaching fellow at Comenius University in Bratislava, Slovakia. Author of monographs on philosophy of corpus linguistics and style of the Slovak judicial decisions in criminal cases and co-author of a book on Slovak verb conjugation, he is interested in terminology, style of legal texts and narratology. He is also a translator of Scandinavian literature.

Index